PEARSON

ALWAYS LEARNING

Edited by
Barry Cartwright

Sociological Explanations of Crime and Deviance: A Reader

Cover art: Coral Panorama by Alisa Harding-Stein.

Pearson Learning Solutions, 501 Boylston Street, Suite 900, Boston, MA 02116
A Pearson Education Company
www.pearsoned.com

000200010270740953

SD/CB

ISBN 10: 1-256-32330-6
ISBN 13: 978-1-256-32330-3

Contents

Preface

I have taught over fifteen university courses on sociological explanations of crime and deviance through the years, and have yet to find a textbook or course reader that deals adequately with this subject area. Most criminology texts or readers try to cover as much territory as possible, including biological, psychological and sociological explanations of crime and deviance, not to mention the Classical School, the Positive School, rational choice theory, deterrence theory, criminal event theory, and low self-control theory. Some try to cover official crime statistics, victimization surveys and the entire criminal justice system as well. There is nothing intrinsically wrong with books and readers that provide a general overview of criminology and criminal justice. However, I find that by the time students have completed several criminology courses, they have usually read any number of such texts and course readers, often going back over the same information time and time again. Moreover, I often come across third and fourth year criminology students who have read numerous text books telling them what Émile Durkheim, Shaw and McKay, Edwin Sutherland, Travis Hirschi and Howard Becker said, yet the students have never read any of the original works of these thinkers.

It is difficult to do justice in one book to all of the extant sociological explanations of crime and deviance. That said, this book is intended to serve as a "stand alone" textbook-course reader. The original reading selections in the book cover a time span of over a hundred years, and are as diverse and comprehensive as possible. In truth, they represent "the classics" of sociological explanations of crime and deviance. They include, for example, Durkheim's analysis of the normal and the pathological in society, Merton's anomie-strain theory, Shaw and McKay's social disorganization theory, Sutherland's differential association theory, Burgess and Akers' reformulation of differential association theory (i.e., social learning theory), and Becker's work on moral entrepreneurship, to name a few. The original readings also encompass a number of recent endeavors in the field, for example, Thornberry's interactional theory, Sampson and Groves's re-test of social disorganization theory, Laub and Sampson's turning points theory, and Messerschmidt's work on masculinities and crime. Each of the original readings—and each of the seven sections in the book—comes with its own individual introduction, contextualizing the theory (or theories) and showing how they relate to or expand upon other theories or perspectives covered in the book.

The seven sections in the book—and the original readings in each of those sections—are organized chronologically. Section I deals with anomie-strain theory, starting with Émile Durkheim's work in the late 1800s, and then progressing through Robert Merton's 1938 article on social structure and anomie, Robert Agnew's general strain theory, and Rosenfeld and Messner's institutional-anomie theory. Section II, on social disorganization theory, begins with Shaw and McKay's 1942 study of delinquency in urban areas of Chicago, followed by Sampson and Groves's retest and reformulation of social disorganization theory based on the British Crime Survey, and finally, Bursik and Grasmick's reformulation of social disorganization theory based on socioeconomic changes in Chicago between 1960 and 1980. Section III starts with Edwin Sutherland's differential association theory, and then moves on to Sykes and Matza's techniques of neutralization and Burgess and Akers' differential-association-reinforcement theory, both of them extensions of (or elaborations on) Sutherland's earlier work. Section IV, on social control theory and life course/developmental theories, starts with Travis Hirschi's social bond theory, and then progresses through Terrence Thornberry's interactional theory and Laub and Sampson's turning points theory, explaining how the latter two theories can be traced back to Hirschi's social bond theory, and ultimately, back to Émile Durkheim. Section V deals with the sociology of deviance, labeling theory and critical constructionism, with Kai Erikson's "notes on the sociology of deviance," Howard Becker's work on "moral entrepreneurs," and Erich Goode's comments on the limits to critical constructionism. Section VI, on conflict and critical criminology, includes William Chambliss' sociological analysis of the vagrancy laws in England and Jock Young's commentary on the state of critical criminology in the 21st century. Section VII builds upon the conflict-critical criminology content of Section VI, with current work by Sally Simpson and James Messerschmidt in the areas of feminist and gender-based theory.

There are several people who contributed significantly to the completion of this project. I would like to thank Dr. Robert Gordon, the Director of the School of Criminology at Simon Fraser University, who encouraged me to write the book, and did his best to ensure that I had sufficient time and space in which to finish it. I am indebted to my friends and colleagues, Sheri Fabian and Jon Heidt, who commented extensively on the content and lay-out of the book during the conceptualization stage, and offered many fine editorial suggestions along the way. I would like to thank Coral Kennett, the Managing Editor for Pearson Learning Solutions, who rode shotgun on this project from beginning to end. Last (and certainly not least), I would like to thank my loving wife Rosa Cartwright, who kept the home fires burning while I wrote this book and continued teaching full-time at Simon Fraser University. I could never have done it without her support and encouragement.

Anomie-Strain Theory

Anomie-strain theory is one of the most well known and most durable sociological explanations of crime and deviance. Section I of this book features four original works by authors whose names are commonly associated with the anomie-strain tradition—Émile Durkheim, Robert Merton, Robert Agnew and Steven Messner and Richard Rosenfeld. As is the case with the following six sections of this book, the four reading selections in this section appear in the chronological order in which they were written in order to help the reader view them from a historical perspective, and understand how anomie-strain theory has evolved over time.

Émile Durkheim derived the term *anomie* from the Greek word *anomia*. The word anomia originally referred to a state of social disorder in which the social norms (or standards of conduct) were weakened or non-existent (Zeitlin, 2001:341). Durkheim first introduced his concept of anomie in his 1893 book, *The Division of Labor in Society*. However, it was not until his 1897 book, *Suicide: A Study in Sociology*, that Durkheim used anomie extensively, to describe a social condition of lawlessness, normlessness and unregulated choice that led certain individuals to commit what he referred to as anomic suicide (Clinard, 1964; Durkheim, 1951).

In his article on "Social Structure and Anomie" (the second reading selection in this part), Robert Merton (1938) borrowed Durkheim's concept of anomie and applied it to American society. Essentially, Merton argued that American society was itself criminogenic (crime-causing), and the main source of anomie. He said this was attributable to the strong emphasis placed on the cultural goals of accumulation of wealth and social advancement, and the lack of institutional means— e.g., access to educational and employment opportunities—by which to attain those goals. Merton's theory came to be referred to as "strain theory" because he pointed out that this disjunction between the cultural goals and the institutional means produced "a strain toward anomie and deviant behavior" (Merton, 1985:128)[1]. Merton observed that there were five ways in which individuals could adapt to this strain—conformity, innovation, ritualism, retreatism and rebellion. To this day, Merton's 1938 article remains amongst the most frequently cited works in both sociology and criminology (Lilly, Cullen, & Ball, 2011:68).

Following in Merton's footsteps, Albert Cohen merged anomie theory with Edwin Sutherland's differential association theory (discussed in Section III of this book), in an effort to identify the types of strain experienced by lower-class males, and demonstrate how this led these individuals to adopt subcultural values and form delinquent subcultures. According to Cohen (1955, 1964:84–87), lower class males had the same aspirations for social status as middle- and upper-class males. However, when they tried to compete for social status in school, they would find that they could not meet the standards of what Cohen referred to as "the middle-class measuring rod." Cohen said that as a consequence, they would develop a sense of "status deprivation" or "status frustration," which could be likened to a sense of anomie or strain. Cohen viewed delinquent behaviour as a "reaction formation"—i.e., a hostile reaction to an adverse environment (Cohen, 1955, 1964:84–87). As well, Cohen viewed delinquency as a collective solution— the delinquent subculture established new norms, redefined the meaning of status, and created new forms of "acceptable" behavior or conduct (Cohen, 1955, 1964:129–131; Cloward & Ohlin, 1960:140–142). Cohen subsequently tried to distance himself somewhat from Merton's anomie theory, saying that Merton was not specific enough about the degree of strain required to generate a deviant response, or the process through which individuals went in order to become deviant (Clinard, 1964; Cohen, 1985).

Another elaboration on Robert Merton's anomie-strain theory and Edwin Sutherland's differential association theory was Cloward and Ohlin's (1960) book, *Delinquency and Opportunity*. While Merton described five ways that individuals could adapt to anomie or strain, Cloward and Ohlin (1960) talked about three different subcultures (or illegitimate opportunity structures)—the criminal subculture, the conflict subculture and the retreatist subculture—which lower class individuals could join in order to deal with their "status discontentment" or sense of "unjust deprivation" (Cloward & Ohlin, 1960:90, 117; Lilly et al., 2011:71).

However, Cloward and Ohlin stressed that individuals could not simply choose whichever one of these illegitimate opportunity structures they wanted— they needed access, which was not always readily available. Criminal subcultures (focused on profit-making) only existed in "organized" slums, where older, more experienced offenders could teach younger, prospective offenders the ropes (e.g., how to pick locks, how to fence stolen goods, etc) (Cloward & Ohlin, 1960:162–165). Conflict subcultures, found in disorganized slums, still rebelled against society and middle class values. However, conflict subcultures placed higher value (status) on a reputation for toughness and willingness to engage in violence, because they lacked access to the profit-making illegitimate opportunity structures of the criminal subculture (Cloward & Ohlin, 1960:171–175). The retreatist subculture, best exemplified by the drug subculture, attracted lower class youth who were "double failures"—they could not attain status, either through legitimate means or through the illegitimate means of the criminal or conflict subculture. Thus, retreatists turned to drugs and other forms of escape to resolve their sense of status discontentment (Cloward & Ohlin, 1960:178–182).

A number of criticisms were levelled against earlier forms of anomie-strain theory. Some claimed that Merton's anomie theory was too specific to American society and its quest for the American Dream. Critics said that not all cultures and societies necessarily had the same aspirations for consumerism, acquisition, and social advancement. Anomie-strain theorists were also criticized for focusing their attention on urban slums and lower-class youth, while ignoring—or failing to offer an adequate explanation for—crimes committed by members of the middle- and upper-class (Vold & Bernard, 1979:224–226). Indeed, questions were raised as to whether or not lower-class youth necessarily subscribed to the American Dream of acquisition and social advancement, or for that matter, actually rejected middle-class values (cf. Lilly et al., 2011:72–73).

Recent advancements in anomie-strain theory, such as relative deprivation theory, general strain theory and institutional-anomie theory have attempted to address some of these criticisms. In his work on relative deprivation theory, for example, Nikos Passas (2003) points out that a sense of anomie can develop in relative (rather than objective) terms, in comparison to reference groups that individuals might aspire to join (e.g., the yacht club), or would prefer to avoid joining (e.g., the homeless). In essence, even middle- or upper-class individuals can experience feelings of relative deprivation when they compare themselves to other individuals in their social milieu who appear to be enjoying higher status or greater levels of achievement. Thus, Passas is able to use an anomie-strain perspective to explain middle- and upper-class crime.

In Section I (on anomie-strain theory), the third original reading selection is concerned specifically with general strain theory, while the fourth is about institutional-anomie theory. Briefly, Robert Agnew's (1985) general strain theory introduces a psychological dimension to anomie-strain theory, by bringing in elements of social learning theory and recent research on frustration-aggression. Messner and Rosenfeld's institutional-anomie theory argues that there is an imbalance in power (or a disjunction) between the major social institutions, whose role it is to facilitate social integration and provide social regulation. Moreover, they point out that the goals or objectives of those institutions are often poorly defined (or misunderstood) by the institutions themselves, thus creating yet another internal disjunction between institutional goals and institutional structure (Messner & Rosenfeld, 2007). It could be said that Agnew's general strain theory is meant to explain individual criminality, whereas Messner and Rosenfeld's institutional-anomie theory is focused more on differences in crime rates. In this sense, the two theories can be seen as complementary. More will be said about general strain theory and institutional-anomie theory in the individual introductions to these two original reading selections.

Notes

1.   Williams III and McShane (2010:84) point out that Merton never actually referred to himself as a "strain" theorist. Rather, this descriptor was given to anomie theory by Ruth Kornhauser in her (1978) book, *The Social Sources of Delinquency*, and then re-used by Travis Hirschi is his (1969) book, *Causes of Delinquency*.

References

Agnew, R. (1985). A revised strain theory of delinquency. *Social Forces, 64*(1), 151–167.

Clinard, M. B. (1964). The theoretical implications of anomie and deviant behavior. In M. B. Clinard (Ed.), *Anomie and deviant behavior: A discussion and critique* (pp. 1–56). New York: Free Press of Glencoe.

Cloward, R. A., & Ohlin, L. E. (1960). *Delinquency and opportunity: A theory of delinquent gangs.* New York: Free Press.

Cohen, A. K. (1955, 1964). *Delinquent boys: The culture of the gang.* Glencoe, IL: Free Press of Glencoe.

Cohen, A. K. (1985). The sociology of the deviant act: Anomie theory and beyond. In S. H. Traub, & C. B. Little (Eds.), *Theories of deviance* (3rd ed., pp. 158–171). Itasca, Ill.: F. E. Peacock Publishers.

Durkheim, E. (1951). *Suicide: A study in sociology* (J. A. Spaulding, G. Simpson Trans.). Glencoe, Ill.: Free Press.

Hirschi, T. (1969). *Causes of delinquency.* Berkeley: University of California Press.

Kornhauser, R. R. (1978). *Social sources of delinquency: An appraisal of analytic models.* Chicago: University of Chicago Press.

Lilly, J. R., Cullen, F. T., & Ball, R. A. (2011). *Criminological theory: Context and consequences* (5th ed.). Thousand Oaks: SAGE Publications.

Merton, R. K. (1938). Social structure and anomie. *American Sociological Review, 3*(5), 672–682.

Merton, R. K. (1985). Social structure and anomie. In S. H. Traub, & C. B. Little (Eds.), *Theories of deviance* (3rd ed., pp. 107–138). Itasca, Ill.: F. E. Peacock Publishers.

Messner, S. F., & Rosenfeld, R. (2007). *Crime and the American dream* (Fourth Edition). Belmont, CA: Thomson Wadsworth.

Passas, N. (2003). Anomie, reference groups, and relative deprivation. In C. M. Renzetti, D. J. Curran & P. J. Carr (Eds.), *Theories of crime: A reader* (pp. 97–113). Boston: Allyn and Bacon.

Vold, G. B., second edition prepared by Thomas J. Bernard. (1979). *Theoretical criminology* (2nd ed.). New York: Oxford University Press.

Williams, F. P., & McShane, M. D. (2010). *Criminological theory* (5th ed.). Upper Saddle River, N.J.: Pearson/Prentice Hall.

Zeitlin, I. M. (2001). *Ideology and the development of sociological theory* (7th ed.). Upper Saddle River, N.J.: Prentice Hall.

1

The Normal and the Pathological

Émile Durkheim was undoubtedly one of the most famous sociologists of all time. He was the founder of academic sociology in France, and the founder of the *L'Année Sociologique* (the French equivalent of the *American Journal of Sociology*). Apart from his influence in the area of anomie-strain theory, Durkheim's thinking underpins various other theoretical perspectives covered later in this book, including Kai Erikson's (1964) work on the sociology of deviance, Travis Hirschi's (1969) social bond theory, and indirectly, Sampson and Laub's (1990) work on the life course perspective and adult social bonds.

While Durkheim was responsible for introducing the concept of anomie to sociological thinking, he did not mention anything in his writings about a specific relationship between anomie and crime (Passas, 1995:92). Rather, he first talked about "the anomic division of labor" in his 1893 book, *The Division of Labor in Society*. According to Durkheim, one of the "abnormal" forms of the division of labor was the "anomic" form, because there was antagonism between labor (the workers) and capital (the businesses). This in turn caused a breakdown in social solidarity (or social cohesion), and impeded the development of social relationships (Clinard, 1964; Durkheim, 1965). Durkheim observed that under an anomic division of labor, the government institutions were unable to effectively regulate the economy and help to integrate the various occupational specializations. In fact, one of Durkheim's main concerns was with social solidarity, and how effectively it was maintained by the forces of integration (e.g., social bonds, shared values and beliefs, etc.) and the forces of regulation (e.g., formal institutions such as the criminal justice system) that would constrain individual behavior if necessary (Lilly, Cullen, & Ball, 2011:91).

Durkheim also wrote about anomic suicide in his 1897 book, *Suicide*, wherein he offered a sociological explanation of suicide rates. Rather than explaining suicide in terms of mental insanity, Durkheim argued that fluctuations in suicide rates were attributable to dramatic economic changes, like major economic depressions, or times of sudden growth and immense prosperity (Clinard, 1964:4–5; Durkheim, 1951:241–243). Major changes of this nature—going in either direction—caused a breakdown in social restraints, and created uncertainty about what was socially acceptable in terms of individual aspirations and expectations. According to Durkheim, these periods of anomie—times of normlessness, lawlessness, and unregulated (or unrestrained) choice—made individuals more susceptible to committing suicide or engaging in deviant behavior (Clinard, 1964:7; Williams & McShane, 2010:77).

The first selection in this book, "The Normal and the Pathological," is a chapter from Émile Durkheim's 1895 book, *The Rules of Sociological Method*. Durkheim's writing may seem to be a bit daunting, but we should bear in mind that this reading selection was written well over a hundred years ago, when sociology was in its infancy. Also, it is worth remembering that all of Durkheim's works were originally written in French, and were translated into English in the early part of the 20th Century. In this particular reading, Durkheim discusses crime, and considers whether it is a normal social phenomenon, or an abnormal (pathological) phenomenon.

To understand Durkheim's approach to normal and abnormal social phenomena, one must clearly understand Durkheim's view of society and how it functioned. Durkheim regarded society much like a functioning organism, with the whole being greater than—but still dependant upon—its constitutive parts. In a sense, society is similar to an organism, consisting of various different organs (e.g., the brain, the heart, the lungs, the stomach, etc.) which all work together to keep the organism alive and healthy. If one or more of these organs ceases to function properly, then all of the other organs (and thus the entire organism) can be endangered. Evidence of Durkheim's thinking can be found in his use of terminology such as "the social organism," "organic solidarity," "the functions of the division of labor" and "the functions of the central organ" (in this latter instance, administrative law) (Durkheim, 1965).

In "The Normal and the Pathological," Durkheim notes that criminologists generally regard crime as "abnormal" or pathological—as a form of "social morbidity" (1964:65–66). However, he also observes that all societies have some level of crime, and therefore, a certain amount of crime must be normal. From a Durkheimian perspective, if crime is normal, then it must perform a necessary social function. According to Durkheim (1964:67–70), crime contributes to social cohesion by bringing individuals together through their sense of indignation or moral outrage. Crime also helps the community to set its boundaries, because crime delineates what it socially acceptable and what is not (Erikson, 2005:9–12).

In Durkheim's work, we also find a "theory of punishment" (Durkheim, 1964:72). For Durkheim, the function of punishment is to defend the collective conscience—to uphold the shared values, beliefs and traditions of the society (Durkheim, 1965:84; Neyer, 1964:34). When members of the society observe a criminal being punished, they also receive confirmation that this type of behavior is "abnormal," and that it is contrary to social convention. Thus, both crime and punishment serve to maintain social cohesion and generate community standards or norms.

The intellectual roots of all of the readings in Section I of this book can be traced back to Émile Durkheim. We will be returning to Durkheimian thinking in Sections IV and V of this book. Therefore, it is important from the outset to acquire a solid understanding of Durkheim's notions of anomie, social bonds, social solidarity, the collective conscience and the forces of integration and regulation.

References

Clinard, M. B. (1964). The theoretical implications of anomie and deviant behavior. In M. B. Clinard (Ed.), *Anomie and deviant behavior: A discussion and critique* (pp. 1–56). New York: Free Press of Glencoe.

Durkheim, É. (1951). *Suicide: A study in sociology* (J. A. Spaulding, G. Simpson Trans.). Glencoe, Ill.: Free Press.

Durkheim, É. (1964). In Catlin G. E. G. (Ed.), *The rules of sociological method* (J. H. Mueller, S. A. Solovay Trans.). (8th ed.). New York: The Free Press of Glencoe.

Durkheim, É. (1965). *The division of labor in society* (G. Simpson Trans.). New York: Free Press.

Erikson, K. T. (1964). Notes on the sociology of deviance. In H. S. Becker (Ed.), *The other side: Perspectives on deviance* (pp. 9–21). New York: Free Press of Glencoe.

Erikson, K. T. (2005). *Wayward puritans: A study in the sociology of deviance.* Boston: Allyn and Bacon.

Hirschi, T. (1969). *Causes of delinquency.* Berkeley: University of California Press.

Lilly, J. R., Cullen, F. T., & Ball, R. A. (2011). *Criminological theory: Context and consequences* (5th ed.). Thousand Oaks: SAGE Publications.

Neyer, J. (1964). Individualism and socialism in Durkheim. In K. H. Wolff (Ed.), *Essays on sociology and philosophy* (pp. 32–76). New York: Harper.

Passas, N. (1995). Continuities in the anomie tradition. In F. Adler, W. S. Laufer & R. K. Merton (Eds.), *The legacy of anomie theory* (pp. 91–112). New Brunswick, U.S.A.: Transaction Publishers.

Sampson, R. J., & Laub, J. H. (1990). Crime and deviance over the life course: The salience of adult social bonds. *American Sociological Review, 55*(5), 609–627. doi:10.2307/2095859

Williams, F. P., & McShane, M. D. (2010). *Criminological theory* (5th ed.). Upper Saddle River, N.J.: Pearson/Prentice Hall.

The Normal and the Pathological

ÉMILE DURKHEIM

All sociological phenomena (as well as all biological phenomena) can assume different forms in different cases while still conserving their essential characteristics. We can distinguish two kinds of such forms. Some are distributed in the entire range of the species; they are to be found, if not in all individuals, at least in the majority of them. If they are not found to be identical in all the cases in question, but vary in different persons, these variations do occur within narrow limits. There are, of course, exceptional variations besides these; but these are, first, to be found only in the minority of cases; and, secondly, where they do occur, they most often do not persist throughout the life of the individual. They are an exception both in time and in space.[1] Here are, then, two distinct varieties of phenomena to which we ought to assign different terms. We shall call "normal" these social conditions that are the most generally distributed, and the others "morbid" or "pathological." If we designate as "average type" that hypothetical being that is constructed by assembling in the same individual, the most frequent forms, one may say that the normal type merges with the average type, and that every deviation from this standard of health is a morbid phenomenon. It is true that the average type cannot be determined with the same distinctness as an individual type, since its constituent attributes are not absolutely fixed but are likely to vary. But the possibility of its constitution is beyond doubt, since, blending as it does with the generic type, it is the immediate subject matter of science. It is the functions of the average organism that the physiologist studies; and the sociologist does the same. Once we know how to distinguish the various social species one from the other—a problem which will be treated below—it is always possible to find the most general form of a phenomenon in a given species.

It is clear that a condition can be defined as pathological only in relation to a given species. The conditions of health and morbidity cannot be defined in the abstract and absolutely. This rule is not denied in biology; it has never occurred to anyone to assume that what is normal for a mollusk is normal also for a vertebrate. Each species has a health of its own, because it has an average type of its own. Hence, there exists a state of health for the lowest species as well as for the highest. The same principle applies to sociology, although it is often misunderstood here. One should completely abandon the still too widespread habit of judging an institution, a practice or a moral standard as if it were good or bad in and by itself, for all social types indiscriminately.

Reprinted from *The Rules of Sociological Method*, translated by S. A. Solovay and J. A. Mueller (1964), Simon & Schuster, Inc.

Since the point of reference for judging health or morbidity varies with the species, it varies also for a single species, if this species itself changes. Thus, from the purely biological point of view, what is normal for the savage is not always normal for the civilized man, and vice versa.[2] There are, especially, the variations depending on age, which are important because they occur regularly in all species. The health of the aged person is not that of the adult, and, similarly, the health of the latter is not that of the child; the same is true of societies.[3] A social fact can, then, be called normal for a given social species only in relation to a given phase of its development; consequently, to know if it has a right to this appellation, it is not enough to observe the form it takes in the generality of societies belonging to this species; we must also take special care to consider them at the corresponding phase of their evolution.

It may seem that we have simply given a definition of terms, for we have only grouped phenomena according to their resemblances and differences, and given names to the groups thus formed. But, in reality, the concepts thus constituted, while having the great advantage of being recognizable by objective and readily perceptible characteristics, do not differ from the lay conception of health and morbidity. Is not morbidity commonly regarded as an accident which the living organism endures but does not itself ordinarily produce? That is what the ancient philosophers meant when they said that it does not originate from the nature of things—that it is the result of some circumstance in the organism. Such a conception is, surely, a negation of all science; for morbidity is no more miraculous than is health: it is equally grounded in the nature of things. But it is not grounded in their normal nature; it is not inherent in their ordinary constitution or bound up with the conditions of existence upon which they generally depend. Conversely, nobody distinguishes the type of the healthy specimen from the type of the species. One cannot, without contradiction, even conceive of a species which would be incurably diseased in itself and by virtue of its fundamental constitution. The healthy constitutes the norm par excellence and can consequently be in no way abnormal.

Health is also commonly thought of as a state generally preferable to morbidity. But this definition is already implied in the preceding one. There must, indeed, have been some reason by virtue of which the characteristics, which in the aggregate form the normal type, have been able to spread to the entire species. This dissemination is itself a fact in need of explanation, and a cause must therefore be assigned to it. It would be incomprehensible if the most widespread forms of organization would not at the same time be, *at least in their aggregate*, the most advantageous. How could they have maintained themselves under so great a variety of circumstances if they had not enabled the individual better to resist the elements of destruction? On the other hand, the reason for the rarity of the other characteristics is evidently that the average organism possessing them has greater difficulty in surviving. The greater frequency of the former is, thus, a proof of their superiority.[4]

II

This last statement furnishes a means of checking the results of the preceding method.

Since the general distribution of normal phenomena is itself an explainable phenomenon, after it has been definitely established by observation it should be explained. Although it is assumed, of course, that it is not without its cause, science demands that we know exactly what this cause is. The normality of the phenomenon will, indeed, be more certain if it is demonstrated that the external sign, which had at first revealed it, is not purely adventitious but grounded in the nature of things—if, in a word, one can erect this normality of fact into a normality by logical necessity. Furthermore, this demonstration will not always consist in showing that the trait is useful to the organism, although this is most frequently the case; but it can also happen, as we have remarked above, that a situation is normal without being at all useful, simply because it is necessarily implied in the nature of the being. Thus, it would perhaps be desirable if parturition did not occasion such violent disturbances in the female organism, but this is impossible; consequently, the normality of the phenomenon is to be explained by the mere fact that it is bound up with the conditions of existence of the species under consideration, either as a mechanically necessary effect of these conditions or as a means permitting the organisms to adapt themselves.[5]

This proof is not simply useful as a check. It must not be forgotten that, if there is any advantage in distinguishing the normal from the abnormal, it is especially helpful in making our practice more intelligent. To act with full knowledge of the facts, we need to know not only the proper procedure but also the reasons for it. Scientific propositions concerning the normal state will be more immediately applicable to individual cases when accompanied by their reasons, for then we shall be better able to recognize in which cases, and in which direction, they should be modified in their application.

There are circumstances in which this verification is absolutely necessary, since the first method, if used alone, might lead to error. This applies to periods of transition, when the entire species is in process of evolution, without having yet become stabilized in its new form. The only normal type that is valid under such circumstances is the type from the previous condition, and yet it no longer corresponds to the new conditions of existence.

A phenomenon can thus persist throughout the entire range of a species although no longer adapted to the requirements of the situation. It is then normal only in appearance. Its universality is now an illusion, since its persistence, due only to the blind force of habit, can no longer be accepted as an index of a close connection with the general conditions of its collective existence. This difficulty is especially peculiar to sociology. It scarcely exists in biology. Very rarely, indeed, are animal species compelled to take on unforeseen forms. The only normal modifications they undergo are those occurring regularly in each individual, principally under the influence of age. Therefore, the norm is easily established, since it can be observed in a great many cases. The normal state can be known at each moment of the development of the animal and even in periods of crisis, and the same is also true in sociology for societies belonging to the lower cultures. Since many of them have already completed their cycle of development, the law of their normal evolution is (or, at least, can be) established. For the highest and most recent societies this law is by definition unknown, since they have not yet accomplished their entire course. Having no point of reference, the sociologist may then be embarrassed in deciding whether a phenomenon is normal or not.

The procedure just indicated will free him from this difficulty. After having established by observation that a particular fact is general, he will go back to the conditions which determined this generality in the past and will then investigate whether these conditions are still given in the present or if, on the contrary, they have changed. In the first case he may properly designate the phenomenon as normal; and, in the second, refuse it this designation. For example, in order to determine whether the present economic state of Europe, with the absence of organization[6] characterizing it, is normal or not, we shall investigate the causes which brought it about. If these conditions still exist in our present-day society, this situation is normal in spite of the dissent it arouses. But if, on the contrary, it is found to be related to the old social structure which we have elsewhere qualified as segmental[7] and which, after having been the essential framework of societies, progressively disappears, we shall have to conclude that the present situation, however universal, is pathological. By the same method should be settled all controversial questions of this kind, such as those concerning the normality of the decline in religious beliefs or of the development of state powers.[8]

Nevertheless, this method can by no means be substituted for the preceding one, nor even be employed as a first resort. In the first place, it raises questions which we shall treat below and which can be approached only at a rather advanced stage of science, for it implies, on the whole, an almost complete explanation of the phenomena concerned, and assumes that either their causes or their functions have already been determined. Now, it is important, from the very beginning of research, to be able to classify facts as normal and abnormal, save for a few exceptional cases, so that the proper domains can be assigned to physiology and pathology, respectively. Further, it is in relation to the normal type that a fact must be useful or necessary, if it is to be designated as normal itself. Otherwise it could be demonstrated that morbidity is indistinguishable from health, since it is merely an outgrowth of the afflicted organism. In this case, however, it is morbid because it does not maintain its proper relation to the average organism. Similarly, since a remedy is useful to the sick, its application could then be considered as a normal phenomenon. The remedy itself possesses this utility. One can, then, use this further method only after the normal type has been determined by some previous method. Finally and above all, if it is true that all that is normal is useful, without being necessary, it is not true that all that is useful is normal. Certainly the states that have become general in the species are more useful than those that have remained exceptional, but they do not possess the maximum of utility that exists or might possibly be brought about. We have no reason to believe that all possible combinations have been tried out in the course of experience; and, among those conceivable but never realized, there are some that are perhaps much more advantageous than those now known to us. The idea of utility is broader than that of normality; it has to the latter the same relation as the genus to the species. It is impossible to deduce the greater from the less, the genus from the species. But the species, since it is contained in the genus, can be discovered in the latter. That is why, once the generality of the phenomenon has been established, one can, by showing its utility, confirm the results of the first method.[9] We may, therefore, formulate the three following rules:

1. A social fact is normal, in relation to a given social type at a given phase of its development, when it is present in the average society of that species at the corresponding phase of its evolution.
2. One can verify the results of the preceding method by showing that the generality of the phenomenon is bound up with the general conditions of collective life of the social type considered.
3. This verification is necessary when the fact in question occurs in a social species which has not yet reached the full course of its evolution.

III

The custom of resolving these difficult questions with a pat phrase and of deciding hastily, from superficial observations supported by syllogisms, whether a social fact is normal or not prevails to such an extent that our procedure will perhaps be judged needlessly complicated. It seems unnecessary to go to such lengths in order to distinguish between morbidity and health. It is true that we make these distinctions every day, but it remains to be seen whether we make them correctly. The fact that the biologist solves these problems with relative ease obscures in our minds the difficulties they involve. We forget that it is much easier for him than for the sociologist to observe how the resistance of the organism is affected by each phenomenon and to determine thereby its normal or abnormal character with sufficient exactness for practical purposes. In sociology the greater complexity and inconstancy of the facts oblige us to take many more precautions, and this is all too evident in the contradictory judgments on the same phenomenon given by different scholars. In order to show clearly the great necessity for circumspection, we shall illustrate by a few examples the errors resulting from the opposite attitude and show in how different a light the most essential phenomena appear when treated methodically.

If there is any fact whose pathological character appears incontestable, that fact is crime. All criminologists are agreed on this point. Although they explain this pathology differently, they are unanimous in recognizing it. But let us see if this problem does not demand a more extended consideration.

We shall apply the foregoing rules. Crime is present not only in the majority of societies of one particular species but in all societies of all types. There is no society that is not confronted with the problem of criminality. Its form changes; the acts thus characterized are not the same everywhere; but, everywhere and always, there have been men who have behaved in such a way as to draw upon themselves penal repression. If, in proportion as societies pass from the lower to the higher types, the rate of criminality, i.e., the relation between the yearly number of crimes and the population, tended to decline, it might be believed that crime, while still normal, is tending to lose this character of normality. But we have no reason to believe that such a regression is substantiated. Many facts would seem rather to indicate a movement in the opposite direction. From the beginning of the [nineteenth] century, statistics enable us to follow the course of criminality. It has everywhere increased. In France the increase is nearly 300 percent. There is, then, no phenomenon that presents more indisputably all the symptoms of normality, since it appears closely connected with the conditions of all collective life. To make of crime a form of social morbidity would be to admit that morbidity is not something accidental, but, on the contrary, that in certain cases it grows out of the fundamental constitution of the living organism; it would result in wiping out all distinction between the physiological and the pathological. No doubt it is possible that crime itself will have abnormal forms, as, for example, when its rate is unusually high. This excess is, indeed, undoubtedly morbid in nature. What is normal, simply, is the existence of criminality, provided that it attains and does not exceed, for each social type, a certain level, which it is perhaps not impossible to fix in conformity with the preceding rules.[10]

Here we are, then, in the presence of a conclusion in appearance quite paradoxical. Let us make no mistake. To classify crime among the phenomena of normal sociology is not to say merely that it is an inevitable, although regrettable phenomenon, due to the incorrigible wickedness of men; it is to affirm that it is a factor in public health, an integral part of all healthy societies. This result is, at first glance, surprising enough to have puzzled even ourselves for a long time. Once this first surprise has been overcome, however, it is not difficult to find reasons explaining this normality and at the same time confirming it.

In the first place crime is normal because a society exempt from it is utterly impossible. Crime, we have shown elsewhere, consists of an act that offends certain very strong collective sentiments. In a society in which criminal acts are no longer committed, the sentiments they offend would have to be found without exception in all individual consciousnesses, and they must be found to exist with the same degree as sentiments contrary to them. Assuming that this condition could actually be realized, crime would not thereby disappear; it would only change its form, for the very cause which would thus dry up the sources of criminality would immediately open up new ones.

Indeed, for the collective sentiments which are protected by the penal law of a people at a specified moment of its history to take possession of the public conscience or for them to acquire a stronger hold where they have an insufficient grip, they must acquire an intensity greater than that which they had hitherto had. The community as a whole must experience them more vividly, for it can acquire from no other source the greater force necessary to control these individuals who formerly were the most refractory. For murderers to disappear, the horror of bloodshed must become greater in those social strata from which murderers are recruited; but, first it must become greater throughout the entire society. Moreover, the very absence of crime would directly contribute to produce this horror; because any sentiment seems much more respectable when it is always and uniformly respected.

One easily overlooks the consideration that these strong states of the common consciousness cannot be thus reinforced without reinforcing at the same time the more feeble states, whose violation previously gave birth to mere infraction of convention—since the weaker ones are only the prolongation, the attenuated form, of the stronger. Thus robbery and simple bad taste injure the same single altruistic sentiment, the respect for that which is another's. However, this same sentiment is less grievously offended by bad taste than by robbery; and since, in addition, the average consciousness has not sufficient intensity to react keenly to the bad taste, it is treated with greater tolerance. That is why the person guilty of bad taste is merely blamed, whereas the thief is punished. But, if this sentiment grows stronger, to the point of silencing in all consciousnesses the inclination which disposes man to steal, he will become more sensitive to the offenses which, until then, touched him but lightly. He will react against them, then, with more energy; they will be the object of greater opprobrium, which will transform certain of them from the simple moral faults that they were and give them the quality of crimes. For example, improper contracts, or contracts improperly executed, which only incur public blame or civil damages, will become offenses in law.

Imagine a society of saints, a perfect cloister of exemplary individuals. Crimes, properly so called, will there be unknown; but faults which appear venial to the layman will create there the same scandal that the ordinary offense does in ordinary consciousnesses. If, then, this society has the power to judge and punish, it will define these acts as criminal and will treat them as such. For the same reason, the perfect and upright man judges his smallest failings with a severity that the majority reserve for acts more truly in the nature of an offense. Formerly, acts of violence against persons were more frequent than they are today, because respect for individual dignity was less strong. As this has increased, these crimes have become more rare; and also, many acts violating this sentiment have been introduced into the penal law which were not included there in primitive times.[11]

In order to exhaust all the hypotheses logically possible, it will perhaps be asked why this unanimity does not extend to all collective sentiments without exception. Why should not even the most feeble sentiment gather enough energy to prevent all dissent? The moral consciousness of the society would be present in its entirety in all the individuals, with a vitality sufficient to prevent all acts offending it—the purely conventional faults as well as the crimes. But a uniformity so universal and absolute is utterly impossible; for the immediate physical milieu in which each one of us is placed, the hereditary antecedents, and the social influences vary from one individual to the next, and consequently diversify consciousnesses. It is impossible for all to be alike, if only because each one has his own organism and that these organisms occupy different areas in space. That is why, even among the lower peoples, where individual originality is very little developed, it nevertheless does exist.

Thus, since there cannot be a society in which the individuals do not differ more or less from the collective type, it is also inevitable that, among these divergences, there are some with a criminal character. What confers this character upon them is not the intrinsic quality of a given act but that definition which the collective conscience lends them. If the collective conscience is stronger, if it has enough authority practically to suppress these divergences, it will also be more sensitive, more exacting; and, reacting against the slightest deviations with the energy it otherwise displays only against more considerable infractions, it will attribute to them the same gravity as formerly to crimes. In other words, it will designate them as criminal.

Crime is, then, necessary; it is bound up with the fundamental conditions of all social life, and by that very fact it is useful, because these conditions of which it is a part are themselves indispensable to the normal evolution of morality and law.

Indeed, it is no longer possible today to dispute the fact that law and morality vary from one social type to the next, nor that they change within the same type if the conditions of life are modified. But, in order that these transformations may be possible, the collective sentiments at the basis of morality must not be hostile to change, and consequently must have but moderate energy. If they were too strong, they would no longer be plastic. Every pattern is an obstacle to new patterns, to the extent that the first pattern is inflexible. The better a structure is articulated, the more it offers a healthy resistance to all modification; and this is equally true of functional, as of anatomical, organization. If there were no crimes, this condition could not have been fulfilled; for such a hypothesis presupposes that collective sentiments have arrived at a degree of intensity unexampled in history. Nothing is good indefinitely and to an unlimited extent. The authority which the moral conscience enjoys must not be excessive; otherwise no one would dare criticize it, and it would too easily congeal into an immutable form. To make progress, individual originality must be able to express itself. In order that the originality of the idealist whose dreams transcend his century may find expression, it is necessary that the originality of the criminal, who is below the level of his time, shall also be possible. One does not occur without the other.

Nor is this all. Aside from this indirect utility, it happens that crime itself plays a useful role in this evolution. Crime implies not only that the way remains open to necessary changes but that in certain cases it directly prepares these changes. Where crime exists, collective sentiments are sufficiently flexible to take on a new form, and crime sometimes helps to determine the form they will take. How many times, indeed, it is only an anticipation of future morality—a step toward what will be! According to Athenian law, Socrates was a criminal, and his condemnation was no more than just. However, his crime, namely, the independence of his thought, rendered a service not only to humanity but to his country. It served to prepare a new morality and faith which the Athenians needed, since the traditions by which they had lived until then were no longer in harmony with the current conditions of life. Nor is the case of Socrates unique; it is reproduced periodically in history. It would never have been possible to establish the freedom of thought we now enjoy if the regulations prohibiting it had not been violated before being solemnly abrogated. At that time, however, the violation was a crime, since it was an offense against sentiments still very keen in the average conscience. And yet this crime was useful as a prelude to reforms which daily became more necessary. Liberal philosophy had as its precursors the heretics of all kinds who were justly punished by secular authorities during the entire course of the Middle Ages and until the eve of modern times.

From this point of view the fundamental facts of criminality present themselves to us in an entirely new light. Contrary to current ideas, the criminal no longer seems a totally unsociable being, a sort of parasitic element, a strange and unassimilable body, introduced into the midst of society.[12] On the contrary, he plays a definite role in social life. Crime, for its part, must no longer be conceived as an evil that cannot be too much suppressed. There is no occasion for self-congratulation when the crime rate drops noticeably below the average level, for we may be certain that this apparent progress is associated with some social disorder. Thus, the number of assault cases never falls so low as in times of want.[13] With the drop in the crime rate, and as a reaction to it, comes a revision, or the need of a revision in the theory of punishment. If, indeed, crime is a disease, its punishment is its remedy and cannot be otherwise conceived; thus, all the discussions it arouses bear on the point of determining what the punishment must be in order to fulfil this role of remedy. If crime is not pathological at all, the object of punishment cannot be to cure it, and its true function must be sought elsewhere.

It is far from the truth, then, that the rules previously stated have no other justification than to satisfy an urge for logical formalism of little practical value, since, on the contrary, according as they are or are not applied, the most essential social facts are entirely changed in character. If the foregoing example is particularly convincing—and this was our hope in dwelling upon it—there are likewise many others which might have been cited with equal profit. There is no society where the rule does not exist that the punishment must be proportional to the offense; yet, for the Italian school, this principle is but an invention of jurists, without adequate basis.[14]

For these criminologists the entire penal system, as it has functioned until the present day among all known peoples, is a phenomenon contrary to nature. We have already seen that, for M. Garofalo, the criminality peculiar to lower societies is not at all natural. For socialists it is the capitalist system, in spite of its wide diffusion, which constitutes a deviation from the normal state, produced, as it was, by violence and fraud. Spencer, on the contrary, maintains that our administrative centralization and the extension of governmental powers are the radical vices of our societies, although both proceed most regularly and generally as we advance in history. We do not believe that scholars have ever systematically endeavored to distinguish the normal or abnormal character of social phenomena from their degree of generality. It is always with a great array of dialectics that these questions are partly resolved.

Once we have eliminated this criterion, however, we are not only exposed to confusions and partial errors, such as those just pointed out, but science is rendered all but impossible. Its immediate object is the study of the normal type. If, however, the most widely diffused facts can be pathological, it is possible that the normal types never existed in actuality; and if that is the case, why study the facts? Such study can only confirm our prejudices and fix us in our errors. If punishment and the responsibility for crime are only the products of ignorance and barbarism, why strive to know them in order to derive the normal forms from them? By such arguments the mind is diverted from a reality in which we have lost interest, and falls back on itself in order to seek within itself the materials necessary to reconstruct its world. In order that sociology may treat facts as things, the sociologist must feel the necessity of studying them exclusively.

The principal object of all sciences of life, whether individual or social, is to define and explain the normal state and to distinguish it from its opposite. If, however, normality is not given in the things themselves—if it is, on the contrary, a character we may or may not impute to them— this solid footing is lost. The mind is then complacent in the face of a reality which has little to teach it; it is no longer restrained by the matter which it is analyzing, since it is the mind, in some manner or other, that determines the matter.

The various principles we have established up to the present are, then, closely interconnected. In order that sociology may be a true science of things, the generality of phenomena must be taken as the criterion of their normality.

Our method has, moreover, the advantage of regulating action at the same time as thought. If the social values are not subjects of observation but can and must be determined by a sort of mental calculus, no limit, so to speak, can be set for the free inventions of the imagination in search of the best. For how may we assign to perfection a limit? It escapes all limitation, by definition. The goal of humanity recedes into infinity, discouraging some by its very remoteness and arousing others who, in order to draw a little nearer to it, quicken the pace and plunge into revolutions. This practical dilemma may be escaped if the desirable is defined in the same way as is health and normality and if health is something that is defined as inherent in things. For then the object of our efforts is both given and defined at the same time. It is no longer a matter of pursuing desperately an objective that retreats as one advances, but of working with steady perseverance to maintain the normal state, of re-establishing it if it is threatened, and of rediscovering its conditions if they have changed. The duty of the statesman is no longer to push society toward an ideal that seems attractive to him, but his role is that of the physician: he prevents the outbreak of illnesses by good hygiene, and he seeks to cure them when they have appeared.[15]

Notes _____

1. Hereby one can distinguish the morbid case from the monstrosity. The second is an exception in space only; it is not met with in the average of the species, but it persists throughout the life of the individual in which it is found. These two orders of facts differ, however, only in degree, and are fundamentally of the same nature; their boundaries are very uncertain, for morbidity is capable of permanence and monstrosity of modification. They can, then, scarcely be rigidly separated in their definitions. The distinction between them cannot be more categorical than that between the morphological and the physiological, since, in short, the morbid is the abnormal in the physiological order as the monstrous is the abnormal in the anatomical order.

2. For example, a savage with the undersized digestive system and the overdeveloped nervous system of the healthy civilized man would be ill in relation to his environment.

3. We cut short this part of our discussion since we can only repeat here, with regard to social facts in general, what we have said elsewhere on the subject of the division of moral facts into normal and abnormal ones. (See *Division du travail social*, pp. 33–39.)

4. M. Garofalo has tried to distinguish between the morbid and the abnormal (*Criminologie*, pp. 109, 110). But he bases this distinction exclusively on the following two arguments: (1) The word "morbidity" always signifies something tending toward the total or partial destruction of the organism; if there is not destruction, there is cure, but never stability, as in some anomalies. But we have just seen that the abnormal is a menace to the living being, on the average. It is true that this is not always the case, but the dangers of morbidity likewise exist only in average cases. And if the absence of stability is taken as the criterion of the morbid, chronic morbidities are overlooked, and the monstrosity is completely separated from the pathological. Monstrosities are fixed. (2) We are told that the normal and the abnormal vary with races, whereas the distinction between the physiological and the pathological holds good for the entire human race. But we have just shown, on the contrary, that often phenomena which are morbid for the savage are not morbid for the civilized man. The conditions of physical health vary with the group.

5. One may well ask whether the necessary derivation of a phenomenon from the general conditions of life does not imply its utility. We cannot treat at length this philosophical question, which will, however, be touched on below.

6. Cf., on this point, the note we published in the *Revue philosophique*, November, 1893, on "La Définition du socialisme."

7. Segmental societies and, more particularly, segmental societies with a territorial basis are those whose essential boundaries correspond to territorial divisions. (See *Division du travail social*, pp. 180–210.)

8. In certain cases, one can proceed in a slightly different way and prove, in the case of a fact whose normality is doubted, the validity or invalidity of this suspicion by showing its close connection with the previous development of the social type under consideration, and even to social evolution in general. Or one can show the opposite, that it contradicts both. In this way we have been able to prove that the present weakening of religious beliefs, and more generally of collective sentiments, is only normal; we have proved that this weakening becomes more and more accentuated as societies approach our present type and as the latter, in its turn, is more highly developed (*ibid.*, pp. 73–182). But, fundamentally, this method is only a particular case of the preceding one. For this demonstration of the normality of the phenomenon in question implies that we relate it to the most general conditions of our collective existence. Indeed, on the one hand, the positive correlation between this regression of religious consciousness and the degree of articulation of the structure of our societies is based not on some accidental cause but on the very constitution of our social milieu. . . Since, on the other hand, the traits characteristic of this constitution are certainly more highly developed today than formerly, it is only normal that the phenomena depending on it be themselves more highly developed. This method differs from the preceding one only in one feature, namely, that the conditions explaining and justifying the generality of the phenomenon are inferred and not directly observed. We know that it is connected with the nature of the social milieu without knowing the nature and mode of this connection.

9.   But it will be said that the determination of the normal type is not the highest objective possible and that, in order to transcend it, science has to be transcended also. We are avowedly not concerned with this question here; let us answer only: (1) that the question is entirely theoretical, for the normal type, the state of health, is difficult enough to determine and rarely enough attained for us to search our imagination in the attempt to find something better; (2) that these improvements of the normal type, although objectively advantageous, are not objectively desirable for that reason, for, if they do not correspond to a latent or actual tendency, they add nothing to happiness, and, if they do, the normal type is not realized; (3) and finally, that in order to improve the normal type, it must be known. One can, then, in any case, only transcend science by first making the best possible use of it.

10.   From the fact that crime is a phenomenon of normal sociology, it does not follow that the criminal is an individual normally constituted from the biological and psychological points of view. The two questions are independent of each other. This independence will be better understood when we have shown, later on, the difference between psychological and sociological facts.

11.   Calumny, insults, slander, fraud, etc.

12.   We have ourselves committed the error of speaking thus of the criminal, because of a failure to apply our rule (*Division du travail social*, pp. 395–96).

13.   Although crime is a fact of normal sociology, it does not follow that we must not abhor it. Pain itself has nothing desirable about it; the individual dislikes it as society does crime, and yet it is a function of normal physiology. Not only is it necessarily derived from the very constitution of every living organism, but it plays a useful role in life, for which reason it cannot be replaced. It would, then, be a singular distortion of our thought to present it as an apology for crime. We would not even think of protesting against such an interpretation, did we not know to what strange accusations and misunderstandings one exposes oneself when one undertakes to study moral facts objectively and to speak of them in a different language from that of the layman.

14.   See Garofalo, *Criminologie*, p. 299.

15.   From the theory developed in this chapter, the conclusion has at times been reached that, according to us, the increase of criminality in the course of the nineteenth century was a normal phenomenon. Nothing is farther from our thought. Several facts indicated by us apropos of suicide (see *Suicide*, pp. 420 ff.) tend, on the contrary, to make us believe that this development is in general morbid. Nevertheless, it might happen that a certain increase of certain forms of criminality would be normal, for each state of civilization has its own criminality. But on this, one can only formulate hypotheses.

2

Social Structure and Anomie

Robert Merton was a Professor of Sociology at Columbia University, and at one time was the President of the American Sociological Association (Lemert, 1993:328; Lilly, Cullen, & Ball, 2011:67). Merton is perhaps best known for taking Durkheim's concept of anomie and using it to explain the high rates of deviancy or non-conformity in America. As noted in the Introduction to Part I of this book, Merton's 1938 article, "Social Structure and Anomie," is still amongst the most frequently cited works in sociology and criminology.

Like Durkheim, Merton could best be described as a structural functionalist (Hinkle, 1964:288; Williams & McShane, 2010:78). This can be seen in his well known (1993) work on "manifest and latent functions," and in his reference to "the malfunctioning of the social structure" in the selected reading, "Social Structure and Anomie" (1938:672). Another common (and very Durkheimian) theme running throughout Merton's article on "Social Structure and Anomie" is the importance of institutional regulation, and the role that social institutions are supposed to play in the integration of cultural goals and institutional means. Unlike Durkheim, however, Merton used the notion of anomie to describe a situation in which the social structure exerted pressure on certain individuals to engage in deviant (rather than conforming) behaviour (Clinard, 1964:10). Because Merton also identified what he considered to be the specific sources of pressure (or strain), his theory came to be known as "strain theory" (Lilly et al., 2011:65).

In "Social Structure and Anomie," Merton (1938:673–674) said that deviant or non-conforming behaviour was caused by a disjunction (or strain) between the "cultural goals and institutional means." According to Merton, American culture placed a strong emphasis on success symbols such as the accumulation of wealth (consumerism and acquisition) and social advancement (getting a more prestigious job and/or climbing the social ladder). At the same time, however, the "malfunctioning" social structure failed to provide many individuals with the conventional means necessary to realize those cultural goals. In other words, not everybody had access to money, power, or a prestigious, high paying job (Merton, 1938:678–679).

In his article, Merton (1938:676–677) described five different ways in which individuals could adapt to this condition of anomie-strain—conformity, innovation, ritualism, retreatism and rebellion:

- *Conformity* was by far and away the most common mode of adaptation. Conformists would try to get a decent education, find a job, work hard to get promoted, and save money to buy things that they wanted. In other words, they would play the game by the rules.
- *Innovation*—i.e., finding an unconventional or non-conforming way in which to achieve the cultural goals—was the mode that Merton thought was most likely to lead to deviance (and criminality). For example, an innovator might very well subscribe to the cultural goals, and believe that he or she did indeed deserve to own a new car, but realizing that they could never afford to buy one, would choose instead to go out and steal one.
- *Ritualism*, the third mode of adaptation, referred to individuals who had essentially given up hope of becoming wealthy or achieving social advancement, but who nevertheless scaled down their aspirations, conformed to the rules, avoided risks, and focused almost exclusively on their day-to-day routines. An example would be somebody who was just going through the motions (as an end unto themselves), without expecting to get anywhere as a result.
- *Retreatism*, the fourth mode of adaptation, referred to individuals (e.g., drug addicts, alcoholics, or street people) who dropped out of society because they had no reason to believe that they could attain the cultural goals, and saw no point in playing the game by the rules (i.e., by conforming to societal conventions).
- *Rebellion*, the fifth and final mode of adaptation, applied to those who rejected both the cultural goals and institutional means, and attempted to replace the rejected goals and institutions with new ones. According to Merton, rebels would attempt to change the established social order, or even try to overthrow the existing government (cf. Lilly et al., 2011:64–65; Williams & McShane, 2010:80–81). Terrorists who blow up airplanes or subways in an effort to achieve political change would be classified under this fifth mode of adaptation.

As we shall see in the last two readings in Section I, Merton's work on social structure and anomie had a profound influence on the thinking of Robert Agnew and Steven Messner and Richard Rosenfeld. With his "general strain theory" Agnew (1985) extended Merton's concept of strain, demonstrating how it could be applied to other types of strain (apart from the strain induced by inability to accumulate wealth or achieve social advancement). With their institutional-anomie theory, Messner and Rosenfeld (1995) returned to Merton's concern with the failure of social institutions to successfully integrate cultural goals and institutional means, and their inability to regulate the behavior of individuals (not to mention the behavior of the institutions themselves). All of these advancements can of course be traced back to Émile Durkheim, who talked about the forces of integration and the forces of regulation, and about the condition of anomie (lawlessness, normlessness, unregulated choice) that would develop when social solidarity broke down.

References

Agnew, R. (1985). A revised strain theory of delinquency. *Social Forces, 64*(1), 151–167.

Clinard, M. B. (1964). The theoretical implications of anomie and deviant behavior. In M. B. Clinard (Ed.), *Anomie and deviant behavior: A discussion and critique* (pp. 1–56). New York: Free Press of Glencoe.

Hinkle, R. C. (1964). Durkheim in American sociology. In K. H. Wolff (Ed.), *Essays on sociology and philosophy* (pp. 267–295). New York: Harper.

Lemert, C. C. (1993). *Social theory: The multicultural and classic readings*. Boulder, Colo.: Westview Press.

Lilly, J. R., Cullen, F. T., & Ball, R. A. (2011). *Criminological theory: Context and consequences* (5th ed.). Thousand Oaks: SAGE Publications.

Merton, R. K. (1938). Social structure and anomie. *American Sociological Review, 3*(5), 672–682.

Merton, R. K. (1993). Manifest and latent functions. In C. C. Lemert (Ed.), *Social theory: The multicultural and classic readings* (pp. 328–334). Boulder, Colo.: Westview Press.

Rosenfeld, R., & Messner, S. F. (1995). Crime and the American dream: An institutional analysis. In F. Adler, W. S. Laufer & R. K. Merton (Eds.), *The legacy of anomie theory* (pp. 159–181). New Brunswick, U.S.A.: Transaction Publishers.

Williams, F. P., & McShane, M. D. (2010). *Criminological theory* (5th ed.). Upper Saddle River, N.J.: Pearson/Prentice Hall.

Social Structure and Anomie

ROBERT K. MERTON

There persists a notable tendency in sociological theory to attribute the malfunctioning of social structure primarily to those of man's imperious biological drives which are not adequately restrained by social control. In this view, the social order is solely a device for "impulse management" and the "social processing" of tensions. These impulses which break through social control, be it noted, are held to be biologically derived. Nonconformity is assumed to be rooted in original nature.[1] Conformity is by implication the result of an utilitarian calculus or unreasoned conditioning. This point of view, whatever its other deficiencies, clearly begs one question. It provides no basis for determining the nonbiological conditions which induce deviations from prescribed patterns of conduct. In this paper, it will be suggested that

Reprinted by permission from *American Sociological Review* 3, no. 5 (1938).

certain phases of social structure generate the circumstances in which infringement of social codes constitutes a "normal" response.[2]

The conceptual scheme to be outlined is designed to provide a coherent, systematic approach to the study of socio-cultural sources of deviate behavior. Our primary aim lies in discovering how some social structures *exert a definite pressure* upon certain persons in the society to engage in nonconformist rather than conformist conduct. The many ramifications of the scheme cannot all be discussed; the problems mentioned outnumber those explicitly treated.

Among the elements of social and cultural structure, two are important for our purposes. These are analytically separable although they merge imperceptibly in concrete situations. The first consists of culturally defined goals, purposes, and interests. It comprises a frame of aspirational reference. These goals are more or less integrated and involve varying degrees of prestige and sentiment. They constitute a basic, but not the exclusive, component of what Linton aptly has called "designs for group living." Some of these cultural aspirations are related to the original drives of man, but they are not determined by them. The second phase of the social structure defines, regulates, and controls the acceptable modes of achieving these goals. Every social group invariably couples its scale of desired ends with moral or institutional regulation of permissible and required procedures for attaining these ends. These regulatory norms and moral imperatives do not necessarily coincide with technical or efficiency norms. Many procedures which from the standpoint of *particular individuals* would be most efficient in securing desired values, e.g., illicit oil-stock schemes, theft, fraud, are ruled out of the institutional area of permitted conduct. The choice of expedients is limited by the institutional norms.

To say that these two elements, culture goals and institutional norms, operate jointly is not to say that the ranges of alternative behaviors and aims bear some constant relation to one another. The emphasis upon certain goals may vary independently of the degree of emphasis upon institutional means. There may develop a disproportionate, at times, a virtually exclusive, stress upon the value of specific goals, involving relatively slight concern with the institutionally appropriate modes of attaining these goals. The limiting case in this direction is reached when the range of alternative procedures is limited only by technical rather than institutional considerations. Any and all devices which promise attainment of the all important goal would be permitted in this hypothetical polar case.[3] This constitutes one type of cultural malintegration. A second polar type is found in groups where activities originally conceived as instrumental are transmuted into ends in themselves. The original purposes are forgotten and ritualistic adherence to institutionally prescribed conduct becomes virtually obsessive.[4] Stability is largely ensured while change is flouted. The range of alternative behaviors is severely limited. There develops a tradition-bound, sacred society characterized by neophobia. The occupational psychosis of the bureaucrat may be cited as a case in point. Finally, there are the intermediate types of groups where a balance between culture goals and institutional means is maintained. These are the significantly integrated and relatively stable, though changing, groups.

An effective equilibrium between the two phases of the social structure is maintained as long as satisfactions accrue to individuals who conform to both constraints, viz., satisfactions from the achievement of the goals and satisfactions emerging directly from the institutionally canalized modes of striving to attain these ends. Success, in such equilibrated cases, is twofold. Success is reckoned in terms of the product and in terms of the process, in terms of the outcome and in terms of activities. Continuing satisfactions must derive from sheer *participation* in a competitive order as well as from eclipsing one's competitors if the order itself is to be sustained. The occasional sacrifices involved in institutionalized conduct must be compensated by socialized rewards. The distribution of statuses and roles through competition must be so organized that positive incentives for conformity to roles and adherence to status obligations are provided *for every position* within the distributive order. Aberrant conduct, therefore, may be viewed as a symptom of dissociation between culturally defined aspirations and socially structured means.

Of the types of groups which result from the independent variation of the two phases of the social structure, we shall be primarily concerned with the first, namely, that involving a disproportionate accent on goals. This statement must be recast in a proper perspective. In no group is there an absence of regulatory codes governing conduct, yet groups do vary in the degree to which these folkways, mores, and institutional controls are effectively integrated with the more diffuse goals which are part of the culture matrix. Emotional convictions may cluster about the complex of socially acclaimed ends, meanwhile shifting their support from the culturally defined implementation of these ends. As we shall see, certain aspects of the social structure may generate countermores and antisocial behavior precisely because of differential emphases on goals and regulations. In the extreme case, the latter may be so vitiated by the goal-emphasis that the range of behavior is limited only by considerations of technical expediency. The sole significant question then becomes, which available means is most efficient in netting the socially approved value?[5] The technically most feasible procedure, whether legitimate or not, is preferred to the institutionally prescribed conduct. As this process continues, the integration of the society becomes tenuous and anomie ensues.

Thus, in competitive athletics, when the aim of victory is shorn of its institutional trappings and success in contests becomes construed as "winning the game" rather than "winning through circumscribed modes of activity," a premium is implicitly set upon the use of illegitimate but technically efficient means. The star of the opposing football team is surreptitiously slugged; the wrestler furtively incapacitates his opponent through ingenious but illicit techniques; university alumni covertly subsidize "students" whose talents are largely confined to the athletic field. The emphasis on the goal has so attenuated the satisfactions deriving from sheer participation in the competitive activity that these satisfactions are virtually confined to a successful outcome. Through the same process, tension generated by the desire to win in a poker game is relieved by successfully dealing oneself four aces, or, when the cult of success has become completely dominant, by sagaciously shuffling the cards in a game of solitaire. The faint twinge of uneasiness in the last instance and the surreptitious nature of public delicts indicate clearly that the institutional rules of the game *are known* to those who evade them, but that the emotional supports of these rules are largely vitiated by cultural exaggeration of the success-goal.[6] They are microcosmic images of the social macrocosm.

Of course, this process is not restricted to the realm of sport. The process whereby exaltation of the end generates a *literal demoralization*, i.e., a deinstitutionalization, of the means is one which characterizes many[7] groups in which the two phases of the social structure are not highly integrated. The extreme emphasis upon the accumulation of wealth as a symbol of success[8] in our own society militates against the completely effective control of institutionally regulated modes of acquiring a fortune.[9] Fraud, corruption, vice, crime, in short, the entire catalogue of proscribed behavior, becomes increasingly common when the emphasis on the *culturally induced* success-goal becomes divorced from a coordinated institutional emphasis. This observation is of crucial theoretical importance in examining the doctrine that antisocial behavior most frequently derives from biological drives breaking through the restraints imposed by society. The difference is one between a strictly utilitarian interpretation which conceives man's ends as random and an analysis which finds these ends deriving from the basic values of the culture.[10]

Our analysis can scarcely stop at this juncture. We must turn to other aspects of the social structure if we are to deal with the social genesis of the varying rates and types of deviate behavior characteristic of different societies. Thus far, we have sketched three ideal types of social orders constituted by distinctive patterns of relations between culture ends and means. Turning from these types of *culture patterning*, we find five logically possible, alternative modes of adjustment or adaptation *by individuals* within the culture-bearing society or group.[11] These are schematically presented in the following table, where (+) signifies "acceptance," (−) signifies "elimination" and (±) signifies "rejection and substitution of new goals and standards."

	Culture Goals	Institutionalized Means
I. Conformity	+	+
II. Innovation	+	−
III. Ritualism	−	+
IV. Retreatism	−	−
V. Rebellion[12]	±	±

Our discussion of the relation between these alternative responses and other phases of the social structure must be prefaced by the observation that persons may shift from one alternative to another as they engage in different social activities. These categories refer to role adjustments in specific situations, not to personality *in toto*. To treat the development of this process in various spheres of conduct would introduce a complexity unmanageable within the confines of this paper. For this reason, we shall be concerned primarily with economic activity in the broad sense, "the production, exchange, distribution and consumption of goods and services" in our competitive society, wherein wealth has taken on a highly symbolic cast. Our task is to search out some of the factors which exert pressure upon individuals to engage in certain of these logically possible alternative responses. This choice, as we shall see, is far from random.

In every society, Adaptation I (conformity to both culture goals and means) is the most common and widely diffused. Were this not so, the stability and continuity of the society could not be maintained. The mesh of expectancies which constitutes every social order is sustained by the modal behavior of its members falling within the first category. Conventional role behavior oriented toward the basic values of the group is the rule rather than the exception. It is this fact alone which permits us to speak of a human aggregate as comprising a group or society.

Conversely, Adaptation IV (rejection of goals and means) is the least common. Persons who "adjust" (or maladjust) in this fashion are, strictly speaking, *in* the society but not *of* it. Sociologically, these constitute the true "aliens." Not sharing the common frame of orientation, they can be included within the societal population merely in a fictional sense. In this category are *some* of the activities of psychotics, psychoneurotics, chronic autists, pariahs, outcasts, vagrants, vagabonds, tramps, chronic drunkards and drug addicts.[13] These have relinquished, in certain spheres of activity, the culturally defined goals, involving complete aim-inhibition in the polar case, and their adjustments are not in accord with institutional norms. This is not to say that in some cases the source of their behavioral adjustments is not in part the very social structure which they have in effect repudiated nor that their very existence within a social area does not constitute a problem for the socialized population.

This mode of "adjustment" occurs, as far as structural sources are concerned, when both the culture goals and institutionalized procedures have been assimilated thoroughly by the individual and imbued with affect and high positive value, but where those institutionalized procedures which promise a measure of successful attainment of the goals are not available to the individual. In such instances, there results a twofold mental conflict insofar as the moral obligation for adopting institutional means conflicts with the pressure to resort to illegitimate means (which may attain the goal) and inasmuch as the individual is shut off from means which are both legitimate *and* effective. The competitive order is maintained, but the frustrated and handicapped individual who cannot cope with this order drops out. Defeatism, quietism and resignation are manifested in escape mechanisms which ultimately lead the individual to "escape" from the requirements of the society. It is an expedient which arises from continued failure to attain the goal by legitimate measures and from an inability to adopt the illegitimate route because of internalized prohibitions and institutionalized compulsives, *during which process the supreme value of the success-goal has as yet not been renounced.* The conflict is resolved by eliminating *both* precipitating elements, the goals and means. The escape is complete, the conflict is eliminated and the individual is socialized.

Be it noted that where frustration derives from the inaccessibility of effective institutional means for attaining economic or any other type of highly valued "success," that Adaptations II, III and V (innovation, ritualism and rebellion) are also possible. The result will be determined by the particular personality, and thus, the *particular* cultural background, involved. Inadequate socialization will result in the innovation response whereby the conflict and frustration are eliminated by relinquishing the institutional means and retaining the success-aspiration; an extreme assimilation of institutional demands will lead to ritualism wherein the goal is dropped as beyond one's reach but conformity to the mores persists; and rebellion occurs when emancipation from the reigning standards, due to frustration or to marginalist perspectives, leads to the attempt to introduce a "new social order."

Our major concern is with the illegitimacy adjustment. This involves the use of conventionally proscribed but frequently effective means of attaining at least the simulacrum of culturally defined success—wealth, power, and the like. As we have seen, this adjustment occurs when the individual has assimilated the cultural emphasis on success without equally internalizing the morally prescribed norms governing means for its attainment. The question arises, Which phases of our social structure predispose toward this mode of adjustment? We may examine a concrete instance, effectively analyzed by Lohman,[14] which provides a clue to the answer. Lohman has shown that specialized areas of vice in the near north side of Chicago constitute a "normal" response to a situation where the cultural emphasis upon pecuniary success has been absorbed, but where there is little access to conventional and legitimate means for attaining such success. The conventional occupational opportunities of persons in this area are almost completely limited to manual labor. Given our cultural stigmatization of manual labor, and its correlate, the prestige of white collar work, it is clear that the result is a strain toward innovational practices. The limitation of opportunity to unskilled labor and the resultant low income can not compete *in terms of conventional standards of achievement* with the high income from organized vice.

For our purposes, this situation involves two important features. First, such antisocial behavior is in a sense "called forth" by certain conventional values of the culture *and* by the class structure involving differential access to the approved opportunities for legitimate, prestige-bearing pursuit of the culture goals. The lack of high integration between the means-and-end elements of the cultural pattern and the particular class structure combine to favor a heightened frequency of antisocial conduct in such groups. The second consideration is of equal significance. Recourse to the first of the alternative responses, legitimate effort, is limited by the fact that actual advance toward desired success-symbols through conventional channels is, despite our persisting open-class ideology,[15] relatively rare and difficult for those handicapped by little formal education and few economic resources. The dominant pressure of group standards of success is, therefore, on the gradual attenuation of legitimate, but by and large ineffective, strivings and the increasing use of illegitimate, but more or less effective, expedients of vice and crime. The cultural demands made on persons in this situation are incompatible. On the one hand, they are asked to orient their conduct toward the prospect of accumulating wealth and on the other, they are largely denied effective opportunities to do so institutionally. The consequences of such structural inconsistency are psychopathological personality, and/or antisocial conduct, and/or revolutionary activities. The equilibrium between culturally designated means and ends becomes highly unstable with the progressive emphasis on attaining the prestige-laden ends by any means whatsoever. Within this context, Capone represents the triumph of amoral intelligence over morally prescribed "failure," when the channels of vertical mobility are closed or narrowed[16] *in a society which places a high premium on economic affluence and social ascent for* all *its members.*[17]

This last qualification is of primary importance. It suggests that other phases of the social structure besides the extreme emphasis on pecuniary success, must be considered if we are to understand the social sources of antisocial behavior. A high frequency of deviate behavior is not generated simply by "lack of opportunity" or by this exaggerated pecuniary emphasis. A comparatively rigidified class structure, a feudalistic or caste order, may limit such opportunities far beyond the point which obtains in our society today. It is only when a system of cultural values extols, virtually above all else, certain *common* symbols of success *for the population at large* while its social structure rigorously restricts or completely eliminates access to approved modes of acquiring these symbols *for a considerable part of the same population*, that antisocial behavior ensues on a considerable scale. In other words, our egalitarian ideology denies by implication the existence of noncompeting groups and individuals in the pursuit of pecuniary success. The same body of success-symbols is held to be desirable for all. These goals are held to *transcend class lines*, not to be bounded by them, yet the actual social organization is such that there exist class differentials in the accessibility of these *common* success-symbols. Frustration and thwarted aspiration lead to the search for avenues of escape from a culturally induced intolerable situation; or unrelieved ambition may eventuate in illicit attempts to acquire the dominant values.[18] The American stress on pecuniary success and ambitiousness for all thus invites exaggerated anxieties, hostilities, neuroses and antisocial behavior.

This theoretical analysis may go far toward explaining the varying correlations between crime and poverty.[19] Poverty is not an isolated variable. It is one in a complex of interdependent social and cultural variables. When viewed in such a context, it represents quite different states of affairs. Poverty as such, and consequent limitation of opportunity, are not sufficient to induce a conspicuously high rate of criminal behavior. Even the often mentioned "poverty in the midst of plenty" will not necessarily lead to this result. Only insofar as poverty and associated disadvantages in competition for the culture values approved for *all* members of the society is linked with the assimilation of a cultural emphasis on monetary accumulation as a symbol of success is antisocial conduct a "normal" outcome. Thus, poverty is less highly correlated with crime in southeastern Europe than in the United States. The possibilities of vertical mobility in these European areas would seem to be fewer than in this country, so that neither poverty *per se* nor its association with limited opportunity is sufficient to account for the varying correlations. It is only when the full configuration is considered, poverty, limited opportunity and a commonly shared system of success symbols, that we can explain the higher association between poverty and crime in our society than in others where rigidified class structure is coupled with *differential class symbols of achievement.*

In societies such as our own, then, the pressure of prestige-bearing success tends to eliminate the effective social constraint over means employed to this end. "The-end-justifies-the-means" doctrine becomes a guiding tenet for action when the cultural structure unduly exalts the end and the social organization unduly limits possible recourse to approved means. Otherwise put, this notion and associated behavior reflect a lack of cultural coordination. In international relations, the effects of this lack of integration are notoriously apparent. An emphasis upon national power is not readily coordinated with an inept organization of legitimate, i.e., internationally defined and accepted, means for attaining this goal. The result is a tendency toward the abrogation of international law, treaties become scraps of paper, "undeclared warfare" serves as a technical evasion, the bombing of civilian populations is rationalized,[20] just as the same societal situation induces the same sway of illegitimacy among individuals.

The social order we have described necessarily produces this "strain toward dissolution." The pressure of such an order is upon outdoing one's competitors. The choice of means within the ambit of institutional control will persist as long as the sentiments supporting a competitive system, i.e., deriving from the possibility of outranking competitors and hence enjoying the favorable response of others, are distributed throughout the entire system of activities and are not confined merely to the final result. A stable social structure demands a balanced distribution of affect among its various segments. When there occurs a shift of emphasis from the satisfactions deriving from competition itself to almost exclusive concern with successful competition, the resultant stress leads to the breakdown of the regulatory structure.[21] With the resulting attenuation of the institutional imperatives, there occurs an approximation of the situation erroneously held by utilitarians to be typical of society generally wherein calculations of advantage and fear of punishment are the sole regulating agencies. In such situations, as Hobbes observed, force and fraud come to constitute the sole virtues in view of their relative efficiency in attaining goals, which were for him, of course, not culturally derived.

It should be apparent that the foregoing discussion is not pitched on a moralistic plane. Whatever the sentiments of the writer or reader concerning the ethical desirability of coordinating the means-and-goals phases of the social structure, one must agree that lack of such coordination leads to anomie. Insofar as one of the most general functions of social organization is to provide a basis for calculability and regularity of behavior, it is increasingly limited in effectiveness as these elements of the structure become dissociated. At the extreme, predictability virtually disappears and what may be properly termed cultural chaos or anomie intervenes.

This statement, being brief, is also incomplete. It has not included an exhaustive treatment of the various structural elements which predispose toward one rather than another of the alternative responses open to individuals; it has neglected, but not denied the relevance of, the factors determining the specific incidence of these responses; it has not enumerated the various concrete responses which are constituted by combinations of specific values of the analytical variables; it has omitted, or included only by implication, any consideration of the social functions performed by illicit responses; it has not tested the full explanatory power of the analytical scheme by examining a large number of group variations in the frequency of deviate and conformist behavior; it has not adequately dealt with rebellious conduct which seeks to refashion the social framework radically; it has not examined the relevance of cultural conflict for an analysis of culture-goal and institutional-means malintegration. It is suggested that these and related problems may be profitably analyzed by this scheme.

Notes

1. E.g., Ernest Jones, *Social Aspects of Psychoanalysis*, 28, London, 1924. If the Freudian notion is a variety of the "original sin" dogma, then the interpretation advanced in this paper may be called the doctrine of "socially derived sin."

2. "Normal" in the sense of a culturally oriented, if not approved, response. This statement does not deny the relevance of biological and personality differences which may be significantly involved in the *incidence* of deviate conduct. Our focus of interest is the social and cultural matrix; hence we abstract from other factors. It is in this sense, I take it, that James S. Plant speaks of the "normal reaction of normal people to abnormal conditions." See his *Personality and the Cultural Pattern*, 248, New York, 1937.

3. Contemporary American culture has been said to tend in this direction. See André Siegfried, *America Comes of Age*, 26–37, New York, 1927. The alleged extreme(?) emphasis on the goals of monetary success and material prosperity leads to dominant concern with technological and social instruments designed to produce the desired result, inasmuch as institutional controls become of secondary importance. In such a situation, innovation flourishes as the *range of means* employed is broadened. In a sense, then, there occurs the paradoxical emergence of "materialists" from an "idealistic" orientation. Cf. Durkheim's analysis of the cultural conditions which predispose toward crime and innovation, both of which are aimed toward efficiency, not moral norms. Durkheim was one of the first to see that "contrairement aux idées courantes le criminel n'apparait plus comme un être radicalement insociable, comme une sorte d'elément parasitaire, de corps étranger et inassimilable, introduit au sein de la société; c'est un agent régulier de la vie sociale." See *Les Règles de la Méthode Sociologique*, 86–89, Paris, 1927.

4. Such ritualism may be associated with a mythology which rationalizes these actions so that they appear to retain their status as means, but the dominant pressure is in the direction of strict ritualistic conformity, irrespective of such rationalizations. In this sense, ritual has proceeded farthest when such rationalizations are not even called forth.

5. In this connection, one may see the relevance of Elton Mayo's paraphrase of the title of Tawney's well known book. "Actually the problem *is not that of the sickness of an acquisitive society; it is that of the acquisitiveness of a sick society." Human Problems of an Industrial Civilization*, 153, New York, 1933. Mayo deals with the process through which wealth comes to be a symbol of social achievement. He sees this as arising from a state of anomie. We are considering the unintegrated monetary-success goal as an element in producing anomie. A complete analysis would involve both phases of this system of interdependent variables.

6. It is unlikely that interiorized norms are completely eliminated. Whatever residuum persists will induce personality tensions and conflict. The process involves a certain degree of ambivalence. A manifest rejection of the institutional norms is coupled with some latent retention of their emotional correlates. "Guilt feelings," "sense of sin," "pangs of conscience" are obvious manifestations of this unrelieved tension; symbolic adherence to the nominally repudiated values or rationalizations constitute a more subtle variety of tensional release.

7. "Many," and not all, unintegrated groups, for the reason already mentioned. In groups where the primary emphasis shifts to institutional means, i.e., when the range of alternatives is very limited, the outcome is a type of ritualism rather than anomie.

8. Money has several peculiarities which render it particularly apt to become a symbol of prestige divorced from institutional controls. As Simmel emphasized, money is highly abstract and impersonal. However acquired, through fraud or institutionally, it can be used to purchase the same goods and services. The anonymity of metropolitan culture, in conjunction with this peculiarity of money, permits wealth, the sources of which may be unknown to the community in which the plutocrat lives, to serve as a symbol of status.

9. The emphasis upon wealth as a success-symbol is possibly reflected in the use of the term "fortune" to refer to a stock of accumulated wealth. This meaning becomes common in the late sixteenth century (Spenser and Shakespeare). A similar usage of the Latin *fortuna* comes into prominence during the first century B.C. Both these periods were marked by the rise to prestige and power of the "bourgeoisie."

10. See Kingsley Davis, "Mental Hygiene and the Class Structure," *Psychiatry*, 1928, I, esp. 62–63; Talcott Parsons, *The Structure of Social Action*, 59–60, New York, 1937.

11. This is a level intermediate between the two planes distinguished by Edward Sapir; namely, culture patterns and personal habit systems. See his "Contribution of Psychiatry to an Understanding of Behavior in Society," *Amer. J. Sociol.*, 1937, 42: 862–70.

12. This fifth alternative is on a plane clearly different from that of the others. It represents a *transitional* response which seeks to *institutionalize* new procedures oriented toward revamped cultural goals shared by the members of the society. It thus involves efforts to *change* the existing structure rather than to perform accommodative actions *within* this structure, and introduces additional problems with which we are not at the moment concerned.

13. Obviously, this is an elliptical statement. These individuals may maintain some orientation to the values of their particular differentiated groupings within the larger society or, in part, of the conventional society itself. Insofar as they do so, their conduct cannot be classified in the "passive rejection" category (IV). Nels Anderson's description of the behavior and attitudes of the bum, for example, can readily be recast in terms of our analytical scheme. See *The Hobo*, 93–98, *et passim*, Chicago, 1923.

14. Joseph D. Lohman, "The Participant Observer in Community Studies," *Amer. Sociol. Rev.*, 1937, 2:890–98.

15. The shifting historical role of this ideology is a profitable subject for exploration. The "office-boy-to-president" stereotype was once in approximate accord with the facts. Such vertical mobility was probably more common then than now, when the class structure is more rigid. (See the following note.) The ideology largely persists, however, possibly because it still performs a useful function for maintaining the *status quo*. For insofar as it is accepted by the "masses," it constitutes a useful sop for those who might rebel against the entire structure, were this consoling hope removed. This ideology now serves to lessen the probability of Adaptation V. In short, the role of this notion has changed from that of an approximately valid empirical theorem to that of an ideology, in Mannheim's sense.

16. There is a growing body of evidence, though none of it is clearly conclusive, to the effect that our class structure is becoming rigidified and that vertical mobility is declining. Taussig and Joslyn found that American business leaders are being *increasingly* recruited from the upper ranks of our society. The Lynds have also found a "diminished chance to get ahead" for the working classes in Middletown. Manifestly, these objective changes are not alone significant; the individual's subjective evaluation of the situation is a major determinant of the response. The extent to which this

change in opportunity for social mobility has been recognized by the least advantaged classes is still conjectural, although the Lynds present some suggestive materials. The writer suggests that a case in point is the increasing frequency of cartoons which observe in a tragi-comic vein that "my old man says everybody can't be President. He says if ya can get three days a week steady on W.P.A. work ya ain't doin' so bad either." See F. W. Taussig and C. S. Joslyn, *American Business Leaders*, New York, 1932; R. S. and H. M. Lynd, *Middletown in Transition*, 67 ff., chap. 12, New York, 1937.

17. The role of the Negro in this respect is of considerable theoretical interest. Certain elements of the Negro population have assimilated the dominant caste's values of pecuniary success and social advancement, but they also recognize that social ascent is at present restricted to their own caste almost exclusively. The pressures upon the Negro which would otherwise derive from the structural inconsistencies we have noticed are hence not identical with those upon lower class whites. See Kingsley Davis, *op. cit.*, 63; John Dollard, *Caste and Class in a Southern Town*, 66 ff., New Haven, 1936; Donald Young, *American Minority Peoples*, 581, New York, 1932.

18. The psychical coordinates of these processes have been partly established by the experimental evidence concerning *Anspruchsniveaus* and levels of performance. See Kurt Lewin, *Vorsatz, Wille und Bedurfnis*, Berlin, 1926; N. F. Hoppe, "Erfolg und Misserfolg," *Psychol. Forschung*, 1930, 14:1–63; Jerome D. Frank, "Individual Differences in Certain Aspects of the Level of Aspiration," *Amer. J. Psychol.*, 1935, 47: 119–28.

19. Standard criminology texts summarize the data in this field. Our scheme of analysis may serve to resolve some of the theoretical contradictions which P. A. Sorokin indicates. For example, "not everywhere nor always do the poor show a greater proportion of crime . . . many poorer countries have had less crime than the richer countries . . . The [economic] improvement in the second half of the nineteenth century, and the beginning of the twentieth, has not been followed by a decrease of crime." See his *Contemporary Sociological Theories*, 560–61, New York, 1928. The crucial point is, however, that poverty has varying social significance in different social structures, as we shall see. Hence, one would not expect a linear correlation between crime and poverty.

20. See M. W. Royse, *Aerial Bombardment and the International Regulation of War*, New York, 1928.

21. Since our primary concern is with the socio-cultural aspects of this problem, the psychological correlates have been only implicitly considered. See Karen Horney, *The Neurotic Personality of Our Time*, New York, 1937, for a psychological discussion of this process.

3

General Strain Theory

A number of criticisms were leveled against Robert Merton's (1938) anomie-strain theory, and also, against Albert Cohen's (1955, 1964) work on status deprivation and Cloward and Ohlin's (1960) work on illegitimate opportunity structures. A major issue was the emphasis they placed on the type of anomie-strain that lower-class individuals suffered as a consequence of being unable to realize monetary success and social advancement (Agnew, 1995:114–115). Thus, critics contended that traditional anomie-strain theories did not offer an adequate explanation for crimes committed by the middle- and upper-classes (Winfree & Abadinsky, 2010:174). Moreover, earlier anomie-strain theories were criticized for their assumption that everybody wanted to achieve "The American Dream." In other words, not all lower-class individuals are preoccupied with getting more money or climbing the social ladder. At the same time, it was noted that some members of the middle- and upper-classes might be more preoccupied with "keeping up with the Joneses" than members of the lower class (e.g., Agnew, 1995:114; Passas, 2003:102–103).

Robert Agnew, a Professor of Sociology at Emory University, attempted to address some of these criticisms of anomie-strain theory by developing what came to be referred to as "general strain theory." Agnew's general strain theory has undergone a number of changes since his original (1985) article, "A Revised Strain Theory of Delinquency" (the one that is found in this book) (cf. Agnew, 2006:359). This earlier (1985) work on general strain theory was selected because it is more concise than many of Agnew's subsequent works, and easier to read and understand.

In "A Revised Strain Theory of Delinquency," Agnew blends elements of psychology and social learning theory with elements of traditional anomie-strain theory, generating a new approach to juvenile delinquency that could best be classified as a form of "social psychology" (Agnew, 1995:113; Winfree & Abadinsky, 2010:169). Agnew takes the position that youth are more concerned about immediate goals—e.g., physical appearance, popularity, success in sports, doing well at school—than they are about longer term goals like accumulation of wealth and social advancement (Agnew, 1985:153). He also says that middle-class youth are just as concerned about popularity and success in sports as lower-class youth, thereby explaining why youth crime is not confined solely to the lower class.

In arriving at his general strain theory, Agnew (1985:154–155) added a number of new sources of strain. For example, Agnew brought into the equation the avoidance of aversive or noxious stimuli, such as conflict with parents, failure at school, or being unpopular with peers. He described this as "pain-avoidance behavior," which if unsuccessful, could lead to "frustration and aggression." Most youth—including middle-and upper-class youth—lack the means to escape from aversive (or strain-inducing) situations of this nature. Younger people do not have money of their own, nor do they have complete control over their own lives. As a consequence, they cannot simply leave home, move to a new neighborhood, or quit or change schools (Agnew, 1985:155–156).

Traditional anomie-strain theory envisioned individuals as running toward socially desirable success symbols, like money, cars and prestigious jobs. General strain theory, on the other hand, envisions individuals as running away from undesirable conditions, like family conflict, lack of popularity, or problems at school (Winfree & Abadinsky, 2010:169). The results of Agnew's study of 2,213 male youth from the Youth In Transition survey (discussed toward the end of the reading selection) confirmed that low socio-economic status did not predict youth delinquency as well as the inability to avoid or escape from such aversive environmental conditions (Agnew, 1985). To this day, Agnew's general strain theory remains one of the most thoroughly researched and well confirmed theories of crime and deviance (Cullen, Wright, & Blevins, 2004:8–9).

References

Agnew, R. (1985). A revised strain theory of delinquency. *Social Forces, 64*(1), 151–167.

Agnew, R. (1995). The contribution of social-psychological strain theory to the explanation of crime and delinquency. In F. Adler, W. S. Laufer & R. K. Merton (Eds.), *The legacy of anomie theory* (pp. 113–137). New Brunswick, U.S.A.: Transaction Publishers.

Agnew, R. (2006). General strain theory: Current status and directions for further research. In F. T. Cullen, J. P. Wright & K. R. Blevins (Eds.), *Taking stock: The status of criminological theory* (pp. 101–123). New Brunswick, N.J.: Transaction Publishers.

Cloward, R. A., & Ohlin, L. E. (1960). *Delinquency and opportunity: A theory of delinquent gangs.* New York: Free Press.

Cohen, A. K. (1955, 1964). *Delinquent boys: The culture of the gang.* Glencoe, IL: Free Press of Glencoe.

Cullen, F. T., Wright, J. P., & Blevins, K. R. (Eds.). (2004). *Taking stock: The status of criminological theory.* New Brunswick, N.J.: Transaction Publishers.

Merton, R. K. (1938). Social structure and anomie. *American Sociological Review, 3*(5), 672–682.

Passas, N. (2003). Anomie, reference groups, and relative deprivation. In C. M. Renzetti, D. J. Curran & P. J. Carr (Eds.), *Theories of crime: A reader* (pp. 97–113). Boston: Allyn and Bacon.

Winfree, L. T., & Abadinsky, H. (2010). *Understanding crime: Essentials of criminological theory* (Third ed.). Belmont, CA: Wadsworth, Cengage Learning.

A Revised Strain Theory of Delinquency*

ROBERT AGNEW

Abstract

Current strain theories argue that delinquency results from the blockage of goal-seeking behavior. Unable to achieve valued goals, individuals become frustrated and may turn to delinquency as a result. This paper points to another major source of frustration and delinquency, the blockage of pain-avoidance behavior. Adolescents are compelled to remain in certain environments, such as family and school. If these environments are painful or aversive, there is little that adolescents can do legally to escape. This blockage of pain-avoidance behavior is likely to be frustrating and may lead to illegal escape attempts or anger-based delinquency. This theory is tested using data from a national sample of adolescent boys. Data indicate that location in aversive school and family environments has a direct effect on delinquency and an indirect effect through anger. These effects hold even after social control and subcultural deviance variables are controlled. Given the weak support for traditional strain theories based on the blockage of goal-seeking behavior, these data suggest a new direction for the development of strain theory.

Strain theory is based on the idea that delinquency results when individuals are unable to achieve their goals through legitimate channels. In such cases, individuals may turn to illegitimate channels of goal achievement or strike out at the source of their frustration in anger. This is an appealing idea and it is not surprising that strain theory has had a major impact on delinquency research and public policy (Liska,b). Recent research, however, has been critical of strain theory or, at best, has provided only mixed support for the theory. This has led a number of researchers to call for either the abandonment or revision of strain theory (Elliott et al.; Hirschi; Kornhauser). This paper reviews the criticisms of current strain theories, examines some recent efforts to revise these theories, and then presents a new revision of strain theory based on the idea that delinquency results from the blockage of pain-avoidance behavior. This new revision is tested using data from a national sample of adolescent boys.

*An earlier version of this paper was presented at the 1983 meetings of the American Sociological Association. Address correspondence to the author, Department of Sociology, Emory University, Atlanta, GA 30322.

Reprinted from *Social Forces* 64, no. 1 (1985), University of North Carolina Press.

Critique of Current Strain Theories

Current strain theories are dominated by Merton, Cohen (a), and Cloward and Ohlin. While these theories differ from one another in many important ways, they all attribute delinquency to the inability of adolescents to achieve conventional goals through legitimate channels. Merton and Cloward and Ohlin focus on the inability of adolescents to achieve the goal of economic success, while Cohen focuses on the somewhat broader goal of middle-class status. In Merton, the inability to achieve one's goals may lead directly to delinquent behavior as the adolescent searches for alternative means of goal achievement. According to Cohen and Cloward and Ohlin, goal-blockage is unlikely to lead to delinquency unless adolescents first form or join delinquent subcultures.

These theories have been criticized on a number of points, with perhaps the most damaging criticism having to do with the research on the disjunction between aspirations and expectations (for summary, see Kornhauser, 174–80). If strain theory were correct, we would expect delinquency to be greatest when aspirations were high and expectations were low. We would, for example, predict that delinquency would be greatest when there was a strong desire for monetary success and a low expectation of fulfilling that desire. Many studies have attempted to test this idea, focusing for the most part on educational and occupational goals. Most of these studies, however, have failed to support strain theory (Elliott and Voss; Gold,a; Hirschi; Johnson; Liska,a).[1] Generally, these studies have found that delinquency is highest when both aspirations and expectations are low, and delinquency is lowest when both aspirations and expectations are high. This finding has been interpreted in terms of social control theory: high aspirations and expectations are said to be indicative of a strong commitment to the conventional order (Hirschi; Kornhauser). Not wishing to jeopardize that commitment, the individual conforms.

A second major criticism of current strain theories deals with the relationship between social class and delinquency. The above strain theories predict that delinquency is concentrated in the lower class, since low-class individuals most often lack the means to achieve economic success or middle-class status. Recent data, however, have seriously challenged this prediction (Hindelang et al.,a,b; Johnson; Krohn et al.; Thornberry and Farnworth; Tittle et al.). While the relationship between social class and delinquency is still a matter of debate (Braithwaite; Elliott and Ageton; Elliott and Huizinga), data indicate that delinquency is quite common in the middle class and that the relationship between class and at least certain types of delinquency is negligible.

These theories have also been criticized because they cannot explain the fact that most delinquents abandon crime in late adolescence (Greenberg,a; Hirschi); they cannot explain why delinquents will often go for long periods of time without committing delinquent acts (Hirschi); and they neglect many variables that are strongly related to delinquency—such as the quality of family relationships. Further criticisms of strain theory can be found in Clinard and Cohen (b). While the validity of certain of these criticisms may be debated, it is clear that there are at least some facts about delinquency that strain theory has trouble explaining. As a result, a number of revisions in the above strain theories have been made.

Revisions in Strain Theory

Most of the revisions challenge the assumption that monetary success or middle-class status is the primary goal of adolescents. Certain theories attempt to specify alternative goals that adolescents pursue (Marwell; Morris). The general theme of most revisions, however, is that adolescents may pursue a variety of goals and that goal commitment should be considered a variable rather than a given (Elliott and Voss; Elliott et al.; Greenberg,a; Simon and Gagnon). Such an approach allows these theories to explain middle-class delinquency. If goal commitment is a variable, one can argue that the middle class has higher aspirations and this offsets whatever advantage they might have in achieving goals (for examples, see Elliott and Voss; Mizruchi).

While most revisions state or imply that goal commitment is a variable, they also suggest that adolescents will be more interested in the achievement of immediate goals rather than long-range goals like monetary success (Coleman; Elliott and Voss; Empey; Greenberg,a; Quicker). The immediate goals of adolescents may include such things as popularity with peers, good grades, doing well in athletics, and getting along with parents. (This focus on immediate goals has been explained in terms of the special structural position of adolescents in our society (Coleman; Greenberg,a)). Focusing on immediate goals also allows strain theory to explain middle-class delinquency, since the achievement of many immediate goals may be independent of social class (see Elliott and Voss). In addition, the focus on immediate goals allows strain theory to explain away those findings dealing with the disjunction between aspirations and expectations. Studies in this area focus on future goals like occupational status. If such goals are unimportant to the adolescent, then we would not expect the disjunction between aspirations and expectations to be related to delinquency. A disjunction between *immediate* goals and the achievement of these goals, however, might result in much delinquency.

Other revisions have been made in strain theory. Much work, in particular, has focused on the factors which may condition the link between strain and delinquency (see especially Elliott et al.). Nevertheless, the major suggested revision is that we treat goal commitment as a variable and focus on the immediate goals of the adolescent. Preliminary tests of this revision, unfortunately, have not been encouraging (Agnew; Elliott and Voss; Greenberg's,b, reanalysis of Quicker; Reiss and Rhodes). While these tests are not definitive (see Agnew), it would nevertheless seem useful to explore other revisions in strain theory. This paper presents a revised version of strain theory that differs from current strain theories and the revised versions of these theories discussed above. This new theory seeks to explain why individuals engage in delinquency, although it also has the potential to explain variations in delinquency rates over time and between groups.

Strain as the Blockage of Pain-Avoidance Behavior

The current and revised strain theories discussed above assume that frustration is due to the blockage of goal-seeking behavior. Individuals, however, not only seek certain goals, they also try to avoid painful or aversive situations. According to Zillman, individuals engage in both reward-seeking and punishment-escaping behaviors. Like goal-seeking efforts, efforts to avoid painful situations may be blocked. Adolescents who find school aversive, for example, may be prevented from quitting school. This blockage of pain-avoidance behavior is likely to be frustrating to the adolescent, irrespective of the goals the adolescent is pursuing. The blockage of pain-avoidance behavior, then, constitutes another major source of strain and it forms the basis for the revised strain theory in this paper. In particular, it is argued that adolescents are often placed in aversive situations from which they cannot legally escape. This blockage of pain-avoidance behavior frustrates the adolescent and may lead to illegal escape attempts or anger-based delinquency.

One way to keep the distinction between the two sources of strain clear is as follows. In the blockage of goal-seeking behavior, the individual is walking *toward* a *valued goal* and his or her path is blocked. In the blockage of pain-avoidance behavior, the individual is walking away from an *aversive situation* and his or her path is blocked.[2] The two sources of strain are not incompatible and the same situation may be related to both types of strain. For example, an adolescent picked on by teachers may be frustrated because there is no escape from this harassment or because the harassment interferes with the achievement of valued goals. Other situations, however, may only be relevant to the blockage of pain-avoidance behavior. Adolescents may find certain situations aversive even though these situations do not interfere with the achievement of valued goals. Certain situations may be intrinsically aversive (e.g., the infliction of physical pain, the deprivation of sensory stimuli); they may be conditioned aversive stimuli (e.g., verbal insults); or the adolescent may simply be taught to experience these situations as aversive. The work of Schachter and Singer and of Becker, for example, indicates that cues provided by the social environment may determine whether individuals experience emotionally arousing situations as pleasant or aversive. The inability to escape from these aversive situations will be frustrating, even though the achievement of valued goals is not threatened.

The idea that the blockage of pain-avoidance behavior may lead to frustration and aggression is common in the physiological literature,[3] and psychological research indicates that exposure to various types of aversive stimuli may lead to aggression, especially when the individual believes that the exposure is undeserved (Zillman). These findings are paralleled in the sociological literature, where data indicate that delinquency is related to such aversive stimuli as parental rejection, unfair or inconsistent discipline, parental conflict (Rodman and Grams), adverse or negative school experiences (Schafer and Polk), and unsatisfactory relations with peers (Short and Strodtbeck). The sociological data, however, have not been interpreted in terms of the blockage of pain-avoidance behavior. The relationship between aversive experiences and delinquency is most commonly explained in terms of social control theory. Punitive disciplinary practices, for example, are said to lead to a breakdown in internalized, indirect, and direct social control (Nye). Subcultural-deviance theory is also used to explain the effect of aversive environments. Punitive discipline, for example, is said to implicitly teach the child that aggression is good (Gold,a).

Occasionally, the effect of aversive environments is explained in terms of strain theory. For example, Cohen (a) argues that aversive school experiences lead to delinquency because they interfere with the attainment of middle-class status. Morris argues that family conflict interferes with the ability of females to satisfy their relational goals. In each case, the aversive situation leads to delinquency because it interferes with the achievement of valued goals. As indicated earlier, however, limited tests of this idea have not produced promising results (Agnew; Elliott and Voss; Reiss and Rhodes). Studies focusing on the disjunction between goals and goal achievement (or the expectation of goal achievement) usually find that these disjunctions are, at best, only weakly related to delinquency. The revised strain theory makes no assumptions about the valued goals of adolescents or how particular situations might interfere with the achievement of these goals. The revised strain theory only assumes that it is frustrating to be unable to escape from an aversive situation. This makes the revised strain theory somewhat more parsimonious than the above strain theories, and it allows the theory to explain the fact that aversive situations affect delinquency even when these situations do not seem to interfere with the achievement of valued goals (e.g., Hirschi).

So while the idea that frustration may result from the blockage of pain-avoidance behavior is not new, this idea has not been used by criminologists to explain delinquency among adolescents. The theory, however, would seem particularly well-suited to this task. One of the distinguishing features of adolescents is that they lack power and are often compelled to remain in situations which they find aversive. They are compelled to live with their family in a certain neighborhood; to go to a certain school; and, within limits, to interact with the same group of peers and neighbors. If any of these contexts is aversive, there is little the adolescent can do legally to escape. Most adults, by contrast, have many legal avenues of escape available, such as divorce, quitting one's job, or moving to another neighborhood. (Certain adults, unable to take advantage of these legal escape routes due to economic hardship or other factors, may resemble adolescents in their lack of power.)

Adolescents located in aversive environments may turn to delinquency for one of two reasons. First, delinquency may be a means to escape from the aversive environment or remove the source of aversion. Adolescents, for example, may escape from an aversive home environment by running away or by stealing to reduce their financial dependency on parents. Or adolescents may fight to end harassment from peers. When escape or removal of the aversive source is not possible, the adolescent may become angry and strike out in rage at the source of aversion or a related target. This second link is less instrumental and more emotional in nature.

Whether the blockage of pain-avoidance behavior actually results in delinquency is undoubtedly influenced by a number of factors. One crucial factor that will be considered in this paper is whether the adolescent believes the aversion being experienced is undeserved (for related discussions, see Bandura; Berkowitz; Elliott et al.). Other factors mentioned in the literature include the beliefs of the adolescent regarding delinquency, the presence of delinquent peers, whether aggression-provoking cues are present, the likelihood that the delinquent act will be punished, and the adolescent's level of social control. This study will not examine the extent to which these additional factors condition the effect of aversion on delinquency. At this early stage of research it would seem most useful to focus on main effects rather than interactions.

If the revised strain theory is correct, we would expect location in an aversive environment to have a direct effect on delinquency since adolescents in such environments would be more likely to engage in illegal escape attempts. We would also expect an indirect effect on delinquency through anger. In examining the effect of aversion on delinquency, however, it is necessary to control for social control and subcultural-deviance variables. This is because part of the direct effect of aversion on delinquency may be due to the fact that aversion causes or is correlated with low social control and deviant beliefs. These connections are summarized in the causal model in Figure 3.1. This model will be estimated using path analysis.

Data and Methods

Data
Data are from the Youth in Transition survey: a national survey of adolescent boys conducted by the Institute for Social Research, University of Michigan. In October and November of 1966, a multi-stage sampling procedure was used to select 2,213 boys who, according to the researchers, constitute "an essentially unbiased representation of 10th grade boys in public high schools throughout the contiguous United States" (Bachman et al.,3). This survey was used since it contained data on the boys' school and family environments, as well as measures of social control, deviant beliefs, and delinquency.

Measures
The survey contained numerous measures of the variables in Figure 3.1. Through the use of factor analysis, these measures were combined to create scales measuring environmental aversion, anger, parental and teacher attachment, commitment to school, and deviant beliefs.[4] The survey already contained scales measuring delinquency.

Environmental Aversion.   The adolescents in the survey were compelled to remain in at least two environments: family and school. Three scales were used to determine whether the adolescents believed these environments were undeservedly aversive.

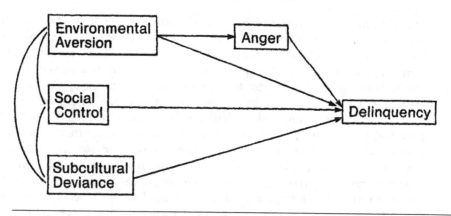

FIGURE 3.1 *A path model of the revised strain theory.*

In particular, scale items asked adolescents such things as whether they were physically punished, verbally harassed, or deprived of adequate sensory stimulation in these environments. (1) *Parental Punitiveness.* High scorers on this 10-item scale report that their parents often scream, slap, threaten, nag, withdraw love, withdraw privileges, and ignore them. High scorers also state that their parents often disagree about whether punishment should be administered and that they "give out undeserved blame." Scores on this scale range from 1 to 5, with a mean of 2.3. (2) *Mean Teacher.* High scorers on this 3-item scale report that their teachers often lose their tempers, make negative comments, and talk down to students. Scores on this scale range from 1 to 5, with a mean of 2.85. (3) *Dissatisfaction with School.* High scorers on this 23-item scale report that they find school boring and a "waste of time," that they would rather be elsewhere, and that they can probably learn more outside of school. Scores on this scale range from 1 to 4 with a mean of 1.78.

While all adolescents were compelled to spend time with parents and teachers, there were undoubtedly differences in the amount of time spent with these agents. The data, unfortunately, did not allow us to obtain accurate measures of these differences. This is not a serious limitation, since most adolescents probably spent a significant amount of time with parents and in school. Nevertheless, future studies should attempt to measure both environmental aversion and the amount of time adolescents are compelled to spend in aversive environments.

Anger.   High scorers on this 9-item scale state that they lose their temper easily, carry a chip on their shoulder, feel like a powder keg ready to explode, are irritated by small things, hold grudges, and "feel like" verbally and physically aggressing against parents and teachers. High scorers, in short, are angry, frustrated individuals. If the revised strain theory is correct, this scale should partly mediate the relationship between aversive environments and delinquency. Scores range from 1 to 5, with a mean of 2.41.

Social Control/Subcultural Deviance Measures.   The data set used in this study is the same used by Wiatrowski et al. in their study of social control theory. This study includes all of the social control variables that Wiatrowski et al. found to be significantly related to delinquency, as well as certain measures of social control not in their study.[5] There are a total of 13 social control and subcultural deviance measures. Two scales measure attachment to parents, a 3-item scale called *Father Attachment* and a 2-item scale called *Mother Attachment*. High scorers report that they feel close to and want to be like their father or mother. One 3-item scale measures *Teacher Attachment*. High scorers report that teachers take a personal interest in them and that they talk privately with teachers about school and non-school matters. Seven scales or single-item measures index commitment to school. These scales and items measure average school *Grades*, the *Value Placed on Academic Achievement* (4 items), the amount of *Time Spent on Homework*, the amount of *Extracurricular Reading*, the adolescent's *Self-Concept of School Ability* (3 items), *Occupational Aspirations*, and the amount of *Time Spent Dating* (3 items). Finally, 3 scales measure the adolescent's values. A 13-item scale called *Nonaggression* measures the value placed on aggression. High scorers report that it is good to be kind and gentle, even if you are provoked or harmed by others. A 4-item scale called *Deviant Beliefs* measures the value placed on other types of deviance. High scorers report that it is good to engage in such deviant acts as charging bills without knowing how to pay for them, borrowing money without expecting to pay it back, and getting hold of a final exam copy. A 5-item scale called *Guilt* measures whether individuals feel guilty about their mistakes or wrongs. The presence of such guilt indicates that the individual possesses some degree of internalized control.

Delinquency.   The blockage of pain-avoidance behavior may lead to any type of delinquency, since any delinquent act can be an escape attempt—however indirect—or an expression of anger. For this reason, a general measure called *Seriousness of Delinquency* is used. The 10 items in this self-report measure were adopted from Gold (b) and they measure the extent of the respondent's delinquent behavior during the prior three years. High scorers on this scale report that they have engaged in minor and serious theft, robbery, arson, and serious fighting (see Appendix for complete scale). Response categories for each item range from "1" (never committed the act) to "5" (committed the act 5 or more times). Scale scores range from "1" (never committed any of the acts) to "5" (committed all acts 5 or more times), with a mean of 1.38 and a standard deviation of .48. Variation in this scale is due largely to the minor theft items (shoplifting, larceny under $50).

While the blockage of pain-avoidance behavior may lead to any type of delinquency, we would expect it to have an especially large effect on aggression and status offenses like truancy and cutting class. Compared to theft, aggression seems more suitable for the expression of anger and the removal of aversive sources. Status offenses like truancy and cutting class represent fairly direct ways of escaping from an aversive environment. An 8-item measure of *Interpersonal Aggression* is used. High scorers on this measure report that they have gotten into serious fights, have been in gang fights, and have hit their mother, father, and teacher. This scale is scored in the same manner as the Seriousness of Delinquency scale. Scale scores range from 1 to 5, with a mean of 1.51 and a standard deviation of .56. Variation in this scale is due largely to the three fighting items (see Appendix). A 4-item scale measuring *Escape Attempts from School* is also used. High scorers on this scale report that they are often late for class and school, and that they often skip class and school. Responses for each item range from "1" (never committed the act) to "5" (almost always committed the act). Scale scores range from 1 to 5, with a mean of 1.66 and a standard deviation of .71.

Methods

Path analytic methods are used to estimate the causal model in Figure 3.1. Through a series of regressions, the effects of the independent variables will be estimated. Path analysis makes a number of assumptions about the data (see Johnson, 96–8 for a discussion), and there are indications that the data violate certain of these assumptions. In particular, the data violate the assumption that variables are perfectly measured.[6] Imperfect measurement will most likely reduce the size of path coefficients. This will reduce the amount of explained variance in delinquency but, to paraphrase Johnson, it should not seriously interfere with our effort to test for the existence and relative magnitude of selected causal processes.

Results

Figures 3.2, 3.3 and 3.4 show the estimated models for Seriousness of Delinquency, Interpersonal Aggression, and Escape Attempts from School. The figures, in particular, show the standardized effects of the independent variables and, in parentheses, the unstandardized effects. Only effects significant at the .05 level are included. Many of the 13 social-control and subcultural-deviance variables are excluded since they did not have a significant effect on delinquency.

All three measures of environmental aversion have a significant positive effect on anger. If we use a sheaf coefficient (Heise) to summarize the combined effect of these variables on anger, it is .53. When aversion rises by one standard deviation unit, anger rises by .53 standard deviation units. Being in an aversive environment, then, clearly makes the individual angry. Anger, in turn, has a significant positive impact on all measures of delinquency. As we might expect, it has a somewhat larger effect on aggression. If we examine the direct and indirect effect of the aversion variables on delinquency, we find a direct effect of .12 on Seriousness of Delinquency and an indirect effect of .11, a direct effect of .21 on aggression and an indirect effect of .16, and a direct effect of .26 on Escape Attempts from School with an indirect effect of .10. As predicted, the total effect of the aversion variables on Interpersonal Aggression (.37) and Escape Attempts from School (.36) is larger than the total effect on Seriousness of Delinquency (.23).

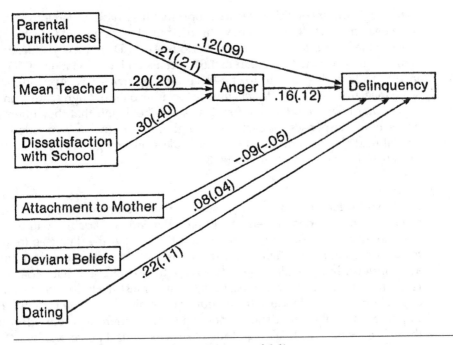

FIGURE 3.2   *The path model for seriousness of delinquency.*

To put the data in better perspective, it is useful to compare the effect of the aversion variables to the effect of the social control and subcultural deviance variables. Focusing on Interpersonal Aggression, we find that each of the aversion variables has a larger total effect than any other variable except dating. These variables have a larger effect than parental attachment, grades, aspirations, and values. Focusing on Escape Attempts from School, we find that Dissatisfaction with School has a larger total effect than all variables except dating, while the effect of Mean Teacher and Parental Punitiveness is only exceeded by dating and grades. The aversion variables also have a relatively large effect on Seriousness of Delinquency. Overall, these data attest to the importance of environmental aversion in the explanation of delinquency.

Conclusions

The data provide strong support for the idea that the blockage of pain-avoidance behavior is a major source of delinquency. Adolescents located in aversive environments from which they cannot escape are more likely to be delinquent. The relationship holds even after social control and subcultural-deviance variables are controlled. These data are important because they suggest a new direction for the development

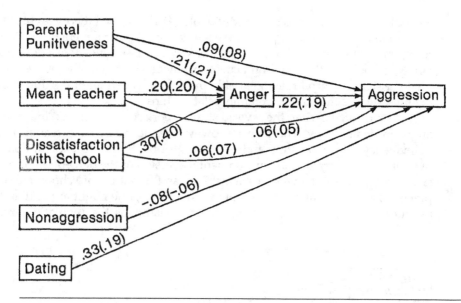

FIGURE 3.3   *The path model for interpersonal aggression.*

of strain theory and they supplement the explanations of delinquency provided by social control and subcultural deviance theory. Social control theory focuses on *neutral* relationships, in which the individual lacks ties to conventional people and institutions. Subcultural deviance theory focuses on *positive* relationships with deviant others. The revised strain theory supplements these theories by describing how *negative* relationships may lead to delinquency. While negative relationships may result in low social control and deviant beliefs in certain cases, the revised strain theory argues that a major effect of location in an aversive environment is frustration. This frustration may lead to illegal escape attempts or anger-based delinquency.

In addition to being supported by the data, the revised theory is able to overcome the major criticisms of current strain theories. (1) The research on the disjunction between aspirations and expectations does not challenge the revised theory, since the revised theory is not based on the idea that delinquency results from the frustration of future goals. (2) The revised strain theory is able to explain the prevalence of middle-class delinquency, since middle-class adolescents may encounter aversive situations from which they cannot escape. In fact, a 5-item measure of SES was only weakly related to Parental Punitiveness ($r = -.09$, $p < .01$), Mean Teacher ($r = -.11$, $p < .01$), and Dissatisfaction with School ($r = -.17$, $p < .01$). Other data confirm that social class is weakly related to many types of environmental aversion (Erlanger). (3) The revised theory is able to explain the decline in delinquency in late adolescence. We would expect such a decline since adolescents are leaving environments that they may have found aversive, such as family and school. Also, as adults, many legal avenues of escape become available to these individuals. (4) The revised theory is able to explain the sporadic nature of delinquency. We would expect environmental aversion to fluctuate, and delinquency should be most likely at those times that adolescents find family, school, or other environments most aversive. (5) Finally, the revised strain theory assigns a central role to variables neglected by certain of the dominant strain theories, such as the quality of family relationships.

As indicated earlier, the revised strain theory seeks to explain individual variations in delinquency. The theory, however, could easily be extended to explain delinquency rates over time and between groups. Efforts to explain delinquency over time would argue that environmental aversion or the perception of such aversion changes with changes in such things as the nature of school, child-rearing practices, and cultural definitions of aversion. Also, one might argue that the legal avenues of escape available to adolescents change as the regulations regarding

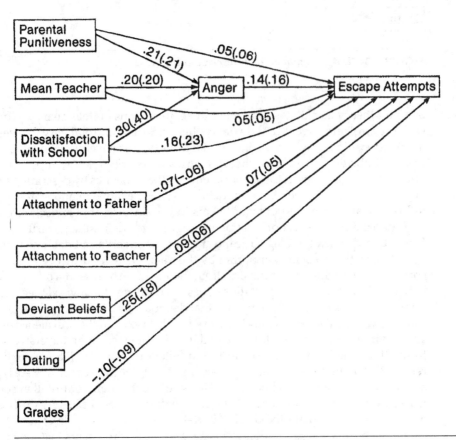

FIGURE 3.4   *The path model for escape attempts from school.*

school attendance change or as norms regarding family obligations are altered. The explanation of group differences in delinquency would revolve around the fact that groups may vary in terms of environmental aversion and the ability to legally escape from such aversion. Aside from SES, however, the data did not allow us to explore group differences in these variables.[7]

Overall, then, the theory has a demonstrated capacity to explain delinquency among individuals and the potential to explain delinquency rates over time and between groups. In addition to exploring the macro implications of the theory, future research should (1) focus on additional forms of environmental aversion, (2) examine the amount of time adolescents are compelled to remain in aversive environments, and (3) examine the factors that condition the link between aversion and delinquency.

Notes

1. A number of studies have found a relationship between perceptions of limited opportunity and delinquency (for example, Aultman; Cernkovich and Giordana). This relationship, however, may be interpreted in terms of social control as well as strain theory. One might argue that perceptions of limited opportunity are indicative of a low commitment to the conventional order. Only studies focusing on the disjunction between aspirations and expectations provide a pure test of strain theory.

2. The difference between goal-seeking and pain-avoidance behavior is, to some extent, a matter of semantics. If we view the desire to escape from an aversive environment as a goal, then pain-avoidance behavior becomes a subcategory of goal-seeking behavior. Nevertheless, there is still a difference. In one case the goal is to escape from negative stimuli, while in the other the goal is the achievement of positively reinforcing stimuli.

3. Elements of this idea can be found in Berkowitz's frustration-aggression theory and Bandura's social learning theory, although Bandura argues that aversion may lead to aggression even if legal avenues of escape are available. The revised strain theory, as indicated, focuses on those situations where legal avenues of escape are unavailable. Since the source of adolescent aversion is often a powerful other—like a parent or teacher—it seems unlikely that adolescents will engage in aggression or illegal escape attempts if legal avenues of escape are accessible.

4. Groups of items similar in content were factor analyzed. For example, 21 items having to do with teacher relations were factored. The eigenvalue was set at one and an orthogonal method of rotation was used. Scale items were equally weighted and scale scores are the average of the item scores. Copies of the resulting scales and the factor loadings of the items in these scales are available from the author.

5. Certain of the scales differ somewhat from those in Wiatrowski et al., since factor analysis was used to create the scales in this study. This, however, should only have the effect of increasing the validity of the scales. Items which did not load highly on a factor or loaded on more than one factor were eliminated.

6. The validity of all multi-item measures was estimated using a procedure developed by Heise and Bohrnstedt. Validity is defined as the correlation between the scale and the true variable that the scale is designed to measure. At a minimum, reliability is equal to the square root of validity. Most of the validities were in the .8 to .9 range, with two exceptions. Mean Teacher had a validity of .75 and Dating had a validity of .77. The effects of these two variables will therefore be underestimated relative to the other variables, and controls for these variables will not be complete.

7. The data set did not contain females, all respondents were of the same age, and the small number of blacks in the sample were not representative of black high school students in the United States.

Appendix

A. Seriousness of Delinquency Scale

1. Taken something not belonging to you worth under $50.
2. Set fire to someone else's property on purpose.
3. Got something by telling a person something bad would happen to him if you did not get what you wanted.
4. Hurt someone badly enough to need bandages or a doctor.
5. Taken something from a store without paying for it.
6. Taken a car that didn't belong to someone in your family without permission of the owner.
7. Taken an expensive part of a car without permission of the owner.
8. Taken an inexpensive part of a car without permission of the owner.
9. Used a knife or gun or some other thing (like a club) to get something from a person.
10. Taken something not belonging to you worth over $50.

B. Interpersonal Aggression Scale

1. Got into a serious fight with a student in school.
2. Got something by telling a person something bad would happen to him if you did not get what you wanted.
3. Hurt someone badly enough to need bandages or a doctor.
4. Hit a teacher.
5. Hit your father.
6. Taken part in a fight where a bunch of your friends are against another bunch.
7. Hit your mother.
8. Used a knife or gun or some other thing (like a club) to get something from a person.

C. Escape Attempts from School

1. How often do you come late to school?
2. How often are you late to class?
3. How often do you skip classes (when against the school rules)?
4. Skipped a day of school without a real excuse.

References

Agnew, R. 1984. "Goal Achievement and Delinquency." *Sociology and Social Research.*
Aultman, M. 1979. "Delinquency Causation: Typological Comparison of Path Models." *Journal of Criminal Law and Criminology* 70:152–63.

Bachman, J., P. O'Malley, and J. Johnston. 1978. *Youth in Transition, Volume 6, Adolescence to Adulthood.* Institute for Social Research.

Bandura, A. 1979. "The Social Learning Perspective: Mechanisms of Aggression." In H. Toch (ed.), *The Psychology of Crime and Criminal Justice.* Holt, Rinehart & Winston.

Becker, H. 1963. *Outsiders: Studies in the Sociology of Deviance.* Free Press.

Berkowitz, L. 1962. *Aggression.* McGraw-Hill.

Braithwaite, J. 1981. "The Myth of Social Class and Criminality Reconsidered." *American Sociological Review* 46:36–58.

Cernkovich, S., and P. Giordano. 1979. "Delinquency, Opportunity, and Gender." *Journal of Criminal Law and Criminology* 70:145–51.

Clinard, M. 1964. *Anomie and Deviant Behavior.* Free Press.

Cloward, R., and L. Ohlin. 1960. *Delinquency and Opportunity.* Free Press.

Cohen, A. a:1955. *Delinquent Boys.* Free Press.

———. b:1965. "The Sociology of the Deviant Act: Anomie Theory and Beyond." *American Sociological Review* 30:5–14.

Coleman, J. 1961. *The Adolescent Society.* Free Press.

Elliott, D., and D. Huizinga. 1983. "Social Class and Delinquent Behavior in a National Youth Panel." *Criminology* 21:149–77.

Elliott, D., and H. Voss. 1974. *Delinquency and Dropout.* Lexington Books.

Elliott, D., and S. Ageton. 1979. "Reconciling Race and Class Differences in Self-reported and Official Estimates of Delinquency." *American Sociological Review* 45:95–110.

Elliott, D., S. Ageton, and R. Canter. 1979. "An Integrated Theoretical Perspective on Delinquent Behavior." *Journal of Research in Crime and Delinquency* 16:3–27.

Empey, L. 1978. *American Delinquency: Its Meaning and Construction.* Dorsey.

Erlanger, H. 1974. "Social Class and Corporal Punishment in Childrearing: a Reassessment." *American Sociological Review* 39:68–85.

Gold, M. a:1963. *Status Forces in Delinquent Boys.* Institute for Social Research.

———. b:1966. "Undetected Delinquent Behavior." *Journal of Research in Crime and Delinquency* 3:27–46.

Greenberg, D. a:1977. "Delinquency and the Age Structure of Society." *Contemporary Crises* 1:66–86.

———. b:1979. *Mathematical Criminology.* Rutgers University Press.

Heise, D., and G. Bohrnstedt. 1970. "Validity, Invalidity, and Reliability." In E. Borgatta and G. Bohrnstedt (eds.), *Sociological Methodology, 1970.* Jossey Bass.

Hindelang, M., T. Hirschi, and J. Weiss. a:1979. "Correlates of Delinquency: The Illusion of Discrepancy Between Self-Report and Official Measures." *American Sociological Review* 44:995–1014.

———. b:1981. *Measuring Delinquency.* Sage.

Hirschi, T. 1969. *Causes of Delinquency.* University of California Press.

Johnson, R. 1979. *Juvenile Delinquency and Its Origins.* Cambridge University Press.

Kornhauser, R. 1978. *Social Sources of Delinquency.* University of Chicago Press.

Krohn, M., R. Akers, M. Radosevich, and L. Lanza-Kaduce. 1980. "Social Status and Deviance." *Criminology* 18:303–18.

Liska, A. a:1971. "Aspirations, Expectations, and Delinquency: Stress and Additive Models." *Sociological Quarterly* 12:99–107.

———. b:1981. *Perspectives on Deviance.* Prentice-Hall.

Marwell, G. 1966. "Adolescent Powerlessness and Delinquent Behavior." *Social Problems* 14:35–47.

Merton, R. 1938. "Social Structure and Anomie." *American Sociological Review* 3:672–82.

Mizruchi, E. 1964. *Success and Opportunity.* Free Press.

Morris, R. 1964. "Female Delinquency and Relational Problems." *Social Forces* 43:82–89.

Nye, I. 1958. *Family Relationships and Delinquent Behavior.* Wiley.

Quicker, J. 1974. "The Effect of Goal Discrepancy on Delinquency." *Social Problems* 22:76–86.

Reiss, A., and A. Rhodes. 1963. "Status Deprivation and Delinquent Behavior." *Sociological Quarterly* 4:135–49.

Rodman, H., and P. Grams. 1967. "Juvenile Delinquency and the Family." In the President's Commission on Law Enforcement and Administration of Justice, Juvenile Delinquency and Youth Crime. GPO.

Schachter, S., and J. Singer. 1962. "Cognitive, Social and Physiological Determinants of Emotional State." *Psychological Review* 69:379–99.

Schafer, W., and K. Polk. 1967. "Delinquency and the Schools." In the President's Commission on Law Enforcement and Administration of Justice, Juvenile Delinquency and Youth Crime. GPO.

Short, J., and F. Strodtbeck. 1965. *Group Process and Gang Delinquency.* University of Chicago Press.

Simon, W., and J. Gagnon. 1976. "The Anomie of Affluence: a Post-Mertonian Conception." *American Journal of Sociology* 82:356–78.

Thornberry, T., and M. Farnworth. 1982. "Social Correlations of Criminal Involvement: Further Evidence on the Relationship Between Social Status and Criminal Behavior." *American Sociological Review* 47:505–18.

Tittle, C., W. Villemez, and D. Smith. 1978. "The Myth of Social Class and Criminality." *American Sociological Review* 43:643–56.

Wiatrowski, M., D. Griswold, and M. Roberts. 1981. "Social Control Theory and Delinquency." *American Sociological Review* 46:525–41.

Zillman, D. 1979. *Hostility and Aggression.* Erlbaum Associates.

4

Crime and the American Dream

In 1994, Steven Messner and Richard Rosenfeld published their book on institutional-anomie theory, entitled *Crime and the American Dream*. In this book, Messner and Rosenfeld (who are both Sociology Professors) set forth their contemporary (macro-level) version of Robert Merton's anomie-strain theory. The next (1995) reading selection, "Crime and the American Dream: An Institutional Analysis," appeared as a chapter in *The Legacy of Anomie Theory*, which itself is one volume in a series of excellent books, called *Advances in Criminological Theory*. This particular reading was chosen because it neatly summarizes the major points of Messner and Rosenfeld's institutional-anomie theory.

Messner and Rosenfeld argue that criminology has become overly preoccupied with the analysis of individuals (e.g., the mentally ill, the intellectually handicapped, etc.), and has not been paying enough attention to social organization and social institutions (Rosenfeld & Messner, 1995:162–163). One of the primary goals of their institutional-anomie theory is to restore to its rightful place the type of macro-level analysis that permeated Merton's original (1938) anomie theory (1995:161). Following Merton, Messner and Rosenfeld argue that crime rates are higher in America due to the criminogenic (crime-causing) nature of American-style capitalism and its unique cultural goals or aspirations. They say this is attributable in part to the American emphasis on individual achievement, measured largely in terms of monetary rewards (Rosenfeld & Messner, 1995:160, 164–165). However, they remind us that "culture and social structure are intimately interconnected" (Rosenfeld & Messner, 1995:161).

Like Merton (and Durkheim before him), Messner and Rosenfeld (Rosenfeld & Messner, 1995:167) are concerned about "the *normal* functions of social institutions" [emphasis added]. They identify four main social institutions that—if they are functioning normally—are supposed to integrate cultural aspirations with the social structure, and at the same time, regulate social behavior (Messner & Rosenfeld, 2006:93, 95). Those four institutions are the economy, the family, the political system (which they refer to as "the polity"), and education (1995:167–168). According to Messner and Rosenfeld (2007), the purpose (or function) of the economy is to provide the basic requirements, such as "food, clothing and shelter." The family is supposed to provide emotional support, and regulate the behavior of individuals through proper socialization. One of the main functions of the polity (or political system) is to provide public safety, by "controlling crime and disorder." Educational institutions are supposed to assist in the socialization process, and at the same time, pass along knowledge and develop human potential.

Throughout this reading selection, Messner and Rosenfeld talk about "the institutional balance of power," and how under American-style capitalism, the economy has come to dominate the other three institutions. Essentially, the other institutions have been forced to accommodate the needs of the economy (Messner & Rosenfeld, 2007:79). In Durkheimian terms, institutional-anomie theory is describing a capitalist economy with unregulated goals and means. Neither the political system (the polity) nor the criminal justice system provide sufficient moral oversight for this deregulated economy. There is a devaluation of the institutional balance of power, with the economy (e.g., large financial institutions) taking precedence over educational institutions, religious institutions and the family. The overwhelming power of the economy, the "culture of competition" and a strong emphasis on monetary rewards results in the pursuit of monetary goals at all costs—a situation where "the ends justify the means" (Rosenfeld & Messner, 1995:164–166).

Recently, Akers and Sellers (2009) have observed that crime rates appear to be going down in America, while rates in other countries have remained stable or have been going up. This of course calls into question just how much the American Dream of accumulation of wealth and achievement of social advancement truly influences crime rates. However, some of the countries that Akers and Sellers mention—e.g., Australia, England, France and Japan—are themselves capitalist countries, where the pursuit of monetary rewards is also encouraged.

In any event, there are elements of Messner and Rosenfeld's institutional-anomie that are simply too compelling to ignore. Institutional-anomie theory explains why governments in capitalist countries always seem to have money to bail out large businesses and/or financial institutions when they get into trouble as a result of their greed and unrestrained (unregulated) ambition, yet rarely seem to have enough money left over to provide desirable levels of public education, public health care, and family services. To see the appeal of institutional-anomie theory, we need look no further than the collapse of the savings and loan industry in the U.S.A. during the 1980s and 1990s. Following that, we witnessed the collapse of World.com and Enron in the very early part of the 21st Century, and the recent (2008–2009) meltdown of the sub-prime mortgage market, which bankrupted or almost bankrupted large financial institutions and governments around the world.

References _____

Akers, R. L., & Sellers, C. S. (2009). *Criminological theories: Introduction, evaluation, and application* (5th, New ed.). New York: Oxford University Press.

Merton, R. K. (1938). Social structure and anomie. *American Sociological Review, 3*(5), 672–682.

Messner, S. F., & Rosenfeld, R. (2006). "Institutionalizing" criminological theory. In R. Rosenfeld (Ed.), *Crime and social institutions* (International library of criminology, criminal justice and penology. Second series. ed., pp. 3–25). Aldershot, England; Burlington, VT: Ashgate.

Messner, S. F., & Rosenfeld, R. (2007). *Crime and the American Dream* (Fourth ed.). Belmont, CA: Thomson Wadsworth.

Rosenfeld, R., & Messner, S. F. (1995). Crime and the American Dream: An institutional analysis. In F. Adler, W. S. Laufer & R. K. Merton (Eds.), *The legacy of anomie theory* (pp. 159–181). New Brunswick, U.S.A.: Transaction Publishers.

Crime and the American Dream: An Institutional Analysis

RICHARD MESSNER AND STEVEN F. ROSENFELD

Freda Adler has called attention to a unique feature of American society—its "obsession" with crime. In her 1983 book published as part of the Comparative Criminal Law Project, Adler offers the following observations based on her travels around the world as a comparative criminologist:

> The preoccupation with crime is not a national past-time in more countries than one. Neither the design of doors and windows, nor the front page stories in the national press, nor the budgetary allocations of municipal and national governments indicate any obsession with crime, the fear of crime, the fear of victimization, or indeed, the national destiny. (Adler 1983: xix)

Despite the myriad changes that have occurred both in the United States and in other countries since the original publication of Adler's book, her comments about the preoccupation with crime in America seem as applicable today as they were a decade ago.

The obsession with crime in the United States cannot be dismissed as an irrational feature of the American character or as a peculiarly American penchant for inventing crime waves or using crime as a stage for enacting other social dramas. Rather, the American obsession with crime is rooted in an objective social reality. Levels of crime in the United States, and more specifically levels of serious crime, are in fact very high in comparative perspective.

A previous draft of this paper was presented at the meeting of the American Society of Criminology, November 1992.

Reprinted by permission from *Advances in Criminological Theory* 6, no. 1 (1994).

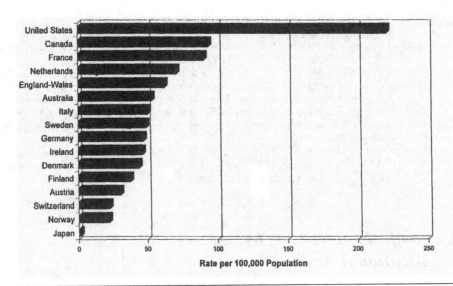

FIGURE 4.1   *Robbery Rates in Selected Nations, 1988.*

Comparisons of the crime rates of different nations must be viewed with considerable caution, and it is best to treat small differences in crime rates between nations as unreliable, especially when comparisons are based on data for a single year.[1] However, the differences in levels of serious crime between the United States and other developed nations are anything but small. Figures 4.1 and 4.2 compare the 1988 U.S. robbery and homicide rates, respectively, with those of 15 other industrial nations.[2] The U.S. robbery rate of 221 robberies per 100,000 residents is more than twice as high as those of the nations with the next highest rates, Canada and France. The robbery rate in the United States is four to five times higher than in most other industrial nations; it is an astounding 158 times higher than the robbery rate in Japan, which reported 1.4 robberies per 100,000 population in 1988, the lowest rate of any of the nations under comparison.

The difference in the homicide rates of the United States and other industrialized nations is even larger. The U.S. homicide rate of 8.9 per 100,000 population is more than three times greater than Finland's rate of 2.8, the next highest among the nations presented in figure 4.2, and is over seven times the rates of most of the other nations. It is important to note that these differences are attenuated, but not eliminated, when race differences in homicide rates within the United States are taken into account. Although homicide rates of black males are six to seven times higher than those of white males, the white male rates are higher than those for males in other developed nations (Fingerhut and Kleinman 1990; Whitaker 1990). Nor are the cross-national differences in levels of homicide fully accounted for by the greater availability of firearms in the United States, because even the U.S. nongun

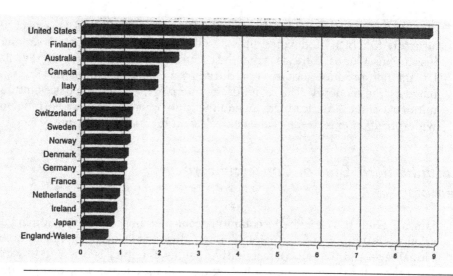

FIGURE 4.2   *Homocide Rates in Selected Nations, 1988.*

homicide rate is higher than the *total* homicide rates of other developed countries (see Messner and Rosenfeld 1994: chap. 2).[3]

We maintain that the comparatively high level of serious criminal behavior in the United States is one of the more important facts about crime to be explained by criminological theory (cf. Braithwaite 1989). Curiously, however, criminologists have devoted relatively little attention to this issue for at least two interrelated reasons: the dominance of individual-level perspectives in contemporary criminology and a corresponding deemphasis on serious forms of criminal behavior. Nonetheless, we propose that the foundations for an explanation of the distinctively high levels of crime in the United States can be found in the arguments advanced by Robert Merton in his classic essay "Social Structure and Anomie" (1938, 1968; hereafter SS&A).

Merton proposes that the sources of crime in the United States lie in the same cultural commitments and social arrangements that are conventionally regarded as part of the American success story. High rates of crime are thus not simply the "sick" outcome of individual pathologies, such as defective personalities or aberrant biological structures. Nor are they the "evil consequence" of individual moral failings.[4] Instead, crime in America derives in significant measure from highly prized cultural and social conditions—indeed, from the American Dream itself.

In this chapter, we offer an explanation of American crime rates that is based on an expanded version of Merton's theory. We amplify the theory in two ways. First, we restore the original macrolevel intent and orientation to SS&A that were removed in the conversion of "anomie theory" into "strain theory." We then extend anomie theory by considering the connections between core elements of the

American Dream, which Merton discussed in some detail, and an aspect of social structure to which he devoted little attention: the interrelationships among social institutions. Our basic thesis is that the anomic tendencies inherent in the American Dream both produce and are reproduced by an *institutional balance of power* dominated by the economy. The result of the interplay between the basic cultural commitments of the American Dream and the companion institutional arrangements is widespread anomie, weak social controls, and high levels of crime.

The Individualistic Bias of Contemporary Criminology

James F. Short has described a common problem of miscommunication in the social sciences resulting from confusion over two different levels of explanation: the individual level and the macrolevel. Individual-level inquiry is oriented toward questions about the determinants of individual actions, such as why one person rather than another commits a given criminal act. Macrolevel inquiry, in contrast, focuses on groups and populations. The relevant questions here are of a different nature: Why do levels of crime vary across social systems (e.g., nations, cities, neighborhoods, etc.), and why is crime patterned in systematic ways across categories within a social system (e.g., by race, class, age, or gender) (Short 1985; see also Cohen 1985)?

The distinction between individual- and macrolevel inquiry is important because neither can be reduced to the other. This point is illustrated very effectively in a recent study of the relationship between mental disorder, intellectual deficiency, and criminal behavior in a Swedish birth cohort (Hodkins 1992). The study reports that persons with mental disorders and intellectual deficits are significantly more likely than others to commit both property and violent crimes. However, the author cautions against generalizing these findings to the macrolevel. Specifically, they cannot account for differences in crime rates between Sweden and the United States because levels of mental disorder and intellectual deficiency are about the same in the two nations. Moreover, "in the United States, given the large amount of crime . . . , the crimes of those with major psychiatric disorders and intellectual handicaps seem insignificant in comparison" (Hodkins 1992: 482). Questions about differences in levels of crime across macrosocial units, such as societies, are distinctively sociological and are best addressed with reference to other macrolevel differences (cf. Cohen 1985: 230).

Inquiry oriented toward both of these levels of analysis is important for the construction of comprehensive explanations of crime and for the development of the discipline of criminology. However, criminological research over the past few decades has been largely preoccupied with individual-level analysis. As Stitt and Giacopassi (1992) report in their review of articles published between 1964 and 1992 in *Criminology*, the official journal of the American Society of Criminology, social control theory, which emphasizes individual restraints against the tempta-tions of crime, has been "by far" the most frequently tested theory in the discipline. The second most frequently tested theory has been social learning theory, another approach that emphasizes the role of individual characteristics (personal experi-ences with reinforcements) in the genesis of crime.

The dominance of these theoretical perspectives has quite understandably ori-ented research toward questions about individual involvement in criminal behav-ior rather than questions about macrosocial variation in levels of crime. In addition, the methodological proclivities of researchers working within these theoretical tra-ditions have encouraged a substantive focus on a domain of criminal behavior for which macrosocial variation may not, in fact, be particularly pronounced. Research-ers pursuing individual-level research have embraced self-report surveys as the preferred data source for measuring criminal offending.[5] The self-report methodol-ogy, however, is not well suited for studying extremely serious and relatively rare forms of behavior, and hence the use of this methodology tends to orient research to the study of rather petty, trivial offenses (Vold and Bernard 1986: 245; Burton and Cullen 1992). This methodologically induced focus on minor offenses thus deflects attention away from precisely those categories of serious criminal behavior for which macrosocial variation in levels of crime is quite striking, as reflected in the comparative data reported above.[6]

The individualistic bias in contemporary criminology has had an ironic con-sequence for anomie theory. Anomie theory has been transformed into "strain theory," thereby converting a macrolevel theory of social organization into a social-psychological theory predicated upon propositions about individual perceptions and feelings (Burton and Cullen 1992). The reduction of anomie theory to an individual-level perspective has occurred in spite of Merton's explicit and self-conscious efforts to address sociological questions about the cultural and structural determinants of variation in *rates* of behavior and not questions about social psychology and individual behavior (Merton 1968: 186).

We do not challenge the utility of individual-level theories of strain. Rather, we object to the virtual substitution of the individual-level version for the original.[7] In our view, the transformation of anomie theory into strain theory has had two unfortunate consequences. First, by reinforcing the dominance of individual-level perspectives in criminology, it has contributed to the neglect of the general question of why crime rates vary across social systems, as well as the specific question of why rates of serious crime are so high in the United States. Second, widespread accep-tance of the individualistic version of SS&A has fostered an underappreciation of those aspects of Merton's arguments that are of greatest assistance in answering macrolevel questions. Most important, criminologists have largely ignored Mer-ton's incisive critique of the anomie tendencies of American culture. A rediscovery of this critique is an essential first step in the formulation of a cogent explanation of the high levels of crime in American society.

The Anomic Tendencies of the American Dream

In SS&A, Merton advances the provocative argument that there are inherent features of American culture, of the American Dream itself, that ultimately contribute to the high rates of crime and deviance observed in the United States. Although Merton does not provide a formal definition of "the American Dream," it is possible to formulate a reasonably concise characterization of this cultural orientation on the basis of his discussion of American culture in general and his scattered references to the American Dream. The American Dream refers to a commitment to the goal of material success, to be pursued by everyone in society, under conditions of open, individual competition.[8]

Merton proposes that the American Dream has been highly functional for society in certain respects. This cultural ethos is particularly effective in satisfying motivational requirements because it encourages high levels of "ambition" (Merton 1968: 200). At the same time, there is a dark side to the American Dream. It tends to promote an anomic imbalance wherein the importance of using the legitimate means is de-emphasized relative to the importance of attaining the desired cultural goals.

Merton explains that this anomic tendency derives ultimately from the very same basic value commitments upon which the American Dream rests.[9] One such commitment is a strong *achievement orientation*. In American society, personal worth tends to be evaluated on the basis of what people have achieved rather than who they are or how they relate to others in social networks. "Success" is to a large extent the ultimate measure of social worth. Quite understandably, then, there are pervasive cultural pressures to achieve at any cost. A strong achievement orientation, at the level of basic cultural values, thus cultivates and sustains a mentality that "it's not how you play the game; it's whether you win or lose."[10]

A second basic value orientation that contributes to the anomic imbalance in American culture is *individualism*. In the pursuit of success, people are encouraged to "make it" on their own. Fellow members of society are thus competitors in the struggle for achievement and the ultimate validation of personal worth. This intense, individual competition to succeed further encourages a tendency to disregard normative restraints on behavior when these restraints interfere with the realization of goals. Andrew Hacker (1992: 29) offers a cogent description of this distinctive feature of American culture:

> America has always been the most competitive of societies. It poises its citizens against one another, with the warning that they must make it on their own. Hence the stress on moving past others, driven by a fear of falling behind. No other nation so rates its residents as winners or losers.

A third component of American culture that is conducive to anomic imbalance is its *universalism*. Everyone is encouraged to aspire to social ascent, and everyone is susceptible to evaluation on the basis of individual achievements. As a consequence, the pressures to "win" are pervasive; no one is exempt from the pursuit of success (Merton, 1968: 200; Orru 1990: 234).

Finally, in American culture, success is signified in a special way: by the accumulation of *monetary rewards*. Merton is keenly aware of the high priority awarded to money in American culture. He observes that "in some large measure, money has been consecrated as a value in itself, over and above its expenditure for articles of consumption or its use for the enhancement of power" (1968: 190). Merton's key point is not that Americans are uniquely materialistic; a strong interest in material well-being can be found in most societies. Rather, the distinctive feature of American culture is the preeminent role of money as the "metric" of success. As Orru puts it, "money is literally, in this context, a *currency* for measuring achievement" (1990: 235).

Merton points to an important implication of the signification of achievement with reference to monetary rewards. Monetary success is inherently open-ended. Because it is always possible in principle to have more money, "in the American Dream there is no final stopping point" (1968: 190). Cultural prescriptions thus mandate "never-ending achievement" (Passas 1990: 159). Relentless pressures to accumulate money, in turn, encourage people to disregard normative restraints when they impede the pursuit of personal goals.

In sum, dominant value patterns of American culture, specifically its achievement orientation, its competitive individualism, its universalism in goal orientations and evaluative standards—when harnessed to the preeminent goal of monetary success—give rise to a distinctive cultural ethos: the American Dream. The American Dream, in turn, encourages members of society to pursue ends, in Merton's words, "limited only by considerations of technical expediency" (1968: 189). One consequence of this open, widespread, competitive, and anomic quest for success by any means necessary is high levels of crime.

Merton's critique of American culture goes a long way to explain high rates of crime in the United States. In the view of one highly influential critic, it goes too far. Ruth Kornhauser maintains that Merton's cultural account is sufficient by itself to explain high levels of crime in American society. If the culture is characterized by a generalized disregard for normative means, high levels of crime and deviance are likely to be observed regardless of the nature of social structural relationships (Kornhauser, 1978: 145–146). Paradoxically, then, social structure might be regarded as superfluous in the thesis of "social structure and anomie." Kornhauser goes even further and asserts that Merton's theory actually "neglects social structure" (1978: 167).

Kornhauser's criticism contains a kernel of truth but is overstated. Merton certainly attends to social structure in his account of the distribution of deviance and crime in the United States. His well-known hypothesis is that the anomic pressures responsible for deviance vary depending on access to legitimate means to attain economic success, which is determined by location in the stratification system. More broadly, the paradox that social structure is unnecessary in Merton's theory can be resolved by remembering an elementary premise about social organization and pursuing its implications. Culture and social structure are intimately interconnected. Culture does not exist in isolation from social structure but rather is expressed in, reproduced by, and occasionally impeded by, social structure. Any theory that emphasizes "culture" as a cause of crime, then, must also consider the full range of structural conditions through which the cultural sources of crime are enacted.

Accepting this, we agree with Kornhauser's criticism that SS&A does not provide a comprehensive account of the impact of social structure on crime rates. Her comment that "there is much more to social structure than stratification" (1978: 178) is particularly relevant to our purposes. Merton's cultural critique represents only a partial explanation of the high levels of crime in the United States considered in comparative perspective. A complete explanation requires identification of the social structural underpinnings of American culture and its associated strains toward anomie. Merton's analysis stops short of an explication of the ways in which specific features of the institutional structure—beyond the class system—interrelate to generate the anomic pressures that are held to be responsible for crime (cf. Cohen 1985: 233). As a consequence, the anomie perspective is best regarded as a "work in progress." In Cohen's words, Merton "has laid the groundwork for an explanation of deviance [and crime] on the sociological level, but the task, for the most part, still lies ahead" (1985: 233).

The Institutional Dynamics of Crime

The Normal Functions of Social Institutions

Social institutions are the building blocks of whole societies. As such, they constitute the fundamental units of macrolevel analysis. Institutions are "relatively stable sets of norms and values, statuses and roles, and groups and organizations" that regulate human conduct to meet the basic needs of a society (Bassis, Gelles, and Levine 1991: 142). These social needs include the need to adapt to the environment, to mobilize and deploy resources for the achievement of collective goals, and to socialize members in the society's fundamental normative patterns.[11]

Adaptation to the environment is the primary responsibility of economic institutions, which organize the production and distribution of goods and services to satisfy the basic material requirements for human existence. The political system, or "polity," mobilizes and distributes power to attain collective goals. One collective purpose of special importance is the maintenance of public safety. Political institutions are responsible for "protecting members of society from invasions from without, controlling crime and disorder within, and providing channels for resolving conflicts of interest" (Bassis, Gelles, and Levine 1991: 142).

The institution of the family has primary responsibility for the maintenance and replacement of members of society. These tasks involve setting the limits of legitimate sexual relations among adults; the physical care and nurturing of children; and the socialization of children into the values, goals, and beliefs of the dominant culture. In addition, a particularly important function of the family in modern societies is to provide emotional support for its members. To a significant degree, the family serves as a refuge from the tensions and stresses generated in other institutional domains. In this idea of the family as a "haven" from the rigors of the public world lies the implicit recognition of the need to counterbalance and temper the harsh, competitive conditions of public life (Lasch 1977).[12]

The institution of education shares many of the socialization functions of the family. Like the family, schools are given responsibility for transmitting basic cultural standards to new generations. In modern industrial societies, schools are also oriented toward the specific task of preparing youth for the demands of adult occupational roles. In addition, education is intended to enhance personal adjustment, facilitate the development of individual human potential, and advance the general "knowledge base" of the culture.

These four social institutions—the economy, polity, family, and education—are the focus of our explanation of crime. They do not, of course, exhaust the institutional structure of modern societies, nor are they the only institutions with relevance to crime. However, the interconnections among these four institutions are central to an institutional analysis of crime in modern societies, in general, and of the exceptionally high levels of crime in the United States, in particular.

Social institutions are to some extent distinct with respect to the primary activities around which they are organized. At the same time, however, the functions of institutions are overlapping and interdependent. For example, the performance of the economy is dependent on the quality of the "human capital" (i.e., the motivations, knowledge, and skills) cultivated in the schools. The capacity of the schools to develop human capital is circumscribed by the individual backgrounds, what Pierre Bourdieu refers to as the "cultural capital," that students bring with them from their families (MacLeod 1987: 11–14). The effective functioning of all three of these institutions—the economy, education, and the family—presupposes an environment with at least a modicum of social order, for which the polity is largely responsible. Finally, the capacity of the polity to promote the collective good depends on the nature and quality of economic and human resources supplied by the other institutions.

The interdependence of major social institutions implies that some coordination and cooperation among institutions is required for societies to "work" at all. The requirements for the effective functioning of any given institution, however, may conflict with the requirements of another. This potential for conflict is illustrated by the particularly stark contrast between the dominant values embodied in two institutions: the economy and the family.

Economic life and family life are supposed to be governed by fundamentally different standards in modern industrial societies. Family relationships are expected to be regulated by the norm of particularism, and positions and roles in the family are allocated; in large measure, on the basis of ascribed characteristics. Each member is entitled to special considerations by virtue of his or her unique identity and position in the family. In contrast, economic relationships, such as transactions in the marketplace, are supposed to entail universalistic orientations, and economic positions are supposed to be filled according to achievement criteria. Persons who occupy the same or functionally equivalent statuses are to be treated similarly, and access to these statuses is supposed to be gained by demonstrating the capacity to successfully perform their duties and responsibilities. There is thus an inevitable tension between the kinds of normative orientations required for the effective functioning of the family and those required for the efficient operation of a market economy.[13]

Any given society will therefore be characterized by a distinctive arrangement of social institutions that reflects a balancing of the sometimes competing claims and requisites of the different institutions, yielding a distinctive institutional balance of power. Further, the nature of the resulting configuration of institutions is itself intimately related to the larger culture. Indeed, our basic premise about social organization is that culture and the institutional balance of power are mutually reinforcing. On the one hand, culture influences the character of institutions and their positions relative to one another. Culture is in a sense "given life" in the institutional structure of society. On the other hand, the patterns of social relationships constituting institutions, which Parsons (1964: 239) terms the "backbone" of the social system, reproduce and sustain cultural commitments. This is, ultimately, where culture "comes from."[14]

In the macrocriminological analysis of a concrete social system, then, the task is to describe the interpenetration of cultural and institutional patterns, to trace the resulting interconnections among institutions that constitute the institutional balance of power, and finally, to show how the institutional balance of power influences levels of crime. In the following sections, we apply this kind of analysis to the relationships among culture, institutional functioning, and crime in the United States.

The American Dream and the Institutional Balance of Power

Who has not reflected on the question of why the Japanese are so different from ourselves? Or the Swedes or the Italians, the French or the Germans? The answer that we give to this question is that their "cultures" are different, which indeed they are, but different in what ways? (Heilbroner 1991: 538–39)

The core elements of the American Dream—a strong achievement orientation, a commitment to competitive individualism, universalism, and most important, the glorification of material success—have their institutional underpinnings in the economy. The most important feature of the economy of the United States is its capitalist nature. The defining characteristics of any capitalist economy are private ownership and control of property, and free market mechanisms for the production and distribution of goods and services.

These structural arrangements are conducive to, and presuppose, certain cultural orientations. For the economy to operate efficiently, the private owners of property must be profit-oriented and eager to invest, and workers must be willing to exchange their labor for wages. The motivational mechanism underlying these conditions is the promise of financial returns. The internal logic of a capitalist economy thus presumes that an attraction to monetary rewards as a result of achievement in the marketplace is widely diffused throughout the population (cf. Passas 1990: 159).

A capitalist economy is also highly competitive for all those involved, property owners and workers alike. Firms that are unable to adapt to shifting consumer demands or to fluctuations in the business cycle are likely to fail. Workers who are unable to keep up with changing skill requirements or who are unproductive in comparison with others are likely to be fired. This intense competition discourages economic actors from being wedded to conventional ways of doing things and instead encourages them to substitute new techniques for traditional ones if they offer advantages in meeting economic goals. In short, a capitalist economy naturally cultivates a competitive, innovative spirit.

These structural and cultural conditions are common to all capitalist societies. What is distinctive about the United States, however, is the *exaggerated* emphasis on monetary success and the *unrestrained* receptivity to innovation. The goal of monetary success overwhelms other goals and becomes the principal measuring rod for achievements. The resulting proclivity and pressures to innovate resist any regulation that is not justified by purely technical considerations. The obvious question that arises is why cultural orientations that express the inherent logic of capitalism have evolved to a particularly extreme degree in American society. The answer, we submit, lies in the inability of other social institutions to tame economic imperatives. In short, the institutional balance of power is tilted toward the economy.

The historical evidence suggests that this distinctive institutional structure has always existed in the United States. In his analysis of American slavery, the historian Stanley Elkins observes that capitalism emerged "as the principal dynamic force in American society," free to develop according to its own institutional logic without interference from "prior traditional institutions, with competing claims of their own" (Elkins 1968: 43). Whereas capitalism developed in European societies (and later in Japan) within powerful preexisting institutional frameworks, the institutional structure of American society emerged simultaneously with, and was profoundly shaped by, the requirements of capitalist economic development. American capitalism thus took on a "purity of form" unknown in other capitalist societies (Elkins 1968: 43). Moreover, other institutions were cast in distinctly sub-sidiary positions in relation to the economy.

In fact, by the 1830s, many Americans could imagine that they had no need for "institutions" as such, which were regarded with suspicion as vestiges of an older oppressive social order (Elkins 1968: 33). Capitalism represented not a new type of social organization, in this view, but a liberation of the individual from social orga-nization itself. The sources of social stability were to be found not in society, but in human nature. The early American could believe that he did not

> "draw from society his traditions, his culture, and all his aspirations; indeed he, the transcendent individual—the new symbol of virtue—now "confronted" society; he challenged it as something of a conspiracy to rob him of his birthright. Miraculously, all society then sprang to his aid in the celebration of that conceit. (Elkins 1968: 33)

It is important to point out that Elkins's thesis does not support the simplistic assertion that "capitalism causes crime." Elkins himself called attention to the fal-lacy in attributing the cultural and social characteristics of capitalist societies simply to the nature of capitalism: "This idea cannot tell us much about the differences between two societies, *both* capitalist, but in one of which the 'means of production' have changed into capitalistic ones and in the other of which the means of produc-tion were never anything *but* capitalistic and in which no other forces were present to resist their development" (43n). All of the societies presented in figures 4.1 and 4.2 are capitalist societies. The pronounced difference in crime rates between the United States and the others, therefore, cannot be accounted for by capitalism alone. The differences in levels of crime and other aspects of these nations are rooted, fol-lowing Elkins, in their contrasting institutional settings.[15]

Elkins's portrait of the barren institutional landscape of early American soci-ety may be somewhat overdrawn, and aspects of his analysis of the North American slave system are controversial (see Lane 1971). Nonetheless, we accept his basic argument that capitalism developed in the United States without the institutional restraints found in other societies. As a consequence, the economy assumed an unusual dominance in the institutional structure of society from the very beginning of the nation's history. This economic dominance, we argue, has continued to the present and is manifested in three somewhat different ways: (1) in the *devaluation* of noneconomic institutional functions and roles; (2) in the *accommodation* to economic requirements by other institutions; and (3) in the *penetration* of economic norms into other institutional domains.

Consider the relative devaluation of the distinctive functions of education and of the social roles that fulfill these functions. Education is regarded largely as a means to occupational attainment, which in turn is valued primarily insofar as it promises economic rewards. The acquisition of knowledge and learning for its own sake is not highly valued.[16] Effective performance of the roles involved with education, accordingly, do not confer particularly high status. The "good student" is not looked up to by his or her peers; the "master teacher" receives meager financial rewards and public esteem in comparison with those to be gained by success in business.

Similar processes are observed in the context of the family, although the tendency toward devaluation is perhaps not as pronounced as in other institutional arenas. There is indeed a paradox here because "family values" are typically extolled in public rhetoric. Nevertheless, the lack of appreciation for tasks such as parenting, nurturing, and providing emotional support to others is manifested in actual social relationships. It is the home owner rather than the homemaker who is widely admired and envied—and whose image is reflected in the American Dream. Indeed, perhaps the most telling evidence of the relative devaluation of family functions is the inferior status in our society of those persons most extensively involved in these activities: women.

The relative devaluation of the family in comparison with the economy is not an inevitable consequence of the emergence of a modern, industrial society, whether capitalist or socialist. Adler (1983: 131) points to nations such as Bulgaria, the (then) German Democratic Republic, Japan, Saudi Arabia, and Switzerland to illustrate the possibilities for maintaining a strong commitment to the family despite the profound social changes that accompany the transformation from agriculturally based economies to industrial economies. Each of these countries has made extensive, and sometimes costly, efforts to preserve the vitality of the family. Furthermore, these are precisely the kinds of societies that exhibit low crime rates and are not, in Adler's words, "obsessed with crime."

The distinctive function of the polity, providing for the collective good, also tends to be devalued in comparison with economic functions. The general public has little regard for politics as an intrinsically valuable activity and confers little social honor on the role of the politician. Perhaps as a result, average citizens are not expected to be actively engaged in public service, which is left to the "career" politician. The contrast with economic activity is illuminating. The citizen who refuses to vote may experience mild social disapproval; the "able-bodied" adult who refuses to work is socially degraded. Economic participation is obligatory for most adults. In contrast, even the minimal form of political participation entailed in voting (which has more in common with shopping than with work) is considered discretionary, and useful primarily to the extent that it leads to tangible economic rewards (e.g., lower taxes).

Moreover, the very purpose of government tends to be conceptualized in terms of its capacity to facilitate the individual pursuit of economic prosperity. A good illustration is the advice given to the Democratic ticket in the 1992 presidential campaign by the conservative columnist, George Will. Will chastised liberal Democrats for allegedly becoming preoccupied with issues of rights based on ethnicity and sexuality and advised the Democratic presidential candidates to remember the following point that two popular presidents—Franklin Roosevelt and Ronald Reagan—understood very well: "Americans are happiest when pursuing happiness, happiness understood as material advancement, pursued with government's help but not as a government entitlement" (Will 1992: E5).

Will's advice to liberal Democrats is revealing, not only of the core content of the American Dream and its effect on popular views of government, but of a particular kind of collective "right" to which Americans *are* entitled: the right to consume (cf. Edsall 1992: 7). Both of the major political parties celebrate the right to acquire material possessions; they differ mainly with respect to the proper degree of governmental involvement in expanding access to the means of consumption. No matter which party is in power, the function of government, at least in the domestic sphere, remains subsidiary to individual economic considerations.

Interestingly, one distinctive function of the polity does not appear to be generally devalued, namely, crime control. There is widespread agreement among the American public that government should undertake vigorous efforts to deal with the crime problem. If anything, Americans want government to do more to control crime. Yet, this apparent exception is quite compatible with the claim of economic dominance. Americans' "obsession" with crime is rooted in fears that crime threatens, according to political analyst Thomas Edsall (1992: 9) "their security, their values, their rights, and their livelihoods and the competitive prospects of their children." In other words, because crime control bears directly on the pursuit of the American Dream, this particular function of the polity receives high priority.

A second way in which the dominance of the economy is manifested is in the *accommodations* that emerge in those situations in which institutional claims are in competition. Economic conditions and requirements typically exert a much stronger influence on the operation of other institutions than vice versa. For example, family routines are dominated by the schedules, rewards, and penalties of the labor market. Consider the resistance of employers (and their representatives in government) to proposals for maternity leaves, flexible hours, or on-the-job child care. The contrast between the United States and another capitalist society with very low crime rates—Japan—is striking in this regard. In Japan, business enterprises are accommodated to the needs of the family, becoming in some respects a "surrogate family," with services ranging from child rearing to burial (Adler 1983: 132).

The most important way that family life is influenced by the economy, however, is through the necessity for paid employment to support a family. Joblessness makes it difficult for families to remain intact and to form in the first place. In the urban underclass, where rates of joblessness are chronically high, so too are rates of separation, divorce, single-parent households, and births to unmarried women (Wilson 1987).

Educational institutions are also more likely to accommodate to the demands of the economy than is the economy to respond to the requirements of education. The timing of schooling reflects occupational demands rather than intrinsic features of the learning process or personal interest in the pursuit of knowledge. People go to school largely to prepare for "good" jobs, and once in the labor market, there is little opportunity to pursue further education for its own sake. When workers do return to school, it is almost always to upgrade skills or credentials to keep pace with job demands, to seek higher-paying jobs, or to "retool" during spells of unemployment. At the organizational level, schools are dependent on the economy for financial resources, and thus it becomes important for school officials to convince business leaders that education is suitably responsive to business needs.

The polity likewise is dependent on the economy for financial support. Governments must accordingly take care to cultivate and maintain an environment hospitable to investment. If they do not, they run the risk of being literally "downgraded" by financial markets, as happened to Detroit in 1992 when Moody's Investors Service dropped the city's credit rating to noninvestment grade. Cities have little choice but to accommodate to market demands in such situations. "A city proposes, Moody's disposes. There is no appeals court or court of last ratings resort" (*New York Times*, 1992: C1). The pursuit of the collective good is thus circumscribed by economic imperatives.

A final way in which the dominance of the economy in the institutional balance of power is manifested is in the *penetration* of economic norms into other institutional areas. Schools rely on grading as a system of extrinsic rewards, like wages, to insure compliance with goals. Learning takes place within the context of individualized competition for these external rewards, and teaching inevitably tends to become oriented toward testing. Economic terminology permeates the very language of education, as in the recent emphasis in higher education on "accountability" conceptualized in terms of the "value-added" to students in the educational production process.

Within the polity, a "bottom-line" mentality develops. Effective politicians are those who deliver the goods. Moreover, the notion that the government would work better if it were run more like a business continues to be an article of faith among large segments of the American public.

The family has probably been most resistant to the intrusion of economic norms. Yet even here, pressures toward penetration are apparent. Contributions to family life tend to be measured against the all-important "breadwinner" role, which has been extended to include women who work in the paid labor force. No corresponding movement of men into the role of "homemaker" has occurred, and a declining number of women desire or can afford to occupy this role on a full-time basis. Here again, shifts in popular terminology are instructive. Husbands and wives are "partners" who "manage" the household "division of labor." We can detect no comparable shifts in kin-based terminology, or primary group norms, from the family to the workplace.

In sum, the social organization of the United States is characterized by a striking dominance of the economy in the institutional balance of power. As a result of this economic dominance, the inherent tendencies of a capitalist economy to orient the members of society toward an unrestrained pursuit of economic achievements are developed to an extreme degree. These tendencies are expressed at the cultural level in the preeminence of monetary success as the overriding goal—the American Dream—and in the relative deemphasis placed on the importance of using normative means to reach this goal—anomie. The anomic nature of the American Dream and the institutional structure of American society are thus mutually supportive and reinforcing. The key remaining question is the impact of this type of social organization on crime.

Anomie, Weak Social Controls, and Crime

The American Dream contributes to high levels of crime in two important ways, one direct and the other indirect. It has a direct effect on crime through the creation of an anomic normative order, that is, an environment in which social norms are unable to exert a strong regulatory force on the members of society. It has an indirect effect on crime by contributing to an institutional balance of power that inhibits the development of strong mechanisms of external social control. The criminogenic tendencies of the American Dream are thus due in part to the distinctive content of the cultural values and beliefs that comprise it and in part to the institutional consequences of these values and beliefs.

One criminogenic aspect of the specific content of the American Dream is the expression of the primary success goal in monetary terms. Because monetary success is an inherently open-ended and elusive, the adequacy of the legitimate means for achieving this particular cultural goal is necessarily suspect. No matter how much money someone is able to make by staying within legal boundaries, illegal means will always offer further advantages in pursuit of the ultimate goal. There is thus a perpetual attractiveness associated with illegal activity that is an inevitable corollary of the goal of monetary success.

This culturally induced pressure to "innovate" by using illegitimate means is exacerbated by the dominance of the economy in the institutional balance of power. There are, of course, important noneconomic tasks carried out in other institutional arenas, tasks associated with goals that might in fact be readily attainable within the confines of the legal order. However, as we have suggested, roles effectively performed in the capacity of being a parent or spouse, a student or scholar, an engaged citizen or public servant are simply not the primary bases upon which success and failure are defined in American society. The dominance of the economy continuously erodes the structural supports for functional alternatives to the goal of economic success.

Nor does the ethos of the American Dream contain within it strong counterbalancing injunctions against substituting more effective illegitimate means for less effective legitimate means. To the contrary, the distinctive cultural "value" accompanying the monetary success goal in the American Dream is the *devaluation* of all but the most technically efficient means.

The American Dream does not completely subsume culture. There are other elements of culture that define socially acceptable modes of behavior and that affirm the legitimacy of social norms, including legal norms. In principle, these other cultural elements could counterbalance the anomic pressures that emanate from the American Dream. However, the very same institutional dynamics that contribute to the pressures to innovate in the pursuit of economic goals also make it less likely that the anomic pressures inherent in the American Dream will in fact be counterbalanced by other social forces.

As noneconomic institutions are relatively devalued, are forced to accommodate to economic needs, and are penetrated by economic standards, they are less able to fulfill their distinctive functions effectively. These functions include socialization into acceptance of the social norms. Weak families and poor schools are handicapped in their efforts to promote allegiance to social rules, including legal prohibitions. As a result, the pressures to disregard normative constraints in the pursuit of the goal of monetary success also tend to undermine social norms more generally. In the absence of the cultivation of strong commitments to social norms, the selection of the means for realizing goals *of any type* is guided mainly by instrumental considerations.

In addition, the relative impotence of noneconomic institutions is manifested in a reduced capacity to exert external social control. The government is constrained in its capacity to provide public goods that would make crime less attractive and in its efforts to mobilize collective resources—including moral resources—to effectively deter criminal choices. Single-parent families or those in which both parents have full-time jobs, all else equal, are less able to provide extensive supervision over children. All families must rely to some extent on other institutions, usually the schools, for assistance in social control. Yet poorly funded or crowded schools also find it difficult to exert effective supervision, especially when students see little or no connection between what is taught in the classroom and what is valued outside of it.

Finally, weak institutions invite challenge. Under conditions of extreme competitive individualism, people actively resist institutional control. They not only fall from the insecure grasp of powerless institutions, sometimes they deliberately, even proudly, push themselves away. The problem of "external" social control, then, is inseparable from the problem of the "internal" regulatory force of social norms, or anomie. Anomic societies will inevitably find it difficult and costly to exert social control over the behavior of people who feel free to use whatever means that prove most effective in reaching personal goals. Hence the very sociocultural dynamics that make American institutions weak also enable and entitle Americans to defy institutional controls. If Americans are exceptionally resistant to social control—and therefore exceptionally vulnerable to criminal temptations—it is because they live in a society that enshrines the unfettered pursuit of individual material success above all other values. In the United States, anomie is a virtue.

Conclusion

This reformulation of Merton's classic theory of social structure and anomie is intended to challenge criminologists and policymakers alike to think about crime in America as a macrolevel product of widely admired cultural and social structures with deep historical roots. Criminological theories that neglect the ironic interdependence between crime and the normal functioning of the American social system will be unable to explain the preoccupation with crime that so dramatically separates the United States from other developed societies. Significant reductions in crime will not result from reforms limited to the criminal justice system, which is itself shaped in important ways by the same cultural and social forces—the same desperate emphasis on ends over means—that produce high rates of crime. Nor will social reforms, whatever their other merits, that widen access to legitimate opportunities for persons "locked out" of the American Dream bring relief from the crimes of those who are "locked in" the American Dream, exposed to its limitless imperatives in the absence of moderating social forces. Reducing these crimes will require fundamental social transformations that few Americans desire, and a rethinking of a dream that is the envy of the world.

Notes

1. See Archer and Gartner (1984) and Kalish (1988) for good discussions of problems associated with cross-national crime comparisons and useful approaches for addressing them.

2. The data on robbery rates are from the International Police Organization (Interpol 1987–88), which defines *robbery* as "violent theft." This definition accords with the general classification of robberies in the United States and elsewhere as thefts (including attempts) accompanied by force or the threat of force. The homicide data are from the World Health Organization (WHO 1990), which defines *homicide* as death by injury purposely inflicted by others (Kalish 1988: 4). Nineteen eighty-eight is the most recent year for which the cross-national data were available. (The robbery rate for the Netherlands is for 1986).

3. Similar comparative data on serious white-collar offending, corporate crime in particular, are not available. This is unfortunate because the aggregate impact of white-collar crime is far greater than that of conventional street crimes in the United States. This applies to both the economic costs of offenses such as fraud, false advertising, and antitrust violations, and the injuries, disease, and deaths resulting from product safety violations, violations of workplace health and safety codes, and other "violent" white-collar offenses (Coleman 1989: 6–12). Although it is not possible to make a comparative assessment of levels of white-collar crime at present, the pervasiveness and injuriousness of such offending in the U.S. seems beyond dispute.

4. For a general discussion of the view that "evil" outcomes must have "evil" causes and of alternative perspectives, see Nisbet (1971: 9–14).

5. Stitt and Giacopassi speculate that the most likely reason for the dominance of social control theory is that "Hirschi's version was directly operationally defined in a survey format" (1992: 4).

6. There are exceptions to the generalization that contemporary criminology has neglected questions about variation in levels of crime across large, macrosocial units. For selected examples of major efforts to address these kinds of questions, see the following: Braithwaite's (1989) general theory of crime, which emphasizes the importance of cultural commitments and social arrangements supportive of "reintegrative shaming"; Adler's (1983) national case studies of "synomie"

and crime; and the work on modernization and crime by Shelley (1981) and Clinard and Abbott (1973). See also the historical studies of Gurr (1981) and Zehr (1976).

7. A good illustration of the explanatory potential of a social-psychological strain perspective is provided by Agnew's (1992) recent work.

8. Very similar characterizations of the American Dream appear in more recent studies of the "success theme" in American literature. See, for example, Hearn (1977) and Long (1985).

9. Our discussion of the anomic tendencies in American culture draws heavily on Orru's (1990) excellent exegesis of Merton's work. See also Passas (1990).

10. See in this regard Gouldner's (1970: 65) arguments concerning the tendency for "bourgeois utilitarian culture" to place a "great stress upon winning or losing, upon success or failure as such. . . . "

11. Our discussion of the needs fulfilled by institutions is based on Parsons' classic description of the functional prerequisites of social systems (Parsons 1951). Parsons identifies a fourth system need, the need to "integrate" the system around its core value orientations, and he locates the legal system within this functional realm. We follow the more common practice of treating the legal system, specifically criminal justice organizations and processes, as part of the political system (see below). We have drawn on Bassis, Gelles, and Levine (1991) in our description of this and other specific institutional activities.

12. These protective functions of the family, it must be noted, traditionally have had greater salience for men. In addition, the family generates its own pressures and conflicts, and these have a special impact on women, the primary caretakers of the domestic domain.

13. The classic discussion of these value patterns is in Parsons (1951).

14. We are well aware of the ideal typical nature of this description of institutional functioning. For example, occupational roles are often filled on the basis of functionally irrelevant criteria (e.g., race and gender) even in societies that proclaim open competition and equal opportunity for all members. Moreover, the persistence of ascriptive inequalities in societies formally committed to the norm of equal opportunity may give rise to feelings of injustice and dissatisfaction that promote criminal behavior (Blau and Blau 1982; Messner and Golden 1992). Our present concern, however, is not with how *departures* from cultural ideals influence crime rates but how crime is produced when societies work pretty much the way they are supposed to (for a similar orientation, see Wright and Hilbert 1980).

15. Similarly, Heilbroner (1991: 539–40) writes that *"American* capitalism, not American *capitalism"* is responsible for the features of American society that distinguish it, for better or worse, from other capitalist societies.

16. A high school student, whose grades dropped when she increased her schedule at her two after-school jobs to 30 hours a week, described her feelings about the intrinsic rewards of education this way: "School's important but so's money. Homework doesn't pay. Teachers say education is your payment, and that just makes me want to puke" (Waldman and Springen 1992: 81).

References

Adler, F. 1983. *Nations Not Obsessed with Crime.* Littleton, CO: Fred. B. Rothman.

Agnew, R. 1992. "Foundation for a General Strain Theory of Crime and Delinquency." *Criminology* 30: 47–48.

Archer, D., and R. Gartner. 1984. *Violence and Crime in Cross-National Perspective.* New Haven, CT: Yale University Press.

Bassis, M. S., R. J. Gelles, and A. Levine. 1991. *Sociology: An Introduction.* 4th ed. New York: McGraw-Hill.

Blau, J. R., and P. M. Blau, 1982. "The Cost of Inequality: Metropolitan Structure and Violent Crime." *American Sociological Review* 47: 114–29.

Braithwaite, J. 1989. *Crime, Shame and Reintegration.* Cambridge: Cambridge University Press.

Burton, V. S., Jr. and F. T. Cullen. 1992. "The Empirical Status of Strain Theory." *Journal of Crime and Justice* 15: 1–30.

Clinard, M. B., and D. J. Abbott. 1973. *Crime in Developing Countries: A Comparative Perspective.* New York: Wiley.

Cohen, A. K. 1985. "The Assumption That Crime Is a Product of Environments: Sociological Approaches." In *Theoretical methods in criminology,* ed. R. F. Meier, 223–243. Beverly Hills, CA: Sage Publications.

Coleman, J. W. 1989. *The Criminal Elite: The Sociology of White Collar Crime.* 2d ed. New York: St. Martin's Press.

Edsall, T. B. 1992, February 13. "Willie Horton's Message." *New York Review,* pp. 7–11.

Elkins, S. M. 1968. *Slavery.* 2d ed. Chicago: University of Chicago Press.

Fingerhut, L. A., and J. C. Kleinman. 1990. "International and Interstate Comparisons of Homicide among Young Males." *Journal of the American Medical Association* 263: 3292–95.

Gouldner, A. W. 1970. *The Coming Crisis of Western Sociology.* New York: Basic Books.

Gurr, T. R. 1981. "Historical Trends in Violent Crimes: A Critical Review of the Evidence." In *Crime and Justice: An Annual Review of Research,* vol. 3, ed. M. Tonry and N. Morris 295–353. Chicago: University of Chicago Press.

Hacker, A. 1992. *Two Nations: Black and White, Separate, Hostile Unequal.* New York: Charles Scribner's.

Hearn, C. 1977. *The American Dream in the Great Depression.* Westport, CT: Greenwood Press.

Heilbroner, R. 1991, November. "A Pivotal Question Unanswered." *The World & I: A Chronicle of our Changing Era,* pp. 538–539.

Hodkins, S. 1992. "Mental Disorder, Intellectual Deficiency, and Crime." *Archives of General Psychiatry* 49: 476–83.

Interpol, 1987–88. *International Crime Statistics.* Saint Cloud, France: International Police Organization.

Kalish, C. B. 1988. *International Crime Rates.* Washington, DC: U.S. Department of Justice.

Kornhauser, R. R. 1978. *Social Sources of Delinquency: An Appraisal of Analytic Models.* Chicago: University of Chicago Press.

Lane, A. J., ed. 1971. *The Debate over Slavery: Stanley Elkins and His Critics.* Urbana, IL: University of Illinois Press.

Lasch, C. 1977. *Haven in a Heartless World.* New York: Basic Books.

Long, E. 1985. *The American Dream and the Popular Novel.* Boston: Routledge & Kegan Paul.

MacLeod, J. 1987. *Ain't No Makin' It: Leveled Aspirations in a Low-Income Neighborhood.* Boulder, CO: Westview.

Merton, R. K. 1938. "Social Structure and Anomie." *American Sociological Review* 3: 672–82.

———. 1968. *Social Theory and Social Structure.* New York: Free Press.

Messner, S. F., and R. M. Golden. 1992. "Racial Inequality and Racially Disaggregated Crime Rates: An Assessment of Alternative Theoretical Explanations." *Criminology* 30: 421–45.

Messner, S. F., and R. Rosenfeld. 1994. *Crime and the American Dream.* Belmont, CA: Wadsworth.

New York Times. 1992, November 3. "A Downgraded Detroit Cries Foul," pp. C1, C4.

Nisbet, R. 1971. "The Study of Social Problems." In *Contemporary Social Problems,* ed. R. K. Merton & R. Nisbet, 1–25. New York: Harcourt Brace Jovanovich.

Orru, M. 1990. "Merton's Instrumental Theory of Anomie." In *Robert K. Merton: Consensus and Controversy,* ed. J. Clark, C. Modgil, and S. Modgil, 231–40. London: Falmer Press.

Parsons, T. 1951. *The Social System.* Glencoe, IL: Free Press.

———. 1964. *Essays in Sociological Theory.* Rev. ed. New York: Free Press.

Passas, N. 1990. "Anomie and Corporate Deviance." *Contemporary Crises* 14: 157–78.

Shelley, L. I. 1981. *Crime and Modernization.* Carbondale, IL: Southern Illinois University Press.

Short, J., Jr. 1985. "The Level of Explanation Problem in Criminology." In *Theoretical methods in criminology,* ed. R. F. Meier, 51–72. Beverly Hills, CA: Sage Publications.

Stitt, B. G., and D. J. Giacopassi. 1992. "Trends in the Connectivity of Theory and Research in *Criminology.*" *The Criminologist* 17(4): 1, 3–6.

Vold, G. B., and T. J. Bernard. 1986. *Theoretical Criminology.* 3d ed. New York: Oxford University Press.

Waldman, S., and K. Springen. 1992, November 16. "Too Old, Too Fast?" *Newsweek*, p. 81.

Whitaker, C. J. 1990. *Black Victims.* Washington, DC: U. S. Department of Justice.

WHO. 1990. *World Health Statistics Annual.* Geneva, Switzerland: World Health Organization.

Will, G. 1992, July 12. "Democrats Can Win If They Remember What Reagan Said." *Albany Times Union*, p. E5.

Wilson, W. J. 1987. *The Truly Disadvantaged.* Chicago: University of Chicago Press.

Wright, C., and R. E. Hilbert. 1980. "Value Implications of the Functional Theory of Deviance." *Social Problems* 28: 205–19.

Zehr, H. 1976. *Crime and the Development of Modern Society: Patterns of Criminality in Nineteenth Century Germany and France.* London: Roman and Littlefield.

Social Disorganization Theory

Social disorganization theory emerged from the renowned "Chicago School" of Sociology. The Chicago School was born when the first department of Sociology in America opened at the University of Chicago in 1892 (Williams & McShane, 2010:46). The Chicago School also came to be known as "The Ecological School," because of its special focus on ecological studies and life histories (Vold & Bernard, 1979:181–182; Williams & McShane, 2010:48–49). Essentially, the Chicago School viewed the urban setting as the natural habitat of human beings. As a consequence, its members actively went out into the city to study humans, much like wildlife researchers might go out into the wilderness to study wildlife. They also regarded the city as a living "organism" (Williams & McShane, 2010:49), similar to Durkheim's (1965) view of society as an organism comprised of various different parts or organs (cf. Traub & Little, 1985:41).

The Chicago School produced a number of ethnographies and life histories, including *The Polish Peasant* by W. I. Thomas and Florian Znaniecki, *The Hobo* by Nels Anderson, *The Professional Thief* by Edwin Sutherland, and *The Jackroller* and *Brothers in Crime* by Clifford R. Shaw, to mention but a few (Mutchnick, Martin, & Austin, 2009; Traub & Little, 1985; Vold & Bernard, 1979). Chicago School thinking also contributed to the development of social disorganization theory, symbolic interactionism (which in turn contributed to the development of labeling theory), differential association (which forms an integral part of social learning theory), and cultural transmission theory (an amalgam of social disorganization theory and differential association theory) (Lilly, Cullen, & Ball, 2011:48–49; Williams & McShane, 2010:50–51). Section III of this book is concerned with differential association theory and social learning theory, while Section V covers the sociology of deviance and labeling theory. In truth, it is difficult to overstate the influence of the Chicago School on the development of both criminological theory and the sociology of deviance.

To understand social disorganization theory (and Chicago School thinking), it is important to appreciate how the City of Chicago evolved over time. As Shaw and McKay (1969:17) point out in the first reading selection in Section II, Chicago grew in a little more than a hundred years from being a small town with around 200 inhabitants to a city with over three million inhabitants. Part of this growth and expansion can be explained by general trends toward industrialization and urbanization that were occurring almost everywhere during the 1800s and 1900s. That said, Chicago grew primarily through successive waves of migrants—African Americans leaving the post-Civil War South to escape racial discrimination and look for better job opportunities in the North, displaced farmers and/or farm workers leaving the American countryside as agriculture and ranching became more commercialized, and overseas immigrants coming to America from places such as Poland, Ireland, Italy, and Germany (Lilly et al., 2011:40; Traub & Little, 1985:41). All of this activity resulted in tremendous overcrowding, and the growth of large urban slums. Many of the people arriving in Chicago had little or no money, and no immediate job prospects. Thus, they had no choice but to live in these slums, where rent was cheapest (Akers & Sellers, 2009:177–179; Lilly et al., 2011:40–41). In these overcrowded slums, they found themselves surrounded by run-down buildings, poverty, unemployment, and people from many different ethnic and cultural backgrounds.

Although Shaw and McKay are the most well known of the early social disorganization theorists, they did not come up with the concept of social disorganization themselves. Moreover, Shaw and McKay did not develop the concentric zone theory upon which social disorganization theory was built. Thomas and Znaniecki described social disorganization in their 1918 book, *The Polish Peasant in Europe and America*. Robert Park, one of the founding members of the Chicago School, also talked about social disorganization at around the same time as Thomas and Znaniecki (Mutchnick et al., 2009:70; Traub & Little, 1985:42). Ernest Burgess, in collaboration with Robert Park, identified the five concentric zones or rings that expanded outward as the City of Chicago grew—the loop (or business center and transportation hub), the zone in transition, the working class zone, the residential zone, and the commuter zone (which we would now call the suburbs) (Traub & Little, 1985:52; Vold & Bernard, 1979:185). More will be said about concentric zone theory in the introduction to the first reading in Section II, by Shaw and McKay.

In their 1931 book *Social Factors in Juvenile Delinquency* and their subsequent 1942 book *Juvenile Delinquency in Urban Areas*, Shaw and McKay expanded upon earlier Chicago School thinking about social disorganization theory. They employed the concentric zone model developed by Park and Burgess to explain why certain areas of Chicago—especially the zone in transition—experienced higher rates of delinquency than other areas of the city (Vold & Bernard, 1979:186–187). Basically, Shaw and McKay described five characteristics of the zone in transition that they said contributed to social disorganization and higher delinquency rates—poverty, overcrowding, residential mobility, ethnic and cultural differences, and broken homes (Lilly et al., 2011:44–45; Williams & McShane, 2010:50).

Shaw and McKay's original research on social disorganization has been the starting point for a number of recent endeavours in this particular direction, including (but not limited to) Robert Bursik's (1988) analysis of the problems and prospects for social disorganization theory, Robert Sampson and Byron Groves's (1989) test of social disorganization theory using data from the British Crime Survey, Bonita Veysey and Steven Messner's further (1999) reassessment of Sampson and Groves's social disorganization study, D. Wayne Osgood and Jeff Chambers' (2000) analysis of social disorganization and youth violence in rural areas of the United States, and Ralph Taylor's (2001) work on social disorganization and collective efficacy. The second and third readings in Section II of this book are in fact written by the aforementioned Robert Sampson and Byron Groves and Robert Bursik. As will be seen shortly, the concept of social disorganization theory remains a vital part of sociological and criminological theory.

References

Akers, R. L., & Sellers, C. S. (2009). *Criminological theories: Introduction, evaluation, and application* (5th , New ed.). New York: Oxford University Press.

Bursik, R. J. Jr. (1988). Social disorganization and theories of crime and delinquency: Problems and prospects. *Criminology, 26*(4), 519–551.

Durkheim, E. (1965). *The division of labor in society* (G. Simpson Trans.). New York: Free Press.

Lilly, J. R., Cullen, F. T., & Ball, R. A. (2011). *Criminological theory: Context and consequences* (5th ed.). Thousand Oaks: SAGE Publications.

Mutchnick, R. J., Martin, R., & Austin, T. W. (2009). *Criminological thought: Pioneers past and present.* Upper Saddle River, NJ: Prentice Hall.

Osgood, D. W., & Chambers, J. M. (2000). Social disorganization outside the metropolis: An analysis of rural youth violence. *Criminology, 38*(1), 81–115.

Sampson, R. J., & Groves, W. B. (1989). Community structure and crime: Testing social-disorganization theory. *American Journal of Sociology, 94*(4), 774–802.

Shaw, C. R., & McKay, H. D. (1969). *Juvenile delinquency and urban areas: A study of rates of delinquency in relation to differential characteristics of local communities in American cities* (Rev. ed.). Chicago: University of Chicago Press.

Taylor, R. B. (2001). The ecology of crime, fear, and delinquency: Social disorganization versus social efficacy. In R. Paternoster, & R. Bachman (Eds.), *Explaining criminals and crime: Essays in contemporary criminological theory* (pp. 124–139). Los Angeles, Calif.: Roxbury Pub. Co.

Traub, S. H., & Little, C. B. (1985). *Theories of deviance* (3rd ed.). Itasca, Ill.: F. E. Peacock Publishers.

Veysey, B. M., & Messner, S. F. (1999). Further testing of social disorganization theory: An elaboration of Sampson and Groves's "community structure and crime." *Journal of Research in Crime and Delinquency, 36*(2), 156–174.

Vold, G. B., & Second edition prepared by Thomas J. Bernard. (1979). *Theoretical criminology* (2nd ed.). New York: Oxford University Press.

Williams, F. P., & McShane, M. D. (2010). *Criminological theory* (5th ed.). Upper Saddle River, N.J.: Pearson/Prentice Hall.

5

Social Disorganization Theory

Clifford Shaw and Henry McKay were graduate students in Sociology at the University of Chicago (Lilly, Cullen, & Ball, 2011:42). Shaw had previously been a probation officer and a parole officer in Chicago (Vold & Bernard, 1979:186–187). Although they were affiliated with—and strongly influenced by—the Chicago School, they were not actually university professors at the Chicago School (Lilly et al., 2011:42). Rather, Clifford Shaw and Henry McKay were practitioners more than they were academicians, and spent most of their time working together at Chicago's Institute for Juvenile Research. With the assistance of graduate students from the University of Chicago, they gathered longitudinal data on juvenile delinquency in Chicago (along with data from Cleveland, Philadelphia, Denver, and various other American cities) (Taylor, 2001:126; Vold & Bernard, 1979:186). The addresses of the known juvenile delinquents were then plotted on city maps, in order to identify the areas where juvenile delinquency was most (and least) concentrated. In addition, Shaw and McKay gathered data on the prevalence of condemned or demolished buildings, which were also plotted on city maps. These maps helped to establish the degree to which juvenile delinquency rates were associated with the run-down areas of the city (Taylor, 2001:126; Vold & Bernard, 1979:187).

Using the concentric zone model of urban growth that had been developed by Robert Park and Ernest Burgess of the Chicago School (see Introduction to Section II), Shaw and McKay were able to demonstrate that juvenile delinquency was most concentrated in the zone in transition, sometimes referred to as the interstitial zone (Vold & Bernard, 1979:195). The zone in transition was adjacent to the central business district, also known as "the Loop" (Shaw & McKay, 1969:31). The business district was the first part of the city to develop—it was where the businesses and major transportation networks (i.e., roads, railways and waterways) came together. The zone in transition (next to the business loop) could best be described as an urban slum or "ghetto" (Lilly et al., 2011:42–43; Vold & Bernard, 1979:186). This zone consisted largely of abandoned or run-down factories and decrepit tenement buildings, many of which were condemned (i.e., slated for demolition, or deemed to be uninhabitable) (Vold & Bernard, 1979:189). The owners of these factories and tenements did not bother to maintain these buildings, and often neglected to do repairs when they were needed. Basically, the owners were hoping that as the city grew and the business center continued to expand outwards, these buildings (and the properties that they were on) would be purchased for higher prices for real estate development purposes. It was expected that the run-down buildings would eventually be demolished, so from a financial point of view, there was little reason to keep them well-maintained (Shaw & McKay, 1969:20; Taylor, 2001:129).

This zone in transition eventually became populated primarily by recently arrived migrants from around the United States, and by immigrants from abroad. Rental prices in the transition zone were much lower than the typical rents in other areas of the city. The inhabitants of the zone in transition were also closer to the heavy industrial areas and factories, where they could search for low-paying (unskilled) laboring jobs. The living conditions in the transition zone were in marked contrast to the conditions in the adjacent working class zone (with its duplexes and row homes), the more distant residential district (with expensive apartments and single-family homes) and the commuter zone on the outskirts of the city (with large houses, far from the noise, industry and pollution).

Shaw and McKay identified five main characteristics of these zones in transition that contributed to (or were symptomatic of) social disorganization:

- Overcrowding, also referred to as residential density. Entire families were living in small, crowded apartments (Sampson & Groves, 1989:781–782).
- Poverty, or low socioeconomic status. Most of the inhabitants of these urban slums or ghettos had arrived in Chicago recently, with no money and no job prospects. Few families owned their own homes, and many were receiving some form of government assistance (Vold & Bernard, 1979:189).
- Ethnic and cultural heterogeneity. There were many different ethnic groups, all crowded together in the zone in transition. These ethnic groups did not speak the same language (some did not speak English at all), they did not follow the same religion, and they did not share the same cultural values (Sampson & Groves, 1989:774–775).
- Residential instability, also referred to as residential mobility. There was a constant turnover of population. People were moving into the zone in transition because of the cheaper rent and the proximity to factories and heavy industry (where they could look for work). However, anyone who was capable of leaving the zone in transition and moving to a better living environment did so as quickly as possible (Lowenkamp, Cullen, & Pratt, 2003:385).

- Family disruption and broken homes. Moving from another country or from distant parts of the United States to the zone in transition put a lot of stress on families. Living in the over-crowded, noisy, run-down and polluted zone in transition only added to this stress (Lilly et al., 2011:44–45; Williams & McShane, 2010:50).

In the socially disorganized zone in transition, the usual sources of social control—the family, neighbors, the schools and religious organizations—broke down and became ineffective . There were large numbers of single-parent homes, where the sole parent was either away at work all day, or on welfare. Even in two-parent homes, both parents were often working in order to make ends meet. Neighbors did not trust one another, because they typically came from different ethnic or cultural backgrounds, and often spoke different languages. Hence, they were unable to communicate, or form friendships with each other. Schools were overwhelmed by the influx of students with differing educational backgrounds, many of whom were unable to communicate in English. There was a wide variety of religious organizations, offering services in a multitude of languages, while promoting widely divergent beliefs.

In essence, social disorganization theory can be seen as the forerunner of social control theory (discussed in Section IV of this book). Shaw and McKay identified what they regarded as a cause-effect relationship between social disorganization and the breakdown of informal social controls (Cullen, Wright, & Blevins, 2004:4; Sampson & Groves, 1989:778). Youth who were living in this zone in transition were freed from social restraints, or controls. These youth were free to gather together on street corners, without adult supervision. This in turn led to the formation of youth gangs, and increased rates of juvenile delinquency.

Social disorganization theory can also be viewed as the forerunner of cultural transmission theory. Shaw and McKay concluded that these disorganized areas produced and sustained criminal values and criminal traditions, and also observed that these values and traditions were passed along from generation to generation (Lilly et al., 2011:45; Williams & McShane, 2010:50–51). Basically, these unrestrained youth banded together to form criminal subcultures with their own set of values and norms that were often in opposition to "conventional" values and norms. These criminal values and norms were then transmitted from gang member to gang member, as well as from older, more experienced gang members to new initiates to the gangs. Any number of subsequent studies—e.g., Albert Cohen's (1955, 1964) work on delinquent boys and the culture of gangs, Cloward and Ohlin's (1960) work on the criminal subculture, the conflict subculture and the retreatist subculture, and Wolfgang and Ferracuti's (1967) study of subcultures of violence—were influenced to one degree or another by Shaw and McKay's observations regarding the transmission of criminal values and criminal traditions.

References

Cloward, R. A., & Ohlin, L. E. (1960). *Delinquency and opportunity: A theory of delinquent gangs.* New York: Free Press.

Cohen, A. K. (1955, 1964). *Delinquent boys: The culture of the gang.* Glencoe, IL: Free Press of Glencoe.

Cullen, F. T., Wright, J. P., & Blevins, K. R. (Eds). (2004). *Taking stock: The status of criminological theory.* New Brunswick, N.J.: Transaction Publishers.

Lilly, J. R., Cullen, F. T., & Ball, R. A. (2011). *Criminological theory: Context and consequences* (5th ed.). Thousand Oaks: SAGE Publications.

Lowenkamp, C. T., Cullen, F. T., & Pratt, T. C. (2003). Replicating Sampson and Groves's test of social disorganization theory: Revisiting a criminological classic. *Journal of Research in Crime and Delinquency, 40*(4), 351–373.

Sampson, R. J., & Groves, W. B. (1989). Community structure and crime: Testing social-disorganization theory. *American Journal of Sociology, 94*(4), 774–802.

Shaw, C. R., & McKay, H. D. (1969). *Juvenile delinquency and urban areas: A study of rates of delinquency in relation to differential characteristics of local communities in American cities* (Rev. ed.). Chicago: University of Chicago Press.

Taylor, R. B. (2001). The ecology of crime, fear, and delinquency: Social disorganization versus social efficacy. In R. Paternoster, & R. Bachman (Eds.), *Explaining criminals and crime: Essays in contemporary criminological theory* (pp. 124–139). Los Angeles, CA: Roxbury Pub. Co.

Vold, G. B., Second edition prepared by Thomas J. Bernard. (1979). *Theoretical criminology* (2nd ed.). New York: Oxford University Press.

Williams, F. P., & McShane, M. D. (2010). *Criminological theory* (5th ed.). Upper Saddle River, NJ: Pearson/Prentice Hall.

Wolfgang, M. E., & Ferracuti, F. (1967). *The subculture of violence: Towards an integrated theory in criminology.* London: Tavistock Publication.

Growth of Chicago and Differentiation of Local Areas

CLIFFORD SHAW AND HENRY MCKAY

Chicago is a large industrial and commercial city located on the western shore of Lake Michigan near its southern extremity. It is the second largest city in the United States and the largest included in this study. Within a period of a little over a century it has grown from a small town, with a population of about 200 and an area of $2\frac{1}{2}$ square miles, to a great industrial metropolis, with a population of over 3,300,000 people and a corporate area of 211 square miles, extending some 25 miles along the lake front and from 8 to 10 miles inland.

During its growth a differentiation of areas has taken place within Chicago. Even a casual observation reveals that certain districts are occupied largely by industry

Reprinted from *Juvenile Delinquency and Urban Areas*, edited by Clifford R. Shaw and Henry D. McKay (1946), University of Chicago Press.

and others used exclusively for residential purposes; that certain areas are occupied by persons of low economic status and others by the very rich; and that certain neighborhoods are characterized by a native white population, and others by the foreign born, whose dominant languages are still those of the Old World. It is generally known, also, that among areas in the city there are wide differences in the rates of truants, of delinquents, and of adult criminals, as well as in disease and mortality rates and other indexes of well-being. More subtle are the differences in standards and cultural values, in community organization, and in the nature of social life; but that they exist there can be no question.

Why do these variations exist? Why has the city assumed this configuration, with this particular distribution of poverty and wealth and of racial and national groups? Why are there such wide differences in standards and cultural values among areas within the city?

This volume is based on the assumption that the best basis for an understanding of the development of differences among urban areas may be gained through study of the processes of city growth. Areas acquire high delinquency rates neither by chance nor by design but rather, it is assumed, as an end-product of processes in American city life over which, as yet, man has been able to exercise little control. This elaboration of the differentiation of areas in city growth is presented, then, as a frame of reference, a basis for analysis of the problem of delinquency not only in relation to the processes of urban expansion but also in relation to the whole complex of urban life.

In the present chapter an effort will be made (1) to outline and describe the processes of growth involved in the differentiation of areas in large cities; (2) to analyze the growth and expansion of Chicago with reference to these processes; and (3) to present some evidence of this differentiation, with the characteristics of the different types of areas resulting.

Processes of City Growth

The general processes of growth underlying segregation and differentiation of areas within cities have long been the subject of investigation by students of urban life. Professor Robert E. Park and others have pointed out the general character of these processes, noting that every American city of the same class tends to reproduce in the course of its expansion all the different types of areas and that these tend to exhibit, from city to city, very similar physical, social, and cultural characteristics, leading to their designation as "natural areas."[1]

In his description of the processes of radial expansion Professor E. W. Burgess has advanced the thesis that, in the absence of opposing factors, the American city tends to take the form of concentric zones.[2] Zone I in this conceptual scheme is the central business and industrial district; Zone II, the "zone in transition," or slum area, in the throes of change from residence to business and industry; Zone III, the zone of workingmen's homes; Zone IV, the residential zone; and Zone V, the outer commuters' zone, beyond the city limits. The same general pattern of areas tends to appear in any major industrial center, even though such a "center" may be on the outskirts of a large city. This ideal or schematic construction furnishes a frame of reference from which the location and characteristics of given city areas may be studied at any moment, as well as the changes that take place as time goes on. In a growing city, zones are continuously expanding, which means that each inner zone must invade[3] the next beyond. The result of this process is observable in our large cities, where the central business and industrial areas, now largely uninhabited except by a transient population, at one time included within their limits all gradations of areas in the city.

The starting-point for a discussion of the processes of expansion and differentiation within the city, as indicated above, is the concentration of industry and commerce, especially the configuration including the central business district. Even if the city were not growing, and its internal organization were assumed to be static, the residential neighborhoods adjacent to industrial and commercial areas would be considered, no doubt, physically less desirable than those farther removed. This would be true especially of residential areas near the central business district, for in most cities these are the sections built up first in the development of the city and for that reason are characterized by the oldest homes. Generally speaking, the largest proportion of new dwellings are to be found in the outlying sections of any city, while the areas with the most old dwellings are close to the points of early settlement.

More directly, the presence of either industrial or commercial districts affects the desirability of adjacent residential areas, making life in them less pleasant, according to prevailing standards. The smoke and soot from heavy industrial plants soon render near-by residential structures dirty and ugly in appearance. Noise from factory machinery may be distracting; and the odors of certain industries, notably slaughtering and rendering, are often very disagreeable. These conditions, together with the fact that they soon become associated with undesirable social status, would tend to create wide differences in the distribution of areas even if the basic structure of the city were permanently fixed.

In an expanding city these differences among areas are exaggerated because invasion or the threat of invasion from inner-city areas results in more active deterioration, with subsequent demolition of the structures in those sections adjacent to industry and commerce. As the city grows, the areas of commerce and light industry near the center encroach upon areas used for residential purposes. The dwellings in such areas, often already undesirable because of age, are allowed to deteriorate when such invasion threatens or actually occurs, as further investment in them is unprofitable. These residences are permitted to yield whatever return can be secured in their dilapidated condition, often in total disregard of the housing laws, until they are demolished to make way for new industrial and commercial structures. Even if invasion has not taken place, these processes are evident when the area is zoned for purposes other than residence.

The same general trends are seen in residential districts adjacent to outlying industrial centers. The distinctions may not be so noticeable, the dwellings so old, or the threat of invasion so active; yet the sections closest to industry are, in general, considered least desirable.

When residential areas are being invaded or threatened by invasion, there is apparently little possibility of reconstruction without public subsidy. The physical undesirability of these areas and the ever present prospect of change in land use make it improbable that any first-class residences will be constructed from private funds without the enactment of some special protective legislation.[4] The result is that persons living in these areas move out as soon as possible. The general effect of this process has been the gradual evacuation of the central areas in all large American cities, leading to the expression frequently heard: "The city is dying at its heart."

The differentiation of areas within the city on the basis of physical characteristics is co-ordinate with a segregation of the population on an economic basis. The relentless pressure of economic competition forces the group of lowest economic status into the areas which are least attractive, because there the rents are low, while the economically most secure groups choose higher-rental residential communities, most of which are near the periphery of the city. Between these two extremes lie communities representing a wide variety of economic levels.

This segregation according to the distribution of economic goods implies also a distribution of the population on an occupational and vocational basis. The persons in those occupations which command the lowest wages—the unskilled and service occupations—are forced to live in the areas of lowest rents, while those in the professions and the more remunerative occupations are concentrated in the more attractive sections of the city.

The segregation of population on an economic and occupational basis results, in turn, in the segregation of racial and nativity groups if, within these groups, different economic levels are represented. In northern industrial cities the group of lowest economic status has, until recently, comprised the most recent immigrants. This fact has resulted in the concentration of the foreign born in areas of lowest economic status and, conversely, in the concentration of native whites in the areas of higher economic status; but this separation does not mean that a given group of their descendants are permanently segregated, when the distinction is based on cultural differences only. The national groups which comprise the foreign born in one era may prosper and move; or they may follow their grown children, most of whom are native born, into outlying areas. Their places are taken by newer immigrant groups, who in turn are replaced by still more recent arrivals, and so on, as long as immigration continues. The result tends to be that, while the segregation of the foreign born in the areas of lowest economic status persists, the nationality groups predominating change from decade to decade. Similarly, the native white population living in areas of high economic status are, at any given time, the descendants of those who constituted the bulk of the foreign born in previous generations.

This segregation of population groups on an economic basis does not always proceed in the manner described, because it may be complicated by conditions which serve as barriers to the free movement of population within the city. In northern cities, barriers of racial prejudice and established custom have prevented the Negroes, the group now in the least advantageous position economically, from occupying certain low-rent areas, into which they otherwise would have been segregated by the economic process, and from moving outward into communities of their choice when economically able to do so. As a result, many have been restricted to neighborhoods which have most of the characteristics of inner-city areas but where often the rentals are disproportionately high, partly because of increased congestion and the resulting demand for homes. In southern cities the segregation of the Negro and white population corresponds in general to differences in economic status but is sustained by more elaborate caste mores and taboos.

The Growth and Expansion of Chicago

An effort will next be made to trace the processes of city growth as they have operated in the city of Chicago and to describe briefly the characteristics of the areas differentiated.

The original plot of Chicago, surveyed about 1830, contained roughly $\frac{1}{2}$ square mile of territory, centered about the forks of the Chicago River. This area was extended to approximately 1 square mile in 1833 and to $2\frac{1}{2}$ square miles in 1835, when the town of Chicago was incorporated. Geographically, the site of Chicago was low and swampy but so level that elevation has been a negligible factor in determining the direction of metropolitan expansion. Two geographic barriers have been important, however—Lake Michigan and the Chicago River.

An effect of Lake Michigan is seen in the fact that the central business district is located on the lake shore—geographically not in the center of the city. The study of the growth of Chicago, diagramed schematically in terms of concentric circles, is at once modified, therefore, to a study in terms of semicircles. The Chicago River, likewise, has been significant both because it has interfered with transportation along the diagonals from the point of original settlement and the present business center and because early in the history of Chicago heavy industry was concentrated along the two branches of the river. This development was accompanied by the location of groups of industries in the areas surrounding this industrial section along the river, while high-class residential districts developed north, south, and west of the central business district.

The internal pattern of Chicago was determined largely by the section lines of the government survey. Dividing the city into square-mile areas, these lines have become the important streets which extend throughout the city from north to south and from east to west, tending to facilitate transportation and, consequently, to accelerate radial expansion along those arterial routes running at right angles and to retard radial expansion in those areas at oblique angles to the streets of the central business district. This basic tendency has been lessened somewhat by the presence of diagonal streets to the northwest and southwest, which originally were Indian trails and later became plank roads leading to Chicago from outlying suburbs.

The growth of Chicago is revealed by the changes between decennial census years. In 1840, 10 years after the original town was plotted, the population numbered 4,470. The population expanded nearly six times between 1840 and 1850, two and one-half times between 1850 and 1860, and nearly three times between 1860 and 1870. It reached 500,000 in 1880, 1,000,000 by 1900, and was well over 2,000,000 by 1910. The rate of increase between 1910 and 1920 was 23.6 per cent; between 1920 and 1930, 24.8 per cent; and between 1930 and 1940, 0.6 per cent. The drop in the rate of increase between 1930 and 1940 is due in part to the fact that during this period the areas of most rapid growth were outside the political boundaries of the city.

The territorial expansion corresponded roughly to population increase. In 1889, when Chicago comprised 44 square miles, an area of 126 square miles was annexed at one time, quadrupling the area of the city and increasing the number of square miles within the political boundaries to 170. This area included Kenwood, Hyde Park, South Chicago, Pullman, and many other small towns, as well as much unoccupied territory. From that time to the present, annexations have been relatively small but have increased the total city area to 211 square miles. Although some of the land within the political boundaries is as yet unpopulated, the metropolitan area extends far beyond these boundaries in every direction and includes many contiguous cities and towns located chiefly along transportation lines toward the north, south, and west.

In the course of this expansion, marked changes have taken place in the character of some sections of the city. This is especially true around the central business district, where early residential areas have been invaded by industrial and commercial developments and have therefore been extended farther and farther out from the center. Similarly, single-family dwellings have been replaced by the characteristic two-flat dwellings in many neighborhoods or by large apartment houses along the important transportation routes. Exclusive residential districts of single homes are now to be found only in the outlying districts and in the suburbs.

The general configuration of Chicago resulting from growth and expansion within the limits set by Lake Michigan, the Chicago River, checkerboard streets, and the early distribution of industry is outlined in Map 1, which shows the areas either occupied by or zoned for industrial and residential purposes.

Today the central business district covers much of the area included in the city as incorporated in March, 1837. This district of approximately 10.6 square miles has primarily a hotel and transient population near its center, but on the outer edge the land is in transition from residential to industrial and commercial uses. This change has not progressed at the same rate in all parts of the area. In some places light industrial plants, business houses, and garages have replaced dwelling-houses

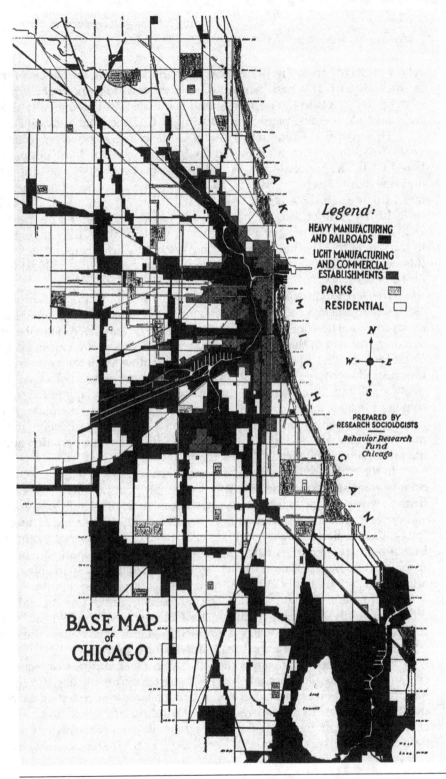

MAP 1 *Zoning Map of Chicago.*

almost completely, while in other parts the land still is used primarily for residential purposes. The fact that it is zoned for light industry and commerce, however, makes it subject to occupancy for these uses as the central business district expands.

While practically all of the exclusive residential neighborhoods of early Chicago now are included in the areas either zoned for or occupied by industry and commerce, one small area on the Near North Side has withstood successfully the threats of industrial and commercial invasion. This district, occupied by large residences and exclusive apartment houses and known locally as the "Gold Coast," stands in vivid contrast to the adjoining areas of deteriorated dwellings and industrial development.

In contrast with the areas zoned for light industry and commerce, located for the most part in a semicircle surrounding the central business district, the districts of heavy industry in Chicago are widely distributed. They tend to be located at points strategic for industrial development because of natural advantages, such as the lake, trunk lines of railroads, or abundance of cheap land. The most extensive industrial areas in Chicago lie along the two forks of the Chicago River. The areas zoned for heavy industry on the North Branch extend some 4 miles northwest from the central business district, while the southern extension follows the south fork to the city limits, after broadening out to include the Union Stock Yards and the so-called "central manufacturing district."

Between these forks of the Chicago River lie two large industrial areas which extend westward from the central business district along railroad trunk lines. These, in turn, are intersected by industrial areas along trunk lines running north and south, so that in a very real sense the Near West Side, the Near Southwest Side, and, to a lesser extent, the Near Northwest Side are bounded by industrial establishments.

The Union Stock Yards and affiliated industries, clearly indicated on Map 1, were opened in 1863. The site was chosen both because of its industrial advantages and because at that time it was far outside the city limits. In the general annexation of 1889, however, this area was brought within the corporate boundary of the city, so that today the Union Stock Yards occupy a position not far from the geographic center of the city.

The South Chicago steel-mill center and the industrial centers indicated by the large areas zoned for industry in the southeastern section were also originally outside the city limits. South Chicago, located on Lake Michigan at the mouth of the Calumet River, was founded almost as early as Chicago, and for several decades remained an independent city. Although annexed to Chicago in 1889, it is still a more or less independent commercial and industrial center. The town of Pullman, located just west of Lake Calumet, likewise was annexed in 1889 and, like South Chicago, has retained its name and essential industrial characteristics. Much of the remaining area zoned for industry in the Calumet district at present is unoccupied waste land. Similarly, on the Southwest Side, the large sections marked in solid black on Map 1 are zoned for, but not yet occupied by, industrial establishments.

Evidences of Differentiation Resulting from City Growth

Demolition of Substandard Housing.—Evidence of physical change and deterioration in Chicago within the general framework of the industrial configuration is seen first in the high proportion of buildings in certain districts which have been condemned either for demolition or for repair. Map 2, showing the location of dilapidated or dangerous buildings demolished as of December, 1935, reveals that a large proportion of these buildings are adjacent to the central business district. It is within this district, known sociologically as an "area in transition," that the change in land use has been most rapid.

Increase and Decrease of Population.—Indirect evidence of the processes of invasion and differentiation in Chicago is seen in the decrease of population in areas adjacent to industry and commerce and the increase in outlying areas. In a rapidly growing city it is natural that a large number of areas should be increasing in population. For purposes of differentiating among communities it is much more significant that, even while the city of Chicago was growing at a very rapid rate, large areas constantly were being depopulated.

Between 1920 and 1930, a period of rapid growth, there were great changes in the distribution of the population in Chicago. The percentage of increase or decrease of population for this period in each of the 113 areas[5] into which the city was divided is shown in Map 3. It will be noted that the areas of decreasing population, delimited by heavy shading, almost completely surround the central business district, while practically all of the areas of rapid increase are near the periphery. Between these two extremes there is a continuous variation. The areas of greatest decrease in population are near the center. Beyond, in order, are the areas where there was a small decrease, then a small increase, then a substantial increase, and finally, at the city's periphery, a zone where the increase was very great. It is this continuum rather than the division into areas of decreasing and increasing population that is significant in showing the essential nature of the processes of city growth.

From Table 5.1 and Map 3 it will be seen that the population in 10 square-mile areas decreased more than 20 per cent between 1920 and 1930, and that in 26 additional areas the drop was between 1 and 20 per cent. The decrease reveals the fact of expansion more vividly when analyzed in conjunction with the rates of increase and decrease of population for the previous and subsequent decades. Between 1910 and 1920 the population decreased in 23 square-mile areas; while between 1930 and 1940, a period of comparatively slight growth in total city population, a drop occurred in 68 out of the 140 square-mile areas. It will be noted that the outward movement from the 36 areas that decreased in population between 1920 and 1930 reduced the proportion of the total population in these areas from 40.0 per cent in 1920 to 27.7 per cent in 1930 and to 25.3 per cent in 1940.

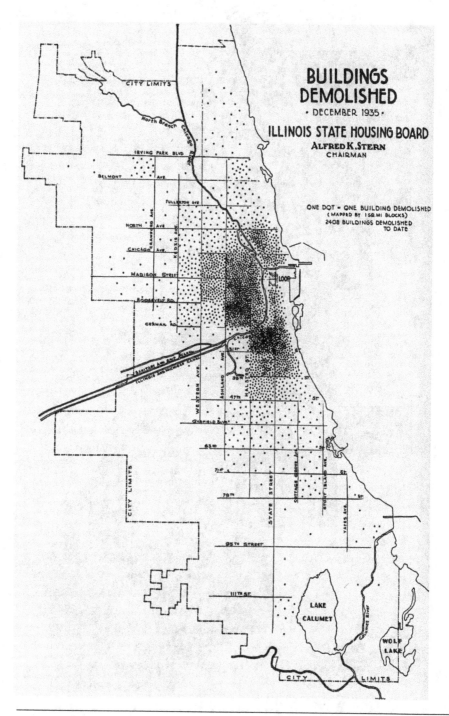

MAP 2   *Distribution of Demolished Buildings, Chicago, 1935.*

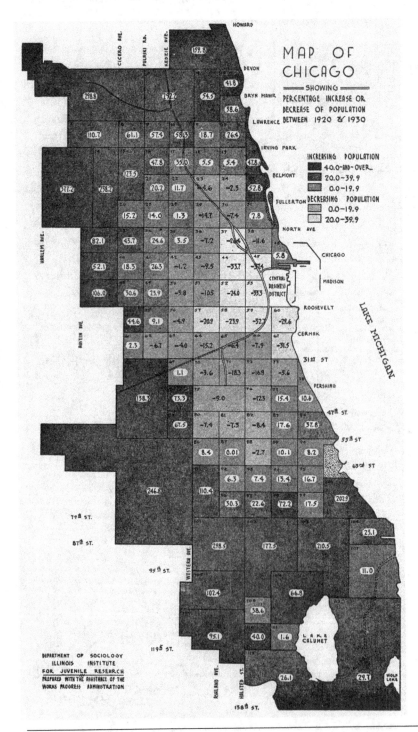

MAP 3 *Increase or Decrease of Population, Chicago, 1920–30.*

TABLE 5.1 *Percentage of City Population, 1920, 1930, 1940, for Square-Mile Areas Grouped by Percentage of Population Increase or Decrease between 1920 and 1930*

Percentage Increase or Decrease in Population 1920–30	Number of Square-Mile Areas	Percentage of City Population		
		1920	1930	1940
Decreasing:				
20–39	10	11.8	6.9	5.9
0–19	26	28.2	20.8	19.4
Increasing:				
0–19	28	29.0	25.4	25.9
20–39	15	11.6	11.9	12.6
40 and over	34	19.4	35.0	36.2

This change in population in the different areas of Chicago establishes the rapidity with which the population is being evacuated from the center of the city. As the areas near the central business district are taken over for industry and commerce, the depopulated district extends farther and farther outward from the Loop; and new residential areas, characterized by very rapid growth of population, are pushed back to the city limits or into the suburbs beyond. On a smaller scale a similar process can be noted in the areas adjacent to each of the major outlying industrial centers.

Although the continuous decrease in population in the inner-city areas indicates a great drop in the number of persons per acre in these areas, this should not be interpreted to mean that there has been any increase in the number of rooms per family or decrease in the number of persons per room. It indicates rather that certain areas are being depopulated as they are abandoned for residential purposes, and either are allowed to remain unoccupied or are taken over for industrial or commercial use.

Segregation of Population on an Economic Basis.—The segregation of groups of low economic status into areas of physical deterioration and decreasing population is clearly indicated when rates of increase and decrease of population are related to indexes of economic status, such as percentage of families on relief, home ownership, median rentals, and occupation. These relationships as of 1930 and 1920 are presented in Table 5.2.

Families on Relief.—Economic segregation in Chicago is likewise indicated by Map 4, which shows the percentage of families on relief in 1934 in each of the 140 square-mile areas. These rates are based on the 115,132 families reported by the Illinois Emergency Relief Commission to be receiving relief and on the total number of families as given in the 1930 census. The range in the percentage of families on relief is from 1.4 in square mile 121 to 55.9 in square mile 87. The median is 10.6, and the percentage for the city 13.7.

TABLE 5.2   Economic Segregation by Areas Grouped According to Increase or Decrease of Population 1930 and 1920

Percentage Increase or Decrease of Population 1920–30	1930				
	Percentage of Families on Relief 1934	Median Rental 1934	Median Rental 1930	Percentage of Families Owning Homes 1930	Percentage of Families Having Radios 1930
Decreasing:					
20–39 (27.5)*	30.0	$16.59	$22.72	16.6	34.2
0–19 (7.9)*	23.3	18.71	35.32	27.2	42.9
Increasing:					
0–19 (9.2)*	16.2	30.05	56.18	23.8	61.2
20–39 (28.4)*	8.6	35.85	62.94	27.6	71.5
40 and over (124.2)*	6.1	41.90	70.62	41.4	76.5

Percentage Increase or Decrease of Population 1910–20	1920					
	Rate of Dependent Families 1921	Percentage of Families Owning Homes 1920	Percentage Manu-facturing	Type of Occupation, 1920		
				Percentage Domestic and Personal Service	Percentage Clerical	Percentage Pro-fessional
Decreasing:						
20–39 (32.5)*	3.2	12.2	50.6	8.6	6.2	2.3
0–19 (8.4)*	1.9	17.9	51.8	6.3	8.1	2.3
Increasing:						
0–19 (10.0)*	1.1	25.6	48.2	4.7	12.2	3.4
20–39 (29.9)*	0.5	28.9	46.8	5.0	13.9	5.0
40 and over (87.5)*	0.4	32.2	39.4	5.9	14.2	6.1

*Percentages for class as a whole.

It will be noted from Map 4 that the areas with the highest percentage of families on relief are the areas of physical deterioration and decreasing population. The lowest percentages, on the other hand, are found in the outlying and newer districts of the city, where the population is increasing and where there is comparatively little deterioration. Between these two extremes the gradations correspond closely with the gradations in the physical characteristics of the areas as already presented. A notable exception to this tendency is seen in certain Negro areas, where the rate of families on relief is high but where the population is increasing, probably as a result of the restrictions to free movement of Negro population into other areas.

Median Rentals.—Another index of economic status is presented in Map 5, which shows for 1930 the median equivalent monthly rental for each of the 140

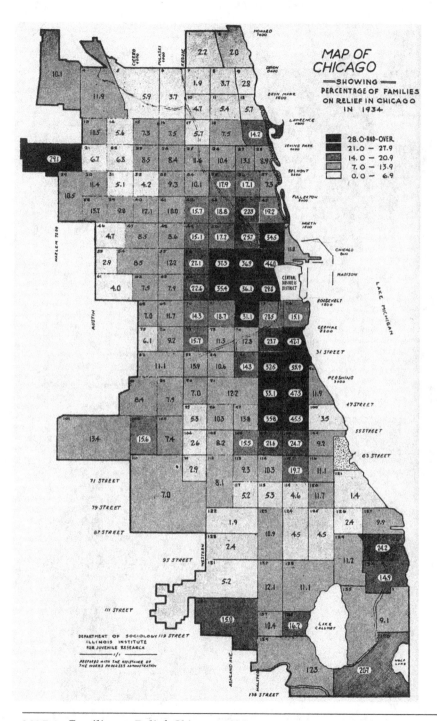

MAP 4   *Families on Relief, Chicago, 1934.*

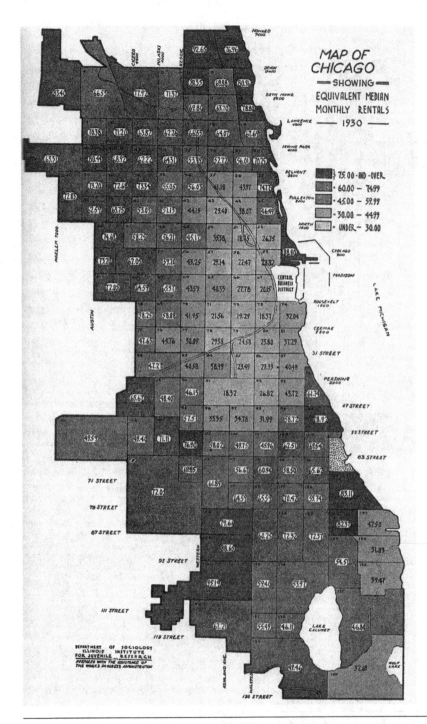

MAP 5   *Median Rentals, Chicago, 1930.*

areas. These rentals are based on the monthly rentals and home values as presented in the 1930 federal census, in relation to the total number of homes in each square mile.[6] From Map 5 it will be seen that the areas of lowest rentals are concentrated around the central business district and the industrial areas along the two forks of the Chicago River. Outside these inner-city areas and in the South Chicago industrial district are the areas of slightly higher rents. In general, the rentals are successively higher as one moves outward from the central business district or away from the heavy industrial centers. With the exception of several Negro areas, where the rentals are disproportionately high, the configuration presented by the variations in median rentals corresponds closely with the variation in the percentage of families on relief as presented in Map 4.

Occupation Groups.[7]—Other evidence of economic segregation is to be seen in the differential distribution of occupation groups. These data are included in Table 5.2. They indicate that a disproportionate number of industrial workers are concentrated in the areas of physical deterioration and decreasing population, and a disproportionate number of professional and clerical workers in outlying residential communities, where the population is increasing most rapidly. Since these occupational groups reflect variations in economic status, the facts constitute further evidence of economic segregation.

Segregation of Racial and Nationality Groups as a Product of Economic Segregation.— The segregation of population on an economic and occupational basis in American society brings about, in turn, a segregation of racial and nativity groups. Throughout most of the history of Chicago the groups of lowest economic status—that is, the foreign born and, more recently, the Negroes—have been concentrated in the areas of physical deterioration and low rentals. On the other hand, the native white population has been centered in the outlying communities, for collectively this group has a higher economic status. Together, the foreign-born and Negro groups furnish a large proportion of the unskilled industrial workers and a comparatively small proportion of the professional and clerical groups. The foreign born have been concentrated, therefore, in the areas adjacent to industrial establishments not only because it is economical and convenient for these workers to live closer to their work but also because they often cannot afford to live elsewhere. The same distribution among low-rent areas would probably characterize the Negroes were it not for the fact that racial barriers prevent their movement into many such areas and, in effect, operate to raise rents in the Negro area.

This segregation of population on an economic basis is again clearly indicated in Table 5.3. Especially noticeable is the concentration of Negro population in the areas where more than 21 per cent of the families are on relief. This concentration was not so apparent in 1920, when the highest proportion of Negro population was found in the areas with intermediate rates of dependent families, based on number receiving relief from private charities.

TABLE 5.3 *Distribution of Racial and Nativity Groups by Areas Grouped According to Relief and Dependency Rates, 1930 and 1920*

	1930		
Percentage of Families on Relief 1934	*Percentage Foreign-born and Negro Heads of Families*	*Percentage Negroes in Total Population*	*Percentage Foreign Born in White Population*
28.0 and over (39.2)*	78.5	38.1	32.9
21.0–27.9 (23.8)*	62.5	15.7	29.5
14.0–20.9 (16.9)*	59.4	3.9	32.4
7.0–13.9 (9.8)*	46.7	0.3	27.1
0.0–6.9 (3.8)*	33.5	0.2	20.8

	1920		
Rates of Dependent Families 1921	*Percentage Foreign-born and Negro Heads of Families*	*Percentage Negroes in Total Population*	*Percentage Foreign Born in White Population*
2.0 and over (2.8)*	80.2	5.4	43.8
1.5–1.9 (1.7)*	71.9	3.5	37.8
1.0–1.4 (1.2)*	67.2	11.3	35.6
0.5–0.9 (0.7)*	54.5	1.6	29.2
0.0–0.4 (0.1)*	42.6	2.2	24.0

*Percentage for class as a whole.

Concentration of Most Recent Immigrants and Migrants.—As indicated by the previous discussion, those nationality groups which represent the newest immigration constitute the largest proportion of the population in areas adjacent to the central business and industrial districts, while the so-called "older immigrant groups" are more widely dispersed. If citizenship is taken as an indication, more positive evidence of the segregation of the newest immigrants is to be seen in the differential distribution of the alien population, both in 1930 and in 1920. These variations in the proportion of aliens in the white population are presented in Table 5.4. This table indicates that the areas of lowest economic status are occupied not only by the highest proportion of foreign born in the white population but also by the highest proportion of aliens in the foreign-born white population 21 years of age and over. The range in 1930 was from 15.9 per cent in the areas of lowest economic status to 3.8 per cent in the areas of highest status.

In his study of the Negro family Frazier similarly found the most recent Negro migrants to the city concentrated in the most deteriorated sections of the Negro areas. He states:

TABLE 5.4 *Distribution of Most Recent Immigrants in Chicago by Areas Grouped According to Relief and Dependency Rates, 1930 and 1920*

	1930		
Percentage of Families on Relief 1934	Percentage Foreign-born in White Population	Percentage Aliens in Foreign-born White Population 21 Years and Over	Percentage Aliens 21 Years and Over in White Population 21 and Over
28.0 and over (39.2)*	32.9	30.5	15.9
21.0–27.9 (23.8)*	29.5	27.3	12.6
14.0–20.9 (16.9)*	32.4	25.6	12.6
7.0–13.9 (9.8)*	27.1	19.7	7.9
0.0–6.9 (3.8)*	20.8	13.0	3.8

	1920		
Rates of Dependent Families 1921	Percentage Foreign-born in White Population	Percentage Aliens in Foreign-born White Population 21 Years and Over	Percentage Aliens 21 Years and Over in White Population 21 and Over
2.0 and over (2.8)*	43.8	41.1	28.7
1.5–1.9 (1.7)*	37.8	32.8	19.6
1.0–1.4 (1.2)*	35.6	26.9	15.0
0.5–0.9 (0.7)*	29.2	22.6	10.1
0.0–0.4 (0.1)*	24.0	16.5	5.4

*Percentage for class as a whole.

Although nearly four-fifths of all the Negroes in Chicago were born in the South, the proportion of southern-born inhabitants in the population diminishes as one leaves those sections of the Negro community nearest the heart of the city. It is in those zones just outside of the Loop where decaying residences and tottering frame dwellings presage the inroads of industry and business that the southern migrant is able to pay the cheap rents that landlords are willing to accept until their property is demanded by the expanding business area.[8]

The results of this process of segregation in Chicago as of 1930 are revealed in Map 6, which shows nativity and race of family heads. In those census tracts where a predominant number of the heads of families were foreign born, the leading nationality group is indicated.[9]

On this map the areas in solid black are those predominantly occupied by Negroes. Since only the numerically dominant group is indicated in each area, it should be remembered that there are Negroes in many of the other tracts in the

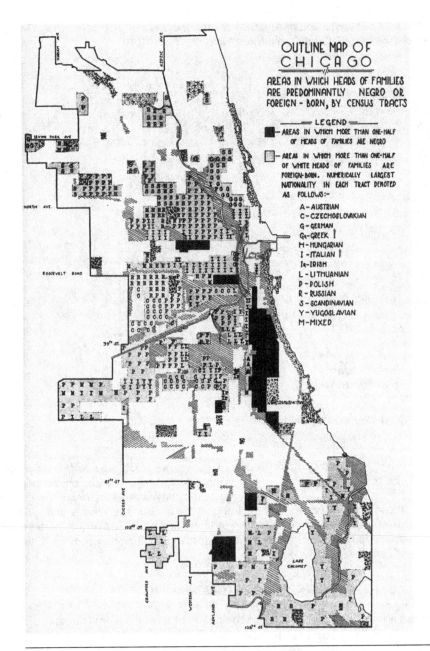

MAP 6   *Predominant Nationality and Race of Family Heads by Nativity Areas, Chicago, 1930*

city. This is especially true on the Near North Side, where large numbers of Negro families are to be found.

Several facts are immediately apparent from Map 6. In the first place, a large proportion of tracts where the foreign-born heads of families constitute the predominant group are clustered around the city's point of original settlement or are distributed in the areas where heavy industry has been located. Secondly, symbols designating the country of birth of the foreign-born heads of families show that in some instances large areas are dominated by one national group and that the most recent immigrants are concentrated in the least desirable sections of the city.

This map represents the distribution of racial and national groups as of 1930, but it does not even suggest the nature of the process that brings about this segregation—the continuous succession of national groups in these immigrant areas. Similar maps for earlier decades would reveal a more decided concentration of foreign born, but the nationalities included would be different.[10] In short, nationality groups have succeeded one another in the areas of lowest economic status, while the concentrations of older immigrant groups are now to be found beyond the inner-city areas. Each new nationality group was segregated into the low-rent areas during the period of its adjustment to the New World. As they have moved out, their places have been taken by other newcomers from abroad until recent years, when part of this inner-city area has been occupied by the newly migrated Negro people.

Thus, in the process of city growth, areas within Chicago have been differentiated in such a way that they can be distinguished from one another by their physical or economic characteristics or, at any given moment, by the composition of the population. Associated with these differences and with the more subtle variations in the attitudes and values which accompany them are found marked variations in child behavior. These are reflected in differential rates of delinquents, as presented in subsequent chapters.

Notes

1. Robert E. Park and E. W. Burgess, *The City* (Chicago: University of Chicago Press, 1925).
2. Ernest W. Burgess (ed.), *The Urban Community* (Chicago: University of Chicago Press, 1926).
3. The terms "invade" and "invasion" are here used in their technical ecological sense, meaning to "encroach upon."
4. Legislation in Illinois in 1941, authorizing privately financed neighborhood redevelopment corporations with limited condemnation powers, has been termed by planning experts as the "first effective attack on the slum problem undertaken in any large city." These experts are confident that "the tide of decentralization can be turned." The question of rentals within reach of low-income groups, however, remains unanswered, constituting the main argument for federal low-rent housing.

5. These areas represent the basic units into which the city of Chicago was divided for the presentation of rates of delinquents and other data based on the 1920 census. In the more densely populated sections of the city these are square-mile areas bounded on all four sides by the section lines of the government survey. In the more sparsely settled outlying areas, it was necessary, in many instances, to combine two or more contiguous square-mile areas until a minimum population base was secured. For the earliest delinquency series further combinations in the outlying areas reduced the number of areas to 106. For 1930 data many of the larger, more populous outlying areas were redivided, and the total number of areas increased to 140. Although some of these units contain more than 1 square mile, they will be referred to throughout this study as "square-mile areas."

6. The computation of the median rental on the basis of the total number of homes was necessary both because in some areas only a small proportion of the homes was rented and because the rented homes often were not representative of the area.

There are probably some inherent errors in these data on monthly rentals. In apartment houses, for example, rentals usually included heat, water, and janitor service, whereas none of these is included in the rental of single homes. These differences may be even greater in furnished-apartment areas where all furnishings, and sometimes gas and light, are included in the rent. It was for the purpose of compensating for these variations that the monthly rentals for homes owned were calculated at 1 per cent of the total value.

These median rentals, calculated from the 1930 federal census, are approximately twice as high as the rentals in the same areas from the Civil Works Administration census for 1934, and it is probable that even these 1934 median rentals are higher than the median rent actually paid. However, for our purpose these variations are not important. We are interested in rentals as indications of the differences among areas rather than in the absolute amount of rent paid.

7. The federal census of 1920 includes the best data for this analysis, since it was a census of occupations, whereas the census of 1930 was a census of gainful workers by industrial groups, in which "all persons whose services are employed in a given industry are classified under that industry." Even the general divisions of occupations used in 1920 are, in several instances, too general to serve as an adequate basis for a study of the differential distribution of occupations. Manufacturing includes, for example, the executives, superintendents, and technicians as well as the unskilled personnel. While it is obvious that, from the point of view of the study of economic segregation, executives should be separated from unskilled workers, these classifications can be used to show general tendencies, because the number of executives and managers is relatively small, as compared with the number of laborers.

8. E. Franklin Frazier, *The Negro Family in Chicago* (Chicago: University of Chicago Press, 1932), pp. 98–100.

9. The effects of a large European immigration on Chicago over a long period of time and of a more recent migration of Negroes are shown in an analysis of the composition of the population. In 1930, 92.3 per cent of the population were white, 6.9 per cent were Negro, and 0.8 per cent were classified as "other races." At the time, 24.9 per cent of the population were foreign born, 39.4 per cent were classified "native white of foreign or mixed parentage," and 29.9 per cent as "native white of native parentage."

Since 1900, significant population changes have taken place. One trend indicating migration of Negroes to Chicago is the increase in the proportion of Negroes in the total population from 2.0 per cent in 1910 to 6.9 per cent in 1930. Another trend is a decrease in the foreign born in the total population from 35.7 to 24.9 per cent, while the percentage classified "native white of native parentage" increased from 20.4 in 1910 to 27.9 in 1930. In spite of this transition, in 1930 the foreign born and the children of the foreign born constituted 69.8 per cent of the total white population in the city. In 1940, 91.7 per cent of the population were white and 8.3 per cent non-white.

Of the foreign-born white, 17.8 per cent were born in Poland; 3.2 per cent in Germany; 13.0 per cent in Russia and Lithuania; 8.8 per cent in Italy; 7.8 per cent in Sweden; 6.5 per cent in the Irish Free State and North Ireland; and 5.8 per cent in Czechoslovakia.

10. Paul F. Cressey, "The Succession of Cultural Groups" (Ph.D. dissertation, Department of Sociology, University of Chicago, 1930).

6

Community Structure and Crime: Testing Social-Disorganization Theory

Robert Sampson is now a Professor of Sociology at Harvard, but he was at one time a Professor of Sociology at the University of Chicago, the home of the famed "Chicago School." Sampson's work in the area of social disorganization is clearly in line with the Chicago School tradition of ecological (community-based) research (Renzetti, Curran, & Carr, 2003:80; Winfree & Abadinsky, 2010:160–161). Robert Sampson was joined in this (1989) study of "community structure and crime" by W. Byron Groves, who is himself a Professor of Sociology and Criminology at the University of Wisconsin.

Sampson and Groves's (1989) re-test of Shaw and McKay's (1969) social disorganization theory has been described as a "criminological classic" (Lilly, Cullen, & Ball, 2011:46; Lowenkamp, Cullen, & Pratt, 2003:382–383). Using data from the 1982 British Crime Survey to produce a sample of 10,905 respondents from 238 different communities, Sampson and Groves (1989:781–783) demonstrated that Shaw and McKay's thinking about social disorganization could still be applied forty years later, to a different society and culture. Sampson and Groves (1989:795) then replicated their study using data from the 1984 British Crime Survey, this time with a sample of 11,030 respondents from 300 different political constituencies. The reason that they drew their first sample from identifiable communities and their second from identifiable political constituencies was to ensure that they were measuring social disorganization at the community or neighborhood level.

According to Sampson and Groves (1989:778), the single most important finding of Shaw and McKay's research was the inability of socially disorganized communities "to supervise and control teenage peer groups." In other words, socially disorganized communities were unable to exercise social control through the usual means of breaking up street corner gangs or effectively supervising teen leisure activities. Another significant factor identified by Shaw and McKay was the inability of community residents to form "social ties" or "local friendship networks" (Sampson & Groves, 1989:778–779). Finally, Sampson and Groves note that Shaw and McKay made the important connection between social disorganization and the low rate of participation by local residents in community organizations, like community centers, churches, committees and social clubs.

Drawing upon Shaw and McKay's original findings, Sampson and Groves (1989:780–781) explain in the following article that the inability of community residents to form strong social ties is attributable to the residential mobility and ethnic and cultural heterogeneity associated with socially disorganized areas. Residential mobility means that people and families are constantly moving in and out of the area. This in turn disrupts the stability of the community, because people are not around long enough to meet their neighbors, join social clubs or form lasting friendships. Ethnic and cultural heterogeneity means that people in these areas come from many different ethnic backgrounds, and have differing cultural values. They may be unable to communicate with each other due to language barriers, and have nothing in common in terms of goals and expectations. Inability to communicate and lack of shared interests further impede their desire to participate in social organizations or form friendships with other local residents.

In their study on community structure and crime in England and Wales, Sampson and Groves (1989:783) measure Shaw and McKay's five main factors in social disorganization—low socioeconomic status (poverty), ethnic and cultural heterogeneity, residential mobility (or residential instability), family disruption (broken homes) and urbanization (as an indication of overcrowding). At the same time, they introduce (and measure) three new intervening or mediating variables—"sparse local friendship networks," "unsupervised teenage peer groups" and "low organizational participation." Sampson and Groves's (1989) research provides general support for the model of social disorganization originally advanced by Shaw and McKay, as well as support for the three new intervening variables that Sampson and Groves themselves introduce in this study.

Using data from the 1994 British Crime Survey, Lowenkamp et al. (2003) set out more than a decade later to re-examine the results of Sampson and Groves's (1989) study of social disorganization in England and Wales. Rather than using data from 238 different communities or 300 different political constituencies—as Sampson and Groves did with the 1982 and 1984 British Crime Surveys—Lowenkamp et al. (2003:387–388) drew their sample of 14,617 respondents from 600 different postal code areas. This was again done to ensure that they were measuring social disorganization at the neighborhood or community level. Like Sampson and Groves, Lowenkamp et al. employed Shaw and McKay's original measures of social disorganization—urbanization, low socioeconomic status, residential mobility, ethnic and cultural heterogeneity and disrupted families. They also used the same three intervening variables that Sampson and Groves introduced in their (1989) study— "local friendship networks," "organizational participation" and "unsupervised peer groups" (Lowenkamp et al., 2003:388–389). Overall, Lowenkamp et al. found a "high level of support for social disorganization theory." Their results were also "generally consistent" with those of Sampson and Groves, albeit with somewhat more modest degrees of correlation (Lowenkamp et al., 2003:397).

In the late 1990s, Robert Sampson went on—in collaboration with Felton Earls and Stephen Raudenbush—to develop what is known as collective efficacy theory (Lilly et al., 2011:52; Taylor, 2001:132–133). Essentially, collective efficacy may be described as the opposite of social disorganization. In neighborhoods that are socially disorganized, people are distrustful of each other, and are unwilling to get involved in dealing with local problems such as graffiti, public drunkenness and general social disorder. In neighborhoods with collective efficacy, there is a higher degree of social cohesion and social control (Bernard, Snipes, & Gerould, 2010:144–145; Lilly et al., 2011:52). In other words, residents will take responsibility for maintaining social order in parks and on streets and sidewalks. If a number of noisy, boisterous teens are congregating on a street corner, the adults will tell them to quiet down. If residents see someone selling drugs in the neighborhood, they will call the police, or perhaps form a neighborhood watch committee (Bernard et al., 2010:144; Lilly et al., 2011:52–53). However, As Robert Sampson cautions in his recent (2006) account of collective efficacy theory, it is not clear whether collective efficacy actually reduces social disorganization, or if social disorganization leads to weakened collective efficacy.

References

Bernard, T. J., Snipes, J. B., & Gerould, A. L. (2010). *Vold's theoretical criminology* (Sixth ed.). New York: Oxford University Press.

Lilly, J. R., Cullen, F. T., & Ball, R. A. (2011). *Criminological theory: Context and consequences* (5th ed.). Thousand Oaks: SAGE Publications.

Lowenkamp, C. T., Cullen, F. T., & Pratt, T. C. (2003). Replicating Sampson and Groves's test of social disorganization theory: Revisiting a criminological classic. *Journal of Research in Crime and Delinquency, 40*(4), 351–373.

Renzetti, C. M., Curran, D. J., & Carr, P. J. (Eds.). (2003). *Theories of crime: A reader*. Boston: Allyn and Bacon.

Sampson, R. J. (2006). Collective efficacy theory: Lessons learned and directions for future inquiry. In F. T. Cullen, J. P. Wright & K. R. Blevins (Eds.), *Taking stock: The status of criminological theory* (pp. 149–167). New Brunswick, N.J.: Transaction Publishers.

Sampson, R. J., & Groves, W. B. (1989). Community structure and crime: Testing social-disorganization theory. *American Journal of Sociology, 94*(4), 774–802.

Shaw, C. R., & McKay, H. D. (1969). *Juvenile delinquency and urban areas: A study of rates of delinquency in relation to differential characteristics of local communities in American cities* (Rev. ed.). Chicago: University of Chicago Press.

Taylor, R. B. (2001). The ecology of crime, fear, and delinquency: Social disorganization versus social efficacy. In R. Paternoster, & R. Bachman (Eds.), *Explaining criminals and crime: Essays in contemporary criminological theory* (pp. 124–139). Los Angeles, Calif.: Roxbury Pub. Co.

Winfree, L. T., & Abadinsky, H. (2010). *Understanding crime: Essentials of criminological theory* (Third ed.). Belmont, CA: Wadsworth, Cengage Learning.

Community Structure and Crime: Testing Social-Disorganization Theory

ROBERT SAMPSON AND W. BYRON GROVES

Shaw and McKay's influential theory of community social disorganization has never been directly tested. To address this, a community-level theory that builds on Shaw and McKay's original model is formulated and tested. The general hypothesis is that low economic status, ethnic heterogeneity, residential mobility, and family disruption lead to community social disorganization, which, in turn, increases crime and delinquency rates. A community's level of social organization is measured in terms of local friendship networks, control of street-corner teenage peer groups, and prevalence of organizational participation. The model is first tested by analyzing data for 238 localities in Great Britain constructed from a 1982 national survey of 10,905 residents. The model is then replicated on an independent national sample of 11,030 residents of 300 British localities in 1984. Results from both surveys support the theory and show that between-community variations in social disorganization transmit much of the effect of community structural characteristics on rates of both criminal victimization and criminal offending.

One of the most fundamental sociological approaches to the study of crime and delinquency emanates from the Chicago-school research of Shaw and McKay. As Bursik (1984) and others (see, e.g., Morris 1970; Short 1969) have argued, few works in criminology have had more influence than *Juvenile Delinquency and Urban Areas* (1942, 1969). In this classic work, Shaw and McKay argued that three structural factors—low economic status, ethnic heterogeneity, and residential mobility—led to the disruption of community social organization, which, in turn, accounted for variations in crime and delinquency (see also Shaw et al. 1929). However, while past researchers have examined Shaw and McKay's predictions concerning community change and extralocal influences on delinquency (Bursik and Webb 1982; Bursik 1986; Heitgerd and Bursik 1987), no one has directly tested their theory of social disorganization.

First, most ecological researchers inspired by Shaw and McKay have examined the effects of such characteristics as median income, racial composition, and residential mobility on crime rates (see, e.g., the reviews in Kornhauser 1978; Bursik 1984; Byrne and Sampson 1986). While useful as a preliminary test, this strategy does little to verify and refine social-disorganization theory since it does not go beyond the steps already taken by Shaw and McKay. As Kornhauser (1978) argues, most delinquency theories begin with the same independent variables—especially socioeconomic status (SES). But the variables that *intervene* between community structure and delinquency are at issue here and to test the theory adequately "it is necessary to establish the relationship to delinquency of the interpretive variables it implies" (Kornhauser 1978, p. 82).

Reprinted from *American Journal of Sociology* 94, no. 4 (1989).

To be sure, the lack of direct tests of the Shaw and McKay thesis does not stem from a lack of theoretical insight. On the contrary, the major problem has been a lack of relevant data. For example, Heitgerd and Bursik (1987) provide an important test of the ecological implications of social-disorganization theory but conclude that traditional ecological studies (including their own) are not well suited to an examination of the formal and informal networks hypothesized to link community social structure and crime. Such an examination requires extensive and prohibitively expensive data collection within each of the communities in the analysis (Heitgerd and Bursik 1987, p. 785). Similarly, Reiss (1986a, pp. 26–27) notes that, since governments gather very little information on the collective properties of administrative units for which they routinely report information, "little causal information is available for those same units."

Thus, the crux of the problem is that previous macro-level research in crime and delinquency has relied primarily on census data that rarely provide measures for the variables hypothesized to mediate the relationship between community structure and crime. Ethnographic research (e.g., Suttles 1968) is an exception to this pattern in that it provides rich descriptive accounts of community processes central to theoretical concerns. But, as Reiss (1986a, p. 27) argues, ethnographies provide limited tests of theories because they focus on a single community or, at most, on a cluster of neighborhoods in which community properties do not display sufficient variation. And while some researchers have examined quantitative dimensions of informal social control (see, e.g., Maccoby, Johnson, and Church 1958; Kapsis 1976; Simcha-Fagan and Schwartz 1986), their studies have been limited to a few select communities, precluding comprehensive multivariate analysis. Consequently, since Shaw and McKay's macrosocial theory is primarily about *between-community* differences in social disorganization (Kornhauser 1978, p. 83), no one has undertaken crucial empirical tests of the community-level implications of the theory.

The second reason that Shaw and McKay's theory has not been tested directly is the overreliance on official crime rates in past research. The general criticisms of official data are well known and need not be repeated here. Suffice it to say that the major issue with respect to community research concerns the extent to which official delinquency rates reflect ecological biases in official reaction to delinquent behavior (Hagan, Gillis, and Chan 1978; Smith 1986; Sampson 1986). For example, conflict theorists argue that lower-economic-status communities may have higher delinquency rates in part because police concentration is greater there compared with higher-status areas. Further, the type of community in which police-citizen encounters occur may influence the actions taken by police (Hagan et al. 1978; Sampson 1986). In support of this idea, Smith (1986) demonstrated that the probability of arrest across communities declines substantially with increasing socioeconomic status—independent of crime type and other correlates of arrest decisions.

The reliance on official data thus leaves open the question of whether Shaw and McKay's findings, and the host of census-based studies following them, are in part artifactual. In the past 20 years or so, self-report and victimization data have been brought to bear on the validity of official statistics (see Hindelang, Hirschi, and Weis 1981), but, to date, these alternative sources of crime measurement have had little effect on the question at issue. For their part, self-report studies have generally been either national in scope (e.g., Elliott and Ageton 1980) or specific to one locale (e.g., Hindelang et al. 1981); between-community estimates of crime rates based on self-reports are thus nonexistent across a representative number of communities. Victimization rates, on the other hand, have been analyzed across 26 cities sampled in the National Crime Survey in the early 1970s (e.g., Decker, Shichor, and O'Brien 1982). But Shaw and McKay's theory is about local community variations in crime rates, not large aggregates such as cities and SMSAs (Bursik 1984). More important, even users of victimization surveys have been forced to rely on census data to measure community structure (see also Sampson 1985).

It is the goal of this article to address these two fundamental limitations of past research. To this end, we use recent data from a large national survey of Great Britain to construct community-level measures of both exogenous structural factors and the mediating dimensions of social disorganization. Using self-reported data on both criminal offending and criminal victimization, we also construct crime and delinquency rates that are not dependent on the official reaction of the criminal-justice system. The unique design of the British Crime Survey (BCS) enables us to create measures of both social disorganization and crime rates for more than 200 local communities and, therefore, to test directly basic hypotheses derived from Shaw and McKay's community-level theory of crime and delinquency.

A Community-Level Theory of Social Disorganization

In general terms, social disorganization refers to the inability of a community structure to realize the common values of its residents and maintain effective social controls (Kornhauser 1978, p. 120; Bursik 1984, p. 12).[1] Empirically, the structural dimensions of community social disorganization can be measured in terms of the prevalence and interdependence of social networks in a community—both informal (e.g., friendship ties) and formal (e.g., organizational participation)—and in the span of collective supervision that the community directs toward local problems (Thomas and Znaniecki 1920; Shaw and McKay 1942; Kornhauser 1978).[2] This approach is grounded in what Kasarda and Janowitz (1974, p. 329) term the *systemic model,* in which the local community is viewed as a complex system of friendship and kinship networks and formal and informal associational ties rooted in family life and ongoing socialization processes (see also Sampson 1988). As Bursik (1984, p. 31) notes, the correspondence of the systemic model with Shaw and McKay's social-disorganization model lies in their shared assumption that structural barriers impede development of the formal and informal ties that promote the ability to solve common problems. Social organization and social *dis*organization are thus seen as different ends of the same continuum with respect to systemic networks of community social control. When formulated in such a way, the notion of social disorganization is clearly separable not only from the processes that may lead to it (e.g., poverty and mobility), but also from the degree of delinquent behavior that may result from it (see Bursik 1984, p. 14).

Intervening Dimensions of Social Disorganization

The first and most important intervening construct in Shaw and McKay's disorganization model was the *ability of a community to supervise and control teenage peer groups* (e.g., gangs). It has been well documented that delinquency is primarily a group phenomenon (Thrasher 1963; Shaw and McKay 1942; Short and Strodtbeck 1965; Reiss 1986b), and hence, according to Shaw and McKay, the capacity of the community to control group-level dynamics is a key mechanism linking community characteristics with delinquency. Indeed, a central fact underlying Shaw and McKay's research was that most gangs developed from unsupervised, spontaneous play groups (Thrasher 1963, p. 25; Bordua 1961, p. 120). Shaw and McKay (1969) thus argued that residents of cohesive communities were better able to control the teenage behaviors that set the context for group-related delinquency (Thrasher 1963, pp. 26–27; Short 1963, p. xxiv; Short and Strodtbeck 1965). Examples of such controls include supervision of leisure-time youth activities, intervention in street-corner congregating (Thrasher 1963, p. 339; Maccoby et al. 1958; Shaw and McKay 1969, pp. 176–85; Bordua 1961), and challenging youth "who seem to be up to no good" (Skogan 1986, p. 217). Theoretically, then, the suggestion is that communities that are unable to control street-corner teenage groups will experience higher rates of delinquency than those in which peer groups are held in check through collective social control.

Socially disorganized communities with extensive street-corner peer groups are also expected to have higher rates of adult crime, especially among younger adults who still have ties to youth gangs. As Thrasher (1963, p. 281) argued: "There is no hard and fast dividing line between predatory gangs of boys and criminal groups of younger and older adults. They merge into each other by imperceptible gradations, and the latter have their real explanation, for the most part, in the former." Similarly, Shaw and McKay pointed to the link between juvenile delinquency and adult criminality, reporting a correlation of .90 between delinquency rates of juveniles aged 10–16 and referral rates of young adults aged 17–20 (1969, p. 95). They further noted the "striking" fact that over 70% of the juveniles in high-gang-delinquency areas were arrested as adults (Shaw and McKay 1969, p. 134). Therefore, the general hypothesis derived from the basic Shaw and McKay model is that street-corner teenage peer groups will have a positive effect on both crime and delinquency rates.

A second dimension of community social organization is informal *local friendship networks*. Systemic theory holds that locality-based social networks constitute the core social fabric of human ecological communities (Hunter 1974; Kasarda and Janowitz 1974). When residents form local social ties, their capacity for community social control is increased because they are better able to recognize strangers and more apt to engage in guardianship behavior against victimization (Skogan 1986, p. 216).

Relatedly, Krohn (1986) has examined the theoretical consequences of social-network theory for delinquency causation. Network density refers to the extent to which all actors in a social network are connected by direct relations. When network density is high, the ability to control delinquency is increased because the behavior of participants in such a network is potentially subject to the reactions of all network members. Hence, the greater the density of networks among persons in a community, the greater the constraint on deviant behavior within the purview of the social network (Krohn 1986, p. 84).

But, as both Krohn (1986) and Freudenberg (1986) point out, the network density of acquaintances and friendships has been largely ignored in past research. To correct for this, we conceptualize local friendship networks as a community-level structural characteristic. On the basis of systemic theory, we expect that local friendship networks will (*a*) increase the capacity of community residents to recognize strangers, thereby enabling them to engage in guardianship behavior against predatory victimization and (*b*) exert structural constraints on the deviant behavior of residents within the community. Hence, local friendship networks are hypothesized to reduce both predatory victimization rates and local crime and delinquency offender rates.

A third component of social organization is the rate of *local participation in formal and voluntary organizations*. Community organizations reflect the structural embodiment of local community solidarity (Hunter 1974, p. 191), and, with this in mind, Kornhauser (1978, p. 79) argues that institutional instability and the isolation of community institutions are key factors underlying the structural dimension of social disorganization. Her argument, in short, is that when links between community institutions are weak, the capacity of a community to defend its local interests is weakened. Shaw and McKay (1969, pp. 184–85), and more recently Simcha-Fagan and Schwartz (1986, p. 688), have also argued that a weak community organizational base serves to attenuate local social-control functions regarding youth.

Taken together, these theorists suggest that efforts to solve common problems (e.g., predatory victimization) and socialize youth against delinquency are to a large degree dependent on a community's organizational base. The key to the success of these efforts hinges on the community's ability to encourage high rates of participation in both formal groups and voluntary associations (Shaw and McKay 1969, pp. 322–26; Kornhauser 1978, p. 81; Simcha-Fagan and Schwartz 1986, p. 688). Consequently, we hypothesize that communities with high rates of participation in committees, clubs, local institutions, and other organizations will have lower rates of victimization and delinquency than communities in which such participation is low.

Exogenous Sources of Social Disorganization

According to Kornhauser's (1978, p. 83) theoretical interpretation of Shaw and McKay, "economic level, mobility, and heterogeneity are, in that order, the variables assumed to account for variations in the capacity of subcommunities within a city to generate an effective system of controls." *Socioeconomic status* (SES) has long been a mainstay ecological correlate of crime and delinquency (Kornhauser 1978; Bursik 1984; Byrne and Sampson 1986), and Shaw and McKay placed a heavy emphasis on how community social disorganization mediated the effects of SES on delinquency. By definition, they argued, communities of low economic status lack adequate money and resources. In conjunction with the well-established positive correlation between SES and participation in formal and voluntary organizations (Tomeh 1973, p. 97), the model suggests that low-socioeconomic-status communities will suffer from a weaker organizational base than higher-status communities. The effects of SES on crime and delinquency rates are thus hypothesized to operate primarily through formal and informal controls as reflected in organizational participation and community supervision of local youth. Most previous ecological research has attempted to establish direct effects of SES on crime (see Kornhauser 1978; Byrne and Sampson 1986) and has consequently failed to measure the hypothesized mediating links necessary to corroborate social-disorganization theory.

In Shaw and McKay's (1942) original model, *residential mobility* was hypothesized to disrupt a community's network of social relations (Kornhauser 1978). In a similar vein, Kasarda and Janowitz (1974, p. 330) argue that, since assimilation of newcomers into the social fabric of local communities is necessarily a temporal process, residential mobility operates as a barrier to the development of extensive friendship networks, kinship bonds, and local associational ties. In this study, we examine a macrosocial conceptualization of systemic theory by focusing on the consequences of residential stability for community organization. The specific hypothesis is that community residential stability has direct positive effects on local friendship networks, which, in turn, reduce crime.

The third source of social disorganization in the Shaw and McKay model was racial and ethnic *heterogeneity*, which was thought to thwart the ability of slum residents to achieve consensus. In Suttles's (1968) account, fear and mistrust accompany heterogeneity, pushing residents into associations selected on the basis of personalistic criteria (e.g., age and sex). As a result of these defensive associations, the social order of the slum becomes segmented, provincial, and personalistic. Hence, while various ethnic groups may share conventional values (e.g., reducing crime), heterogeneity impedes communication and patterns of interaction.

Again, like mobility and SES, heterogeneity has usually been assessed only in terms of its direct effects on crime. In contrast, we test the basic disorganization postulate by hypothesizing that variations in ethnic heterogeneity will also increase delinquency by weakening the mediating components of social organization—especially control of disorderly peer groups.

Family disruption.—In a recent contribution to this *Journal*, Sampson (1987) argued that marital and family disruption may decrease informal social controls at the community level. The basic thesis was that two-parent households provide increased supervision and guardianship not only for their own children and household property (Cohen and Felson 1979), but also for general activities in the community. From this perspective, the supervision of peer-group and gang activity is not simply dependent on one child's family, but on a network of collective family control (Thrasher 1963, pp. 26, 65, 339; Reiss 1986a). In support of this theoretical model, Sampson (1987) showed that macro-level family disruption had large direct effects on rates of juvenile crime by both whites and blacks. However, the analysis was based on city-level rather than local community data, and empirical measures of hypothesized intervening constructs (e.g., informal community supervision of peer groups) were not available. Sampson (1987, p. 376) thus emphasized that "definitive resolution of the mechanisms linking family disruption with crime rates must await further research."

The present study addresses this limitation by examining the mediating effects of community social organization on crime. In particular, we hypothesize that community-level family disruption has a direct positive effect on the prevalence of street-corner teenage peer groups, which, in turn, increases rates of crime and delinquency.

Urbanization.—The fifth and final exogenous variable to be examined is level of urbanization. Although Shaw and McKay (1942) were primarily concerned with intracity patterns of delinquency, their theoretical framework is consistent with the idea that urban communities have a decreased capacity for social control, compared with suburban and rural areas. In particular, urbanization may weaken local kinship and friendship networks and impede social participation in local affairs (see, e.g., Fischer 1982). To provide a strict test of our hypothesized effects of community structure on crime, we thus control for between-community variations in urbanization.

In sum, our extended model of Shaw and McKay relies on the theoretical explication of Kornhauser (1978), recent contributions of systemic and social-network theory (Kasarda and Janowitz 1974; Krohn 1986), and a macrosocial conceptualization of family disruption and crime (Sampson 1987). The general causal structure of the direct and indirect effects of community theoretical constructs is represented in Figure 6.1.[3]

Data and Methodology

The main data analyzed in this study come from the first British Crime Survey (BCS), a nationwide survey of England and Wales conducted in 1982 under the auspices of the Research and Planning Unit of the Home Office. The unique advantage of the BCS for present purposes is that, unlike most survey research, it facilitates

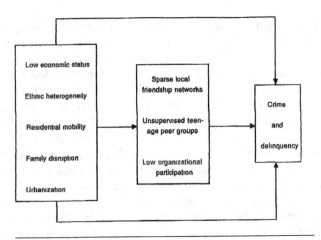

FIGURE 6.1 *Causal Model of Extended Version of Shaw and McKay's Theory of Community Systemic Structure and Rates of Crime and Delinquency.*

macro-level community analysis. The reason for this is that sampling procedures resulted in the proportionate selection of 60 addresses in *each* of 238 ecological areas in Great Britain.[4] A favorable 80% response rate from persons 16 and older randomly selected from 13,702 nonempty households generated the final sample (*N* = 10,905), distributed across the 238 localities. The sample drawn from each geographical unit is representative of a relatively small locality that reasonably approximates the concept of "local community."[5]

Most national samples include too few persons in any one geographic area for the construction of community-level variables (Reiss 1986a). In contrast, the within-area BCS samples are large enough (average = 46), and the survey instrument so comprehensive, that one can construct theoretically relevant and reliable community variables that are not dependent on census data. Therefore, using the geographical area identifiers for each household, we aggregated responses to selected survey questions within each of the 238 areas and constructed structural variables (e.g., means and percentages).

On the basis of the theoretical model developed above, we constructed empirical measures of the three endogenous dimensions of community social organization. The indicator of local friendship networks is derived from a question in which respondents were asked how many of their friends (on a five-point scale ranging from none to all) resided in the local community, which was defined as the area within a 15-minute walk of the respondent's home. Note that the "15-minute walk" survey definition meshes well with the relatively compact geographical size of each sampled area. Our community indicator is empirically defined as the mean level of local friendships and is intended to reflect the extent of local ties and friendship networks among community residents.

The macro-level indicator of organizational participation was created from a question in which respondents were asked about their social and leisure activities for each night of the week, broken down by type of activity. One of the categories was attendance at the meetings of committees and clubs. The resulting structural measure refers to the percentage of residents who participated in such meetings in the week before the interview. Although a more detailed measure is unavailable, we believe that variations across communities in attendance at committee, club, and other organizational activities provide a reasonable indicator of mobilization capacity and organizational base (see Kornhauser 1978, pp. 79–80).

A direct indicator of the social control and supervision of youth peer groups is typically hard to come by in macro-level data. However, the BCS provides a fairly straightforward indicator of youth-supervision patterns that is conceptually and empirically independent of crime itself. Specifically, each respondent was asked how common it was (on a four-point scale) for groups of teenagers to hang out in public in the neighborhood and make nuisances of themselves. Separate questions were asked regarding crime—including common youth crimes such as vandalism. The problem of disorderly teenage youth hanging about in groups in public thus has face validity as an indicator of the extent to which the community is unable to control peer-group dynamics (see Maccoby et al. 1958; Bordua 1961; Thrasher 1963). We therefore aggregated the individual responses in each area and computed the percentage of residents who reported that disorderly teenage peer groups were a "very common" neighborhood problem.

The three exogenous community characteristics from the original Shaw and McKay model are SES, residential stability, and ethnic heterogeneity. To measure SES, we constructed a scale by summing z-scores of the major dimensions of social class—education (percentage college educated), occupation (percentage in professional and managerial positions), and income (percentage with high incomes). Residential stability is defined as the percentage of residents brought up in the area within a 15-minute walk from home. Race/ethnicity in the BCS sample is distributed across five categories: white, West Indian or African black, Pakistani or Bangladeshi Indian, other nonwhite, and mixed. To capture fully the range of heterogeneity, we use an index employed in recent research on intergroup relations (Blau 1977, p. 78). The index is $(1 - \Sigma p_i^2)$, where p_i is the fraction of the population in a given group. Note that the measure takes into account both the relative size and number of groups in the population, with a score of one reflecting maximum heterogeneity.

On the basis of our theoretical extension of Shaw and McKay derived from Sampson (1987), family disruption is included as a fourth exogenous community characteristic. Family disruption is measured by summing z-scores of two related dimensions—the proportion of divorced and separated adults among those who had ever married and the percentage of households with single parents with children. And the final exogenous variable, urbanization, is controlled for by our assigning all communities located in central-city locations a dummy variable of one and all others a zero (see Hough and Mayhew 1983).[6]

The most general test of social-disorganization theory concerns its ability to explain total crime rates. Accordingly, to serve as an overall indicator of crime, we constructed the *total victimization rate*. To reflect between-community variations in serious predatory crimes against persons, we also constructed measures of *mugging/ street robbery* and *stranger violence* (assault and rape). The mugging/robbery variable was derived from aggregation of the responses to a question in which respondents were asked how prevalent such crimes were in their local community. Knowledge of criminal victimization of other than respondents is thus reflected in the measure (see Skogan 1986). Conversely, both the stranger violence and total victimization rates were constructed from respondents' reports of their victimization experiences during the previous year, aggregated to the community level. Specifically, each victim of assaultive violence (rape or assault) was asked if the offender(s) was a stranger or acquaintance. The resulting rate of stranger violence reflects the prevalence of predatory attacks by stranger(s). Total victimization refers to the prevalence of all personal and household crimes. To the extent that these indicators of victimization measured in different ways yield similar patterns, they give us more confidence in the validity of results.

To measure property and household victimization, we constructed three measures from victim reports—*burglary, motor vehicle theft*, and *vandalism* to home or property. Note that juveniles are involved in property crimes much more than in violent crimes (Flanagan and McLeod 1983, p. 402). Vandalism, in particular, may be seen as a general proxy for juvenile delinquency.

The theory of social disorganization speaks not only to the ability of a community to achieve common values (e.g., to defend itself against predatory victimization), but also to community processes that produce offenders. Indeed, Shaw and McKay's (1942, 1969) analyses focused mostly on rates of delinquent offending (e.g., court referral rates per 1,000 local youth). We also examine offending rates, but to counteract official reaction biases, we derived rates of offending from *self-reported* data. Using show-card methods, the interviewer asked each respondent to report his or her involvement in various deviant and illegal activities. Many of these acts are not germane to the present study (e.g., drunk driving and occupational theft) and many serious crimes occurred too infrequently to study reliably (e.g., major theft and burglary). We thus constructed two measures tapping behaviors that are directly relevant to this study and that permit reliable analysis. Specifically, measures of self-reported *personal violence* (e.g., started a fight with someone outside the family, deliberately injured someone outside the family, or carried a weapon in a fight) and *property theft/vandalism* (e.g., defaced wall, did deliberate property damages to car, house, phone booth; took things from shops, stores, etc. without paying for them) were created for each person. Because even these offenses were relatively infrequent, the resulting rates represent between-community variations in the prevalence of self-reported offending against persons and property.[7]

Findings

The most notable feature of the descriptive statistics displayed in Table 6.1 is that communities do vary significantly along theoretically relevant dimensions. For example, although a third of residents were brought up in the community, residential stability varies from a low of zero to almost 75%. The variables tapping the three intervening community factors also vary widely: for example, the prevalence of unsupervised peer groups in a community ranges from zero to over 75%, while organizational participation of community residents ranges from none to over a third. We now address the nature of these variations with respect to the theory.

The first two columns in Table 6.2 reveal clear support for our linkage of Shaw and McKay's (1942) social-disorganization theory with Kasarda and Janowitz's (1974) systemic model of community attachment.[8] Net of urbanization, SES, heterogeneity, and family disruption, residential stability has a large direct effect ($B = .42$) on local friendship networks. Urbanization also has a negative effect on friendship networks, as expected, but its magnitude is considerably smaller than residential stability.

TABLE 6.1 *Descriptive Statistics for Major Variables,
238 British Local Communities (1982)*

Variable	Mean	SD	Min.	Max.
Exogenous:				
Socioeconomic status*	.00	2.48	−4.02	9.69
Ethnic heterogeneity	.08	.14	.00	.65
Residential stability	32.99	15.06	.00	72.50
Family disruption*	.00	1.72	−2.09	6.66
Urbanization	.20	.40	.00	1.00
Intervening:				
Local friendship networks	2.52	.38	1.56	3.73
Unsupervised peer groups	37.38	14.44	.00	76.40
Organizational participation	8.66	6.94	.00	34.60
Victimization rates:				
Mugging/street robbery[†]	2.13	1.35	.00	4.48
Stranger violence[†]	.96	.79	.00	3.07
Total crime	41.99	16.55	9.10	93.30
Burglary[†]	1.54	.87	.00	3.39
Motor-vehicle theft[†]	1.18	1.02	.00	3.32
Vandalism	7.03	5.48	.00	28.60
Offending rates:				
Personal violence[†]	1.31	.96	.00	3.08
Theft/vandalism[†]	.42	.79	.00	2.59

*Scale based on z-scores.
[†]Natural log transformation.

TABLE 6.2   WLS Regression Estimates of Effects of Community Structure on Dimensions of Social Disorganization in 238 British Local Communities (1982)

	Local Friendship Networks		Unsupervised Peer Groups		Organizational Participation	
	B	t-ratio	B	t-ratio	B	t-ratio
Socioeconomic status	−.06	−.91	−.34	−5.31**	.17	2.33**
Ethnic heterogeneity	.02	.34	.13	2.04**	−.06	−.83
Residential stability	.42	6.35**	.12	1.90*	−.09	−1.26
Family disruption	−.03	−.45	.22	3.73**	−.02	−.28
Urbanization	−.27	−3.91**	.15	2.21**	−.10	−1.32
R^{2a}	.26		.30		.07	

[a]$P < .01$ for these values.
*$P < .10$.
**$P < .05$.

The data in columns 3 and 4 provide support for the most crucial mediating variable in the social-disorganization model. As hypothesized by Shaw and McKay, lower-class communities with fewer resources are apparently unable to control or supervise youths' congregating to the extent that upper-class communities can. Note that the standardized direct effect of SES is substantial (−.34). And in support of the macro-level social-control model proposed by Sampson (1987), communities with elevated levels of family disruption experience higher levels of disorderly peer-group behavior by teenagers than communities with lower levels of family disruption. Also in consistency with the Shaw and McKay model, urbanization and ethnic heterogeneity have significant positive effects on the inability of a community to control its youth. The only unexpected finding is the marginally significant positive effect of residential stability.

The results for organizational participation (cols. 5 and 6) indicate weaker predictive power of community structural context, but the pattern of effects is still consistent with the theory. As Shaw and McKay hypothesized, community-level SES is the strongest determinant of organizational participation ($B = .17$; $P < .05$). Overall, the data support the model and, in the process, the construct validity of key endogenous dimensions of community social disorganization.

Rates of Personal Violence and Total Victimization

The structural-equation results in Table 6.3 indicate that the level of unsupervised teenage peer groups has the largest independent effect on all three forms of victimization. Specifically, net of all other community characteristics, the indicator of unsupervised peer groups is substantially related to mugging and robbery (.35), stranger violence (.19), and the total victimization rate (.34). Furthermore, community SES

TABLE 6.3 *WLS Regression Estimates of Effects of Community Structure and Social Disorganization on Rates of Personal Violence and Total Victimization in 238 British Local Communities (1982)*

| | Personal Violence and Total Victimization | | | | | |
| | Mugging/Street Robbery | | Stranger Violence | | Total Victimization | |
	B	t-ratio	B	t-ratio	B	t-ratio
Socioeconomic status	−.01	−.20	.10	1.30	−.03	−.48
Ethnic heterogeneity	.29	5.79**	.02	.26	.08	1.23
Residential stability	.08	1.53	−.09	−1.11	.03	.53
Family disruption	.08	1.78*	.14	2.02**	.20	3.61**
Urbanization	.26	5.01**	.11	1.36	.21	3.26**
Local friendship networks	−.19	−4.01**	−.03	−.48	−.12	−2.12**
Unsupervised peer groups	.35	7.01**	.19	2.60**	.34	5.58**
Organizational participation	−.07	−1.70*	−.14	−2.11**	−.11	−2.00**
R^{2a}	.61		.15		.42	

[a]$P < .01$ for these values.
*$P < .10$.
**$P < .05$.

has insignificant effects on all three types of victimization. These data thus provide an illustration of the misleading inferences that could be drawn from an attempt to identify only direct effects of social-stratification factors, such as SES. Indeed, 80% of the total effect of SES on mugging and street robbery is mediated by the indicator of unsupervised teenage youth. Similarly, 34% and 68% of the total effect of community SES on stranger violence and total victimization, respectively, is mediated by level of unsupervised peer groups.[9] And while ethnic heterogeneity has a fairly large direct effect on mugging/robbery (.29), the indicator of unsupervised peer groups transmits 47% of the effect of heterogeneity on stranger violence and 33% of its effect on total-victimization rates.

The extent of community friendship ties is inversely related to both street robbery (−.19) and total victimization (−.12). The direct effect of residential stability on victimization is insignificant, and when we combine that result with the results in Table 6.2, we conclude that the total effect of such stability on crime is accounted for in large part by local social networks. This conclusion confirms a key hypothesis linking the disorganization framework with recent developments in social-network theory (Krohn 1986). More precisely, we find that 39% of the total effect of community stability on mugging is mediated through local friendship networks, while the corresponding figure for total victimization is 38%.

Although modest in magnitude, the pattern of results for organizational participation also supports theoretical predictions. For example, organizational participation has significant ($P < .05$) negative effects on stranger violence and total

TABLE 6.4 *WLS Regression Estimates of the Effects of Community Structure and Social Disorganization on Rates of Household and Property Victimization in 238 British Local Communities (1982)*

| | Household and Property Victimization | | | | | |
| | Burglary | | Auto Theft | | Vandalism | |
	B	t-ratio	B	t-ratio	B	t-ratio
Socioeconomic status	.12	1.87*	−.13	−1.87*	−.16	−2.20**
Ethnic heterogeneity	.21	3.35**	.03	.52	−.10	−1.44
Residential stability	.05	.74	−.13	−1.83*	−.15	−1.96**
Family disruption	.15	2.68**	.13	2.14**	.09	1.35
Urbanization	.19	2.78**	.19	2.62**	−.00	−.03
Local friendship networks	−.20	−3.35**	−.03	−.53	−.07	−.97
Unsupervised peer groups	.18	2.82**	.26	3.92**	.38	5.32**
Organizational participation	−.15	−2.85**	−.18	−3.19**	−.04	−.65
R^{2a}	.61		.15		.42	

[a]$P < .01$ for these values.
*$P < .10$.
**$P < .05$.

personal crime and a marginally significant negative effect ($P < .10$) on rates of street mugging. Of the total effect of community socioeconomic status on stranger violence and total crime, organizational participation mediates about 12%.

Family disruption has indirect effects on all three types of victimization through its effect on disorderly teenage peer groups. The proportion of the total effects of family disruption accounted for by unsupervised youth is 50%, 23%, and 27% for mugging, stranger violence, and total victimization, respectively. Family disruption also has fairly substantial direct effects on the last two rates, a finding consistent with the argument that single-adult households provide increased opportunities for crime (Cohen and Felson 1979; Sampson 1987).

Rates of Household and Property Victimization

Columns 1 and 2 in Table 6.4 reveal that all three mediating dimensions of community social organization have independent effects on burglary. In particular, the data suggest that communities characterized by extensive friendship networks, high organizational participation, and effective control of teenage peer groups have lower than average rates of burglary. It is especially interesting to note the important role of friendship networks, the variable with the second largest effect (−.20) on burglary. In conjunction with the fact that residential stability has an insignificant direct effect on burglary, the results again establish empirical support for the systemic, social-organizational approach. Specifically, one-half of the effect of community residential stability on burglary rates is mediated by friendship ties among local residents.

The indicator of disorderly peer groups has a significant positive effect on burglary (.18), motor-vehicle theft (.26), and vandalism (.38). The large effect on vandalism is particularly supportive of the theory since it is one of the most typical juvenile offenses and is usually committed in groups (Thrasher 1963; Shaw and McKay 1942). Note also that, if only direct effects were considered, we would conclude that community SES increases burglary—not an unreasonable finding since wealthier communities offer more to steal than poorer ones. But almost a third (28%) of the total effect of SES on burglary is mediated by disorderly peer groups; that is, SES reduces burglary indirectly through its effects on local control of teenage peer groups.

Organizational participation has a relatively strong negative effect on two out of the three property crimes: burglary (–.15) and motor-vehicle theft (–.18). This indicator of the structural embodiment of community social control also mediates a small part of the effect of community SES (approximately 12%). Only vandalism is unaffected by either friendship networks or organizational participation.

In short, our analyses support the view that community social disorganization accounts for much of the effect of community-level SES, residential stability, family disruption, and heterogeneity on rates of both personal and property victimization. Indeed, taken together, the three dimensions of community social disorganization mediate over one-half of the effects of Shaw and McKay's three structural factors (SES, mobility, heterogeneity) on the most general indicator of crime (i.e., total victimization rate) in the predicted manner. And while family disruption has direct effects on every crime but vandalism, on average, one-third of its effects on victimization are transmitted by teenage peer groups.

Rates of Offending

Thus far we have examined rates of survey-reported victimization that are independent of the selection mechanisms of the criminal-justice system. We now turn to an alternative window that is also free of criminal-justice distortions in order to view the criminal process—estimates of the rate of offending in each area for common crimes against persons (e.g., fighting and assault) and property (e.g., vandalism and larceny) generated from self-reported survey data.

As shown in Table 6.5, the pattern of relative effects provides support for the major hypothesis concerning variations in macro-level social control. Namely, the level of unsupervised peer groups has direct positive effects on rates of both violent (.17) and property (.16) offending. Moreover, none of the three exogenous factors in Shaw and McKay's original model (SES, heterogeneity, and residential stability) have significant (P < .05) direct effects on offending rates. Rather, as predicted by the theory, their effects are largely mediated by unsupervised teenage peer groups.[10] For example, of the total effect of SES on rates of personal violence and property theft/vandalism, a substantial portion (64% and 46%, respectively) is mediated by unsupervised teenage peer groups. Further, some 97% of the total effect of family disruption on violent offending is mediated by unsupervised peer groups. Note,

TABLE 6.5   WLS Regression Estimates of the Effects of Community Structure and Social Disorganization on Self-reported Offending Rates in 238 British Local Communities (1982)

	Offending Rates			
	Personal Violence		Poverty Theft/ Vandalism	
	B	t-ratio	B	t-ratio
Socioeconomic status	−.03	−.40	.04	.54
Ethnic heterogeneity	.14	1.79*	−.10	−1.27
Residential stability	−.02	−.30	.10	1.24
Family disruption	−.00	−.08	.18	2.56**
Urbanization	−.00	−.11	−.10	−1.23
Local friendship networks	.02	.20	−.17	−2.26**
Unsupervised peer groups	.17	2.20**	.16	2.16**
Organizational participation	.01	.16	.08	1.27
R^2		.06[a]		.06[b]

[a]$P < .07$ for this value.
[b]$P < .01$ for this value.
*$P < .10$.
**$P < .05$.

however, that family disruption has the largest direct effect on involvement in property offending. Areas with cohesive family structures appear able to control crimes such as vandalism through means other than supervision of youth (e.g., increased guardianship of property).

Of the other two intervening factors, the density of local friendship networks has a significant negative effect on rates of property offending ($B = -.17$). The lack of an effect of organizational participation on either property or violent offending rates is somewhat surprising, given its significant negative effect on victimization rates (tables 6.3 and 6.4). This suggests that well-organized communities (or communities with high mobilization capacities) may be effective in countering threats to personal safety by neighborhood victimization, but that such efforts do not necessarily reduce the propensity to offend among community residents. In this vein, note that offenders may be committing crimes outside the community.[11]

Consistency Tests and Verification

We performed a series of tests to detect possible influential observations, multicollinearity, and misspecification error. First, all regression models in tables 6.2–6.5 were examined for influential observations through inspection of residuals and the statistic Cook's D (see Cook and Weisberg 1982). In all models, no one community in Great Britain had a disproportionate influence on the parameter estimates. In fact, the largest Cook's D value was .10, well below traditional levels of concern (typically 1.0). Second, we examined empirically the issue of multicollinearity. The correlations among independent variables were moderate—out of 28, only four were greater than .30, and, of these, the largest was .51. Variance-inflation factors were thus much below levels of concern (less than 2.0).

Third, we explored the possibility of whether our measure of unsupervised peer groups was confounded with age structure. It is possible that both high concentrations of unsupervised peer groups and high crime rates could be the result of there being many youths in the community. To assess this, we re-ran all models with a control for the proportion of households with juveniles. This control for age structure did not alter the major findings: the effect of unsupervised peer groups on rates of robbery, stranger violence, total victimization, burglary, auto theft, vandalism, self-reported (SR) violence and SR theft/vandalism was .36, .19, .33, .17, .26, .38, .15, and .16, respectively (cf. tables 6.3 and 6.4).

Fourth, we reestimated each regression model by (*a*) deleting insignificant predictors from tables 6.2–6.5 and (*b*) entering a new vector of four other potentially confounding characteristics. These included two traditional factors—percentage of unemployed and percentage of homeowners—and an alternative indicator of urbanization (building density). For the crime regressions, we also entered a variable tapping the "routine activity" patterns of community residents (Cohen and Felson 1979), defined as the mean number of nights spent outside the home for leisure activities. However, these new specifications did not change the major substantive results, thus increasing confidence in the validity and robustness of the original models.

Finally, it is possible that, in communities where crime rates are high, residents are afraid to venture outside their homes. In particular, fear of crime may inhibit the formation of local friendship groups and participation in community organizations (Skogan 1986; Sampson 1988). If this were true, it would confound the effects of friendship ties and organizational participation on crime with the consequences of fear of crime. To assess this, we re-ran the models and controlled for the extent to which residents felt unsafe walking in their neighborhoods at night. This is a strict test of the independent effects of theoretical measures because crime rates and fear overlap, both conceptually and empirically (.52). Nevertheless, the results were consistent with those presented above. It is important that the effects of local friendship networks and organizational participation on total victimization remained unchanged ($B = -.12$ and $-.11$, respectively; $P < .05$).

Replication and External Validation

Despite the supportive empirical results thus far, there are two specific limitations to the 1982 BCS data that bear on major theoretical concerns. The first relates to the key indicator of unsupervised teenage peer groups. Recall that respondents were asked about groups of teenagers who made nuisances of themselves in the community. Although most of the victimization rates referred to quite serious crimes (e.g., robbery, stranger violence, burglary), it is nonetheless possible that respondents used these crimes as the criterion for defining nuisance behavior by teens. Were this the case, our measure of unsupervised peer groups may be in part definitionally confounded with crime itself.

The second issue pertains to the macro-level indicator of local friendship networks. Given that the survey question asked how many of the respondent's personal friends resided in the area (from none to all), a respondent with only one friend could be viewed as having strong local ties if his or her only friend lived in the community. On the other hand, those with an unusually large number of friends could be defined as having weak local ties even if they had several friends in the community. The question thus partly confounds variation in the number of friends each respondent has with their location.

While we do not believe that these two limitations pose a significant threat to the validity of findings, they do raise questions that merit empirical answers.[12] An answer is therefore provided through replication on a separate study that specifically addresses the two measurement issues—the second British Crime Survey. Conducted in 1984, the second BCS was not a follow-up but rather an independent nationally representative sample of 11,030 British residents. Approximately 37 randomly selected household respondents aged 16 and over were interviewed in each of 300 political constituencies of England and Wales, thus permitting the construction of macro-level measures in a fashion analogous to that in 1982.[13]

Despite similarities in design, the 1984 BCS is not as germane as the 1982 BCS for community-level analysis. First, political constituencies reflect ecological units that are much larger and more heterogeneous than those used for 1982. Second, because more areas were sampled, there are about 10 fewer respondents per area; consequently, aggregated community measures are less reliable. Third, the detailed activity question that served as the basis for our measure of organizational participation was not asked, and none of the relevant self-reported offending items (e.g., personal violence, theft, and vandalism) in the 1982 BCS were repeated. Accordingly, the 1984 BCS cannot be used to replicate the offending-rate results or the organizational-participation results, nor are the sampling units as valid as those from 1982 for approximating local communities.

Fortunately, however, the strengths of the 1984 BCS directly address the weaknesses in the 1982 BCS for our two main indicators of social disorganization. First, the wording of the peer-group question was changed to ask about "teenagers hanging around on the streets." No mention was made of nuisance behavior, and, unlike the 1982 BCS, the question specifically taps the dimension of group-oriented *street-corner* behavior. This is directly relevant to the ideas of both Shaw and McKay (1969) and Thrasher (1963) concerning teenagers "hanging out" on the street in groups. The new measure is defined as the proportion of residents who said that local street-corner teens were common.

Second, the friendship question was changed to restrict the respondent's universe of friends to the immediate area. Each resident was asked, "Thinking of the people who live in this area, how many would you regard as friends or acquaintances?" (ranging from none to most). Hence, instead of confounding the number of total friends, this question measures only the ties among local residents (e.g., a person with only one friend in the area would score low on this dimension). Note also that the question asks about acquaintances—thus merging friendships with the idea of density of acquaintanceship to form a more general measure tapping local associational ties and networks (see Freudenberg 1986). The community-level measure is defined as the proportion of residents who reported that most of the people in the area were either friends or acquaintances.

In short, the 1984 BCS allows us to replicate the fundamental portion of our social-disorganization model. Where the 1982 BCS is weak, the 1984 BCS is strong, and vice versa. Therefore, if the results converge in light of these divergent limitations, we will have strong empirical support for the theory in the form of external validation (see Selltiz, Wrightsman, and Cook 1976, p. 577).

1984 BCS Results

Table 6.6 presents the WLS regression model.[14] In panel A we observe that the exogenous community characteristics predict the endogenous dimensions of social disorganization in much the same manner as in 1982. For example, SES has a significant negative effect on teenage street-corner groups, while heterogeneity and, especially, family disruption have significant positive effects. The pattern of results for local informal networks is also congruent with that in 1982, in that the strongest predictor of the density of friendships/acquaintanceships is residential stability. In fact, the effect of residential stability (.32) is more than double that of any other variable. Panel A thus replicates on an independent sample our extended version of Shaw and McKay's model of the structural sources of community social disorganization.

Panel B of Table 6.6 turns to the estimates of the full theoretical model. The primary question is whether the newly defined street-corner peer group and local network variables have the predicted effects on victimization rates. The answer is clear: the indicator of street-corner teenage peer groups has a significant effect on all four victimization rates. In fact, of all the variables in the model, the level of street-corner youth has by far the largest effect on vandalism and assault. In conjunction with the 1982 results, the large effect on vandalism underscores the connection between "hanging out" (Thrasher 1963) and delinquent acts. It thus appears that poor heterogeneous communities with pronounced family disruption foster street-corner teenage groups, which, in turn, leads to increased delinquency and ultimately to a pattern of adult crime.

The results for friendship networks are similarly supportive. The density of friendships/acquaintanceships has significant inverse effects on three out of four crimes, despite controls for six important community characteristics. It is

TABLE 6.6   *WLS Regression Estimates for Replication of Social Disorganization Model on Independent Validation Sample: 300 British Constituencies (1984)*

A. Social Disorganization

	Street-Corner Peer Groups		Density of Friendship/ Acquaintanceship	
	B	t-ratio	B	t-ratio
Socioeconomic status	-.17	-3.02**	-.13	-2.49**
Ethnic heterogeneity	.11	1.82*	-.15	-2.64**
Residential stability	.07	1.18	.32	5.98**
Family disruption	.19	3.21**	-.09	-1.68*
Urbanization	.09	1.44	-.14	-2.31**
R^{2a}	.12		.24	

B. Victimization Rates

	Property				Personal			
	Burglary		Vandalism		Robbery		Assault	
	B	t-ratio	B	t-ratio	B	t-ratio	B	t-ratio
Socioeconomic status	.14	2.60**	-.16	-2.87**	.06	1.23	-.00	-.11
Ethnic heterogeneity	.02	.42	.00	.04	.34	6.49**	.14	2.23**
Residential stability	.02	.29	.03	.57	.06	1.07	-.08	-1.40
Family disruption	.11	1.91*	.04	.68	.12	2.40**	.10	1.68*
Urbanization	.27	4.55**	-.05	-.76	.15	2.73**	.02	.35
Street-corner peer groups	.17	3.01**	.35	6.26**	.13	2.65**	.23	4.01**
Density of friendship/acquaintanceship	-.15	-2.61**	-.09	-1.43	-.20	-3.62**	-.10	-1.65*
R^{2a}	.24		.19		.37		.16	

[a]$P < .01$ for these values.
*$P < .10$.
**$P < .05$.

particularly noteworthy that informal associational ties have the second largest effect on robbery. It seems that communities with sparse ties among friends and neighbors generate a weakened system of social control, which, in turn, facilitates predatory crime.

In brief, macro-level empirical analysis of the 1984 BCS replicates almost fully the theoretical picture painted in the 1982 BCS. Replication in this case is especially compelling because of the differing nature of limitations associated with each survey.[15] Our confidence is therefore increased that the indicators of unsupervised peer groups and local friendship networks in *both* surveys are tapping important and distinct dimensions of community levels of social disorganization.

Conclusions

Relying on recent insights from social-network theory and a macro-level conceptualization of family structure and crime, we have presented evidence from two large national surveys of England and Wales that replicate and significantly extend Shaw and McKay's systemic model of community social disorganization. Specifically, our empirical analysis established that communities characterized by sparse friendship networks, unsupervised teenage peer groups, and low organizational participation had disproportionately high rates of crime and delinquency. Moreover, variations in these dimensions of community social disorganization were shown to mediate in large part the effects of community structural characteristics (i.e., low socioeconomic status, residential mobility, ethnic heterogeneity, and family disruption) in the manner predicted by our theoretical model. We have thus demonstrated that social-disorganization theory has vitality and renewed relevance for explaining macro-level variations in crime rates (see also Bursik 1984, 1986). In particular, the fact that Shaw and McKay's model explains crime and delinquency rates in a culture other than the United States (cf. Clinard and Abbott 1976, p. 201) is testimony to its power and generalizability (see Kohn 1987).

Nevertheless, our analysis does not constitute a definitive test of social-disorganization theory. First, the proportion of variance explained in crime and delinquency was, at times, quite modest. Second, only three dimensions of community organization were examined, and these were, of necessity, measured with single items. In this regard, note that while local friendship networks, organizational participation, and control of teenage peer groups are all dimensions of a systemic concept of social organization, they are conceptually distinct and hence not different measures of the same variable. Consequently, we were unable to model measurement error with unobservable-variable methods. Third, the organizational-participation variable was imprecise—for example, we do not know which organizations respondents were involved with, and in fact we cannot guarantee that they were located in the community. Finally, better measures of both friendship networks (see, e.g., Fischer 1982; Freudenberg 1986) and street-corner gangs (see, e.g., Short and Strodtbeck 1965) are needed at the community level.

But despite these limitations, the overall empirical results were theoretically consistent and robust for a variety of model specifications. Indeed, 12 different victimization and offending rates were analyzed across a large number of local communities (238, 300, and 599) for two independent samples at different time periods, all with convergent results. And most important, we believe that the ability to measure dimensions of social disorganization at the community level represents an essential first step in directly testing macrosocial control theory. Without such empirical identification of mediating links, the theory is open to charges that it is conceptually redundant with crime itself and, what is perhaps more crucial, that traditional ecological studies are compatible with almost any theoretical speculation. We therefore hope that future research will improve on the present effort by directing attention toward more precise measures of the salient dimensions of community social disorganization.

Notes

1. As Janowitz (1975) emphasizes, social control should not be equated with social repression but rather with the collective pursuit of shared values that are rewarding and meaningful. In this regard, we assume that residents of an area value a relatively crime-free existence (Bursik 1984, p. 12). Given the consistent findings on public rankings of the seriousness of crime, this does not seem problematic (see Kornhauser 1978, pp. 214–18).

2. Because of data and space constraints, our focus in this paper is on the structural dimensions of social disorganization. For an extensive discussion of the cultural components of social disorganization and the cultural-deviance portion of Shaw and McKay's "mixed model" of delinquency, see Kornhauser (1978, pp. 62–78).

3. Before we test fig. 6.1, we should emphasize that Shaw and McKay's theory was primarily about *indigenous* community social control. It is quite possible that weak local ties among residents are counterbalanced by strong ties to external institutions and larger (e.g., national) friendship networks (see Granovetter 1973). But while extralocal ties among many urbanites may be strong (Fischer 1982), they do not necessarily bear on local social control (see Shaw and McKay 1969, p. 185).

4. Specifically, in the first stage of enumeration, 238 of the 552 parliamentary constituencies in England and Wales (including London) were selected with probability proportional to the electorate (Hough and Mayhew 1983, p. 38). Then, in 119 of the constituencies, 119 electoral wards were sampled with probability proportional to the electorate. In the other 119 areas, two polling districts were selected, also with probability proportional to the electorate. Finally, within each sampling unit, addresses were chosen with probability proportional to the number of electors listed there (60 in each ward, 30 in each of the two polling districts). Preliminary analysis showed no meaningful design effects of wards vs. polling districts on the substantive results, and we therefore examine all 238 areas.

5. The average size of wards in England and Wales is just over 5,000 (see Office of Population Censuses and Surveys 1984, pp. xi, 2). While areal boundaries were administratively defined, we believe that the geographical size of sampling units, in conjunction with the sampling procedures, justifies using the 238 ecological areas to approximate local communities.

6. At the aggregate level, the dummy variable for urbanization also serves to control for the overrepresentation of inner-city communities in the sample (see Hough and Mayhew 1983, p. 38).

7. Preliminary inspection of descriptive data revealed that rates of the most serious crimes (e.g., robbery, stranger violence, burglary) were highly skewed. For example, in raw form, the rate of stranger violence had skewness and kurtosis values of 2.4 and 10.1, respectively. To induce normality, we took the natural logarithms (+1) of victimization rates that had skewness and kurtosis values greater than one. Self-reported offending rates were also skewed, and, hence, they too were logged. Further, it should be noted that the six self-reported delinquency items, along with the two questions about local friendships and organizational participation, were asked in a follow-up interview of all victims and a random selection (40%) of nonvictims ($N = 6,329$). Hence, the structural variables referring to friendship networks, organizational participation, and the two offending rates are based on an average within-area sample size of 27. Because victims were oversampled in the follow-up (see Hough and Mayhew 1983, pp. 39–40), the individual-level responses were weighted to restore representativeness before community variables were constructed. All other aggregate measures were constructed from the full sample of 10,905 persons.

8. Because the number of individual cases used to create the aggregate measures varied slightly by community, the variance of the residuals is not constant. Therefore, weighted-least-squares (WLS) regression is used to induce homoscedasticity of error variances: each case is weighted by the square root of the unweighted sample size (Hanushek and Jackson 1977, pp. 143, 152).

9. Space limitations preclude the tabular presentation of reduced-form results and indirect effects in the structural equations for all eight crime rates. For simplicity, we present the direct effects in tables and discuss in the text the indirect-effect estimates and the proportion of the absolute value of total effects (see Alwin and Hauser 1981, p. 140) mediated by the intervening variables, as specified in the theoretical model.

10. As noted earlier, the link, between gang delinquency and adult criminal careers in socially disorganized areas was suggested by both Thrasher (1963) and Shaw and McKay (1942, 1969). Nonetheless, the effect of unsupervised teenage peer groups should be stronger on juvenile delinquency than on adult crime (Thrasher 1963, p. 281). This expectation appears supported by the data in that the indicator of unsupervised peer groups has stronger effects on victimization rates—which include a substantial proportion of offenses by juveniles—than on rates of self-reported offending by respondents, most of whom are adults.

11. The lower overall explained variance in Table 6.5, as opposed to Tables 6.3 and 6.4, suggests that there may be more measurement error in self-reported offending rates than victimization rates. If true, this is probably due to greater unreliability in measuring offending than victimization and also to the overall infrequent nature of offending among adults in the BCS sample.

12. We thank an anonymous *AJS* reviewer for raising these issues, spurring the idea of external validation.

13. Within the 300 selected constituencies, further clustering of the sample was required, leading to the selection of two wards. The final sampling unit from which names and addresses were drawn was a polling district within each ward. In this design, there were only 18 interviews conducted in each polling district for the main questionnaire and 11 for the follow-up. With fewer than 20 respondents per area, community-level measures may be unreliable. Therefore, the decision was made to base the main replication on macro-level measures for the 300 political constituencies. Although larger than polling districts, the samples within constituencies are representative of the population and they are sufficient in number—the average number of completed main interviews per area is 37 (22 for follow-up). For complete details of the 1984 BCS design and interview format, see Hough and Mayhew (1985, app. B).

14. To achieve replication, we constructed indicators of SES, heterogeneity, residential stability, family disruption, and urbanization parallel to those in 1982. And while parallel self-reported offending rates were unavailable for analysis, we were able to construct four victimization rates

similar to 1982—two personal (robbery and assault) and two property (burglary and vandalism). As in 1982, we included not only retrospective reports of victimization but, where possible, ratings of the crime problem in the local area (burglary, vandalism, and robbery). Also, parallel to 1982, the WLS regression models are weighted by the differential sample sizes across communities.

15. Further analysis revealed that the major findings in Table 6.6 were not affected by influential observations, multicollinearity, or alternative model specifications. And as a final check on the results, we repeated the entire 1984 BCS analysis on equivalent measures constructed for each of 599 polling districts. The results showed that the proportion of variance explained was generally lower for the polling districts, most likely because of increased measurement error associated with the smaller sample sizes used to construct aggregate measures (see n. 14). However, the structural-parameter estimates were almost equivalent. In particular, the direct effect of the major theoretical variable—street-corner peer groups—was .12, .34, .16, and .23 (all $P < .01$) on rates of burglary, vandalism, robbery, and assault, respectively (cf. Table 6.6). These convergent results solidify the substantive conclusions based on the 1984 data.

References

Alwin, Duane, and Robert Hauser. 1981. "The Decomposition of Effects in Path Analysis," Pp. 123–40 in *Linear Models in Social Research,* edited by Peter Marsden. Beverly Hills: Sage.

Blau, Peter. 1977. *Inequality and Heterogeneity.* New York: Free Press.

Bordua, David. 1961. "Delinquent Subcultures: Sociological Interpretations of Gang Delinquency." *Annals of the American Academy of Political and Social Science* 338:119–36.

Bursik, Robert J., Jr. 1984. "Ecological Theories of Crime and Delinquency since Shaw and McKay." Paper presented at the annual meetings of the American Society of Criminology, Cincinnati.

———. 1986. "Ecological Stability and the Dynamics of Delinquency." Pp. 35–66 in *Communities and Crime,* edited by A. J. Reiss, Jr., and M. Tonry. Chicago: University of Chicago Press.

Bursik, Robert J., Jr., and Jim Webb. 1982. "Community Change and Patterns of Delinquency." *American Journal of Sociology* 88:24–42.

Byrne, James, and Robert J. Sampson. 1986. "Key Issues in the Social Ecology of Crime." Pp. 1–22 in *The Social Ecology of Crime,* edited by James Byrne and Robert J. Sampson. New York: Springer-Verlag.

Clinard, Marshall, and Daniel Abbott. 1976. "Community Organization and Property Crime: A Comparative Study of Social Control in the Slums of an African City." Pp. 186–206 in *Delinquency, Crime, and Society,* edited by James F. Short, Jr. Chicago: University of Chicago Press.

Cohen, Lawrence, and Marcus Felson. 1979. "Social Change and Crime Rate Trends: A Routine Activities Approach." *American Sociological Review* 44:588–607

Cook, Dennis, and Sanford Weisberg. 1982. "Criticism and Influence Analysis in Regression." Pp. 313–61 in *Sociological Methodology,* edited by S. Leinhardt. San Francisco: Jossey-Bass.

Decker, David, David Shichor, and Robert O'Brien. 1982. *Urban Structure and Victimization.* Lexington, Mass.: Heath.

Elliott, Delbert, and Suzanne Ageton. 1980. "Reconciling Race and Class Differences in Self-reported and Official Estimates of Delinquency." *American Sociological Review* 45:95–110.

Fischer, Claude. 1982. *To Dwell among Friends: Personal Networks in Town and City.* Chicago: University of Chicago Press.

Flanagan, Timothy, and Maureen McLeod, eds. 1983. *Sourcebook of Criminal Justice Statistics—1982.* Washington, D.C.: Government Printing Office.

Freudenberg, William. 1986. "The Density of Acquaintanceship: An Overlooked Variable in Community Research?" *American Journal of Sociology* 92:27–63.

Granovetter, Mark. 1973. "The Strength of Weak Ties." *American Journal of Sociology* 78:1360–80.

Hagan, John, A. R. Gillis, and Janet Chan. 1978. "Explaining Official Delinquency: A Spatial Study of Class, Conflict, and Control." *Sociological Quarterly* 19:386–98.

Hanushek, Eric, and John Jackson. 1977. *Statistical Methods for Social Scientists.* New York: Academic.

Heitgerd, Janet L., and Robert J. Bursik, Jr. 1987. "Extracommunity Dynamics and the Ecology of Delinquency," *American Journal of Sociology* 92:775–87.

Hindelang, Michael, Travis Hirschi, and Joseph Weis. 1981. *Measuring Delinquency.* Beverly Hills: Sage.

Hough, Mike, and Pat Mayhew. 1983. *The British Crime Survey: First Report.* London: Her Majesty's Stationery Office.

———. 1985. *Taking Account of Crime: Key Findings from the Second British Crime Survey.* Home Office Research Report no. 85. London: Her Majesty's Stationery Office.

Hunter, Albert. 1974, *Symbolic Communities: The Persistence and Change of Chicago's Local Communities.* Chicago: University of Chicago Press.

Janowitz, Morris. 1975. "Sociological Theory and Social Control." *American Journal of Sociology* 81:82–108.

Kapsis, Robert. 1976. "Continuities in Delinquency and Riot Patterns in Black Residential Areas." *Social Problems* 23:567–80.

Kasarda, John, and Morris Janowitz. 1974. "Community Attachment in Mass Society." *American Sociological Review* 39:328–39.

Kohn, Melvin. 1987, "Cross-National Research as an Analytic Strategy." *American Sociological Review* 52:713–31.

Kornhauser, Ruth. 1978. *Social Sources of Delinquency.* Chicago: University of Chicago Press.

Krohn, Marvin. 1986. "The Web of Conformity: A Network Approach to the Explanation of Delinquent Behavior." *Social Problems* 33:81–93.

Maccoby, Eleanor, Joseph Johnson, and Russell Church. 1958. "Community Integration and the Social Control of Juvenile Delinquency." *Journal of Social Issues* 14:38–51.

Morris, T. 1970. Review of *Juvenile Delinquency and Urban Areas,* 2d ed., by Clifford Shaw and Henry McKay. *British Journal of Criminology* 10:194–96.

Office of Population Censuses and Surveys. 1984. *Census, 1981: Key Statistics for Local Authorities, Great Britain.* London: Her Majesty's Stationery Office.

Reiss, Albert J., Jr. 1986a. "Why Are Communities Important in Understanding Crime?" Pp. 1–33 in *Communities and Crime,* edited by A. J. Reiss, Jr., and M. Tonry. Chicago: University of Chicago Press.

———. 1986b. "Co-Offender Influences on Criminal Careers." Pp. 121–60 in *Criminal Careers and "Career Criminals,"* edited by Alfred Blumstein, Jacqueline Cohen, Jeffrey Roth, and Christy Visher. Washington, D.C.: National Academy.

Sampson, Robert J. 1985. "Neighborhood and Crime: The Structural Determinants of Personal Victimization." *Journal of Research in Crime and Delinquency* 22:7–40.

———. 1986. "Effects of Socioeconomic Context on Official Reaction to Juvenile Delinquency." *American Sociological Review* 51:876–85.

———. 1987. "Urban Black Violence: The Effect of Male Joblessness and Family Disruption." *American Journal of Sociology* 93:348–82.

———. 1988. "Local Friendship Ties and Community Attachment in Mass Society: A Multilevel Systemic Model." *American Sociological Review* 53:766–79.

Selltiz, Claire, Lawrence Wrightsman, and Stuart Cook. 1976. *Research Methods in Social Relations,* 3d ed. New York: Halt, Rinehart & Winston.

Shaw, Clifford, and Henry McKay. 1942. *Juvenile Delinquency and Urban Areas.* Chicago: University of Chicago Press.

———. 1969. *Juvenile Delinquency and Urban Areas,* rev ed. Chicago: University of Chicago Press.

Shaw, Clifford, Frederick Zorbaugh, Henry McKay, and Leonard Cottrell. 1929. *Delinquency Areas.* Chicago: University of Chicago Press.

Short, James F., Jr. 1963. "Introduction to the Abridged Edition." Pp. xv–liii in *The Gang: A Study of 1,313 Gangs in Chicago*, by Frederic Thrasher. Chicago: University of Chicago Press.

———. 1969. "Introduction to the Revised Edition." Pp. xxv–liv in *Juvenile Delinquency and Urban Areas*, by Clifford Shaw and Henry McKay. Chicago: University of Chicago Press.

Short, James F., and Fred Strodtbeck. 1965. *Group Process and Gang Delinquency*. Chicago: University of Chicago Press.

Simcha-Fagan, Ora, and Joseph Schwartz. 1986. "Neighborhood and Delinquency: An Assessment of Contextual Effects." *Criminology* 24:667–703.

Skogan, Wesley. 1986. "Fear of Crime and Neighborhood Change." Pp. 203–29 in *Communities mid Crime*, edited by A. J. Reiss, Jr., and M. Tonry. Chicago: University of Chicago Press.

Smith, Douglas R. 1986. "The Neighborhood Context of Police Behavior." Pp. 313–41 in *Communities and Crime*, edited by A. J. Reiss, Jr., and M. Tonry. Chicago: University of Chicago Press.

Suttles, Gerald. 1968. *The Social Order of the Slum*. Chicago: University of Chicago Press.

Thomas, W. I., and F. Znaniecki. 1920. *The Polish Peasant in Europe and America*, vol. 4. Boston: Gorham.

Thrasher, Frederic. 1963. *The Gang: A Study of 1,313 Gangs in Chicago*, rev. ed. Chicago: University of Chicago Press.

Tomeh, Aida. 1973. "Formal Voluntary Organizations: Participation, Correlates, and Interrelationships." *Sociological Inquiry* 43:89–121.

7

Economic Deprivation and Neighborhood Crime Rates

Robert J. Bursik Jr. did his MA and Ph.D in Sociology at the University of Chicago. His connection to Chicago School thinking can be seen in the following (1993) article entitled "Economic Deprivation and Neighborhood Crime Rates." In this article, he extends upon Shaw and McKay's social disorganization theory by analyzing demographic and crime rate data from the City of Chicago for the years 1960 through 1980 (Williams & McShane, 2010:57–58). Although Harold G. Grasmick (the co-author of this article) did not study at the University of Chicago, he did his BA, MA and Ph.D in Sociology, and has co-authored over twenty articles, book chapters and books with Robert J. Bursik Jr. As is the case with following article, most of the work on which Bursik and Grasmick have collaborated falls under the rubric of social disorganization theory or ecological criminology (cf. Akers & Sellers, 2009:180; Winfree & Abadinsky, 2010:161).

In an earlier (1988:520) article, Bursik reviewed some of the problems with (and prospects for) social disorganization theory. He observed that following the end of World War II in 1945—shortly after Shaw and McKay's original time series studies of social disorganization in Chicago during the 1930s and 1940s—the ecological patterns and demographics of the City of Chicago changed quite dramatically. Bursik and Grasmick investigate this in considerable depth in the following article, which describes the transformation of the City of Chicago between 1960 and 1980.

In his 1988 article (mentioned above), Bursik stressed that there were exogenous forces—outside of the control of the community—that could have a deleterious effect on community stability. For example, Bursik (1988:537–538) noted that city planning and the construction of government-sponsored public housing could attract impoverished individuals or families who otherwise would be unable to afford to live in a particular community. Similarly, the manipulation of real estate values by developers and speculators could influence the number and type of people moving into—or moving out of—a community.

Perhaps most importantly, Bursik recognized in his 1988 article that higher reported rates of crime and delinquency could be a reflection of police bias toward a particular community, rather than a fair and accurate representation of the criminal proclivities of the local inhabitants themselves. As Bursik pointed out, areas that were characterized by low socioeconomic status and high residential density were more likely to attract the attention of the police, which in turn would result in more police reports and higher arrest rates (Bursik, 1988:533). If true, then the claimed relationship between social disorganization and criminality could be spurious.

In their 1993 article, Bursik and Grasmick report on the large demographic shift that occurred in the inner city areas of Chicago between 1960 and 1980. There was a tremendous influx of African-Americans, accompanied by an even greater outflow of affluent White residents, as people fled the inner cities in droves (Bursik & Grasmick, 1993:264, 273). Apart from suffering net population losses, these inner city areas lost residents who had been living there for a period of time, and in return, gained residents who were strangers to the area. At the same time, many of the manufacturing industries moved to industrial parks on the outskirts of the city (or closed down altogether), making it even more difficult for the inner city residents to find work. The population turnover and loss of gainful employment resulted in a weakening of social ties and a breakdown in social cohesion (1993:264, 266). This in turn led to a weakening of the informal social controls that would normally be exercised by families, neighbors, schools and community organizations.

The results of this study of the demographic transformation of the City of Chicago are consistent with a number of Shaw and McKay's original (1969) observations regarding social disorganization. However, Bursik and Grasmick (1993:276) note that low socioeconomic status on its own does not have a large effect, either on delinquency rates, or on the capacity of the neighborhoods to regulate themselves. Rather, Bursik and Grasmick find that severe economic deprivation has the strongest influence on delinquency and social disorder. They conclude that the combination of severe economic deprivation (as indicated by low income, high unemployment, and the number of people on social assistance) and residential instability (as indicated by owner occupancy, the number of movers and net population loss) offers the best explanation for high rates of crime and delinquency (1993:271–272).

Toward the end of their (1993) article, Bursik and Grasmick engage in a lengthy discussion about the importance of private, parochial and public controls. This way of characterizing the various levels of social control was first introduced by Albert J. Hunter in his (1985) article, "Private, Parochial and Public Social Order: The Problem of Crime and Incivility in Urban Communities." Like Robert J. Bursik Jr, Albert Hunter did his MA and Ph.D at the University of Chicago, and has written extensively on community change, the Chicago School and the social ecology of Chicago. Private controls are exercised by informal primary groups such as family and friends (Bursik & Grasmick, 1993:278). Parochial controls come from neighbors and local institutions such as "schools, churches and voluntary associations" (Hunter, 1985:233). Public controls involve bureaucracies or agencies that are legally permitted to use coercion and force to achieve social control (Hunter, 1985:234). However, the notion of public controls can also be extended to the community's ability to obtain services or resources from these public agencies—e.g., traffic calming measures, bike patrols, or money for crime control measures (Bursik & Grasmick, 1993:279; Taylor, 2001:129). The presence and strength of these private, parochial and public controls are themselves a measure of how much collective efficacy a community has.

References

Akers, R. L., & Sellers, C. S. (2009). *Criminological theories: Introduction, evaluation, and application* (5th , New ed.). New York: Oxford University Press.

Bursik, R. J. Jr., & Grasmick, H. G. (1993). Economic deprivation and neighborhood crime rates, 1960–1980. *Law & Society Review*, 27(2), 263–283.

Bursik, R. J. Jr. (1988). Social disorganization and theories of crime and delinquency: Problems and prospects. *Criminology*, 26(4), 519–551.

Hunter, A. J. (1985). Private, parochial and public social order: The problem of crime and incivility in urban communities. In M. Janowitz, G. D. Suttles & M. N. Zald (Eds.), *The challenge of social control: Citizenship and institution building in modern society: Essays in honor of Morris Janowitz* (pp. 230–242). Norwood, NJ: Ablex Pub.

Shaw, C. R., & McKay, H. D. (1969). *Juvenile delinquency and urban areas: A study of rates of delinquency in relation to differential characteristics of local communities in American cities* (Rev. ed.). Chicago: University of Chicago Press.

Taylor, R. B. (2001). The ecology of crime, fear, and delinquency: Social disorganization versus social efficacy. In R. Paternoster, & R. Bachman (Eds.), *Explaining criminals and crime: Essays in contemporary criminological theory* (pp. 124–139). Los Angeles, Calif.: Roxbury Pub. Co.

Williams, F. P., & McShane, M. D. (2010). *Criminological theory* (5th ed.). Upper Saddle River, N.J.: Pearson/Prentice Hall.

Winfree, L. T., & Abadinsky, H. (2010). *Understanding crime: Essentials of criminological theory* (Third ed.). Belmont, CA: Wadsworth, Cengage Learning.

Economic Deprivation and Neighborhood Crime Rates, 1960–1980

ROBERT J. BURSIK JR. AND HAROLD G. GRASMICK

The social disorganization model of crime and delinquency generally has argued that the socioeconomic composition of neighborhoods is related to rates of illegal behavior only to the extent that it increases the likelihood of residential turnover and racial/ethnic heterogeneity. Such an orientation reflects the traditional assumption

Reprinted from *Law & Society Review* 27, no. 2 (1993), The Law and Society Association.

of human ecology that urban areas are characterized by continual processes of residential upgrading as groups become progressively assimilated into the economic structure of the community and have more economic resources at their disposal. However, the validity of the indirect effect hypothesis may have become questionable in the many cities that have experienced a significant economic decline during the last few decades, thereby leading to the creation of an immobile underclass population. We examine here the relative validity of the indirect effect hypothesis in Chicago's neighborhoods during 1960 and 1980. While the findings generally support the traditional indirect effect assumption of social disorganization, they also emphasize the need to consider the economic and political contexts in which these communities are embedded.

The presumed relationship between economic deprivation and the number of crimes committed by the residents of a particular neighborhood is one of the lasting legacies of the research of Clifford Shaw, Henry McKay, and associates (1929, 1942, 1969). As noted by the theoretical explications of Kornhauser (1978), Tittle (1983), and Bursik and Grasmick (1993), their social disorganization framework assumed that this relationship was an indirect one, mediated in turn by the residential instability and heterogeneity of the neighborhood and by the regulatory capacity of the area. Nevertheless, despite the indirect nature of its effect on crime rates, the economic composition of local urban communities was the key ecological factor that set in operation the dynamics associated with social disorganization.

The pivotal role of economic factors in the development of social disorganization is derived from the Park and Burgess (1924) model of human ecology which assumed that residential mobility was a function of the degree of assimilation of local populations into the occupational structure of urban areas. Since the initial occupations of immigrant groups were assumed to be relatively low paying, these groups tended to be concentrated in economically deprived areas. However, over time, occupational mobility would lead to resettlement in more desirable neighborhoods characterized by higher economic status, greater stability, and less heterogeneity.[1]

The availability of unskilled jobs in goods-production industries played an important role in shaping these ecological dynamics, for they provided a relatively open entree into the occupational structure. Unfortunately, as industries have been enticed into suburban and rural locations, many residents of modern central-city neighborhoods no longer have easy access to the type of jobs that traditionally provided the opportunity for occupational mobility, especially in the older, Northern cities. Wilson (1987:100), for example, notes that the number of manufacturing jobs declined by 701,700 in the Northeast and North Central regions of the United States between 1970 and 1980.

The authors would like to acknowledge the very helpful, constructive and insightful comments of John Hagan, Al Liska, and Susan Silbey on an earlier version of this article. Address correspondence to Robert J. Bursik, Department of Sociology, University of Oklahoma, 900 Asp Avenue, Norman, Oklahoma 73019-0250.

At the same time, dramatic changes have occurred in the racial composition of many cities. For example, while Wilson (1987:101) notes that the black population of the 33 largest central cities increased by more than 5,000,000 between 1950 and 1980, the white population declined by more than 9,000,000 during the same period. The coupling of such demographic shifts with the noted trend in urban economies has resulted in the concentration and isolation of the most disadvantaged segments of minority populations in central-city neighborhoods of older industrial cities (p. 58), leading to the emergence of an extremely poor "underclass" population that is structurally prohibited from any significant degree of residential upgrading (see Sampson & Wilson 1991). Such dramatic alterations in the ecological structures and dynamics of many urban areas suggest that the relationship between economic deprivation and crime rates may have changed significantly from the indirect effect envisioned by Shaw and McKay. On the other hand, the association may have remained fairly stable despite these new ecological dynamics. We here compare the structure of relationships between the ecological dynamics associated with crime in Chicago during 1960 and 1980 and interpret the results within the contemporary systemic reformulation of the social disorganization framework (Sampson & Groves 1989; Bursik & Grasmick 1993).

The Role of Economic Deprivation in Social Disorganization Models

The literature that has considered the degree to which neighborhood economic composition is related to crime has been characterized by two conceptually distinct approaches. The first has emphasized the degree of economic inequality within local communities. While such internal variation in the availability of economic resources has been recognized within urban sociology at least since the publication of Zorbaugh's classic *The Gold Coast and the Slum* in 1929, surprisingly few recent studies have examined the effects of economic inequality at the neighborhood level.[2] The important exceptions, Messner and Tardiff (1986) and Patterson (1991), have failed to find a significant relationship between inequality and crime. Given Wilson's (1987) argument concerning the flight of affluent families from the central city, such findings are not theoretically unexpected since these dynamics should lead to a decreasing level of inequality within urban neighborhoods over time.

Many more studies have focused on a conceptually different approach to the economic issue that operationalizes deprivation relative to some fixed physical or physiological standards of well-being (Braithwaite 1979; Messner 1982) rather than to the overall distribution of economic status. Whereas the inequality frameworks generally are referred to as relative approaches, the fixed-standard orientation typically is referred to as an absolute approach. Not only do we consider such an orientation to be much more consistent with Wilson's underclass hypothesis, but it is identical to the conceptualization underlying Shaw and McKay's traditional social disorganization framework.

Many contemporary discussions of the relationship of absolute deprivation to crime entail neighborhood dynamics much like those found in Shaw and McKay and, therefore, represent variations of the indirect effect hypothesis. Wacquant and Wilson (1989), for example, argue that the economic marginalization and deterioration of black neighborhoods has had devastating effects on the ability of local communities to act as agents of social control. In support of this position, they present data (pp. 22–24) suggesting that there is a decline in attachment to and identification with the neighborhood, fewer social ties with other community residents, and an overall loss of strength within such economic contexts. Similarly, Bluestone and Harrison (1982) note that the closing of manufacturing plants typically is accompanied by strained family and social relationships and a general decline in social cohesion in the affected communities.[3]

On the other hand, a growing body of work suggests that the economic and political dynamics associated with the emergence of the underclass are reflected in a direct effect of absolute deprivation on crime. The possibility that deprivation has such an effect presents a historically fascinating challenge to the traditional social disorganization model, for it suggests that it may be necessary to supplant Park and Burgess's "desirable space" ecological model with the "sustenance activity" orientation found in the ecological theory of Amos Hawley (1944, 1950).[4] While Hawley acknowledged that the dynamics emphasized by Park and Burgess should be part of a general ecological model (see, e.g., Hawley 1944:404), and discussed the regulatory capacities of commensalistic relationships (1950: 219), he expanded their orientation by emphasizing the distribution of sustenance activities that give rise to an urban structure of interdependent relationships (ibid., p. 180). From this perspective, crime is an alternative means of gaining economic and social sustenance from the environment (see Bursik & Grasmick 1993:65–70).

Sullivan's (1989) discussion of a Brooklyn neighborhood during the late 1970s and early 1980s provides a rich description of how attempts to derive economic sustenance from the social environment can lead directly to criminal involvement. Many youths in that community were skeptical of the relevance of education to their future in the labor market and left school to obtain work prior to graduation. However, given their relative lack of conventional employment credentials, the positions that were available tended to be unstable, with undesirable working conditions and no chance for advancement. Since a significant proportion of these jobs were never officially recorded, many of these youths did not qualify for unemployment compensation if a position was terminated suddenly (Sullivan 1989:60–64). As a result, many of the local youths became involved in a systematic series of thefts and other economically motivated illegal activities that were coordinated through membership in local gangs (p. 117).

Moore (1988:8) also has argued that the shrinking number of employment opportunities can lead to the institutionalization of gang activities in economically deprived neighborhoods. While a significant proportion of gang members may mature out of such behavior (as also noted by Sullivan), some fraction retain their gang affiliation well into adulthood due to the lack of financial alternatives. Some of the children from this fraction are recruited into gangs during adolescence, and the process of gang formation and maintenance continues to reproduce itself.

The findings of recent studies testing the viability of the direct effect hypothesis are inconsistent.[5] Curry and Spergel (1988) conclude that the degree of poverty in a neighborhood is directly related to both the general delinquency rate and the rate of gang-related homicides; these findings are supported by the research of Taylor and Covington (1988) concerning homicides in general. Yet the direct relationship between percentage poor and the homicide rate presented in Messner and Tardiff (1986) is not significant. Likewise, Sampson and Groves (1989) present evidence that the socioeconomic composition of a local community has no direct effect on community rates of personal violence and property theft/vandalism. Therefore, there has been a great deal of divergence in the findings of studies that have examined this issue.

A number of reasons may be proposed for such differences.[6] As noted by Patterson (1991:761), the unit of analysis used in neighborhood studies presents very severe operational problems. Traditional studies in the social disorganization framework have defined the neighborhood in a wide variety of ways, such as local community areas, census tracts, police districts, and electoral wards (see Bursik & Grasmick 1993:chs. 1–2). For example, in the four studies discussed in the preceding paragraph, the units of analysis include empirically delineated neighborhoods (Taylor & Covington), neighborhoods that are assumed to be symbolically meaningful (Messner & Tardiff), officially/administratively defined communities (Curry & Spergel), and electoral wards and polling districts (Sampson & Groves). As Bailey (1985) has clearly illustrated, the level of aggregation used in an analysis of crime rates can dramatically affect the statistical patterns that emerge. Therefore, some of the differences found in these studies may simply represent the effects of variation in the unit of analysis.

A second source of divergence may represent the nature of the urban systems in which these neighborhoods are embedded (Taylor & Covington, Baltimore; Messner & Tardiff, New York City; Curry & Spergel, Chicago; Sampson & Groves, England and Wales, including London). The economic and ecological upheavals Wilson discussed are not consistently distributed among U.S. or British cities. Frey and Speare (1988) note that while many U.S. areas lost manufacturing jobs during the 1970s, other areas experienced significant growth in both population and the number of such jobs. For example, Los Angeles was a growing metropolis between 1950 and 1980, increasing from 1,970,358 residents to 2,968,258, while the population of Chicago declined from 3,360,962 to 3,005,072 people during that period. While manufacturing continued to play a central role in Los Angeles's economy during that period (the number of manufacturing establishments grew from 7,502 to 8,647 and the number of workers they employed increased from 268,800 to 327,600 between 1954 and 1984), this has not been the case in Chicago (which experienced a decrease from 10,288 to 5,203 establishments and from 615,700 to 277,000 employed workers during the same period). However, while such a consideration may serve as an appropriate caution against the validity of generalizations that sometimes have been drawn from findings derived from neighborhoods within a single urban system, it does not appear to provide much of a basis for resolving the differences observed between Chicago, Baltimore, and New York, for all these cities experienced significant declines in the number of manufacturing establishments and related employees between 1967 and 1982 (U.S. Bureau of the Census 1973, 1983).

A third basis of incomparability is the one we feel is most crucial for understanding the inconsistencies appearing in the literature—the measurement of economic deprivation and related dynamics of social disorganization. We turn our attention to this issue in the next section.

The Measurement of the Model Components

Two measurement issues have been especially problematic in the analysis of economic deprivation, social disorganization, and crime. The first entails deprivation itself. Many researchers have utilized very general measures of socioeconomic status. Sampson and Groves, for example, derive a scale of neighborhood SES that combines the percentage who have gone to college, the percentage employed in professional or managerial positions, and the percentage with a high income.

While they conclude that socioeconomic composition is unrelated to crime, it often has been noted that the variation most pertinent to the analysis of economic deprivation and crime may be concentrated in the lowest tail of the economic distribution (Gordon 1967; Clelland & Carter 1980). This especially is the case if the statistical associations related to the emergence of an underclass are the focus of one's research, for it is by definition the most disadvantaged segment of the population. Thus, it is interesting to note that Curry and Spergel's scale combines the unemployment rate and the percentage below the poverty level with more general indicators of socioeconomic status; likewise, a central component of Taylor and Covington's scale involves the distribution of poverty. Recall that both studies present evidence of a significant direct effect of economic deprivation on crime. Therefore, there is some evidence that the characteristics associated with underclass neighborhood status are related to neighborhood crime and delinquency rates. Thus, a valid examination of the issues must be based on indicators that measure such deprivation in a reliable and valid manner.

The second measurement issue is much trickier to address, yet on it rests the resolution of the competing direct and indirect hypotheses. A complete evaluation of the relative validity of these two models requires that they are specified as fully as possible; included are not only the appropriate indicators of economic deprivation but also measures that represent the full range of neighborhood regulatory capacities that lie at the heart of the social disorganization framework (see the related argument of Land et al. 1990:934).

Although the works of Smith and Jarjoura (1988) and Patterson (1991) are based on victimization rates, their findings exemplify the inferential problems that may arise due to an incomplete specification. Both studies utilize the same set of data gathered from 57 neighborhoods in three SMSAs. At the zero-order level, there is a significant correlation of .374 between the burglary rate and the percentage of residents with low income levels (Smith & Jarjoura 1988:58).

The effect of economic deprivation on burglary continues to be significant when indicators of residential mobility and racial heterogeneity are introduced into the model (Smith & Jarjoura 1988:Table 3). If Smith and Jarjoura had considered only these three variables, they would have been forced to conclude that deprivation has a direct effect on burglary. However, the introduction of additional ecological variables (such as population density, age structure, and household composition) reduces the direct effect of deprivation to zero, while the direct effects of mobility and heterogeneity continue to be significant. Patterson's analysis also concludes that there is no direct effect of deprivation on burglary rates. However, using a specification of the full model that is minimally different from that of Smith and Jarjoura (reflecting the inclusion of the Gini coefficient), Patterson concludes that racial heterogeneity also is unrelated to burglary, a conclusion clearly departing from that of Smith and Jarjoura despite the fact that it is based on the same data set.

This illustration highlights the variation in conclusions that may result simply from a failure to fully specify a model. However, while the solution is extremely simple theoretically, it poses enormous practical problems. It is fairly easy to collect indicators of the ecological dynamics pertinent to the social disorganization framework (i.e., socioeconomic composition, economic deprivation, residential instability, and population heterogeneity) from published census materials. However, data pertaining to the regulatory capacity of the neighborhood are not readily available from published sources (see Bursik & Grasmick 1993:ch. 2). Thus, most large-scale studies of urban systems have been forced to assume that processes of neighborhood control intervene between the ecological dynamics and crime, and many of the inferences drawn from such research are based on "conjecture and speculation" (Sampson 1987:100).

The findings of Sampson and Groves (1989) have a special importance within the context of this limitation, for they are able to incorporate variables into their model that represent the breadth of local friendship networks, the rate of organization participation, and the supervisory capacity of the neighborhood. Therefore, their conclusion that socioeconomic composition has no direct effect on rates of personal and property crime, thereby supporting the indirect hypothesis, are very persuasive. Yet recall that they do not incorporate indicators of economic deprivation per se. In addition, the cross-sectional nature of their study precludes an analysis of the effects of a changing urban economy on the relevance of the social disorganization model. As a result, while their findings are exciting, they certainly cannot be considered conclusive.

Data and Measurement

Our examination of the viability of the direct and indirect hypotheses within the context of contemporary urban economies is based on the rates of male referrals to the Cook County, Illinois, juvenile court (computed per 1,000 male juveniles ages 10–17) for the years 1960 and 1980 in each of Chicago's officially recognized local community areas.[7] The years 1960 and 1980 were chosen because they seem to bracket nicely the development of the economic processes discussed by Wilson (1987:3–7) and a wide variety of consistently defined variables were available for these periods.

Our measures of socioeconomic composition and deprivation were selected to be as congruent with Wilson's argument as possible. The indicators of general socioeconomic status (SES) are identical to those that often have been used in past research; the percentage of the population with professional/managerial occupations, the median education level, and the median family income. Three of the measures of severe economic deprivation (DEP) are also straightforward: the percentage of families with incomes below the poverty level (for 1960 this is measured as the percentage with incomes below $3,000), the unemployment rate, and the rate of public assistance allocations per 100 residents.[8]

We have included one other indicator in our scale of economic deprivation, although it does not represent financial considerations per se: the percentage of the population that is black. Wilson has argued that this minority population tends to be concentrated in economically deprived neighborhoods, and as will be seen in the subsequent analyses, a very large proportion of its individual variation is shared in common with the other economic indicators. Therefore, its separate incorporation into the model would have led to an intolerably high level of multicollinearity and very unstable estimates of its effects.

Unfortunately, the selection of indicators to represent the regulatory capacity (RC) element of the social disorganization model was limited by the same paucity of data that other studies have confronted; information on the breadth and depth of relational networks in all these neighborhoods during 1960 and 1980 is not available. Therefore, we have been forced to rely on more indirect measures drawn from census data. Two of these, the rates of owner occupancy and residential mobility, have often appeared in other research within this tradition. However, the mobility indicator is somewhat problematic given the way the variable is defined by the Bureau of the Census (the percentage of residents who have not lived at the same address for five or more years). While this gives some sense of the rate of turnover, it is possible for very unstable communities to have scores nearing 0% on this item. Such a situation would occur when a large number of residents have left a neighborhood, essentially abandoning those who cannot (or will not) leave. If the remaining population has resided in the area for more than five years, the neighborhood will appear to be highly stable, even if a majority of the population has left the area. To compensate for this source of inferential complexity, we have also included community-specific measures of net migration, defined as the percentage

TABLE 7.1 *Factor Structures of Socioeconomic Status, Economic Deprivation, and Social Disorganization, 1960–1980*

Indicator	1960	1980
	Socioeconomic Status (SES)	
% professional	.897	.869
Median education	.773	.928
Median income	.844	.718
Eigenvalue	2.114	2.133
	Economic Deprivation (DEP)	
% below poverty	.971	.943
Unemployment rate	.981	.957
Rate of public aid	.981	.968
% black	.936	.865
Eigenvalue	3.742	3.491
	Regulatory Capacity (RC)	
% owner occupancy	.943	.942
Residential mobility	−.785	−.536
Net migration (%)	.608	.720
% children with parents	.888	.843
Eigenvalue	2.665	2.405

change in population size during the preceding decade that cannot be accounted for by births or deaths, as an additional indicator of stability.[9] The final indicator of regulatory capacity is the percentage of children who live in husband-wife households, for Sampson (1987) has argued persuasively that this compositional element is intrinsically related to a neighborhood's ability to supervise the nature of the activities occurring within its borders.

Each set of variables was combined into the relevant scale through a principal components model (see Table 7.1). Two aspects of this table are particularly interesting. First, while the factor loadings all are relatively strong, the shared variations of the all-deprivation indicators are extraordinarily high; the communalities range from .88 to .96 for 1960 and from .75 to .94 for 1980. These findings confirm Wilson's argument concerning the pronounced concentration of these social characteristics within urban neighborhoods.

Second, the factor structures underlying these three dimensions during 1960 and 1980 are strikingly similar. Therefore, the generally invariant ecological structure described by Bursik (1984) for Chicago during 1960 and 1970 appears to also characterize the city during 1980. This finding calls for a slight modification of Wilson's (1987) argument, which implies that recent trends in urban economies

TABLE 7.2   *Chicago Neighborhood Characteristics, 1960–1980*

| | 1960 | | 1980 | | |
	Mean	S.D.	Mean	S.D.	t^a
Delinquency rate	15.57	12.12	56.83	36.93	11.55
% professional	8.67	5.12	18.05	10.20	10.40
Median income	$6,913	$1,595	$19,180	$6,136	$22.05
% below poverty	13.30	10.46	16.54	14.31	4.04
Unemployment rate	5.09	3.61	10.61	6.12	11.72
Rate of public aid	6.62	10.33	37.89	38.02	9.11
% black	20.06	33.76	39.69	42.86	5.36
% owner-occupancy	45.45	27.31	45.58	24.78	0.21
Residential mobility	50.46	10.73	38.42	11.25	8.34
Net migration (%)	0.34	52.11	–13.44	15.30	2.41
% children with parents	84.49	12.45	65.88	22.06	12.61

[a]N = 74 for all variables. The t-test was computed on the basis of a paired comparison between years.

have led to an increasing concentration of "the most disadvantaged segments of the urban black population" (p. 58). Rather, our findings suggest that the five indicators of economic deprivation we have used in our analysis generally have been concentrated in particular neighborhood settings since at least 1960.

However, while the nature of concentration is similar for these two decades, the number of neighborhoods characterized by extreme economic deprivation has increased dramatically and in a fashion consistent with Wilson's discussion. Table 7.2 presents the univariate statistics for the variables that formed the basis of our three scales. A simple inspection of these distributions confirms Wilson's argument concerning recent urban dynamics. There appears to have been a bifurcated process of economic change during this 20-year period: while there was an increase in the percentage of residents employed in professional occupations, there also were significant increases in the poverty and unemployment rates, and a more than fivefold jump in the rate of public aid.

It is also interesting that the mean levels and variations of owner occupancy did not change significantly between 1960 and 1980 even though the levels of residential mobility significantly decreased. In addition, note that while the in- and out-migration flows tended to balance one another between 1950 and 1960, Chicago's neighborhoods on the average suffered a net loss of more than 13% in their residential populations between 1970 and 1980 due to migration. In fact, an inspection of the frequencies for the 1980 levels of this variable indicates that only 5 of the 74 neighborhoods were characterized by a positive level of inmigration (compared to 21 growing neighborhoods during 1960). When this trend is placed in the context of the noted patterns for owner occupancy and residential mobility, the findings suggest that Chicago's real estate market stagnated during this period and that the central city during 1980 was populated to a large degree by residents who had been "abandoned" in their neighborhoods.

TABLE 7.3   *Changes in Neighborhood Economic Deprivation, 1960–1980*

			1960				
			Low Deprivation			High Deprivation	Row %
			1	2	3	4	
1980	Low Deprivation	1	21.1	0.0	0.0	0.0	5.4
		2	31.6	11.8	0.0	0.0	10.8
		3	26.3	29.4	11.1	0.0	16.2
	High Deprivation	4	21.1	58.8	88.9	100.0	67.6
	Total		100.1	100.0	100.0	100.0	100.0
	Column %		25.7	23.0	24.3	27.0	N = 74

The full extent of Chicago's economic transformation can be provided by examining the changes in the neighborhood levels of economic deprivation during this 20-year period. Unfortunately, this relatively simple analytic question is trickier than it appears. Since a factor score reflects the weighted sum of the Z scores for each of the indicators reflected in that factor, a community's score for a particular decade reflects only its relative standardized position within the overall distribution of scores for that year. Because of the significant differences in the means of the deprivation variables in 1960 and 1980, a straightforward comparison of the DEP scores for these years is inappropriate because the raw scores have been standardized on the basis of inconsistent distributional characteristics. For example, if all the neighborhoods declined to the same degree between 1960 and 1980, the relative ordering of neighborhoods still would be identical for both decades, resulting in a rank correlation of 1 despite the growing level of deprivation.

Our goal was to transform both sets of variables on the basis of a consistent and comparable metric. Therefore, we "quasi-standardized" the 1980 data on the basis of the raw 1960 distributions by subtracting the 1960 mean from each 1980 observation and then dividing by the 1960 standard deviation. The five transformed variables were then combined by using the factor score coefficients that were used to create the DEP scale for 1960. This transformation enabled us to examine the level of economic deprivation of each neighborhood in 1980 relative to what it was in 1960, not just to other neighborhoods during 1980.[10]

Table 7.3 provides two very clear indications of the general economic decline of Chicago's neighborhoods. First, note from the marginal distributions that nearly 70% of the areas had the same level of economic deprivation during 1980 as the lowest 25% of the 1960 neighborhoods. In fact, over one-fifth of the least deprived 1960 neighborhoods were in the most deprived category by 1980. Second, economic decline during this period was a unidirectional process; none of the neighborhoods could be classified as moving from a more deprived to a less deprived status during this period.

In sum, Chicago is a city that clearly has undergone the economic transformations Wilson discussed. This is an important difference from the image of Chicago envisioned by Shaw and McKay and by Park and Burgess, in which the functional role of the neighborhood in the ecological system was assumed to be in a general state of equilibrium. The central question facing contemporary social disorganization research, therefore, is the degree to which these changes may have affected the viability of the basic hypothesis that economic deprivation has a primarily indirect, rather than direct, effect on the crime rate.

Findings

One of the most important findings that can be derived from our regression analyses (Table 7.4) is the absolute necessity of differentiating between economic deprivation and more general measures of socioeconomic composition that are not nearly as sensitive to variation in the low end of the economic distribution. In both 1960 and 1980, SES has a nonsignificant effect on both the delinquency rate and regulatory capacity that characterize Chicago's neighborhoods. The level of economic deprivation, on the other hand, plays a major role in shaping these two aspects of the local community even after the effects of the other variables in the model are controlled for. This pattern may explain the contradictory conclusions of Sampson and Groves (who found no direct effects of economic factors on crime on the basis of variables similar to SES) and Curry and Spergel and Taylor and Covington (who document such effects using variables similar to DEP).

Nearly as important a finding is that despite the dramatic changes in the distribution of economic deprivation that occurred between the beginning and end of this 20-year period, the patterns of relationships for 1960 and 1980 are strikingly similar, including the magnitudes of the significant standardized coefficients. The only departure from this similarity is that the models explained somewhat less of the variation in regulatory capacity and delinquency rates in 1980 than in 1960. Nevertheless, the model is fairly powerful during both periods and in general can be considered to be robust.

Most important, the predictions of the traditional social disorganization model receive strong but mixed support during both periods. As expected, economic deprivation is strongly associated with the regulatory capacity of an area, which in turn has the strongest direct effect on delinquency during both periods. In addition, the indirect effects of economic deprivation on delinquency during 1960 (.376) and 1980 (.406) are greater than the direct effects in the full models (.335 and .321, respectively).[11] Therefore, our findings indicate that economic factors affect delinquency, at least primarily, in a manner consistent with the traditional Shaw and McKay framework.

TABLE 7.4   *Regression Models for Chicago's Neighborhoods, 1960 and 1980*

| Independent Variables | Dependent Variables | | |
	Delinquency	Regulatory Capacity	Delinquency
	1960		
Constant	15.568	0.000	15.568
DEP	8.623	−.789	4.059
	(7.867)	(−9.187)	(2.789)
	.711	−.789	.335
SES	−1.817	.070	−1.411
	(−1.658)	(0.817)	(−1.428)
	−.150	.070	−.116
RC	—	—	−5.782
			(−4.254)
			−.477
Adjusted R^2	.659	.692	.725
	1980		
Constant	56.830	0.000	56.830
DEP	26.845	−.775	11.844
	(7.316)	(−7.998)	(2.704)
	.727	−.775	.321
SES	−0.310	.051	−1.292
	(−0.084)	(−0.524)	(−0.406)
	−.008	−.05170	−.035
RC	—	—	−19.349
			(−4.975)
			−.524
Adjusted R^2	.522	.546	.642

Note: For each effect, the first entry is the unstandardized beta coefficient, followed by the *t*-value (in parentheses) and the standardized coefficient.

Nevertheless, economic deprivation has a significant direct effect on delinquency during both periods. It certainly is possible that this effect would have been further attenuated if we had incorporated additional indicators of the internal regulatory capacity of these neighborhoods into the model. Yet, on the basis of these findings, we must consider the possibility that there are additional neighborhood dynamics relevant to delinquency that are not reflected in the traditional theoretical specification of social disorganization. In the final section of this article, we discuss such an extension of the social disorganization framework that may account for these findings in a manner which is logically consistent with the underlying theoretical assumptions of the model.

Discussion

The findings represented in Table 7.4 certainly do not represent the only time empirical patterns have departed from those predicted by the traditional social disorganization model. In fact, the viability of the framework as a whole was prematurely dismissed by many criminologists because of its notorious inability to account for the presence of stable, working-class communities that nonetheless were characterized by relatively high rates of crime and delinquency. Likewise, the existence of a direct effect of economic deprivation on delinquency is inconsistent with the core assumptions of the model. In addition, many observers have criticized its general failure to consider the political and economic contexts of the larger urban systems in which local neighborhoods are embedded.

Recently, however, there have been several attempts to reformulate the social disorganization framework in terms of a broader systemic approach that emphasizes the breadth and depth of institutional and personal relational networks within a community and the capacities of such networks as sources of social control (see Sampson & Groves 1989; Bursik & Grasmick 1993). These capacities have been most fully addressed by Hunter (1985), who identifies three dimensions of neighborhood social order. The *private* level is grounded in the intimate, informal primary groups in a community, and control is exerted primarily through the allocation or threatened withdrawal of sentiment, social support, and mutual esteem (Hunter 1985:233). The second, *parochial* level of control reflects the nonintimate relationships among neighbors who do not have a deep sentimental attachment and the interlocking of local institutions such as schools, churches, and voluntary organizations (ibid.). At this level, the regulatory capacity of an area reflects the ability of residents to supervise activities within the community and the degree to which local institutions are integrated into the fabric of everyday community life.

While the concepts of private and parochial control formalize several of the key dynamics of the social disorganization model that were left implicit by Shaw and McKay, we do not feel they totally can account for our observed direct effect of economic deprivation on delinquency. Likewise, they are totally unable to account for the existence of stable, high-delinquency areas. In our opinion, this is due to the primary emphasis of these two levels of control on the internal dynamics of the community. Spergel and Korbelik (1979:109) have shown that there are externally determined contingencies that mediate the ability of local networks and institutions to control the threat of crime. In fact, some local associations initially arise due to the intervention of external organizations who may seek legitimacy for projects they are considering in a particular community (Taub et al. 1977). Therefore, it is also necessary to consider the *public* level of social control (Hunter 1985:233), which focuses on a community's ability to secure the public goods and services allocated by agencies located outside the neighborhood that are necessary for the development of an effective regulatory capacity.

The potential importance of the public dimension of neighborhood crime control is highlighted by the resource mobilization research which shows consistently that a social movement is more likely to be successful if it is able to develop linkages among representatives of the movement and other groups in the environment (see McCarthy & Zald 1987; Bursik & Grasmick 1993:156–57). For example, Mayer (1983:155–56) has argued that ties to established community organizations in other neighborhoods that share an interest in crime control can be crucial to the success of a locally based crime control program, for these groups may already have established relationships with local politicians and business leaders who may be able to provide the resources necessary to an association's success.

Such resources are not necessarily monetary or even tangible. Molotch (1976; see also Logan & Molotch 1987) characterizes cities as a system of competing neighborhood-based land interests that are capable of strategic coalition and action vis-à-vis other neighborhoods in that system. Therefore, the development of broad-based networks of association can also increase the capacity of local communities to influence the processes of urban political decisionmaking so that the outcomes foster their regulatory capacities. For example, Bursik (1989) has presented evidence suggesting that political decisions about the location of the public housing constructed in Chicago between 1970 and 1980 were not made on the basis of market considerations relating to the costs of acquiring the necessary tracts of land. Rather, the projects were most likely to be located in neighborhoods that already were unstable and presumably unable to organize and negotiate an effective defense against their construction. It is important to note that the construction that resulted from these externally generated decisions tended to increase the existing rate of residential turnover and, in turn, delinquency.

We feel that the greatest shortcoming of the traditional social disorganization model has been the failure to consider the relational networks that pertain to this public sphere of control, for as many urban analysts have noted (see, e.g., Lewis & Salem 1986), it is very difficult to significantly affect the nature of neighborhood life solely through indigenous neighborhood processes. Therefore, a central assumption underlying the systemic reformulation of social disorganization is that crime is more likely in areas in which the networks of public control cannot effectively provide services to the neighborhood.

Therefore, we would argue that the effect of economic deprivation on crime and delinquency is, in fact, an indirect one, mediated by the capacity of a neighborhood to solicit human and economic resources from external institutional actors. Such an assumption is supported by the work of Moore (1978:21–26), who notes the general absence of political "brokers" who can intercede between underclass Chicago communities with relatively high rates of gang behavior and major institutional agencies, such as those connected with health and welfare, education, migration, and most importantly, criminal justice. Thus, she concludes that residents of such neighborhoods are poorly equipped to deal with such institutions. As a result, the potential ability of an economically marginal neighborhood to exercise effective public control is very limited.

Unfortunately, it is very difficult to collect the requisite data concerning the relational networks implicit to the public-level control of crime on a large scale basis (i.e., for every neighborhood in a large urban system). However, there is at least anecdotal evidence to illustrate the powerful potential for these trans-neighborhood networks to foster a community's capacity for the control of crime. For example, Dawley's (1992) excellent history of the Conservative Vice Lords (one of Chicago's supergangs) describes a period during 1968 and 1969 when the Lords were able to solicit funds successfully from outside of their community (most notably from the Rockefeller and Ford Foundations) to develop a series of neighborhood-based community improvement programs. Although the central area of their territory generally was considered to be one of the most dangerous in Chicago, Dawley (1992) has argued that important changes in neighborhood life occurred during this period, including a significant decline in gang activity and a reduction in the fear of crime.[12] Similar patterns have been noted by Erlanger (1979) in Los Angeles during a period in which many gang members became involved in a local political movement

In sum, we do not feel that the findings pertaining to economic deprivation presented here and in other related research necessarily contradict the assumptions of a systemic model of social disorganization. Rather, we believe that a simultaneous consideration of all three levels of control—the private, the parochial, and the public—can account for these patterns in a logically consistent manner. Unfortunately, the validity of these conclusions must await the collection and analysis of very sophisticated network-based data. If such data do, in fact, become more widely available, we believe that social disorganization research will enter a new, exciting, and theoretically provocative era.

Notes

1. The Park and Burgess model assumed the existence of an open market in which housing was available to anyone with sufficient financial resources or credit. However, this has never been the case for many minority groups (see Bursik 1986) and declined generally as a valid assumption since World War II (see Bursik 1989).

2. There certainly are many more studies of neighborhood inequality in the corpus of criminological literature. However, since the underclass argument of Wilson is highly period dependent, we have restricted our attention to the most recent work. The same consideration will be reflected in our discussion of absolute deprivation.

3. Taylor and Covington (1988) present an alternative indirect model in which absolute deprivation is assumed to increase the levels of perceived relative deprivation. However, they do not include measures of the prevalence of such perceptions in their model. Therefore, it is impossible to determine whether their data more fully support the existence of a primarily indirect or direct effect of absolute deprivation on crime rates.

4. Despite the ecological intellectual heritage of the social disorganization perspective, the theoretical implications of the urban dynamics that underlie Hawley's model of human ecology

rarely have been considered from within the disorganization context, although they lie at the heart of the routine activities model as developed by Felson and Cohen (1980).

5. A number of studies have examined the effect of economic deprivation on neighborhood rates of victimization (see, e.g., Smith & Jarjoura 1988; Sampson & Groves 1989; Patterson 1991). However, since the focus of this article is on rates of offending behavior, these findings are not considered in detail.

6. For a similar discussion of divergent findings concerning economic deprivation at the city, SMSA, and state level, see Land et al. 1990.

7. Chicago had 76 community areas during 1960 and 77 during 1980. Since the additional neighborhood for 1980 was created by splitting one of the original 76, we reaggregated the data to make the two decades comparable. Of these 76 units of analysis, two had very small juvenile populations (the Loop and O'Hare), thereby making the estimated rates highly unreliable. They have been eliminated from the analysis, resulting in our use of 74 consistently defined neighborhoods in the analysis.

8. This indicator represents all financial allocations made through the tax-supported programs of Aid to Dependent Children, Aid to the Blind, Disability Assistance, and General Assistance. Since residents can qualify simultaneously under more than one program, it is possible that the total number of allocations provided by these four programs is greater than the number of residents (and this is the case in several neighborhoods). Therefore it is more appropriate to consider it to represent a rate rather than a percentage. All noncensus materials have been drawn from Kitagawa and Taeuber (1963) and the Chicago Fact Book Consortium (1984).

9. Although it would be desirable to have such information on a race-specific basis, the material available to us suppressed the data if the population during the base year (i.e., 1950 for 1960 estimates, and 1970 for 1980 estimates) was less than 1,500. This especially was the case for the size of the black population in many of Chicago's neighborhoods during the 1950–60 period.

10. Based on the means and standard deviations presented in Table 7.2, this transformation is:

$$\text{Transformed 1980 DEP} = .26207*[(1980 \text{ unemployment} - 5.092)/3.606] +$$
$$.25954*[(1980 \text{ poverty} - 13.303)/10.455)] +$$
$$.26206*[(1980 \text{ public aid} - 6.616)/10.330)] +$$
$$.24997*[(1980 \text{ black composition} - 20.065)/33.757)].$$

The cutting points for the categorized distribution were chosen so that the 1960 DEP values were roughly divided into quartiles. The same intervals were then used to categorize the transformed 1980 DEP values. This transformation was only utilized to facilitate the 1960–80 comparisons. The 1980 DEP values incorporated into the regression models presented in Table 7.4 represent the original factor scores based on the analysis shown in Table 7.1.

11. The indirect effects are computed by multiplying the direct effect of DEP on RC by the direct effect of RC on the delinquency rate.

12. Unfortunately, the Lords became involved in a series of intense clashes with City Hall and encountered problems with their tax-exempt status as an organization. As a result, the funding disappeared, and 10 years later most of the gang were either reinvolved in serious crime or dead, and the neighborhood regained its former status as an "urban cemetery" (Dawley 1992:190).

References

Bailey, William C. (1985) "Aggregation and Disaggregation in Cross-sectional Analyses of Crime Patterns." Presented at Annual Meetings of American Society of Criminology, San Diego.

Bluestone, Barry, & Bennett Harrison (1982) *The De-industrialization of America: Plant Closings, Community Abandonment, and the Dismantling of Basic Industry.* New York: Basic Books.

Braithwaite, John (1979) *Inequality, Crime, and Public Policy*. London: Routledge & Kegan Paul.

Bursik, Robert J., Jr. (1984) "Urban Dynamics and Ecological Studies of Delinquency," 63 *Social Forces* 393.

——— (1986) "Ecological Stability and the Dynamics of Delinquency," in A. J. Reiss & M. Tonry, eds., *Communities and Crime*. Chicago: Univ. of Chicago Press.

——— (1989) "Political Decisionmaking and Ecological Models of Delinquency: Conflict and Consensus," in S. F. Messner, M. D. Krohn, & A. E. Liska, eds., *Theoretical Integration in the Study of Deviance and Crime*. Albany: State Univ. of New York Press.

Bursik, Robert J., Jr., & Harold G. Grasmick (1993) *Neighborhoods and Crime: The Dimensions of Effective Community Control*. New York: Lexington Books.

Chicago Fact Book Consortium, ed. (1984) *Local Community Fact Book: Chicago Metropolitan Area*. Chicago: Chicago Review Press.

Clelland, Donald, & Timothy J. Carter (1980) "The New Myth of Class and Crime," 18 *Criminology* 319.

Curry, G. David, & Irving A. Spergel (1988) "Gang Homicide, Delinquency and Community," 26 *Criminology* 381.

Dawley, David (1992) *A Nation of Lords*. 2d ed. Prospect Heights, IL: Waveland Press.

Erlanger, Howard S. (1979) "Estrangement, Machismo, and Gang Violence," 60 *Social Science Q.* 235.

Felson, Marcus, & Lawrence E. Cohen (1980) "Human Ecology and Crime: A Routine Activity Approach," 8 *Human Ecology* 389.

Frey, William H., & Alden Speare (1988) *Regional and Metropolitan Growth and Decline in the United States*. New York: Russell Sage Foundation.

Gordon, Robert A. (1967) "Issues in the Ecological Study of Delinquency," 32 *American Sociological Rev.* 927.

Hawley, Amos H. (1944) "Ecology and Human Ecology," 23 *Social Forces* 398.

——— (1950) *Human Ecology: A Theory of Community Structure*. New York: Ronald Press.

Hunter, Albert J. (1985) "Private, Parochial and Public Social Orders: The Problem of Crime and Incivility in Urban Communities," in G. D. Suttles & M. N. Zald, eds., *The Challenge of Social Control: Citizenship and Institution Building in Modern Society*. Norwood, NJ: Ablex Publishing.

Jankowski, Martin Sanchez (1991) *Islands in the Street: Gangs and American Urban Society*. Berkeley: Univ. of California Press.

Kitagawa, Evelyn M., & Karl E. Taeuber, eds. (1963) *Local Community Fact Book. Chicago Metropolitan Area, 1960*. Chicago: Univ. of Chicago Press.

Kornhauser, Ruth Rosner (1978) *Social Sources of Delinquency*. Chicago: Univ. of Chicago Press.

Land, Kenneth C., Patricia L. McCall, & Lawrence E. Cohen (1990) "Structural Covariates of Homicide Rates: Are There Any Invariances across Time and Social Space?" 87 *American J. of Sociology* 413.

Lewis, Dan A., & Greta Salem (1986) *Fear of Crime, Incivility, and the Production of a Social Problem*. New Brunswick, NJ: Transaction Books.

Logan, John R., & Harvey L. Molotch (1987) *Urban Fortunesrontiers: The Political Economy of Place*. Berkeley: Univ. of California Press.

Mayer, Neil S. (1983) "How Neighborhood Development Programs Succeed and Grow: A Survey," in P. L. Clay & R. M. Hollister, eds., *Neighborhood Policy and Planning*. Lexington, MA: Lexington Books.

McCarthy, John D., & Mayer N. Zald (1987) "Resource Mobilization and Social Movements: A Partial Theory," in M. N. Zald & J. D. McCarthy, eds., *Social Movements in an Organizational Society*. New Brunswick, NJ: Transaction Books.

Messner, Steven F. (1982) "Poverty, Inequality, and the Urban Homicide Rate," 20 *Criminology* 103.

Messner, Steven F., & Kenneth Tardiff (1986) "Economic Inequality and Levels of Homicide: An Analysis of Urban Neighborhoods," 24 *Criminology* 297.

Molotch, Harvey (1976) "The City as a Growth Machine: Toward a Political Economy of Place," 82 *American J. of Sociology* 309.

Moore, Joan W. (1978) *Homeboys*. Philadelphia: Temple Univ. Press.

——— (1988) "Introduction: Gangs and the Underclass: A Comparative Perspective," in J. M. Hagedorn, ed., *People and Folks: Gangs, Crime and the Underclass in a Rustbelt City*. Chicago: Lake View Press.

Park, Robert E., & Ernest W. Burgess (1924) *Introduction to the Science of Sociology*. 2d ed. Chicago: Univ. of Chicago Press.

Patterson, E. Britt (1991) "Poverty, Income Inequality, and Community Crime Rates," 29 *Criminology* 755.

Sampson, Robert J. (1987) "Communities and Crime," in M. R. Gottfredson & T. Hirschi, eds., *Positive Criminology*. Beverly Hills, CA: Sage Publications.

Sampson, Robert J., & W. Byron Groves (1989) "Community Structure and Crime: Testing Social-Disorganization Theory," 94 *American J. of Sociology* 774.

Sampson, Robert J., & William Julius Wilson (1991) "Toward a Theory of Race, Crime, and Urban Inequality." Presented at Annual Meetings of American Society of Criminology, San Francisco.

Shaw, Clifford R., & Henry D. McKay (1942) *Juvenile Delinquency and Urban Areas*. Chicago: Univ. of Chicago Press.

——— (1969) *Juvenile Delinquency and Urban Areas*. 2d ed. Chicago: Univ. of Chicago Press.

Shaw, Clifford R., Frederick M. Zorbaugh, Henry D. McKay, & Leonard S. Cottrell (1929) *Delinquency Areas*. Chicago: Univ. of Chicago Press.

Smith, Douglas A., & G. Roger Jarjoura (1988) "Social Structure and Criminal Victimization," 25 *J. of Research in Crime & Delinquency* 27.

Spergel, Irving A., & John Korbelik (1979) "The Local Community Service System and ISOS: An Interorganizational Analysis." Executive Report to the Illinois Law Enforcement Commission. Chicago: Illinois Law Enforcement Commission.

Sullivan, Mercer L. (1989) *"Getting Paid": Youth Crime and Work in the Inner City*. Ithaca, NY: Cornell Univ. Press.

Taub, Richard P., George P. Surgeon, Sara Lindholm, Phyllis Betts Ottim, & Amy Bridges (1977) "Urban Voluntary Associations, Locality Based and Externally Induced," 83 *American J. of Sociology* 425.

Taylor, Ralph B., & Jeanette Covington (1988) "Neighborhood Changes in Ecology and Violence," 26 *Criminology* 553.

Tittle, Charles R. (1983) "Social Class and Criminal Behavior: A Critique of the Theoretical Foundation," 62 *Social Forces* 334.

U.S. Bureau of the Census (1972) *County and City Fact Book 1972*. Washington, DC: U.S. Department of Commerce.

——— (1984) *County and City Fact Book 1983*. Washington, DC: U.S. Department of Commerce.

Wacquant, Loic J. D., & William Julius Wilson (1989) "The Cost of Racial and Class Exclusion in the Inner City," 501 *Annals of the American Academy of Political and Social Science* 8.

Wilson, William Julius (1987) *The Truly Disadvantaged*. Chicago: Univ. of Chicago Press.

Zorbaugh, Harvey W. (1929) *The Gold Coast and the Slum*. Chicago: Univ. of Chicago Press.

Differential Association Theory and Social Learning Theory

As is the case with social disorganization theory (see Section II of this book), differential association theory emerged from the Chicago School. Edwin Sutherland, the originator of differential association theory, did his Ph.D in Sociology and Political Economy at the University of Chicago, and subsequently held a research professorship position at the university for five years (Adler & Adler, 2003:xxvii; Mutchnick, Martin, & Austin, 2009:96). Edwin Sutherland has been described as "the most important criminologist of the 20th Century" (Akers & Sellers, 2009:85; cf. Mutchnick et al., 2009:96). Sutherland's renowned book, *Principles of Criminology* (first published in 1924) was the leading criminological text for decades, and has been re-printed and updated many times over the years (Akers & Sellers, 2009:86; Warr, 2001:182). However, it was not until the 1939 edition of *Principles of Criminology* that Sutherland first laid out his differential association theory, and not until the 1947 edition that all nine propositions of the theory were fully enunciated (Akers & Sellers, 2009; Warr, 2001). These nine propositions of differential association theory are set out in detail in the first reading selection in Section III.

Edwin Sutherland was a close friend of Henry McKay, who—along with Clifford Shaw—used the concentric zone model developed by Park and Burgess to explain why socially disorganized areas of Chicago (especially the zone in transition) experienced higher rates of delinquency than other areas of the city (Mutchnick et al., 2009:97; Vold & Bernard, 1979:186–187). In addition to the influence of Shaw and McKay, differential association theory was also shaped by Sutherland's affiliation with W. I. Thomas, an earlier member of the Chicago School. Thomas actually employed the concept of social disorganization well before Shaw and McKay expanded upon it in their oft-cited social disorganization study. W. I. Thomas was—alongside George Hebert Mead—one of the founders of the symbolic interactionist perspective (Williams & McShane, 2010:64). George Herbert Mead joined the philosophy department at the University of Chicago in the late 1890s, at around the same time that the sociology department (The Chicago School) was in its infancy (Lemert, 1993:243). Although Mead started off as a philosopher, he became most well known for his work in the areas of sociology and social psychology in general, and symbolic interactionism in particular (Lemert, 1993:243; Zeitlin, 2001:426). Briefly, symbolic interactionist theory states that meaning and reality are constructed through social interaction, and through the sharing or communication of symbols that take on a significance of their own (Akers & Sellers, 2009:89; Zeitlin, 2001:427–428). More will be said about symbolic interactionism in the introductions to the selected readings by Sutherland and Cressey on differential association theory and Burgess and Akers on social learning theory. For now, it is important to recognize that W. I. Thomas, George Herbert Mead and Henry McKay—all well known Chicago School theorists—had a profound influence on the thinking of Edwin Sutherland, who in turn had a similar influence on the thinking of Gresham Sykes and David Matza and Robert Burgess and Ronald Akers.

Edwin Sutherland's differential association theory proposes that "criminal behavior is learned," and that it is "learned in interaction with other persons in a process of communication." Differential association theory further states that the learning includes "the techniques of committing the crime" and the "motives, drives, rationalizations, and attitudes" that go along with criminal behavior (Sutherland & Cressey, 1985:180). Gresham Sykes and David Matza's (1957) subsequent work on "techniques of neutralization" (the second reading selection in Section III) elaborates on the learning of criminality, by describing in detail the motives, rationalizations and attitudes criminals actually learn, and how they employ them to justify or "neutralize" their criminal behavior. Robert Burgess and Ronald Akers' (1966) "differential association-reinforcement theory" (the third reading in Section III) is more commonly referred to as "social learning theory." Burgess and Akers build upon Sutherland's notion that criminal behavior is learned, by introducing elements of classical and operant conditioning (or behavior modification), thereby specifying the mechanisms that contribute to the learning of criminal behavior (Akers & Sellers, 2009:88).

The three reading selections in Section III represent a branch of differential association/social learning theory that is closely aligned with the sociological (and symbolic interactionist) perspective. Another well-known theorist, C. Ray Jeffery, argued in favor of a more psychological or biological social learning theory. Jeffery actually published his (1965) article on "Criminal Behavior and Learning Theory" a year before Burgess and Akers published their (1966) "Differential Association-Reinforcement Theory of Criminal Behavior." Like Burgess and Akers, C. Ray Jeffery intended his learning theory to be an elaboration on Edwin

Sutherland's differential association theory and B. F. Skinner's work on operant conditioning. Indeed, C. Ray Jeffery did his graduate studies in sociology under the supervision of Edwin Sutherland (Jeffery, 1965:294; Jeffery, 1978:149). However, Jeffery moved away from symbolic interactionism and sociological explanations of crime and deviance, placing progressively greater emphasis on genetic and brain variables, in search of what he referred to as a "biosocial model of learning" (Jeffery, 1978:158; cf. Williams & McShane, 2010:168). Ronald Akers, on the other hand, continued to work on his sociological version of social learning theory, which was (and still is) more in keeping with Chicago School thinking, the symbolic interactionist perspective, and Edwin Sutherland's original theory of differential association (Akers, 1990:666; Williams & McShane, 2010:169). Over the past three decades, the term "social learning theory" has come to be associated primarily with the thinking of Ronald Akers, and the bulk of the empirical research has in fact been directed toward Akers' version of social learning theory (cf. Lilly, Cullen, & Ball, 2011:56–57; Winfree & Abadinsky, 2010:193–199).

As is true with anomie-strain theory and social disorganization theory (see Sections I and II), it is difficult to over-state the importance of differential association theory and the wide variety of social learning theories and research studies that have developed over the years as a result. Indeed, Cullen, Wright and Blevins (2004:3–4) state that "differential association/social learning theory" is one of the three core theories that have dominated criminological thinking for the past seventy years. (The other two "core" theories they mention are anomie-strain theory, discussed in Section I of this book, and social control theory, discussed in Section IV of this book). Differential association/social learning theory is certainly one of the most well-researched—if not the most researched—criminological theories in existence, and its applicability and validity have been well documented all over the world (Jensen & Akers, 2003; Winfree & Abadinsky, 2010:200). Unlike may other sociological and criminological theories, differential association/social learning theory has also been a mainstay of correctional treatment programs, and compared to other theories, has fared very well in outcome assessments of such treatment programs (Cullen, Wright, Gendreau, & Andrews, 2003; Winfree & Abadinsky, 2010:203–204).

References

Adler, P., & Adler, P. (Eds.). (2003). *Constructions of deviance: Social power, context and interaction* (Fourth ed.). Belmont, CA: Thomson Wadsworth.

Akers, R. L. (1990). Rational choice, deterrence, and social learning theory in criminology: The path not taken. *The Journal of Criminal Law & Criminology, 81*(3), 653–676.

Akers, R. L., & Sellers, C. S. (2009). *Criminological theories: Introduction, evaluation, and application* (5th , New ed.). New York: Oxford University Press.

Burgess, R. L., & Akers, R. L. (1966). A differential association-reinforcement theory of criminal behavior. *Social Problems, 14*(2), 128–147.

Cullen, F. T., Wright, J. P., & Blevins, K. R. (Eds.). (2004). *Taking stock: The status of criminological theory*. New Brunswick, N.J.: Transaction Publishers.

Cullen, F. T., Wright, J. P., Gendreau, P., & Andrews, D. A. (2003). What correctional treatment can tell us about criminological theory: Implications for social learning theory. In R. L. Akers, & G. F. Jensen (Eds.), *Social learning theory and the explanation of crime: A guide for the new century* (pp. 339–362). New Brunswick, N.J.: Transaction.

Jeffery, C. R. (1965). Criminal behavior and learning theory. *Journal of Criminal Law, Criminology, and Police Science, 56*(3), 294–300.

Jeffery, C. R. (1978). Criminology as an interdisciplinary behavioral science. *Criminology, 16*(2), 149–169.

Jensen, G. F., & Akers, R. L. (2003). "Taking social learning global": Micro-macro transitions in criminological theory. In R. L. Akers, & G. F. Jensen (Eds.), *Social learning theory and the explanation of crime: A guide for the new century* (pp. 9–37). New Brunswick, N.J.: Transaction.

Lemert, C. C. (1993). *Social theory: The multicultural and classic readings*. Boulder, Colo.: Westview Press.

Lilly, J. R., Cullen, F. T., & Ball, R. A. (2011). *Criminological theory: Context and consequences* (5th ed.). Thousand Oaks: SAGE Publications.

Mutchnick, R. J., Martin, R., & Austin, T. W. (2009). *Criminological thought: Pioneers past and present*. Upper Saddle River, NJ: Prentice Hall.

Sutherland, E. H., & Cressey, D. R. (1985). The theory of differential association. In S. H. Traub, & C. B. Little (Eds.), *Theories of deviance* (3rd ed., pp. 176–182). Itasca, Ill.: F. E. Peacock Publishers.

Sykes, G. M., & Matza, D. (1957). Techniques of neutralization: A theory of delinquency. *American Sociological Review, 22*(6), 664–670.

Vold, G. B., & Thomas J. Bernard. (1979). *Theoretical criminology* (2nd ed.). New York: Oxford University Press.

Warr, M. (2001). The social origins of crime: Edwin Sutherland and the theory of differential association. In R. Paternoster, & R. Bachman (Eds.), *Explaining criminals and crime: Essays in contemporary criminological theory* (pp. 182–191). Los Angeles, Calif.: Roxbury Pub. Co.

Williams, F. P., & McShane, M. D. (2010). *Criminological theory* (5th ed.). Upper Saddle River, N.J.: Pearson/Prentice Hall.

Winfree, L. T., & Abadinsky, H. (2010). *Understanding crime: Essentials of criminological theory* (Third ed.). Belmont, CA: Wadsworth, Cengage Learning.

Zeitlin, I. M. (2001). *Ideology and the development of sociological theory* (7th ed.). Upper Saddle River, N.J.: Prentice Hall.

8

The Theory of Differential Association

As noted in the Introduction to Section III, Edwin Sutherland has been described as "the most important criminologist of the 20th Century" (Akers & Sellers, 2009:85). It has also been said that Sutherland made sociology "the centerpiece . . . of American criminology" (Akers & Matsueda, 1989:424). In particular, Sutherland was known for steadfastly fighting against the (then popular) characterization of criminals as being feebleminded or psychopathic, or being the products of poverty and poor childrearing (Lilly, Cullen, & Ball, 2011:47; Sutherland, 1940:1; Vold & Bernard, 1979:193). Instead, he argued that criminals were not substantially different from non-criminals, except that they had learned criminal attitudes, skills and behaviors, in much the same way that other (non-criminal) attitudes, skills and behaviors were learned (Sutherland & Cressey, 1985:179–181; Winfree & Abadinsky, 2010).

The first reading in this section, by Edwin Sutherland and Donald Cressey, outlines the nine main propositions of Sutherland's theory of differential association. Edwin Sutherland completed his Ph.D at the University of Chicago, and also taught at the University of Chicago (The Chicago School) for five years (Mutchnick, Martin, & Austin, 2009:96; Williams & McShane, 2010:65). Although Donald Cressey co-authored this particular explication of differential association theory, Edwin Sutherland had been working on and refining this theory on his own since the late 1930s (Vold & Bernard, 1979:180; Warr, 2001:183). Donald Cressey was one of Edwin Sutherland's Ph.D students when Sutherland was teaching sociology at Indiana University (Akers & Matsueda, 1989:424). After finishing his doctoral dissertation in 1950 (at around the time of Sutherland's death), Cressey became a Sociology Professor at the University of California—first at UCLA, and then at Santa Barbara—until his own death in 1987. Between 1955 and 1978, Cressey co-authored six editions of Sutherland's renowned textbook, *Principles of Criminology* (Mutchnick et al., 2009:96). Apart from his collaboration with Edwin Sutherland, Donald Cressey was a highly respected scholar in his own right, recognized for his work on white collar crime, organized crime, and the sociology of corrections (Akers & Matsueda, 1989:424, 429).

The selected reading by Sutherland and Cressey offers what is an "historical" or "developmental" theory of criminal behavior (Sutherland & Cressey, 1985:178–179). In other words, it focuses less on the immediate situation and the criminal opportunities that it may offer, and more on how past experiences—especially learning experiences—shape criminal behavior. While there are nine propositions in all, differential association theory can be summarized as follows:

1. Criminal behavior is learned through a process of interaction and communication, usually occurring "within intimate personal groups."
2. Criminals learn the techniques (i.e., skills or aptitudes) for committing crimes, and also, the "motives, drives, rationalizations and attitudes" that go along with committing crimes.
3. Individuals are exposed to definitions of "legal codes as favorable or unfavorable"—i.e., that the law should be obeyed, or that the law should be disobeyed. The more often they hear that is acceptable to disobey the law, the more likely it is that they will come to see criminal behavior as normal and acceptable.
4. The frequency, duration and intensity of differential associations—differing degrees of exposure to criminal peers and to pro-criminal attitudes—will influence the likelihood of somebody engaging in criminal behavior. If an individual associates often with criminal peers, and does so over a protracted period of time, and holds these criminal peers in high regard, then he or she is more likely to become a criminal.
5. The type of learning that goes into criminal behavior is no different than that associated with learning other kinds of behavior. Moreover, criminals are not all that different than non-criminals, except that they have learned to become criminal through frequent, lengthy and intense exposure to criminal peers and pro-criminal attitudes (Sutherland & Cressey, 1985:179–181).

A number of new ideas or directions emerged from Sutherland's differential association theory. In his formulations, Sutherland replaced the earlier Chicago School notion of "social disorganization" (see Section II of this book) with the concept of "differential social organization" (Vold & Bernard, 1979:182; Williams & McShane, 2010:68). By differential social organization, Sutherland meant that there were a number of different or divergent groups or cultures within society, some of them law-abiding, some of them not so law-abiding, and others falling somewhere in between (Vold & Bernard, 1979:182; Williams & McShane, 2010:68–69). Sutherland's thinking was influenced by Thorsten Sellin's cultural conflict theory, and in return, Sutherland's contributions spurred further developments in the cultural conflict area (Mutchnick et al., 2009:97; Winfree & Abadinsky, 2010:190). Essentially, cultural conflict theory takes the position that different groups (or cultures) have differing norms and values, and that these divergent norms and values may result in conflict when these groups or cultures come into contact with each other (Sellin, 1994:188–189; Williams & McShane, 2010:70). Sutherland's differential association theory also underpins the type of cultural deviance theory exemplified by Walter Miller's work on the unique cultural concerns of lower-class street corner gangs, and by Wolfgang and Ferracuti's work on subcultures of violence (Lilly et al., 2011:53; Vold & Bernard, 1979:184–185). All of these theoretical developments ultimately tie back into the symbolic interactionist perspective of W. I. Thomas and George Herbert Mead, and the notion that human behavior is shaped by the "definitions", meanings or identities that individuals and groups acquire through the process of social interaction (Vold & Bernard, 1979:181; Warr, 2001:184).

Although Sutherland was best known for his differential association theory, he was also well known for his life history of *The Professional Thief*, and for his work on white collar crime (Lilly et al., 2011:49; Mutchnick et al., 2009:110). *The Professional Thief* was written in 1937, before Sutherland first introduced differential association theory in the 1939 edition of his textbook *Principles of Criminology*. This life history or ethnography was consistent with The Chicago School's emphasis on ecological studies—i.e., getting out into the urban setting in order to study human beings in their natural habitat (Lilly et al., 2011:49; Warr, 2001:184). The life history was about Chic Conwell, who had learned—through a process of "differential association" with other professional thieves–how to plan and execute crimes, how to dispose of stolen goods, and, if caught, how to deal with the police and the courts (Sutherland, 1994:9–12). In his article on "White-Collar Criminality," Sutherland pointed out that the cost of white collar crime—e.g., embezzlement, bribery of government officials, false advertising, manipulation of stock values, etc.—was many times greater than the cost of all street crime combined (1940:4–6). Sutherland further recognized that white collar criminals were mostly able to avoid criminal prosecution because: a) their behavior was regulated by government agencies or commissions, or b) their victims were more interested in seeking damages and restitution through lawsuits in civil court (Sutherland, 1940:6, 8). The breadth and depth of Sutherland's influence on sociological and criminological theory is further evidenced by Sykes and Matza's "Techniques of Neutralization" (the second reading in Section III) and Burgess and Akers' "Differential Association-Reinforcement Theory" (the third reading in Section III).

References

Akers, R. L., & Matsueda, R. L. (1989). Donald R. Cressey: An intellectual portrait of a criminologist. *Sociological Inquiry, 59*(4), 423–438.

Akers, R. L., & Sellers, C. S. (2009). *Criminological theories: Introduction, evaluation, and application* (5th, New ed.). New York: Oxford University Press.

Lilly, J. R., Cullen, F. T., & Ball, R. A. (2011). *Criminological theory: Context and consequences* (5th ed.). Thousand Oaks: SAGE Publications.

Mutchnick, R. J., Martin, R., & Austin, T. W. (2009). *Criminological thought: Pioneers past and present.* Upper Saddle River, NJ: Prentice Hall.

Sellin, T. (1994). Culture conflict and crime. In J. E. Jacoby (Ed.), *Classics of criminology* (2nd ed., pp. 188–192). Prospect Heights, Illinois: Waveland Press Inc.

Sutherland, E. H. (1940). White-collar criminality. *American Sociological Review, 5*(1), 1–12.

Sutherland, E. H., & Cressey, D. R. (1985). The theory of differential association. In S. H. Traub, & C. B. Little (Eds.), *Theories of deviance* (3rd ed., pp. 176–182). Itasca, Ill.: F. E. Peacock Publishers.

Sutherland, E. H. (1994). The professional thief. In J. E. Jacoby (Ed.), *Classics of criminology* (2nd ed., pp. 9–12). Prospect Heights, Illinois: Waveland Press Inc.

Vold, G. B., & Second edition prepared by Thomas J. Bernard. (1979). *Theoretical criminology* (2nd ed.). New York: Oxford University Press.

Warr, M. (2001). The social origins of crime: Edwin Sutherland and the theory of differential association. In R. Paternoster, & R. Bachman (Eds.), *Explaining criminals and crime: Essays in contemporary criminological theory* (pp. 182–191). Los Angeles, Calif.: Roxbury Pub. Co.

Williams, F. P., & McShane, M. D. (2010). *Criminological theory* (5th ed.). Upper Saddle River, N.J.: Pearson/Prentice Hall.

Winfree, L. T., & Abadinsky, H. (2010). *Understanding crime: Essentials of criminological theory* (Third ed.). Belmont, CA: Wadsworth, Cengage Learning.

The Theory of Differential Association

EDWIN H. SUTHERLAND AND DONALD R. CRESSEY

The Problem for Criminological Theory

If criminology is to be scientific, the heterogeneous collection of multiple factors known to be associated with crime and criminality must be organized and integrated by means of explanatory theory which has the same characteristics as the scientific theory in other fields of study. That is, the conditions which are said to cause crime should be present when crime is present, and they should be absent when crime is absent. Such a theory or body of theory would stimulate, simplify, and give direction to criminological research, and it would provide a framework for understanding the significance of much of the knowledge acquired about crime and criminality in the past. Furthermore, it would be useful in minimizing crime rates, provided it could be "applied" in much the same way that the engineer "applies" the scientific theories of the physicist.

There are two complementary procedures which may be used to put order into criminological knowledge. The first is logical abstraction. Blacks, males,

Reprinted from *Theories of Deviance*, edited by Stuart H. Traub and Craig B. Little (1985).

urban-dwellers, and young adults all have comparatively high crime rates. What do they have in common that results in these high crime rates? Research studies have shown that criminal behavior is associated, in greater or lesser degree, with such social and personal pathologies as poverty, bad housing, slum-residence, lack of recreational facilities, inadequate and demoralized families, mental retardation, emotional instability, and other traits and conditions. What do these conditions have in common which apparently produces excessive criminality? Research studies have also demonstrated that many persons with those pathological traits and conditions do not commit crimes and that persons in the upper socioeconomic class frequently violate the law, although they are not in poverty, do not lack recreational facilities, and are not mentally retarded or emotionally unstable. Obviously, it is not the conditions or traits themselves which cause crime, for the conditions are sometimes present when criminality does not occur, and they also are sometimes absent when criminality does occur. A generalization about crime and criminal behavior can be reached by logically abstracting the conditions and processes which are common to the rich and the poor, the males and the females, the blacks and the whites, the urban- and the rural-dwellers, the young adults and the old adults, and the emotionally stable and the emotionally unstable who commit crimes.

In developing such generalizations, criminal behavior must be precisely defined and carefully distinguished from noncriminal behavior. Criminal behavior is human behavior, and has much in common with noncriminal behavior. An explanation of criminal behavior should be consistent with a general theory of other human behavior, but the conditions and processes said to produce crime and criminality should be specific. Many things which are necessary for behavior are not important to criminality. Respiration, for instance, is necessary for any behavior, but the respiratory process cannot be used in an explanation of criminal behavior, for it does not differentiate criminal behavior from noncriminal behavior.

The second procedure for putting order into criminological knowledge is differentiation of levels of analysis. The explanation or generalization must be limited, largely in terms of chronology, and in this way held at a particular level. For example, when Renaissance physicists stated the law of falling bodies, they were not concerned with the reasons why a body began to fall except as this might affect the initial momentum. Galileo did not study the "traits" of falling objects themselves, as Aristotle might have done. Instead, he noted the relationship of the body to its environment while it was falling freely or rolling down an inclined plane, and it made no difference to his generalization whether a body began to fall because it was dropped from the hand of an experimenter or because it rolled off the ledge of a bridge due to vibration caused by a passing vehicle. Also, a round object would roll off the bridge more readily than a square object, but this fact was not significant for the law of falling bodies. Such facts were considered as existing on a different level of explanation and were irrelevant to the problem of explaining the behavior of falling bodies.

Much of the confusion regarding crime and criminal behavior stems from a failure to define and hold constant the level at which they are explained. By analogy, many criminologists and others concerned with understanding and defining crime would attribute some degree of causal power to the "roundness" of the object in the above illustration. However, consideration of time sequences among the conditions associated with crime and criminality may lead to simplicity of statement. In the heterogeneous collection of factors associated with crime and criminal behavior, one factor often occurs prior to another (in much the way that "roundness" occurs prior to "vibration," and "vibration" occurs prior to "rolling off a bridge"), but a theoretical statement can be made without referring to those early factors. By holding the analysis at one level, the early factors are combined with or differentiated from later factors or conditions, thus reducing the number of variables which must be considered in a theory.

A motion picture made several years ago showed two boys engaged in a minor theft; they ran when they were discovered; one boy had longer legs, escaped, and became a priest; the other had shorter legs, was caught, committed to a reformatory, and became a gangster. In this comparison, the boy who became a criminal was differentiated from the one who did not become a criminal by the length of his legs. But "length of legs" need not be considered in a criminological theory because it is obvious that this condition does not determine criminality and has no necessary relation to criminality. In the illustration, the differential in the length of the boys' legs apparently was significant to subsequent criminality or noncriminality only to the degree that it determined the subsequent experiences and associations of the two boys. It is in these experiences and associations, then, that the mechanisms and processes which are important to criminality or noncriminality are to be found.

Two Types of Explanations of Criminal Behavior

Scientific explanations of criminal behavior may be stated either in terms of the processes which are operating at the moment of the occurrence of crime or in terms of the processes operating in the earlier history of the criminal. In the first case, the explanation may be called "mechanistic," "situational," or "dynamic"; in the second, "historical" or "developmental." Both types of explanation are desirable. The mechanistic type of explanation has been favored by physical and biological scientists, and it probably could be the more efficient type of explanation of criminal behavior. As Gibbons said:

> In many cases, criminality may be a response to nothing more temporal than the provocations and attractions bound up in the immediate circumstances. It may be that, in some kinds of lawbreaking, understanding of the behavior may require detailed attention to the concatenation of events immediately preceding it. Little or nothing may be added to this understanding from a close scrutiny of the early development of the person.[1]

However, criminological explanations of the mechanistic type have thus far been notably unsuccessful, perhaps largely because they have been formulated in connection with an attempt to isolate personal and social pathologies among criminals. Work from this point of view has, at least, resulted in the conclusion that the immediate determinants of criminal behavior lie in the person-situation complex.

The objective situation is important to criminality largely to the extent that it provides an opportunity for a criminal act. A thief may steal from a fruit stand when the owner is not in sight but refrain when the owner is in sight; a bank burglar may attack a bank which is poorly protected but refrain from attacking a well-protected bank. A corporation which manufactures automobiles seldom violates the pure food and drug laws, but a meat-packing corporation might violate these laws with great frequency. But in another sense, a psychological or sociological sense, the situation is not exclusive of the person, for the situation which is important is the situation as defined by the person who is involved. That is, some persons define a situation in which a fruit-stand owner is out of sight as a "crime-committing" situation, while others do not so define it. Furthermore, the events in the person-situation complex at the time a crime occurs cannot be separated from the prior life experiences of the criminal. This means that the situation is defined by the person in terms of the inclinations and abilities which he or she has acquired. For example, while a person could define a situation in such a manner that criminal behavior would be the inevitable result, past experiences would, for the most part, determine the way in which he or she defined the situation. An explanation of criminal behavior made in terms of these past experiences is a historical or developmental explanation.

The following paragraphs state such a developmental theory of criminal behavior on the assumption that a criminal act occurs when a situation appropriate for it, as defined by the person, is present. The theory should be regarded as tentative, and it should be tested by the factual information presented in the later chapters and by all other factual information and theories which are applicable.

Developmental Explanation of Criminal Behavior

The following statements refer to the process by which a particular person comes to engage in criminal behavior:

1. *Criminal behavior is learned.* Negatively, this means that criminal behavior is not inherited, as such; also, the person who is not already trained in crime does not invent criminal behavior, just as a person does not make mechanical inventions unless he has had training in mechanics.

2. *Criminal behavior is learned in interaction with other persons in a process of communication.* This communication is verbal in many respects but includes also "the communication of gestures."

3. *The principal part of the learning of criminal behavior occurs within intimate personal groups.* Negatively, this means that the impersonal agencies of communication, such as movies and newspapers, play a relatively unimportant part in the genesis of criminal behavior.

4. *When criminal behavior is learned, the learning includes (a) techniques of committing the crime, which are sometimes very complicated, sometimes very simple; (b) the specific direction of motives, drives, rationalizations, and attitudes.*

5. *The specific direction of motives and drives is learned from definitions of the legal codes as favorable or unfavorable.* In some societies an individual is surrounded by persons who invariably define the legal codes as rules to be observed, while in others he is surrounded by persons whose definitions are favorable to the violation of the legal codes. In our American society these definitions are almost always mixed, with the consequence that we have culture conflict in relation to the legal codes.

6. *A person becomes delinquent because of an excess of definitions favorable to violation of law over definitions unfavorable to violation of law.* This is the principle of differential association. It refers to both criminal and anticriminal associations and has to do with counteracting forces. When persons become criminal, they do so because of contact with criminal patterns and also because of isolation from anticriminal patterns. Any person inevitably assimilates the surrounding culture unless other patterns are in conflict; a southerner does not pronounce *r* because other southerners do not pronounce *r*. Negatively, this proposition of differential association means that associations which are neutral so far as crime is concerned have little or no effect on the genesis of criminal behavior. Much of the experience of a person is neutral in this sense, for instance, learning to brush one's teeth. This behavior has no negative or positive effect on criminal behavior except as it may be related to associations which are concerned with the legal codes. This neutral behavior is important especially as an occupier of the time of a child so that he or she is not in contact with criminal behavior during the time the child is so engaged in the neutral behavior.

7. *Differential associations may vary in frequency, duration, priority, and intensity.* This means that associations with criminal behavior and also associations with anticriminal behavior vary in those respects. Frequency and duration as modalities of associations are obvious and need no explanation. Priority is assumed to be important in the sense that lawful behavior developed in early childhood may persist throughout life, and also that delinquent behavior developed in early childhood may persist throughout life. This tendency, however, has not been adequately demonstrated, and priority seems to be important principally through its selective influence. Intensity is not precisely defined, but it has to do with such things as the prestige of the source of a criminal or anticriminal pattern and with emotional reactions related to the associations. In a precise description of the criminal behavior of a person, these modalities would be rated in quantitative form and a mathematical ratio would be reached. A formula in this sense has not been developed, and the development of such a formula would be extremely difficult.

8. *The process of learning criminal behavior by association with criminal and anti-criminal patterns involves all of the mechanisms that are involved in any other learning.* Negatively, this means that the learning of criminal behavior is not restricted to the process of imitation. A person who is seduced, for instance, learns criminal behavior by association, but this process would not ordinarily be described as imitation.

9. *While criminal behavior is an expression of general needs and values, it is not explained by those general needs and values, since noncriminal behavior is an expression of the same needs and values.* Thieves generally steal in order to secure money, but likewise honest laborers work in order to secure money. The attempts by many scholars to explain criminal behavior by general drives and values, such as the happiness principle, striving for social status, the money motive, or frustration, have been, and must continue to be, futile, since they explain lawful behavior as completely as they explain criminal behavior. They are similar to respiration, which is necessary for any behavior, but which does not differentiate criminal from noncriminal behavior.

It is not necessary, at this level of explanation, to explain why persons have the associations they have; this certainly involves a complex of many things. In an area where the delinquency rate is high, a boy who is sociable gregarious, active, and athletic is very likely to come in contact with the other boys in the neighborhood, learn delinquent behavior patterns from them, and become a criminal; in the same neighborhood the psychopathic boy who is isolated, introverted, and inert may remain at home, now become acquainted with the other boys in the neighborhood, and now become delinquent. In another situation, the sociable, athletic, aggressive boy may become a member of a scout troop and not become involved in delinquent behavior. The person's associations are determined in a general context of social organization. A child is ordinarily reared in a family; the place of residence of the family is determined largely by family income; and the delinquency rate is in many respects related to the rental value of the houses. Many other aspects of social organization affect the associations of a person.

The preceding explanation of criminal behavior purports to explain the criminal and noncriminal behavior of individual persons. As indicated earlier, it is possible to state sociological theories of criminal behavior which explain the criminality of a community, nation, or other group. The problem, when thus stated, is to account for variations in crime rates, which involves a comparison of the crime rates of various groups or the crime rates of a particular group at different times. The explanation of a crime rate must be consistent with the explanation of the criminal behavior of the person, since the crime rate is a summary statement of the number of persons in the group who commit crimes and the frequency with which they commit crimes. One of the best explanations of crime rates from this point of view is that a high crime rate is due to social disorganization. The term *social disorganization* is not entirely satisfactory, and it seems preferable to substitute for it the term *differential social organization*. The postulate on which this theory is based, regardless of the name, is that crime is rooted in the social organization and is an expression of that social organization. A group may be organized for criminal behavior or organized against criminal behavior. Most communities are organized for both criminal and anticriminal behavior, and, in that sense, the crime rate is an expression of the differential group organization. Differential group organization as an explanation of variations in crime rates is consistent with the differential association theory of the processes by which persons become criminals.

Note

1. Don C. Gibbons, "Observations on the Study of Crime Causation," *American Journal of Sociology*, 77:262–78, 1971.

9

Techniques of Neutralization

Gresham Sykes and David Matza begin their (1957) article "Techniques of Neutralization" by acknowledging Edwin Sutherland's "classic statement" that delinquent or criminal behavior "is learned in the process of social interaction" (p. 664). Sykes and Matza observe, however, that when they published their article in the *American Sociological Review* in 1957, there had been little follow-up research or theoretical elaboration on Sutherland's contention that part of the process involved learning the "motives, drives, rationalizations and attitudes" that go along with being a criminal (Sutherland & Cressey, 1985:180; Sykes & Matza, 1957:664). Their article, "Techniques of Neutralization," is an explanation of—or an elaboration on—the types of rationalizations or excuses that criminals actually learn during this process (Lilly, Cullen, & Ball, 2011:103).

In this article, Sykes and Matza go to considerable lengths to distinguish their work from that of Albert Cohen, whose 1955 book, *Delinquent Boys: The Culture of the Gang*, was discussed in the Introduction to Section I on Anomie-Strain Theory. Albert Cohen merged Robert Merton's anomie theory with Edwin Sutherland's differential association theory, in order to identify the types of strain experienced by lower-class males, and show how this led certain individuals to adopt subcultural values and form delinquent subcultures. Cohen argued that lower-class males had the same aspirations for social status as middle- and upper-class males. However, he said that when they tried to compete for status in school, they could not meet the standards of "the middle-class measuring rod." Cohen said that as a consequence, they would develop "status deprivation" or "status frustration," similar to a sense of anomie or strain (Cohen, 1955, 1964:84–87). It is noteworthy that Cohen viewed delinquency as a collective solution—delinquent subcultures reacted to status deprivation by redefining the meaning of status, establishing new norms, and creating new forms of "acceptable" behavior or conduct for the members of their own subculture (cf. Cloward & Ohlin, 1960; Cohen, 1955, 1964). According to this interpretation, the new subcultural norms and standards would permit members of these subcultures to engage in criminal behavior without the usual feelings of shame or guilt (Williams & McShane, 2010:153).

Sykes and Matza, on the other hand, say that it is unlikely—as Albert Cohen claimed—that delinquents substitute a new set of unconventional norms for the conventional norms that are widely accepted by most members of society (Akers & Sellers, 2009:191; Sykes & Matza, 1957:665–666). Rather, they say that delinquents subscribe to some degree to the dominant social norms. They point out that delinquents may even admire and respect law-abiding people like their parents or the neighborhood priest, and will actually be disappointed if these respected role models break the law (Sykes & Matza, 1957:665). Delinquents also have a keen sense of what is fair game and what is not—they do not steal from their friends, nor do they vandalize their own churches.

Sykes and Matza (1957:665–666) argue that delinquents *do* experience feelings of shame and guilt. Delinquents know what they are doing is wrong, and knowing this, attempt to justify their behavior by employing defenses that are somewhat similar to those used on occasion in the criminal justice system—e.g., insanity, duress, provocation, self-defense, etc. While the defenses or "techniques of neutralization" used by delinquents would not likely be recognized in a court of law, they nevertheless enable these delinquents to rationalize or justify their criminal behavior—if not to others, than at least to themselves and to their delinquent peers. Thus, these rationalizations neutralize the social controls that would normally inhibit delinquent or criminal behavior (Sykes & Matza, 1957:667–669).

The five techniques of neutralization identified by Sykes and Matza (1957: 667–669) are as follows:

1. "Denial of responsibility". . . saying that the delinquent act was unintentional, or due to circumstances beyond the delinquent's control (e.g., due to poverty, or to a poor upbringing, etc.).
2. "Denial of injury". . . defining vandalism as "mischief," auto theft as "borrowing," or criminal misdemeanors as "pranks."
3. "Denial of the victim". . . describing the offense as a justifiable form of retaliation; re-casting the victim as the wrongdoer or transgressor, and portraying the offender as the heroic avenger.
4. "Condemnation of the condemners". . . calling the accusers hypocrites, or saying that the accusers are acting out of personal spite.
5. "Appeal to higher loyalties". . . saying that the offenders were defending their family or friends, or protecting the honor of their gang.

Techniques of neutralization have been researched extensively throughout the years, with both juvenile and adult offender populations. Some studies have focused on pedophiles, others on children who shoplift, and still others on students who cheat at school (Williams & McShane, 2010:153). One prison study of

114 convicted rapists, conducted by Diana Scully and Joseph Marolla, found that offenders did indeed attempt to justify or excuse their behavior. Those who denied being rapists described "women as seductresses" (denial of the victim), claimed that "women say no when they mean yes" (denial of injury, denial of the victim), said that "women eventually relax and enjoy it" (denial of injury, denial of the victim), said that "nice girls don't get raped" (denial of the victim), or insisted that "it was only a minor wrongdoing" (denial of injury) (Scully & Marolla, 2003:248–253). Those who admitted to rape minimized the level of violence involved, or downplayed the seriousness of the injuries that they inflicted on their victim (denial of injury). They often blamed forces beyond their control, like alcohol or drug use, or emotional problems and stress, saying that essentially, they were nice guys who had made a bad mistake (denial of responsibility) (Scully & Marolla, 2003:254–258).

Another (2005) study of 133 MBA students, conducted by Piquero, Tibbetts and Blankenship, specifically set out to evaluate Sutherland's notion that criminal behavior is learned in intimate peer groups, plus the applicability of Sykes and Matza's five techniques of neutralization. The MBA students filled out a questionnaire regarding the sale of Panalba, a hypothetical drug that was banned by the Food and Drug Administration—in other words, a potential corporate or white collar crime. The average student was in favor of continuing to sell existing inventories of the banned drug, continuing to sell to doctors who wanted the drug, or selling to other countries that were not subject to FDA oversight (Piquero et al., 2005:170–172). Most felt that their co-workers and business directors would agree with their decisions—hence the significance of receiving symbolic reinforcement from their intimate peer group (Piquero et al., 2005:176–177). As techniques of neutralization, the MBA students indicated that governments exaggerated the dangers to consumers, that regulations just impeded normal business practices, that profit was more important, and that buyers should beware (Piquero et al., 2005:170–171). Explanations of criminality that combine Sutherland's differential association theory and Sykes and Matza's techniques of neutralization have been shown to work across a variety of settings and offence types.

References

Akers, R. L., & Sellers, C. S. (2009). *Criminological theories : Introduction, evaluation, and application* (5th, New ed.). New York: Oxford University Press.

Cloward, R. A., & Ohlin, L. E. (1960). *Delinquency and opportunity: A theory of delinquent gangs.* New York: Free Press.

Cohen, A. K. (1955, 1964). *Delinquent boys: The culture of the gang.* Glencoe, IL: Free Press of Glencoe.

Lilly, J. R., Cullen, F. T., & Ball, R. A. (2011). *Criminological theory: Context and consequences* (5th ed.). Thousand Oaks: SAGE Publications.

Piquero, N. L., Tibbetts, S. G., & Blankenship, M. B. (2005). Examining the role of differential association and techniques of neutralization in explaining corporate crime. *Deviant Behavior,* 26(2), 159–188.

Scully, D., & Marolla, J. (2003). "Convicted rapists' vocabulary of motive." In P. Adler, & P. Adler (Eds.), *Constructions of deviance: Social power, context and interaction* (Fourth ed., pp. 247–271). Belmont, CA: Thomson Wadsworth.

Sutherland, E. H., & Cressey, D. R. (1985). The theory of differential association. In S. H. Traub, & C. B. Little (Eds.), *Theories of deviance* (3rd ed., pp. 176–182). Itasca, Ill.: F. E. Peacock Publishers.

Sykes, G. M., & Matza, D. (1957). Techniques of neutralization: A theory of delinquency. *American Sociological Review*, 22(6), 664–670.

Williams, F. P., & McShane, M. D. (2010). *Criminological theory* (5th ed.). Upper Saddle River, N.J.: Pearson/Prentice Hall.

Techniques of Neutralization: A Theory of Delinquency

GRESHAM M. SYKES AND DAVID MATZA

In attempting to uncover the roots of juvenile delinquency, the social scientist has long since ceased to search for devils in the mind or stigma of the body. It is now largely agreed that delinquent behavior, like most social behavior, is learned and that it is learned in the process of social interaction.

The classic statement of this position is found in Sutherland's theory of differential association, which asserts that criminal or delinquent behavior involves the learning of (a) techniques of committing crimes and (b) motives, drives, rationalizations, and attitudes favorable to the violation of law.[1] Unfortunately, the specific content of what is learned—as opposed to the process by which it is learned—has received relatively little attention in either theory or research. Perhaps the single strongest school of thought on the nature of this content has centered on the idea of a delinquent subculture. The basic characteristic of the delinquent subculture, it is argued, is a system of values that represents an inversion of the values held by respectable, law-abiding society. The world of the delinquent is the world of the law-abiding turned upside down and its norms constitute a countervailing force directed against the conforming social order. Cohen[2] sees the process of developing a delinquent sub-culture as a matter of building, maintaining, and reinforcing a code for behavior which exists by opposition, which stands in point by point contradiction to dominant values, particularly those of the middle class. Cohen's portrayal of delinquency is executed with a good deal of sophistication, and he carefully avoids overly simple explanations such as those based on the principle of "follow the leader" or easy generalizations about "emotional disturbances." Furthermore, he does not accept the delinquent sub-culture as something given, but instead systematically examines the function of delinquent values as a viable solution to the lower-class, male child's problems in the area of social status. Yet in spite

Reprinted from *American Sociological Review* 22, no. 6 (1957).

of its virtues, this image of juvenile delinquency as a form of behavior based on competing or countervailing values and norms appears to suffer from a number of serious defects. It is the nature of these defects and a possible alternative or modified explanation for a large portion of juvenile delinquency with which this paper is concerned.

The difficulties in viewing delinquent behavior as springing from a set of deviant values and norms—as arising, that is to say, from a situation in which the delinquent defines his delinquency as "right"—are both empirical and theoretical. In the first place, if there existed in fact a delinquent sub-culture such that the delinquent viewed his illegal behavior as morally correct, we could reasonably suppose that he would exhibit no feelings of guilt or shame at detection or confinement. Instead, the major reaction would tend in the direction of indignation or a sense of martyrdom.[3] It is true that some delinquents do react in the latter fashion, although the sense of martyrdom often seems to be based on the fact that others "get away with it" and indignation appears to be directed against the chance events or lack of skill that led to apprehension. More important, however, is the fact that there is a good deal of evidence suggesting that many delinquents *do* experience a sense of guilt or shame, and its outward expression is not to be dismissed as a purely manipulative gesture to appease those in authority. Much of this evidence is, to be sure, of a clinical nature or in the form of impressionistic judgments of those who must deal first hand with the youthful offender. Assigning a weight to such evidence calls for caution, but it cannot be ignored if we are to avoid the gross stereotype of the juvenile delinquent as a hardened gangster in miniature.

In the second place, observers have noted that the juvenile delinquent frequently accords admiration and respect to law-abiding persons. The "really honest" person is often revered, and if the delinquent is sometimes overly keen to detect hypocrisy in those who conform, unquestioned probity is likely to win his approval. A fierce attachment to a humble, pious mother or a forgiving, upright priest (the former, according to many observers, is often encountered in both juvenile delinquents and adult criminals) might be dismissed as rank sentimentality, but at least it is clear that the delinquent does not necessarily regard those who abide by the legal rules as immoral. In a similar vein, it can be noted that the juvenile delinquent may exhibit great resentment if illegal behavior is imputed to "significant others" in his immediate social environment or to heroes in the world of sport and entertainment. In other words, if the delinquent does hold to a set of values and norms that stand in complete opposition to those of respectable society, his norm-holding is of a peculiar sort. While supposedly thoroughly committed to the deviant system of the delinquent sub-culture, he would appear to recognize the moral validity of the dominant normative system in many instances.[4]

In the third place, there is much evidence that juvenile delinquents often draw a sharp line between those who can be victimized and those who cannot. Certain social groups are not to be viewed as "fair game" in the performance of supposedly approved delinquent acts while others warrant a variety of attacks. In general, the potentiality for victimization would seem to be a function of the social distance between the juvenile delinquent and others and thus we find implicit maxims in the world of the delinquent such as "don't steal from friends" or "don't commit vandalism against a church of your own faith." [5] This is all rather obvious, but the implications have not received sufficient attention. The fact that supposedly valued behavior tends to be directed against disvalued social groups hints that the "wrongfulness" of such delinquent behavior is more widely recognized by delinquents than the literature has indicated. When the pool of victims is limited by considerations of kinship, friendship, ethnic group, social class, age, sex, etc., we have reason to suspect that the virtue of delinquency is far from unquestioned.

In the fourth place, it is doubtful if many juvenile delinquents are totally immune from the demands for conformity made by the dominant social order. There is a strong likelihood that the family of the delinquent will agree with respectable society that delinquency is wrong, even though the family may be engaged in a variety of illegal activities. That is, the parental posture conducive to delinquency is not apt to be a positive prodding. Whatever may be the influence of parental example, what might be called the "Fagin" pattern of socialization into delinquency is probably rare. Furthermore, as Redl has indicated, the idea that certain neighborhoods are completely delinquent, offering the child a model for delinquent behavior without reservations, is simply not supported by the data.[6]

The fact that a child is punished by parents, school officials, and agencies of the legal system for his delinquency may, as a number of observers have cynically noted, suggest to the child that he should be more careful not to get caught. There is an equal or greater probability, however, that the child will internalize the demands for conformity. This is not to say that demands for conformity cannot be counteracted. In fact, as we shall see shortly, an understanding of how internal and external demands for conformity are neutralized may be crucial for understanding delinquent behavior. But it is to say that a complete denial of the validity of demands for conformity and the substitution of a new normative system is improbable, in light of the child's or adolescent's dependency on adults and encirclement by adults inherent in his status in the social structure. No matter how deeply enmeshed in patterns of delinquency he may be and no matter how much this involvement may outweigh his associations with the law-abiding, he cannot escape the condemnation of his deviance. Somehow the demands for conformity must be met and answered; they cannot be ignored as part of an alien system of values and norms.

In short, the theoretical viewpoint that sees juvenile delinquency as a form of behavior based on the values and norms of a deviant sub-culture in precisely the same way as law-abiding behavior is based on the values and norms of the larger society is open to serious doubt. The fact that the world of the delinquent is embedded in the larger world of those who conform cannot be overlooked nor can the delinquent be equated with an adult thoroughly socialized into an alternative way of life. Instead, the juvenile delinquent would appear to be at least partially committed to the dominant social order in that he frequently exhibits guilt or shame when he violates its proscriptions, accords approval to certain conforming figures, and distinguishes between appropriate and inappropriate targets for his deviance. It is to an explanation for the apparently paradoxical fact of his delinquency that we now turn.

As Morris Cohen once said, one of the most fascinating problems about human behavior is why men violate the laws in which they believe. This is the problem that confronts us when we attempt to explain why delinquency occurs despite a greater or lesser commitment to the usages of conformity. A basic clue is offered by the fact that social rules or norms calling for valued behavior seldom if ever take the form of categorical imperatives. Rather, values or norms appear as *qualified* guides for action, limited in their applicability in terms of time, place, persons, and social circumstances. The moral injunction against killing, for example, does not apply to the enemy during combat in time of war, although a captured enemy comes once again under the prohibition. Similarly, the taking and distributing of scarce goods in a time of acute social need is felt by many to be right, although under other circumstances private property is held inviolable. The normative system of a society, then, is marked by what Williams has termed *flexibility*; it does not consist of a body of rules held to be binding under all conditions.[7]

This flexibility is, in fact, an integral part of the criminal law in that measures for "defenses to crimes" are provided in pleas such as nonage, necessity, insanity, drunkenness, compulsion, self-defense, and so on. The individual can avoid moral culpability for his criminal action—and thus avoid the negative sanctions of society—if he can prove that criminal intent was lacking. *It is our argument that much delinquency is based on what is essentially an unrecognized extension of defenses to crimes, in the form of justifications for deviance that are seen as valid by the delinquent but not by the legal system or society at large.*

These justifications are commonly described as rationalizations. They are viewed as following deviant behavior and as protecting the individual from self-blame and the blame of others after the act. But there is also reason to believe that they precede deviant behavior and make deviant behavior possible. It is this possibility that Sutherland mentioned only in passing and that other writers have failed to exploit from the viewpoint of sociological theory. Disapproval flowing from internalized norms and conforming others in the social environment is neutralized, turned back, or deflected in advance. Social controls that serve to check or inhibit deviant motivational patterns are rendered inoperative, and the individual is freed to engage in delinquency without serious damage to his self image. In this sense, the delinquent both has his cake and eats it too, for he remains committed to the dominant normative system and yet so qualifies its imperatives that violations are "acceptable" if not "right." Thus the delinquent represents not a radical opposition to law-abiding society but something more like an apologetic failure, often more sinned against than sinning in his own eyes. We call these justifications of deviant behavior techniques of neutralization; and we believe these techniques make up a crucial component of Sutherland's "definitions favorable to the violation of law." It is by learning these techniques that the juvenile becomes delinquent, rather than by learning moral imperatives, values or attitudes standing in direct contradiction to those of the dominant society. In analyzing these techniques, we have found it convenient to divide them into five major types.

The Denial of Responsibility

In so far as the delinquent can define himself as lacking responsibility for his deviant actions, the disapproval of self or others is sharply reduced in effectiveness as a restraining influence. As Justice Holmes has said, even a dog distinguishes between being stumbled over and being kicked, and modern society is no less careful to draw a line between injuries that are unintentional, i.e., where responsibility is lacking, and those that are intentional. As a technique of neutralization, however, the denial of responsibility extends much further than the claim that deviant acts are an "accident" or some similar negation of personal accountability. It may also be asserted that delinquent acts are due to forces outside of the individual and beyond his control such as unloving parents, bad companions, or a slum neighborhood. In effect, the delinquent approaches a "billiard ball" conception of himself in which he sees himself as helplessly propelled into new situations. From a psychodynamic viewpoint, this orientation toward one's own actions may represent a profound alienation from self, but it is important to stress the fact that interpretations of responsibility are cultural constructs and not merely idiosyncratic beliefs. The similarity between this mode of justifying illegal behavior assumed by the delinquent and the implications of a "sociological" frame of reference or a "humane" jurisprudence is readily apparent.[8] It is not the validity of this orientation that concerns us here, but its function of deflecting blame attached to violations of social norms and its relative independence of a particular personality structure.[9] By learning to view himself as more acted upon than acting, the delinquent prepares the way for deviance from the dominant normative system without the necessity of a frontal assault on the norms themselves.

The Denial of Injury

A second major technique of neutralization centers on the injury or harm involved in the delinquent act. The criminal law has long made a distinction between crimes which are *mala in se* and *mala prohibita*—that is between acts that are wrong in themselves and acts that are illegal but not immoral—and the delinquent can make the same kind of distinction in evaluating the wrongfulness of his behavior. For the delinquent, however, wrongfulness may turn on the question of whether or not anyone has clearly been hurt by his deviance, and this matter is open to a variety of interpretations. Vandalism, for example, may be defined by the delinquent simply as "mischief"—after all, it may be claimed, the persons whose property has been destroyed can well afford it. Similarly, auto theft may be viewed as "borrowing," and gang fighting may be seen as a private quarrel, an agreed upon duel between two willing parties, and thus of no concern to the community at large. We are not suggesting that this technique of neutralization, labelled the denial of injury, involves an explicit dialectic, rather, we are arguing that the delinquent frequently, and in a hazy fashion, feels that his behavior does not really cause any great harm despite the fact that it runs counter to law. Just as the link between the individual and his acts may be broken by the denial of responsibility, so may the link between acts and their consequences be broken by the denial of injury. Since society sometimes agrees with the delinquent, e.g., in matters such as truancy, "pranks," and so on, it merely reaffirms the idea that the delinquent's neutralization of social controls by means of qualifying the norms is an extension of common practice rather than a gesture of complete opposition.

The Denial of the Victim

Even if the delinquent accepts the responsibility for his deviant actions and is willing to admit that his deviant actions involve an injury or hurt, the moral indignation of self and others may be neutralized by an insistence that the injury is not wrong in light of the circumstances. The injury, it may be claimed, is not really an injury; rather, it is a form of rightful retaliation or punishment. By a subtle alchemy the delinquent moves himself into the position of an avenger and the victim is transformed into a wrong-doer. Assaults on homosexuals or suspected homosexuals, attacks on members of minority groups who are said to have gotten "out of place," vandalism as revenge on an unfair teacher or school official, thefts from a "crooked" store owner—all may be hurts inflicted on a transgressor, in the eyes of the delinquent. As Orwell has pointed out, the type of criminal admired by the general public has probably changed over the course of years and Raffles no longer serves as a hero; [10] but Robin Hood, and his latter day derivatives such as the tough detective seeking justice outside the law, still capture the popular imagination, and the delinquent may view his acts as part of a similar role.

To deny the existence of the victim, then, by transforming him into a person deserving injury is an extreme form of a phenomenon we have mentioned before, namely, the delinquent's recognition of appropriate and inappropriate targets for his delinquent acts. In addition, however, the existence of the victim may be denied for the delinquent, in a somewhat different sense, by the circumstances of the delinquent act itself. Insofar as the victim is physically absent, unknown, or a vague abstraction (as is often the case in delinquent acts committed against property), the awareness of the victim's existence is weakened. Internalized norms and anticipations of the reactions of others must somehow be activated, if they are to serve as guides for behavior; and it is possible that a diminished awareness of the victim plays an important part in determining whether or not this process is set in motion.

The Condemnation of the Condemners

A fourth technique of neutralization would appear to involve a condemnation of the condemners or, as McCorkle and Korn have phrased it, a rejection of the rejectors.[11] The delinquent shifts the focus of attention from his own deviant acts to the motives and behavior of those who disapprove of his violations. His condemners, he may claim, are hypocrites, deviants in disguise, or impelled by personal spite. This orientation toward the conforming world may be of particular importance when it hardens into a bitter cynicism directed against those assigned the task of enforcing or expressing the norms of the dominant society. Police, it may be said, are corrupt, stupid, and brutal. Teachers always show favoritism and parents always "take it out" on their children. By a slight extension, the rewards of conformity—such as material success—become a matter of pull or luck, thus decreasing still further the stature of those who stand on the side of the law-abiding. The validity of this jaundiced viewpoint is not so important as its function in turning back or deflecting the negative sanctions attached to violations of the norms. The delinquent, in effect, has changed the subject of the conversation in the dialogue between his own deviant impulses and the reactions of others; and by attacking others, the wrongfulness of his own behavior is more easily repressed or lost to view.

The Appeal to Higher Loyalties

Fifth, and last, internal and external social controls may be neutralized by sacrificing the demands of the larger society for the demands of the smaller social groups to which the delinquent belongs such as the sibling pair, the gang, or the friendship clique. It is important to note that the delinquent does not necessarily repudiate the imperatives of the dominant normative system, despite his failure to follow them. Rather, the delinquent may see himself as caught up in a dilemma that must be resolved, unfortunately, at the cost of violating the law. One aspect of this situation has been studied by Stouffer and Toby in their research on the conflict between particularistic and universalistic demands, between the claims of friendship and general social obligations, and their results suggest that "it is possible to classify people according to a predisposition to select one or the other horn of a dilemma in role conflict."[12] For our purposes, however, the most important point is that deviation from certain norms may occur not because the norms are rejected but because other norms, held to be more pressing or involving a higher loyalty, are accorded precedence. Indeed, it is the fact that both sets of norms are believed in that gives meaning to our concepts of dilemma and role conflict.

The conflict between the claims of friendship and the claims of law, or a similar dilemma, has of course long been recognized by the social scientist (and the novelist) as a common human problem. If the juvenile delinquent frequently resolves his dilemma by insisting that he must "always help a buddy" or "never squeal on a friend," even when it throws him into serious difficulties with the dominant social order, his choice remains familiar to the supposedly law-abiding. The delinquent is unusual, perhaps, in the extent to which he is able to see the fact that he acts in behalf of the smaller social groups to which he belongs as a justification for violations of society's norms, but it is a matter of degree rather than of kind.

"I didn't mean it." "I didn't really hurt anybody." "They had it coming to them." "Everybody's picking on me." "I didn't do it for myself." These slogans or their variants, we hypothesize, prepare the juvenile for delinquent acts. These "definitions of the situation" represent tangential or glancing blows at the dominant normative system rather than the creation of an opposing ideology; and they are extensions of patterns of thought prevalent in society rather than something created *de novo*.

Techniques of neutralization may not be powerful enough to fully shield the individual from the force of his own internalized values and the reactions of conforming others, for as we have pointed out, juvenile delinquents often appear to suffer from feelings of guilt and shame when called into account for their deviant behavior. And some delinquents may be so isolated from the world of conformity that techniques of neutralization need not be called into play. Nonetheless, we would argue that techniques of neutralization are critical in lessening the effectiveness of social controls and that they lie behind a large share of delinquent behavior. Empirical research in this area is scattered and fragmentary at the present time, but the work of Redl,[13] Cressy,[14] and others has supplied a body of significant data that has done much to clarify the theoretical issues and enlarge the fund of supporting evidence. Two lines of investigation seem to be critical at this stage. First, there is need for more knowledge concerning the differential distribution of techniques of neutralization, as operative patterns of thought, by age, sex, social class, ethnic group, etc. On a *priori* grounds it might be assumed that these justifications for deviance will be more readily seized by segments of society for whom a discrepancy between common social ideals and social practice is most apparent. It is also possible however, that the habit of "bending" the dominant normative system—if not "breaking" it—cuts across our cruder social categories and is to be traced primarily to patterns of social interaction within the familiar circle. Second, there is need for a greater understanding of the internal structure of techniques of neutralization, as a system of beliefs and attitudes, and its relationship to various types of delinquent behavior. Certain techniques of neutralization would appear to be better adapted to particular deviant acts than to others, as we have suggested, for example, in the case of offenses against property and the denial of the victim. But the issue remains far from clear and stands in need of more information.

In any case, techniques of neutralization appear to offer a promising line of research in enlarging and systematizing the theoretical grasp of juvenile delinquency. As more information is uncovered concerning techniques of neutralization, their origins, and their consequences, both juvenile delinquency in particular, and deviation from normative systems in general may be illuminated.

Notes _____

1. E. H. Sutherland, *Principles of Criminology*, revised by D. R. Cressey, Chicago: Lippincott, 1955, pp. 77–80.

2. Albert K. Cohen, *Delinquent Boys*, Glencoe, Ill.: The Free Press, 1955.

3. This form of reaction among the adherents of a deviant subculture who fully believe in the "rightfulness" of their behavior and who are captured and punished by the agencies of the dominant social order can be illustrated, perhaps, by groups such as Jehovah's Witnesses, early Christian sects, nationalist movements in colonial areas, and conscientious objectors during World Wars I and II.

4. As Weber has pointed out, a thief may recognize the legitimacy of legal rules without accepting their moral validity. Cf. Max Weber, *The Theory of Social and Economic Organization* (translated by A. M. Henderson and Talcott Parsons), New York: Oxford University Press, 1947, p. 125. We are arguing here, however, that the juvenile delinquent frequently recognizes *both* the legitimacy of the dominant social order and its moral "rightness."

5. Thrasher's account of the "Itschkies"—a juvenile gang composed of Jewish boys—and the immunity from "rolling" enjoyed by Jewish drunkards is a good illustration. Cf. F. Thrasher, *The Gang*, Chicago: The University of Chicago Press, 1947, p. 315.

6. Cf. Solomon Kobrin, "The Conflict of Values in Delinquency Areas," *American Sociological Review*, 16 (October, 1951), pp. 653–661.

7. Cf. Robin Williams, Jr., *American Society*, New York: Knopf, 1951, p. 28.

8. A number of observers have wryly noted that many delinquents seem to show a surprising awareness of sociological and psychological explanations for their behavior and are quick to point out the causal role of their poor environment.

9. It is possible, of course, that certain personality structures can accept some techniques of neutralization more readily than others, but this question remains largely unexplored.

10. George Orwell, *Dickens, Dali, and Others*, New York: Reynal, 1946.

11. Lloyd W. McCorkle and Richard Korn, "Resocialization Within Walls," *The Annals of the American Academy of Political and Social Science*, 293, (May, 1954), pp. 88–98.

12. See Samuel A. Stouffer and Jackson Toby, "Role Conflict and Personality," in *Toward a General Theory of Action*, edited by Talcott Parsons and Edward A. Shils, Cambridge: Harvard University Press, 1951, p. 494.

13. See Fritz Redl and David Wineman, *Children Who Hate*, Glencoe: The Free Press, 1956.

14. See D. R. Cressey, *Other People's Money*, Glencoe: The Free Press, 1953.

10

Differential Association-Reinforcement Theory

Robert Burgess and Ronald Akers' 1966 "differential association-reinforcement theory" was the forerunner to what is now known as "social learning theory." Ronald Akers met Robert Burgess in 1965, when he (Akers) accepted a faculty position at the University of Washington (in Seattle) (Lilly, Cullen, & Ball, 2011:56). At that time, Ronald Akers was still finishing his Ph.D in the sociology of law at the University of Kentucky. Robert Burgess was also a recently-hired faculty member in the Department of Sociology at the University of Washington in Seattle. When they met, Burgess was still working on his Ph.D in sociology and social psychology at the University of Washington in St. Louis, Missouri. Akers was intrigued by Burgess' knowledge of behavioral psychology, and together, they collaborated on a reformulation of Sutherland's theory of differential association, introducing some key elements of B. F. Skinner's work on operant conditioning (Akers & Sellers, 2009:88; Lilly et al., 2011:56).

Burgess and Akers begin their 1966 article by recognizing that Edwin Sutherland's differential association theory is in fact a learning theory, and accepting the notion that criminal behavior is—as Sutherland originally asserted—learned in the same manner that conforming behavior is learned (cf. Akers, 1998:51–52). However, they observe that up to the point in time when they were reformulating Sutherland's propositions, differential association theory had proven to be difficult to validate empirically (Burgess & Akers, 1966:128–129). Moreover, they note that Sutherland did not clearly specify the mechanisms or processes through which criminal behavior was learned. Burgess and Akers (1966:132) contend in this reading selection that the "modern behavior theory" (operant conditioning) of B. F. Skinner is capable of explaining the mechanisms involved in the learning of behavior.

Operant conditioning states that behaviors are learned (conditioned) as a consequence of exposure to positive and negative (or aversive) stimuli, also referred to as positive and negative reinforcers (Burgess & Akers, 1966:132–133; Winfree & Abadinsky, 2010:139). Unlike "classical conditioning," it is called "operant conditioning" because the individual operates on his or her environment, and/or on other people (Cassel & Bernstein, 2001:102). If a certain behavior results in positive reinforcement, then the frequency of that behavior is likely to increase. If a behavior results in negative reinforcement, or punishment, then the frequency of that behavior is likely to decrease (Burgess & Akers, 1966:133). A central tenet of operant conditioning is that behavior can be modified—if the behavior no longer produces the desired stimuli, or instead produces undesired (and possibly painful) stimuli, then the behavior will become "extinct" (Burgess & Akers, 1966:133; Cassel & Bernstein, 2001:102).

In their "differential association-reinforcement theory," Burgess and Akers re-state Edwin Sutherland's nine propositions regarding how behavior is learned. Rather than simply saying that "criminal behavior is learned," they say that it is learned in accordance with "the principles of operant conditioning" (Burgess & Akers, 1966:137). While Sutherland (1985:179–180) said that criminal behavior was learned through a process of interaction and communication, usually occurring "within intimate personal groups," Burgess and Akers (1966:138) say that it can also be learned through imitation and modeling. This is consistent with Albert Bandura's (1977:22, 117) work on social learning theory, and his assertion that human behavior can be learned vicariously, through observing whether other individuals have had their behavior reinforced or punished. In other words, it is not essential for individuals to "operate" on their environment directly—they can observe the cause-effect relationship indirectly, watching others operate on the environment. Sutherland's theory focused on the frequency, duration and intensity of exposure to criminal peers and to pro-criminal attitudes (differential associations) as the key determinants in the learning of criminal behavior (Sutherland, 1985:180–181). Burgess and Akers, on the other hand, state that "the strength of criminal behavior is a direct function of the amount, frequency, and probability of its reinforcement" (Burgess & Akers, 1966:144).

Over the years, Ronald Akers gradually took "ownership" of "differential association-reinforcement theory" and developed it into what has commonly come to be known as "social learning theory" (Akers, 1990:657; Akers, 1998:139; Akers, 2001:194). In the process, Akers moved away from B. F. Skinner's operant conditioning, and aligned himself more closely with Albert Bandura's work on imitation and modeling behavior. B. F. Skinner's operant conditioning and Albert Bandura's imitation and modeling were both psychological in origin (cf. Akers, 2001:194), and thus, it could be argued that Ronald Akers' social learning theory is more "social-psychological" than it is "sociological." That said, Akers has continued to stress the influence of the social structure (e.g., social organization or disorganization, social class, socio-demographic factors, social groups, etc.) and the importance of "differential social reinforcement" in the learning of criminal behavior (Akers & Sellers, 2009:96–97). He has also stated that:

> Social learning theory retains a strong element of the symbolic interactionism found in the concepts of differential association. . . . Symbolic interactionism is the theory that social interaction is mainly the exchange of meaning and symbols; individuals have the cognitive capacity to imagine themselves in the roles of others and incorporate this into their conceptions of themselves (R. L. Akers & Sellers, 2009:89).

As noted in the Introduction to Section III, differential association/social learning theory is one of the most thoroughly researched criminological theories (Lilly et al., 2011:57; Winfree & Abadinsky, 2010:200). The tenets of social learning theory have been critical to the success of the long-standing Oregon Social Learning Center's crime prevention program, which works with families to modify the behavior of parents and children (Akers & Jensen, 2006:49–50; Winfree & Abadinsky, 2010:201). In a recent re-assessment of a well-known 1967 meta-analysis of 231 evaluations of correctional treatment programs, Cullen, Wright, Gendreau and Andrews (2003:348) found that those correctional programs that employed elements of differential association/social learning theory reduced recidivism by 20 to 30 percent. A more recent meta-analysis of 133 studies conducted on social learning theory between 1974 and 2003 found that—as proposed by differential association/social learning theory—antisocial behavior of peers, antisocial behavior of parents and exposure to antisocial attitudes did indeed have a substantial effect size on criminal and deviant behavior (Pratt et al., 2010:771, 777).

References

Akers, R. L. (1990). Rational choice, deterrence, and social learning theory in criminology: The path not taken. *The Journal of Criminal Law & Criminology, 81*(3), 653–676.

Akers, R. L. (1998). *Social learning and social structure: A general theory of crime and deviance.* Boston: Northeastern University Press.

Akers, R. L. (2001). Social learning theory. In R. Paternoster, & R. Bachman (Eds.), *Explaining criminals and crime: Essays in contemporary criminological theory* (pp. 192–210). Los Angeles, Calif.: Roxbury Pub. Co.

Akers, R. L., & Jensen, G. F. (2006). The empirical status of social learning theory of crime and deviance: The past, present and future. In F. T. Cullen, J. P. Wright & K. R. Blevins (Eds.), *Taking stock: The status of criminological theory* (pp. 37–76). New Brunswick, N.J.: Transaction Publishers.

Akers, R. L., & Sellers, C. S. (2009). *Criminological theories: Introduction, evaluation, and application* (5th, New ed.). New York: Oxford University Press.

Bandura, A. (1977). *Social learning theory.* Englewood Cliffs, NJ: Prentice-Hall.

Burgess, R. L., & Akers, R. L. (1966). A differential association-reinforcement theory of criminal behavior. *Social Problems, 14*(2), 128–147.

Cassel, E., & Bernstein, D. A. (2001). *Criminal behavior.* Needham Heights, MA: Allyn and Bacon.

Cullen, F. T., Wright, J. P., Gendreau, P., & Andrews, D. A. (2003). What correctional treatment can tell us about criminological theory: Implications for social learning theory. In R. L. Akers, & G. F. Jensen (Eds.), *Social learning theory and the explanation of crime: A guide for the new century* (pp. 339–362). New Brunswick, N.J.: Transaction.

Lilly, J. R., Cullen, F. T., & Ball, R. A. (2011). *Criminological theory: Context and consequences* (5th ed.). Thousand Oaks: SAGE Publications.

Pratt, T. C., Cullen, F. T., Sellers, C. S., Winfree, L. T., Madensen, T. D., Daigle, L. E., & Gau, J. M. (2010). The empirical status of social learning theory: A meta-analysis. *Justice Quarterly,* 27(6), 765–802.

Sutherland, E. H., & Cressey, D. R. (1985). The theory of differential association. In S. H. Traub, & C. B. Little (Eds.), *Theories of deviance* (3rd ed., pp. 176–182). Itasca, Ill.: F. E. Peacock Publishers.

Winfree, L. T., & Abadinsky, H. (2010). *Understanding crime: Essentials of criminological theory* (Third ed.). Belmont, CA: Wadsworth, Cengage Learning.

A Differential Association-Reinforcement Theory of Criminal Behavior

ROBERT L. BURGESS AND RONALD L. AKERS

Introduction

In spite of the body of literature that has accumulated around the differential association theory of criminal behavior,[1] it has yet to receive crucial empirical test or thorough restatement beyond Sutherland's own revision in 1947. Recognizing that the theory is essentially a learning theory, Sutherland rephrased it to state explicitly that criminal behavior is learned as any behavior is learned. In Cressey's two revisions of the textbook, the theory has been deliberately left unchanged from Sutherland's revision. Thus, the theory as it stands now is postulated upon the knowledge of the learning process extant 20–25 years ago.[2]

Sutherland, himself, never was able to test directly or find specific empirical support for his theory, but he was convinced that the two-edged theory—(1) genetic, differential association and (2) structural, differential social organization—accounted for the known data on the full range of crimes, including conventional violations and white-collar crimes.[3] The theory has received some other empirical support,[4] but negative cases have also been found.[5] The attempts to subject the theory to empirical test are marked by inconsistent findings both within the same study and between studies, as well as by highly circumscribed and qualified findings and conclusions. Whether the particular researcher concludes that his findings do or do not seem

Reprinted by permission from *Social Problems* 14, no. 2 (1966).

to support the theory, nearly all have indicated difficulty in operationalizing the concepts and recommend that the theory be modified in such a way that it becomes more amenable to empirical testing.

Suggested theoretical modifications have not been lacking, but the difficulty with these restatements is that they are no more readily operationalized than Sutherland's.[6] One recent paper, however, by DeFleur and Quinney,[7] offers new promise that the theory can be adequately operationalized. They have presented a detailed strategy for making specific deductions for empirical testing. But while they have clarified the problems in the derivation and generation of testable hypotheses from differential association, they still see its empirical validation as a very difficult, though not impossible task.

Regardless of the particular criticisms, the exceptions taken, and the difficulties involved in testing and reformulating the theory that have been offered, few take exception to the central learning assumptions in differential association. If we accept the basic assumption that criminal behavior is learned by the same processes and involves the same mechanisms as conforming behavior, then we need to recognize and make use of the current knowledge about these processes and mechanisms. Neither the extant statement of the theory nor the reformulations of it make explicit the nature of the underlying learning process involved in differential association. In short, no major revisions have been made utilizing established learning principles.

That this type of revision of the theory is needed has been recognized and some criticism of differential association has revolved around the fact that it does not adequately portray the process by which criminal behavior is learned. But as Cressey explains:

> It is one thing to criticise the theory for failure to specify the learning process accurately and another to specify which aspects of the learning process should be included and in what way.[8]

Sutherland, of course, was as interested in explaining the "epidemiology" of crime as in explaining how the individual comes to engage in behavior in violation of the law and insisted that the two explanations must be consistent.[9] Differential social organization (normative conflict) has been successful in "making sense" of variations in crime rates. But differential association has been less successful in explicating the process by which this differential organization produces individual criminality. This seems to be due not to the lack of importance of associations for criminal behavior but:

> . . . rather to the fact that the theory outran the capacity of either psychology or social psychology to give adequate, scientific answers to the question of why there are such qualitative (selective) differences in human association.[10]

It now appears, however, that there is a body of verified theory which is adequate to the task of accurately specifying this process. Modern learning theory seems capable of providing insights into the problem of uniting structural and genetic formulations. While sociologists know a great deal about the structure of the environment from which deviants come, we know very little about the determining variables operating within this environment. The burden of criminological theory today is to combine knowledge of structural pressures with explanations of "why only *some* of the persons on whom this pressure is exerted become non-conformists."[11]

It is for this reason that the recent effort by C. R. Jeffery to re-examine differential association in light of modern learning theory marks a new departure in the abundance of thinking and writing that has characterized the intellectual history of this theory.[12] In spite of their intricate axiomatization of the theory, DeFleur and Quinney, for example, recognize that even they have left the learning process in differential association unspecified. But, they note, "modern reinforcement learning theory would handle this problem. . . . "[13] This is precisely what Jeffery proposed to do and to the extent that this objective is served by discussing learning theory and criminal behavior together, he is at least partially successful. However, Jeffery does not in fact make it clear just how Sutherland's differential association theory may be revised. His explanation incorporates differential reinforcement:

> . . . [A] criminal act occurs in an environment in which in the past the actor has been reinforced for behaving in this manner, and the aversive consequences attached to the behavior have been of such a nature that they do not control or prevent the response.[14]

This statement, as it stands, bears no obvious or direct relation to Sutherland's differential association, and nowhere else does Jeffery make it clear how differential reinforcement is a reformulation of differential association. Jeffery does discuss modern learning principles, but he does not show how these principles may be incorporated within the framework of Sutherland's theory, nor how these principles may lead to explanations of past empirical findings.

Jeffery's theory and his discussion of criminal behavior and learning theory remains not so much incorrect as unconvincing. His presentation of learning principles is supported wholly by reference to experiments with lower organisms and his extension to criminal behavior is mainly through anecdotal and illustrative material. The potential value and impact of Jeffery's article is diminished by not calling attention to the already large and growing body of literature in experimental behavioral science, especially evidence using human subjects, that has direct implications for differential association theory. We are basically in agreement with Jeffery that learning theory has progressed to the point where it seems likely that differential association can be restated in a more sophisticated and testable form in the language of modern learning theory. But that restatement must be attempted in a thorough fashion before we can expect others to accept it. Jeffery begins to do this and his thoughts are significant, but they do not take into account the theory as a whole.

The amount of empirical research in the social psychology of learning clearly has shown that the concepts in learning theory are susceptible to operationalization. Therefore, applying an integrated set of learning principles to differential association theory should adequately provide the revision needed for empirical testing. These learning principles are based on literally thousands of experimental hours covering a wide range of the phylogenetic scale and more nearly constitute empirically derived *laws* of behavior than any other set of principles. They enable the handling of a great variety of observational as well as experimental evidence about human behavior.

It is the purpose of this paper to take the first step in the direction to which Jeffery points. A restatement of the theory, not an alternative theory, will be presented, although, of necessity, certain ideas not intrinsic to differential association will have to be introduced and additions will be made to the original propositions. It should be pointed out that DeFleur and Quinney have been able to demonstrate that Sutherland's propositions, when stated in the form of set theory, appear to be internally consistent. By arranging the propositions in axiomatic form, stating them in logical rather than verbal symbols, they have brought the theoretical grammar up to date.[15] Such is not our intention in this paper, at all. We recognize and appreciate the importance of stating the propositions in a formal, deductive fashion. We do feel, however, that this task is, at the present time, subsidiary to the more urgent task of: (1) making explicit the learning process, as it is now understood by modern behavioral science, from which the propositions of differential association can be derived; (2) fully reformulating the theory, statement by statement, in light of the current knowledge of this learning process; and (3) helping criminologists become aware of the advances in learning theory and research that are directly relevant to an explanation of criminal behavior.[16] No claim is made that this constitutes a final statement. If it has any seminal value at all, that is, if it provokes a serious new look at the theory and encourages further effort in this direction, our objective will have been served.

Differential Association and Modern Behavior Theory

In this section the nine formal propositions in which Sutherland expressed his theory will be analyzed in terms of behavior theory and research and will be reformulated as seven new propositions. (See Table 10.1.)

I. "Criminal behavior is learned." VIII. "The process of learning criminal behavior by association with criminal and anti-criminal patterns involves all of the mechanisms that are involved in any other learning."

Since both the first and eighth sentences in the theory obviously form a unitary idea, it seems best to state them together. Sutherland was aware that these statements did not sufficiently describe the learning process,[17] but these two items leave no doubt that differential association theory was meant to fit into a general explanation of human behavior and, as much is unambiguously stated in the prefatory remarks of the theory; an "explanation of criminal behavior should be a specific part of a general theory of behavior."[18] Modern behavior theory as a general theory provides us with a good idea of what the mechanisms are that are involved in the process of acquiring behavior.[19]

According to this theory, there are two major categories of behavior. On the one hand, there is reflexive or *respondent* behavior which is behavior that is governed by the stimuli that elicit it. Such behaviors are largely associated with the autonomic system. The work of Pavlov is of special significance here. On the other hand, there is *operant* behavior: behavior which involves the central nervous system. Examples of operant behavior include verbal behavior, playing ball, driving a car, and buying a new suit. It has been found that this class of behavior is a function of its past and present environmental consequences. Thus, when a particular operant is followed by certain kinds of stimuli, that behavior's frequency of occurrence will increase in the future. These stimuli are called reinforcing stimuli or reinforcers[20] and include food, money, clothes, objects of various sorts, social attention, approval, affection and social status. This entire process is called positive reinforcement. One distinguishing characteristic of operant behavior as opposed to respondent behavior, then, is that the latter is a function of its antecedent stimuli, whereas the former is a function of its antecedent environmental consequences.

Typically, operant and respondent behaviors occur together in an individual's everyday behavior, and they interact in extremely intricate ways. Consequently, to fully understand any set of patterned responses, the investigator should observe the effects of the operants on the respondents as well as effects of the respondents on the operants. The connections between operant and respondent behaviors are especially crucial to an analysis of attitudes, emotional and conflict behaviors.

In everyday life, different consequences are usually contingent upon different classes of behavior. This relationship between behavior and its consequences functions to alter the rate and form of behavior as well as its relationship to many features of the environment. The process of operant reinforcement is the most important process by which behavior is generated and maintained. There are, in fact, six possible environmental consequences relative to the Law of Operant Behavior. (1) A behavior may produce certain stimulus events and thereby increase in frequency. As we have indicated above, such stimuli are called positive reinforcers and the process is called positive reinforcement. (2) A behavior may remove, avoid, or terminate certain stimulus events and thereby increase in frequency. Such stimuli are termed negative reinforcers and the process, negative reinforcement. (3) A behavior may produce certain stimulus events and thereby decrease in frequency. Such stimuli are called aversive stimuli or, more recently, punishers.[21] The entire behavioral process is called positive punishment. (4) A behavior may remove or terminate certain stimulus events and thereby decrease in frequency. Such stimuli are positive reinforcers and the process is termed negative punishment. (5) A behavior may produce or remove certain stimulus events which do not change the behavior's frequency at all. Such stimuli are called neutral stimuli. (6) A behavior may no longer produce customary stimulus events and thereby decrease in frequency. The stimuli which are produced are neutral stimuli, and the process, extinction. When a reinforcing stimulus no longer functions to increase the future probability of the behavior which produced it, we say the individual is satiated. To restore the reinforcing property of the stimulus we need only deprive the individual of it for a time.[22]

The increase in the frequency of occurrence of a behavior that is reinforced is the very property of reinforcement that permits the fascinating variety and subtlety that occur in operant as opposed to respondent behavior. Another process producing the variety we see in behavior is that of *conditioning*. When a primary or unconditioned reinforcing stimulus such as food is repeatedly paired with a neutral stimulus, the latter will eventually function as a reinforcing stimulus as well. An illustration of this would be as follows. The milk a mother feeds to her infant is an unconditioned reinforcer. If the food is repeatedly paired with social attention, affection, and approval, these latter will eventually become reinforcing as will the mother herself as a stimulus object. Later these *conditioned reinforcers* can be used to strengthen other behaviors by making these reinforcers contingent upon those new behaviors.

Differential reinforcement may also alter the form of a response. This process is called *shaping or response differentiation*. It can be exemplified by a child learning to speak. At first, the parent will reinforce any vocalization, but as time wears on, and as the child grows older, the parent will differentially reinforce only those responses which successfully approximate certain criteria. The child will be seen to proceed from mere grunts to "baby-talk" to articulate speech.[23]

Of course, organisms, whether pigeons, monkeys or people, do not usually go around behaving in all possible ways at all possible times. In short, behavior does not occur in a vacuum; a given behavior is appropriate to a given situation. By appropriate we mean that reinforcement has been forthcoming only under certain conditions and it is under these conditions that the behavior will occur. In other words, differential reinforcement not only increases the probability of a response, it also makes that response more probable upon the recurrence of conditions the same as or similar to those that were present during previous reinforcements. Such a process is called *stimulus control* or *stimulus discrimination*. For example, a child when he is first taught to say "daddy" may repeat it when any male is present, or even, in the very beginning, when any adult is present. But through differential reinforcement, the child will eventually only speak the word "daddy" when his father is present or in other "appropriate" conditions. We may say that the father, as a stimulus object, functions as a discriminative stimulus (S^D) setting the occasion for the operant verbal response "daddy" because in the past such behavior has been reinforced under such conditions.

It has also been discovered that the pattern or schedule of reinforcement is as important as the amount of reinforcement. For example, a *fixed-interval* schedule of reinforcement, where a response is reinforced only after a certain amount of time has passed, produces a lower rate of response than that obtained with reinforcement based on a *fixed-ratio* schedule where a response is reinforced only after a certain number of responses have already been emitted. Similarly a response rate obtained with a fixed-ratio schedule is lower than that obtained with a *variable-ratio* schedule, where reinforcement occurs for a certain proportion of responses randomly varied about some central value. A schedule of reinforcement, then, refers to the response *contingencies* upon which reinforcement depends. All of the various schedules of reinforcement, besides producing lawful response characteristics, produce lawful extinction rates, once reinforcement is discontinued. Briefly, behavior reinforced on an intermittent schedule takes longer to extinguish than behavior reinforced on a continuous schedule.

This concept, schedules of reinforcement, is one the implications of which are little understood by many behavioral scientists, so a few additional words are in order. First of all, social reinforcements are for the most part intermittent. One obvious result of this fact is the resistance to extinction and satiation of much social behavior, desirable as well as undesirable. This is not peculiar to human social behavior, for even lower organisms seldom are faced with a continuous reinforcement schedule. Nevertheless, reinforcements mediated by another organism are probably much less reliable than those produced by the physical environment. This is the case because social reinforcement depends upon behavioral processes in the reinforcer which are not under good control by the reinforcee. A more subtle, though essentially methodological, implication of this is that because most social behaviors are maintained by complex intermittent schedules which have been shaped over a long period of time, a social observer, newly entering a situation may have extreme difficulty in immediately determining exactly what is maintaining a particular behavior or set of behaviors. Nor can the individual himself be expected to be able to identify his own contingencies of reinforcement.[24]

An important aspect of this theory is the presentation of the general ways that stimuli and responses can be formed into complex constellations of stimulus-response events. Although the basic principles are simple and must be separated to distinguish and study them, in actual life the principles function in concert, and consist of complex arrays and constellations.[25] Such complexity can be seen in the fact that single S-R events may be combined into sequences on the basis of conditioning principles. That is, responses can be thought to have stimulus properties. In addition, more than one response may come under the control of a particular stimulus. Thus, when the stimulus occurs, it will tend to set the occasion for the various responses that have been conditioned to it. These responses may be competitive, that is, only one or the other can occur. When this is so, the particular response which does occur may also depend upon other discriminative stimuli present in the situation that control only one or the other response. Finally, while some of the stimuli to which an individual responds emanate from the external environment, social and otherwise, some come from his own behavior. An individual is, then, not only a source of responses, he is also a source of some stimuli—stimuli that can effect his own behavior.

The most general behavioral principle is the Law of Operant Behavior which says that behavior is a function of its past and current environmental consequences. There have been numerous studies with children[26] as well as adults[27] which indicate that individual behavior conforms to this law. Of much more interest to sociologists is an experiment designed by Azrin and Lindsley in 1956[28] to investigate coopera- tive social behavior. Their study demonstrated that cooperative behavior could be developed, maintained, eliminated and reinstated solely through the manipulation of the contingency between reinforcing stimuli and the cooperative response. This basic finding has received much subsequent support. It has also been demonstrated that not only cooperative behavior, but also competitive behavior and leading and following behavior are a function of their past and present consequences.

Another of the behavioral principles we mentioned was that of stimulus dis- crimination. A discriminative stimulus is a stimulus in the presence of which a particular operant response is reinforced. Much of our behavior has come under the control of certain environmental, including social stimuli because in the past it has been reinforced in the presence of those stimuli. In an experiment by Don- ald Cohen,[29] a normal 13-year-old boy named Justin, when placed under identical experimental conditions emitted different behaviors depending upon whether his partner was his mother, brother, sister, friend, or a stranger. The results of this inves- tigation demonstrated that Justin's social behavior was differentially controlled by reinforcement; but it also demonstrated that his behavior was different depend- ing upon the social stimuli present, thus reaffirming the principle of stimulus dis- crimination. In other words, the dynamic properties of his social behavior, whether cooperative, competitive, leading or following, were controlled by his previous extra-experimental history with his teammates, although the experimenter could change those behaviors by experimentally altering the contingencies of reinforce- ment. It is, of course, almost a truism to say that an individual behaves differently in the presence of different people. The significance of this experiment, however, is that the investigator was able to isolate the determining variables and the principles by which they operated to produce this common phenomenon.

While this is by no means a complete survey of the relevant experimental tests of the behavioral principles outlined above, it may serve to point out that many forms of "normal" social behavior function according to the Law of Operant Behav- ior. But what about "deviant" behavior? Can we be sure these same principles are operating here? Unfortunately there have been no studies which attempt to test directly the relevance of these behavioral principles to criminal behavior. But there have been several experimental investigations of deviant behaviors emitted by men- tal patients. For example, in a study by Ayllon and Michael,[30] it was shown that the bizarre behaviors of psychotics functioned according to these learning principles. In this particular study various behavioral problems of psychotic patients were "cured" through the manipulation of reinforcement contingencies. Such principles as extinction, negative and positive reinforcement, and satiation were effectively utilized to eliminate the unwanted behaviors.[31] This study was one of the first experimental tests of the contention that not only conforming but also many unusual, inappropriate, or undesirable behaviors are shaped and maintained through social reinforcement. In another experiment Isaacs, Thomas, and Goldiamond[32] demonstrate that complex adjustive behaviors can be operantly conditioned in longterm psychotics by manipulating available reinforcers.

In yet another investigation,[33] the personnel of a mental hospital ward for schizophrenics recorded the behavior of the patients and provided consequences to it according to certain pre-established procedures. Without going into the many important details of this long investigation, we may note that in each of the six experiments that were carried out, the results demonstrate that reinforcement was effective in maintaining desired performances, even though these were "backward" psychotics who had resisted all previous therapy, including psychoanalysis, electroshock therapy, lobotomies and so forth.

> In each experiment, the performance fell to a near zero level when the established response-reinforcement relation was discontinued. . . . The standard procedure for reinforcement had been to provide tokens. . . . [exchanged] for a variety of reinforcers. Performance decreased when this response-reinforcement relation was disrupted (1) by delivering tokens independently of the response while still allowing exchange of tokens for the reinforcers (Exp II and III), (2) by discontinuing the token system entirely but providing continuing access to the reinforcers (Exp IV), or (3) by discontinuing the delivery of tokens for a previously reinforced response while simultaneously providing tokens for a different, alternative response (Exp I and VI). Further, the effectiveness of the reinforcement procedure did not appear to be limited to an all-or-none basis. Patients selected and performed the assignment that provided the larger number of tokens when reinforcement was available for more than one assignment (Exp V).[34]

Again, we cannot review all of the relevant literature, yet perhaps the three investigations cited will serve to emphasize that many forms of deviant behavior are shaped and maintained by various contingencies of reinforcement.[35] Given this experimental evidence we would amend Sutherland's first and eighth propositions to read:

I. *Criminal behavior is learned according to the principles of operant conditioning.*

II. "Criminal behavior is learned in interaction with other persons in the process of communication."

As DeFleur and Quinney have noted, the major implication of this proposition is that symbolic interaction is a necessary condition for the learning of criminal behavior.[36] Of direct relevance to this is an experiment designed to test the relative significance of verbal instructions and reinforcement contingencies in generating and maintaining a certain class of behaviors.[37] In brief, the results indicated that behavior could not be maintained solely through verbal instructions. However, it was also discovered that it was an extremely arduous task to shape a set of complex behaviors without using verbal instructions as discriminative stimuli. Behavior was quickly and effectively developed and maintained by a combination of verbal instructions *and* reinforcement consequences. Symbolic interaction is, then, not enough, contingencies of reinforcement must also be present.

From the perspective of modern behavior theory, two aspects of socialization are usually considered to distinguish it from other processes of behavioral change: (1) Only those behavioral changes occurring through learning are considered relevant; (2) only the changes in behavior having their origins in interaction with other persons are considered products of socialization.[38] Sutherland's theory may, then, be seen to be a theory of differential socialization since he, too, restricted himself to learning having its origin in interaction with other persons. While social learning is, indeed, important and even predominant, it certainly does not exhaust the learning process. In short, we may learn (and, thus, our behavior would be modified) without any direct contact with another person. As such, Sutherland's theory may be seen to suffer from a significant lacuna in that it neglected the possibility of deviant behavior being learned in nonsocial situations. Consequently, to be an adequate theory of deviant behavior, the theory must be amended further to include those forms of deviant behavior that are learned in the absence of social reinforcement. Other people are not the only source of reinforcement although they are the most important. As Jeffery[39] has aptly noted, stealing is reinforcing in and by itself whether other people know about it and reinforce it socially or not. The same may be said to apply to many forms of aggressive behaviors.[40]

There are many studies which are relevant to social interaction and socialization on the one hand, and Sutherland's second proposition on the other. For example, in a study by Lott and Lott[41] it was found that when child A was reinforced in the presence of child B, child A would later select child B as a companion. The behavior of selecting child B was not the behavior that was reinforced. The experimental conditions simply paired child B with positive reinforcement. In accordance with the principle of conditioning, child B had become a conditioned positive reinforcer. As such any behavior which produced the presence of child B would be strengthened, such behaviors, for example, as verbal responses requesting child B's company. Thus, as Staats[42] has noted, the results of this study indicate that the concepts of reinforcing stimuli and group cohesion are related when analyzed in terms of an integrated set of learning principles.

Glaser[43] has attempted to reformulate Sutherland's differential association theory in terms of social identification. It should be recognized, however, that identification as well as modeling and imitative behavior (which are usually associated with identification) comprise just one feature of the socialization process.

Furthermore, such behavior may be analyzed quite parsimoniously with the principles of modern behavior theory. For example, in a study by Bandura and Ross,[44] a child experienced the pairing of one adult with positive reinforcers. Presumably this adult would become a conditioned reinforcer. And indeed, later it was found that the child imitated this adult more than he did an adult who was not paired with positive reinforcers. That is, the one adult, as he became a stronger reinforcer, had also become a stronger S^D for imitating or following behavior. Thus, Bandura's and Ross's results demonstrate that imitating or following behavior is at least in part a function of the reinforcing value of people as social stimuli.

> On the basis of these results it is suggested that a change in the reinforcing value of an individual will change his power as a stimulus controlling other people's behavior in various ways. An increase in the reinforcing value of an individual will increase verbal and motor approach, or companionable responses, respectful responses, affectionate behavior, following behavior, smiling, pleasant conversation, sympathetic responses and the like.[45]

The relevance of these studies is that they have isolated some of the determining variables whereby the behavior of one person is influenced or changed by the behavior of another as well as the principles by which these variables operate. We have, of course, only scratched the surface. Many other variables are involved. For instance, not all people are equally effective in controlling or influencing the behavior of others. The person who can mediate the most reinforcers will exercise the most power. Thus, the parent, who controls more of his child's reinforcers, will exercise more power than an older sibling or the temporary "baby sitter." As the child becomes older and less dependent upon the parent for many of his reinforcers, other individuals or groups such as his peers may exercise more power. Carrying the analysis one step further, the person who has access to a large range of aversive stimuli will exert more power than one who has not. Thus a peer group may come to exercise more power over a child's behavior than the parent even though the parent may still control a large share of the child's positive reinforcers.

In addition to the reinforcing function of an individual or group, there is, as seen in the Cohen and the Bandura and Ross studies, the discriminative stimulus function of a group. For example, specific individuals as physical stimuli may acquire discriminative control over an individual's behavior. The child in our example above is reinforced for certain kinds of behaviors in the presence of his parent, thus the parent's presence may come to control this type of behavior. He is reinforced for different behaviors in the presence of his peers, who then come to set the occasion for this type of behavior. Consequently this proposition must be amended to read: II. *Criminal behavior is learned both in nonsocial situations that are reinforcing or discriminative, and through that social interaction in which the behavior of other persons is reinforcing or discriminative for criminal behavior.*

III. "The principal part of the learning of criminal behavior occurs within intimate personal groups."

In terms of our analysis, the primary group would be seen to be the major source of an individual's social reinforcements. The bulk of behavioral training which the child receives occurs at a time when the trainers, usually the parents, possess a very powerful system of reinforcers. In fact, we might characterize a primary group as a generalized reinforcer (one associated with many reinforcers, conditioned as well as unconditioned). And, as we suggested above, as the child grows older, groups other than the family may come to control a majority of an individual's reinforcers, e.g., the adolescent peer group.

To say that the primary group is the principal molder of an individual's behavioral repertoire is not to ignore social learning which may occur in other contexts. As we noted above, learning from social models can be adequately explained in terms of these behavioral principles. The analysis we employed there can also be extended to learning from the mass media and from "reference" groups. In any case, we may alter this proposition to read: III. *The principal part of the learning of criminal behavior occurs in those groups which comprise the individual's major source of reinforcements.*

IV. "When criminal behavior is learned, the learning includes (a) techniques of committing the crime, which are sometimes very complicated, sometimes very simple; (b) the specific direction of motives, drives, rationalizations, and attitudes."

A study by Klaus and Glaser[46] as well as many other studies[47] indicate that reinforcement contingencies are of prime importance in learning various behavioral techniques. And, of course, many techniques, both simple and complicated, are specific to a particular deviant act such as jimmying, picking locks of buildings and cars, picking pockets, short- and big-con techniques, counterfeiting and safe-cracking. Other techniques in criminal behavior may be learned in conforming or neutral contexts, e.g., driving a car, signing checks, shooting a gun, etc. In any event, we need not alter the first part of this proposition.

The second part of this proposition does, however, deserve some additional comments. Sutherland's major focus here seems to be motivation. Much of what we have already discussed in this paper often goes under the general heading of motivation. The topic of motivation is as important as it is complex. This complexity is related to the fact that the same stimulus may have two functions: it may be both a reinforcing stimulus and a discriminative stimulus controlling the behavior which is followed by reinforcement.[48] Thus, motivation may be seen to be a function of the processes by which stimuli acquire conditioned reinforcing value and become discriminative stimuli. Reinforcers and discriminative stimuli here would become the dependent variables; the independent variables would be the conditioning procedures previously mentioned and the level of deprivation. For example, when a prisoner is deprived of contact with members of the opposite sex, such sex reinforcers will become much more powerful. Thus, those sexual reinforcers that are available, such as homosexual contact, would come to exert a great deal of influence and would shape behaviors that would be unlikely to occur without such deprivation. And, without going any further into this topic, some stimuli may be more reinforcing, under similar conditions of deprivation, for certain individuals or groups than for others. Furthermore, the satiation of one or more of these reinforcers would allow for an increase in the relative strength of others.

Much, therefore, can be learned about the distinctive characteristics of a group by knowing what the available and effective reinforcers are and the behaviors upon which they are contingent. Basically, we are contending that the nature of the reinforcer system and the reinforcement contingencies are crucial determinants of individual and group behavior. Consequently, a description of an individual's or group's reinforcers, and an understanding of the principles by which reinforcers affect behavior, would be expected to yield a great deal of knowledge about individual and group deviant behavior.

Finally, the rationalizations which Cressey identifies with regard to trust violators and the peculiar extensions of "defenses to crimes" or "techniques of neutralization" by which deviant behavior is justified, as identified by Sykes and Matza,[49] may be analyzed as operant behaviors of the escape or avoidance type which are maintained because they have the effect of avoiding or reducing the punishment that comes from social disapproval by oneself as well as by others. We may, therefore, rewrite this proposition to read: IV. *The learning of criminal behavior, including specific techniques, attitudes, and avoidance procedures, is a function of the effective and available reinforcers, and the existing reinforcement contingencies.*

V. "The specific direction of motives and drives is learned from definitions of the legal codes as favorable or unfavorable."

In this proposition, Sutherland appears to be referring, at least in part, to the concept "norm" which may be defined as a statement made by a number of the members of a group, not necessarily all of them, prescribing or proscribing certain behaviors at certain times.[50] We often infer what the norms of a group are by observing reaction to behavior, i.e., the sanctions applied to, or reinforcement and punishment consequences of, such behavior. We may also learn what a group's norms are through verbal or written statements. The individual group member also learns what is and is not acceptable behavior on the basis of verbal statements made by others, as well as through the sanctions (i.e., the reinforcing or aversive stimuli) applied to his behavior (and other norm violators) by others.

Behavior theory specifies the place of normative statements and sanctions in the dynamics of acquiring "conforming" or "normative" behavior. Just as the behavior and even the physical characteristics of the individual may serve discriminative functions, verbal behavior, and this includes normative statements, can be analyzed as S^D's. A normative statement can be analyzed as an S^D indicating that the members of a group ought to behave in a certain way in certain circumstances. Such "normative" behavior would be developed and maintained by social reinforcement. As we observed in the Ayllon-Azrin study[51] of instructions and reinforcement contingencies, such verbal behavior would not maintain any particular class of behaviors if it were not at least occasionally backed by reinforcement consequences. Extending their analysis, an individual would not "conform" to a norm if he did not have a past history of reinforcement for such conforming behavior. This is important, for earlier we stated that we can learn a great deal about a group by knowing what the effective reinforcers are and the behaviors upon which they are contingent. We may now say that we can learn a great deal about an individual's or a group's behavior when we are able to specify, not only what the effective reinforcers are, but also what the rules or norms are by which these reinforcers are applied.[52] For these two types of knowledge will tell us much about the types of behavior that the individual will develop or the types of behaviors that are dominant in a group.

For example, it has often been noted that most official criminal acts are committed by members of minority groups who live in slums. One distinguishing characteristic of a slum is the high level of deprivation of many important social reinforcers. Exacerbating this situation is the fact that these people, in contrast to other groups, lack the behavioral repertoires necessary to produce reinforcement in the prescribed ways. They have not been and are not now adequately reinforced for lawful or normative behavior. And as we know from the Law of Operant Reinforcement, a reinforcer will increase the rate of occurrence of any operant which produces it. Furthermore, we would predict that given a large number of individuals under similar conditions, they are likely to behave in similar ways. Within such groups, many forms of social reinforcement may become contingent upon classes of behaviors which are outside the larger society's normative requirements. Norms and legal codes, as discriminative stimuli, will only control the behavior of those who have experienced the appropriate learning history. If an individual has been, and is, reinforced for such "normative" behavior, that behavior will be maintained in strength. If he has not been, and is not now reinforced for such behaviors they would be weak, if they existed in his repertoire at all. And, importantly, the reinforcement system may shape and maintain another class of behaviors which do result in reinforcement and such behaviors may be considered deviant or criminal by other members of the group. Thus we may formulate this proposition to read:
V. *The specific class of behaviors which are learned and their frequency of occurrence are a function of the reinforcers which are effective and available, and the rules or norms by which these reinforcers are applied.*

VI. "A person becomes delinquent because of an excess of definitions favorable to violation of law over definitions unfavorable to violation of law."

This proposition is generally considered the heart of Sutherland's theory; it is the principle of differential association. It follows directly from proposition V, and we must now refer back to that proposition. In proposition V, the use of the preposition "from" in the phrase, "learned from definitions of the legal codes as favorable or unfavorable," is somewhat misleading. The meaning here is not so much that learning results *from* these definitions as it is that they form part of the *content* of one's learning, determining which direction one's behavior will go in relation to the law, i.e., law-abiding or lawbreaking.

These definitions of the law make lawbreaking seem either appropriate or inappropriate. Those definitions which place lawbreaking in a favorable light in a sense can be seen as essentially norms of evasion and/or norms directly conflicting with conventional norms. They are, as Sykes and Matza and Cressey note, "techniques of neutralization," "rationalizations," or "verbalizations" which make criminal behavior seem "all right" or justified, or which provide defenses against self-reproach and disapproval from others.[53] The principle of negative reinforcement would be of major significance in the acquisition and maintenance of such behaviors.

This analysis suggests that it may not be an "excess" of one kind of definition over another in the sense of a cumulative ratio, but rather in the sense of the relative amount of discriminative stimulus value of one set of verbalizations or normative statements over another. As we suggested in the last section, normative statements are, themselves, behaviors that are a function of reinforcement consequences. They, in turn, may serve as discriminative stimuli for other operant behaviors (verbal and nonverbal). But recall that reinforcement must be forthcoming, at least occasionally, before a verbal statement can continue as a discriminative stimulus. Bear in mind, also, that behavior may produce reinforcing consequences even in the absence of any accompanying verbal statements.

In other terms, a person will become delinquent if the official norms or laws do not perform a discriminative function and thereby control "normative" or conforming behavior. We know from the Law of Differential Reinforcement that that operant which produces the most reinforcement will become dominant if it results in reinforcement. Thus, if lawful behavior did not result in reinforcement, the strength of the behavior would be weakened, and a state of deprivation would result, which would, in turn, increase the probability that other behaviors would be emitted which are reinforced, and such behaviors would be strengthened. And, of course, these behaviors, though common to one or more groups, may be labelled deviant by the larger society. And such behavior patterns, themselves, may acquire conditioned reinforcing value and, subsequently, be enforced by the members of a group by making various forms of social reinforcement, such as social approval, esteem, and status contingent upon that behavior.

The concept "excess" in the statement, "excess of definitions favorable to violation of law," has been particularly resistant to operationalization. A translation of this concept in terms of modern behavior theory would involve the "balance" of reinforcement consequences, positive and negative. The Law of Differential Reinforcement is crucial here. That is, a person would engage in those behaviors for which he had been reinforced most highly in the past. (The reader may recall that in the Ayllon-Azrin study with schizophrenics, it was found that the patients selected and performed those behaviors which provided the most reinforcers when reinforcement was available for more than one response.) Criminal behavior would, then, occur under those conditions where an individual has been most highly reinforced for such behavior, and the aversive consequences contingent upon the behavior have been of such a nature that they do not perform a "punishment function."[54] This leads us to a discussion of proposition VII. But, first, let us reformulate the sixth proposition to read: VI. *Criminal behavior is a function of norms which are discriminative for criminal behavior, the learning of which takes place when such behavior is more highly reinforced than non-criminal behavior.*

VII. "Differential associations may vary in frequency, duration, priority, and intensity."

In terms of our analysis, the concepts frequency, duration, and priority are straightforward enough. The concept *intensity* could be operationalized to designate the number of the individual's positive and negative reinforcers another individual or group controls, as well as the reinforcement value of that individual or group. As previously suggested the group which can mediate the most positive reinforcers and which has the most reinforcement value, as well as access to a larger range of aversive stimuli, will exert the most control over an individual's behavior.

There is a good reason to suspect, however, that Sutherland was not so much referring to differential associations with other persons, as differential associations with criminal *patterns.* If this supposition is correct, then this proposition can be clarified by relating it to differential contingencies of reinforcement rather than differential social associations. From this perspective, the experimental evidence with regard to the various schedules of reinforcement is of major importance. There are three aspects of the schedules of reinforcement which are of particular importance here: (1) the *amount* of reinforcement: the greater the amount of reinforcement, the higher the response rate; (2) the *frequency* of reinforcement which refers to the number of reinforcements per given time period: the shorter the time period between reinforcements, the higher the response rate; and (3) the *probability* of reinforcement which is the reciprocal of responses per reinforcement: the lower the ratio of responses per reinforcement, the higher the rate of response.[55]

Priority, frequency, duration, and intensity of association with criminal persons and groups are important to the extent that they insure that deviant behavior will receive greater amounts of reinforcement at more frequent intervals or with a higher probability than conforming behavior. But the frequency, probability, and amount of reinforcement are the crucial elements. This means that it is the coming under the control of contingencies of reinforcement that selectively produces the criminal definitions and behavior. Consequently, let us rewrite this proposition to read: VII. *The strength of criminal behavior is a direct function of the amount, frequency, and probability of its reinforcement.*

IX. "While criminal behavior is an expression of general needs and values, it is not explained by those general needs and values since noncriminal behavior is an expression of the same needs and values."

In this proposition, Sutherland may have been reacting, at least in part, to the controversy regarding the concept "need." This controversy is now essentially resolved. For, we have finally come to the realization that "needs" are unobservable, hypothetical, fictional inner-causal agents which were usually invented on the spot to provide spurious explanations of some observable behavior. Futhermore, they were inferred from precisely the same behavior they were supposed to explain.

While we can ignore the reference to needs, we must discuss values. Values may be seen as reinforcers which have salience for a number of the members of a group or society. We agree with Sutherland to the extent that he means that the nature of these general reinforcers do not necessarily determine which behavior they will strengthen. Money, or something else of general value in society, will reinforce any behavior that produces it. This reinforcement may depend upon noncriminal behavior, but it also may become contingent upon a set of behaviors that are labelled as criminal. Thus, if Sutherland can be interpreted as meaning that criminal and noncriminal behavior cannot be maintained by the same set of reinforcers, we must disagree. However, it may be that there are certain reinforcing consequences which only criminal behavior will produce, for the behavior finally shaped will depend upon the reinforcer that is effective for the individual. Nevertheless, it is the reinforcement, not the specific nature of the reinforcer, which explains the rate and form of behavior. But since this issue revolves around contingencies of reinforcement which are handled elsewhere, we will eliminate this last proposition.

Concluding Remarks

The purpose of this paper has been the application of the principles of modern behavior theory to Sutherland's differential association theory. While Sutherland's theory has had an enduring effect upon the thinking of students of criminal behavior, it has, till now, undergone no major theoretical revision despite the fact that there has been a steady and cumulative growth in the experimental findings of the processes of learning.

There are three aspects of deviant behavior which we have attempted to deal with simultaneously, but which should be separated. First, how does an individual *become* delinquent, or how does he learn delinquent behavior? Second, what *sustains* this delinquent behavior? We have attempted to describe the ways in which the principles of modern behavior theory are relevant to the development and maintenance of criminal behavior. In the process, we have seen that the principle of differential reinforcement is of crucial importance. But we must also attend to a third question, namely, what sustains the pattern or *contingency* of reinforcement?

TABLE 10.1 *A Differential Association-Reinforcement Theory of Criminal Behavior*

Sutherland's Statements	Reformulated Statements
1. "Criminal behavior is learned." 8. "The process of learning criminal behavior by association with criminal and anti-criminal patterns involves all of the mechanisms that are involved in any other learning."	1. Criminal behavior is learned according to the principles of operant conditioning.
2. "Criminal behavior is learned in interaction with other persons in a process of communication."	2. Criminal behavior is learned both in nonsocial situations that are reinforcing or discriminative and through that social interaction in which the behavior of other persons is reinforcing or discriminative for criminal behavior.
3. "The principal part of the learning of criminal behavior occurs within intimate personal groups."	3. The principal part of the learning of criminal behavior occurs in those groups which comprise the individual's major source of reinforcements.
4. "When criminal behavior is learned, the learning includes (a) techniques of committing the crime, which are sometimes very complicated, sometimes very simple; (b) the specific direction of motives, drives, rationalizations, and attitudes."	4. The learning of criminal behavior, including specific techniques, attitudes, and avoidance procedures, is a function of the effective and available reinforcers, and the existing reinforcement contingencies.
5. "The specific direction of motives and drives is learned from definitions of the legal codes as favorable or unfavorable."	5. The specific class of behaviors which are learned and their frequency of occurrence are a function of the reinforcers which are effective and available, and the rules or norms by which these reinforcers are applied.
6. "A person becomes delinquent because of an excess of definitions favorable to violation of law over definitions unfavorable to violation of law."	6. Criminal behavior is a function of norms which are discriminative for criminal behavior, the learning of which takes place when such behavior is more highly reinforced than noncriminal behavior.
7. "Differential associations may vary in frequency, duration, priority, and intensity."	7. The strength of criminal behavior is a direct function of the amount, frequency, and probability of its reinforcement.
9. "While criminal behavior is an expression of general needs and values, it is not explained by those general needs and values since noncriminal behavior is an expression of the same needs and values."	9. (Omit from theory.)

We only have hinted at some of the possibly important variables. We have mentioned briefly, for example, structural factors such as the level of deprivation of a particular group with regard to important social reinforcers, and the lack of effective reinforcement of "lawful" behavior[56] and the concomitant failure to develop the appropriate behavioral repertoires to produce reinforcement legally.[57] We have also suggested that those behaviors which do result in reinforcement may, themselves, gain reinforcement value and be enforced by the members of the group through the manipulation of various forms of social reinforcement such as social approval and status, contingent upon such behaviors.[58] In short, new norms may develop and these may be termed delinquent by the larger society.

There are many other topics that are of direct relevance to the problem of deviant behavior which we have not been able to discuss given the requirements of space. For instance, no mention has been made of some outstanding research in the area of punishment. This topic is, of course, of prime importance in the area of crime prevention. To illustrate some of this research and its relevance, it has been found experimentally that the amount of behavior suppression produced by response-contingent aversive stimuli is a direct function of the intensity of the aversive stimulus, but that a mild aversive stimulus may produce a dramatic behavior-suppression if it is paired with reinforcement for an alternative and incompatible behavior. Furthermore, it has been discovered that if an aversive stimulus is repeatedly paired with positive reinforcement, and reinforcement is not available otherwise, the aversive stimulus may become a discriminative stimulus (S^D) for reinforcement and, consequently, not decrease the behavior's frequency of occurrence.

There are, in conclusion, numerous criteria that have been used to evaluate theories. One such set is as follows:

1. The amount of empirical support for the theory's basic propositions.
2. The "power" of the theory, i.e., the amount of data that can be derived from the theory's higher-order propositions.
3. The controlling possibilities of the theory, including (a) whether the theory's propositions are, in fact, causal principles, and (b) whether the theory's propositions are stated in such a way that they suggest possible *practical* applications.

What dissatisfaction there has been with differential association can be attributed to its scoring low on these criteria, especially (1) and (3). We submit that the reformulated theory presented here answers some of these problems and better meets each of these criteria. It is our contention, moreover, that the reformulated theory not only specifies the conditions under which criminal behavior is learned, but also some of the conditions under which deviant behavior in general is acquired. Finally, while we have not stated our propositions in strictly axiomatic form, a close examination will reveal that each of the later propositions follow from, modify, or clarify earlier propositions.

Notes

1. By 1960, Cressey had collected a 70-item bibliography on the theory; see Edwin H. Sutherland and Donald R. Cressey, *Principles of Criminology*, 6th ed., Chicago: J. B. Lippincott Co., 1960, p. vi. He has presented an exhaustive review of the mistaken notions, criticisms, attempted reformulations, and empirical tests of the theory contained in a sizable body of literature. Donald R. Cressey, "Epidemiology and Individual Conduct: A Case from Criminology," *Pacific Sociological Review*, 3 (Fall, 1960), pp. 47–58. For more recent literature see Donald R. Cressey, "The Theory of Differential Association: An Introduction," *Social Problems*, 8 (Summer, 1960), pp. 2–5. James F. Short, Jr., "Differential Association as a Hypothesis: Problems of Empirical Testing," *Social Problems*, 8 (Summer, 1960), pp. 14–25. Henry D. McKay, "Differential Association and Crime Prevention: Problems of Utilization," *Social Problems*, 8 (Summer, 1960), pp. 25–37. Albert J. Reiss, Jr., and A. Lewis Rhodes, "An Empirical Test of Differential Association Theory," *The Journal of Research in Crime and Delinquency*, 1 (January, 1964), pp. 5–18. Harwin L. Voss, "Differential Association and Reported Delinquent Behavior: A Replication," *Social Problems*, 12 (Summer, 1964), pp. 78–85. Siri Naess, "Comparing Theories of Criminogenesis," *The Journal of Research in Crime and Delinquency*, 1 (July, 1964), pp. 171–180. C. R. Jeffery, "Criminal Behavior and Learning Theory," *The Journal of Criminal Law, Criminology and Police Science*, 56 (September, 1965), pp. 294–300.

2. The original formal statement appeared in Edwin H. Sutherland, *Principles of Criminology*, 3rd ed., Philadelphia: J. B. Lippincott Co., 1939, pp. 4–8. The terms, "systematic" and "consistency" along with some statements referring to social disorganization and culture conflict were deleted in the revised theory. Two sentences stating that criminal behavior is learned were added and the terms "learned" and "learning" were included in other sentences. The modalities of duration, priority, and intensity were added. The revised theory is in Sutherland and Cressey, *op. cit.*, pp. 77–79. For Cressey's discussion of why he left the theory in its 1947 form see *ibid.*, p. vi.

3. *Ibid.*, pp. 77–80. Edwin H. Sutherland, *White Collar Crime*, New York: Holt, Rinehart and Winston, 1961, pp. 234–256 (originally published 1949). See also Cressey's "Foreword," *ibid.*, p. x.

4. John C. Ball, "Delinquent and Non-Delinquent Attitudes Toward the Prevalence of Stealing," *The Journal of Criminal Law, Criminology and Police Science*, 48 (September–October, 1957), pp. 259–274. James F. Short, "Differential Association and Delinquency," *Social Problems*, 4, (January, 1957), pp. 233–239. Short, "Differential Association with Delinquent Friends and Delinquent Behavior," *Pacific Sociological Review*, 1 (Spring, 1958), pp. 20–25. Short, "Differential Association as a Hypothesis," *op. cit.* Voss, *op. cit.* Donald R. Cressey, "Application and Verification of the Differential Association Theory," *The Journal of Criminal Law, Criminology and Police Science*, 43 (May–June, 1952), pp. 47–50. Cressey, *Other People's Money*, Glencoe, Ill.: The Free Press, 1953, pp. 147–149. Glaser, *op. cit.*, pp. 7–10.

5. Marshall Clinard, *The Black Market*, New York: Rinehart Co., 1952, pp. 285–329. Marshall Clinard, "Rural Criminal Offenders," *American Journal of Sociology*, 50 (July, 1944), pp. 38–45. Edwin M. Lemert, "An Isolation and Closure Theory of Naive Check Forgery," *The Journal of Criminal Law, Criminology and Police Science*, 44, (September–October, 1953), pp. 293–307. Reiss and Rhodes, *op. cit.* Cressey, "Application and Verification of the Differential Association Theory," *op. cit.*, pp. 51–52. Cressey, *Other People's Money, op. cit.*, pp. 149–151. Glaser, *op. cit.*, pp. 12–13.

6. See Daniel Glaser, "Criminality Theories and Behavioral Images," *American Journal of Sociology*, 61 (March, 1956), pp. 433–444. Glaser, "Differential Association and Criminological Prediction," *op. cit.*, pp. 10–13. Naess, *op. cit.*, pp. 174–179.

7. Melvin DeFleur and Richard Quinney, "A Reformulation of Sutherland's Differential Association Theory and a Strategy for Empirical Verification," *Journal of Research in Crime and Delinquency*, 3 (January, 1966), p. 13.

8. Cressey, "Epidemiology and Individual Conduct," *op. cit.*, p. 54.

    9. Sutherland and Cressey, *op. cit.*, p. 80. Albert K. Cohen, Alfred R. Lindesmith, and Karl F. Schuessler (eds.), *The Sutherland Papers*, Bloomington: Indiana University Publications, Social Science Series, No. 15, 1956, pp. 5–42. That Sutherland intended an explanation of the two-fold problem of rates of crime and individual criminal behavior is, of course, the basic point of Cressey's paper, "Epidemiology and Individual Conduct," *op. cit.*

    10. George B. Vold, *Theoretical Criminology*, New York: Oxford University Press, 1958, p. 198.

    11. Cressey, "The Theory of Differential Association," *op. cit.*, p. 5.

    12. Jeffery, *op. cit.*

    13. DeFleur and Quinney, *op. cit.*, p. 3.

    14. *Ibid.*, p. 295.

    15. DeFleur and Quinney, *op. cit.*

    16. Our main concern here, of course, is with the nine statements of the theory as a genetic explanation of the process by which the individual comes to engage in illegal behavior. We do not lose sight of the fact, however, that this must be integrated with explanations of the variation and location of crime.

    17. Cressey, 1960, *op. cit.*, p. 54.

    18. Sutherland and Cressey, *op. cit.*, p. 75.

    19. It should be mentioned at the outset that there is more than one learning theory. The one we will employ is called Behavior Theory. More specifically, it is that variety of behavior theory largely associated with the name of B. F. Skinner. (*Science and Human Behavior*, New York: Macmillan, 1953.) It differs from other learning theories in that it restricts itself to the relations between observable, measurable behavior and observable, measurable conditions. There is nothing in this theory that denies the existence, or importance, or even the inherent interest of the nervous system or brain. However, most behavioral scientists in this area are extremely careful in hypothesizing intervening variables or constructs, whether they are egos, personalities, response sets, or some sort of internal computers. Generally they adopt the position that the only real value of a construct is its ability to improve one's predictions. If it does not, then it must be excluded in accordance with the rule of parsimony.

    20. It has been said by some that a tautology is involved here. But there is nothing tautological about classifying events in terms of their effects. As Skinner, *op. cit.*, pp. 72–73, has noted, this criterion is both empirical and objective. There is only one sure way of telling whether or not a given stimulus event is reinforcing to a given individual under given conditions and that is to make a direct test: observe the frequency of a selected behavior, then make a stimulus event contingent upon it and observe any change in frequency. If there is a change in frequency then we may classify the stimulus as reinforcing to the individual under the stated conditions. Our reasoning would become circular, however, if we went on to assert that a given stimulus strengthens the behavior *because* it is reinforcing. Furthermore, not all stimuli, when presented, will increase the frequency of the behavior which *produced* them. Some stimuli will increase the frequency of the behavior which *removes* them, still others will neither strengthen nor weaken the behavior which produced them. See Robert L. Burgess, Ronald L. Akers, "Are Operant Principles Tautological?" *The Psychological Record*, 16 (July, 1966), pp. 305–312.

    21. N. H. Azrin and D. F. Hake, "Conditioned Punishment," *Journal of the Experimental Analysis of Behavior*, 8 (September, 1965), pp. 279–293.

    22. See Jacob L. Gewirtz and Donald M. Baer, "Deprivation and Satiation of Social Reinforcers as Drive Conditions," *Journal of Abnormal and Social Psychology*, 57, 1958, pp. 165–172.

    23. This seems to be the process involved in learning to become a marihuana user. By successive approximations, the user learns (from others) to close on the appropriate techniques and effects of using marihuana. See Howard S. Becker, *Outsiders*, Glencoe, Ill.: The Free Press, 1963, pp. 41–58.

    24. Cressey encountered this problem in trying to get trust violators to reconstruct past associations. Cressey, *Other People's Money*, op. cit., p. 149.

    25. Arthur Staats, "An Integrated-Functional Learning Approach to Complex Human Behavior," *Technical Report 28*, Contract ONR and Arizona State University, 1965.

26. See, for example, S. W. Bijou and P. T. Sturges, "Positive Reinforcers for Experimental Studies with Children—Consumables and Manipulatables," *Child Development*, 30, 1959, pp. 151–170.

27. J. G. Holland, "Human Vigilance," *Science*, 128, 1959, pp. 61–67; Harold Weiner, "Conditioning History and Human Fixed-Interval Performance," *Journal of the Experimental Analysis of Behavior*, 7 (September, 1964), pp. 383–385.

28. N. H. Azrin and O. R. Lindsley, "The Reinforcement of Cooperation Between Children," *The Journal of Abnormal and Social Psychology*, 52 (January, 1956).

29. Donald J. Cohen, "Justin and His Peers: an Experimental Analysis of a Child's Social World," *Child Development*, 33, 1962.

30. T. Ayllon and J. Michael, "The Psychiatric Nurse as a Behavioral Engineer," *Journal of the Experimental Analysis of Behavior*, 2, 1959, pp. 323–334.

31. There is, of course, no intention on out part to equate "mental" illness or similarly severe behavior problems with criminal behavior. The only connection that we are making is that both may be seen to function according to the same basic behavioral principles and both may be in opposition to established norms.

32. W. Isaacs, J. Thomas, and I. Goldiamond, "Application of Operant Conditioning to Reinstate Verbal Behavior in Psychotics," *Journal of Speech and Disorders*, 25, 1960, pp. 8–12.

33. T. Ayllon and N. Azrin, "The Measurement and Reinforcement of Behavior of Psychotics," *Journal of the Experimental Analysis of Behavior*, 8 (November, 1965), pp. 357–383.

34. *Ibid.*, p. 381.

35. See also J. J. Eysenck (ed.), *Experiments in Behaviour Therapy*, New York: Pergamon Press, The Macmillan Company, 1964. I. Krasner and L. Ullman, *Research in Behavior Modification*, New York: Holt, Rinehart and Winston, 1965. L. Ullman and L. Krasner, *Case Studies in Behavior Modification*, New York: Holt, Rinehart and Winston, 1964.

36. DeFleur and Quinney, *op. cit.*, p. 3.

37. T. Ayllon and N. Azrin, "Reinforcement and Instructions with Mental Patients," *Journal of the Experimental Analysis of Behavior*, 7, 1964, pp. 327–331.

38. Paul E. Secord and Carl W. Backman, *Social Psychology*, New York: McGraw-Hill, 1964.

39. Jeffery, *op. cit.*

40. For some evidence that aggressive behavior may be of a respondent as well as an operant nature, see N. Azrin, R. Hutchinson, and R. McLaughlin, "The Opportunity for Aggression as an Operant Reinforcer during Aversive Stimulation," *Journal of the Experimental Analysis of Behavior*, 8 (May, 1965), pp. 171–180.

41. B. E. Lott and A. J. Lott, "The Formation of Positive Attitudes Toward Group Members," *The Journal of Abnormal and Social Psychology*, 61, 1960, pp. 297–300.

42. Arthur Staats, *Human Learning*, New York: Holt, Rinehart and Winston, 1964, p. 333.

43. Glaser, "Criminality Theories and Behavioral Images," *op. cit.*

44. A. Bandura, D. Ross, and S. Ross, "A Comparative Test of the Status Envy, Social Power and the Secondary Reinforcement Theories of Identification Learning," *Journal of Abnormal and Social Psychology*, 67, 1963, pp. 527–534.

45. Staats, 1964, *op. cit.*, p. 333.

46. D. J. Klaus and R. Glaser, "Increasing Team Proficiency Through Training," Pittsburg: American Institute of Research, 1960.

47. See Robert L. Burgess, "Communication Networks and Behavioral Consequences," forthcoming

48. A central principle underlying this analysis is that reinforcing stimuli, both positive and negative, elicit certain respondents. Unconditioned reinforcers elicit these responses without training, conditioned reinforcers elicit such responses through respondent conditioning. Staats and Staats (*Complex Human Behavior*, New York: Holt, Rinehart and Winston, 1964) have characterized such respondents as "attitude" responses. Thus, a positive reinforcer elicits a positive attitude. Furthermore, these respondents have stimulus characteristics which may become discriminative stimuli setting the occasion for a certain class of operants called "striving" responses for positive

reinforcers and escape and/or avoidance behaviors for negative reinforcers. These respondents and their attendant stimuli may be generalized to other reinforcing stimuli. Thus, striving responses can be seen to generalize to new positive reinforcers since these also will elicit the respondent responses and their characteristic stimuli which have become S^D's for such behavior.

49. Cressey, *Other People's Money*, op. cit., pp. 93–138. G. M. Sykes and David Matza, "Techniques of Neutralization: A Theory of Delinquency," *American Sociological Review*, 22 (December, 1957), pp. 664–670.

50. George C. Homans, *Social Behavior: Its Elementary Forms*, New York: Harcourt, Brace and World, 1961.

51. Ayllon-Azrin, 1964, *op. cit.*

52. Staats and Staats, *op. cit.*

53. Sykes and Matza, *op. cit.*, Cressey, *Other People's Money*, *op. cit.*, pp. 93–138; Donald R. Cressey, "The Differential Association Theory and Compulsive Crimes," *Journal of Criminal Law, Criminology and Police Science*, 45 (May-June, 1954), pp. 29–40; Donald R. Cressey, "Social Psychological Foundations for Using Criminals in the Rehabilitation of Criminals," *Journal of Research in Crime and Delinquency*, 2 (July, 1965), pp. 45–59. See revised proposition IV.

54. This, then, is essentially differential reinforcement as Jeffery presents it. We have attempted to show how this is congruent with differential association. Further, while Jeffery ignores the key concepts of "definitions" and "excess" we have incorporated them into the reformulation. These definitions, viewed as verbalizations, become discriminative stimuli; and "excess" operates to produce criminal behavior in two related ways: (1) verbalizations conducive to law violation have greater discriminative stimulus value than other verbalizations, and (2) criminal behavior has been more highly reinforced and has produced fewer aversive outcomes than has law abiding behavior in the conditioning history of the individual.

55. R. T. Kelleher and L. R. Gollub, "A Review of Positive Conditioned Reinforcement," *Journal of the Experimental Analysis of Behavior* (October, 1962), pp. 543–597. Because the emission of a fixed ratio or variable ratio of responses requires a period of time, the rate of responding will indirectly determine the frequency of reinforcement.

56. Robert K. Merton, *Social Theory and Social Structure*, Glencoe, Ill.: The Free Press, pp. 161–195. For a more complete discussion of social structure in terms relevant to this paper, see Robert L. Burgess and Don Bushell, Jr., *Behavioral Sociology*, Parts IV and V, forthcoming, 1967.

57. *Ibid.*, and Richard A. Cloward, "Illegitimate Means, Anomie, and Deviant Behavior," *American Sociological Review*, 24 (April, 1959), pp. 164–177.

58. Albert K. Cohen, *Delinquent Boys: The Culture of the Gang*, Glencoe, Ill.: The Free Press, 1955.

Social Control Theory and Developmental Life Course Theories

The origins of social control theory can be traced back to French sociologist Émile Durkheim (discussed in Section I, on Anomie-Strain Theory), and also to the Chicago School of Sociology (discussed in Sections II and III, on Social Disorganization Theory and Differential Association/Social Learning Theory) (Cullen, Wright, & Blevins, 2004:4; Kornhauser, 1978:48, 70). As is true for anomie-strain theory and differential association/social learning theory, social control theory is listed by Cullen, Wright and Blevins (2004:3–4) as one of the three core theories that have dominated criminological thinking over the past seventy years. In fact, social control theory has gained steadily in popularity since the mid-1970s, to the point where it is probably now *the* predominant—or at least most popular—criminological theory (Garland, 2001:102; Williams & McShane, 2010:157, 205).

Émile Durkheim felt that individual aspirations and appetites knew no natural bounds—that without civilization, humans would be unrestrained and lacking in moral standards (Durkheim, 1951:246–247; Durkheim, 1964:325–327; Paternoster & Bachman, 2001:73–75). Thus, Durkheim thought that social controls were necessary if individuals were to understand the boundaries between acceptable and unacceptable behavior (Williams & McShane, 2010:150–151). Travis Hirschi—probably the most well known of all social control theorists—premised much of his social bond theory on the Durkheimian notion that many individuals would be inclined to engage in deviance in the absence of effective social controls, or social bonds (Hirschi, 2002:10–11; Paternoster & Bachman, 2001a:77).

As noted in the Introduction to Section II (on Social Disorganization Theory), and again in the introductory comments to Reading 5 (by Shaw and McKay), members of The Chicago School—e.g., Shaw and McKay—were amongst the fore-runners of contemporary social control theory (Cullen et al., 2004:4; Sampson & Groves, 1989:778). Shaw and McKay identified a cause-effect relationship between social disorganization and the breakdown of informal social controls. Youth in the zone in transition were freed from social restraints. They were permitted to gather together on street corners, without adult supervision, which in turn led to the formation of youth gangs and juvenile delinquency. Albert Reiss, who finished his Ph.D at the University of Chicago and who also taught at The Chicago School, published an article in the *American Sociological Review* in 1951, entitled "Delinquency as a Failure of Personal and Social Controls." In this article, Reiss distinguished between personal controls and social controls. He said that personal controls came from within, and consisted of an individual's internalization of (and conformance with) the rules and norms of society (Reiss, 1951:196, 203). Following Shaw and McKay, Reiss emphasized the importance of the informal social controls exercised by parents and by community institutions such as recreational facilities and schools (Reiss, 1951:198–199, 201).

Walter Reckless was another well-known social control theorist from the Chicago School tradition. Reckless did his Ph.D at the University of Chicago during the 1920s, where he worked with Robert Park and Ernest Burgess, the early Chicago School thinkers who developed the concentric zone model upon which Shaw and McKay's social disorganization theory was premised (Lilly, Cullen, & Ball, 2011:96–97). In his "containment theory," Reckless (1973:55–56) talked about inner and outer containment and internal pushes and external pulls. Inner containment included such personal characteristics as self-control, a good self-image, and the ability to tolerate frustration. Outer containment referred to external factors such as family morals and values, plus institutional reinforcement from schools and religious organizations. Internal pushes, which came from within the individual, included restlessness, impatience and anger. These would push individuals toward delinquency. External pulls, such as poverty, unemployment, media influences and delinquent peers, were found in the surrounding environment. These would pull individuals toward delinquency (Reckless, 1973:55–56). According to Reckless's containment theory, if the inner and outer containments were weakened or absent, the internal pushes and external pulls would probably overcome societal restraints and end up pushing or pulling individuals toward delinquency. On the other hand, Reckless felt that if inner and outer containments were functioning as they should, they would have a restraining (or constraining) effect on these internal pushes and external pulls (Williams & McShane, 2010:152).

Travis Hirschi's social bond theory is the most well known of all the social control theories (Williams & McShane, 2010:205; Winfree & Abadinsky, 2010:209). At one point, if the notion of "social control theory" was mentioned, people would automatically think of Hirschi's social bond theory. "A Control Theory of Delinquency," the first reading selection in Section IV, is the second chapter from Travis Hirschi's book, *Causes of Delinquency*. In this reading, Hirschi (2002) sets out the four main elements of the social bond—attachment, commitment, involvement and belief. The second and third readings in Section IV—Terence Thornberry's "Toward an Interactional Theory of Deviance" and Laub and Sampson's "Turning Points in the Life Course"—are both life course (or developmental) theories. However, both employ elements of Travis Hirschi's social bond theory, and both are concerned with the effectiveness of informal social controls over the life course (Sampson & Laub, 1992:73–74; Williams & McShane, 2010:211). Thus, Thornberry's interactional theory and Laub and Sampson's turning points or life course theory have been included in this section on social control theory.

References

Cullen, F. T., Wright, J. P., & Blevins, K. R. (Eds.). (2004). *Taking stock: The status of criminological theory*. New Brunswick, N.J.: Transaction Publishers.

Durkheim, E. (1951). *Suicide: A study in sociology* (J. A. Spaulding, G. Simpson Trans.). Glencoe, Ill.: Free Press.

Durkheim, E. (1964). The dualism of human nature and its social conditions. In K. H. Wolff (Ed.), *Essays on sociology & philosophy by Émile Durkheim et al.* (C. Blend Trans.). (pp. 325–340). New York: Harper & Row.

Garland, D. (2001). *The culture of control: Crime and social order in contemporary society*. Chicago: University of Chicago Press.

Hirschi, T. (2002). *Causes of delinquency*. New Brunswick, N.J.: Transaction Publishers.

Kornhauser, R. R. (1978). *Social sources of delinquency: An appraisal of analytic models*. Chicago: University of Chicago Press.

Lilly, J. R., Cullen, F. T., & Ball, R. A. (2011). *Criminological theory: Context and consequences* (5th ed.). Thousand Oaks: SAGE Publications.

Paternoster, R., & Bachman, R. (2001). Control theories of crime. In R. Paternoster, & R. Bachman (Eds.), *Explaining criminals and crime: Essays in contemporary criminological theory* (pp. 80–191). Los Angeles, Calif.: Roxbury Pub. Co.

Reckless, W. C. (1973). *The crime problem* (5th ed.). New York: Appleton-Century-Crofts.

Reiss, A. J. (1951). Delinquency as the failure of personal and social controls. *American Sociological Review, 16*(2), 196–207.

Sampson, R. J., & Groves, W. B. (1989). Community structure and crime: Testing social-disorganization theory. *American Journal of Sociology, 94*(4), 774–802.

Sampson, R. J., & Laub, J. H. (1992). Crime and deviance in the life course. *Annual Review of Sociology, 18*(1), 63–84.

Williams, F. P., & McShane, M. D. (2010). *Criminological theory* (5th ed.). Upper Saddle River, N.J.: Pearson/Prentice Hall.

Winfree, L. T., & Abadinsky, H. (2010). *Understanding crime: Essentials of criminological theory* (Third ed.). Belmont, CA: Wadsworth, Cengage Learning.

11

A Control Theory of Delinquency

Travis Hirschi spent much of his academic career criticizing sociological explanations of crime and deviance (Lilly, Cullen, & Ball, 2011:110–112; Williams & McShane, 2010:155). In the 1969 edition of his book, *Causes of Delinquency* (and again in the 2002 edition), Hirschi went to great lengths to criticize what he mischaracterized as Robert Merton's "strain theory" and what he inaccurately—and perhaps intentionally—referred to as Edwin Sutherland's "cultural deviance theory" (Bernard, 1995:81–82; Hirschi, 1969:6–15). In their 1977 article entitled "Intelligence and Delinquency: A Revisionist Review," Travis Hirschi and Michael Hindelang complained: "Few groups in American society have been defended more diligently by sociologists against allegations of difference than ordinary delinquents" (Hirschi & Hindelang, 1977:571). In his 1980 critique of labelling theory, Hirschi expended considerable effort challenging the 1938 symbolic interactionist work of Frank Tannenbaum (Hirschi, 1980:271–278)—a work that was actually published several decades before the term labelling theory even appeared on the horizon. In their 1990 book, *A General Theory of Crime*, Michael Gottfredson and Travis Hirschi lamented that: "Criminology is taught in American universities today mainly under the auspices of departments of sociology." Gottfredson and Hirschi went on to complain that sociology had "claimed criminology as a subfield for most of the twentieth century," before they attacked Merton's anomie-strain theory and social disorganization theory (Gottfredson & Hirschi, 1990:75).

Despite his persistent assaults on sociological explanations of crime and deviance, Travis Hirschi in fact completed his Ph.D in Sociology at the University of California at Berkeley, and was a Sociology professor for many years (Mutchnick,

Martin, & Austin, 2009:285–286). In "A Control Theory of Delinquency" (the first reading in Section IV), in which he sets out his social bond theory, Hirschi clearly acknowledges the contributions of the French sociologist Émile Durkheim, as well as the influence of Chicago School sociologists such as Albert Reiss and Walter Reckless (2002:4, 16–19). In later years, Hirschi (reluctantly) admitted that he was also influenced by Chicago School perspectives regarding social disorganization and the breakdown of informal social controls (Williams & McShane, 2010:155). Indeed, Hirschi's social bond theory was clearly rooted in Durkheim's sociologically-driven notions of social integration and the "social bonds" that attach individuals to society (Durkheim, 1951:214; Lilly et al., 2011:90–91).

Travis Hirschi's social bond theory consists of four elements—attachment, commitment, involvement and belief. They can be summarized as follows:

- Attachment refers to "the attachment of the individual to others"—to parents, schoolteachers and other significant role models (Hirschi, 2002:18; Williams & McShane, 2010:155). The individual identifies with and respects these conventional role models, and at the same time, values their opinions and seeks their respect.
- Commitment means commitment to conventional activities, such as getting good grades at school, obtaining a higher level of education, finding a good job or career, and maintaining a good reputation (Hirschi, 2002:20–21; Lilly et al., 2011:116–117). If an individual has invested a lot of time and energy in social commitments such as these, then he or she has something meaningful to lose by engaging in delinquency.
- Involvement means being involved in conventional, pro-social activities, for example, recreation, sports, pursuing a hobby, or doing homework. In essence, this comes down to the notion that "idle hands are the devil's workshop"—if you are busy in the evening doing homework or playing organized sports, then you do not have time to engage in delinquent behavior (Hirschi, 2002:22; Winfree & Abadinsky, 2010:206).
- Belief refers to belief in the law and conventional norms, and respect for authority. This relates to the issue of morality, the development of a social conscience, and the individual being able to distinguish right from wrong (T. Hirschi, 2002:23–26; Williams & McShane, 2010:155; Winfree & Abadinsky, 2010:206).

Along with Akers' social learning theory (discussed in Section III), Travis Hirschi's social bond theory has been one of the most thoroughly tested sociological explanations of crime and deviance (Akers & Sellers, 2009:132–134; Lilly et al., 2011:119–121). While the results have at times been "mixed," social bond theory still fares reasonably well in empirical testing when compared to many other criminological theories (Lilly et al., 2011:119–121; Winfree & Abadinsky, 2010:210–212). Social bond theory has certainly had a significant impact on the development of intervention programs, such as the Seattle Social Development Project (which was designed to promote commitment to education) (Lilly et al., 2011:136), the Police Athletic League (intended to facilitate non-confrontational social bonding between police officers and youth), and Drug Abuse Resistance Education (which focuses on "attachments to police," involvement "in conventional activities," and the "development of pro-social beliefs") (Winfree & Abadinsky, 2010:217). In addition, elements of Hirschi's social bond theory have found their way into any number of other theories, including (but not limited to) Agnew's (1985) general strain theory, Thornberry's interactional (1987) theory, and Laub and Sampson's (1993) turning points theory.

References

Agnew, R. (1985). A revised strain theory of delinquency. *Social Forces, 64*(1), 151–167.

Akers, R. L., & Sellers, C. S. (2009). *Criminological theories: Introduction, evaluation, and application* (5th , New ed.). New York: Oxford University Press.

Bernard, T. J. (1995). Merton versus Hirschi: Who is faithful to Durkheim's heritage? In F. Adler, W. S. Laufer & R. K. Merton (Eds.), *The legacy of anomie theory* (pp. 81–90). New Brunswick, U.S.A.: Transaction Publishers.

Durkheim, É. (1951). *Suicide: A study in sociology* (J. A. Spaulding, G. Simpson Trans.). Glencoe, Ill.: Free Press.

Gottfredson, M. R., & Hirschi, T. (1990). *A general theory of crime.* Stanford, Calif.: Stanford University Press.

Hirschi, T. (1969). *Causes of delinquency.* Berkeley: University of California Press.

Hirschi, T. (1980). Labelling theory and juvenile delinquency: An assessment of the evidence. In W. R. Gove (Ed.), *The labelling of deviance: Evaluating a perspective* (2nd ed., pp. 271–293). Beverly Hills, Calif.: Sage Publications.

Hirschi, T. (2002). *Causes of delinquency.* New Brunswick, N.J.: Transaction Publishers.

Hirschi, T., & Hindelang, M. J. (1977). Intelligence and delinquency: A revisionist review. *American Sociological Review, 42*(4), 571–586.

Laub, J. H., & Sampson, R. J. (1993). Turning points in the life course: Why change matters to the study of crime. *Criminology, 31*(3), 301–325.

Lilly, J. R., Cullen, F. T., & Ball, R. A. (2011). *Criminological theory: Context and consequences* (5th ed.). Thousand Oaks: SAGE Publications.

Mutchnick, R. J., Martin, R., & Austin, T. W. (2009). *Criminological thought: Pioneers past and present.* Upper Saddle River, NJ: Prentice Hall.

Thornberry, T. (1987). Toward an interactional theory of delinquency. *Criminology, 25*(4), 863–891.

Williams, F. P., & McShane, M. D. (2010). *Criminological theory* (5th ed.). Upper Saddle River, N.J.: Pearson/Prentice Hall.

Winfree, L. T., & Abadinsky, H. (2010). *Understanding crime: Essentials of criminological theory* (Third ed.). Belmont, CA: Wadsworth, Cengage Learning.

A Control Theory of Delinquency

TRAVIS HIRSCHI

> "The more weakened the groups to which [the individual] belongs, the less he depends on them, the more he consequently depends only on himself and recognizes no other rules of conduct than what are founded on his private interests."[1]

Control theories assume that delinquent acts result when an individual's bond to society is weak or broken. Since these theories embrace two highly complex concepts, the *bond* of the individual to *society*, it is not surprising that they have at one time or another formed the basis of explanations of most forms of aberrant or unusual behavior. It is also not surprising that control theories have described the elements of the bond to society in many ways, and that they have focused on a variety of units as the point of control.

I begin with a classification and description of the elements of the bond to conventional society. I try to show how each of these elements is related to delinquent behavior and how they are related to each other. I then turn to the question of specifying the unit to which the person is presumably more or less tied, and to the question of the adequacy of the motivational force built into the explanation of delinquent behavior.

Elements of the Bond

Attachment

In explaining conforming behavior, sociologists justly emphasize sensitivity to the opinion of others.[2] Unfortunately, they tend to suggest that man is sensitive to the opinion of others and thus exclude sensitivity from their explanations of deviant behavior. In explaining deviant behavior, psychologists, in contrast, emphasize insensitivity to the opinion of others.[3] Unfortunately, they too tend to ignore variation, and, in addition, they tend to tie sensitivity inextricably to other variables, to make it part of a syndrome or "type," and thus seriously to reduce its value as an explanatory concept. The psychopath is characterized only in part by "deficient attachment to or affection for others, a failure to respond to the ordinary motivations founded in respect or regard for one's fellows";[4] he is also characterized by such things as "excessive aggressiveness," "lack of superego control," and "an infantile level of response."[5] Unfortunately, too, the behavior that psychopathy is used to explain often becomes part of the *definition* of psychopathy. As a result,

Reprinted by permission from *Causes of Delinquency*, edited by Travis Hirschi (2002).

in Barbara Wootton's words: "[The psychopath] is . . . *par excellence,* and without shame or qualification, the model of the circular process by which mental abnormality is inferred from anti-social behavior while anti-social behavior is explained by mental abnormality."[6]

The problems of diagnosis, tautology, and name-calling are avoided if the dimensions of psychopathy are treated as causally and therefore problematically interrelated, rather than as logically and therefore necessarily bound to each other. In fact, it can be argued that all of the characteristics attributed to the psychopath follow from, are effects of, his lack of attachment to others. To say that to lack attachment to others is to be free from moral restraints is to use lack of attachment to explain the guiltlessness of the psychopath, the fact that he apparently has no conscience or superego. In this view, lack of attachment to others is not merely a symptom of psychopathy, it *is* psychopathy; lack of conscience is just another way of saying the same thing; and the violation of norms is (or may be) a consequence.

For that matter, given that man is an animal, "impulsivity" and "aggressiveness" can also be seen as natural consequences of freedom from moral restraints. However, since the view of man as endowed with natural propensities and capacities like other animals is peculiarly unpalatable to sociologists, we need not fall back on such a view to explain the amoral man's aggressiveness.[7] The process of becoming alienated from others often involves or is based on active interpersonal conflict. Such conflict could easily supply a reservoir of *socially derived* hostility sufficient to account for the aggressiveness of those whose attachments to others have been weakened.

Durkheim said it many years ago: "We are moral beings to the extent that we are social beings."[8] This may be interpreted to mean that we are moral beings to the extent that we have "internalized the norms" of society. But what does it mean to say that a person has internalized the norms of society? The norms of society are by definition shared by the members of society. To violate a norm is, therefore, to act contrary to the wishes and expectations of other people. If a person does not care about the wishes and expectations of other people—that is, if he is insensitive to the opinion of others—then he is to that extent not bound by the norms. He is free to deviate.

The essence of internalization of norms, conscience, or superego thus lies in the attachment of the individual to others.[9] This view has several advantages over the concept of internalization. For one, explanations of deviant behavior based on attachment do not beg the question, since the extent to which a person is attached to others can be measured independently of his deviant behavior. Furthermore, change or variation in behavior is explainable in a way that it is not when notions of internalization or superego are used. For example, the divorced man is more likely after divorce to commit a number of deviant acts, such as suicide or forgery. If we explain these acts by reference to the superego (or internal control), we are forced to say that the man "lost his conscience" when he got a divorce; and, of course, if he remarries, we have to conclude that he gets his conscience back.

This dimension of the bond to conventional society is encountered in most social control-oriented research and theory. F. Ivan Nye's "internal control" and "indirect control" refer to the same element, although we avoid the problem of explaining changes over time by locating the "conscience" in the bond to others rather than making it part of the personality.[10] Attachment to others is just one aspect of Albert J. Reiss's "personal controls"; we avoid his problems of tautological empirical *observations* by making the relationship between attachment and delinquency problematic rather than definitional.[11] Finally, Scott Briar and Irving Piliavin's "commitment" or "stake in conformity" subsumes attachment, as their discussion illustrates, although the terms they use are more closely associated with the next element to be discussed.[12]

Commitment

"Of all passions, that which inclineth men least to break the laws, is fear. Nay, excepting some generous natures, it is the only thing, when there is the appearance of profit or pleasure by breaking the laws, that makes men keep them."[13] Few would deny that men on occasion obey the rules simply from fear of the consequences. This rational component in conformity we label commitment. What does it mean to say that a person is committed to conformity? In Howard S. Becker's formulation it means the following:

> First, the individual is in a position in which his decision with regard to some particular line of action has consequences for other interests and activities not necessarily [directly] related to it. Second, he has placed himself in that position by his own prior actions. A third element is present though so obvious as not to be apparent: the committed person must be aware [of these other interests] and must recognize that his decision in this case will have ramifications beyond it.[14]

The idea, then, is that the person invests time, energy, himself, in a certain line of activity—say, getting an education, building up a business, acquiring a reputation for virtue. When or whenever he considers deviant behavior, he must consider the costs of this deviant behavior, the risk he runs of losing the investment he has made in conventional behavior.

If attachment to others is the sociological counterpart of the superego or conscience, commitment is the counterpart of the ego or common sense. To the person committed to conventional lines of action, risking one to ten years in prison for a ten-dollar holdup is stupidity, because to the committed person the costs and risks obviously exceed ten dollars in value. (To the psychoanalyst, such an act exhibits failure to be governed by the "reality-principle.") In the sociological control theory, it can be and is generally assumed that the decision to commit a criminal act may well be rationally determined—that the actor's decision was not irrational given the risks and costs he faces. Of course, as Becker points out, if the actor is capable of in some sense calculating the costs of a line of action, he is also capable of calculational errors: ignorance and error return, in the control theory, as possible explanations of deviant behavior.

The concept of commitment assumes that the organization of society is such that the interests of most persons would be endangered if they were to engage in criminal acts. Most people, simply by the process of living in an organized society, acquire goods, reputations, prospects that they do not want to risk losing. These accumulations are society's insurance that they will abide by the rules. Many hypotheses about the antecedents of delinquent behavior are based on this premise. For example, Arthur L. Stinchcombe's hypothesis that "high school rebellion . . . occurs when future status is not clearly related to present performance"[15] suggests that one is committed to conformity not only by what one has but also by what one hopes to obtain. Thus "ambition" and/or "aspiration" play an important role in producing conformity. The person becomes committed to a conventional line of action, and he is therefore committed to conformity.

Most lines of action in a society are of course conventional. The clearest examples are educational and occupational careers. Actions thought to jeopardize one's chances in these areas are presumably avoided. Interestingly enough, even nonconventional commitments may operate to produce conventional conformity. We are told, at least, that boys aspiring to careers in the rackets or professional thievery are judged by their "honesty" and "reliability"—traits traditionally in demand among seekers of office boys.[16]

Involvement

Many persons undoubtedly owe a life of virtue to a lack of opportunity to do otherwise. Time and energy are inherently limited: "Not that I would not, if I could, be both handsome and fat and well dressed, and a great athlete, and make a million a year, be a wit, a bon vivant, and a lady killer, as well as a philosopher, a philanthropist, a statesman, warrior, and African explorer, as well as a 'tone-poet' and saint. But the thing is simply impossible."[17] The things that William James here says he would like to be or do are all, I suppose, within the realm of conventionality, but if he were to include illicit actions he would still have to eliminate some of them as simply impossible.

Involvement or engrossment in conventional activities is thus often part of a control theory. The assumption, widely shared, is that a person may be simply too busy doing conventional things to find time to engage in deviant behavior. The person involved in conventional activities is tied to appointments, deadlines, working hours, plans, and the like, so the opportunity to commit deviant acts rarely arises. To the extent that he is engrossed in conventional activities, he cannot even think about deviant acts, let alone act out his inclinations.[18]

This line of reasoning is responsible for the stress placed on recreational facilities in many programs to reduce delinquency, for much of the concern with the high school dropout, and for the idea that boys should be drafted into the Army to keep them out of trouble. So obvious and persuasive is the idea that involvement in conventional activities is a major deterrent to delinquency that it was accepted even by Sutherland: "In the general area of juvenile delinquency it is probable that the most significant difference between juveniles who engage in delinquency and those who do not is that the latter are provided abundant opportunities of a conventional type for satisfying their recreational interests, while the former lack those opportunities or facilities."[19]

The view that "idle hands are the devil's workshop" has received more sophisticated treatment in recent sociological writings on delinquency. David Matza and Gresham M. Sykes, for example, suggest that delinquents have the values of a leisure class, the same values ascribed by Veblen to *the* leisure class: a search for kicks, disdain of work, a desire for the big score, and acceptance of aggressive toughness as proof of masculinity.[20] Matza and Sykes explain delinquency by reference to this system of values, but they note that adolescents at all class levels are "to some extent" members of a leisure class, that they "move in a limbo between earlier parental domination and future integration with the social structure through the bonds of work and marriage."[21] In the end, then, the leisure of the adolescent produces a set of values, which, in turn, leads to delinquency.

Belief

Unlike the cultural deviance theory, the control theory assumes the existence of a common value system within the society or group whose norms are being violated. If the deviant is committed to a value system different from that of conventional society, there is, within the context of the theory, nothing to explain. The question is, "Why does a man violate the rules in which he believes?" It is not, "Why do men differ in their beliefs about what constitutes good and desirable conduct?" The person is assumed to have been socialized (perhaps imperfectly) into the group whose rules he is violating; deviance is not a question of one group imposing its rules on the members of another group. In other words, we not only assume the deviant *has* believed the rules, we assume he believes the rules even as he violates them.

How can a person believe it is wrong to steal at the same time he is stealing? In the strain theory, this is not a difficult problem. (In fact, the strain theory was devised specifically to deal with this question.) The motivation to deviance adduced by the strain theorist is so strong that we can well understand the deviant act even assuming the deviator believes strongly that it is wrong.[22] However, given the control theory's assumptions about motivation, if both the deviant and the nondeviant believe the deviant act is wrong, how do we account for the fact that one commits it and the other does not?

Control theories have taken two approaches to this problem. In one approach, beliefs are treated as mere words that mean little or nothing if the other forms of control are missing. "Semantic dementia," the dissociation between rational faculties and emotional control which is said to be characteristic of the psychopath, illustrates this way of handling the problem.[23] In short, beliefs, at least insofar as they are expressed in words, drop out of the picture; since they do not differentiate between deviants and non-deviants, they are in the same class as "language" or any other characteristic common to all members of the group. Since they represent no real obstacle to the commission of delinquent acts, nothing need be said about how they are handled by those committing such acts. The control theories that do not mention beliefs (or values), and many do not, may be assumed to take this approach to the problem.

The second approach argues that the deviant rationalizes his behavior so that he can at once violate the rule and maintain his belief in it. Donald R. Cressey has advanced this argument with respect to embezzlement,[24] and Sykes and Matza have advanced it with respect to delinquency.[25] In both Cressey's and Sykes and Matza's treatments, these rationalizations (Cressey calls them "verbalizations," Sykes and Matza term them "techniques of neutralization") occur prior to the commission of the deviant act. If the neutralization is successful, the person is free to commit the act(s) in question. Both in Cressey and in Sykes and Matza, the strain that prompts the effort at neutralization also provides the motive force that results in the subsequent deviant act. Their theories are thus, in this sense, strain theories. Neutralization is difficult to handle within the context of a theory that adheres closely to control theory assumptions, because in the control theory there is no special motivational force to account for the neutralization. This difficulty is especially noticeable in Matza's later treatment of this topic, where the motivational component, the "will to delinquency" appears *after* the moral vacuum has been created by the techniques of neutralization.[26] The question thus becomes: Why neutralize?

In attempting to solve a strain theory problem with control theory tools, the control theorist is thus led into a trap. He cannot answer the crucial question. The concept of neutralization assumes the existence of moral obstacles to the commission of deviant acts. In order plausibly to account for a deviant act, it is necessary to generate motivation to deviance that is at least equivalent in force to the resistance provided by these moral obstacles. However, if the moral obstacles are removed, neutralization and special motivation are no longer required. We therefore follow the implicit logic of control theory and remove these moral obstacles by hypothesis. Many persons do not have an attitude of respect toward the rules of society; many persons feel no moral obligation to conform regardless of personal advantage. Insofar as the values and beliefs of these persons are consistent with their feelings, and there should be a tendency toward consistency, neutralization is unnecessary; it has already occurred.

Does this merely push the question back a step and at the same time produce conflict with the assumption of a common value system? I think not. In the first place, we do not assume, as does Cressey, that neutralization occurs in order to make a specific criminal act possible.[27] We do not assume, as do Sykes and Matza, that neutralization occurs to make many delinquent acts possible. We do not assume, in other words, that the person constructs a system of rationalizations in order to justify commission of acts he *wants* to commit. We assume, in contrast, that the beliefs that free a man to commit deviant acts are *unmotivated* in the sense that he does not construct or adopt them in order to facilitate the attainment of illicit ends. In the second place, we do not assume, as does Matza, that "delinquents concur in the conventional assessment of delinquency."[28] We assume, in contrast, that there is *variation* in the extent to which people believe they should obey the rules of society, and, furthermore, that the less a person believes he should obey the rules, the more likely he is to violate them.[29]

In chronological order, then, a person's beliefs in the moral validity of norms are, for no teleological reason, weakened. The probability that he will commit delinquent acts is therefore increased. When and if he commits a delinquent act, we may justifiably use the weakness of his beliefs in explaining it, but no special motivation is required to explain either the weakness of his beliefs or, perhaps, his delinquent act.

The keystone of this argument is of course the assumption that there is variation in belief in the moral validity of social rules. This assumption is amenable to direct empirical test and can thus survive at least until its first confrontation with data. For the present, we must return to the idea of a common value system with which this section was begun.

The idea of a common (or, perhaps better, a single) value system is consistent with the fact, or presumption, of variation in the strength of moral beliefs. We have not suggested that delinquency is based on beliefs counter to conventional morality; we have not suggested that delinquents do not believe delinquent acts are wrong. They may well believe these acts are wrong, but the meaning and efficacy of such beliefs are contingent upon other beliefs and, indeed, on the strength of other ties to the conventional order.[30]

Relations Among the Elements

In general, the more closely a person is tied to conventional society in any of these ways, the more closely he is likely to be tied in the other ways. The person who is attached to conventional people is, for example, more likely to be involved in conventional activities and to accept conventional notions of desirable conduct. Of the six possible combinations of elements, three seem particularly important and will therefore be discussed in some detail.

Attachment and Commitment

It is frequently suggested that attachment and commitment (as the terms are used here) tend to vary inversely. Thus, according to delinquency research, one of the lower-class adolescent's "problems" is that he is unable to sever ties to parents and peers, ties that prevent him from devoting sufficient time and energy to educational and occupational aspirations. His attachments are thus seen as getting in the way of conventional commitments.[31] According to stratification research, the lower-class boy who breaks free from these attachments is more likely to be upwardly mobile.[32] Both research traditions thus suggest that those bound to *conformity* for instrumental reasons are less likely to be bound to conformity by emotional ties to conventional others. If the unattached compensate for lack of attachment by commitment to achievement, and if the uncommitted make up for their lack of commitment by becoming more attached to persons, we could conclude that neither attachment nor commitment will be related to delinquency.

Actually, despite the evidence apparently to the contrary, I think it safe to assume that attachment to conventional others and commitment to achievement tend to vary together. The common finding that middle-class boys are likely to choose instrumental values over those of family and friendship while the reverse is true of lower-class boys cannot, I think, be properly interpreted as meaning that middle-class boys are less attached than lower-class boys to their parents and peers. The zero-sum methodological model that produces such findings is highly likely to be misleading.[33] Also, although many of the characteristics of the upwardly mobile alluded to by Seymour M. Lipset and Reinhard Bendix could be accounted for as consequences rather than causes of mobility, a methodological critique of these studies is not necessary to conclude that we may expect to find a positive relation between attachment and commitment in the data to be presented here. The present study and the one study Lipset and Bendix cite as disagreeing with their general conclusion that the upwardly mobile come from homes in which interpersonal relations were unsatisfactory are both based on high school samples.[34] As Lipset and Bendix note, such studies necessarily focus on aspirations rather than actual mobility. For the present, it seems, we must choose between studies based on hopes for the occupational future and those based on construction or reconstruction of the familial past. Interestingly enough, the former are at least as likely to be valid as the latter.

Commitment and Involvement

Delinquent acts are events. They occur at specific points in space and time. For a delinquent act to occur, it is necessary, as is true of all events, for a series of causal chains to converge at a given moment in time. Events are difficult to predict, and specification of some of the conditions necessary for them to occur often leaves a large residue of indeterminacy. For example, to say that a boy is free of bonds to conventional society is not to say that he will necessarily commit delinquent acts; he may and he may not. All we can say with certainty is that he is *more likely* to commit delinquent acts than the boy strongly tied to conventional society.

It is tempting to make a virtue of this defect and espouse "probabilistic theory," since it, and it alone, is consistent with "the facts."[35] Nevertheless, this temptation should be resisted. The primary virtue of control theory is not that it relies on conditions that make delinquency possible while other theories rely on conditions that make delinquency necessary. On the contrary, with respect to their logical framework, these theories are superior to control theory, and, if they were as adequate empirically as control theory, we should not hesitate to advocate their adoption in preference to control theory.

But they are not as adequate, and we must therefore seek to reduce the indeterminacy within control theory. One area of possible development is with respect to the link between elements of the bond affecting the probability that one will yield to temptation and those affecting the probability that one will be exposed to temptation.

The most obvious link in this connection is between educational and occupational aspirations (commitment) and involvement in conventional activities. We can attempt to show how commitment limits one's opportunities to commit delinquent acts and thus get away from the assumption implicit in many control theories that such opportunities are simply randomly distributed through the population in question.

Attachment and Belief

That there is a more or less straightforward connection between attachment to others and belief in the moral validity of rules appears evident. The link we accept here and which we shall attempt to document is described by Jean Piaget:

> It is not the obligatory character of the rule laid down by an individual that makes us respect this individual, it is the respect we feel for the individual that makes us regard as obligatory the rule he lays down. The appearance of the sense of duty in a child thus admits of the simplest explanation, namely that he receives commands from older children (in play) and from adults (in life), and that he respects older children and parents.[36]

In short, "respect is the source of law."[37] Insofar as the child respects (loves and fears) his parents, and adults in general, he will accept their rules. Conversely, insofar as this respect is undermined, the rules will tend to lose their obligatory character. It is assumed that belief in the obligatory character of rules will to some extent maintain its efficacy in producing conformity even if the respect which brought it into being no longer exists. It is also assumed that attachment may produce conformity even in the face of beliefs favorable to nonconformity. In short, these two sources of moral behavior, although highly and complexly related, are assumed to have an independent effect that justifies their separation.

The Bond to What?

Control theorists sometimes suggest that attachment to any object outside one's self, whether it be the home town, the starry heavens, or the family dog, promotes moral behavior.[38] Although it seems obvious that some objects are more important than others and that the important objects must be identified if the elements of the bond are to produce the consequences suggested by the theory, a priori rankings of the objects of attachment have proved peculiarly unsatisfactory. Durkheim, for example, concludes that the three groups to whom attachment is most important in producing morality are the family, the nation, and humanity. He further concludes that, of these, the nation is most important.[39] All of which, given much contemporary thinking on the virtues of patriotism,[40] illustrates rather well the difficulty posed by such questions as: Which is more important in the control of delinquency, the father or the mother, the family or the school?

Although delinquency theory in general has taken a stand on many questions about the relative importance of institutions (for example, that the school is more important than the family), control theory has remained decidedly eclectic, partly because each element of the bond directs attention to different institutions. For these reasons, I shall treat specification of the units of attachment as a problem in the empirical interpretation of control theory, and not attempt at this point to say which should be more or less important.

Where Is the Motivation?

The most disconcerting question the control theorist faces goes something like this: "Yes, but *why* do they do it?" In the good old days, the control theorist could simply strip away the "veneer of civilization" and expose man's "animal impulses" for all to see. These impulses appeared to him (and apparently to his audience) to provide a plausible account of the motivation to crime and delinquency. His argument was *not* that delinquents and criminals alone are animals, but that we are all animals, and thus all naturally capable of committing criminal acts. It took no great study to reveal that children, chickens, and dogs occasionally assault and steal from their fellow creatures; that children, chickens, and dogs also behave for relatively long periods in a perfectly moral manner. Of course the acts of chickens and dogs are not "assault" or "theft," and such behavior is not "moral"; it is simply the behavior of a chicken or a dog. The chicken stealing corn from his neighbor knows nothing of the moral law; he does not *want* to violate rules; he wants merely to eat corn. The dog maliciously destroying a pillow or feloniously assaulting another dog is the moral equal of the chicken. No motivation to deviance is required to explain his acts. So, too, no special motivation to crime within the human animal was required to explain his criminal acts.

Times changed. It was no longer fashionable (within sociology, at least) to refer to animal impulses. The control theorist tended more and more to deemphasize the motivational component of his theory. He might refer in the beginning to "universal human needs," or some such, but the driving force behind crime and delinquency was rarely alluded to. At the same time, his explanations of crime and delinquency increasingly left the reader uneasy. What, the reader asked, is the control theorist assuming? Albert K. Cohen and James F. Short answer the question this way:

> . . . it is important to point out one important limitation of both types of theory. They [culture conflict and social disorganization theories] are both *control* theories in the sense that they explain delinquency in terms of the *absence* of effective controls. They appear, therefore, to imply a model of motivation that assumes that the impulse to delinquency is an inherent characteristic of young people and does not itself need to be explained; it is something that erupts when the lid—i.e., internalized cultural restraints or external authority—is off.[41]

There are several possible and I think reasonable reactions to this criticism. One reaction is simply to acknowledge the assumption, to grant that one is assuming what control theorists have always assumed about the motivation to crime—that it is constant across persons (at least within the system in question): "There is no reason to assume that only those who finally commit a deviant act usually have the impulse to do so. It is much more likely that most people experience deviant impulses frequently. At least in fantasy, people are much more deviant than they appear."[42] There is certainly nothing wrong with *making* such an assumption. We are free to assume anything we wish to assume; the truth of our theory is presumably subject to empirical test.[43]

A second reaction, involving perhaps something of a quibble, is to defend the logic of control theory and to deny the alleged assumption. We can say the fact that control theory suggests the absence of something causes delinquency is not a proper criticism, since negative relations have as much claim to scientific acceptability as do positive relations.[44] We can also say that the present theory does not impute an inherent impulse *to delinquency* to anyone.[45] That, on the contrary, it denies the necessity of such an imputation: "The desires, and other passions of man, are in themselves no sin. No more are the actions, that proceed from those passions, till they know a law that forbids them."[46]

A third reaction is to accept the criticism as valid, to grant that a complete explanation of delinquency would provide the necessary impetus, and proceed to construct an explanation of motivation consistent with control theory. Briar and Piliavin provide situational motivation: "We assume these acts are prompted by short-term situationally induced desires experienced by all boys to obtain valued goods, to portray courage in the presence of, or be loyal to peers, to strike out at someone who is disliked, or simply to 'get kicks.' "[47] Matza, too, agrees that delinquency cannot be explained simply by removal of controls:

Delinquency is only epiphenomenally action. . . . [It] is essentially infraction. It is rule-breaking behavior performed by juveniles aware that they are violating the law and of the nature of their deed, and made permissible by the neutralization of infractions [!] elements. Thus, Cohen and Short are fundamentally right when they insist that social control theory is incomplete unless it provides an impetus by which the potential for delinquency may be realized.[48]

The impetus Matza provides is a "feeling of desperation," brought on by the "mood of fatalism," "the experience of seeing one's self as effect" rather than cause. In a situation in which manliness is stressed, being pushed around leads to the mood of fatalism, which in turn produces a sense of desperation. In order to relieve his desperation, in order to cast off the mood of fatalism, the boy "makes things happen"—he commits delinquent acts.[49]

There are several additional accounts of "why they do it" that are to my mind persuasive and at the same time generally compatible with control theory.[50] But while all of these accounts may be compatible with control theory, they are by no means deducible from it. Furthermore, they rarely impute built-in, unusual motivation to the delinquent: he is attempting to satisfy the same desires, he is reacting to the same pressures as other boys (as is clear, for example, in the previous quotation from Briar and Piliavin). In other words, if included, these accounts of motivation would serve the same function in the theory that "animal impulses" traditionally served: they might add to its persuasiveness and plausibility, but they would add little else, since they do not differentiate delinquents from nondelinquents.

In the end, then, control theory remains what it has always been: a theory in which deviation is not problematic. The question "Why do they do it?" is simply not the question the theory is designed to answer. The question is, "Why don't we do it?" There is much evidence that we would if we dared.

Notes

1. Émile Durkheim, *Suicide*, trans. John A. Spaulding and George Simpson (New York: The Free Press, 1951), p. 209.

2. Books have been written on the increasing importance of interpersonal sensitivity in modern life. According to this view, controls from within have become less important than controls from without in producing conformity. Whether or not this observation is true as a description of historical trends, it is true that interpersonal sensitivity has become more important in *explaining* conformity. Although logically it should also have become more important in explaining nonconformity, the opposite has been the case, once again showing that Cohen's observation that an explanation of conformity should be an explanation of deviance cannot be translated as "an explanation of conformity has to be an explanation of deviance." For the view that interpersonal sensitivity currently plays a greater role than formerly in producing conformity, see William J. Goode, "Norm Commitment and Conformity to Role-Status Obligations," *American Journal of Sociology*, LXVI (1960), 246–258. And, of course, also see David Riesman, Nathan Glazer, and Reuel Denney, *The Lonely Crowd* (Garden City, New York: Doubleday, 1950), especially Part I.

3. The literature on psychopathy is voluminous. See William McCord and Joan McCord, *The Psychopath* (Princeton: D. Van Nostrand, 1964).

4. John M. Martin and Joseph P. Fitzpatrick, *Delinquent Behavior* (New York: Random House, 1964), p. 130.

5. *Ibid.* For additional properties of the psychopath, see McCord and McCord, *The Psychopath*, pp. 1–22.

6. Barbara Wootton, *Social Science and Social Pathology* (New York: Macmillan, 1959), p. 250.

7. "The logical untenability [of the position that there are forces in man 'resistant to socialization'] was ably demonstrated by Parsons over 30 years ago, and it is widely recognized that the position is empirically unsound because it assumes [!] some universal biological drive system distinctly separate from socialization and social context—a basic and intransigent human nature" (Judith Blake and Kingsley Davis, "Norms, Values, and Sanctions," *Handbook of Modern Sociology*, ed. Robert E. L. Faris [Chicago: Rand McNally, 1964], p. 471).

8. Émile Durkheim, *Moral Education*, trans. Everett K. Wilson and Herman Schnurer (New York: The Free Press, 1961), p. 64.

9. Although attachment alone does not exhaust the meaning of internalization, attachments and beliefs combined would appear to leave only a small residue of "internal control" not susceptible in principle to direct measurement.

10. F. Ivan Nye, *Family Relationships and Delinquent Behavior* (New York: Wiley, 1958), pp. 5–7.

11. Albert J. Reiss, Jr., "Delinquency as the Failure of Personal and Social Controls," *American Sociological Review*, XVI (1951), 196–207. For example, "Our observations show … that delinquent recidivists are less often persons with mature ego ideals or nondelinquent social roles" (p. 204).

12. Scott Briar and Irving Piliavin, "Delinquency, Situational Inducements, and Commitment to Conformity," *Social Problems*, XIII (1965), 41–42. The concept "stake in conformity" was introduced by Jackson Toby in his "Social Disorganization and Stake in Conformity: Complementary Factors in the Predatory Behavior of Hoodlums," *Journal of Criminal Law, Criminology and Police Science*, XLVIII (1957), 12–17. See also his "Hoodlum or Business Man: An American Dilemma," *The Jews*, ed. Marshall Sklare (New York: The Free Press, 1958), pp. 542–550. Throughout the text, I occasionally use "stake in conformity" in speaking in general of the strength of the bond to conventional society. So used, the concept is somewhat broader than is true for either Toby or Briar and Piliavin, where the concept is roughly equivalent to what is here called "commitment."

13. Thomas Hobbes, *Leviathan* (Oxford: Basil Blackwell, 1957), p. 195.

14. Howard S. Becker, "Notes on the Concept of Commitment," *American Journal of Sociology* LXVI (1960), 35–36.

15. Arthur L. Stinchcombe, *Rebellion in a High School* (Chicago: Quadrangle, 1964), p. 5.

16. Richard A. Cloward and Lloyd E. Ohlin, *Delinquency and Opportunity* (New York: The Free Press, 1960), p. 147, quoting Edwin H. Sutherland, ed., *The Professional Thief* (Chicago: University of Chicago Press, 1937), pp. 211–213.

17. William James, *Psychology* (Cleveland: World Publishing Co., 1948), p. 186.

18. Few activities appear to be so engrossing that they rule out contemplation of alternative lines of behavior, at least if estimates of the amount of time men spend plotting sexual deviations have any validity.

19. *The Sutherland Papers*, ed. Albert K. Cohen et al. (Bloomington: Indiana University Press, 1956), p. 37.

20. David Matza and Gresham M. Sykes, "Juvenile Delinquency and Subterranean Values," *American Sociological Review*, XXVI (1961), 712–719.

21. *Ibid.*, p. 718.

22. The starving man stealing the loaf of bread is the image evoked by most strain theories. In this image, the starving man's belief in the wrongness of his act is clearly not something that must be explained away. It can be assumed to be present without causing embarrassment to the explanation.

23. McCord and McCord, *The Psychopath*, pp. 12–15.

24. Donald R. Cressey, *Other People's Money* (New York: The Free Press, 1953).

25. Gresham M. Sykes and David Matza, "Techniques of Neutralization: A Theory of Delinquency," *American Sociological Review*, XXII (1957), 664–670.

26. David Matza, *Delinquency and Drift* (New York: Wiley, 1964), pp. 181–191.

27. In asserting that Cressey's assumption is invalid with respect to delinquency, I do not wish to suggest that it is invalid for the question of embezzlement, where the problem faced by the deviator is fairly specific and he can reasonably be assumed to be an upstanding citizen. (Although even here the fact that the embezzler's nonshareable financial problem often results from some sort of hanky-panky suggests that "verbalizations" may be less necessary than might otherwise be assumed.)

28. *Delinquency and Drift*, p. 43.

29. This assumption is not, I think, contradicted by the evidence presented by Matza against the existence of a delinquent subculture. In comparing the attitudes and actions of delinquents with the picture painted by delinquent subculture theorists, Matza emphasizes—and perhaps exaggerates—the extent to which delinquents are tied to the conventional order. In implicitly comparing delinquents with a supermoral man, I emphasize—and perhaps exaggerate—the extent to which they are not tied to the conventional order.

30. The position taken here is therefore somewhere between the "semantic dementia" and the "neutralization" positions. Assuming variation, the delinquent is, at the extremes, freer than the neutralization argument assumes. Although the possibility of wide discrepancy between what the delinquent professes and what he practices still exists, it is presumably much rarer than is suggested by studies of articulate "psychopaths."

31. The idea that the middle-class boy is less closely tied than the lower-class boy to his peers has been widely adopted in the literature on delinquency. The middle-class boy's "cold and rational" relations with his peers are in sharp contrast with the "spontaneous and warm" relations of the lower-class boy. See, for example, Albert K. Cohen, *Delinquent Boys* (New York: The Free Press, 1955), pp. 102–109.

32. The evidence in favor of this proposition is summarized in Seymour M. Lipset and Reinhard Bendix, *Social Mobility in Industrial Society* (Berkeley: University of California Press, 1959), especially pp. 249–259. For example: "These [business leaders] show strong traits of independence, they are characterized by an inability to form intimate relations and are consequently often socially isolated men" (p. 251).

33. Relations between measures of attachment and commitment are examined in Chapter VIII.

34. *Social Mobility*, p. 253.

35. Brair and Piliavin, "Situational Involvements," p. 45.

36. Jean Piaget, *The Moral Judgment of the Child*, trans. Marjorie Gabain (New York: The Free Press, n.d.), p. 101.

37. *Ibid.*, p. 379.

38. Durkheim, *Moral Education*, p. 83.

39. *Ibid.*, pp. 73–79.

40. In the end, Durkheim distinguishes between a patriotism that leads to concern for domestic problems and one that emphasizes foreign relations (especially that variety which puts "national sentiment in conflict with commitments of mankind").

41. See their "Juvenile Delinquency," in *Contemporary Social Problems*, ed. Robert K. Merton and Robert A. Nisbet (New York: Harcourt, Brace and World, 1961), p. 106.

42. Howard S. Becker, *Outsiders* (New York: The Free Press, 1963), p. 26. See also Kate Friedlander, *The Psycho-Analytic Approach to Juvenile Delinquency* (New York: International Universities Press, 1947), p. 7.

43. Cf. Albert K. Cohen, *Deviance and Control* (Englewood Cliffs, N.J.: Prentice-Hall, 1966), pp. 59–62.

44. I have frequently heard the statement "it's an absence of something explanation" used as an apparently damning criticism of a sociological theory. While the origins of this view are unknown to me, the fact that such a statement appears to have some claim to plausibility suggests one of the sources of uneasiness in the face of a control theory.

45. The popular "it's-an-id-argument" dismissal of explanations of deviant behavior assumes that the founding fathers of sociology somehow proved that the blood of man is neither warm nor red, but spiritual. The intellectual trap springs shut on the counterassumption that innate aggressive-destructive impulses course through the veins, as it should. The solution is not to accept both views, but to accept neither.

46. Thomas Hobbes, *Leviathan*, p. 83. Given the history of the sociological response to Hobbes, it is instructive to compare Hobbes' picture of the motivation behind the deviant act with that painted by Talcott Parsons. According to Parsons, the motive to deviate is a psychological trait or need that the deviant carries with him at all times. This need is itself deviant: *it cannot be satisfied by conformity*. Social controls enter merely as reality factors that determine the form and manner in which this need will be satisfied. If one path to deviant behavior is blocked, the deviant will continue searching until he finds a path that is open. Perhaps because this need arises from interpersonal conflict, and is thus socially derived, the image it presents of the deviant as fundamentally immoral, as doing evil because it is evil, has been largely ignored by those objecting to the control theorist's tendency to fall back on natural propensities as a source of the energy that results in the activities society defines as wrong. See Talcott Parsons, *The Social System* (New York: The Free Press, 1951), Chapter 7.

47. Briar and Piliavin, "Situational Inducements," p. 36.

48. *Delinquency and Drift*, p. 182.

49. Matza warns us that we cannot take the fatalistic mood out of context and hope to find important differences between delinquents and other boys: "That the subcultural delinquent is not significantly different from other boys is precisely the point" (*ibid.*, p. 89).

50. For example: Carl Werthman, "The Function of Social Definitions in the Development of Delinquent Careers," *Juvenile Delinquency and Youth Crime*, Report of the President's Commission on Law Enforcement and Administration of Justice (Washington: USGPO, 1967), pp. 155–170; Jackson Toby, "Affluence and Adolescent Crime," *ibid.*, pp. 132–144; James F. Short, Jr., and Fred L. Strodtbeck, *Group Process and Gang Delinquency* (Chicago: University of Chicago Press, 1965), pp. 248–264.

12

Toward an Interactional Theory of Deviance

Terence Thornberry begins this reading, "Toward an Interactional Theory of Deviance," by observing that two of the most important sociological perspectives for explaining crime and deviance—as noted in Sections III and IV of this book—are social control theory and social learning theory (Thornberry, 1987:864). Thornberry notes, however, that control theory and learning theory start with quite different assumptions regarding the causes of crime and deviance. Social control theory assumes that there is widespread motivation to engage in criminal or deviant behavior. It also takes the position that most individuals would engage in such behavior from time to time, if the social controls or social restraints were not in place to prevent them from doing so (Kornhauser, 1978:48; Lilly, Cullen, & Ball, 2011:110–111; Thornberry, 1987:863). Social learning theory, on the other hand, assumes that widespread motivation to engage in criminal or deviant behavior does not necessarily exist. Rather, social learning theory posits that nonconforming behavior must be learned, in much the same manner that conforming behavior is learned (Burgess & Akers, 1966:129; Thornberry, 1987:863; Williams & McShane, 2010:169–170).

Thornberry identifies what he considers the three main limitations or weaknesses of social control theory and social learning theory. First, he says that both theories are unidirectional, rather than reciprocal (1987:864). What Thornberry means is that the cause-effect relationships go in one direction. Control theorists assume that a breakdown in social controls—whether they are called inner containments and outer containments, or attachment, commitment, involvement and belief—will lead to criminal and deviant behavior. Social learning theorists assume that the learning of criminal or deviant behavior, and having that behavior reinforced, will ultimately lead to criminality and deviance. Second, Thornberry says that both social control theory and social learning theory are "non-developmental," in the sense that they are concerned primarily with the type of criminality—more

229

commonly referred to as "delinquency"—that occurs during mid-adolescence (1987:864). Third, he argues that social control theory and social learning theory do not adequately take into consideration the effects of the social structure on crime and deviance (1987:864). In other words, he is saying that an individual's position in the social structure (i.e., his or her social class) can have as much of an effect on criminality and deviance as the presence or absence of social controls, or the learning and reinforcement (or punishment) of such behavior.

Terence Thornberry's interactional theory is rooted in Durkheimian notions of social control, social bonds and social constraints (Thornberry & Krohn, 2005:194–195; Thornberry, 1987:865). It is also a "life course" or "developmental" theory, in that it examines how social bonds—and the propensity for delinquency and criminality—change as individuals transition through the life stages of childhood, adolescence, young adulthood and adulthood (Sampson & Laub, 2001:155; Thornberry & Krohn, 2005:192–196; Williams & McShane, 2010:211). Interactional theory could arguably be characterized as an "integrated theory," because it employs elements of social bond theory, social learning theory, anomie-strain theory and social disorganization theory (Thornberry, 1987:865, 884). However, Thornberry himself has warned against theoretical integration, preferring instead to describe his interactional theory as an elaboration on or extension of social control theory (Paternoster & Bachman, 2001:312–313; Williams & McShane, 2010:225). That said, the prominence of social learning variables in Thornberry's interactional theory seems more or less equivalent to the prominence of social control variables (cf. Akers & Sellers, 2009:310–311).

In this reading selection, Thornberry uses three of the main elements of Travis Hirschi's social bond theory—"*attachment* to parents," "*commitment* to school," and "*belief* in conventional values" [emphasis added] (Thornberry, 1987:866, 875). He also employs a number of the major components of differential association theory and/or social learning theory—the interaction with "delinquent peers," the learning of "delinquent values," and the reinforcement of "delinquent behavior" (Thornberry, 1987:866, 870, 873). Thornberry views these elements of social control and social learning as part of a causal or reciprocal loop, wherein the variables interact with and influence each other over the life course (Paternoster, Dean, Piquero, Mazerolle, & Brame, 2001:286; Thornberry, 1987:867, 869). In this causal or reciprocal loop, weakened attachment to parents, lack of commitment to school and weakened belief in conventional values can indeed lead to increased interaction with delinquent peers, the learning of delinquent values, and involvement in delinquent behavior. Thornberry observes, however, that this process can just as easily go in the opposite direction—interaction with delinquent peers, the learning of delinquent values and involvement in delinquent behavior can lead to weakened attachment to parents, lack of commitment to school, and weakened belief in conventional values (Thornberry, 1987:876). Seen from this vantage point, delinquency is not merely an end product of the social environment and social institutions; rather, delinquency in turn influences the social environment and the strength (or weakness) of social institutions (Lilly et al., 2011:390).

Thornberry takes the position that social bonds vary over the life course—i.e., social bonds are not fixed in place, and can change quite dramatically as individuals age and mature. During childhood, children are more attached to—and influenced or controlled by—their parents and school teachers (Thornberry & Krohn, 2005:197–198; Thornberry, 1987:879). When they reach mid-adolescence, individuals are more likely to be attached to (and influenced by) their teenage peers. Many teenagers seek approval or "reinforcement" from their peer group, while resenting or rejecting parental controls. Doing poorly at school, or disavowing the conventional values espoused by schools, may actually result in greater approval from teen peers. This is, as Thornberry points out, the peak time for involvement in delinquent behavior (1987:877). In later adolescence (or young adulthood), the nature of social bonds often change again, as individuals start planning their lives around careers, long-term relationships and having children. At this point, they tend to become more attached and committed to their employers and fellow employees, their spouses, and their children (Thornberry, 1987:881). As Thornberry says, this may explain the well-documented phenomenon of "maturational reform"—i.e., the high rate of desistance from delinquent behavior in late adolescence and young adulthood. Adolescents and young adults who do not outgrow these delinquent teen peer groups and move on to establish these new (adult) social bonds may turn out to be chronic and persistent criminal offenders (Thornberry, 1987:881, 883).

Thornberry sees this developmental process as playing out against a backdrop of social structure and social class, along the lines of that described by "strain and social disorganization theories" (Thornberry, 1987:884). Members of the lower class are more likely than members of the lower working class or middle class to have experienced family disruption, poverty, and exposure to higher rates of crime and delinquency. Consequently, they tend to be "less bonded to conventional society," and thus, more likely to end up on a life course trajectory toward delinquency and criminality (Thornberry, 1987:885). Middle class youth, on the other hand, come from more economically stable backgrounds, have brighter future prospects, and tend to be more conforming (and more socially bonded). Lower working class youth fall somewhere in between the lower class and middle class youth in terms of their socio-economic backgrounds and the strength of their attachments to parents and teachers, commitment to school, and belief in conventional values (Thornberry, 1987:884–885). As a result, the life course trajectory of lower working class youth is more difficult to predict than the life course trajectories for lower and middle class youth.

References

Akers, R. L., & Sellers, C. S. (2009). *Criminological theories: Introduction, evaluation, and application* (5th, New ed.). New York: Oxford University Press.

Burgess, R. L., & Akers, R. L. (1966). A differential association-reinforcement theory of criminal behavior. *Social Problems, 14*(2), 128–147.

Kornhauser, R. R. (1978). *Social sources of delinquency: An appraisal of analytic models.* Chicago: University of Chicago Press.

Lilly, J. R., Cullen, F. T., & Ball, R. A. (2011). *Criminological theory: Context and consequences* (5th ed.). Thousand Oaks: SAGE Publications.

Paternoster, R., & Bachman, R. (Eds.). (2001). *Explaining criminals and crime: Essays in contemporary criminological theory*. Los Angeles, Calif.: Roxbury Pub. Co.

Paternoster, R., Dean, C. W., Piquero, A., Mazerolle, P., & Brame, R. (2001). Generality, continuity and change in offending. In A. Piquero, & P. Mazerolle (Eds.), *Life-course criminology: Contemporary and classic readings* (pp. 283–316). Toronto: Wadsworth Thomson Learning.

Sampson, R. J., & Laub, J. H. (2001). A life-course theory of cumulative disadvantage and the stability of delinquency. In A. Piquero, & P. Mazerolle (Eds.), *Life-course criminology: Contemporary and classic readings* (pp. 146–169). Toronto: Wadsworth Thomson Learning.

Thornberry, T. (1987). Toward an interactional theory of delinquency. *Criminology, 25*(4), 863–891.

Thornberry, T. P., & Krohn, M. D. (2005). Applying interactional theory to the explanation of continuity and change in antisocial behavior. In D. P. Farrington (Ed.), *Integrated developmental & life-course theories of offending* (pp. 183–209). New Brunswick, NJ: Transaction Publishers.

Williams, F. P., & McShane, M. D. (2010). *Criminological theory* (5th ed.). Upper Saddle River, N.J.: Pearson/Prentice Hall.

Toward an Interactional Theory of Delinquency*

TERENCE THORNBERRY

Contemporary theories of delinquency are seen as limited in three respects: they tend to rely on unidirectional causal structures that represent delinquency in a static rather than dynamic fashion, they do not examine developmental progressions, and they do not adequately link processual concepts to the person's position in the social structure. The present article develops an interactional theory of delinquency that addresses each of these issues. It views delinquency as resulting from the freedom afforded by the weakening of the person's bonds to conventional society and from an interactional setting in which delinquent behavior is learned and reinforced. Moreover, the control, learning, and delinquency variables are seen as reciprocally interrelated, mutually affecting one another over the person's life. Thus, delinquency is viewed as part of a larger causal network, aflected by social factors but also aflecting the development of those social factors over time.

A variety of sociological theories have been developed to explain the onset and maintenance of delinquent behavior. Currently, three are of primary importance: social control theory (Hirschi, 1969), social learning theory (Akers, 1977), and

*The present work was supported in part by the Office of Juvenile Justice and Delinquency Prevention, grant number 86-JN-CX-0007; the views expressed are those of the author and not necessarily those of the funding agency. I would like to thank Drs. Robert A. Silverman of the University of Alberta and Margaret Farnworth, Alan Lizotte, and Hans Toch of the University at Albany for providing helpful comments on earlier drafts of this article.

Reprinted from *Criminology* 25, no. 4 (1987), American Society of Criminology.

integrated models that combine them into a broader body of explanatory principals (Elliott, Ageton, and Canter, 1979; Elliott, Huizinga, and Ageton, 1985).

Control theory argues that delinquency emerges whenever the social and cultural constraints over human conduct are substantially attenuated. As Hirschi states in his classic presentation (1969), control theory assumes that we would all be deviant if only we dared. Learning theory, on the other hand, posits that there is no natural impulse toward delinquency. Indeed, delinquent behavior must be learned through the same processes and mechanisms as conforming behavior. Because of these different starting points, control and learning models give causal priority to somewhat different concepts, and integrated models capitalize on these complementary approaches. Muting the assumptive differences, integrated theories meld together propositions from these (and sometimes other theories—for example, strain) to explain delinquent behavior.

Although these approaches have substantially informed our understanding of the causes of delinquency, they and other contemporary theories suffer from three fundamental limitations. First, they rely on unidirectional rather than reciprocal causal structures. By and large, current theories ignore reciprocal effects in which delinquent behavior is viewed as part of a more general social nexus, affected by, but also affecting, other social factors. Second, current theories tend to be nondevelopmental, specifying causal models for only a narrow age range, usually mid-adolescence. As a result, they fail to capitalize on developmental patterns to explain the initiation, maintenance, and desistance of delinquency. Finally, contemporary theories tend to assume uniform causal effects throughout the social structure. By ignoring the person's structural position, they fail to provide an understanding of the sources of initial variation in both delinquency and its presumed causes. In combination, these three limitations have led to theories that are narrowly conceived and which provide incomplete and, at times, misleading models of the causes of delinquency.

The present article develops an interactional theory of delinquency that addresses and attempts to respond to each of these limitations. The model proposed here pays particular attention to the first issue, recursive versus reciprocal causal structures, since the development of dynamic models is seen as essential to represent accurately the interactional settings in which delinquency develops.

Origins and Assumptions

The basic premise of the model proposed here is that human behavior occurs in social interaction and can therefore best be explained by models that focus on interactive processes. Rather than viewing adolescents as propelled along a unidirectional pathway to one or another outcome—that is, delinquency or conformity—it argues that adolescents interact with other people and institutions and that behavioral outcomes are formed by that interactive process. For example, the delinquent behavior of an adolescent is formed in part by how he and his parents *interact* over time, not simply by the child's perceived, and presumably invariant, *level* of attachment to parents. Moreover, since it is an interactive system, the behaviors of others—for example, parents and school officials—are influenced both by each other and by the adolescent, including his or her delinquent behavior. If this view is correct, then interactional effects have to be modelled explicitly if we are to understand the social and psychological processes involved with initiation into delinquency, the maintenance of such behavior, and its eventual reduction.

Interactional theory develops from the same intellectual tradition as the theories mentioned above, especially the Durkheimian tradition of social control. It asserts that the fundamental cause of delinquency lies in the weakening of social constraints over the conduct of the individual. Unlike classical control theory, however, it does not assume that the attenuation of controls leads directly to delinquency. The weakening of controls simply allows for a much wider array of behavior, including continued conventional action, failure as indicated by school dropout and sporadic employment histories, alcoholism, mental illness, delinquent and criminal careers, or some combination of these outcomes. For the freedom resulting from weakened bonds to be channeled into delinquency, especially serious prolonged delinquency, requires an interactive setting in which delinquency is learned, performed, and reinforced. This view is similar to Cullen's structuring perspective which draws attention to the indeterminancy of deviant behavior. "It can thus be argued that there is an *indeterminate* and not a determinate or etiologically specific relationship between motivational variables on the one hand and any particular form of deviant behavior on the other hand" (Cullen, 1984: 5).

Although heavily influenced by control and learning theories, and to a lesser extent by strain and culture conflict theories, this is not an effort at theoretical integration as that term is usually used (Elliott, 1985). Rather, this paper is guided by what we have elsewhere called theoretical elaboration (Thornberry, 1987). In this instance, a basic control theory is extended, or elaborated upon, using available theoretical perspectives and empirical findings to provide a more accurate model of the causes of delinquency. In the process of elaboration, there is no requirement to resolve disputes among other theories—for example, their different assumptions about the origins of deviance (Thornberry, 1987: 15–18); all that is required is that the propositions of the model developed here be consistent with one another and with the assumptions about deviance stated above.

Organization

The presentation of the interactional model begins by identifying the central concepts to be included in the model. Next, the underlying theoretical structure of the proposed model is examined and the rationale for moving from unidirectional to reciprocal causal models is developed. The reciprocal model is then extended to include a developmental perspective, examining the theoretical saliency of different variables at different developmental stages. Finally, the influence of the person's position in the social structure is explored. Although in some senses the last issue is logically prior to the others, since it is concerned with sources of initial variation in the causal variables, it is discussed last so that the reciprocal relationships among the concepts—the heart of an interactional perspective—can be more fully developed.

Theoretical Concepts

Given these basic premises, an interactional model must respond to two overriding issues. First, how are traditional social constraints over behavior weakened and, second, once weakened, how is the resulting freedom channelled into delinquent patterns? To address these issues, the present article presents an initial version of an interactional model, focusing on the interrelationships among six concepts: attachment to parents, commitment to school, belief in conventional values, associations with delinquent peers, adopting delinquent values, and engaging in delinquent behavior. These concepts form the core of the theoretical model since they are central to social psychological theories of delinquency and since they have been shown in numerous studies to be strongly related to subsequent delinquent behavior (see Elliott et al., 1985, Chs. 1–3, for an excellent review of this literature).

The first three derive from Hirschi's version of control theory (1969) and represent the primary mechanisms by which adolescents are bonded to conventional middle-class society. When those elements of the bond are weakened, behavioral freedom increases considerably. For that freedom to lead to delinquent behavior, however, interactive settings that reinforce delinquency are required. In the model, those settings are represented by two concepts—associations with delinquent peers and the formation of delinquent values—which derive primarily from social learning theory.

For the purpose of explicating the overall theoretical perspective, each of these concepts is defined quite broadly. Attachment to parents includes the affective relationship between parent and child, communication patterns, parenting skills such as monitoring and discipline, parent-child conflict, and the like. Commitment to school refers to the stake in conformity the adolescent has developed and includes such factors as success in school, perceived importance of education, attachment to teachers, and involvement in school activities. Belief in conventional values represents the granting of legitimacy to such middle-class values as education, personal industry, financial success, deferral of gratification, and the like.

Three delinquency variables are included in the model. Association with delinquent peers includes the level of attachment to peers, the delinquent behavior and values of peers, and their reinforcing reactions to the adolescent's own delinquent or conforming behavior. It is a continuous measure that can vary from groups that are heavily delinquent to those that are almost entirely nondelinquent. Delinquent values refer to the granting of legitimacy to delinquent activities as acceptable modes of behavior as well as a general willingness to violate the law to achieve other ends.

Delinquent behavior, the primary outcome variable, refers to acts that place the youth at risk for adjudication; it ranges from status offenses to serious violent activities. Since the present model is an interactional one, interested not only in explaining delinquency but in explaining the effects of delinquency on other variables, particular attention is paid to prolonged involvement in serious delinquency.

Theoretical Structure

The present section develops the reciprocal structure of the interactional model by examining the interplay of the concepts just defined. It begins by describing (Figure 12.1) the way in which these variables are typically represented in predominately recursive theories of delinquency (see, for example, Johnson, 1979; Weis and Sederstrom, 1981; Elliott et al., 1985).

In these models, all the variables are temporally ordered; earlier ones affect later ones, but there is no provision for feedback or reciprocal causal paths. The unidirectional specification can be illustrated by examining the relationship between attachment to parents and associations with delinquent peers. According to the model, attachment to parents reduces the extent to which the child associates with delinquent peers, an assertion consistent with common observation and empirical research (for example, Poole and Regoli, 1979). Yet, by implication, the model also states that associations with delinquent peers *exerts no causal influence* on the extent to which the child is attached to parents. If peer associations were thought to influence attachment to parents, then this effect would have to be specified and estimated. As seen in Figure 12.1, reciprocal effects of this type are excluded by design.

The second feature to note about this model is that it treats delinquency entirely as an outcome of a social process rather than as an integral part of that process. Models such as this assert that various social factors cause delinquent behavior but ignore the possibility that delinquency and its presumed causes are part of a reciprocal causal structure, mutually influencing one another over the person's life span. For example, these models state that associations with delinquent peers increase the likelihood of delinquent conduct, an obviously reasonable assertion, but ignore the possibility that delinquent conduct affects the likelihood and intensity of associations with delinquent peers. Similar statements can be made for the other relationships in which delinquency is embedded.

It should be noted at the outset that there is nothing inherently incorrect with recursive models; if the causal processes are unidirectional, recursive models offer a correct specification and should be used. It is only when the causal processes are in fact reciprocal that models such as these lead to problems of misspecification and incorrect interpretations of causal effects.

The remainder of this section develops the argument that unidirectional models are inadequate and that reciprocal models are required to understand the

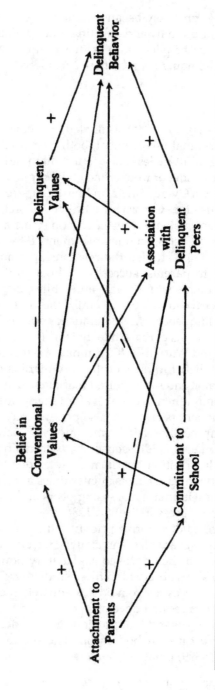

FIGURE 12.1   *A typical recursive causal model of delinquency.*

causes of delinquency, precisely because delinquency is embedded in an inter-active social process, affected by and affecting other variables. As a starting point, the findings of three recent panel studies that examine both unidirectional and reciprocal models of delinquent conduct are considered.

Empirical Findings

Thornberry and Christenson (1984) estimated a reciprocal causal structure for unemployment and criminal involvement, both measured at the individual level, for a sample of young adult males. They found that unidirectional models, either from unemployment to crime or from crime to unemployment, were inadequate to model the causal process. Overall, their findings offer strong support for a recipro-cal model of crime causation. Consistent with our theoretical specification, unem-ployment has significant instantaneous effects on crime and crime has significant effects, primarily lagged effects, on unemployment (1984: 408).

Liska and Reed (1985) studied the relationship among three control theory variables, attachment to parents, success in school, and delinquency. Although their results differed somewhat for blacks and whites, these variables appear to be embedded in a reciprocal causal loop. Overall, "the analysis suggests that parental attachment affects delinquency, that delinquency affects school attachment, and that school attachment affects parental attachment" (Liska and Reed, 1985: 556–557).

Finally, Burkett and Warren (1987) estimate a panel model for four variables: religious commitment, belief in the sinfulness of marijuana use, associations with peers who use marijuana, and self-reported marijuana use. Their basic finding sug-gests that religious commitment and belief affect marijuana use indirectly, through association with delinquent peers. They also present consistent evidence that these four variables are reciprocally related over time. Marijuana use increases associa-tions with delinquent peers, and associations with delinquent peers reduce reli-gious commitments. In addition, marijuana use at one time significantly affects both religious commitment and beliefs at later times and "this, in turn, contributes to deeper involvement with marijuana-using peers and subsequent continued use in response to direct peer pressure" (1987: 123).

All three of these studies derive primarily from a social control framework, but use different data sets, variables, and analytic techniques. Nevertheless, all pro-vide empirical support for the improved explanatory power of reciprocal models. The pattern of relationships observed in these studies strongly suggests that recip-rocal causal models are necessary to model adequately the social settings in which delinquent behavior emerges and develops.

These findings also suggest that previous tests of delinquency theories based on recursive causal structures are both incomplete and misleading. As Thornberry and Christenson (1984: 399) point out, such tests

> are incomplete since estimates for reciprocal paths simply cannot be obtained. More importantly, recursive tests can produce misleading results since estimates of uni-directional effects obtained from them may be in substantial error. Conceivably,

recursive tests could indicate a unidirectional effect between two variables, i.e., X→Y, when the actual relationship (as estimated from a nonrecursive model) could indicate either that the variables are reciprocally related, i.e., X⇄Y, or that the direction of the causality is actually reversed, i.e., X←Y (see Heise, 1975: 191–93; Hanushek and Jackson, 1977: 79–86).

If any or all of these errors exist, and results of recent research suggest they do, then current theories of delinquency, which have been strongly influenced by the results of recursive studies, are inadequate to describe the actual processes in which delinquency is embedded. Because of this, it is important to develop and test interactional models that allow for reciprocal effects.

Model Specification

A causal model allowing for reciprocal relationships among the six concepts of interest—attachment to parents, commitment to school, belief in conventional values, association with delinquent peers, delinquent values, and delinquent behavior—is presented in Figure 12.2. This model refers to the period of early adolescence, from about ages 11 to 13, when delinquent careers are beginning, but prior to the period at which delinquency reaches its apex in terms of seriousness and frequency. In the following sections the model is extended to later ages.

The specification of causal effects begins by examining the three concepts that form the heart of social learning theories of delinquency—delinquent peers, delinquent values, and delinquent behavior. For now we focus on the reciprocal nature of the relationships, ignoring until later variations in the strength of the relationships.

Traditional social learning theory specifies a causal order among these variables in which delinquent associations affect delinquent values and, in turn, both produce delinquent behavior (Akers, Krohn, Lanza-Kaduce, and Radosevich, 1979; Matsueda, 1982). Yet, for each of the dyadic relationships involving these variables, other theoretical perspectives and much empirical evidence suggest the appropriateness of reversing this causal order. For example, social learning theory proposes that associating with delinquents, or more precisely, people who hold and reinforce delinquent values, increases the chances of delinquent behavior (Akers, 1977). Yet, as far back as the work of the Gluecks (1950) this specification has been challenged. Arguing that "birds of a feather flock together," the Gluecks propose that youths who are delinquent seek out and associate with others who share those tendencies. From this perspective, rather than being a cause of delinquency, associations are the result of delinquents seeking out and associating with like-minded peers.

An attempt to resolve the somewhat tedious argument over the temporal priority of associations and behavior is less productive theoretically than capitalizing on the interactive nature of human behavior and treating the relationship as it probably is: a reciprocal one. People often take on the behavioral repertoire of their

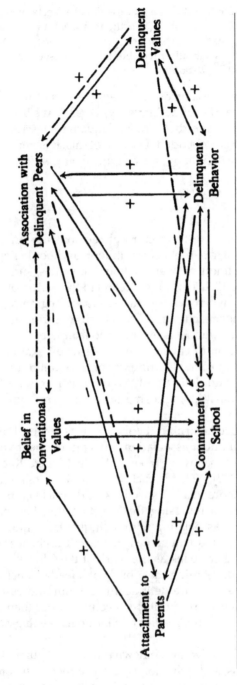

FIGURE 12.2   *A reciprocal model of delinquent involvement at early adolescence.*[a]

[a]Solid lines represent stronger effects; dashed lines represent weaker effects.

associates but, at the same time, they often seek out associates who share their behavioral interests. Individuals clearly behave this way in conventional settings, and there is no reason to assume that deviant activities, such as delinquency, are substantially different in this regard.

Similar arguments can be made for the other two relationships among the delinquency variables. Most recent theories of delinquency, following the lead of social learning theory, posit that delinquent associations lead to the formation of delinquent values. Subcultural theories, however, especially those that derive from a cultural deviance perspective (Miller, 1958) suggest that values precede the formation of peer groups. Indeed, it is the socialization of adolescents into the "lower-class culture" and its particular value system that leads them to associate with delinquent peers in the first place. This specification can also be derived from a social control perspective as demonstrated in Weis and Sederstrom's social development model (1981) and Burkett and Warren's social selection model (1987).

Finally, the link between delinquent values and delinquent behavior restates, in many ways, the basic social psychological question of the relationship between attitudes and behavior. Do attitudes form behavior patterns or does behavior lead to attitude formation? Social psychological research, especially in cognitive psychology and balance models (for example, Festinger, 1957; Brehm and Cohen, 1962) points to the reciprocal nature of this relationship. It suggests that people indeed behave in a manner consistent with their attitudes, but also that behavior is one of the most persuasive forces in the formation and maintenance of attitudes.

Such a view of the relationship between delinquent values and behavior is consistent with Hindelang's findings:

> This general pattern of results indicates that one can "predict" a respondent's self approval [of illegal behaviors] from knowledge of that respondent's involvement/ non-involvement [in delinquency] with fewer errors than vice-versa (1974: 382).

It is also consistent with recent deterrence research which demonstrates that the "experiential effect," in which behavior affects attitudes, is much stronger than the deterrent effect, in which attitudes affect behavior (Paternoster, Saltzman, Waldo, and Chiricos, 1982; Paternoster, Saltzman, Chiricos, and Waldo 1983).

Although each of these relationships appears to be reciprocal, the predicted strengths of the associations are not of equal strength during the early adolescent period (see Figure 12.2). Beliefs that delinquent conduct is acceptable and positively valued may be emerging, but such beliefs are not fully articulated for 11- to 13-year-olds. Because of their emerging quality, they are viewed as more effect than cause, produced by delinquent behavior and associations with delinquent peers. As these values emerge, however, they have feedback effects, albeit relatively weak ones at these ages, on behavior and associations. That is, as the values become more fully articulated and delinquency becomes positively valued, it increases the likelihood of such behavior and further reinforces associations with like-minded peers.

Summary: When attention is focused on the interrelationships among associations with delinquent peers, delinquent values, and delinquent behavior, it appears that they are, in fact, reciprocally related. The world of human behavior is far more complex than a simple recursive one in which a temporal order can be imposed on interactional variables of this nature. Interactional theory sees these three concepts as embedded in a causal loop, each reinforcing the others over time. Regardless of where the individual enters the loop, the following obtains: delinquency increases associations with delinquent peers and delinquent values; delinquent values increase delinquent behavior and associations with delinquent peers; and associations with delinquent peers increases delinquent behavior and delinquent values. The question now concerns the identification of factors that lead some youth, but not others, into this spiral of increasing delinquency.

Social Control Effects

As indicated at the outset of this essay, the premise of interactional theory is that the fundamental cause of delinquency is the attenuation of social controls over the person's conduct. Whenever bonds to the conventional world are substantially weakened, the individual is freed from moral constraints and is at risk for a wide array of deviant activities, including delinquency. The primary mechanisms that bind adolescents to the conventional world are attachment to parents, commitment to school, and belief in conventional values, and their role in the model can now be examined.

During the early adolescent years, the family is the most salient arena for social interaction and involvement and, because of this, attachment to parents has a stronger influence on other aspects of the youth's life at this stage than it does at later stages of development. With this in mind, attachment to parents[1] is predicted to affect four other variables. Since youths who are attached to their parents are sensitive to their wishes (Hirschi, 1969: 16–19), and, since parents are almost universally supportive of the conventional world, these children are likely to be strongly committed to school and to espouse conventional values. In addition, youths who are attached to their parents, again because of their sensitivity to parental wishes, are unlikely to associate with delinquent peers or to engage in delinquent behavior.

In brief, parental influence is seen as central to controlling the behavior of youths at these relatively early ages. Parents who have a strong affective bond with their children, who communicate with them, who exercise appropriate parenting skills, and so forth, are likely to lead their children towards conventional actions and beliefs and away from delinquent friends and actions.

On the other hand, attachment to parents is not seen as an immutable trait, impervious to the effects of other variables. Indeed, associating with delinquent peers, not being committed to school, and engaging in delinquent behavior are so contradictory to parental expectations that they tend to diminish the level of attachment between parent and child. Adolescents who fail at school, who associate with delinquent peers, and who engage in delinquent conduct are, as a consequence, likely to jeopardize their affective bond with their parents, precisely because these behaviors suggest that the "person does not care about the wishes and expectations of other people . . ." (Hirschi, 1969: 18), in this instance, his or her parents.

Turning next to belief in conventional values, this concept is involved in two different causal loops. First, it strongly affects commitment to school and in turn is affected by commitment to school. In essence, this loop posits a behavioral and attitudinal consistency in the conventional realm. Second, a weaker loop is posited between belief in conventional values and associations with delinquent peers. Youths who do not grant legitimacy to conventional values are more apt to associate with delinquent friends who share those views, and those friendships are likely to attenuate further their beliefs in conventional values. This reciprocal specification is supported by Burkett and Warren's findings concerning religious beliefs and peer associations (1987). Finally, youths who believe in conventional values are seen as somewhat less likely to engage in delinquent behavior.

Although belief in conventional values plays some role in the genesis of delinquency, its impact is not particularly strong. For example, it is not affected by delinquent behavior, nor is it related to delinquent values. This is primarily because belief in conventional values appears to be quite invariant; regardless of class of origin or delinquency status, for example, most people strongly assert conventional values (Short and Strodtbeck, 1965: Ch. 3). Nevertheless, these beliefs do exert some influence in the model, especially with respect to reinforcing commitment to school.

Finally, the impact of commitment to school is considered. This variable is involved in reciprocal loops with both of the other bonding variables. Youngsters who are attached to their parents are likely to be committed to and succeed in school, and that success is likely to reinforce the close ties to their parents. Similarly, youths who believe in conventional values are likely to be committed to school, the primary arena in which they can act in accordance with those values, and, in turn, success in that arena is likely to reinforce the beliefs.

In addition to its relationships with the other control variables, commitment to school also has direct effects on two of the delinquency variables. Students who are committed to succeeding in school are unlikely to associate with delinquents or to engage in substantial amounts of serious, repetitive delinquent behavior. These youths have built up a stake in conformity and should be unwilling to jeopardize that investment by either engaging in delinquent behavior or by associating with those who do.

Low commitment to school is not seen as leading directly to the formation of delinquent values, however. Its primary effect on delinquent values is indirect, via associations with delinquent peers and delinquent behavior (Conger, 1980: 137). While school failure may lead to a reduced commitment to conventional values, it does not follow that it directly increases the acceptance of values that support delinquency.

Commitment to school, on the other hand, is affected by each of the delinquency variables in the model. Youths who accept values that are consistent with delinquent behavior, who associate with other delinquents, and who engage in delinquent behavior are simply unlikely candidates to maintain an active commitment to school and the conventional world that school symbolizes.

Summary: Attachment to parents, commitment to school, and belief in conventional values reduce delinquency by cementing the person to conventional institutions and people. When these elements of the bond to conventional society are strong, delinquency is unlikely, but when they are weak the individual is placed at much greater risk for delinquency. When viewed from an interactional perspective, two additional qualities of these concepts become increasingly evident.

First, attachment to parents, commitment to school, and belief in conventional values are not static attributes of the person, invariant over time. These concepts interact with one another during the developmental process. For some youths the levels of attachment, commitment, and belief increase as these elements reinforce one another, while for other youths the interlocking nature of these relationships suggests a greater and greater attenuation of the bond will develop over time.

Second, the bonding variables appear to be reciprocally linked to delinquency, exerting a causal impact on associations with delinquent peers and delinquent behavior; they also are causally effected by these variables. As the youth engages in more and more delinquent conduct and increasingly associates with delinquent peers, the level of his bond to the conventional world is further weakened. Thus, while the weakening of the bond to conventional society may be an initial cause of delinquency, delinquency eventually becomes its own indirect cause precisely because of its ability to weaken further the person's bonds to family, school, and conventional beliefs. The implications of this amplifying causal structure is examined below. First, however, the available support for reciprocal models is reviewed and the basic model is extended to later developmental stages.

Support for Reciprocal Structures

The previous section developed a theoretical rationale for moving from recursive to reciprocal causal structures of delinquency. Using an interactional perspective, delinquent behavior, especially sustained involvement with serious delinquent behavior, was viewed as part of an ongoing social process rather than simply a product of other social variables. The present section reviews sources of theoretical and empirical support for this perspective.

First, this model is logically consistent with the approaches of many other theoretical models; see, for example, those proposed by Hirschi (1969), Akers (1977), Elliott et al. (1979, 1985), Weis and Sederstrom (1981), and Snyder and Patterson (in press). Indeed, the present model can be viewed as a logical extension of those theories since it explicitly specifies reciprocal effects that have, until recently, remained largely implicit in criminological theory and research.

Second, as indicated above, recent panel studies that estimate reciprocal effects produce consistent support for this perspective. Whether concerned with unemployment and crime (Thornberry and Christenson, 1984), attachment to parents, commitment to school and delinquency (Liska and Reed, 1985),or religion, peers, and marijuana use (Burkett and Warren, 1987), each of these analyses suggest that there are substantial feedback effects involving delinquency and its presumed causes.

Third, using data from the National Youth Survey, Huizinga and Elliott (1986) report a number of significant reciprocal effects. Although they did not observe feedback effects from delinquent behavior to the conventional bonding variables posited by interactional theory, they do report reciprocal effects among the elements of the bond. They also report that delinquent behavior and associations with delinquent peers are mutually reinforcing (Huizinga and Elliott, 1986: 12). Finally, they report that exposure to delinquent friends has significant feedback effects on a wide range of variables, including "internal deviant bonds, perceived sanctions, normlessness, prosocial aspirations, and involvement in prosocial roles" (Huizinga and Elliott, 1986: 14).

Fourth, a large number of studies have found that delinquent behavior (including drug use) measured at one time has significant effects on the presumed "causes" of delinquency measured at a later time. Among the variables found to be affected by prior delinquency are educational and occupational attainment (Bachman, O'Malley, and Johnston, 1978; Kandel and Logan, 1984); dropping out of high school (Elliott and Voss, 1974; Bachman et al., 1978; Polk et al., 1981; Thornberry, Moore, and Christenson, 1985); unemployment (Bachman et al., 1978; Thornberry and Christenson, 1984); attachment to parents (Paternoster et al., 1983); commitment to school (Paternoster et al., 1983; Liska and Reed, 1985; Agnew, 1985); and belief in conventional values (Hindelang, 1974; Paternoster et al., 1983; Agnew, 1985). These empirical findings are quite consistent with a theory that posits that delinquent behavior is not only produced by other social variables, but also exerts a significant causal influence on those variables.

Developmental Extensions

The previous section developed a strategy for addressing one of the three major limitations of delinquency theories mentioned in the introduction—namely, their unidirectional causal structure. A second limitation is the nondevelopmental posture of most theories which tend to provide a cross-sectional picture of the factors associated with delinquency at one age, but which do not provide a rationale for understanding how delinquent behavior develops over time. The present section offers a developmental extension of the basic model.

Middle Adolescence

First, a model for middle adolescence, when the youths are approximately 15 or 16 years of age is presented (Figure 12.3). This period represents the highest rates of involvement in delinquency and is the reference period, either implicitly or explicitly, for most theories of delinquent involvement. Since the models for the early and middle adolescent periods have essentially the same structure and causal relationships (Figures 12.2 and 12.3), discussion focuses on the differences between them and does not repeat the rationale for individual causal effects.

Perhaps the most important difference concerns attachment to parents which is involved in relatively few strong relationships. By this point in the life cycle, the most salient variables involved in the production of delinquency are likely to be external to the home, associated with the youth's activities in school and peer networks. This specification is consistent with empirical results for subjects in this age range (Johnson, 1979: 105; and Schoenberg, 1975, quoted in Johnson). Indeed, Johnson concludes that "an adolescent's public life has as much or more to do with his or her deviance or conformity than do 'under-the-roof' experiences" (1979: 116).

This is not to say that attachment to parents is irrelevant; such attachments are involved in enhancing commitment to school and belief in conventional values, and in preventing associations with delinquent peers. It is just that the overall strength of parental effects are weaker than at earlier ages when the salience of the family as a locus of interaction and control was greater.

The second major change concerns the increased importance of delinquent values as a causal factor. It is still embedded in the causal loop with the other two delinquency variables, but now it is as much cause as effect. Recall that at the younger ages delinquent values were seen as emerging, produced by associations with delinquent peers and delinquent behavior. Given their emergent nature, they were not seen as primary causes of other variables. At midadolescence, however, when delinquency is at its apex, these values are more fully articulated and have stronger effects on other variables. First, delinquent values are seen as major reinforcers of both delinquent associations and delinquent behavior. In general, espousing values supportive of delinquency tends to increase the potency of this causal loop. Second, since delinquent values are antithetical to the conventional settings of school and family, youths who espouse them are less likely to be committed to school and attached to parents. Consistent with the reduced saliency of family at these ages, the feedback effect to school is seen as stronger than the feedback effect to parents.

By and large, the other concepts in the model play the same role at these ages as they do at the earlier ones. Thus, the major change from early to middle adolescence concerns the changing saliency of some of the theoretical concepts. The family declines in relative importance while the adolescent's own world of school and peers takes on increasing significance. While these changes occur, the overall structure of the theory remains constant. These interactive variables are still seen as mutually reinforcing over time.

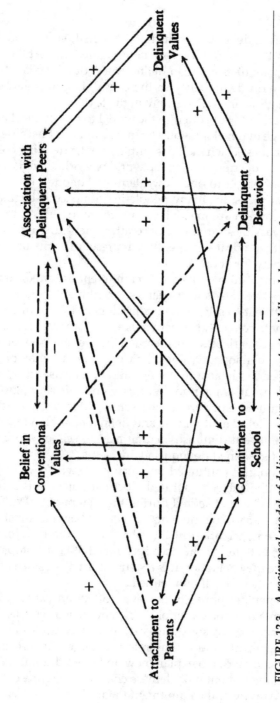

FIGURE 12.3   *A reciprocal model of delinquent involvement at middle adolescence.*[a]

[a]Solid lines represent stronger effects; dashed lines represent weaker effects.

Later Adolescence

Finally, the causes of delinquency during the transition from adolescence to adulthood, about ages 18 to 20, can be examined (Figure 12.4). At these ages one should more properly speak of crime than delinquency, but for consistency we will continue to use the term delinquency in the causal diagrams and employ the terms delinquency and crime interchangeably in the text.

Two new variables are added to the model to reflect the changing life circumstances at this stage of development. The more important of these is commitment to conventional activities which includes employment, attending college, and military service. Along with the transition to the world of work, there is a parallel transition from the family of origin to one's own family. Although this transition does not peak until the early 20s, for many people its influence is beginning at this stage. Included in this concept are marriage, plans for marriage, and plans for childrearing. These new variables largely replace attachment to parents and commitment to school in the theoretical scheme; they represent the major sources of bonds to conventional society for young adults.

Both attachment to parents and commitment to school remain in the model but take on the cast of exogenous variables. Attachment to parents has only a minor effect on commitment to school, and commitment to school is proposed to affect only commitment to conventional activities and, more weakly, delinquent behavior.

The other three variables considered in the previous models—association with delinquent peers, delinquent values, and delinquent behavior—are still hypothesized to be embedded in an amplifying causal loop. As indicated above, this loop is most likely to occur among adolescents who, at earlier ages, were freed from the controlling influence of parents and school. Moreover, via the feedback paths delinquent peers, delinquent values, and delinquent behavior further alienate the youth from parents and diminish commitment to school. Once this spiral begins, the probability of sustained delinquency increases.

This situation, if it continued uninterrupted, would yield higher and higher rates of crime as the subjects matured. Such an outcome is inconsistent with the desistance that has been observed during this age period (Wolfgang, Thornberry, and Figlio, 1987). Rates of delinquency and crime begin to subside by the late teenage years, a phenomenon often attributed to "maturational reform." Such an explanation, however, is tautological since it claims that crime stops when adolescents get older, because they get older. It is also uninformative since the concept of maturational reform is theoretically undefined.

A developmental approach, however, offers an explanation for desistance. As the developmental process unfolds, life circumstances change, developmental milestones are met (or, for some, missed), new social roles are created, and new networks of attachments and commitments emerge. The effects of these changes enter the processual model to explain new and often dramatically different behavioral patterns. In the present model, these changes are represented by commitment to conventional activity and commitment to family.

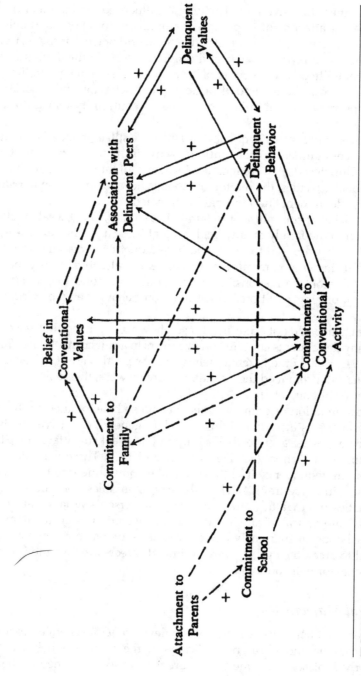

FIGURE 12.4 *A reciprocal model of delinquent involvement at later adolescence.*[a]

[a]Solid lines represent stronger effects; dashed lines represent weaker effects.

Commitment to conventional activity is influenced by a number of variables, including earlier attachment to parents, commitment to school, and belief in conventional values. And once the transition to the world of work is made, tremendous opportunities are afforded for new and different effects in the delinquency model. Becoming committed to conventional activities—work, college, military service, and so on—reduces the likelihood of delinquent behavior and associations with delinquent peers because it builds up a stake in conformity that is antithetical to delinquency.

Moreover, since the delinquency variables are still embedded in a causal loop, the effect of commitment to conventional activities tends to resonate throughout the system. But, because of the increased saliency of a new variable, commitment to conventional activities, the reinforcing loop is now set in motion to *reduce* rather than increase delinquent and criminal involvement.

The variable of commitment to family has similar, albeit weaker, effects since the transition to the family is only beginning at these ages. Nevertheless, commitment to family is proposed to reduce both delinquent associations and delinquent values and to increase commitment to conventional activity. In general, as the individual takes on the responsibilities of family, the bond to conventional society increases, placing additional constraints on behavior and precluding further delinquency.

These changes do not occur in all cases, however, nor should they be expected to since many delinquents continue on to careers in adult crime. In the Philadelphia cohort of 1945, 51% of the juvenile delinquents were also adult offenders, and the more serious and prolonged the delinquent careers were, the greater the odds of an adult career (Wolfgang et al., 1987: Ch. 4).

The continuation of criminal careers can also be explained by the nature of the reciprocal effects included in this model. In general, extensive involvement in delinquency at earlier ages feeds back upon and weakens attachment to parents and commitment to school (see Figures 12.2 and 12.3). These variables, as well as involvement in delinquency itself, weaken later commitment to family and to conventional activities (Figure 12.4). Thus, these new variables, commitment to conventional activities and to family, are affected by the person's situation at earlier stages and do not "automatically" alter the probability of continued criminal involvement. If the initial bonds are extremely weak, the chances of new bonding variables being established to break the cycle towards criminal careers are low and it is likely that criminal behavior will continue.

Behavioral Trajectories

The manner in which reciprocal effects and developmental changes are interwoven in the interactional model can be explicated by the concept of behavioral trajectories. At early adolescence, some youths are very weakly attached to their parents, very weakly committed to school, and do not grant legitimacy to conventional values. As indicated above, they are the most likely youngsters for high delinquency involvement. (The term delinquency involvement summarizes the causal loop containing delinquent behavior, delinquent values, and association with delinquent peers.) In turn, the high delinquency involvement further attenuates the bonding to parents and to school. This early adolescent situation continues during middle adolescence and substantially reduces the chances of the person reestablishing (or perhaps establishing) bonds to conventional society during late adolescence.

In brief, a behavioral trajectory is established that predicts increasing involvement in delinquency and crime. The initially weak bonds lead to high delinquency involvement, the high delinquency involvement further weakens the conventional bonds, and in combination both of these effects make it extremely difficult to reestablish bonds to conventional society at later ages. As a result, all of the factors tend to reinforce one another over time to produce an extremely high probability of continued deviance.

On the other hand, one can imagine many young adolescents who, at the outset, are strongly attached to their parents, highly committed to school, and believe in conventional values. The theoretical model predicts that this high level of bonding buffers them from the world of delinquency. Moreover, the reciprocal character of this loop establishes a behavioral trajectory for these youths that tends towards increasing conformity. Their initial strong conventional bonds reduce the chances of involvement in delinquency and thereby increase the chances of commitment to conventional activities and the like at later ages.

Thus, we can conceive of at least two types of adolescents with differing and diverging behavioral trajectories. In one trajectory, social bonds become progressively weaker and delinquent behavior progressively more likely, while in the other commitment to conformity becomes progressively stronger and delinquent behavior progressively less likely.

Of course, if there are these extremes, there are also intermediate cases. In many ways they are the most interesting since their eventual outcome is much more in doubt. For example, there are some youths who have a relatively high level of attachment to parents but low commitment to school (or vice versa). These adolescents are more likely candidates for delinquency involvement than are youths with both high attachment and commitment. But, should the delinquent involvement occur, its feedback effect on the bonding variables is less certain. While the delinquency may further reduce the already weak commitment to school, the strong attachment to parents may serve as a buffer to offset some of the negative feedback. Such a situation, in which the initial bonding variables are neither extremely high nor extremely low, allows for rather varied patterns of interactive effects as the developmental process unfolds. Moreover, the prediction of the eventual outcome for such youths awaits more direct empirical evidence establishing the relative strength of these competing effects.

The concept of behavioral trajectories raises an important theoretical issue. It suggests that the initial values of the process variables play a central role in the entire process since they set the basic path of the behavioral trajectories. Because of this, it is theoretically important to account for variation in those initial values. In the present paper the role of one general class of variables, position in the social structure, is used to illustrate this issue.

Structural Effects

Structural variables, including race, class, sex, and community of residence, refer to the person's location in the structure of social roles and statuses. The manner in which they are incorporated in the interactional model is illustrated here by examining only one of them, social class of origin.

Although social class is often measured continuously, a categorical approach is more consistent with the present model and with most theories of delinquency that incorporate class as a major explanatory variable—for example, strain and social disorganization theories. For our purposes, the most important categories are the lower class, the working lower class, and the middle class.

The lower class is composed of those who are chronically or sporadically unemployed, receive welfare, and subsist at or below the poverty level. They are similar to Johnson's "underclass" (1979). The working lower class is composed of those with more stable work patterns, training for semiskilled jobs, and incomes that allow for some economic stability. For these families, however, the hold on even a marginal level of occupational and economic security is always tenuous. Finally, the middle class refers to all families above these lower levels. Middle-class families have achieved some degree of economic success and stability and can reasonably expect to remain at that level or improve their standing over time.

The manner in which the social class of origin affects the interactional variables and the behavioral trajectories can be demonstrated by comparing the life expectancies of children from lower-and middle-class families. As compared to children from a middle-class background, children from a lower-class background are more apt to have (1) disrupted family processes and environments (Conger, McCarty, Wang, Lahey, and Kroop, 1984; Wahler, 1980); (2) poorer preparation for school (Cloward and Ohlin, 1960); (3) belief structures influenced by the traditions of the American lower class (Miller, 1958; Anderson, 1976); and (4) greater exposure to neighborhoods with high rates of crime (Shaw and McKay, 1942; Braithwaite, 1981). The direction of all these effects is such that we would expect children from lower-class families to be *initially* less bonded to conventional society and more exposed to delinquent values, friends, and behaviors.

As one moves towards the working lower class, both the likelihood and the potency of the factors just listed decrease. As a result, the initial values of the interactional variables improve but, because of the tenuous nature of economic and social stability for these families, both the bonding variables and the delinquency variables are still apt to lead to considerable amounts of delinquent conduct. Finally, youths from middle-class families, given their greater stability and economic security, are likely to start with a stronger family structure, greater stakes in conformity, and higher chances of success, and all of these factors are likely to reduce the likelihood of initial delinquent involvement.

In brief, the initial values of the interactional variables are systematically related to the social class of origin. Moreover, since these variables are reciprocally related, it follows logically that social class is systematically related to the behavioral trajectories described above. Youngsters from the lowest classes have the highest probability of moving forward on a trajectory of increasing delinquency. Starting from a position of low bonding to conventional institutions and a high delinquency environment, the reciprocal nature of the interrelationships leads inexorably towards extremely high rates of delinquent and criminal involvement. Such a view is consistent with prevalence data which show that by age 18, 50%, and by age 30, 70% of low SES minority males have an official police record (Wolfgang et al., 1987).

On the other hand, the expected trajectory of middle-class youths suggests that they will move toward an essentially conforming life-style, in which their stakes in conformity increase and more and more preclude serious and prolonged involvement in delinquency. Finally, because the initial values of the interactional variables are mixed and indecisive for children from lower-working-class homes, their behavioral trajectories are much more volatile and the outcome much less certain.

Summary: Interactional theory asserts that both the initial values of the process variables and their development over time are systematically related to the social class of origin. Moreover, parallel arguments can be made for other structural variables, especially those associated with class, such as race, ethnicity, and the social disorganization of the neighborhood. Like class of origin, these variables are systematically related to variables such as commitment to school and involvement in delinquent behavior, and therefore, as a group, these structural variables set the stage on which the reciprocal effects develop across the life cycle.

Conclusion

The present article has developed an interactional theory of delinquent behavior. Unlike traditional theories of delinquency, interactional theory does not view delinquency merely as an outcome or consequence of a social process. On the contrary, it views delinquent behavior as an active part of the developmental process, interacting with other social factors over time to determine the person's ultimate behavioral repertoire.

The initial impetus towards delinquency comes from a weakening of the person's bond to conventional society, represented, during adolescence, by attachment to parents, commitment to school, and belief in conventional values. Whenever these three links to conformity are attenuated, there is a substantially increased potential for delinquent behavior.

For that potential to be converted to delinquency, especially prolonged serious delinquency, however, a social setting in which delinquency is learned and reinforced is required. This setting is represented by associations with delinquent peers and delinquent values. These two variables, along with delinquent behavior itself, form a mutually reinforcing causal loop that leads towards increasing delinquency involvement over time.

Moreover, this interactive process develops over the person's life cycle, and the saliency of the theoretical concepts varies as the person ages. During early adolescence, the family is the most influential factor in bonding the youth to conventional society and reducing delinquency. As the youth matures and moves through middle adolescence, the world of friends, school, and youth culture becomes the dominant influence over behavior. Finally, as the person enters adulthood, new variables, especially commitment to conventional activities and to family, offer a number of new avenues to reshape the person's bond to society and involvement with delinquency.

Finally, interactional theory posits that these process variables are systematically related to the person's position in the social structure. Class, minority-group status, and the social disorganization of the neighborhood of residence all affect the initial values of the interactive variables as well as the behavioral trajectories. Youths from the most socially disadvantaged backgrounds begin the process least bonded to conventional society and most exposed to the world of delinquency. Furthermore, the reciprocal nature of the process increases the chances that they will continue on to a career of serious criminal involvement. On the other hand, youths from middle-class families enter a trajectory which is strongly oriented toward conformity and away from delinquency.

But, regardless of the initial starting points or the eventual outcome, the essential point of an interactional theory is that the causal process is a dynamic one that develops over the person's life. And delinquent behavior is a vital part of that process; it is clearly affected by, but it also affects, the bonding and learning variables that have always played a prominent role in sociological explanations of delinquency.

Epilogue

The version of interactional theory presented here is an initial statement of this perspective and does not represent a complete model of all the factors that are associated with delinquency. For example, the role of other structural variables, especially race and sex, which are so strongly correlated with delinquency, has to be fully explicated to better understand the sources of both the delinquency and bonding variables. Similarly, greater attention needs to be paid to the influence of early childhood behaviors and family processes since it is increasingly clear that delinquency is part of a progressive sequence that begins at much earlier ages (Patterson and Dishion, 1985; Loeber and Stouthamer-Loeber, 1986).

In addition, other process variables similar to those incorporated in Figure 12.2 through 12.4 need to be considered. For example, the general issue of gang membership and co-offending should be examined in an interactional setting as should concepts such as self-concept and self-efficacy. Finally, developmental stages have been represented here by rough age categories, and they require more careful and precise definition in terms of physical maturation and psychological growth.

Despite these, and no doubt other, limitations, this article accurately represents the basic structure of an interactional theory of delinquency. It has identified the theory's core concepts and described the manner in which they are reciprocally related to account for the initiation of delinquency and its development over time. In the coming years, the theory described here will be developed theoretically and tested empirically.[2]

Notes

1. The term "attachment to parents" is used throughout the text, but it is clear that parent surrogates—for example foster parents or guardians—can also perform this function.

2. The Rochester Youth Development Study, supported by the Office of Juvenile Justice and Delinquency Prevention and directed with my colleagues Alan Lizotte, Margaret Farnworth, and Susan Stern, is designed to examine the basic causes and correlates of delinquency from this perspective.

References

Agnew, Robert. 1985. Social control theory and delinquency: A longitudinal test. Criminology 23: 47–62.

Akers, Ronald. 1977. Deviant Behavior: A Social Learning Perspective. Belmont: Wadsworth.

Akers, Ronald L., Marvin D. Krohn, Lonn Lanza-Kaduce, and Marcia Radosevich. 1979. Social learning theory and deviant behavior. American Sociological Review 44: 635–655.

Anderson, Elijah. 1976. A Place on the Corner. Chicago: University of Chicago Press.

Bachman, Jerald G., Patrick M. O'Malley, and John Johnston. 1978. Youth in Transition: Adolescence to Adulthood—Change and Stability in the Lives of Young Men. Ann Arbor: Institute for Social Research.

Braithwaite, John. 1981. The myth of social class and criminality reconsidered. American Sociological Review 46: 36–58.

Brehm, J.W., and Arthur R. Cohen. 1962. Explorations in Cognitive Dissonance. New York: Wiley.

Burkett, Steven R., and Bruce O. Warren. 1987. Religiosity, peer influence, and adolescent marijuana use: A panel study of underlying causal structures. Criminology 25: 109–131.

Cloward, Richard A., and Lloyd E. Ohlin. 1960. Delinquency and Opportunity: A Theory of Delinquent Gangs. Glencoe: Free Press.

Conger, Rand D. 1980. Juvenile delinquency: Behavior restraint or behavior facilitation? In Travis Hirschi and Michael Gottfredson (eds.), Understanding Crime. Beverly Hills: Sage.

Conger, Rand D., John A. McCarty, Raymond K. Wang, Benjamin B. Lahey, and Joseph P. Kroop. 1984. Perception of child, child-rearing values, and emotional distress as mediating links between environmental stressors and observed maternal behavior. Child Development 55: 2,234–2,247.

Cullen, Francis T. 1984. Rethinking Crime and Deviance Theory: The Emergence of a Structuring Tradition. Totowa, NJ: Rowman and Allanheld.

Elliott, Delbert S. 1985. The assumption that theories can be combined with increased explanatory power: Theoretical integrations. In Robert F. Meier (ed.), Theoretical Methods in Criminology. Beverly Hills: Sage.

Elliott, Delbert S., Suzanne S. Ageton, and Rachelle J. Canter. 1979. An integrated theoretical perspective on delinquent behavior. Journal of Research on Crime and Delinquency 16: 3–27.

Elliott, Delbert S., David Huizinga, and Suzanne S. Ageton. 1985. Explaining Delinquency and Drug Use. Beverly Hills: Sage.

Elliott, Delbert S., and Harwin L. Voss. 1974. Delinquency and Dropout. Lexington: Lexington Books.

Festinger, Leon. 1957. A Theory of Cognitive Dissonance. Stanford: Stanford University Press.

Glueck, Sheldon, and Eleanor Glueck. 1950. Unraveling Juvenile Delinquency. Cambridge: Harvard University Press.

Hanushek, Eric A., and John E. Jackson. 1977. Statistical Methods for Social Scientists. New York: Academic Press.

Heise, David R. 1975. Causal Analysis. New York: Wiley.

Hindelang, Michael J. 1974. Moral evaluations of illegal behaviors. Social Problems 21: 370–384.

Hindelang, Michael J., Travis Hirschi, and Joseph G. Weis. 1981. Measuring Delinquency. Beverly Hills: Sage.

Hirschi, Travis. 1969. Causes of Delinquency. Berkeley: University of California Press.

Huizinga, David, and Delbert S. Elliott. 1986. The Denver High-Risk Delinquency Project. Proposal Submitted to the Office of Juvenile Justice and Delinquency Prevention.

Johnson, Richard E. 1979. Juvenile Delinquency and Its Origins. Cambridge: Cambridge University Press.

Kandel, Denise B., and John A. Logan. 1984. Patterns of drug use from adolescence to young adulthood I: Periods of risk for initiation, continued risk and discontinuation. American Journal of Public Health 74: 660–667.

Krohn, Marvin D., and James Massey. 1980. Social and delinquent behavior: An examination of the elements of the social bond. Sociological Quarterly 21: 529–543.

LaGrange, Randy L., and Helene Raskin White. 1985. Age differences in delinquency: A test of theory. Criminology 23: 19–46

Loeber, Rolf, and Magda Stouthamer-Loeber. 1986. Family factors as correlates and predictors of juvenile conduct problems and delinquency. In Norval Morris and Michael Tonry (eds.), Crime and Justice: An Annual Review of Research. Chicago: University of Chicago Press.

Liska, Allen, and Mark Reed. 1985. Ties to conventional institutions and delinquency. American Sociological Review 50: 547–560.

Matsueda, Ross. 1982. Testing social control theory and differential association. American Sociological Review 47: 489–504.

Miller, Walter B. 1958. Lower class culture as a generating milieu of gang delinquency. Journal of Social Issues 14: 5–19.

Paternoster, Raymond, Linda E. Saltzman, Gordon P. Waldo, and Theodore G Chiricos. 1982. Perceived risk and deterrence: Methodological artifacts in perceptual deterrence research. Journal of Criminal Law and Criminology 73: 1,238–1,258.

Paternoster, Raymond, Linda E. Saltzman, Theodore G. Chiricos, and Gordon P. Waldo. 1983. Perceived risk and social control: Do sanctions really deter? Law and Society Review 17: 457–479.

Patterson, Gerald R., and Thomas S. Dishion. 1985. Contributions of families and peers to delinquency. Criminology 23: 63–80.

Polk, Kenneth, Christine Adler, Gordon Bazemore, Gerald Blake, Sheila Cordray, Garry Coventry, James Galvin, and Mark Temple. 1981. Becoming Adult: An Analysis of Maturational Development from Age 16 to 30 of a Cohort of Young Men. Final Report of the Marion County Youth Study. Eugene: University of Oregon.

Poole, Eric D., and Robert M. Regoli. 1979. Parental Support, delinquent friends and delinquency: A test of interactional effects. Journal of Criminal Law and Criminology 70: 188–193.

Schoenberg, Ronald J. 1975. A Structural Model of Delinquency. Unpublished doctoral dissertation, Seattle: University of Washington.

Shaw, Clifford R., and Henry D. McKay. 1942. Juvenile Delinquency and Urban Areas. Chicago: University of Chicago Press.

Short, James F., Jr., and Fred L. Strodtbeck. 1965. Group Processes and Gang Delinquency. Chicago: University of Chicago Press.

Snyder. J., and Gerald Patterson. In Press. Family interactions and delinquent behavior. Child Development.

Thornberry, Terence P. 1987. Reflections on the advantages and disadvantages of theoretical integration. Presented at the Albany Conference on Theoretical Integration in the Study of Crime and Deviance.

Thornberry, Terence P., and R.L. Christenson. 1984. Unemployment and criminal involvement: An investigation of reciprocal causal structures. American Sociological Review 49: 398–411.

Thornberry, Terence P., Margaret Farnworth, and Alan Lizotte. 1986. A Panel Study of Reciprocal Causal Model of Delinquency. Proposal submitted to the Office of Juvenile Justice and Delinquency Prevention.

Thornberry, Terence P., Melanie Moore, and R.L. Christenson. 1985. The effect of dropping out of high school on subsequent delinquent behavior. Criminology 23: 3–18.

Wahler, R. 1980. The insular mother: Her problems in parent-child treatment. Journal of Applied Behavior Analysis 13: 207–219.

Weis, Joseph G., and John Sederstrom. 1981. The Prevention of Serious Delinquency: What to Do? Washington, D.C.: U.S. Department of Justice.

Wolfgang, Marvin E., Terence P. Thornberry, and Robert M. Figlio. 1987. From Boy to Man—From Delinquency to Crime: Followup to the Philadelphia Birth Cohort of 1945. Chicago: University of Chicago Press.

13

Turning Points in the Life Course: Why Change Matters to the Study of Crime

John Laub and Robert Sampson's turning points theory is another form of "life course" or "developmental" theory, similar in a number of respects to Terence Thornberry's interactional theory (see the previous reading by Thornberry). Both theories talk about "reciprocal" causal paths, wherein weakened social bonds contribute to delinquency, and delinquency in turn contributes to weakened social bonds (Laub & Sampson, 1993:303, 311; Thornberry, 1987:867, 873). Both are also rooted in Durkheimian tradition, and in Travis Hirschi's social bond theory (Paternoster & Bachman, 2001:73, 79; Sampson & Laub, 1990:611; Thornberry, 1987:865). However, Laub, Sampson and Thornberry (amongst others) have disagreed with Travis Hirschi when it comes to the stability of criminality over the life course. Travis Hirschi and Michael Gottfredson (amongst others) have argued for many years that crime is stable over the life course—i.e., that problem children become teenage delinquents, who then go on to become adult criminals (Gottfredson & Hirschi, 1990:107–108; Hirschi & Gottfredson, 2001:232–235). Laub, Sampson and Thornberry, on the other hand, argue that crime is not necessarily stable over the life course. They say that social bonds and informal social controls can change for the better over time, and that as a consequence, many individuals who appear to have embarked upon an inevitable pathway toward criminality veer off and become "normal," law-abiding adults (Laub, Sampson, & Allen, 2001:97; Paternoster & Bachman, 2001:78–80; Thornberry & Krohn, 2005:200–202).

Laub and Sampson describe this process of change in terms of "trajectories," "transitions" and "turning points" (Laub & Sampson, 1993:304). Trajectories are the life pathways that individuals are on. These pathways may go in various different directions. For example, if an individual was skipping out of school and shoplifting during childhood, and engaging in serious delinquency (e.g., gang fighting, breaking into houses, selling drugs, etc.) as a teenager, we might say that he or she appeared to be on a pathway (or trajectory) toward a life time of criminality. Transitions are changes in status, for example, graduating from high school, moving from adolescence into adulthood, going from being single to being married, or finding a first job (Williams & McShane, 2010:209). These transitions may lead to turning points, where the pathway comes to a fork in the road. If the individual chooses the right fork in the road, then he or she may be deflected away from a lifetime of crime. This notion of trajectories, transitions and turning points is not, by the way, unique to—or an original invention of—Sampson and Laub. Terence Thornberry talks about trajectories and transitions in his interactional theory (Thornberry & Krohn, 2005; Thornberry, 1987), and these terms were used previously by Glen Elder in his work on human agency, social change and the life course perspective (Elder, 2001:4–5).

In this article, "Turning Points in the Life Course," Laub and Sampson discuss attachment, commitment, and social bonds (1993:304; cf. Sampson & Laub, 1990: 614, 616). Attachment and commitment are of course the first two components of Travis Hirschi's social bond theory. However, Laub and Sampson redefine the development of prosocial adult bonds as the acquisition of "social capital" (1993:309–310; cf. Sampson & Laub, 1992:73–74). Social capital refers to the social resources that individuals have available to them—their social relationships, neighborhood networks, and the degree of social support which they receive from family, friends and employers (Coleman, 1988). The connection between social capital, social bond theory and Durkheimian thinking is captured well in Robert Putnam's Johan Skytte prize lecture on social capital and social diversity, delivered at Uppsala University in Sweden. In this lecture, he talks simultaneously about "commpunity," "social cohesion," "social solidarity," and the importance of both "bridging social capital" and "bonding social capital" (Putnam, 2007).

As they reach adulthood, many individuals enter into good, stable marriages, where they develop a strong sense of attachment and commitment to their partners (and to their children, if they have any). As importantly, many find well-paying, stable jobs, where they develop ties to (and have respect for) their employer and workplace colleagues. Through this process, they make a social investment in their future, whilst simultaneously acquiring social capital (Laub & Sampson, 1993:310–311, 313–314). Once individuals have acquired social capital like this, they are reluctant to risk it by engaging in criminal activity. Going to prison or getting a criminal record can lead to the break–up of a marriage, or to the loss of employment. In other words, individuals who might have been on a pathway to prison suddenly find that they have something at stake if they continue in that direction. According to Sampson and Laub, this acquisition of social capital acts as a new source of informal social control, and helps in large part to explain why the majority of young offenders do not go on to become adult offenders (1993:319–320).

References

Coleman, J. S. (1988). Social capital in the creation of human capital. *American Journal of Sociology, 94* (Supplement: Organizations and Institutions: Sociological and Economic Approaches to the Analysis of Social Structure), S95–S120.

Elder, G. H. (2001). Time, human agency and social change: Perspectives on the life course. In A. Piquero, & P. Mazerolle (Eds.), *Life-course criminology: Contemporary and classic readings* (pp. 3–20). Toronto: Wadsworth Thomson Learning.

Gottfredson, M. R., & Hirschi, T. (1990). *A general theory of crime.* Stanford, Calif.: Stanford University Press.

Hirschi, T., & Gottfredson, M. R. (2001). Control theory and the life course perspective. In A. Piquero, & P. Mazerolle (Eds.), *Life-course criminology: Contemporary and classic readings* (pp. 229–241). Toronto: Wadsworth Thomson Learning.

Laub, J. H., & Sampson, R. J. (1993). Turning points in the life course: Why change matters to the study of crime. *Criminology, 31*(3), 301–325.

Laub, J. H., Sampson, R. L., & Allen, L. C. (2001). Explaining crime over the life course: Toward a theory of age-graded informal social control. In R. Paternoster, & R. Bachman (Eds.), *Explaining criminals and crime: Essays in contemporary criminological theory* (pp. 97–112). Los Angeles, Calif.: Roxbury Pub. Co.

Paternoster, R., & Bachman, R. (2001). Control theories of crime. In R. Paternoster, & R. Bachman (Eds.), *Explaining criminals and crime: Essays in contemporary criminological theory* (pp. 80–191). Los Angeles, Calif.: Roxbury Pub. Co.

Putnam, R. D. (2007). E pluribus unum: Diversity and community in the Twenty-First Century the 2006 Johan Skytte prize lecture. *Scandinavian Political Studies, 30*(2), 137–174. doi:10.1111/j.1467–9477.2007.00176.x

Sampson, R. J., & Laub, J. H. (1990). Crime and deviance over the life course: The salience of adult social bonds. *American Sociological Review, 55*(5), 609–627. doi:10.2307/2095859

Sampson, R. J., & Laub, J. H. (1992). Crime and deviance in the life course. *Annual Review of Sociology, 18*(1), 63–84.

Thornberry, T. (1987). Toward an interactional theory of delinquency. *Criminology, 25*(4), 863–891.

Thornberry, T. P., & Krohn, M. D. (2005). Applying interactional theory to the explanation of continuity and change in antisocial behavior. In D. P. Farrington (Ed.), *Integrated developmental & life-course theories of offending* (pp. 183–209). New Brunswick, NJ: Transaction Publishers.

Williams, F. P., & McShane, M. D. (2010). *Criminological theory* (5th ed.). Upper Saddle River, N.J.: Pearson/Prentice Hall.

Turning Points in the Life Course: Why Change Matters to the Study of Crime*

JOHN H. LAUB AND ROBERT J. SAMPSON

This article examines conceptual issues relating to continuity and change in crime over the life course. Building on past efforts, we first distinguish self-selection from a cumulative, developmental process whereby delinquent behavior attenuates adult social bonds (e.g., labor force attachment, marital cohesion). We then conceptualize various types of change and argue that social capital and turning points are crucial in understanding processes of change in the adult life course. These concepts are illustrated by examining person-based, life-history data drawn from the Gluecks' longitudinal study of 1,000 men. Although adult crime is clearly connected to childhood behavior, these qualitative data suggest that both incremental and abrupt change are structured by changes in adult social bonds. We conclude with some hypotheses and implications for future research on subjective contingencies, opportunity structures, and chance encounters as potential turning points for change, especially as they interact with race, class location, and historical context.

Several years ago we uncovered 60 cartons of case files in the basement of the Harvard Law School Library. These data constituted the classic longitudinal study of 500 delinquents and 500 nondelinquents initiated by Sheldon and Eleanor Glueck in 1940 (see Glueck and Glueck, 1950, 1968). While we were organizing and reconstructing the Gluecks' data, two important books rocked the field of criminology—*Crime and Human Nature* by James Q. Wilson and Richard Herrnstein (1985), and *A General Theory of Crime* by Michael Gottfredson and Travis Hirschi (1990). Although certainly different, the thrust of these books was to redirect criminological attention to the importance of childhood. For example, Gottfredson and Hirschi (1990) argue that effective child rearing in the early formative years of a child's development produces high self-control, which in turn is a stable phenomenon that inhibits crime throughout the life course. The work of Wilson and Herrnstein (1985) pushed the explanation of crime back even earlier in life to constitutional differences (e.g., impulsiveness and temperament) in interaction with familial factors (see also Grasmick et al., 1993; Nagin and Paternoster, 1991).

Ironically, then, as we were resurrecting the Gluecks' data, new life was breathed into the primary thesis of the Gluecks—childhood temperament and family socialization matter most, and thus the "past is prologue" (Glueck and Glueck, 1968:167).

*An earlier version of this article was presented at the annual meeting of the American Society of Criminology, New Orleans, 1992. We thank the reviewers for constructive criticisms on an earlier draft. Life-history data were derived from the Sheldon and Eleanor Glueck archives of the Harvard Law School Library, currently on long-term loan to the Henry A. Murray Research Center of Radcliffe College.

Reprinted from *Criminology* 31, no. 3 (1993), American Society of Criminology.

Although attracted to this renewed emphasis on the importance of children and families to the explanation of delinquency, we were troubled by the profound questions raised by the childhood-stability argument. Are differences in child rearing and temperament all we need to know to understand patterns of adult crime? Are childhood differences in antisocial behavior invariably stable? Why does continuity in deviant behavior exist? Perhaps most important, what about individual change, salient life events, and turning points in adulthood?

Challenged by these and other questions, we set out to examine crime and deviance in childhood, adolescence, and adulthood in a way that recognized the significance of both continuity and change over the life course. To do so we synthesized and integrated the criminological literature on childhood antisocial behavior, adolescent delinquency, and adult crime with theory and research on the life course (Sampson and Laub, 1992). By also rethinking the findings produced by longitudinal research, we were eventually led to develop an age-graded theory of informal social control to explain crime and deviance over the life span. We then tested this theory on the longitudinal data we reconstructed from the Gluecks' study (Sampson and Laub, 1993).

Building on these efforts, we turn to an examination of conceptual issues relating to continuity and change in antisocial behavior over the life course. With respect to continuity, we highlight the distinction between self-selection and cumulative continuity. We then unite the ideas of state dependence (Nagin and Paternoster, 1991) and cumulative continuity (Caspi and Moffitt, 1993a; Moffitt, 1993) in delineating a developmental, sequential model of crime across the life course. With respect to change, we explicate the relevance of the adult life course and the various meanings of change. Our major thesis is that social capital and turning points are important concepts in understanding processes of change in the adult life course. We illustrate these concepts using qualitative life-history data drawn from the Gluecks' study. Overall, our goal is to advance a framework that challenges theories of crime which "presuppose a developmental determinism in which childhood experiences set the course of later development" (Bandura, 1982:747). To set the stage, we briefly highlight the theoretical framework on change from our recent study (Sampson and Laub, 1993).

An Age-Graded Theory of Informal Social Control

The central idea of social control theory—that crime and deviance are more likely when an individual's bond to society is weak or broken—is an organizing principle in our theory of social bonding over the life course.[1] Following Elder (1975, 1985), we differentiate the life course of individuals on the basis of age and argue that the important institutions of both formal and informal social control vary across the life span. However, we emphasize the role of age-graded, *informal* social control as reflected in the structure of interpersonal bonds linking members of society to one another and to wider social institutions (e.g., work, family, school). Unlike formal sanctions that originate in purposeful efforts to control crime, informal social controls "emerge as by-products of role relationships established for other purposes and are components of role reciprocities" (Kornhauser, 1978:24).

Although rejecting the "ontogenetic" approach dominant in developmental psychology (see Dannefer, 1984), our theoretical framework nonetheless follows a developmental strategy (Loeber and LeBlanc, 1990; Patterson et al., 1989). The specific developmental approach we take views causality as "best represented by a developmental network of causal factors" in which dependent variables become independent variables over time (Loeber and LeBlanc, 1990:433). Moreover, developmental criminology recognizes both continuity and within-individual changes over time, focusing on "life transitions and developmental covariates . . . which may mediate the developmental course of offending" (Loeber and LeBlanc, 1990:451). This strategy has also been referred to as a "stepping-stone approach" whereby factors are time ordered by age and assessed with respect to outcome variables (see Farrington, 1986).

A similar orientation can be found in interactional theory as proposed by Thornberry (1987). Interactional theory embraces a developmental approach and argues convincingly that causal influences are reciprocal over the life course and that delinquency may contribute to the weakening of social bonds over time. Thornberry's perspective is also consistent with a person-centered approach to development as propounded by Magnusson and Bergman (1988:47). Namely, by focusing explicitly on "persons" rather than "variables" and examining individual life histories over time (see Magnusson and Bergman, 1988, 1990), this strategy offers insight into the social processes of intra-individual developmental change in criminal behavior over the life course.

Although beyond the scope of this analysis, the first building block in our "sociogenic" developmental theory focuses on the mediating role of informal family and school social bonds in explaining childhood and adolescent delinquency (Sampson and Laub, 1993: Ch. 4–5). As elaborated more below, the second building block incorporates the subsequent continuity in childhood and adolescent antisocial behavior that extends throughout adulthood across a variety of life's domains (e.g., crime, alcohol abuse, divorce, unemployment).

Having provided a role for continuity, we nonetheless believe that salient life events and social ties in adulthood can counteract, at least to some extent, the trajectories of early child development. Hence, a third and major thesis of our work is that social bonds in adulthood—especially *attachment to the labor force* and *cohesive marriage* (or cohabitation)—explain criminal behavior regardless of prior differences in criminal propensity. In other words, we contend that pathways to both crime and conformity are modified by key institutions of social control in the transition to adulthood (e.g., employment, military service, and marriage).

In contrast to many life-course models, we emphasize the quality or strength of social ties in these transitions more than the occurrence or timing of discrete life events (cf. Loeber and LeBlanc, 1990:430–432). For example, marriage per se may not increase social control, but close emotional ties and mutual investment increase the social bond between individuals and, all else equal, should lead to a reduction in criminal behavior (cf. Shover, 1985:94). Employment by itself also does not necessarily increase social control. It is employment coupled with job stability, commitment to work, and mutual ties binding workers and employers that should increase social control and, all else equal, lead to a reduction in criminal behavior.

In short, our theory attempts to unite continuity and change within the context of a sociological understanding of crime in the life course. A major concept in our framework is the dynamic process whereby the interlocking nature of trajectories and transitions generates *turning points* or a change in life course (Elder, 1985:32). Adaptation to life events is crucial because the same event or transition followed by different adaptations can lead to different trajectories (Elder, 1985:35). That is, despite the connection between childhood events and experiences in adulthood, turning points can modify life trajectories—they can "redirect paths." For some individuals, turning points are abrupt—radical "turnarounds" or changes in life history that separate the past from the future (Elder et al., 1991:215). For most individuals, however, we conceptualize turning points as "part of a process over time and not as a dramatic lasting change that takes place at any one time" (Pickles and Rutter, 1991:134; see also Clausen, 1990; McAdam, 1989:745; Rutter, 1989a, 1989b). The process-oriented nature of turning points leads us to focus on incremental change embedded in informal social controls.

To evaluate the refine our theory, we analyzed the natural histories of two groups of boys that differed dramatically in childhood antisocial behavior and delinquency that were followed into adulthood. More specifically, we reconstructed and examined the life histories originally gathered by Glueck and Glueck (1950, 1968) of 500 delinquents and 500 control subjects matched on age, IQ, ethnicity, and neighborhood deprivation. An exhaustive body of data (e.g., official records, observations, and personal interviews with subjects, parents, spouses, neighbors, and employers) was collected on these individuals in childhood, adolescence, young adulthood, and adulthood. Our analyses involved a multi-method, multi-measurement scheme that used quantitative and qualitative data (see Sampson and Laub, 1993, for details).

Distinguishing Self-Selection from Cumulative Continuity

Critics will argue that individual differences combine with self-selection to account for patterns of behavior across the life course. In brief, this counter-argument goes as follows: Individuals with an early propensity to crime (e.g., low self-control) determined mainly by family socialization and individual differences (e.g., impulsiveness) systematically sort themselves throughout adulthood into states consistent with this latent trait. For instance, Gottfredson and Hirschi (1990: 166–167) argue that delinquent and impulsive youths will choose deviant spouses, unstable jobs, and continue their delinquent ways in adulthood. If true, the adult life course is merely a setting within which predetermined lives are played out.

In one sense the self-selection thesis was supported in the Gluecks' study—adolescent delinquents and nondelinquents displayed significant behavioral consistency well into adulthood. Delinquency and other forms of antisocial conduct in childhood were related not only to adult crime, but also to troublesome behaviors across a variety of adult domains (e.g., AWOL in the military, economic dependence, marital discord). This continuity persisted despite the fact that delinquents and controls were originally matched case-by-case on age, intelligence, neighborhood, and ethnicity.

The hypothesis of self-selection, however, leads to a more fundamental methodological implication—correlations among adult behaviors (e.g., job instability and crime) are completely spurious and should disappear once controls are introduced for prior individual-level differences in criminal propensity or low self-control (see Gottfredson and Hirschi, 1990: 154–168). Although rarely examined directly, we believe the data do not support this spuriousness hypothesis. In particular, our quantitative analyses revealed independent effects of marital attachment and job stability on adult crime. These results were consistent for a wide variety of outcome measures, control variables (e.g., childhood and adolescent antisocial behavior; individual-difference constructs, such as IQ, self-control, mesomorphy, and personality), and analytic techniques—including methods that account for persistent unobserved heterogeneity in criminal propensity (see Nagin and Paternoster, 1991). Rutter et al. (1990) have also shown the independent explanatory power of adult marital cohesion on adult deviance, self-selection notwithstanding.

At the same time, our theory incorporates the causal role of prior delinquency in facilitating adult crime by integrating the concept of *state dependence* (Nagin and Paternoster, 1991) with that of *cumulative continuity* (Moffitt, 1993). Although this role is potentially direct, we emphasize a developmental model wherein delinquent behavior has a systematic, attenuating effect on the social and institutional bonds linking adults to society (e.g., labor force attachment, marital cohesion). More specifically, the idea of cumulative continuity posits that delinquency incrementally mortgages the future by generating negative consequences for the life chances of stigmatized and institutionalized youths. For example, arrest and incarceration may spark failure in school, unemployment, and weak community bonds, in turn increasing adult crime (Tittle, 1988:80). Serious delinquency in particular leads to the "knifing off" (Caspi and Moffitt, 1993a; Moffitt, 1993) of future opportunities such that participants have fewer options for a conventional life. The cumulative continuity of disadvantage is thus not only a result of stable individual differences in criminal propensity, but a dynamic process whereby childhood antisocial behavior and adolescent delinquency foster adult crime through the severance of adult social bonds. In this view, weak social bonding is a mediating and, hence, causal sequential link in a chain of adversity between childhood delinquency and adult criminal behavior.

The thesis of cumulative continuity was supported in our quantitative analyses. As noted above, job stability and marital attachment in adulthood were significantly related to changes in adult crime—the stronger the adult ties to work and family, the less crime and deviance among delinquents and controls. Moreover, social bonds to employment were directly influenced by state sanctions—incarceration as a juvenile and as a young adult had a negative effect on later job stability, which in turn was negatively related to continued involvement in crime over the life course. Although we found little direct effect of incarceration on subsequent criminality, the indirect "criminogenic" effects through job stability were substantively important. Recent research by Nagin and Waldfogel (1992) also supports the cumulative continuity thesis in showing a destabilizing effect of convictions on the labor market prospects of a cohort of London boys.

Our synthesis of cumulative continuity and state dependence recasts in a structural and developmental framework the original contentions of labeling theory—that official reactions to primary deviance (e.g., arrest) may create problems of adjustment (e.g., unemployment) that foster additional crime in the form of secondary deviance (Becker, 1963; Lemert, 1951; Tittle, 1988). As Becker (1963: 24–39) has argued, the concept of a deviant career suggests a stable pattern of deviant behavior, which is sustained by the labeling process. More recently, Hagan and Palloni (1990) suggested that continuity in delinquent behavior may result from a structural imputation process that begins early in childhood (see also Tittle, 1988:78–81). They show that this process may even extend across generations, thereby explaining the effects of parental conviction on sons' delinquency regardless of family background and propensity to crime.

Cumulative Disadvantage and Structural Background

Hagan's (1991) research further suggests that the deleterious effect of adolescent deviance on adult stratification outcomes is greatest among lower-class boys, especially as mediated by police contacts. Middle-class boys who escaped the negative consequences of official labeling did not suffer impairment in adult occupational outcomes as a result of their adolescent delinquency. In other words, avoiding the snares of arrest and institutionalization provided opportunities for prosocial attachments among middle-class youths to take firm hold in adulthood. Similarly, Jessor et al. (1991) show that for middle-class youths, delinquency is not a major handicap with respect to adult outcomes. These studies suggest that the concepts of knifing off and cumulative continuity are most salient in explaining the structurally constrained life chances of the disadvantaged urban poor.

In short, there is evidence that cumulative disadvantage, state-dependence, and location in the class structure may interact. Among those in advantaged positions that provide continuity in social resources over time, nondelinquents and delinquents alike are presumably not just more motivated, but better able structurally to establish binding ties to conventional lines of adult activity. If nothing else, incumbency in prosocial middle-class roles provides advantages in maintaining the status quo and counteracting negative life events (e.g., last hired, first fired). Race, class, and crime also pervade the consciousness of American society more generally and employers in particular. Consider the widespread perceptions of blacks as "dangerous" and "criminal" as rationales by employers for discrimination in hiring (Kirschenman and Neckerman, 1991). We therefore merge the state-dependence thesis that historical time matters with a concern for structural location. Quite simply, the context of where *and* how long one has been in prior states is crucial in understanding later adult development.

Self-Selection Reconsidered

Our theoretical conceptualization of cumulative continuity and the causal role of the adult life course does not negate the potential direct or unmediated effect of self-selection through individual differences. In other words, by distinguishing self-selection from cumulative continuity, we incorporate the independent effects of early delinquency (or individual propensity) and the dimensions of adult social bonding on adult crime. This distinction is consistent with recent research on homophily in social choices across the life course. For example, Kandel et al. (1990) studied mate selection and found considerable homophily—deviant individuals tend to select deviant marriage or cohabitation partners (see also Caspi et al., 1990). Nevertheless, social causation emerges as a crucial factor even in the face of such social selection. As Kandel et al. (1990:221) state, "Although individual choices are made, in part, as a function of the individual's prior attributes, values, and personality characteristics, involvement in the new relationship has further effects and influences on that individual." Similarly, Rutter et al. (1990) found homophily in the choice of marital partners but also a substantial effect of marital cohesion that held after taking planning of marriage partners into account.

The emergence of significant social causation in tandem with homophily (or self-selection) undermines the theoretical individualism that pervades social scientific thought. We believe that an overemphasis on self-selection stems from a "broadly perpetuated fiction in modem society" (Coleman, 1990:300):

> This fiction is that society consists of a set of independent individuals, each of whom acts to achieve goals that are independently arrived at, and that the functioning of the social system consists of the combinations of the actions of independent individuals.

Consistent with our theory, social interdependence arises from the fact that actors have social investments in events and relationships that are partially under the control of other actors. Hence, the interdependent web of relations characteristic of social collectivities ensures the operation of constraints and opportunities in shaping behavior notwithstanding individual intentions.[2]

Why Change Still Matters

Whether generated by self-selection or cumulative continuity, a focus on stability is nonetheless insufficient for understanding crime in the adult life course. First, the stability of antisocial behavior is far from perfect. As the literature on prediction shows, childhood variables tend to be rather modest prognostic devices. In fact, a large percentage of false positives and false negatives is a common result (see, e.g., Loeber and Stouthamer-Loeber, 1987; Farrington and Tarling, 1985). The prediction literature thus reinforces the futility of an invariant or deterministic conception of human development (Jessor et al., 1991; Sampson and Laub, 1992).

Second, and equally important, rank-order correlations and other common measures of stability refer to the consistency of between-individual differences over time and consequently rely on an aggregate picture of relative standing. As Huesmann et al. (1984:1131) note, what remains stable over time is the position of an individual relative to the population. Stability coefficients do not measure the heterogeneity of individual behaviors over time and, hence, do not capture within-individual change.

Life is dynamic; change is clearly possible. Yet the theoretical conceptualization of change has been surprisingly neglected, not just in criminology (see Farrington, 1988; Sampson and Laub, 1992) but in developmental psychology as well. Indeed, in searching the literature, we found little conceptual work that directly confronts the problem.[3] Moreover, Caspi and Bem (1990:569) have argued that when the term change does appear, it frequently refers to the mere absence of continuity. We thus consider more explicitly the meaning of change and how it comes about.

Social Capital and Turning Points

Much of the confusion regarding change centers on the various meanings the concept conveys. According to the 1992 edition of *The American Heritage Dictionary of the English Language*, one definition of change is "to cause to be different"—to give a completely different form or appearance, to wholly transform or alter. This definition is most closely related to Caspi and Moffitt's (1993b) notion of "deep" or "real" change (e.g., a high-rate offender who suddenly desists and becomes a productive citizen). But change can also mean a modification, reshaping, or transition from one state, condition, or phase to another. For instance, a high-rate offender who begins to commit fewer crimes than expected based on age and prior criminal propensity changes because his or her trajectory has been modified. A third meaning of change is exchange or replacement with another, usually of the same kind or category. An individual may change from use of beer and wine to use of marijuana and cocaine. Or offenders may change from burglary to robbery.

All of this leads us to think of change along a continuum and to investigate the underlying processes that enable people to change the course of their lives. We believe this may be accomplished by viewing the life course as a probabilistic linkage or chain of events (Rutter et al., 1990) and by unraveling the mechanisms that operate at key turning points (e.g., when a risk trajectory is recast to a more adaptive path [Rutter, 1987:329]).

In our view, "deep" change and "modified" change are of most interest; both are enhanced when changing roles and environments lead to social investment or *social capital* (Coleman, 1988, 1990; Nagin and Paternoster, 1992) in institutional relationships (e.g., family, work, community). As Coleman (1990:302) argues, the distinguishing feature of social capital lies in the structure of interpersonal relations and institutional linkages. Social capital is created when these relations change in ways that facilitate action. In other words, "social capital is productive, making possible the achievements of certain ends that in its absence would not be possible" (Coleman, 1988:98). By contrast, physical capital is wholly tangible, being embodied in observable material form (1990:304), and human capital is embodied in the skills and knowledge acquired by an individual. Social capital is even less tangible, for it is embodied in the relations among persons (1990:304). A core idea, then, is that independent of the forms of physical and human capital available to individuals (e.g., income, occupational skill), social capital is a central factor in facilitating effective ties that bind a person to societal institutions.[4]

Linking Coleman's notion of social capital to social control theory, we have argued that the lack of social capital or investment is one of the primary features of weak social bonds (Sampson and Laub, 1993; see also Coleman, 1990:307; Nagin and Paternoster, 1992). The theoretical task is to identify the characteristics of social relations that facilitate the social capital available to individuals, families, employers, and other social actors. One of the most important factors is the closure (i.e., "connectedness") of networks among actors in a social system (Coleman, 1990:318–320). In a system involving employers and employees, for example, relations characterized by an extensive set of obligations, expectations, and interdependent social networks are better able to facilitate social control than are jobs characterized by purely utilitarian objectives and nonoverlapping social networks. Similarly, the mere presence of a relationship (e.g., marriage) among adults is not sufficient to produce social capital, and hence, the idea of social capital goes beyond simple structural notions of role change (i.e., married versus not married) to capture the idea of embeddedness.

Our theory thus maintains that adult social ties are important insofar as they create interdependent systems of obligation and restraint that impose significant costs for translating criminal propensities into action. In this scheme, adults will be inhibited from committing crime to the extent that over time they accumulate social capital in their work and family lives, regardless of delinquent background. By contrast, those subject to weak systems of interdependency (see also Braithwaite, 1989) and informal social control as an adult (e.g., weak attachment to the labor force or noncohesive marriage) are freer to commit deviance—even if nondelinquent as a youth. This dual premise enables us to explain desistance from crime as well as late onset, and it is consistent with Jessor et al.'s (1991:160) argument that change is "as much an outcome of the person's embeddedness in a socially organized and structured context of age-related roles, expectations, demands, and opportunities as it is of internal dispositions and intentions."

We also emphasize the reciprocal nature of social capital invested by employers and spouses. For example, employers often take chances in hiring workers, hoping that their investment will pay off. Similarly, a prospective marriage partner may be aware of a potential spouse's deviant background but may nonetheless invest his or her future in that person. This investment by the employer or spouse may in turn trigger a return investment in social capital by the employee or other spouse. The key theoretical point is that social capital and interdependency are reciprocal and embedded in the social ties that exist between individuals and social institutions. This conception may help explain how change in delinquent behavior is initiated (e.g., an employer's taking a chance on a former delinquent, fostering a return investment in that job, which in turn inhibits the deviant behavior of the employee).

Sullivan's (1989) research on gangs in New York also provides insight into racial, ethnic, and community differences in the influence of social capital on transitions to work. As they entered young adulthood, the men in the low-income white neighborhood that Sullivan studied secured better-quality jobs than men in African-American or Hispanic neighborhoods. Whites were also better able to hold onto these jobs, in part because of their familiarity with the "discipline of the workplace" gained through personal networks and intergenerational ties (1989: 100–105). Networks with the adult community thus differentiated the chances of white youths' escaping environmental adversity from those of their minority counterparts. In a similar vein, Anderson's *Streetwise: Race, Class and Change in an Urban Community* (1990) points to the importance of racial differences in intergenerational ties and the salience of those ties in facilitating employment among young males as they enter adulthood. Anderson (1990) focuses in particular on the sharp decrease over time in African-American "old heads," who socialized boys in the world of work and adulthood more generally. These ethnographies underscore variations by race, ethnicity, and structural context in social capital and its role in promoting successful transitions to young adulthood (see also Short, 1990).

Thus, because individual-difference constructs and childhood antisocial behavior are independent of adult social capital and structural context in fundamental respects, another key aspect of our theory is the partial *exogenous* nature of the adult life course. This conceptualization opens the door for turning points that can redirect behavioral trajectories in the transition to adulthood. To be sure, we are not implying that individuals in our study became completely different or that they transformed their total personality as a result of social bonding in adulthood. We do not have the data to assess such transformations, nor would we expect that kind of change to occur given what we know about continuities over the life course. But we strongly contend that behavioral changes do occur and that adult life-course patterns are not solely the result of childhood socialization (Bandura, 1982).[5]

A Person-Based, Life-History Approach to Change

Our research program has included an intensive qualitative analysis of the life-history records for a subset of men from the Gluecks' study (see Sampson and Laub, 1993: Ch. 9). In contrast to the traditional "variables oriented" approach dominant in criminology and the social sciences at large (see especially, Abbott, 1992; Katz, 1988), we have adopted a "person oriented" strategy that allows us to explore "patterns or configurations of relevant person characteristics in a developmental perspective" (Magnusson and Bergman, 1990:101). This approach enables one to investigate person-environment interactions, sequences of action, and individual change over time (see Abbott, 1992; Cairns, 1986; Magnusson and Bergman, 1988:47).

Consistent with our goal of integrating quantitative and qualitative methods, we used quantitative results to identify cases for in-depth qualitative analysis. For example, based on the finding that job stability was an important predictor of desistance from crime, we selected cases that displayed high job stability (e.g., upper 15% of the frequency distribution) in combination with no arrest experiences as an adult. Similarly, we selected cases exhibiting low job stability (e.g., bottom quartile of the distribution) and arrest experiences as an adult. When there was a sufficient number of cases in a cell (usually on the diagonal), we randomly selected them for in-depth analysis (e.g., strong job stability and no offending in adulthood). We used a similar selection procedure for marital attachment. In total, we reconstructed and examined 70 life histories from the delinquent sample (see Sampson and Laub, 1993, for details).

Integrating divergent sources of life-history data (e.g., narratives, interviews), our qualitative analysis was consistent with the hypothesis that the major turning points in the life course for men that refrained from crime and deviance in adulthood were stable employment and good marriages. As an illustration of our thesis, consider the case history of a subject we call Charlie.[6] Although Charlie had no official arrests during adulthood (ages 17–32), this pattern sharply contrasted with his criminal experiences in childhood and adolescence. As a juvenile, Charlie had 10 arrests, primarily for larcenies and burglaries. His first arrest occurred at the age of eight. Moreover, he was incarcerated three times (his first commitment took place when he was 11), and he spent a total of 30 months confined in reform schools.

At the age of 18, Charlie joined the U.S. Maritime Service. He was employed by the same shipping line for two and a half years, working the eastern seaboard from Canada to Cuba. Once every three months, he returned home. Charlie gave virtually all of his earnings to his mother to bank for him. His parole officer speculated that Charlie joined the merchant service to remove himself from detrimental neighborhood influences that were leading him to delinquency and crime. During this same period (ages 18–20), Charlie began a relationship with a woman who would eventually become his wife. Although classmates together in high school, they began "an active courtship via letters" while Charlie was in the merchant service.

At age 25, Charlie was living with his wife in East Boston. (He was almost 21 at the time of marriage and his wife was 19.) According to interview data, Charlie was devoted to his wife, and the couple appeared especially united in their mutual desire to advance economically. Their goal was to build their own home. Charlie was appreciative of his wife's cooperation and her enduring help and desire to advance economically. When asked for reasons for his reformation, he offered, "I'm married, older, and settled down now."

This portrait of Charlie's life did not change very much at his age-32 interview. He was living with his wife and two children in a suburb close to Boston. Charlie appeared happy and was especially devoted to his two children. In his spare time, he worked on home improvement. Throughout the age 25–32 period, Charlie worked at one job and had recently been promoted to foreman. He had been a machine operator at the factory where he now acted as the foreman. From interviewer notes, Charlie was described as an industrious worker with no problems on the job whatsoever.

In this article, we further advance the life-history, person-based approach to uncovering turning points and processes of change. Specifically, we selected cases for qualitative analyses that demonstrated a change in social bonds (a general measure combining job stability and marital attachment) from age 25 to age 32. Our analysis revealed evidence of both incremental and abrupt change. Incremental change usually occurred over a period of time in the context of an ongoing relationship or institutional affiliation (e.g., marriage); abrupt change was linked to a single event (e.g., entering the military). We also examined the investment processes that are involved as social capital is formed through the development of strong marital ties. Marital investment is a reciprocal process between husbands and wives that, if successful, encourages desistance from crime because of the strength of the social relations that are built up in the family. The life history of the subject we call Tony illustrates these investment processes.

Tony had five arrests during the age 17–25 period, including arrests for serious crimes such as armed robbery and burglary. He also served considerable time in penal institutions—32 months from age 20 to 25. Tony's marital situation at ages 17–25 was also rocky. At the time of his marriage, Tony was 22 and his wife was 17. His wife was in high school when she became pregnant, an event that precipitated their marriage. Shortly after the marriage, the couple separated on and off. They continued to experience poor conjugal relations throughout the early period of their marriage.

Despite marital discord and a record of crime as a young adult, Tony had no criminal activity (official or unofficial) during the age 25–32 period. What accounted for this change in behavior? Inspection of his life-history material reveals a distinct change in the marital relationship. At Tony's age-32 interview, his family situation had changed dramatically, to the point that the couple's conjugal relations were cohesive. Tony was described as a rather dependent type who clung to his wife. She was portrayed as a strong, sensible person whose interests were in the home and in her family. The couple had two sons, and overall there was a strong "we feeling" in the household.

According to Tony, his reasons for reformation included: (1) "I have steady work," (2) "I have family responsibilities now," and (3) "I have learned my lesson"—he feared returning to prison. According to detailed interviewer notes and additional narratives, the strong influence of Tony's wife was the most important reason for his reform. Indeed, in what appears to be a form of marital social control seen in other cases described below, the interviewer wrote that Tony's wife "gives him good counsel and she sees to it that the subject follows her advice."

Other cases we examined revealed more abrupt change. For instance, one subject, Fred, had no arrests as an adult although he experienced five arrests as a juvenile, mainly for burglaries and larcenies. Fred was incarcerated in reform school for a period of nine months for his crimes. At the age of 16, he left school to go to work in order to support his mother and five siblings. Fred served in the U.S. Maritime Service for about 18 months at ages 17–18. He worked on oil tankers along the East Coast.

Throughout the age 17–25 period, Fred remained single. He was living with his mother and siblings in Boston at the age-25 interview. Fred fully supported his mother and two siblings who were still in high school. According to narrative data in the case file, Fred had refrained from marriage until his younger siblings were out of high school. He worked in several unskilled jobs (e.g., an oil and coal truck helper, an apprentice welder, and a factory worker) over this period. Fred stated that his "home responsibilities forced him to be a stable and regular worker."

A similar pattern is revealed in Frank's life history. Although he had eight arrests during the age 17–25 period, Frank emphasized at age 25 that he intended to marry later that year and was making an earnest effort to reform. He noted how hard it was for him to get a steady job because of his record. At the age-32 interview, Frank had no official or unofficial record of criminal behavior. He married and was living with his wife and child. He worked in a warehouse and, by all accounts, was a reliable worker (e.g., he had held the same job for the past five years). Frank did admit to some excessive drinking during the period, but he claimed that his drinking had tapered off since his marriage. He stated that his reformation stemmed from a variety of factors: (1) the influence of his wife—according to the interviewer, "she exerts pressure on the subject to conform and holds in check his aggression," (2) family responsibilities, (3) a long period of probation, (4) fairly steady work since 1957, and (5) fear of being "put away."

For George, a more incremental process of change was evident; it consisted of several circumstances, including leaving the city of Boston, becoming a parent, and finding a steady job. In his interview, George remarked: "Well, for one thing, I got out of Boston—I began to work steadily, and now I have a family—a son whom I always wanted. My father helped me to get back on the road to respectability and he has lived with us since we moved here. My wife always wanted me to do the right thing and I try to follow her advice. I got away from the old gang and the bookie racket which my uncle runs in the city. In a small town such as this, you have to go straight."

Another set of cases we examined pointed to the military as a "settling influence" or turning point in the life course (see also Elder, 1986). Given the available information in the Gluecks' case files, it is hard to uncover exactly what it was about the military experience that facilitated a change in behavior. Also, our finding of a positive influence is somewhat surprising given our results on the continuity of antisocial behavior from adolescence into adult domains, including misconduct in the military (see Sampson and Laub, 1993: Ch. 6). However, it is not inconsistent that the military can function to turn some men's lives around, even as it disrupts other men's lives (Elder, 1986) or provides yet another setting for some men to continue their criminal and deviant behavior (Gottfredson and Hirschi, 1990:165).

At his age-25 and age-32 interviews, Mickey was living with his wife and children. The subject married when he was almost 22 and his wife was nearly 21. A strong marital attachment between Mickey and his spouse centered around their home and children. Mickey joined the U.S. Navy while on parole from reform school and remained there for 13 years. According to narrative data, the subject stated that his enlistment in the military changed his outlook on life. "In the navy I was thrown in with guys from all over the country; some of them were well educated and had good backgrounds. I began to see that my thinking was way out of line and that I was probably wrong. I began to do things their way and things have gone well ever since."

This experience parallels that of another subject who spent a considerable period of time in the navy (seven and a half years) and had strong bonds to his wife and two sons. Similarly, other subjects in the study reported that they "matured in the service" or that the "army taught me a few things." Like Elder (1986), we find that for some men serving in the military can help surmount childhood disadvantage by recasting the past. Bandura (1982:753) argues that encounters in a closed milieu such as the military "have the greatest potential for branching persons abruptly into new trajectories of life."

We also examined a subset of men who experienced a significant decline in social bonding from ages 25 to 32. In these cases, it was difficult to detect clear turning points, but nevertheless certain patterns did emerge. For some men, a decline in job stability was due to changes in the labor market. Not surprisingly, layoffs, seasonal work, and factory closings all contributed to the weakening of ties to work. For one subject, his troubles in adulthood started when the company he was working for "folded." All employees were let go and his "good job" was simply gone. Macro-level transformations of the economy clearly bear on individual lives.

For several other cases the following scenario emerged. The subject married young, and often the marriage was forced due to pregnancy. Although prior to marriage there was some evidence of excessive drinking by the subject, the subject's wife claimed that the subject had matured into his familial responsibilities, and initially the couple got along well. Work was typically of a seasonal nature (e.g., construction work) and weather dependent. But as the men became older (and while one would normally expect an increasing "conformity" or settling down), ties to marriage and work unraveled. There were separations, followed by reconciliations, followed by further separations. There was often evidence of physical abuse and nonsupport of children. The subject's wife objected to the subject's drinking and was not pleased by the financial uncertainty of seasonal work. The subject resented what he perceived to be "overprotectiveness" on the part of his wife and claimed she "nagged" him. Often the subject's drinking continued to be a problem, exacerbated in part by the fact that in certain jobs drinking seemed to be tolerated or even encouraged so long as one did not drink on the job (Vaillant, 1983:96–97). As a result, crime and deviance became more pronounced over time due to the severing of social ties to work and family.

Implications for Future Research

As Clausen (1990) argues, the idea of turning points is an important concept in the study of lives. Turning points are closely linked to role transitions, and conceptually, they are helpful in understanding change in human behavior over the life course. We adapted this perspective to explore turning points in the lives of a sample of disadvantaged, persistent adolescent delinquents. Some positive turning points in the course of their lives were cohesive marriage, meaningful work, and serving in the military. Clear negative turning points were prolonged incarceration, heavy drinking, and subsequent job instability during the transition to young adulthood.

Having established that change does in fact occur, the key research question for the future becomes: Why do some individuals change while others do not? Learning more about turning points—especially in the transition from adolescence to adulthood—is critical for understanding the development of social capital and the facilitation of change in life trajectories. For example, what predicts strong marital attachment in adulthood? How do troubled youths achieve job stability and a strong commitment to work as adults? Is military service an effective vehicle for reshaping the life course of disadvantaged youths? What roles do structural factors and historical context play in determining strong bonds to family and work? More generally, how does one explain differential change among individuals?

Although these questions are complex and form the basis of our current work, we advance some tentative hypotheses. One is simply that there is an element of luck, randomness, or chance operating throughout the course of life. Bandura (1982) argues that chance encounters play a prominent role in shaping life paths. Namely, chance encounters introduce an element of unpredictability in life-course trajectories and thereby opportunities for change to emerge. As Bandura (1982:749) writes, "Although the separate chains of events in a chance encounter have their own causal determinants, their intersection occurs fortuitously rather than through deliberate plan." A more explicit theorizing of the roles of chance, "adventitious happenings" (Rutter, 1989b:33) or what Short and Strodtbeck (1965) many years ago called "aleatory" elements, may thus help to capture dynamic etiological processes.

The confluence of objective and subjective contingencies is also important in understanding the change process. In all likelihood, transitions involving structural role change, like marriage and employment, do not have the same meaning for everyone (Rutter, 1989a:20). For example, marriage and full-time work provided an opportunity for men in our study to change the direction of their life-course trajectory, but not every man saw it that way (see also Clausen, 1990; Elder et al., 1991). In other words, structural role changes only provide the possibility for change to occur—its realization is mediated by individual contingencies. Hence, there is a need to conceptualize and measure objective and subjective elements of turning points.

Although beyond the scope of this analysis, macro opportunity structures for marriage and the labor market also play central roles. As recent research on work and occupations shows, employment outcomes have as much to do with structural features of the labor market (e.g., vacancy chains, segmentation of the labor market, ethnic enclaves) as it does with individual predispositions to work (Rosenbaum, 1984; Rosenfeld, 1992). Similarly, network and exchange theory emphasize the importance of role multiplexity and interdependence that combine with other structural features of collective life to introduce numerous avenues for positive and negative change (Cook and Whitmeyer, 1992). As Dannefer (1987:216) argues, most research on life-course transitions is too quick to attribute continuity to social-psychological processes of "accentuation" rather than "structured mechanisms of social allocation producing similar differentiating tendencies in successive cohorts." The channeling of prior differences and the tendency toward cumulation of advantage and disadvantage in employment (e.g., increasing inequality over time) are so general that they have been referred to as the "Matthew effect" (see Dannefer, 1987:216). Labor market research thus motivates a deeper appreciation of contextual forces and opportunity structures in the shaping of the life transitions of young adults.

Relatedly, variations in criminal propensity (e.g., low self-control) are incomplete as an explanation of adult crime because the latter's realization is dependent on criminal opportunity (e.g., lack of guardianship or surveillance; suitable targets). Ties to work and family in adulthood restrict many criminal opportunities and thus reduce the probability that criminal propensities will be translated into action. For example, those in stable employment and marital relations are typically subject to more structured routine activities and less free time than those in unstable roles (see the discussion of free time, types of employment, and opportunities that facilitate drinking in Vaillant, 1983:96–97). Some turning points in life may also reflect changes in the availability or profitability of criminal strategies (see Cohen and Machalek, 1988).[7]

As noted earlier, cumulative continuity and processes of change are likely to interact with race and structural location (Hagan, 1991; Jessor et al., 1991). In particular, there is increasing evidence that the probability of adolescent risks becoming transmuted into adverse adult circumstances is greatest among those in disadvantaged racial and economic positions. Whether it be environmental traps in the form of unemployment or arrest, research is needed to specify the dependence of trajectories on structural location.

Turning points and developmental change are bounded by historical context as well. The men in the Gluecks' study grew to young adulthood in a period of expanding economic opportunities during the 1950s and 1960s. They were also in a position to take advantage of numerous opportunities offered by the G.I. Bill. Prospects for current cohorts may not be as promising. The industrial base in America has changed dramatically over the past 20 years (Wilson, 1987), and there has been an increase in global competition and a decline in expectations for upward social mobility. There is a sense that good jobs are harder to find and keep today than in previous decades. Moreover, the military may not be the vehicle out of poverty in the 1990s as it was during the 1940s and 1950s (Elder, 1986). Consistent with the life-course perspective, we thus stress the importance of conceptualizing and measuring secular change at the macrosocial level, especially through explicit cohort comparisons (see Ryder, 1965). In this regard we believe a central topic for future research is the interaction of turning points with the varying structural locations and historical contexts within which individuals make the transition to young adulthood.

Conclusion

Our dynamic conceptualization of social capital and informal social control at once incorporates stability and change in criminal behavior. Change is central to our model because we propose that variations in adult crime unexplained by childhood behavior are directly related to the strength of adult social bonds. Yet, we incorporate the link between childhood and adult outcomes, positing a cumulative, developmental process wherein delinquent behavior attenuates the social and institutional bonds linking adults to society (e.g., labor force attachment, marital cohesion). As such, we theorize that adult social bonds not only have important effects on adult crime in and of themselves, but help to explain the probabilistic links in the chain connecting early childhood differences and later adult crime.

Perhaps the key idea is ultimately a simple one—the adult life course matters, regardless of how one gets there. We do not deny the reality of self-selection or that persons may sometimes "create" their own environment. But once in place, those environments take on a history of their own in a way that invalidates a pure spuriousness or self-selection argument. Moreover, the self-selection view of the world is, in our opinion, much too deterministic and neglects the role of state sanctions, chance, luck, structural location, historical context, and opportunity structure in shaping the life course.

In sum, by redirecting attention to the significance of both pathways and turning points in the life course, we are optimistic about the possibilities for a new research agenda that has the potential to unify heretofore divergent conceptions of stability and change in human development. For example, Gottfredson and Hirschi (1990:177–178; Hirschi and Gottfredson, 1993) explicitly incorporate the role of opportunity in explaining criminal events. If opportunity matters for criminal events, surely it matters for the establishment of strong employment and marital bonds. More important, at one point Gottfredson and Hirschi (1990:115) allow for *social* control in explaining adolescent delinquency. In this sense we see some compatibility between our theory and Gottfredson and Hirschi's theory, especially if one conceptualizes variations in social control as partly influenced by variations in self-control (see also Hirschi, 1992; Hirschi and Gottfredson, 1993; Nagin and Paternoster, 1992). Therefore, while Gottfredson and Hirschi (1990) and Wilson and Herrnstein (1985) start off with a similar premise, they offer quite different possibilities for potential integration with our focus on change and informal social control across the adult life course. Future research is needed to examine these possibilities, especially the relative importance of stability and change throughout lives in varying contexts.

References

Abbott, Andrew. 1992. From causes to events: Notes on narrative positivism. Sociological Methods and Research 20:428–455.

Anderson, Elijah. 1990. Streetwise: Race, Class, and Change in an Urban Community. Chicago: University of Chicago Press.

Bandura, Albert. 1982. The psychology of chance encounters and life paths. American Psychologist 37:747–755.

Becker, Howard. 1963. The Outsiders. New York: Free Press.

Braithwaite, John. 1989. Crime, Shame, and Reintegration. New York: Cambridge University Press.

Cairns, Robert B. 1986. Phenomena lost: Issues in the study of development. In Jaan Valsiner (ed.), The Individual Subject and Scientific Psychology. New York: Plenum.

Caspi, Avshalom and Daryl Bern. 1990. Personality continuity and change across the life course. In Lawrence Pervin (ed.), Handbook of Personality: Theory and Research. New York: Guilford.

Caspi, Avshalom and Terrie E. Moffitt. 1993a. The continuity of maladaptive behavior: From description to understanding in the study of antisocial behavior. In Dante Cicchetti and Donald Cohen (eds.), Manual of Developmental Psychopathology. New York: John Wiley KL Sons, in press.

———. 1993b. Continuity amidst change: A paradoxical theory of personality coherence. Psychological Inquiry, in press.

———. Caspi, Avshalom, Glen H. Elder, Jr., and Ellen S. Herbener.

———. 1990. Childhood personality and the prediction of life-course patterns. In Lee Robins and Michael Rutter (eds.), Straight and Devious Pathways from Childhood to Adulthood. New York: Cambridge University Press.

Clausen, John. 1990. Turning point as a life course concept: Meaning and measurement. Paper presented at the annual meeting of the American Sociological Association, Washington, D.C.

Cohen, Lawrence and Richard Machalek. 1988. A general theory of expropriative crime: An evolutionary ecological approach. American Journal of Sociology 94:465–50 1.

Coleman, James S. 1988. Social capital in the creation of human capital. American Journal of Sociology 94:S95–120.

———. 1990. Foundations of Social Theory. Cambridge, Mass.: Harvard University Press.

Cook, Karen and Joseph Whitmeyer. 1992. Two approaches to social structure: Exchange theory and network analysis. Annual Review of Sociology 18:109–127.

Dannefer, Dale. 1984. Adult development and social theory: A paradigmatic reappraisal. American Sociological Review 49: 100–116.

———. 1987. Aging as intracohort differentiation: Accentuation, the Matthew effect, and the life course. Sociological Forum 2:211–236.

DiMaggio, Paul and John Mohr. 1985. Cultural capital, educational attainment and marital selection. American Journal of Sociology 90:1231–1261.

Ebaugh, Helen Rose Fuchs. 1988. Becoming an EX: The Process of Role Exit. Chicago: University of Chicago Press.

Elder, Glen H., Jr. 1975. Age differentiation and the life course. Annual Review of Sociology 1:165–190.

———. 1985. Perspectives on the life course. In Glen H. Elder, Jr. (ed.), Life Course Dynamics. Ithaca, N.Y.: Cornell University Press.

———. 1986. Military times and turning points in men's lives. Developmental Psychology 22:233–245.

Elder, Glen H., Jr., Cynthia Gimbel, and Rachel Ivie. 1991. Turning points in life: The case of military service and war. Military Psychology 3:215–231.

Farrington, David P. 1986. Stepping stones to adult criminal careers. In Dan Olweus, Jack Block, and Marian Radke-Yarrow (eds.), Development of Antisocial and Prosocial Behavior. New York: Academic Press.

———. 1988. Studying changes within individuals: The causes of offending. In Michael Rutter (ed.), Studies of Psychosocial Risk: The Power of Longitudinal Data New York: Cambridge University Press.

Farrington, David P. and Roger Tarling. 1985. Prediction in Criminology. Albany: State University of New York Press.

Glueck, Sheldon and Eleanor Glueck. 1950. Unraveling Juvenile Delinquency. New York: Commonwealth Fund.

———. 1968. Delinquents and Nondelinquents in Perspective. Cambridge, Mass.: Harvard University Press.

Gottfredson, Michael and Travis Hirschi. 1990. A General Theory of Crime. Stanford, Calif.: Stanford University Press.

Grasmick, Harold, Charles R. Tittle, Robert J. Bursik, Jr., and Bruce Arneklev. 1993. Testing the core empirical implications of Gottfredson and Hirschi's general theory of crime. Journal of Research in Crime and Delinquency 30:5–29.

Hagan, John. 1991. Destiny and drift: Subcultural preferences, status attainments, and the risks and rewards of youth. American Sociological Review 56:567–582.

Hagan, John and Alberto Palloni. 1990. The social reproduction of a criminal class in working-class London, circa 1950–1980. American Journal of Sociology 96:265–299.

Hirschi, Travis. 1992. From social control to self control. Paper presented at the annual meeting of the American Society of Criminology, New Orleans.

Hirschi, Travis and Michael Gottfredson. 1993. Commentary: Testing the general theory of crime. Journal of Research in Crime and Delinquency 30:47–54.

Huesmann, Rowell, Leonard Eron, Monroe Lefkowitz, and Leopold Walder. 1984. Stability of aggression over time and generations. Developmental Psychology 20:1120–1134.

Jessor, Richard, John E. Donovan, and Frances M. Costa. 1991. Beyond Adolescence: Problem Behavior and Young Adult Development. New York: Cambridge University Press.

Kandel, Denise, Mark Davies, and Nazli Baydar. 1990. The creation of interpersonal contexts: Homophily in dyadic relationships in adolescence and young adulthood. In Lee Robins and Michael Rutter (eds.), Straight and Devious Pathways from Childhood to Adulthood. New York: Cambridge University Press.

Katz, Jack. 1988. Seductions of Crime. New York: Basic Books.

Kessler, Ronald and David Greenberg. 1981. Linear Panel Analysis. New York: Academic Press.

Kirschenman, Joleen and Kathryn Neckerman. 1991. "We'd love to hire them, but . . .:" The meaning of race for employers. In Christopher Jencks and Paul Peterson (eds.), The Urban Underclass. Washington, D.C.: Brookings Institution.

Kornhauser, Ruth. 1978. Social Sources of Delinquency. Chicago: University of Chicago Press.

Lemert, Edwin. 1951. Social Pathology. New York: McGraw-Hill.

Loeber, Rolf and Marc LeBlanc. 1990. Toward a developmental criminology. In Michael Tonry and Norval Morris (eds.), Crime and Justice. Chicago: University of Chicago Press.

Loeber, Rolf and Magda Stouthamer-Loeber. 1987. Prediction. In Herbert C. Quay (ed.),Handbook of Juvenile Delinquency. New York: John Wiley & Sons.

Magnusson, David and Lars R. Bergman. 1988. Individual and variable-based approaches to longitudinal research on early risk factors. In Michael Rutter (ed.), Studies of Psychosocial Risk: The Power of Longitudinal Data. New York: Cambridge University Press.

———. 1990. A pattern approach to the study of pathways from childhood to adulthood. In Lee Robins and Michael Rutter (eds.), Straight and Devious Pathways from Childhood to Adulthood. New York: Cambridge University Press.

McAdam, Doug. 1989. The biographical consequences of activism. American Sociological Review 54:744–760.

Moffitt, Terrie E. 1993. Adolescence-limited and life-course-persistent antisocial behavior: A developmental taxonomy. Psychological Review, in press.

Nagin, Daniel and Raymond Paternoster. 1991. On the relationship of past and future participation in delinquency. Criminology 29:163–190.

———. 1992. Social capital and social control: The deterrence implications of a theory of individual differences in criminal offending. Unpublished manuscript. Carnegie Mellon University, Pittsburgh.

Nagin, Daniel and Joel Waldfogel. 1992. The effects of criminality and conviction on the labour market status of young British offenders. Unpublished manuscript. Carnegie Mellon University, Pittsburgh.

Patterson, Gerald R., Barbara D. DeBaryshe, and Elizabeth Ramsey. 1989. A developmental perspective on antisocial behavior. American Psychologist 44:329–335.

Pickles, Andrew and Michael Rutter. 1991. Statistical and conceptual models of "turning points" in developmental processes. In David Magnusson, Lars Bergman, Georg Rudinger, and Bertil Torestad (eds.), Problems and Methods in Longitudinal Research: Stability and Change. New York: Cambridge University Press.

Rogosa, David, David Brandt, and Michele Zimowski. 1982. A growth curve approach to the measurement of change. Psychological Bulletin 92:726–748.

Rosenbaum, James. 1984. Career Mobility in a Corporate Hierarchy. Orlando, Fla.: Academic Press.

Rosenfeld, Rachel A. 1992. Job mobility and career processes. Annual Review of Sociology 18:39–61.

Rutter, Michael. 1987. Psychosocial resilience and protective mechanisms. American Journal of Orthopsychiatry 57:316333.

———. 1989a. Age as an ambiguous variable in developmental research: Some epidemiological considerations from developmental psychopathology. International Journal of Behavioral Development 12: 1–34.

———. 1989b. Pathways from childhood to adult life. Journal of Child Psychology and Psychiatry 30:23–51.

Rutter, Michael, David Quinton, and Jonathan Hill. 1990. Adult outcomes of institution-reared children: Males and females compared. In Lee Robins and Michael Rutter (eds.), Straight and Devious Pathways from Childhood to Adulthood. New York: Cambridge University Press.

Ryder, Norman. 1965. The cohort as a concept in the study of social change. American Sociological Review 30:843–861.

Sampson, Robert J. and John H. Laub. 1992. Crime and deviance in the life course. Annual Review of Sociology 18:63–84.

———. 1993. Crime in the Making: Pathways and Turning Points Through Life. Cambridge, Mass.: Harvard University Press.

Short, James F., Jr. 1990. Gangs, neighborhoods, and youth crime. Criminal Justice Research Bulletin 5:1–11.

Short, James F., Jr., and Fred Strodtbeck. 1965. Group Process and Gang Delinquency. Chicago: University of Chicago Press.

Shover, Neal. 1985. Aging Criminals. Beverly Hills, Calif.: Sage.

Sullivan, Mercer. 1989. "Getting Paid:" Youth Crime and Work in the Inner City. Ithaca, N.Y.: Cornell University Press.

Thornberry, Terence P. 1987. Toward an interactional theory of delinquency. Criminology 25:863–891.

Tittle, Charles R. 1988. Two empirical regularities (maybe) in search of an explanation: Commentary on the age-crime debate. Criminology 26:75–86.

Tuma, Nancy and Michael Hannan. 1984. Social Dynamics: Models and Methods. Orlando, Fla.: Academic Press

Vaillant, George. 1983. The Natural History of Alcoholism. Cambridge, Mass: Harvard University Press.

Wilson, James Q. and Richard Herrnstein. 1985. Crime and Human Nature. New York: Simon & Schuster.

Wilson, William Julius. 1987. The Truly Disadvantaged: The Inner City, the Underclass, and Public Policy. Chicago: University of Chicago Press.

John H. Laub is Professor in the College of Criminal Justice at Northeastern University and Visiting Scholar at the Henry A. Murray Research Center of Radcliffe College. He is also editor of the *Journal of Quantitative Criminology.*

Robert J. Sampson is Professor of Sociology at the University of Chicago and Research Associate at the Ogburn-Stouffer Center for the Study of Social Organization, NORC.

Notes _____

1. The life course has been defined as "pathways through the age differentiated life span" (Elder, 1985: 17), in particular the "sequence of culturally defined age-graded roles and social transitions that are enacted over time" (Caspi et al., 1990:15). Two central concepts underlie the analysis of life-course dynamics. A *trajectory* is a pathway or line of development over the life span, such as work life, parenthood, and criminal behavior. Trajectories refer to long-term patterns of behavior and are marked by a sequence of transitions. *Transitions* are marked by life events (e.g., first job or first marriage) that are embedded in trajectories and evolve over shorter time spans (Elder, 1985:31–32). See also Sampson and Laub (1992).

2. Ecological constancy (e.g., community constraints) and continuities in the interpersonal environment may also underlie individual-level stability. In other words, behavioral patterns may show stability simply because the contextual environment remains stable. Hence, behavioral stability does not necessarily imply causal forces operating solely at the level of the individual (Sampson and Laub, 1992:78).

3. There is no doubt that substantial breakthroughs have been made in the statistical study of change (see especially, Kessler and Greenberg, 1981; Rogosa et al., 1982; Tuma and Hannan, 1984). However, as indicated by the subtitle of Tuma and Hannan (1984), this work has focused on "models and methods." Our motivation is the development of a conceptual framework on types of change and the social mechanisms underlying change processes.

4. Although space limitations preclude extended consideration, we also believe that *cultural* capital is central to understanding change. Cultural capital emerges in the form of adolescent cultural preferences that reflect transitional experiences in the life course (DiMaggio and Mohr, 1985). Cultural deficits stemming from identification with delinquent subcultures appear to diminish educational achievement and, hence, occupational outcomes in the transition to young adulthood (Hagan, 1991).

5. A similar perspective on change is found in the literature on social movements. In studying the biographical consequences of activism, McAdam (1989) distinguishes between a radical transformation of one's life—conversion—and the more common form of personal change—"alternation." The latter is not as drastic as a conversion; it refers instead to changes in life that grow out of prior programs of behavior. Specifically, "the crucial difference between conversion and alternation centers on the degree to which the change is continuous with the individual's previous life and conception of self" (1989:745). Although alternation does not entail a radical break with the past, McAdam correctly notes that "it is not an insignificant social process. On the contrary, it is associated with most of life's turning points" (p. 745). McAdam's conceptualization of alternation parallels our discussion of "incremental" change. For additional discussion of change processes involved in conversions and role exits see Ebaugh (1988).

6. For the life histories we describe herein, potentially revealing information has been altered slightly in order to protect the confidentiality of subjects (e.g., the names of the subjects are fictitious). There did not seem to be any pattern in the selection of these cases with respect to IQ, personality traits such as aggressiveness, and early childhood experiences.

7. We further recognize that some turning points may provide the opportunity for exposure to criminal and deviant peer networks. Moreover, it is possible that as social ties to criminal and deviant networks become stronger over time, the less likely one is to abandon them. More research is needed on the competing roles of conventional and deviant peer networks in generating social capital and the effect of turning points in reshaping the structure and relative influence of associational networks.

The Sociology of Deviance, the Labeling Perspective and Critical Constructionism

In Sections II, III, and IV of this book, we saw that social disorganization theory, differential association theory, cultural transmission theory, cultural conflict theory, social learning theory and social control theory all had their intellectual roots in the Chicago School tradition. The same can be said with respect to the sociology of deviance, the labeling perspective and critical constructionism. Howard Becker and Kai Erikson, unquestionably two of the foremost thinkers in the sociology of deviance and the labeling perspective, both did their graduate studies in sociology at the University of Chicago (Matsueda, 2001:223; Plummer, 1979:86–87). While others associated with the labeling perspective and the sociology of deviance—e.g., Frank Tannenbaum, Edwin Lemert, John Kitsuse, and Thomas Scheff—did not study at the University of Chicago, their work was influenced by Chicago School thinking. In particular, they were influenced by the symbolic interactionist paradigm advanced by such Chicago School theorists as W. I. Thomas, George Herbert Mead and Charles Horton Cooley (Akers & Sellers, 2009:152; Matsueda, 2001:223).

The first indications of the development of the social reaction or labeling perspective can be found in Frank Tannenbaum's 1938 work on the dramatization of evil (Akers & Sellers, 2009:153; Paternoster & Bachman, 2001:218–219). Tannenbaum observed that once young offenders were apprehended and processed through the youth criminal justice system, they ended up being tagged as "juvenile delinquents." Tannenbaum said that as a consequence of this social reaction to deviance, these youth would come to view themselves as juvenile delinquents—they would start to act in accordance with their new role or status, and begin to associate with other delinquents (Pfohl, 1985:285; Tannenbaum, 1985:282–283). It has been argued that Tannenbaum was not truly a labeling theorist, and that the first major foray into the field of labeling and the social reaction to deviance was undertaken by Edwin Lemert, in his 1951 discussion of primary and secondary deviance (Paternoster & Bachman, 2001:219; Spector & Kitsuse, 1977:61). According to Lemert, individuals may engage in primary deviance without seeing their behavior as deviant or abnormal. In other words, they may self-identify as being normal and conforming, even though other members of society may not share their self-perceptions or self-definitions (Lemert, 2005:75–76). Secondary deviance results from the social reaction process, wherein the individual comes to be identified by others as deviant. The individual adjusts to this social reaction, and comes to see himself or herself as deviant. Thus, secondary deviance occurs when the individual continues (or amplifies) his or her deviant behavior on the basis of these new self-perceptions or self-definitions, as well as on the basis of the new societal perceptions and definitions (Williams & McShane, 2010:115–116).

As was the case with Frank Tannenbaum, it has been suggested that Edwin Lemert was not really a labeling theorist (Goode, 2005:97; Lilly, Cullen, & Ball, 2011:145). Rather, it is widely held that the labeling perspective came into its own in the early 1960s, with publications by Kai Erikson, Howard Becker and John Kitsuse in the areas of labeling, the sociology of deviance, moral entrepreneurship (or claimsmaking) and the construction of social problems (Goode, 2005:97; Lilly et al., 2011:145). Kai Erikson's (1962) "Notes on the Sociology of Deviance" and Howard Becker's (1963) "Moral Entrepreneurs" (taken from Becker's book, *Outsiders: Studies in the Sociology of Deviance*) are the first two reading selections in this section.

The labeling perspective became the predominant explanation of crime and deviance during the 1960s, and held its own into the mid-1970s (Goode, 2005:96; Matsueda, 2001:226). Essentially, the labeling perspective takes the position that once an individual is labeled as a deviant or criminal, this becomes his or her master status, which in turn becomes a self-fulfilling prophecy (Becker, 1963:34; Lilly et al., 2011:145; Pfohl, 1985:291). Moreover, it is held that crime and deviance are often socially constructed—i.e., that social groups make up rules and then apply them to individuals or groups who come to be regarded as "outsiders" or social outcasts (Becker, 1964:3; Kitsuse, 1964:87–88). For those rules to be enforced, there must be social groups who assume the role of whistleblowers, claimsmakers, moral crusaders or moral entrepreneurs—they demand that action be taken against those whom they perceive to be deviant (Becker, 1963:122; Spector & Kitsuse, 1977:78–81). Generally speaking, those who do the labeling possess greater social or political power, whereas those who end up on the receiving end are marginalized, and powerless to resist the label (Matsueda, 2001:227; Paternoster & Bachman, 2001:215).

Those who found themselves being labeled as labeling theorists also found themselves on the receiving end of a great deal of criticism from mainstream and radical criminologists alike (Paternoster & Bachman, 2001:220; Renzetti, Curran, &

Carr, 2003:176). It has been said that the propositions of the labeling perspective are difficult to test, and that there is no empirical support for the notion that labeling (or the social reaction to deviance) causes or increases criminal behavior (Gove, 1980:14–15; Tittle, 1980:257–259). It has also been argued that labeling theorists did not pay sufficient attention to the role of power and social inequality in the labeling process, or to the ability of the rich and powerful to avoid being labeled themselves (Liazos, 2005:119; Plummer, 1979:108–109). Perhaps one of the most telling blows to the labeling perspective and to the sociology of deviance was the accusation that its adherents were seemingly preoccupied with the study of "nuts, sluts and preverts"—mental patients, strippers, prostitutes, drug users, alcoholics and "flat-earthers" (Liazos, 2005:112, 118; Plummer, 1979:108–109).

In defense of the labeling perspective and the sociology of deviance, it must be said that most of its adherents themselves rejected the types of labels that others were attempting to impose upon them (Plummer, 1979:87, 90–91). It is debatable that Frank Tannenbaum or Edwin Lemert could ever be described as "labeling theorists" in the first place. Both Tannenbaum and Lemert arrived on the scene long before the hey-day of the labeling perspective, and Lemert—who focused much of his attention on primary rather than secondary deviance—actually rejected some of the main propositions associated with the perspective (Goode, 2005:96; Spector & Kitsuse, 1977:61–62). Kai Erikson was as much a structural functionalist and a Durkheimian social control theorist as he was a labeling theorist, while Howard Becker preferred to describe himself as an "interactionist" (Goode, 2005:97; Plummer, 1979:87). Moreover, claims by critics that there is no supporting evidence for the labeling perspective are not necessarily accurate. Over the past twenty years, a number of studies have found a positive correlation between formal (justice system) and informal (community-level) labeling and subsequent delinquent or criminal behavior (Bernburg, 2009:345–349; Matsueda, 2001:233–235). There is no question that the labeling perspective had (and continues to have) a significant impact on criminal justice policy. Most diversion programs, restorative justice programs and deinstitutionalization or decriminalization initiatives were influenced to one extent or another by the notion that official labeling and stigmatization often led to further delinquent and criminal behavior (Akers & Sellers, 2009:158–160; Lilly et al., 2011:153–156).

The labeling perspective and the sociology of deviance also gave rise to what has come to be known as critical constructionism, a field that studies the construction of social problems (Best, 1995:6–7; Matsueda, 2001:229). The third reading selection in this section, "Round Up the Usual Suspects: Crime, Deviance and the Limits of Constructionism," is written by Erich Goode. As it happens, Erich Goode is himself a critical constructionist, and a recognized authority on the subject of social problems and moral panics (Burns & Crawford, 1999:148–150; Sacco & Kennedy, 2008:227–230). In this reading selection, Goode (1994) reminds us that where there's smoke, there's sometimes fire—that there are indeed real criminals in the world, and that not all of the crime we hear about is simply the end result of media-fueled moral panics or socially constructed problems.

References

Akers, R. L., & Sellers, C. S. (2009). *Criminological theories: Introduction, evaluation, and application* (5th , New ed.). New York: Oxford University Press.

Becker, H. S. (1963). *Outsiders: Studies in the sociology of deviance.* London: Free Press of Glencoe.

Becker, H. S. (1964). Introduction. In H. S. Becker (Ed.), *The other side: Perspectives on deviance* (pp. 1–6). New York: Free Press of Glencoe.

Bernburg, J. G. (2009). Labeling and secondary deviance. In H. Copes, & V. Topalli (Eds.), *Criminological theory: Readings and retrospectives* (pp. 340–350). New York: McGraw-Hill.

Best, J. (1995). Typification and social problems construction. In J. Best (Ed.), *Images of issues: Typifying contemporary social problems* (Second ed., pp. 3–10). New York: Aldine de Gruyter.

Burns, R., & Crawford, C. (1999). School shootings, the media and public fear: Ingredients for a moral panic. *Crime, Law and Social Change, 32*(2), 147–168.

Erikson, K. T. (1962). Notes on the sociology of deviance. *Social Problems, 9*(4), 307–314.

Goode, E. (1994). Round up the usual suspects: Crime, deviance, and the limits of constructionism. *The American Sociologist, 25*(4), 90–104.

Goode, E. (2005). On behalf of labeling theory. In H. N. Pontell (Ed.), *Social deviance: Readings in theory and research* (Fifth ed., pp. 96–106). Upper Saddle River, NJ: Pearson Prentice Hall.

Gove, W. (1980). The labelling perspective: An overview. In W. R. Gove (Ed.), *The labelling of deviance: Evaluating a perspective* (2nd ed., pp. 9–26). Beverly Hills, Calif.: Sage Publications.

Kitsuse, J. I. (1964). Societal reaction to deviant behavior: Problems of theory and method. In H. S. Becker (Ed.), *The other side: Perspectives on deviance* (pp. 87–102). New York: Free Press of Glencoe.

Lemert, E. M. (2005). Primary and secondary deviation. In H. N. Pontell (Ed.), *Social deviance: Readings in theory and research* (Fifth ed., pp. 74–77). Upper Saddle River, NJ: Pearson Prentice Hall.

Liazos, A. (2005). The poverty of the sociology of deviance: Nuts, sluts and preverts. In H. N. Pontell (Ed.), *Social deviance: Readings in theory and research* (Fifth ed., pp. 112–126). Upper Saddle River, NJ: Pearson Prentice Hall.

Lilly, J. R., Cullen, F. T., & Ball, R. A. (2011). *Criminological theory: Context and consequences* (5th ed.). Thousand Oaks: SAGE Publications.

Matsueda, R. L. (2001). Labeling theory: Historical roots, implications, and recent developments. In R. Paternoster, & R. Bachman (Eds.), *Explaining criminals and crime: Essays in contemporary criminological theory* (pp. 223–241). Los Angeles, Calif.: Roxbury Pub. Co.

Paternoster, R., & Bachman, R. (2001). Labeling or social reaction theories of crime. In R. Paternoster, & R. Bachman (Eds.), *Explaining criminals and crime: Essays in contemporary criminological theory* (pp. 211–222). Los Angeles, Calif.: Roxbury Pub. Co.

Pfohl, S. J. (1985). *Images of deviance and social control: A sociological history.* New York: McGraw-Hill.

Plummer, K. (1979). Misunderstanding labelling perspectives. In D. M. Downes, & P. E. Rock (Eds.), *Deviant interpretations* (pp. 85–121). Oxford: Martin Robertson.

Renzetti, C. M., Curran, D. J., & Carr, P. J. (2003). Crime and stigma: Labeling theory. In C. M. Renzetti, D. J. Curran & P. J. Carr (Eds.), *Theories of crime: A reader* (pp. 166–167). Boston: Allyn and Bacon.

Sacco, V. F., & Kennedy, L. W. (2008). *The criminal event: An introduction to criminology in Canada* (Fourth ed.). Toronto: Thomson Nelson.

Spector, M., & Kitsuse, J. I. (1977). *Constructing social problems.* Menlo Park, Calif.: Cummings Pub. Co.

Tannenbaum, F. (1985). The dramatization of evil. In S. H. Traub, & C. B. Little (Eds.), *Theories of deviance* (3rd ed., pp. 280–284). Itasca, Ill.: F. E. Peacock Publishers.

Tittle, C. R. (1980). Labelling and crime: An empirical evaluation. In W. R. Gove (Ed.), *The labelling of deviance: Evaluating a perspective* (2nd ed., pp. 241–269). Beverly Hills, Calif.: Sage Publications.

Williams, F. P., & McShane, M. D. (2010). *Criminological theory* (5th ed.). Upper Saddle River, N.J.: Pearson/Prentice Hall.

14

Notes on the Sociology of Deviance

The following reading selection by Kai Erikson, "Notes on the Sociology of Deviance", appeared under the same name on two different occasions—first as an article in a 1962 edition of the journal *Social Problems*, and then again as a slightly re-worked chapter in Howard Becker's 1964 book, *The Other Side: Perspectives on Deviance*. Parts of this article also re-surfaced in "On the Sociology of Deviance", which served as the first chapter in Kai Erikson's 1966 book, *Wayward Puritans: A Study in the Sociology of Deviance*. In this particular instance, we are examining Erikson's "Notes on the Sociology of Deviance" as they first appeared in his 1962 article in the journal *Social Problems*.

As noted in the introduction to this section of the course reader, Kai Erikson did his PhD in sociology at the University of Chicago, and consequently, was influenced by the symbolic interactionist paradigm advanced by George Herbert Mead and Charles Horton Cooley (Akers & Sellers, 2009:152; Matsueda, 2001:223). Charles Horton Cooley talked about "the looking-glass self", and about our ability to see ourselves as others see us (Cooley, 2005:72–73). George Herbert Mead talked about "the social self", and discussed how meaning was created during the process of social interaction, through the sharing of commonly understood symbols and gestures (e.g., "shaking a fist in anger") (Zeitlin, 2001:426–429). Kai Erikson mentioned and cited George Herbert Mead in the modified version of "Notes on the Sociology of Deviance" which was published two years later in Howard Becker's book (Erikson, 1964:12), but did not cite Mead in the 1962 article included in this course reader. Erikson did, however, cite other symbolic interactionists with Chicago School connections in his 1962 article, including Erving Goffman and Harold Garfinkel (cf. Erikson, 1962:311). Goffman wrote about the spoiled social identity that resulted from stigmatization, and about how individuals attempted to cope with this spoiled identity (Goffman, 2005:80–83). Garfinkel wrote about the type of status degradation ceremonies that can be found in most societies. These ceremonies function as outlets for the expression of moral indignation, and as forums for public denunciation and shaming or those who violate social norms (Garfinkel, 1956:420–423).

More than anything, Kai Erikson was influenced by Émile Durkheim's notion—expressed in "The Normal and the Pathological" (the first reading in this course reader)—that crime and deviance function to keep the social order intact (Durkheim, 1964; Erikson, 1962). According to Durkheim's structural functionalist view, crime functioned to maintain social cohesion, by bringing individuals together through their sense of indignation or moral outrage. Crime also helped the community to set its boundaries, because crime delineated what was socially acceptable and what was not (Durkheim, 1964:72, 84; Erikson, 2005:9–12). For Durkheim, the function of punishment was to defend the collective conscience—to uphold the shared values, beliefs and traditions of the society (Durkheim, 1964:72; Durkheim, 1965:84; Neyer, 1964:34).

Kai Erikson is himself a structural functionalist (Goode, 2005:97; Matsueda, 2001:227–228). This can be seen in his "Notes on the Sociology of Deviance", where he describes the manner in which deviance functions to promote conformity and demarcate social boundaries (Erikson, 1962:309–310, 312). The influence of Harold Garfinkel's (1956) symbolic interactionist thinking with respect to status degradation ceremonies is also in evidence here. Like Garfinkel, Erikson talks about the structure of status degradation ceremonies, starting with a confrontation between the deviant and community, followed by a judgment as to the deviant's guilt or mental illness, and ending with some sort of disposition or placement (e.g., prison, or a psychiatric institution) (Erikson, 1962:311). Following another symbolic interactionist, Erving Goffman, Erikson remarks on the stigmatization (labeling) that occurs at these status degradation ceremonies (Goffman, 2005:78–81). Erikson notes that the stigma (or label) is affixed at the end of a dramatic and highly public event, for example, at a court trial or an insanity hearing. He adds that no similar process exists for the removal of the stigma once the stigmatized individual has completed his or her term of imprisonment or period of treatment (Erikson, 1962:311–312). Thus, the individual remains stigmatized permanently, which may in turn contribute to their ongoing involvement in criminal or deviant behavior.

Kai Erikson builds upon these themes in his sociological classic, *Wayward Puritans: A Study in the Sociology of Deviance*. In this book, Erikson recounts how the Puritans—who migrated from England to Massachusetts in the early 1600s in search of a new place to practice their Christian beliefs—seemed to find themselves surrounded by deviance and sin in their "community of saints" (Durkheim, 1964:68–69; Erikson, 2005:61, 85). They staggered from one crisis—or crime wave—to another. First there was the "Antinomian crisis," where a number of Puritans (led by a woman) dared to challenge the authority of the clergy and question the clergy's interpretation of Biblical law (Erikson, 2005:71–74). These deviant Puritans were charged with sedition and heresy, and were brought to trial. Some of them—including their leader, Ann Hutchinson—were found guilty, excommunicated from the church, and banished from the community of saints (Erikson, 2005:87-88, 102–105). Next came the "Quaker crisis." The Quakers were a Christian sect that, much like the Puritans, migrated from England to Massachusetts in the 1600s (shortly after the Puritans) in search of a new place to practice their Christian beliefs (Erikson,

2005:107–108). The Puritans decided that the somewhat different religious beliefs and practices of the Quakers were heretical; thus, being a Quaker quickly came to be an offense punishable by whipping, branding, mutilation, banishment, and in some cases execution (Erikson, 2005:116–117, 120–123). After the Quaker crisis, there was the witchcraft crisis. During this period of fear and panic, nineteen "witches" were executed. Another 150 accused "witches" were still in custody when the Governor finally interceded and put an end to the witch trials (Erikson, 2005:149–152).

Erikson views the events in the Puritan colony as evidence of Durkheim's contention that even in "a society of saints," where crime would theoretically be unheard of, small faults that might otherwise be ignored would come to be identified as deviant, and ultimately, as criminal (Durkheim, 1964:68–69). Erikson also views these events as evidence of his own contention that societies will generally experience "a stable 'quota' of deviation," more or less in line with the ability of the agencies of social control—e.g., the police, the courts, the prisons, the psychiatric hospitals, etc—to handle the volume (Erikson, 1962:311–312; Erikson, 2005:163–164). In the following reading, "Notes on the Sociology of Deviance," Erikson points out that these agencies of social control are not known for their success when it comes to rehabilitating or treating the deviants with whom they regularly deal. He argues that the function of these agencies is not to rehabilitate or treat, but rather, to promote conformity by drawing a "symbolic set of parentheses" around what the community considers to be acceptable behavior (Erikson, 1962:311–312; Erikson, 2005:10).

References

Akers, R. L., & Sellers, C. S. (2009). *Criminological theories: Introduction, evaluation, and application* (5th , New ed.). New York: Oxford University Press.

Cooley, C. H. (2005). The social self. In H. N. Pontell (Ed.), *Social deviance: Readings in theory and research* (Fifth ed., pp. 72–73). Upper Saddle River, NJ: Pearson Prentice Hall.

Durkheim, É. (1964). In Catlin G. E. G. (Ed.), *The rules of sociological method* (J. H. Mueller, S. A. Solovay Trans.). New York: The Free Press of Glencoe. (8th ed.).

Durkheim, É. (1965). *The division of labor in society* (G. Simpson Trans.). New York: Free Press.

Erikson, K. T. (1962). Notes on the sociology of deviance. *Social Problems, 9*(4), 307–314.

Erikson, K. T. (1964). Notes on the sociology of deviance. In H. S. Becker (Ed.), *The other side: Perspectives on deviance* (pp. 9–21). New York: Free Press of Glencoe.

Erikson, K. T. (2005). *Wayward puritans: A study in the sociology of deviance*. Boston: Allyn and Bacon.

Garfinkel, H. (1956). Conditions of successful degradation ceremonies. *American Journal of Sociology, 61*(5), 420–424.

Goffman, E. (2005). Stigma and social identity. In H. N. Pontell (Ed.), *Social deviance: Readings in theory and research* (Fifth ed., pp. 77–96). Upper Saddle River, NJ: Pearson Prentice Hall.

Goode, E. (2005). On behalf of labeling theory. In H. N. Pontell (Ed.), *Social deviance: Readings in theory and research* (Fifth ed., pp. 96–106). Upper Saddle River, NJ: Pearson Prentice Hall.

Matsueda, R. L. (2001). Labeling theory: Historical roots, implications, and recent developments. In R. Paternoster, & R. Bachman (Eds.), *Explaining criminals and crime: Essays in contemporary criminological theory* (pp. 223–241). Los Angeles, Calif.: Roxbury Pub. Co.

Neyer, J. (1964). Individualism and socialism in Durkheim. In K. H. Wolff (Ed.), *Essays on sociology and philosophy* (pp. 32–76). New York: Harper.

Zeitlin, I. M. (2001). *Ideology and the development of sociological theory* (7th ed.). Upper Saddle River, N.J.: Prentice Hall.

NOTES ON THE SOCIOLOGY
OF DEVIANCE

KAI T. ERIKSON

It is general practice in sociology to regard deviant behavior as an alien element in society. Deviance is considered a vagrant form of human activity, moving outside the more orderly currents of social life. And since this type of aberration could only occur (in theory) if something were wrong within the social organization itself, deviant behavior is described almost as if it were leakage from machinery in poor condition: it is an accidental result of disorder and anomie, a symptom of internal breakdown.

The purpose of the following remarks will be to review this conventional outlook and to argue that it provides too narrow a framework for the study of deviant behavior. Deviation, we will suggest, recalling Durkheim's classic statement on the subject, can often be understood as a normal product of stable institutions, a vital resource which is guarded and preserved by forces found in all human organizations.[1]

I

According to current theory, deviant behavior is most likely to occur when the sanctions governing conduct in any given setting seem to be contradictory.[2] This would be the case, for example, if the work rules posted by a company required one course of action from its employees and the longer-range policies of the company required quite another. Any situation marked by this kind of ambiguity, of course, can pose a serious dilemma for the individual: if he is careful to observe one set of demands imposed upon him, he runs the immediate risk of violating some other, and thus may find himself caught in a deviant stance no matter how earnestly he tries to avoid it. In this limited sense, deviance can be regarded a "normal" human response to "abnormal" social conditions, and the sociologist is therefore invited

Paper read at the 55th annual meetings of the American Sociological Association, New York, 1960.

Reprinted from *Social Problems* 9, no. 4 (spring 1962), University of California Press.

to assume that some sort of pathology exists within the social structure whenever deviant behavior makes an appearance.

This general approach is clearly more concerned with the *etiology* of deviant behavior than with its continuing social *history*—and as a result it often draws sociological attention away from an important area of inquiry. It may be safe to assume that naive acts of deviance, such as first criminal offenses, are provoked by strains in the local situation. But this is only the beginning of a much longer story, for deviant activities can generate a good deal of momentum once they are set into motion: they develop forms of organization, persist over time, and sometimes remain intact long after the strains which originally produced them have disappeared. In this respect, deviant activities are often absorbed into the main tissue of society and derive support from the same forces which stabilize other forms of social life. There are persons in society, for example, who make career commitments to deviant styles of conduct, impelled by some inner need for continuity rather than by any urgencies in the immediate social setting. There are groups in society which actively encourage new deviant trends, often prolonging them beyond the point where they represent an adaptation to strain. These sources of support for deviant behavior are difficult to visualize when we use terms like "strain," "anomie," or "breakdown" in discussions of the problem. Such terms may help us explain how the social structure creates fresh deviant potential, but they do not help us explain how that potential is later shaped into durable, persisting social patterns.[3] The individual's need for self continuity and the group's offer of support are altogether normal processes, even if they are sometimes found in deviant situations; and thus the study of deviant behavior is as much a study of social organization as it is a study of *dis*organization and anomie.

II

From a sociological standpoint, deviance can be defined as conduct which is generally thought to require the attention of social control agencies—that is, conduct about which "something should be done." Deviance is not a property *inherent in* certain forms of behavior; it is a property *conferred upon* these forms by the audiences which directly or indirectly witness them. Sociologically, then, the critical variable in the study of deviance is the social *audience* rather than the individual *person*, since it is the audience which eventually decides whether or not any given action or actions will become a visible case of deviation.

This definition may seem a little indirect, but it has the advantage of bringing a neglected sociological issue into proper focus. When a community acts to control the behavior of one of its members, it is engaged in a very intricate process of selection. Even a determined miscreant conforms in most of his daily behavior—using the correct spoon at mealtime, taking good care of his mother, or otherwise observing the mores of his society—and if the community elects to bring sanctions against him for the occasions when he does act offensively, it is responding to a few deviant details set within a vast context of proper conduct. Thus a person may be jailed or hospitalized for a few scattered moments of misbehavior, defined as a full-time deviant despite the fact that he had supplied the community with countless other indications that he was a decent, moral citizen. The screening device which sifts these telling details out of the individual's over-all performance, then, is a sensitive instrument of social control. It is important to note that this screen takes a number of factors into account which are not directly related to the deviant act itself: it is concerned with the actor's social class, his past record as an offender, the amount of remorse he manages to convey, and many similar concerns which take hold in the shifting moods of the community. This is why the community often overlooks behavior which seems technically deviant (like certain kinds of white collar graft) or takes sharp exception to behavior which seems essentially harmless (like certain kinds of sexual impropriety). It is an easily demonstrated fact, for example, that working class boys who steal cars are far more likely to go to prison than upper class boys who commit the same or even more serious crimes, suggesting that from the point of view of the community lower class offenders are somehow more deviant. To this extent, the community screen is perhaps a more relevant subject for sociological research than the actual behavior which is filtered through it.

Once the problem is phrased in this way, we can ask: how does a community decide what forms of conduct should be singled out for this kind of attention? And why, having made this choice, does it create special institutions to deal with the persons who enact them? The standard answer to this question is that society sets up the machinery of control in order to protect itself against the "harmful" effects of deviance, in much the same way than an organism mobilizes its resources to combat an invasion of germs. At times, however, this classroom convention only seems to make the problem more complicated. In the first place, as Durkheim pointed out some years ago, it is by no means clear that all acts considered deviant in a culture are in fact (or even in principle) harmful to group life.[4] And in the second place, specialists in crime and mental health have long suggested that deviance can play an important role in keeping the social order intact—again a point we owe originally to Durkheim.[5] This has serious implications for sociological theory in general.

III

In recent years, sociological theory has become more and more concerned with the concept of "social system"—an organization of society's component parts into a form which sustains internal equilibrium, resists change, and is boundary maintaining. Now this concept has many abstract dimensions, but it is generally used to describe those forces in the social order which promote a high level of uniformity among human actors and a high degree of symmetry within human institutions. In this sense, the concept is normatively oriented since it directs the observer's attention toward those centers in social space where the core values of society are figuratively located. The main organizational principle of a system, then, is essentially a centripetal one: it draws the behavior of actors toward the nucleus of the system, bringing it within range of basic norms. Any conduct which is neither attracted toward this nerve center by the rewards of conformity nor compelled toward it by other social pressures is considered "out of control," which is to say, deviant.

This basic model has provided the theme for most contemporary thinking about deviance, and as a result little attention has been given to the notion that systems operate to maintain boundaries. Generally speaking, boundaries are controls which limit the fluctuation of a system's component parts so that the whole retains a defined range of activity—a unique pattern of constancy and stability—within the larger environment.[6] The range of human behavior is potentially so great that any *social* system must make clear statements about the nature and location of its boundaries, placing limits on the flow of behavior so that is circulates within a given cultural area. Thus boundaries are a crucial point of reference for persons living within any system, a prominent concept in the group's special language and tradition. A juvenile gang may define its boundaries by the amount of territory it defends, a professional society by the range of subjects it discusses, a fraternal order by the variety of members it accepts. But in each case, members share the same idea as to where the group begins and ends in social space and know what kinds of experience "belong" within this domain.

For all its apparent abstractness, a social system is organized around the movements of persons joined together in regular social relations. The only material found in a system for marking boundaries, then, is the behavior of its participants; and the form of behavior which best performs this function would seem to be deviant almost by definition, since it is the most extreme variety of conduct to be found within the experience of the group. In this respect, transactions taking place between deviant persons on the one side and agencies of control on the other are boundary maintaining mechanisms. They mark the outside limits of the area in which the norm has jurisdiction, and in this way assert how much diversity and variability can be contained within the system before it begins to lose its distinct structure, its unique shape.

A social norm is rarely expressed as a firm rule or official code. It is an abstract synthesis of the many separate times a community has stated its sentiments on a given issue. Thus the norm has a history much like that of an article of common law: it is an accumulation of decisions made by the community over a long period of time which gradually gathers enough moral influence to serve as a precedent for future decisions. Like an article of common law, the norm retains its validity only if it is regularly used as a basis for judgment. Each time the community censures some act of deviance, then, it sharpens the authority of the violated norm and reestablishes the boundaries of the group.

One of the most interesting features of control institutions, in this regard, is the amount of publicity they have always attracted. In an earlier day, correction of deviant offenders took place in the public market and gave the crowd a chance to display its interest in a direct, active way. In our own day, the guilty are no longer paraded in public places, but instead we are confronted by a heavy flow of newspaper and radio reports which offer much the same kind of entertainment. Why are these reports considered "newsworthy" and why do they rate the extraordinary attention they receive? Perhaps they satisfy a number of psychological perversities among the mass audience, as many commentators have suggested, but at the same time they constitute our main source of information about the normative outlines of society. They are lessons through which we teach one another what the norms mean and how far they extend. In a figurative sense, at least, morality and immorality meet at the public scaffold, and it is during this meeting that the community declares where the line between them should be drawn.

Human groups need to regulate the routine affairs of everyday life, and to this end the norms provide an important focus for behavior. But human groups also need to describe and anticipate those areas of being which lie beyond the immediate borders of the group—the unseen dangers which in any culture and in any age seem to threaten the security of group life. The universal folklore depicting demons, devils, witches and evil spirits may be one way to give form to these otherwise formless dangers, but the visible deviant is another kind of reminder. As a trespasser against the norm, he represents those forces excluded by the group's boundaries: he informs us, as it were, what evil looks like, what shapes the devil can assume. In doing so, he shows us the difference between kinds of experience which belong within the group and kinds of experience which belong outside it.

Thus deviance cannot be dismissed as behavior which *disrupts* stability in society, but is itself, in controlled quantities, an important condition for *preserving* stability.

IV

This raises a serious theoretical question. If we grant that deviant behavior often performs a valuable service in society, can we then assume that society as a whole actively tries to promote this resource? Can we assume, in other words, that some kind of active recruitment process is going on to assure society of a steady volume of deviance? Sociology has not yet developed a conceptual language in which this sort of question can be discussed without a great deal of circularity, but one observation can be made which gives the question an interesting perspective—namely, that deviant activities often seem to derive support from the very agencies designed to suppress them. Indeed, the institutions devised by human society for guarding against deviance sometimes seem so poorly equipped for this task that we might well ask why this is considered their "real" function at all.

It is by now a thoroughly familiar argument that many of the institutions built to inhibit deviance actually operate in such a way as to perpetuate it. For one thing, prisons, hospitals, and other agencies of control provide aid and protection for large numbers of deviant persons. But beyond this, such institutions gather marginal people into tightly segregated groups, give them an opportunity to teach one another the skills and attitudes of a deviant career, and even drive them into using these skills by reinforcing their sense of alienation from the rest of society.[7] This process is found not only in the institutions which actually confine the deviant, but in the general community as well.

The community's decision to bring deviant sanctions against an individual is not a simple act of censure. It is a sharp rite of transition, at once moving him out of his normal position in society and transferring him into a distinct deviant role.[8] The ceremonies which accomplish this change of status, usually, have three related phases. They arrange a formal *confrontation* between the deviant suspect and representatives of his community (as in the criminal trial of psychiatric case conference); they announce some *judgment* about the nature of his deviancy (a "verdict" or "diagnosis," for example); and they perform an act of social *placement*, assigning him to a special deviant role (like that of "prisoner" or "patient") for some period of time. Such ceremonies tend to be events of wide public interest and ordinarily take place in a dramatic, ritualized setting.[9] Perhaps the most obvious example of a commitment ceremony is the criminal trial, with its elaborate ritual and formality, but more modest equivalents can be found almost anywhere that procedures are set up for judging whether or not someone is officially deviant.

An important feature of these ceremonies in our culture is that they are almost irreversible. Most provisional roles conferred by society—like those of the student or citizen soldier, for instance—include some kind of terminal ceremony to mark the individual's movement back out of the role once its temporary advantages have been exhausted. But the roles allotted to the deviant seldom make allowance for this type of passage. He is ushered into the special position by a decisive and dramatic ceremony, yet is retired from it with hardly a word of public notice. As a result, the deviant often returns home with no proper license to resume a normal life in the community. From a ritual point of view, nothing has happened to cancel out the stigmas imposed upon him by earlier commitment ceremonies: the original verdict or diagnosis is still formally in effect. Partly for this reason, the community is apt to place the returning deviant on some form of probation within the group, suspicious that he will return to deviant activity upon a moment's provocation.

A circularity is thus set into motion which has all the earmarks of a "self-fulfilling prophecy," to use Merton's fine phrase. On the one hand, it seems obvious that the apprehensions of the community help destroy whatever chances the deviant might otherwise have for a successful return to society. Yet, on the other hand, everyday experience seems to show that these apprehensions are altogether reasonable, for it is a well-known and highly publicized fact that most ex-convicts return to prison and that a large proportion of mental patients require additional treatment after once having been discharged. The community's feeling that deviant persons cannot change, then, may be based on a faulty premise, but it is repeated so frequently and with such conviction that it eventually creates the facts which "prove" it correct. If the returned deviant encounters this feeling of distrust often enough, it is understandable that he too many begin to wonder if the original verdict of diagnosis is still in effect—and respond to this uncertainty by resuming deviant activity. In some respects, this solution may be the only way for the individual and his community to agree what forms of behavior are appropriate for him.

Moreover, this prophecy is found in the official policies of even the most advanced agencies of control. Police departments could not operate with any real effectiveness if they did not regard ex-convicts as an almost permanent population of offenders, a constant pool of suspects. Nor could psychiatric clinics do a reasonable job if they did not view former patients as a group unusually susceptible to mental illness. Thus the prophecy gains currency at many levels within the social order, not only in the poorly informed attitudes of the community at large, but in the best informed theories of most control agencies as well.

In one form or another, this problem has been known to Western culture for many hundreds of years, and this simple fact is a very important one for sociology. For if the culture has supported a steady flow of deviant behavior throughout long periods of historical evolution, then the rules which apply to any form of functionalist thinking would suggest that strong forces must be at work to keep this flow intact. This may not be reason enough to assert that deviant behavior is altogether "functional"—in any of the many senses of that term—but it should make us reluctant to assume that the agencies of control are somehow organized to prevent deviant acts from occurring or to "cure" deviant offenders of their misbehavior.[10]

This in turn might suggest that our present models of the social system, with their clear emphasis on harmony and symmetry in social relations, only do a partial job of representing reality. Perhaps two different (and often conflicting) currents are found within any well-functioning system: those forces which promote a high overall degree of conformity among human actors, and those forces which encourage some degree of diversity so that actors can be deployed throughout social space to mark the system's boundaries. In such a scheme, deviant behavior would appear as a variation on normative themes, a vital form of activity which outlines the area within which social life as such takes place.

As Georg Simmel wrote some years ago:

> An absolutely centripetal and harmonious group, a pure "unification," not only is empirically unreal, it could show no real life process. . . . Just as the universe needs "love and hate," that is, attractive and repulsive forces, in order to have any form at all, so society, too, in order to attain a determinate shape, needs some quantitative ratio of harmony and disharmony, of association and competition, of favorable and unfavorable tendencies. . . . Society, as we know it, is the result of both categories of interaction, which thus both manifest themselves as wholly positive.[11]

V

In summary, two new lines of inquiry seem to be indicated by the argument presented above.

First, this paper attempts to focus our attention on an old but still vital sociological question: how does a social structure communicate its "needs" or impose its "patterns" on human actors? In the present case, how does a social structure enlist actors to engage in deviant activity? Ordinarily, the fact that deviant behavior is more common in some sectors of society than in others is explained by declaring that something called "anomie" or "disorganization" prevails at these sensitive spots. Deviance leaks out where the social machinery is defective; it occurs where the social structure *fails* to communicate its needs to human actors. But if we consider the possibility that deviant persons are responding to the same social forces that elicit conformity from others, then we are engaged in another order of inquiry altogether. Perhaps the stability of some social units is maintained only if juvenile offenders are recruited to balance an adult majority; perhaps some families can remain intact only if one of their members becomes a visible deviant or is committed to a hospital or prison. If this supposition proves to be a useful one, sociologists should be interested in discovering how a social unit manages to differentiate the roles of its members and how certain persons are "chosen" to play the more deviant parts.

Secondly, it is evident that cultures vary in the way they regulate traffic moving back and forth from their deviant boundaries. Perhaps we could begin with the hypothesis that the traffic pattern known in our own culture has a marked Puritan cast: a defined portion of the population, largely drawn from young adult groups and from the lower economic classes, is stabilized in deviant roles and generally expected to remain there for indefinite periods of time. To this extent, Puritan attitudes about predestination and reprobation would seem to have retained a significant place in modern criminal law and public opinion. In other areas of the world, however, different traffic patterns are known. There are societies in which deviance is considered a natural pursuit for the young, an activity which they can easily abandon when they move through defined ceremonies into adulthood. There are societies which give license to large groups of persons to engage in deviant behavior for certain seasons or on certain days of the year. And there are societies in which special groups are formed to act in ways "contrary" to the normal expectations of the culture. Each of these patterns regulates deviant traffic differently, yet all of them provide some institutionalized means for an actor to give up a deviant "career" without permanent stigma. The problem for sociological theory in general might be to learn whether or not these varying patterns are functionally equivalent in some meaningful sense; the problem for applied sociology might be to see if we have anything to learn from those cultures which permit re-entry into normal social life to persons who have spent a period of "service" on society's boundaries.

Notes

1. Emile Durkheim, *The Rules of Sociological Method* (translated by S. A. Solovay and J. H. Mueller), Glencoe: The Free Press, 1958.

2. The best known statements of this general position, of course, are by Robert K. Merton and Talcott Parsons. Merton, *Social Theory and Social Structures* (revised edition), Glencoe: The Free Press, 1957; and Parsons, *The Social System*, Glencoe: The Free Press, 1951.

3. Cf. Daniel Glaser and Kent Rice, "Crime, Age, and Employment," *American Sociological Review*, 24 (1959), pp. 679–86.

4. Emile Durkheim, *The Division of Labor in Society* (translated by George Simpson), Glencoe: The Free Press, 1952. See particularly Chapter 2, Book 1.

5. Emile Durkheim, *The Rules of Sociological Method, op. cit.*

6. Cf. Talcott Parsons, *The Social System, op. cit.*

7. For a good description of this process in the modern prison, see Gresham Sykes, *The Society of Captives*, Princeton: Princeton University Press, 1958. For views of two different types of mental hospital settings, see Erving Goffman, "The Characteristics of Total Institutions," *Symposium on Preventative and Social Psychiatry*, Washington, D. C.: Walter Reed Army Institute of Research, 1957; and Kai T. Erikson, "Patient Role and Social Uncertainty: A Dilemma of the Mentally Ill," *Psychiatry*, 20 (1957), pp. 263–74.

8. Talcott Parsons, *op cit.*, has given the classical description of how this role transfer works in the case of medical patients.

9. Cf. Harold Garfinkel, "Successful Degradation Ceremonies," *American Journal of Sociology*, 61 (1956), pp. 420–24.

10. Albert K. Cohen, for example, speaking for most sociologists, seems to take the question for granted: "It would seem that the control of deviant behavior is, by definition, a culture goal." In "The Study of Social Disorganization and Deviant Behavior," Merton, et al., editors, *Sociology Today*, New York: Basic Books, 1959, p. 465.

11. Georg Simmel, *Conflict* (translated by Kurt H. Wolff), Glencoe: The Free Press, 1955, pp. 15–16.

15

Moral Entrepreneurs

Howard Becker is unquestionably the most well known of the "labeling theorists." Becker was born in Chicago, received his PhD in Sociology from the University of Chicago, and also taught sociology at the University of Chicago for two years (Mutchnick, Martin, & Austin, 2009:241–242). In addition, he was an accomplished jazz pianist. His interest in the music scene is reflected in a number of his earlier works, such as his (1951) article "The Professional Dance Musician and his Audience" and his (1953) article "Becoming a Marihuana User," both published in the *American Journal of Sociology*. Large portions of these articles subsequently formed two chapters in Becker's (1963) book, *Outsiders: Studies in the Sociology of Deviance*. The following reading, "Moral Entrepreneurs," was also a chapter in his 1963 book *Outsiders*.

Howard Becker was by no means the first or only thinker to pinpoint the significant role that moral entrepreneurs play in rule creation and rule enforcement. In 1950, Edwin Sutherland (the originator of differential association theory) detailed the influence that interest groups such as the media, the politicians, the FBI, the PTA and the medical profession had when they rose up (seemingly in unison) to demand the introduction of sexual psychopath laws throughout the United States (Sutherland, 1950). In 1955, Joseph Gusman classified efforts by the Christian Woman's Temperance Union to criminalize the sale and consumption of alcohol in the United States as "moral reformism" (Gusman, 1955:221–232). Spector and Kitsuse have also undertaken substantive work in the area of claims-making and moral crusading (Pfohl, 1985; 1977:306).

To appreciate Howard Becker's view of moral entrepreneurship, it is important to understand how Becker saw deviance as being socially constructed (Lilly, Cullen, & Ball, 2011:140–142). He talked about the subjective (as opposed to objective) nature of social problems, and explored how they came to be defined as social problems through the process of social reaction (Matsueda, 2001:226; Mutchnick et al., 2009:244). In other words, deviance was in the eye of the beholder. Unless a certain behavior was identified as being deviant by some other individual or group in society, it would likely be ignored altogether. In his 1963 book *Outsiders: Studies in the Sociology of Deviance*, Becker observed:

> Social groups create deviance by making rules whose infraction constitutes deviance, and by applying those rules to particular people and labeling them as outsiders. From this point of view, deviance is *not* a quality of the act the person commits, but rather a consequence of the application by others of rules and sanctions to an "offender." The deviant is one to whom the label has been successfully applied; deviant behavior is behavior that people so label.

Becker characterized moral entrepreneurs as "crusaders," because they act as though they are on a holy mission to stamp out evil. They believe that their views are the right ones, and feel that it is their moral duty to impose their views on others, whether the others agree with those views or not (Becker, 1963:148). Moral crusades are typically led by well-to-do individuals (or groups) with the money and political connections necessary to further their own agenda. If the crusade is successful, then it usually results in new rules, along with the officials and agencies necessary to enforce those rules (Becker, 1963:152–153). Thus, the crusade may transform itself from a reform movement into a social institution. In order to ensure its survival, the new social institution must then search for and identify other "urgent" social problems that require its attention (Becker, 1963:155–157; Kitsuse, 1964:96).

Moral entrepreneurship was just one of a number of important issues that Becker touched upon. Although he was not the first to talk about it, Becker was known for his work on master status and auxiliary status (Williams & McShane, 2010:116; Winfree & Abadinsky, 2010:227). According to Becker, a person's master status—e.g., drug addict, criminal, mentally ill, etc.—would override his or her auxiliary or secondary status (Becker, 1963:32–33). They might possess positive characteristics such as intelligence, kindness or artistic ability, but people would find it difficult to see beyond the negative master status of "deviant" or "criminal." Becker also spoke about retrospective introspection, a process which takes place after a person has been labeled as deviant or criminal (Williams & McShane, 2010:117). Once the label (or master status) was assigned, people who knew the person previously would begin to wonder why they did not recognize the deviance long ago. They would go back though their recollections of past experiences, and reinterpret them in order to find consistency between the individual's new master status and their previous behavior (Williams & McShane, 2010:117).

The labeling perspective led to the development of critical constructionism, accompanied by various studies of social problems and how they resulted in extreme social reactions known as moral panics (Best, 2003:91; Lilly et al., 2011:140–141). More will be said about these topics in the introduction to the last reading in this section, "Round Up the Usual Suspects: The Limits to Constructionism." Elements of the labeling tradition are still evident in the recent works of Lawrence Sherman,

Ross Matsueda, and John Braithwaite, to name a few (Lilly et al., 2011:157–158; Paternoster & Bachman, 2001:221). Ross Matsueda, for example, has been studying the effects of informal labeling by peers, teachers and parents, employing an integrated approach that includes labeling theory, control theory and social learning theory (Matsueda, 2001:235). John Braithwaite's reintegrative shaming theory talks about the effects of stigmatization and disintegrative shaming, and also uses an integrated approach that includes labeling theory, control theory, learning theory, opportunity theory and subcultural theory (Ahmed, Harris, Braithwaite, & Braithwaite, 2001:39–41; Braithwaite, 2001:245–247). Despite its seeming fall from grace during the 1980s, it is difficult to over-state the role that the labeling perspective played in drawing attention away from the individual offender and his or her immediate environment, and in re-directing the attention toward the rule makers and enforcers and the societal reaction to deviance.

References

Ahmed, E., Harris, N., Braithwaite, J., & Braithwaite, V. (2001). *Shame management through reintegration.* Cambridge: Cambridge University Press.

Becker, H. S. (1951). The professional dance musician and his audience. *American Journal of Sociology, 57*(2), 136–144.

Becker, H. S. (1953). Becoming a marihuana user. *American Journal of Sociology, 59*(3), 235–242.

Becker, H. S. (1963). *Outsiders: Studies in the sociology of deviance.* London: Free Press of Glencoe.

Best, J. (2003). Deviance: The constructionist stance. In P. Adler, & P. Adler (Eds.), *Constructions of deviance: Social power, context and interaction* (Fourth ed., pp. 90–105). Belmont, CA: Thomson Wadsworth.

Braithwaite, J. (2001). Reintegrative shaming. In R. Paternoster, & R. Bachman (Eds.), *Explaining criminals and crime: Essays in contemporary criminological theory* (pp. 242–251). Los Angeles, Calif.: Roxbury Pub. Co.

Gusman, J. R. (1955). Social structure and moral reform: A study of the Woman's Christian Temperance Union. *American Journal of Sociology, 6*(3), 221–223.

Kitsuse, J. I. (1964). Societal reaction to deviant behavior: Problems of theory and method. In H. S. Becker (Ed.), *The other side: Perspectives on deviance* (pp. 87–102). New York: Free Press of Glencoe.

Lilly, J. R., Cullen, F. T., & Ball, R. A. (2011). *Criminological theory: Context and consequences* (5th ed.). Thousand Oaks: SAGE Publications.

Matsueda, R. L. (2001). Labeling theory: Historical roots, implications, and recent developments. In R. Paternoster, & R. Bachman (Eds.), *Explaining criminals and crime: Essays in contemporary criminological theory* (pp. 223–241). Los Angeles, Calif.: Roxbury Pub. Co.

Mutchnick, R. J., Martin, R., & Austin, T. W. (2009). *Criminological thought: Pioneers past and present.* Upper Saddle River, NJ: Prentice Hall.

Paternoster, R., & Bachman, R. (Eds.). (2001). *Explaining criminals and crime: Essays in contemporary criminological theory.* Los Angeles, Calif.: Roxbury Pub. Co.

Pfohl, S. J. (1985). *Images of deviance and social control: A sociological history.* New York: McGraw-Hill.

Spector, M., & Kitsuse, J. I. (1977). *Constructing social problems.* Menlo Park, Calif.: Cummings Pub. Co.

Sutherland, E. H. (1950). The diffusion of sexual psychopath laws. *American Journal of Sociology, 56*(2), 142–148.

Williams, F. P., & McShane, M. D. (2010). *Criminological theory* (5th ed.). Upper Saddle River, N.J.: Pearson/Prentice Hall.

Winfree, L. T., & Abadinsky, H. (2010). *Understanding crime: Essentials of criminological theory* (Third ed.). Belmont, CA: Wadsworth, Cengage Learning.

Moral Entrepreneurs

HOWARD BECKER

Rules are the products of someone's initiative and we can think of the people who exhibit such enterprise as *moral entrepreneurs*. Two related species—rule creators and rule enforcers—will occupy our attention.

Rule Creators

The prototype of the rule creator, but not the only variety as we shall see, is the crusading reformer. He is interested in the content of rules. The existing rules do not satisfy him because there is some evil which profoundly disturbs him. He feels that nothing can be right in the world until rules are made to correct it. He operates with an absolute ethic; what he sees is truly and totally evil with no qualification. Any means is justified to do away with it. The crusader is fervent and righteous, often self-righteous.

It is appropriate to think of reformers as crusaders because they typically believe that their mission is a holy one. The prohibitionist serves as an excellent example, as does the person who wants to suppress vice and sexual delinquency or the person who wants to do away with gambling.

These examples suggest that the moral crusader is a meddling busybody, interested in forcing his own morals on others. But this is a one-sided view. Many moral crusades have strong humanitarian overtones. The crusader is not only interested in seeing to it that other people do what he thinks right. He believes that if they do what is right it will be good for them. Or he may feel that his reform will prevent certain kinds of exploitation of one person by another. Prohibitionists felt that they were not simply forcing their morals on others, but attempting to provide the conditions for a better way of life for people prevented by drink from realizing a truly good life. Abolitionists were not simply trying to prevent slave owners from doing the wrong thing; they were trying to help slaves to achieve a better life. Because of the importance of the humanitarian motive, moral crusaders (despite

Reprinted from *Outsiders: Studies in The Sociology of Deviance*, edited by Howard S. Becker (1963), Simon & Schuster, Inc.

their relatively single-minded devotion to their particular cause) often lend their support to other humanitarian crusades. Joseph Gusfield has pointed out that:

> The American temperance movement during the 19th century was a part of a general effort toward the improvement of the worth of the human being through improved morality as well as economic conditions. The mixture of the religious, the equalitarian, and the humanitarian was an outstanding facet of the moral reformism of many movements. Temperance supporters formed a large segment of movements such as sabbatarianism, abolition, woman's rights, agrarianism, and humanitarian attempts to improve the lot of the poor. . . .
>
> In its auxiliary interests the WCTU revealed a great concern for the improvement of the welfare of the lower classes. It was active in campaigns to secure penal reform, to shorten working hours and raise wages for workers, and to abolish child labor and in a number of other humanitarian and equalitarian activities. In the 1880's the WCTU worked to bring about legislation for the protection of working girls against the exploitation by men.[1]

As Gusfield says,[2] "Moral reformism of this type suggests the approach of a dominant class toward those less favorably situated in the economic and social structure." Moral crusaders typically want to help those beneath them to achieve a better status. That those beneath them do not always like the means proposed for their salvation is another matter. But this fact—that moral crusades are typically dominated by those in the upper levels of the social structure—means that they add to the power they derive from the legitimacy of their moral position, the power they derive from their superior position in society.

Naturally, many moral crusades draw support from people whose motives are less pure than those of the crusader. Thus, some industrialists supported Prohibition because they felt it would provide them with a more manageable labor force.[3] Similarly, it is sometimes rumored that Nevada gambling interests support the opposition to attempts to legalize gambling in California because it would cut so heavily into their business, which depends in substantial measure on the population of Southern California.[4]

The moral crusader, however, is more concerned with ends than with means. When it comes to drawing up specific rules (typically in the form of legislation to be proposed to a state legislature or the Federal Congress), he frequently relies on the advice of experts. Lawyers, expert in the drawing of acceptable legislation, often play this role. Government bureaus in whose jurisdiction the problem falls may also have the necessary expertise, as did the Federal Bureau of Narcotics in the case of the marihuana problem.

As psychiatric ideology, however, becomes increasingly acceptable, a new expert has appeared—the psychiatrist. Sutherland, in his discussion of the natural history of sexual psychopath laws, pointed to the psychiatrist's influence.[5] He suggests the following as the conditions under which the sexual psychopath law, which provides that a person "who is diagnosed as a sexual psychopath may be confined for an indefinite period in a state hospital for the insane,"[6] will be passed.

First, these laws are customarily enacted after a state of fear has been aroused in a community by a few serious sex crimes committed in quick succession. This is illustrated in Indiana, where a law was passed following three or four sexual attacks in Indianapolis, with murder in two. Heads of families bought guns and watch dogs, and the supply of locks and chains in the hardware stores of the city was completely exhausted. . . . .

A second element in the process of developing sexual psychopath laws is the agitated activity of the community in connection with the fear. The attention of the community is focused on sex crimes, and people in the most varied situations envisage dangers and see the need of and possibility for their control. . . .

The third phase in the development of these sexual psychopath laws has been the appointment of a committee. The committee gathers the many conflicting recommendations of persons and groups of persons, attempts to determine "facts," studies procedures in other states, and makes recommendations, which generally include bills for the legislature. Although the general fear usually subsides within a few days, a committee has the formal duty of following through until positive action is taken. Terror which does not result in a committee is much less likely to result in a law.[7]

In the case of sexual psychopath laws, there usually is no government agency charged with dealing in a specialized way with sexual deviations. Therefore, when the need for expert advice in drawing up legislation arises, people frequently turn to the professional group most closely associated with such problems:

In some states, at the committee stage of the development of a sexual psychopath law, psychiatrists have played an important part. The psychiatrists, more than any others, have been the interest group back of the laws. A committee of psychiatrists and neurologists in Chicago wrote the bill which became the sexual psychopath law of Illinois; the bill was sponsored by the Chicago Bar Association and by the state's attorney of Cook County and was enacted with little opposition in the next session of the State Legislature. In Minnesota all the members of the governor's committee except one were psychiatrists. In Wisconsin the Milwaukee Neuropsychiatric Society shared in pressing the Milwaukee Crime Commission for the enactment of a law. In Indiana the attorney-general's committee received from the American Psychiatric Association copies of all of the sexual psychopath laws which had been enacted in other states.[8]

The influence of psychiatrists in other realms of the criminal law has increased in recent years.

In any case, what is important about this example is not that psychiatrists are becoming increasingly influential, but that the moral crusader, at some point in the development of his crusade, often requires the services of a professional who can draw up the appropriate rules in an appropriate form. The crusader himself is often not concerned with such details. Enough for him that the main point has been won; he leaves its implementation to others.

By leaving the drafting of the specific rule in the hands of others, the crusader opens the door for many unforeseen influences. For those who draft legislation for crusaders have their own interests, which may affect the legislation they prepare. It is likely that the sexual psychopath laws drawn by psychiatrists contain many features never intended by the citizens who spearheaded the drives to "do something about sex crimes," features which do however reflect the professional interests of organized psychiatry.

The Fate of Moral Crusades

A crusade may achieve striking success, as did the Prohibition movement with the passage of the Eighteenth Amendment. It may fail completely, as has the drive to do away with the use of tobacco or the anti-vivisection movement. It may achieve great success, only to find its gains whittled away by shifts in public morality and increasing restrictions imposed on it by judicial interpretations; such has been the case with the crusade against obscene literature.

One major consequence of a successful crusade, of course, is the establishment of a new rule or set of rules, usually with the appropriate enforcement machinery being provided at the same time. I want to consider this consequence at some length later. There is another consequence, however, of the success of a crusade which deserves mention.

When a man has been successful in the enterprise of getting a new rule established—when he has found, so to speak, the Grail—he is out of a job. The crusade which has occupied so much of his time, energy, and passion is over. Such a man is likely, when he first began his crusade, to have been an amateur, a man who engaged in a crusade because of his interest in the issue, in the content of the rule he wanted established. Kenneth Burke once noted that a man's occupation may become his preoccupation. The equation is also good the other way around. A man's preoccupation may become his occupation. What started as an amateur interest in a moral issue may become an almost full-time job; indeed, for many reformers it becomes just this. The success of the crusade, therefore, leaves the crusader without a vocation. Such a man, at loose ends, may generalize his interest and discover something new to view with alarm, a new evil about which something ought to be done. He becomes a professional discoverer of wrongs to be righted, of situations requiring new rules.

When the crusade has produced a large organization devoted to its cause, officials of the organization are even more likely than the individual crusader to look for new causes to espouse. This process occurred dramatically in the field of health problems when the National Foundation for Infantile Paralysis put itself out of business by discovering a vaccine that eliminated epidemic poliomyelitis. Taking the less constraining name of The National Foundation, officials quickly discovered other health problems to which the organization could devote its energies and resources.

The unsuccessful crusade, either the one that finds its mission no longer attracts adherents or the one that achieves its goal only to lose it again, may follow one of two courses. On the one hand, it may simply give up its original mission and concentrate on preserving what remains of the organization that has been built up. Such, according to one study, was the fate of the Townsend Movement.[9] Or the failing movement may adhere rigidly to an increasingly less popular mission, as did the Prohibition Movement. Gusfield has described present-day members of the WCTU as "moralizers-in-retreat."[10] As prevailing opinion in the United States becomes increasingly anti-temperance, these women have not softened their attitude toward drinking. On the contrary, they have become bitter at the formerly "respectable" people who no longer will support a temperance movement. The social class level from which WCTU members are drawn has moved down from the upper-middle class to the lower-middle class. The WCTU now turns to attack the middle class it once drew its support from, seeing this group as the locus of acceptance of moderate drinking. The following quotations from Gusfield's interviews with WCTU leaders give some of the flavor of the "moralizer-in-retreat":

> When this union was first organized, we had many of the most influential ladies of the city. But now they have got the idea that we ladies who are against taking a cocktail are a little queer. We have an undertaker's wife and a minister's wife, but the lawyer's and the doctor's wives shun us. They don't want to be thought queer.
>
> We fear moderation more than anything. Drinking has become so much a part of everything—even in our church life and our colleges.
>
> It creeps into the official church boards. They keep it in their iceboxes. . . . The minister here thinks that the church has gone far, that they are doing too much to help the temperance cause. He's afraid that he'll stub some influential toes.[11]

Only some crusaders, then, are successful in their mission and create, by creating a new rule, a new group of outsiders. Of the successful, some find they have a taste for crusades and seek new problems to attack. Other crusaders fail in their attempt and either support the organization they have created by dropping their distinctive mission and focusing on the problem of organizational maintenance itself or become outsiders themselves, continuing to espouse and preach a doctrine which sounds increasingly queer as time goes on.

Rule Enforcers

The most obvious consequence of a successful crusade is the creation of a new set of rules. With the creation of a new set of rules we often find that a new set of enforcement agencies and officials is established. Sometimes, of course, existing agencies take over the administration of the new rule, but more frequently a new set of rule enforcers is created. The passage of the Harrison Act presaged the creation of the Federal Narcotics Bureau, just as the passage of the Eighteenth Amendment led to the creation of police agencies charged with enforcing the Prohibition Laws.

With the establishment of organizations of rule enforcers, the crusade becomes institutionalized. What started out as a drive to convince the world of the moral necessity of a new rule finally becomes an organization devoted to the enforcement of the rule. Just as radical political movements turn into organized political parties and lusty evangelical sects become staid religious denominations, the final outcome of the moral crusade is a police force. To understand, therefore, how the rules creating a new class of outsiders are applied to particular people we must understand the motives and interests of police, the rule enforcers.

Although some policemen undoubtedly have a kind of crusading interest in stamping out evil, it is probably much more typical for the policeman to have a certain detached and objective view of his job. He is not so much concerned with the content of any particular rule as he is with the fact that it is his job to enforce the rule. When the rules are changed, he punishes what was once acceptable behavior just as he ceases to punish behavior that has been made legitimate by a change in the rules. The enforcer, then, may not be interested in the content of the rule as such, but only in the fact that the existence of the rule provides him with a job, a profession, and a *raison d'être*.

Since the enforcement of certain rules provides justification for his way of life, the enforcer has two interests which condition his enforcement activity: first, he must justify the existence of his position and, second, he must win the respect of those he deals with.

These interests are not peculiar to rule enforcers. Members of all occupations feel the need to justify their work and win the respect of others. Musicians, as we have seen, would like to do this but have difficulty finding ways of successfully impressing their worth on customers. Janitors fail to win their tenants' respect, but develop an ideology which stresses the quasi-professional responsibility they have to keep confidential the intimate knowledge of tenants they acquire in the course of their work.[12] Physicians, lawyers, and other professionals, more successful in winning the respect of clients, develop elaborate mechanisms for maintaining a properly respectful relationship.

In justifying the existence of his position, the rule enforcer faces a double problem. On the one hand, he must demonstrate to others that the problem still exists: the rules he is supposed to enforce have some point, because infractions occur. On the other hand, he must show that his attempts at enforcement are effective and worthwhile, that the evil he is supposed to deal with is in fact being dealt with adequately. Therefore, enforcement organizations, particularly when they are seeking funds, typically oscillate between two kinds of claims. First, they say that by reason of their efforts the problem they deal with is approaching solution. But, in the same breath, they say the problem is perhaps worse than ever (though through no fault of their own) and requires renewed and increased effort to keep it under control. Enforcement officials can be more vehement than anyone else in their insistence that the problem they are supposed to deal with is still with us, in fact is more with us than ever before. In making these claims, enforcement officials provide good reason for continuing the existence of the position they occupy.

We may also note that enforcement officials and agencies are inclined to take a pessimistic view of human nature. If they do not actually believe in original sin, they at least like to dwell on the difficulties in getting people to abide by rules, on the characteristics of human nature that lead people toward evil. They are skeptical of attempts to reform rule-breakers.

The skeptical and pessimistic outlook of the rule enforcer, of course, is reinforced by his daily experience. He sees, as he goes about his work, the evidence that the problem is still with us. He sees the people who continually repeat offenses, thus definitely branding themselves in his eyes as outsiders. Yet it is not too great a stretch of the imagination to suppose that one of the underlying reasons for the enforcer's pessimism about human nature and the possibilities of reform is that fact that if human nature were perfectible and people could be permanently reformed, his job would come to an end.

In the same way, a rule enforcer is likely to believe that it is necessary for the people he deals with to respect him. If they do not, it will be very difficult to do his job; his feeling of security in his work will be lost. Therefore, a good deal of enforcement activity is devoted not to the actual enforcement of rules, but to coercing respect from the people the enforcer deals with. This means that one may be labeled as deviant not because he has actually broken a rule, but because he has shown disrespect to the enforcer of the rule.

Westley's study of policemen in a small industrial city furnishes a good example of this phenomenon. In his interview, he asked policemen, "When do you think a policeman is justified in roughing a man up?" He found that "at least 37% of the men believed that it was legitimate to use violence to coerce respect."[13] He gives some illuminating quotations from his interviews:

> Well, there are cases. For example, when you stop a fellow for a routine questioning, say a wise guy, and he starts talking back to you and telling you you are no good and that sort of thing. You know you can take a man in on a disorderly conduct charge, but you can practically never make it stick. So what you do in a case like that is to egg the guy on until he makes a remark where you can justifiably slap him and, then, if he fights back, you can call it resisting arrest.
>
> Well, a prisoner deserves to be hit when he goes to the point where he tries to put you below him.
>
> You've gotta get rough when a man's language becomes very bad, when he is trying to make a fool of you in front of everybody else. I think most policemen try to treat people in a nice way, but usually you have to talk pretty rough. That's the only way to set a man down, to make him show a little respect.[14]

What Westley describes is the use of an illegal means of coercing respect from others. Clearly, when a rule enforcer has the option of enforcing a rule or not, the difference in what he does may be caused by the attitude of the offender toward him. If the offender is properly respectful, the enforcer may smooth the situation over. If the offender is disrespectful, then sanctions may be visited on him. Westley has shown that this differential tends to operate in the case of traffic offenses, where the policeman's discretion is perhaps at a maximum.[15] But it probably operates in other areas as well.

Ordinarily, the rule enforcer has a great deal of discretion in many areas, if only because his resources are not sufficient to cope with the volume of rule-breaking he is supposed to deal with. This means that he cannot tackle everything at once and to this extent must temporize with evil. He cannot do the whole job and knows it. He takes his time, on the assumption that the problems he deals with will be around for a long while. He establishes priorities, dealing with things in their turn, handling the most pressing problems immediately and leaving others for later. His attitude toward his work, in short, is professional. He lacks the naïve moral fervor characteristic of the rule creator.

If the enforcer is not going to tackle every case he knows of at once, he must have a basis for deciding when to enforce the rule, which persons committing which acts to label as deviant. One criterion for selecting people is the "fix." Some people have sufficient political influence or know-how to be able to ward off attempts at enforcement, if not at the time of apprehension then at a later stage in the process. Very often, this function is professionalized; someone performs the job on a full-time basis, available to anyone who wants to hire him. A professional thief described fixers this way:

> There is in every large city a regular fixer for professional thieves. He has no agents and does not solicit and seldom takes any case except that of a professional thief, just as they seldom go to anyone except him. This centralized and monopolistic system of fixing for professional thieves is found in practically all of the large cities and many of the small ones.[16]

Since it is mainly professional thieves who know about the fixer and his operations, the consequence of this criterion for selecting people to apply the rules to is that amateurs tend to be caught, convicted, and labeled deviant much more frequently than professionals. As the professional thief notes:

> You can tell by the way the case is handled in court when the fix is in. When the copper is not very certain he has the right man, or the testimony of the copper and the complainant does not agree, or the prosecutor goes easy on the defendant, or the judge is arrogant in his decisions, you can always be sure that someone has got the work in. This does not happen in many cases of theft, for there is one case of a professional to twenty-five or thirty amateurs who know nothing about the fix.

These amateurs get the hard end of the deal every time. The coppers bawl out about the thieves, no one holds up his testimony, the judge delivers an oration, and all of them get credit for stopping a crime wave. When the professional hears the case immediately preceding his own, he will think, "He should have got ninety years. It's the damn amateurs who cause all the heat in the stores." Or else he thinks, "Isn't it a damn shame for that copper to send that kid away for a pair of hose, and in a few minutes he will agree to a small fine for me for stealing a fur coat?" But if the coppers did not send the amateurs away to strengthen their records of convictions, they could not sandwich in the professionals whom they turn loose.[17]

Enforcers of rules, since they have no stake in the content of particular rules themselves, often develop their own private evaluation of the importance of various kinds of rules and infractions of them. This set of priorities may differ considerably from those held by the general public. For instance, drug users typically believe (and a few policemen have personally confirmed it to me) that police do not consider the use of marihuana to be as important a problem or as dangerous a practice as the use of opiate drugs. Police base this conclusion on the fact that, in their experience, opiate users commit other crimes (such as theft or prostitution) in order to get drugs, while marihuana users do not.

Enforcers, then, responding to the pressures of their own work situation, enforce rules and create outsiders in a selective way. Whether a person who commits a deviant act is in fact labeled a deviant depends on many things extraneous to his actual behavior: whether the enforcement official feels that at this time he must make some show of doing his job in order to justify his position, whether the misbehaver shows proper deference to the enforcer, whether the "fix" has been put in, and where the kind of act he has committed stands on the enforcer's list of priorities.

The professional enforcer's lack of fervor and routine approach to dealing with evil may get him into trouble with the rule creator. The rule creator, as we have said, is concerned with the content of the rules that interest him. He sees them as the means by which evil can be stamped out. He does not understand the enforcer's long-range approach to the same problems and cannot see why all the evil that is apparent cannot be stamped out at once.

When the person interested in the content of a rule realizes or has called to his attention the fact that enforcers are dealing selectively with the evil that concerns him, his righteous wrath may be aroused. The professional is denounced for viewing the evil too lightly, for failing to do his duty. The moral entrepreneur, at whose instance the rule was made, arises again to say that the outcome of the last crusade has not been satisfactory or that the gains once made have been whittled away and lost.

Deviance and Enterprise: A Summary

Deviance—in the sense I have been using it, of publicly labeled wrongdoing—is always the result of enterprise. Before any act can be viewed as deviant, and before any class of people can be labeled and treated as outsiders for committing the act, someone must have made the rule which defines the act as deviant. Rules are not made automatically. Even though a practice may be harmful in an objective sense to the group in which it occurs, the harm needs to be discovered and pointed out. People must be made to feel that something ought to be done about it. Someone must call the public's attention to these matters, supply the push necessary to get things done, and direct such energies as are aroused in the proper direction to get a rule created. Deviance is the product of enterprise in the largest sense; without the enterprise required to get rules made, the deviance which consists of breaking the rule could not exist.

Deviance is the product of enterprise in the smaller and more particular sense as well. Once a rule has come into existence, it must be applied to particular people before the abstract class of outsiders created by the rule can be peopled. Offenders must be discovered, identified, apprehended and convicted (or noted as "different" and stigmatized for their nonconformity, as in the case of legal deviant groups such as dance musicians). This job ordinarily falls to the lot of professional enforcers who, by enforcing already existing rules, create the particular deviants society views as outsiders.

It is an interesting fact that most scientific research and speculation on deviance concerns itself with the people who break rules rather than with those who make and enforce them. If we are to achieve a full understanding of deviant behavior, we must get these two possible foci of inquiry into balance. We must see deviance, and the outsiders who personify the abstract conception, as a consequence of a process of interaction between people, some of whom in the service of their own interests, make and enforce rules which catch others who, in the service of their own interests, have committed acts which are labeled deviant.

Notes

1. Joseph R. Gusfield, "Social Structure and Moral Reform: A Study of the Woman's Christian Temperance Union," *American Journal of Sociology*, LXI (November, 1955), 223.

2. *Ibid.*

3. See Raymond G. McCarthy, editor, *Drinking and Intoxication* (New Haven and New York: Yale Center of Alcohol Studies and The Free Press of Glencoe, 1959), pp. 395–396.

4. This is suggested in Oscar Lewis, *Sagebrush Casinos: The Story of Legal Gambling in Nevada* (New York: Doubleday and Co., 1953), pp. 233–234.

5. Edwin H. Sutherland, "The Diffusion of Sexual Psychopath Laws," *American Journal of Sociology*, LVI (September, 1950), 142–148.

6. *Ibid.*, p. 142.

7. *Ibid.*, pp. 143–145.

8. *Ibid.*, pp. 145–146.

9. Sheldon Messinger, "Organizational Transformation: A Case Study of a Declining Social Movement," *American Sociological Review*, XX (February, 1955), 3–10.

10. Gusfield, *op, cit.*, pp. 227–228.

11. *Ibid.*, pp. 227, 229–230.

12. See Ray Gold, "Janitors Versus Tenants: A Status-Income Dilemma," *American Journal of Sociology*, LVII (March, 1952), 486–493.

13. William A. Westley, "Violence and the Police," *American Journal of Sociology*, LIX (July, 1953), 39.

14. *Ibid.*

15. See William A. Westley, "The Police: A Sociological Study of Law, Custom, and Morality" (unpublished Ph.D. dissertation, University of Chicago, Department of Sociology, 1951).

16. Edwin H. Sutherland (editor), *The Professional Thief* (Chicago: University of Chicago Press, 1937), pp. 87–88.

17. *Ibid.*, pp. 91–92.

16

Round Up the Usual Suspects: Crime, Deviance, and the Limits of Constructionism

In the first two readings in this section—"Notes on the Sociology of Deviance" by Kai Erikson and "Moral Entrepreneurs" by Howard Becker—we saw how earlier developments in the sociology of deviance and labeling theory contributed to ongoing efforts to study and document the construction of social problems and moral panics (Best, 1999:91; Matsueda, 2001:226). It is not possible to do justice to all of the "social problems" and "moral panics" literature in a short space, so we will focus briefly on two of the most well known works in this genre.

Stanley Cohen is generally recognized as the thinker who first coined the term "moral panic" (Goode & Ben-Yehuda, 1994:155). In *Folk Devils and Moral Panics*, Cohen (1987) described how the Mods and Rockers—two relatively small, disorganized youth "gangs" that had been in existence in England for years—suddenly attracted widespread media and public attention, leading to police crackdowns, stiffer sentencing, and calls for new legislative initiatives to deal with the "problem." Cohen observed that the Mods and Rockers actually caused relatively little in the way of measurable harm, and that they soon disappeared altogether from the public imagination. In *Threatened Children*, Best (1990) analyzed the development of the "missing children" problem in the US, demonstrating how it led to *The Missing Children's Act* of 1982, The US Attorney's Advisory Board on Missing Children, The National Center for Missing and Exploited Children, and to the establishment of such organizations as Child Find and the Child Stealing Research Center. Best pointed out that claims regarding the number of "missing" children were highly exaggerated, that nobody actually knew where the numbers came from, and that the bulk of the so-called "missing children" were either runaways or had been abducted by non-custodial parents. The emergence of such "social problems" or "moral panics" has at times been attributed by critical constructionists to society's perennial preoccupation with "youth misconduct," "child-victims" and "at-risk youth" (Best, 1994; Schissel, 1997).

Eric Goode, the author of the following reading, "Round Up the Usual Suspects", is well known for his work in the areas of critical constructionism, social problems and moral panics (Burns & Crawford, 1999; Sacco & Kennedy, 2008). Just prior to publishing "Round Up the Usual Suspects," Erich Goode co-authored another paper with Nachman Ben-Yehuda, entitled "Moral Panics: Culture, Politics and Social Construction." The abstract for Goode and Ben-Yehuda's article on moral panics and social construction provides an excellent summary of the critical constructionist perspective:

> Social problems may fruitfully be looked at as constructed phenomenon, that is, what constitutes a problem is the concern that segments of the public feel about a given condition. From the constructionist perspective, that concern need not bear a close relationship with the concrete harm or damage that the condition poses or causes. At times, substantial numbers of the members of societies are subject to intense feelings of concern about a given threat which a sober assessment of the evidence suggests is either nonexistent or considerably less than would be expected from the concrete harm posed by the threat. Such over-heated periods of intense concern are typically short-lived (Goode & Ben-Yehuda, 1994:149).

In this article, Goode and Ben-Yehuda set out the main criteria for identifying a socially constructed "problem" or "moral panic." They said that moral panics were characterized by widespread concern about the "problem" behavior, increased hostility toward the source of the problem, a general social consensus that the "threat" was real, and a disproportionate social reaction to the supposed threat. They also noted that social problems or moral panics were volatile—they appeared suddenly, were of short duration, and then disappeared as suddenly as they had appeared (Goode & Ben-Yehuda, 1994:157–158).

In "Round Up the Usual Suspects: Crime, Deviance and the Limits of Constructionism," Erich Goode warns against simplistic applications of the constructionist perspective to social problems that might in fact be genuinely threatening. According to Goode, we should avoid automatic assumptions that the police round up suspects randomly, round them up because they are underdogs, or round them up because they are easy "social control" targets who have already been labeled as criminals on prior occasions (1994:91–92). Goode recounts a (true) story about Norman Mailer, Gary Gilmore and Jack Henry Abbott. Norman Mailer, a famous author, was writing a book about Gary Gilmore, who was facing the death penalty in Utah during the late 1970s. Goode does not explain in this particular article why Gary Gilmore was facing the death penalty. However, it is worth noting that by age 35, Gilmore had spent 18 years of his life in prison, and that he had an extremely lengthy criminal record for assault and armed robbery. Gilmore was executed by firing squad in Utah because (while on parole) he shot and killed a gas station attendant and a motel operator in two separate incidents within a two day time span. Norman Mailer seemingly came to like Gary Gilmore, and did not feel that the death penalty was an appropriate outcome in this case (Mailer, 1979).

While Norman Mailer was writing his book about Gary Gilmore (entitled *The Executioner's Song*), he started to receive letters from another prisoner. Jack Henry Abbot was 37 years old, and had spent even more of his life in prison than Gary Gilmore. Over the years, Abbot had assaulted a prison doctor, attempted to strangle a witness in court, and had stabbed and killed another prisoner (Goode, 1994:95–96). Norman Mailer and some of his literary friends were persuaded that Jack Henry Abbott had a great future as a writer, and successfully advocated for his early release from prison. Several weeks following his release from prison, Jack Henry Abbott stabbed and killed a waiter who made the mistake of telling Abbott that he could not use the restaurant washroom because it was designated for employee use only (Goode, 1994:97). While accounts of reality may indeed be socially constructed, Goode points out that they often have some sort of factual grounding in the real world. While it is true that both Gary Gilmore and Jack Henry Abbott were labeled as "criminals" at a fairly early age, and were frequently targeted by the agents of social control, it is also true that both of them were extremely violent and dangerous career criminals.

References

Best, J. (1990). *Threatened children: Rhetoric and concern about child-victims.* Chicago: University of Chicago Press.

Best, J. (1994). *Troubling children: Studies of children and social problems.* New York: Aldine de Gruyter.

Best, J. (1999). *Random violence: How we talk about new crimes and new victims.* Berkeley; London: University of California Press.

Burns, R., & Crawford, C. (1999). School shootings, the media and public fear: Ingredients for a moral panic. *Crime, Law and Social Change, 32*(2), 147–168.

Cohen, S. (1987). *Folk devils & moral panics: The creation of the Mods and Rockers.* Oxford: Basil Blackwell.

Goode, E. (1994). Round up the usual suspects: Crime, deviance, and the limits of constructionism. *The American Sociologist, 25*(4), 90–104.

Goode, E., & Ben-Yehuda, N. (1994). MORAL PANICS: Culture, politics, and social construction. *Annual Review of Sociology, 20*(1), 149–171. doi:10.1146/annurev.so.20.080194.001053

Mailer, N. (1979). *The executioner's song.* Boston: Little, Brown.

Matsueda, R. L. (2001). Labeling theory: Historical roots, implications, and recent developments. In R. Paternoster, & R. Bachman (Eds.), *Explaining criminals and crime: Essays in contemporary criminological theory* (pp. 223–241). Los Angeles, Calif.: Roxbury Pub. Co.

Sacco, V. F., & Kennedy, L. W. (2008). *The criminal event: An introduction to criminology in Canada* (Fourth ed.). Toronto: Thomson Nelson.

Schissel, B. (1997). *Blaming children: Youth crime, moral panic and the politics of hate.* Halifax, N.S.: Fernwood.

Round Up the Usual Suspects: Crime, Deviance, and the Limits of Constructionism

ERICH GOODE

> In the 1960s and early 1970s, the sociological study of deviance underwent a sharp break in orientation; many observers in the field began to shift their focus away from an examination of etiology to the study of social control. Examining the social construction of deviance and crime to the exclusion of crucial and unavoidable material features that cannot be defined away lead to certain conclusions that could not be sustained and were vulnerable to successful challenge from later approaches. The lives and work of Frank Tannenbaum, Jack Henry Abbott, and Alvin Gouldner, as well as the work of other labelists and Marxists, offer testimony to the limits of constructionism in the sociological study of deviance and crime.

The last scene of *Casablanca* is set in the city's airport. Major Strasser, a Nazi commanding officer, discovers that Victor Lazlo, a partisan fighter in the anti-Nazi underground and an escapee from a concentration camp, is on a plane bound for Lisbon. Strasser attempts to telephone the radio tower to stop the plane. Rick Blaine, the Humphrey Bogart character, shoots and kills him, at which point, Captain Reynaud, a police commander, played by Claude Raines, turns to one of his assistants and utters the classic line, "Round up the usual suspects."

The sentiment expressed by that self-consciously cynical line is both similar to and yet different from one that emerges from another film, directed, some 15 years later, by Orson Welles—*A Touch of Evil.* Welles plays a law enforcement officer, a sheriff in a town near the United States-Mexican border. For years, he had framed suspects by planting fraudulent evidence on them on his intuition that they were guilty anyway. At first, this might seem to convey the same "Round up the usual suspects" message as the one presented in *Casablanca,* that is, that innocent suspects are being railroaded by the criminal justice system. But it turns out that Welles's final suspect, the one whose case puts an end to his illegal evidence-planting, is actually guilty of the crime of which he was charged. The sheriff framed a guilty man! In a way, this is the *reverse* of "Round up the usual suspects." Instead of railroading innocent suspects, this seems to be a case in which, no matter how much you tinker with the niceties of the evidence—that is, just *how* suspects come to be "rounded up"—if *they're guilty, they'll be rounded up!* Or, even better: If *they're rounded up, they must be guilty!* The cynicism expressed in *A Touch of Evil* makes the message conveyed by Claude Raines's order seem almost naive and idealistic in comparison.

Erich Goode is a professor in the department of sociology, State University of New York, Stony Brook, NY 11794-4356.

Reprinted from *The American Sociologist* 25, no. 4 (1994), Springer Publishing.

The line, "Round up the usual suspects," spoken in a popular film in the 1940s, provided something of an unstated metaphor for several schools in the sociology of deviance and crime that were launched in the 1960s and early 1970s. Beginning at that time, questions about the etiology of deviance and crime became less interesting to many of the field's younger and avant garde practitioners. Instead, what required explaining was: How did certain behavior or actors come to be *regarded* as deviant? How did they attract a deviant or criminal *label* or *judgment*? More broadly, the "new" perspective argued that, in interesting and reveal ways, the relationship between action and reaction is problematic, that is, it is the *invocation* of social control that requires explaining. Today, these approaches are covered by the broad umbrella of constructionism. Behavior can be thought of as being *constructed* as deviant and criminal, and individuals are constructed as deviants and criminals. The question is, how are these constructions *accomplished*? And why? More generally, what these theorists were discussing is how something can be made out of nothing, how categories are created or constructed by the human mind, how putative representatives of these categories are treated *as if* they shared something in common. The constructionist-essentialist debate has been going on for thousands of years, of course, but as it applies specifically to sanctionable behavior, its systematic exploration does not stretch back much more than a generation or two.

In one way or another, these so-called "new" perspectives (Gibbs 1966) shifted their focus away from the traditional question of what causes certain individuals to engage in deviance and crime, or what social structures, contexts, or experiences make for a higher incidence of deviance and crime than others, toward an interest in social control. But note: The uncoupling of the link between the nature of the behavior or condition and the label they attracted does not—intrinsically at least—address the issue of whether the target of the label *deserves* the condemnation. To say that social control is problematic is *not* to imply that injustice is (necessarily) afoot. It *is* to say that social reaction is not a simple reflection of the concrete features of the action or condition, that the relationship between the two is far from automatic; it requires an explanation. Yet, this slide from seeing social control as *problematic* to seeing social control as *unjust*—based on no concrete wrongdoing or harm whatsoever—is easy to make. Constructionists have occasionally taken that slide, and their critics have frequently made the assumption that constructionism is based on making that slide.

One major thrust of the constructionist enterprise was to raise the possibility that social control is exercised in a fashion that is, to a degree, independent of whether its target, if an individual, actually committed the act or offense in question, or, if a category of behavior, actually causes significant social harm. Individuals, or categories of individuals, were being "rounded up" not because they did anything wrong or caused any harm, but simply because they were convenient or acceptable targets of social control. The individuals who were "rounded up": didn't do it; or did it, but so did other individuals; or they did it a little—while others got away—but having gotten caught, they end up doing it a lot more; or didn't cause any harm; or they caused some harm, but others caused more. In short, targets of social control didn't *deserve* to become so targeted. Indeed, it was the football of injustice that many constructionists grabbed and ran downfield with.

Variations on a Ruling Metaphor

In its most literal form, "round up the usual suspects" can be understood as arguing that social control is random; it swoops down and dredges up candidates for punishment *without regard* for whether or not they engaged in sanctionable behavior—indeed, without regard for any identifiable behavior or characteristic whatsoever. This is to say: One seeming implication of the "new" perspective toward deviance was that there is nothing *wrong* or even *different* in the behavior of individuals who are labeled deviant. The epigram to Howard Becker's *Outsiders* (1963), from William Faulkner's *As I Lay Dying*, includes the line: "It's like it ain't so much what a fellow does, but it's the way the majority of folks is looking at him when he does it," implying that behavior may be irrelevant to the deviant label. It is possible that no labeling theorist ever literally advocated this view, although members of the labeling school were sometimes charged with advocating it. "One sometimes gets the impression from reading the literature on labeling," says Ronald Akers—admitting that his characterization represents an exaggeration—"that people mind their own business until bad society comes along and slaps a stigmatized labeling on them" (1985:31). Talking to undergraduates who have read the labelists a bit too hastily and superficially often yields an impression not appreciably different from the "random sanctioning" variant of our ruling metaphor.

A second possible reading of the "Round up the usual suspects" metaphor is that, given that there is a pool of potentially sanctionable candidates, all of whom have engaged in behavior that would be recognized as deviant or criminal, social control swoops down, apprehends, and punishes some, but not others, in this pool. This is not a random process, of course; it is systematically related to key sociological factors or variables. Here, having committed the deviant or criminal behavior is assumed, but it is not the key determining factor in the application of social control. What counts is a variety of *contingencies*—ancillary or auxiliary characteristics in which agents of social control seem far more interested, or at least, are influenced by. Certainly central among these contingencies is a lack of power and status. The primary qualification here is that sanctionable individuals are relatively marginal to mainstream society, relatively vulnerable to punishment, incapable of retaliating or resisting social control. Again, the process is not random; it is sociologically patterned. And actors judged deviant and criminal actually "did it." But, given their deviant behavior, what actually caused them to be punished and condemned is a set of factors that are *extraneous* to the behavior itself, factors that, logically speaking, shouldn't determine the outcome of the sanctioning process, but actually do.

For instance, Goffman argues, to the extent that mentally ill persons outside mental hospitals "numerically approach or surpass those inside hospitals, one could say that mental patients distinctively suffer not from mental illness, but from contingencies" (1961:135). Some of the contingencies Goffman mentions: "socio-economic status, visibility of the offense, proximity to a mental hospital, amount of treatment facilities available, [and] community regard for the type of treatment given in available hospitals" (1961:134–135). In arguing that former arrestees make up a permanent pool of potentially arrestable suspects, David Matza (1969:182–183) certainly comes very close to this position. Here, former arrest—however it was earned—represents a contingency. In one of the most frequently cited and reprinted articles in the deviance literature, William Chambliss (1973) tells us that the "Saints," a group of middle-class, college-oriented adolescent boys who engaged in illegal, delinquent actions, were not arrested, but were dealt with informally by law enforcement, while the "Roughnecks," a group of lower and working-class boys who engaged in much the same behavior, were routinely arrested. In this case, socioeconomic status is the key contingency determining arrest.

To the positivist, who adopts the strict natural science model in studying the social world, and the essentialist, who argues that deviance and crime are more than a mere label—indeed, they represent identifiable forms of behavior caused by an identifiable set of mechanisms and factors—contingencies are a distraction, a fly in the ointment, a speck on the lens, a minor deviation from a strong and unambiguous relationship between act and label, condition and construction. What causes social actors, especially agents of social control, to label deviants, the positivist says, is the nature of their behavior, not contingencies. Gwynn Nettler tells us, in a blistering attack on Scheff's labeling theory of mental illness (1966): "Some people *are* more crazy than others; we can tell the difference; and calling lunacy a name does not *cause* it" (1974:894). With respect to crime, Nettler (1984:282–286) tells us that individuals get caught in the criminal justice "sieve" because they have committed more serious crimes more often, not because of the impact of contingencies; Wellford (1975) argues that acts are criminalized to the extent that they are harmful, and actors are arrested and prosecuted to the extent that they have engaged in serious crimes and that, contrary to what labeling theory says, contingencies play no role in this process; and Jeffery (1990:267) states that there is "little or no proof" for the proposition that "deviants are labeled because they are minorities who are powerless." Labeling is neither capricious nor directed at individuals with the—from the point of view of agents of social control—wrong social characteristics.

A third variation on our ruling metaphor argues that, *however* and *regardless* of why punishment was inflicted, it has the consequence of reinforcing deviant behavior and a deviant identity among the individuals who are punished. This is, of course, the view that is stereotypically associated with the work of the labeling theorists, the view that has become enshrined in many textbooks on deviance and crime. (For a representative few, see Holman and Quinn 1992:152–157; Siegel

1992:239–240; and Mannle and Hirschel 1988:93–94.) The writings of labeling theorists do not support such a simple and unambiguous proposition (Becker 1963:61; Lemert 1951:63). Still, the labelists did *emphasize* the "self-fulfilling prophecy" feature of deviance labeling over effective social control, and that is the proposition for which they are known. It is a great deal more interesting than the proposition that social control usually works, which is commonsensical and unoriginal. Moreover, the figure who is regarded as the most influential theoretical ancestor of labeling theory, Frank Tannenbaum, *did* focus almost entirely on law enforcement as an amplifier of deviance, crime, and delinquency.

And a fourth variation on our "Round up the usual suspects" metaphor is utopian and Marxist. It is that there are persons who might in some way be troublesome to the existing social order but, because the social order is itself illegitimate and repressive, they do not "deserve" to be punished. The putative harm they inflict, or the danger they pose, rests entirely on the nature of this regime. They do not pose any danger to the well-being of the community as such, but to the existing power structure—which does not deserve to rule anyway. The genuine culprits, those who inflict real damage on the society as a whole—the ruling class, the "top dogs," the "fat cats," polluters and warmongers, the manufacturers and politicians, the corporate and white collar criminals—use specific categories of deviance and crime, powerless deviants and criminals, as a scapegoating mechanism to divert attention away from the evil and damaging actions of which they themselves are guilty. It is the "fat cats" who are the true deviants, this perspective argued. In this sense, the punishment of the concrete targets of social control is unfair, unjust, and illegitimate (Gouldner 1968; Liazos 1972; Quinney 1979). Ironically, here, the radical criminologists charged the labeling theorists with the very sin that formed the foundation of their own perspective. That is, the exclusive focus of sociologists of deviance on unconventional, powerless individuals—"nuts, sluts, and deviated preverts"—simply shows that they were colluding in this self-same process: Rounding up the usual suspects. We'll look at this argument shortly.

Frank Tannenbaum

Universally regarded as the most influential precursor of labeling theory, Frank Tannenbaum's family emigrated to the United States from Austria in 1895, when he was two years old. Bridling under his father's authoritarian hand, young Frank ran away from home at the age of 13 (although he returned from time to time), worked at a variety of manual jobs, and became involved with the International Workers of the World (the IWW). In 1914, 21-year-old Frank Tannenbaum led a demonstration of homeless, unemployed men into St. Alphonsis Church in New York City. He was arrested, charged with unlawful assembly, and sentenced to a year in prison in an institution that was located on what is now Welfare Island. Tannenbaum served the entire sentence, including two months in solitary confinement. In prison, he became friendly with Thomas Mott Osborne, warden at Sing Sing prison, who gave him a strong recommendation to Columbia College, which he attended upon his release and from which he graduated Phi Beta Kappa, with highest honors, in 1921. After a stint in the army, Tannenbaum attended, then received a Ph.D. in economics from the Brookings Institution in Washington. He spent nearly his entire academic career, until his retirement, at Columbia University (Delpar 1988).

Frank Tannenbaum was on the side of the little guy, the underdog, and against the massive institutions that were crushing human freedoms and liberties. In *Crime and the Community* (1938:17–20), Tannenbaum argued that in a lower class neighborhood, most adolescent boys engage in a variety of mischievous behavior, such as stealing, truancy from school, and breaking windows. These actions, which are acceptable and conventional to these boys, are often regarded as seriously delinquent by the community—by authorities, teachers, social workers, truant officers, the police, and the courts. The community demands a "suppression" of these activities. A shift takes place from seeing the acts as evil to seeing the boys as evil, so that all their acts "come to be looked at with suspicion." What were once boys engaged in mischievous behavior are now boys who are regarded and treated as "bad and irredeemable." In turn, these boys resent the fact that they have been treated unjustly; they react with antagonism and rebellion. When caught, they encounter a series of agents and agencies of social control: the police, jails, attorneys, courts, judges. The boy who is caught "has been tagged" as a delinquent; he responds by "becoming the thing he is described as being," by escalating the seriousness of the illegal deeds he commits (1938:17–20). On the other hand, the boys who escape apprehension and therefore escape being labeled as deviants, criminals, and delinquents, in time abandon their adolescent high jinks and, for the most part, eventually grow up to become respectable, law-abiding citizens. The difference between them is the labeling process, Tannenbaum argued (1938:71). Hence, social control is self-defeating; the harder agents of social control work "to reform the evil, the greater the evil grows under their hands" (1938:20). Those mischievous boys are just misunderstood and mistakenly stigmatized, Tannenbaum seemed to be saying. It is social control that is doing the real damage, he argued, not the boys themselves. Don't "dramatize" the evil of their behavior, and they'll grow up to be just fine. If any author's work on deviance and crime expresses a view of social control, which is captured in the phrase, "Round up the usual suspects," it is Tannenbaum's.

The labeling theorists loved irony: Witness their focus on the escalation process as a possible outcome of negative labeling. What labeling theorist could have imagined that irony would have haunted the life and death of Frank Tannenbaum? His last years were "marred by a near fatal mugging attack" (Ross 1970). Was Tannenbaum's attacker aware of his theory of crime? Had he been a victim of "Round up the usual suspects"? Was he a misunderstood underdog? Was he, perhaps, a mischievous adolescent, engaged in exuberant high jinks? Or did he, perhaps, *start out* as a mischievous youngster, only to be unjustly and capriciously labeled? As a result, was he forced to see himself as a true criminal? Is this why he mugged and nearly killed a 75-year-old man, blighting the final year or so of his life? Irony can be cruel, and it was especially cruel with the work and death of Frank Tannenbaum.

The Saga of Jack Henry Abbott

In 1977, while working on his book, *The Executioner's Song,* about the life and death of Gary Gilmore, a convicted murderer, author Norman Mailer was sent a series of letters from a prison inmate named Jack Henry Abbott. In these letters, Abbott focused mainly on his prison experiences and his reaction to them. That Mailer would have been impressed by these letters was almost a foregone conclusion. Abbott wrote with a passion and fury with which Mailer had tried, with uneven success, to energize his own work. Mailer had in his younger and even middle-aged years written eloquently about what he referred to as "existential violence"—the beauty of acting in a righteous frenzy in a world that attempts to crush the human will. Once, he heaped (albeit qualified) praise on three adolescents who murdered a candy store owner, arguing that they displayed not only virility but creativity and moral courage (1959:347). Violence, Mailer wrote, is a an act bursting with energy and vitality, a catharsis that prepares for growth. In *An American Dream,* a novel, Mailer's protagonist frees himself from the pious dishonesty of contemporary life by committing a murder, moreover, of a woman with whom he has just had sex. Mailer likened crime and violence to a religious experience. He insisted that not only the worst of the young were being sent to prison, but also the best, "the proudest, the bravest, the most daring, the most enterprising, and the most undefeated of the poor" (1981:xii).

Prison has been used as a literary metaphor in Western society for more than a century; in the United States, Billy the Kid, Butch Cassidy, Bonnie and Clyde, Al Capone, Jesse James, and John Dillinger, became romantic heroes. It should not be surprising that American literary figures generally, and Norman Mailer specifically, should have been attracted to the writings of Jack Henry Abbott. What's more exciting than hearing or reading about underdogs struggling against an oppressive establishment? And if they break a few bones along the way, so much the better!

At the age of 12 Abbott was sent to reform school; at 19, while he was free, he was convicted of burglary and stealing checks which he then made out to himself. Three years into a five-year maximum sentence, Abbott stabbed and killed a fellow inmate and was given a 3-to-20-year sentence. He escaped from prison, committed armed robbery, was arrested and convicted, and was given a 19-year sentence. His prison record shows many disciplinary infractions. Abbott served time in a half-dozen prisons. From the age of 12 until his release at the age of 37, Abbott had been free a total of only nine-and-a-half months; 14 of those years were spent in solitary confinement. His years in prison were marked by many violent incidents. In one, Abbott leaped from the witness stand into the jury box and grabbed the throat of a witness, who said something he didn't like, and began throttling him. In another, when a prison physician was stitching up his wrist after a slashing by another inmate, Abbott inexplicably stabbed the doctor in the face with a sharpened ballpoint pen.

After reading and being profoundly impressed by Abbott's prison letters, Mailer contacted his friends in the literary establishment, including the editor of *The New York Review of Books*, Robert Silvers, and Jason Epstein, a major Random House editor. *The New York Review of Books* published several of Abbott's letters and Random House collected them into a book (1981). These writings, along with endorsements by Mailer and other literary figures, sufficiently impressed prison authorities that these Abbott advocates were able to secure his early release in 1981. Mailer told the Utah Board of Corrections that Abbott had "the makings of a powerful and important American writer." Abbie Hoffman likened Abbott to unjustly imprisoned political prisoners such as Jacobo Timmerman and Alexander Solzhenitsyn (Kakutani, 1981:1).

After his release, Abbott was signed on by the prestigious literary agent Scott Meredith. He was wined and dined by a diverse array of literary figures and was accorded interviews and given writing assignments by a number of leading newspapers and magazines. Abbott was the guest of honor at a dinner thrown by Mailer; in attendance were many of the major literary figures of the day. All assembled, Abbott included, were referred to as men (and women, although they didn't say so at the time) of letters; collectively, they toasted their discovery's literary success.

After being released from prison only a few weeks, while dining in the BiniBon restaurant in New York City, accompanied by two young women, Abbott asked a waiter, 22-year-old Richard Adan, a Cuban-born aspiring actor and playwright, where the BiniBon's rest rooms were located. Adan explained that the only restaurant's toilet was off the kitchen and, as it had no accident insurance for customers, only employees could walk through the kitchen. This restriction on his freedom struck Abbott as infuriating, and he challenged Adan to step outside. After a brief exchange of words, with a single thrust of a knife between the ribs to his heart, Adan lay dead on the sidewalk (Farber 1981a, 1981b; Montgomery 1981; for Abbott's version of the killing, see Manso, 1985:631–632 and Rollyson, 1991:312–313). Abbott quickly made himself a fugitive. He was apprehended working at a Louisiana oil field seven weeks later, was convicted of manslaughter, and sentenced to a 15-year-to-life term; Abbott may be imprisoned for the rest of his life.

The literary figures who had supported Abbott were stunned, shocked, traumatized; somehow, they felt betrayed. Aside from a few brief platitudes, Mailer—otherwise so eloquent on any subject that confronted him—was incapable of formulating a detailed, coherent response to this tragic event. At a press conference held soon after Abbott's arrest, Mailer was defensive, arrogant, belligerent, self-righteous, and inarticulate; Mailer terminated the conference after he and a reporter began shouting obscenities at one another. On his part, Abbott claimed that the killing was simply the result of a misunderstanding.

Michiko Kakutani, in a major review of the Jack Henry Abbott saga in *The New York Times Book Review* (1981), wrote that Mailer and his friends had suffered from a confusion between metaphor and reality. They were deluded into thinking that talent could act as a redeemer, that "the act of writing can somehow transform a violent man into a philosopher of violence" (1981:1). Mailer specifically had spent years "nurturing a theory of violence, only to find out that if an individual lives by such principles, the consequences can be terrible indeed" (1981:38). Said Joyce Carol Oates, a novelist, certain circles of upper-middle class intellectuals can romanticize criminals such as Abbott because they are personally unacquainted with them (Kakutani 1981:36). They see violence as a metaphor for a struggle against a repressive bourgeois society without bothering to understand its real-life motivations and consequences. They want literary and metaphorical violence, not real violence—clean, sanitary, purely ideological violence, violence with all the politically correct accoutrements; they wanted violence with all the warts removed.

Of all literary figures who came into contact with Abbott, perhaps Jerzy Kosinski (who, some 20 years before, had been a graduate student in Columbia's department of sociology) saw him in the most clear-headed and perceptive a fashion. Kosinski began a correspondence with Abbott while he was in prison, but it ended with recrimination and even hatred, judging from the letters, on both sides. Kosinski, who had more than his share of brutal, horrifying experiences—notwithstanding the fact that his claim that his first novel, *The Painted Bird*, was based on factual events has been challenged—wrote to Abbott, prophetically, years before the stabbing incident to the effect that Abbott seemed to believe that, since he was hurt as a child, he had the right "to hurt and kill and molest and torture others in the name of that once-felt pain and rage." However, though he broke off all correspondence with Abbott, and still recognized that he was a violent man, Kosinski nonetheless joined in the dinner honoring and welcoming him into the literary establishment. "By toasting him," Kosinski said somewhat guiltily after the killing, "I endorsed his philosophy. . . . I blame myself for becoming a part of 'radical chic.' I went to welcome a writer, to celebrate his intellectual birth. But instead, I should have been welcoming a just-freed prisoner. . . , a man from another planet who needed to know how to control [his] negative emotions" (Kakutani 1981:38).

Abbott's writings in his prison letters, collected in *In the Belly of the Beast*, display the "Round up the usual suspects," but with an important twist. *He* didn't do anything wrong, or at least, not terribly heinous, not worthy of the lengthy sentences he received—but he was punished anyway. In fact, he was punished *because he was virtuous* (at least by his code). If "you behave like a man," Abbott writes, "you are doomed; you are feared and hated" (1981:13). I have never been indoctrinated with the belief that I should please Caesar, he says; I'm not going to "whine all the way to my death. . . . That is the only reason I have been in prison this long" (1981:15). I am not guilty of the crimes of which I was charged, Abbott writes; of those of which I was technically guilty, I did what was right. I was punished because I was a man, because I stood up for my rights, because I refused to knuckle under to oppression, injustice, and cruelty, because I insisted on asserting my dignity and self-respect. What others define as a vice is really a virtue. "It is a maxim," Abbott writes, "that the morally strongest and the most intelligent among an oppressed people are to be found on the scaffolds and in the prisons of the oppressors" (1981:138–139). Thus, in Abbott's scheme of things, not only is punishment unrelated to the heinousness of one's offense, in an upside-down fashion—and in a fashion only a few of the academic supporters of the "Round up the usual suspects" formula were likely to endorse—certain *virtues* attract punishment. To many observers at the time of his release from prison, Abbott's claim to martyrdom seemed extremely convincing.

Post hoc, some commentators have seen in the Abbott tragedy support for at least one version of the "Round up the usual suspects" theme—that labeling leads to a reinforcement of deviant behavior and a deviant identity. (See, for instance, Franklin 1986:xiii–xiv.) This was the Tannenbaum thesis, of course, and in a more qualified and complex manner, that of the labeling generation of the 1960s. (However, consider the fact that these observers would *not* have opposed Abbott's release on the grounds that, having been mistreated in prison, as a free man, he was likely to be violent and dangerous.) But, as we have observed, life is full of cruel ironies, and this was not the lesson that most observers drew from the notorious case of Jack Henry Abbott. Riding a crest of 1980s "lock 'em up and throw away the key" law-and-order penology, the Abbott case confirmed what much of the public and most criminal justice practitioners had come to suspect anyway: that criminals are *not* incarcerated unjustly, they *do* harm the community in very real and not merely symbolic ways, *do* deserve to be imprisoned—their punishment flowing not from contingency but from objective harm—and they should *not* be treated leniently for their crimes. Certainly, many reasoned, letting a violent offender out on the street simply because he wrote eloquently and passionately about the many (supposed) injustices that had been inflicted upon him was an irresponsible, dangerous and, as it turns out, fatal error. Richard Adan's murder at the hands of Jack Henry Abbott verified the view that the "Round up the usual suspects" critics of deviance and crime labeling had no meaningful contact with behavior taking place in the real world of the prisons and the streets, and that any policy based on this line of criticism could safely be ignored.

Was Jack Henry Abbott "rounded up"—in his case, punished—unjustly, on phony charges? Abbott's writings, we have learned in the decade or more since their publication, are not to be entirely trusted. According to at least one acquaintance, an inmate of the Utah state penitentiary system (Sheffield 1990), much of Abbott's account in *In the Belly of the Beast* was deceptive, a self-serving, overdramatized tract served up with a massive helping of fabrication. Abbott takes credit for taking part in events he had only heard about from other inmates; he claimed to have been the "first" or the "only" inmate to have done certain things (for instance, escape from a maximum security prison) when others also did it, or did it before him; he characterized certain events in a misleading or completely false light (he snuck up on and killed a defenseless inmate "snitch," then claimed to have killed him in "combat," in self-defense); he fails to mention the favors and acts of kindness guards showed him during his inmate career; and he fails to mention that much of his plight (being sent to solitary confinement) was a product of his own making (for instance, striking or screaming insults or obscenities at guards). In short, guards and inmates "know that the book is a fiction. . . . The book is essentially a false literature which deliberately creates a misrepresentation of reality" (Sheffield 1990:13).

Alvin Gouldner and the "New" Criminologists

In the late 1960s and early 1970s, the Marxist, radical, and "new" criminologists turned the tables on the labeling theorists. In one form or another, the labelists advanced at least two versions of the "Round up the usual suspects"—one, that labeling (or being "rounded up") is heavily dependent on contingencies and two, that labeling often reinforces deviant tendencies and a deviant identity. And yet, the radicals accused the labelists of collaborating in the very process they appeared to critique. The behaviors the labeling theorists chose to focus on as deviant implied agreement with the dominant definition. By examining "the world of hip, drug addicts, jazz musicians, cab drivers, prostitutes, night people, drifters, grifters, and skidders"—the "cool world" (Gouldner, 1968:104)—the labelists were endorsing the view that the denizens of this world *deserved* to be regarded as deviant and that the truly harmful actors, the fat cats and members of the corporate elite, should be ignored and permitted to pursue their nefarious practices. Instead, these utopians insisted, deviance should be redefined as violations of human rights—imperialism, racism, sexism, exploitation, oppression. By studying categories of actors *conventionally understood* to be deviants, the radicals argued, the labelists were actually engaged in the very endeavor they appeared to denounce—rounding up the usual suspects.

Alvin Gouldner was the first to make this argument (1968). His hostility to research into the "cool world" of deviance was so intense that he and an acolyte of Becker's, Laud Humphreys (1970), then a graduate student in his department, engaged in a fistfight over the issue. The tale is both sordid and well-known (Hamblin, 1989–90; Pittman and Boden, 1989–90), but it does address our central metaphor. What infuriated Gouldner so much was the issue of who and what should be regarded as deviant. The wrong suspects were being "rounded up," he felt. And by studying the interface between street deviants and the social control functionaries who dealt with them, the labelists ignored the more massive and influential processes taking place at the upper reaches of the power structure. Gouldner felt that Humphreys' study should never have been conducted; it represented an exercise in triviality, a glorification of the esoteric and the exotic. Commenting on the C. Wright Mills award granted to *Tearoom Trade* by the Society for the Study of Social Problems, Gouldner fumed: "And look at what we get: papers on. . . . homosexuals diddling one another in public toilets! When we gave the C. Wright Mills award for that trivia, one had to suspect it was all over for the Society" (Aurbach et al. 1976:41).

Yet, even before the decade of the 1970s was out, the radicals, Marxists, and "new" criminologists faced precisely the same charge of "rounding up"—or, in this case, failing to round up—suspects from a novel source: feminism. Gouldner betrayed his insensitivity to women's issues even in his phallocentric metaphors. He attacks Becker's "Whose Side Are We On?" (1967) by describing it as having been written in a "nonpolemical and flaccid style" (1968:105). To make sure his metaphor is clearly grasped, he refers to Becker's style as characterized by a "limp sobriety" (1968:105). In contrast, he refers to his own style as characterized by a "passionate or erect partisanship" (1968:105). In what is regarded as his most outstanding work, Gouldner writes: "it is my strong but undocumented impression that when some sociologists change their work interests, problems, or styles, they also change their mistresses or wives" (1970:57). The fact is, Gouldner, like the left-leaning criminologists who attacked labeling theory, were somewhat shaky on the issue of sex and gender. Liazos, in his critique of what he sees as the dominant approach in the sociology of deviance—mainly although not exclusively labeling theory—mentions homosexuality (1972:104) and rape (1972:106) as examples of "nuts and sluts" deviance that have received altogether too much attention from sociologists. His failure to see either sexual oppression or the structural dimension in such behaviors reflected a bias one cannot help but refer to as androcentric from today's vantage point. In all of their voluminous writings on deviance and crime, the major Marxist criminologists literally ignored sex and gender. Taylor, Walton, and Young's massive critique of criminology (1973) "does not contain *one word* about women" (Leonard 1982:176); the authors "never notice the limited applicability" of their theories to women. "Likewise, Qunney is all but blind to distinctions between the conditions of males and females in capitalist society" (1982:176).

In short, in making their "Round up the usual suspects" argument, the Marxists and radicals now seem most vulnerable on the gender issue. And they displayed their inability to understand the political implications of the sexual dimension perhaps most in their glorification of proletarian crime. In fact, their argument was not wildly different from Jack Henry Abbott's: The true criminal can be seen as a rebel, a challenge to the status quo, a potential revolutionary—practically a comrade in arms. Although not in itself a revolutionary act, crime has revolutionary implications, they said. It can be a threat to the capitalist system; crime and criminals can be a positive force in the class struggle. Predatory crimes such as robbery are, at once, both a "reproduction" of the capitalist system and "antagonistic to" the capitalist order (Quinney 1980:60, 61). Deviance and crime can be seen as a "challenge to authority" in a repressive system (Taylor, Walton, and Young 1973:169); they represent "the acts of men in the process of actively making, rather than passively taking, the external world" (1973:221). In short, much deviance "is in itself a political act" (1973:221). This seems a clear-cut case of one of our "Round up the usual suspects" metaphors. Does this mean that criminals shouldn't be rounded up? Or that their actions do not have true victims?

Just as the Marxists turned the tables on the labeling theorists on the "Round up the usual suspects" issue, the feminists turned the tables on the Marxists. It was *they* who were colluding in "rounding up" the wrong suspects. Or, more properly, they were colluding in *not* rounding up suspects that in fact *should* be rounded up.

They ignored real crimes—more specifically, real crimes against real women—as truly victimless and illegitimately punished. In imagining that crime represents a kind of primitive struggle against the capitalist system, little or no attention was paid "to the ordinary, abundant suffering which working-class crime inflicts on the working class. The criminal has been romanticized and the victim liquidated" (Downes and Rock 1988:269). Most street crime entails one poor, powerless person exploiting and brutalizing another poor, relatively powerless person. Moreover, and more directly to the point, crime treated as romantic, class-conscious rebellion leaves the gender issue out of the picture; phallocentric crimes as rape, domestic violence, and sexual harassment are condoned. Almost in spite of itself, feminism found itself launching a devastating critique of Marxist and radical criminology (Smart, 1976; Leonard, 1982). Feminists "reproached radical criminology for ignoring the politics of gender, for forgetting the extensive victimization of women, and for celebrating what seemed to be patriarchal oppression" (Downes and Rock 1988:269). In a significant way, a feminist approach to deviance and crime was *forged* in a critique of the Marxist perspective. Feminism forced a systematic reevaluation of just who, and what, the field of the sociology of deviance and crime is—and is not—"rounding up."

Coda

Of necessity, the empirically based constructionist must be compromised, impure, tormented by the contradictions and dilemmas in the perspective. (Woolgar and Powluch 1985, and Best 1993, make related points.) We remain troubled by attempts to define away the concrete world. Just before the Gulf War, Jean Baudrillard, a fashionable French philosopher, declared that there would be no war; after the outbreak of the war, Baudrillard declared that there had been no war, that it was in fact all a social construction (1991). If the Gulf War didn't happen, what about the Holocaust? Or the history of slavery? There are some extremely troubling implications of radical, extreme, or *strict* constructionism, which does not even permit us to ask questions about the material world—the phenomena whose reality we have, presumably, constructed. *Of course* we construct reality; *all* accounts of reality are constructed. And yet, those constructs are typically based *in some way* on what's "out there" in the material world. Often, these constructs bear an extremely loose and oblique relationship to the phenomena they supposedly categorize. An investigation of the discrepancy constructs and material world is frequently instructive. (Correction: the discrepancy between *one set of constructs*—say, popular notions of what's true—and *another* set of constructs—the results of a systematic, empirical investigation of a given phenomenon.)

There are also, as we saw, troubling implications of the more old-fashioned brands of constructionism, discussed here—such as Marxism and certain interpretations of labeling theory—which *do* privilege certain versions of material reality, but insist these discrepancies by their very nature and of necessity fit their models. But every construct need not display such discrepancies. Or be a product of systematic injustice, capriciousness, arbitrariness, the motive to protect elite interests, or downright prudishness. Some of the theoretically pure constructionist arguments made in the past may have been a lot more interesting than more moderate ones. But most of them simply haven't stood the test of time. As we grope around in the world out there, trying to discern what it's like, we can't help but bump into creatures—phenomena—that have to be explained. I feel a greater obligation to those creatures than I do to the purity of a special perspective. The more radical constructionists are terribly distressed by theoretical impurity, but I, for one, am not. Holding an impure, compromised theoretical position is a small price to pay for keeping those creatures out there in the world that I keep bumping into happy.

Acknowledgments

I would like to thank the Lady Davis Fellowship Trust for granting me a visiting professorship at The Hebrew University of Jerusalem for the spring semester of 1993, during which, among other things, I wrote this paper. I would also like to thank Nachman Ben-Yehuda for his encouragement and support, and Stanley Cohen for his comments on an earlier version of this paper.

References

Abbott, Jack Henry. 1981. *In the Belly of the Beast: Letters From Prison.* New York: Random House.

Akers, Ronald L. 1985. *Deviant Behavior: A Social Learning Approach* (3rd ed.). Belmont, CA: Wadsworth.

Aurbach, Herbert A., et al. 1976. "SSSP as the Organization of a Social Movement: Comments and Suggestions," *Social Problems,* 24(1):37–53.

Baudrillard, Jean. 1991. "The Reality Gulf." *The Guardian,* January 11:25.

Becker, Howard S. 1963. *Outsiders: Studies in the Sociology of Deviance.* New York: Free Press.

Becker, Howard S. 1967. "Whose Side Are We On?" *Social Problems,* 14(3):239–247.

Best, Joel. 1993. "But Seriously Folks: The Limitations of the Strict Constructionist Interpretation of Social Problems." In Gale Miller and James A. Holstein, eds., *Constructionist Controversies: Issues in Social Problems Theory.* New York: Aldine de Gruyter, 109–127.

Chambliss, William J. 1973. "The Saints and the Roughnecks." *Society,* 11(Dec.):24–31.

Delpar, Helen. 1988. "Frank Tannenbaum, 1914–1933." *The Americas: A Quarterly Review of Inter-American Cultural History,* 45(2):153–171.

Downes, David, and Paul Rock. 1988. *Understanding Deviance: A Guide to the Sociology of Crime and Rule Breaking* (2nd ed.). Oxford, England: Clarendon Press.

Erikson, Kai T. 1964. "Notes on the Sociology of Deviance." In Howard S. Becker, ed., *The Other Side.* New York: Free Press, 9–21.

Farber, M.A. 1981a. "Convict-author Known by Mailer is Being Sought in Fatal Stabbing." *The New York Times,* July 20:B3.

Farber, M.A. 1981b. "Killing Clouds Ex-convict Writer's New Life." *The New York Times,* July 26:1, 26.

Franklin, H. Bruce. 1986. *Prison Literature in America: The Victim as Criminal and Artist* (expanded ed.). New York: Oxford University Press.

Gibbs, Jack P. 1966. "Conceptions of Deviant Behavior: The Old and the New." *Pacific Sociological Review*, 9(1):9–14.

Goffman, Erving. 1961. *Asylums*. Garden City, N.Y.: Doubleday-Anchor.

Gouldner, Alvin W. 1968. "The Sociologist as Partisan: Sociology and the Welfare State." *The American Sociologist*, 3(2):103–116.

Gouldner, Alvin W. 1970. *The Coming Crisis of American Sociology*. New York: Basic Books.

Hamblin, Robert L. 1989–90. "Sociology and a Developing Administrative Tradition at Washington University: 1957–1971." *The American Sociologist*, 20(4):324–329.

Holman, John E., and James F. Quinn. 1992. *Criminology: Applying Theory*. St. Paul, Minn.: West.

Humphreys, Laud. 1970. *Tearoom Trade: Impersonal Sex in Public Places*. Chicago: Aldine.

Jeffery, C. Ray. 1990. *Criminology: An Interdisciplinary Approach*. Englewood Cliffs, N.J.: Prentice-Hall.

Kakutani, Michiko. 1981. "The Strange Case of the Writer and the Criminal." *The New York Times Book Review*, September 20:1, 36, 39.

Lemert, Edwin M. 1991. *Social Pathology: A Systematic Approach to the Theory of Sociopathic Behavior*. New York: McGraw-Hill.

Leonard, Eileen B. 1982. *Women, Crime, and Society. A Critique of Criminological Theory*. New York: Longman.

Liazos, Alexander. 1972. "The Poverty of the Sociology of Deviance: Nuts, Sluts, and Preverts." *Social Problems*, 20(1):103–120.

Mailer, Norman. 1959. "The White Negro: Superficial Reflections on the Hipster." In *Advertisements for Myself*, New York: G. P. Putnam, 337–358.

Mailer, Norman. 1981. "Introduction." In *In the Belly of the Beast: Letters from Prison, Jack Henry Abbott*. New York: Random House, ix–xvi.

Mannle, Henry W., and J. David Hirschel. 1988. *Fundamentals of Criminology* (2nd ed.). Englewood Cliffs, N.J.: Prentice-Hall.

Manso, Peter. 1985. *Mailer: His Life and Times*. New York: Viking.

Matza, David. 1969. *Becoming Deviant*. Englewood Cliffs, N.J.: Prentice-Hall.

Montgomery, Paul L. 1981. "Convict-author Sought to Staying in New York is Seized in Louisiana." *The New York Times*, September 24:A1, D27.

Nettler, Gwynn. 1974. "On Telling Who's Crazy." *American Sociological Review*, 39(6):893–894.

Nettler, Gwyan. 1984. *Explaining Crime* (3rd ed.). New York: McGraw-Hill.

Pittman, David J., and Dierdre Boden. 1989–90. "Sociology at Washington University in St. Louis: History and Reflections, 1906–1989." *The American Sociologist*, 20(4):305–321.

Quinney, Richard. 1979. *Criminology* (2nd ed.). Boston: Little. Brown.

Quinney, Richard. 1980. *Class, State, and Crime* (2nd ed.) New York: Longman.

Rollyson, Carl. 1991. *The Lives of Norman Mailer: A Biography*. New York: Paragon House.

Ross, Stanley R. 1970. Obituary, Frank Tannenbaum. *Hispanic-American Historical Review*, 50(2):345–348.

Scheff, Thomas J. 1966. *Being Mentally Ill: A Sociological Theory*. Chicago: Aldine.

Sheffield, Paul Ray. 1990. "Slitting Open the Belly of the Beast." *The Threepenny Review*, Winter:13–15.

Siegel, Larry J. 1992. *Criminology*. St. Paul, Minn.: West.

Smart, Carol. 1976. *Women, Crime and Criminology: A Feminist Critique*. London: Routledge & Kegan Paul.

Tannenbaum, Frank. 1938. *Crime and the Community*. New York: Ginn.

Taylor, Ian, Paul Walton, and Jock Young. 1973. *The New Criminology: For a Social Theory of Deviance*. London: Routledge & Kegan Paul.

Wellford, Charles. 1975. "Labelling Theory and Criminology: An Assessment." *Social Problems*, 22(3):332–344.

Woolgar, Steve, and Dorothy Pawluch. 1985. "Ontological Gerrymandering: The Anatomy of Social Problems Explanations." *Social Problems*, 32(3):214–227.

Conflict Criminology
and Critical Criminology

Conflict criminology and critical criminology have been included in the same section of this book for a number of reasons. While certain (less radical) strains of conflict theory can be traced back to Georg Simmel and George Vold (Akers & Sellers, 2009:215; Vold & Bernard, 1979:283), the more radicalized versions of conflict and critical criminology that came to prominence during the 1970s and early 1980s generally had their intellectual roots in the thinking of Karl Marx (Renzetti, Curran, & Carr, 2003:177; Williams & McShane, 2010:134). In contrast to the consensus view of law as representing our shared social values and beliefs, conflict criminologists and critical criminologists alike view law as resulting from social conflict (Arrigo & Williams, 2009:402). They stress the impact of economic power and social inequality on law formation. Conflict and critical criminologists examine the manner in which criminal sanctions are applied primarily to marginalized members of the under-class, while pointing out that crimes by the rich and powerful often go unsanctioned (Quinney, 2003:85–86; Spitzer, 2005:109; Winfree & Abadinsky, 2010:281).

There are only two reading selections in this particular section of the book. This is not, however, because conflict and critical criminology are unimportant. Rather, it is because a number of the thinkers referred to in Sections V and VII of this book (the preceding section and the following section) would themselves be regarded as conflict or critical criminologists. Stanley Cohen, the author of the 1972 book *Folk Devils and Moral Panics: The Creation of the Mods and Rockers* (see the introduction to Reading 16 in Section V) also co-edited a book in 1973 with Jock Young, entitled *The Manufacture of News: Social Problems, Deviance and the Mass Media*. Jock Young, along with Ian Taylor and Paul Walton, was a co-author of the 1973 book *The New Criminology* and a co-editor of the 1975 book *Critical Criminology*—two of the most well known and influential books in the areas of conflict and critical criminology. In fact, the second of the two reading selections in this section is written by the same Jock Young who worked with Stanley Cohen on *The Manufacture of News* and with Taylor and Walton on *The New Criminology* and *Critical Criminology*. Sally Simpson, the author of the first reading in Section VII, talks about Marxian theories of crime, socialist feminism and "underclass" Black females (Simpson, 1991:116).

The first reading in this section, "A Sociological Analysis of the Law of Vagrancy," is an example of a conflict-oriented approach to the sociology of law. It was written in 1964, before the term "critical criminology" appeared on the horizon. The author of the article, William Chambliss, later came to be considered one of the "critical criminologists," and went on to write a chapter in Taylor, Walton and Young's well known book, *Critical Criminology* (Lilly, Cullen, & Ball, 2011:184-185; Winfree & Abadinsky, 2010:286–287). The second reading selection in this section, by Jock Young, is representative of what came to be known as "left realism." Left realism was an outgrowth (or modification) of some of the more radicalized strains of conflict and critical criminology that emerged during the 1970s (Williams & McShane, 2010:137).

There are a number of conflict or critical criminologists whose works span the entire spectrum, from conflict criminology to critical criminology to left realism (Williams & McShane, 2010:134). When he published his 1970 book *The Social Reality of Crime*, Richard Quinney was thought of as a conflict criminologist (Arrigo & Williams, 2009:403). By 1975, Quinney became more closely aligned with the critical criminologists. In this regard, he contributed a chapter on "Crime Control in Capitalist Society" to Taylor, Walton and Young's book *Critical Criminology* (Quinney, 1975). In his (1977) book, *Class, State and Crime*, Richard Quinney talked about crimes of domination (committed by the capitalist class and its crime control agencies), crimes of accommodation (committed by members of the working class in order to cope with the conditions of capitalism) and crimes of resistance (committed by those who were attempting to resist or overthrow the capitalist system) (Winfree & Abadinsky, 2010:283–285). In later years, Richard Quinney began writing about peacemaking criminology, a form of left realism that—while still critical of the ills of capitalist society—accepted the continued existence of the present socioeconomic system and sought new ways to make the society less violent and the criminal justice system more humane (Renzetti et al., 2003:200–201).

Essentially, "critical criminology" became known as such because of its "critical" analysis of the law, its criticism of the inegalitarian nature of capitalist society, and its criticisms of mainstream criminologists and their correctionalist attitudes toward criminals (Young, 2002). Conflict and critical criminologists argued that crime and deviance were produced by the social structure of capitalist society (Lynch & Stretesky, 2001:270–273; Spitzer, 2005:108–109). They also sought to demystify the origins and purposes of law, by showing that is was economically driven, and usually served the interests of those who had money and power (Quinney, 1975:199). The following reading selection by William Chambliss is an historical analysis of how and why vagrancy laws were originally introduced in England, and how such laws worked to the benefit of the upper classes of English society.

References

Akers, R. L., & Sellers, C. S. (2009). *Criminological theories: Introduction, evaluation, and application* (5th ed.). New York: Oxford University Press.

Arrigo, B. A., & Williams, C. R. (2009). Conflict criminology: Developments, directions, and destinations past and present. In H. Copes, & V. Topalli (Eds.), *Criminological theory: Readings and retrospectives* (pp. 401–412). New York: McGraw-Hill.

Lilly, J. R., Cullen, F. T., & Ball, R. A. (2011). *Criminological theory: Context and consequences* (5th ed.). Thousand Oaks: SAGE Publications.

Lynch, M. J., & Stretesky, P. B. (2001). Radical criminology. In R. Paternoster, & R. Bachman (Eds.), *Explaining criminals and crime: Essays in contemporary criminological theory* (pp. 267–286). Los Angeles, Calif.: Roxbury Pub. Co.

Quinney, R. (1975). Crime control in capitalist society: A critical philosophy of legal order. In I. Taylor, P. Walton & J. Young (Eds.), *Critical criminology* (pp. 181–201). London: Routledge & Kegan Paul.

Quinney, R. (1977). *Class, state and crime: On the theory and practice of criminal justice*. New York: David McKay Company, Inc.

Quinney, R. (2003). Conflict theory of crime. In P. Adler, & P. Adler (Eds.), *Constructions of deviance: Social power, context and interaction* (Fourth ed., pp. 84–89). Belmont, CA: Thomson Wadsworth.

Renzetti, C. M., Curran, D. J., & Carr, P. J. (Eds.). (2003). *Theories of crime: A reader*. Boston: Allyn and Bacon.

Simpson, S. S. (1991). Caste, class and violent crime: Explaining difference in female offending. *Criminology, 29*(1), 115–135.

Spitzer, S. (2005). Toward a Marxian theory of deviance. In H. N. Pontell (Ed.), *Social deviance: Readings in theory and research* (Fifth ed., pp. 108–112). Upper Saddle River, NJ: Pearson Prentice Hall.

Vold, G. B., & Thomas J. Bernard. (1979). *Theoretical criminology* (2nd ed.). New York: Oxford University Press.

Williams, F. P., & McShane, M. D. (2010). *Criminological theory* (5th ed.). Upper Saddle River, N.J.: Pearson/Prentice Hall.

Winfree, L. T., & Abadinsky, H. (2010). *Understanding crime: Essentials of criminological theory* (Third ed.). Belmont, CA: Wadsworth, Cengage Learning.

Young, J. (2002). Critical criminology in the twenty-first century: Critique, irony and the always unfinished. In K. Carrington, & R. Hogg (Eds.), *Critical criminology: Issues, debates and challenges* (pp. 251–274). Cullompton, Devon: Willan Publishers.

17

A Sociological Analysis
of the Law of Vagrancy

William Chambliss completed his PhD in Sociology at the University of Indiana, and subsequently pursued postdoctoral studies at the University of Wisconsin. It is noteworthy that Richard Quinney, another well known conflict theorist and critical criminologist, completed his PhD in Sociology at the University of Wisconsin at approximately the same time (Lilly, Cullen, & Ball, 2011:179–180; Mutchnick, Martin, & Austin, 2009:263–264).

The thinking of William Chambliss changed considerably over the years. His (1964) analysis of vagrancy laws in England (the next reading selection) is clearly consistent with the conflict criminology tradition, in that it focuses on how social and economic changes and class conflict can lead to changes in the law. That said, there is no mention whatsoever in this earlier work of Karl Marx, or of Marxian thinking. In his 1973 study of "The Saints and the Roughnecks," Chambliss observes that The Saints—a group of higher class boys who engaged in frequent truancy and delinquency—were well respected by the community, and treated leniently by school teachers and the police. On the other hand, the Roughnecks—a group of lower class boys from the same town who engaged in less truancy and the same amount of delinquency—were regarded as troublesome by school teachers and the community, and were often arrested by the police (Chambliss, 2003). While Chambliss demonstrates the relevance of social class and the effects of labeling on life outcomes in this study of The Saints and the Roughnecks, there is again no mention of Karl Marx or Marxian thinking.

In his 1974 article, "Toward a Political Economy of Crime," Chambliss begins by announcing that he is "attempting to develop a Marxist theory of crime and criminal law." In this article, he uses Marian terminology in referring to capitalists as "the ruling class" and to workers as "the proletariat" (Chambliss, 1985:423–427). In "The Political Economy of Crime," which appeared as a chapter in Taylor, Walton and Young's 1975 book *Critical Criminology*, Chambliss examines crime data from Nigeria and Seattle, and concludes that in both countries, "criminal acts which serve the interests of the ruling class will go unsanctioned whilst those that do not will be punished" (Chambliss, 1975:177). Clearly, Chambliss underwent a major shift in thinking between 1973 and 1974 (cf. Lilly et al., 2011:180–184).

William Chambliss' sociological analysis of the vagrancy laws in England sets out to demonstrate how social settings, economic changes and interest groups all contribute to changes in the law. It is, he says, an attempt to develop "a mature sociology of law" (Chambliss, 1964:67, 70, 77). Chambliss notes that his approach is in contrast to the consensus perspective, which regards laws as a "reflection of public opinion" (Chambliss, 1964:77).

Chambliss reports that the first vagrancy law appeared in England in 1349. This was just after The Black Death, when half of the English population died as a result of the bubonic plague epidemic. The law also came on the heels of The Crusades and a number of other wars, which forced the wealthy to sell off or sell freedom to some of their serfs in order to pay for their war-related expenses (Chambliss, 1964:69). The vagrancy law of 1349 threatened imprisonment for anyone who provided sane, able-bodied individuals with food, shelter or monetary support. It also required sane, able-bodied individuals to look for work, and if they did not, threatened them with imprisonment until such time as they found work (Chambliss, 1964:68–69). The group targeted by this law included beggars, minstrels, jugglers, pedlars and the like. Chambliss argues that the main thrust of this law was to force able-bodied workers to accept low-paying work, to ensure that landowners had a steady supply of cheap labor (1964:69). In other words, the vagrancy law of 1349 came into existence as the result of the then current social circumstances (high death rates and unpaid war costs) and the economic needs of the wealthy landowners.

Chambliss observes that subsequent amendments to the vagrancy law were intended to make it progressively more punitive. The 1388 amendment stipulated that social loafers were to be placed in the stocks (the pillory) until such time as they secured employment. The 1495 amendment stipulated that such individuals were to spend three days in the stocks, and then be ordered to avoid town altogether (Chambliss, 1964:70). By 1530, first time offenders would be tied to a cart naked and whipped at various locations around town until they were bloody, second time offenders would be whipped in a similar fashion for two days, spend a night in the stocks and have an ear cut off, while third time offenders would be whipped, placed in the stocks, and have their other ear cut off. Five years later, being a third time offender resulted in the death penalty (Chambliss, 1964:71–72).

According to Chambliss, the increasing severity of penalties for vagrancy was attributable to a number of major changes that were occurring in the economy and the social structure. The system of feudalism—where landlords owned the land and the serfs were virtually "bound" to them—was breaking down. Serfs who had not already purchased their freedom—or simply left the land in search of better prospects in the towns—were emancipated in 1575. Commerce and industry were beginning to flourish in the urban centers, thus generating the need to transport an ever-increasing volume of goods by road (Chambliss, 1964:71–72). This in turn led to new opportunities for "highway robbery." Chambliss says that the vagrancy law gained renewed strength at this time, primarily to protect the interests of merchants whose goods were being stolen. Vagrants or "loiterers" came to be referred to as "vagabonds". For a first offense, the vagabond would be branded with the letter "V," and be enslaved for two years to his or her accuser. If the vagabond ran away, then he or she would be branded with the letter "S," and enslaved for life (Chambliss, 1964:72–73).

Chambliss' analysis of the vagrancy law in 13th–15th Century England is a prime example of conflict criminology, and how sociology can be applied to the study of law. While this work could not be described as Marxist criminology or "critical criminology," it is nevertheless possible to see its connection to both. It is also possible to sense from this earlier work that Chambliss might eventually turn toward the more radical, class-based explanations offered by Marxist criminology and critical criminology.

References

Chambliss, W. J. (1964). A sociological analysis of the law of vagrancy. *Social Problems, 12*(1), 67–77.

Chambliss, W. J. (1975). The political economy of crime: A comparative study of Nigeria and the USA. In I. Taylor, P. Walton & J. Young (Eds.), *Critical criminology* (pp. 167–179). London: Routledge & Kegan Paul.

Chambliss, W. J. (1985). Toward a political economy of crime. In S. H. Traub, & C. B. Little (Eds.), *Theories of deviance* (3rd ed., pp. 423–441). Itasca, Ill.: F. E. Peacock Publishers.

Chambliss, W. J. (2003). The Saints and The Roughnecks. In P. Adler, & P. Adler (Eds.), *Constructions of deviance: Social power, context and interaction* (Fourth ed., pp. 169–182). Belmont, CA: Thomson Wadsworth.

Lilly, J. R., Cullen, F. T., & Ball, R. A. (2011). *Criminological theory: Context and consequences* (5th ed.). Thousand Oaks: SAGE Publications.

Mutchnick, R. J., Martin, R., & Austin, T. W. (2009). *Criminological thought: Pioneers past and present.* Upper Saddle River, NJ: Prentice Hall.

A Sociological Analysis of the Law of Vagrancy

WILLIAM J. CHAMBLISS

With the outstanding exception of Jerome Hall's analysis of theft[1] there has been a severe shortage of sociologically relevant analyses of the relationship between particular laws and the social setting in which these laws emerge, are interpreted, and take form. The paucity of such studies is somewhat surprising in view of widespread agreement that such studies are not only desirable but absolutely essential to the development of a mature sociology of law.[2] A fruitful method of establishing the direction and pattern of this mutual influence is to systematically analyze particular legal categories, to observe the changes which take place in the categories and to explain how these changes are themselves related to and stimulate changes in the society. This paper is an attempt to provide such an analysis of the law of vagrancy in Anglo-American Law.

Legal Innovation: The Emergence of the Law of Vagrancy in England

There is general agreement among legal scholars that the first full fledged vagrancy statute was passed in England in 1349. As is generally the case with legislative innovations, however, this statute was preceded by earlier laws which established a climate favorable to such change. The most significant forerunner to the 1349 vagrancy statute was in 1274 when it was provided:

> Because that abbies and houses of religion have been overcharged and sore grieved, by the resort of great men and other, so that their goods have not been sufficient for themselves, whereby they have been greatly hindered and impoverished, that they cannot maintain themselves, nor such charity as they have been accustomed to do; it is provided, that none shall come to eat or lodge in any house of religion, or any other's foundation than of his own, at the costs of the house, unless he be required by the governor of the house before his coming hither.[3]

Unlike the vagrancy statutes this statute does not intend to curtail the movement of persons from one place to another, but is solely designed to provide the religious houses with some financial relief from the burden of providing food and shelter to travelers.

For a more complete listing of most of the statutes dealt with in this report the reader is referred to Burn, *The History of the Poor Laws*. Citations of English statutes should be read as follows: 3 Ed. 1. c. 1. refers to the third act of Edward the first, chapter one, etc.

Reprinted by permission from *Social Problems* 12, no. 1 (1964).

The philosophy that the religious houses were to give alms to the poor and to the sick and feeble was, however, to undergo drastic change in the next fifty years. The result of this changed attitude was the establishment of the first vagrancy statute in 1349 which made it a crime to give alms to any who were unemployed while being of sound mind and body. To wit:

> Because that many valiant beggars, as long as they may live of begging, do refuse to labor, giving themselves to idleness and vice, and sometimes to theft and other abominations; it is ordained, that none, upon pain of imprisonment shall, under the colour of pity or alms, give anything to such which may labour, or presume to favour them towards their desires; so that thereby they may be compelled to labour for their necessary living.

It was further provided by this statute that:

> . . . every man and woman, of what condition he be, free or bond, able in body, and within the age of threescore years, not living in merchandize nor exercising any craft, nor having of his own whereon to live, nor proper land whereon to occupy himself, and not serving any other, if he in convenient service (his estate considered) be required to serve, shall be bounded to serve him which shall him require . . . And if any refuse, he shall on conviction by two true men, . . . be commited to gaol till he find surety to serve.
>
> And if any workman or servant, of what estate or condition he be, retained in any man's service, do depart from the said service without reasonable cause or license, before the term agreed on, he shall have pain of imprisonment.[5]

There was also in this statute the stipulation that the workers should receive a standard wage. In 1351 this statute was strengthened by the stipulation:

> An none shall go out of the town where he dwelled in winter, to serve the summer, if he may serve in the same town.[6]

By 34 Ed 3 (1360) the punishment for these acts became imprisonment for fifteen days and if they "do not justify themselves by the end of that time, to be sent to gaol till they do."

A change in official policy so drastic as this did not, of course, occur simply as a matter of whim. The vagrancy statutes emerged as a result of changes in other parts of the social structure. The prime-mover for this legislative innovation was the Black Death which struck England about 1348. Among the many disastrous consequences this had upon the social structure was the fact that it decimated the labor force. It is estimated that by the time the pestilence had run its course at least fifty per cent of the population of England had died from the plague. This decimation of the labor force would necessitate rather drastic innovations in any society but its impact was heightened in England where, at this time, the economy was highly dependent upon a ready supply of cheap labor.

Even before the pestilence, however, the availability of an adequate supply of cheap labor was becoming a problem for the landowners. The crusades and various wars had made money necessary to the lords and, as a result, the lord frequently agreed to sell the serfs their freedom in order to obtain the needed funds. The serfs, for their part, were desirous of obtaining their freedom (by "fair means" or "foul") because the larger towns which were becoming more industrialized during this period could offer the serf greater personal freedom as well as a higher standard of living. This process is nicely summarized by Bradshaw:

> By the middle of the 14th century the outward uniformity of the manorial system had become in practice considerably varied . . . for the peasant bad begun to drift to the towns and it was unlikely that the old village life in its unpleasant aspects should not be resented. Moreover the constant wars against France and Scotland were fought mainly with mercenaries after Henry III's time and most villages contributed to the new armies. The bolder serfs either joined the armies or fled to the towns, and even in the villages the free men who held by villein tenure were as eager to commute their services as the serfs were to escape. Only the amount of 'free' labor available enabled the lord to work his demense in many places.[7]

And he says regarding the effect of the Black Death:

> . . . in 1348 the Black Death reached England and the vast mortality that ensued destroyed that reserve of labour which alone had made the manorial system even nominally possible.[8]

The immediate result of these events was of course no surprise: Wages for the "free" man rose considerably and this increased, on the one hand, the landowners problems and, on the other hand, the plight of the unfree tenant. For although wages increased for the personally free laborers, it of course did not necessarily add to the standard of living of the serf, if anything it made his position worse because the landowner would be hard pressed to pay for the personally free labor which he needed and would thus find it more and more difficult to maintain the standard of living for the serf which he had heretofore supplied. Thus the serf had no alternative but flight if he chose to better his position. Furthermore, flight generally meant both freedom and better conditions since the possibility of work in the new weaving industry was great and the chance of being caught small.[9]

It was under these conditions that we find the first vagrancy statutes emerging. There is little question but that these statutes were designed for one express purpose: to force laborers (whether personally free or unfree) to accept employment at a low wage in order to insure the landowner an adequate supply of labor at a price he could afford to pay. Caleb Foote concurs with this interpretation when he notes:

> The anti-migratory policy behind vagrancy legislation began as an essential complement of the wage stabilization legislation which accompanied the breakup of

feudalism and the depopulation caused by the Black Death. By the Statutes of Labourers in 1349–1351, every ablebodied person without other means of support was required to work for wages fixed at the level preceding the Black Death; it was unlawful to accept more, or to refuse an offer to work, or to flee from one county to another to avoid offers of work or to seek higher wages, or go give alms to able-bodied beggars who refused to work.[10]

In short, as Foote says in another place, this was an "attempt to make the vagrancy statutes a substitute for serfdom."[11] This same conclusion is equally apparent from the wording of the statute where it is stated:

> Because great part of the people, and especially of workmen and servants, late died in pestilence; many seeing the necessity of masters, and great scarcity of servants, will not serve without excessive wages, and some rather willing to beg in idleness than by labour to get their living: it is ordained, that every man and woman, of what condition he be, free or bond, able in body and within the age of threescore years, not living in merchandize, (etc.) be required to serve . . .

The innovation in the law, then, was a direct result of the afore-mentioned changes which had occurred in the social setting. In this case these changes were located for the most part in the economic institution of the society. The vagrancy laws were designed to alleviate a condition defined by the lawmakers as undesirable. The solution was to attempt to force a reversal, as it were, of a social process which was well underway; that is, to curtail mobility of laborers in such a way that labor would not become a commodity for which the landowners would have to compete.

Statutory Dormancy: A Legal Vestige. In time, of course, the curtailment of the geographical mobility of laborers was no longer requisite. One might well expect that when the function served by the statute was no longer an important one for the society, the statutes would be eliminated from the law. In fact, this has not occurred. The vagrancy statutes have remained in effect since 1349. Furthermore, as we shall see in some detail later, they were taken over by the colonies and have remained in effect in the United States as well.

The substance of the vagrancy statutes changed very little for some time after the first ones in 1349–1351 although there was a tendency to make punishments more harsh than originally. For example, in 1360 it was provided that violators of the statute should be imprisoned for fifteen days[12] and in 1388 the punishment was to put the offender in the stocks and to keep him there until "he find surety to return to his service."[13] That there was still, at this time, the intention of providing the landowner with labor is apparent from the fact that this statute provides:

> and he or she which use to labour at the plough and cart, or other labour and service of husbandry, till they be of the age of 12 years, from thenceforth shall abide at the same labour without being put to any mistery or handicraft: and any covenant of apprenticeship to the contrary shall be void.[14]

The next alteration in the statutes occurs in 1495 and is restricted to an increase in punishment. Here it is provided that vagrants shall be "set in stocks, there to remain by the space of three days and three nights, and there to have none other sustenance but bread and water; and after the said three days and nights, to be had out and set at large, and then to be commanded to avoid the town."[15]

The tendency to increase the severity of punishment during this period seems to be the result of a general tendency to make finer distinctions in the criminal law. During this period the vagrancy statutes appear to have been fairly inconsequential in either their effect as a control mechanism or as a generally enforced statute.[16] The processes of social change in the culture generally and the trend away from serfdom and into a "free" economy obviated the utility of these statutes. The result was not unexpected. The judiciary did not apply the law and the legislators did not take it upon themselves to change the law. In short, we have here a period of dormancy in which the statute is neither applied nor altered significantly.

A Shift in Focal Concern

Following the squelching of the Peasant's Revolt in 1381, the services of the serfs to the lord " . . . tended to become less and less exacted, although in certain forms they lingered on till the seventeenth century . . . By the sixteenth century few knew that there were any bondmen in England . . . and in 1575 Queen Elizabeth listened to the prayers of almost the last serfs in England . . . and granted them manumission."[17]

In view of this change we would expect corresponding changes in the vagrancy laws. Beginning with the lessening of punishment in the statute of 1503 we find these changes. However, instead of remaining dormant (or becoming more so) or being negated altogether, the vagrancy statutes experienced a shift in focal concern. With this shift the statutes served a new and equally important function for the social order of England. The first statute which indicates this change was in 1530. In this statute (22 H.8.c. 12 1530) it was stated:

> If any person, being whole and mighty in body, and able to labour, be taken in begging, or be vagrant and can give no reckoning how he lawfully gets his living; . . . and all other idle persons going about, some of them using divers and subtle crafty and unlawful games and plays, and some of them feigning themselves to have knowledge of . . . crafty sciences . . . shall be punished as provided.

What is most significant about this statute is the shift from an earlier concern with laborers to a concern with *criminal* activities. To be sure, the stipulation of persons "being whole and mighty in body, and able to labour, be taken in begging, or be vagrant" sounds very much like the concerns of the earlier statutes. Some important differences are apparent however when the rest of the statute includes those who " . . . can give no reckoning how he lawfully gets his living"; "some of them using divers subtil and unlawful games and plays." This is the first statute which specifically focuses upon these kinds of criteria for adjudging someone a vagrant.

It is significant that in this statute the severity of punishment is increased so as to be greater not only than provided by the 1503 statute but the punishment is more severe than that which had been provided by *any* of the pre-1503 statutes as well. For someone who is merely idle and gives no reckoning of how he makes his living the offender shall be:

> . . . had to the next market town, or other place where they [the constables] shall think most convenient, and there to be tied to the end of a cart naked, and to be beaten with whips throughout the same market town or other place, till his body be bloody by reason of such whipping.[18]

But, for those who use "divers and subtil crafty and unlawful games and plays," etc., the punishment is ". . . whipping at two days together in manner aforesaid."[19] For the second offense, such persons are:

> . . . scourged two days, and the third day to be put upon the pillory from nine of the clock till eleven before noon of the same day and to have one of his ears cut off.[20]

And if he offend the third time ". . . to have like punishment with whipping, standing on the pillory and to have his other ear cut off."

This statute (1) makes a distinction between types of offenders and applies the more severe punishment to those who are clearly engaged in "criminal" activities, (2) mentions a specific concern with categories of "unlawful" behavior, and (3) applies a type of punishment (cutting off the ear) which is generally reserved for offenders who are defined as likely to be a fairly serious criminal.

Only five years later we find for the first time that the punishment of death is applied to the crime of vagrancy. We also note a change in terminology in the statute:

> and if any ruffians . . . after having been once apprehended . . . shall wander, loiter, or idle use themselves and play the vagabonds . . . shall be eftfoons not only whipped again, but shall have the gristle of his right ear clean cut off. And if he shall again offend, he shall be committed to gaol till the next sessions; and being there convicted upon indictment, he shall have judgment to suffer pains and execution of death, as a felon, as an enemy of the commonwealth.[21]

It is significant that the statute now makes persons who repeat the crime of vagrancy a felon. During this period then, the focal concern of the vagrancy statutes becomes a concern for the control of felons and is no longer primarily concerned with the movement of laborers.

These statutory changes were a direct response to changes taking place in England's social structure during this period. We have already pointed out that feudalism was decaying rapidly. Concomitant with the breakup of feudalism was an increased emphasis upon commerce and industry. The commercial emphasis in England at the turn of the sixteenth century is of particular importance in the development of vagrancy laws. With commercialism came considerable traffic bearing valuable items. Where there were 169 important merchants in the middle of the fourteenth century there were 3,000 merchants engaged in foreign trade alone at the beginning of the sixteenth century.[22] England became highly dependent upon commerce for its economic support. Italians conducted a great deal of the commerce of England during this early period and were held in low repute by the populace. As a result, they were subject to attacks by citizens and, more important, were frequently robbed of their goods while transporting them. "The general insecurity of the times made any transportation hazardous. The special risks to which the alien merchant was subjected gave rise to the royal practice of issuing formally executed covenants of safe conduct through the realm."[23]

Such a situation not only called for the enforcement of existing laws but also called for the creation of new laws which would facilitate the control of persons preying upon merchants transporting goods. The vagrancy statutes were revived in order to fulfill just such a purpose. Persons who had committed no serious felony but who were suspected of being capable of doing so could be apprehended and incapacitated through the application of vagrancy laws once these laws were refocused so as to include ". . . any ruffians . . . [who] shall wander, loiter, or idle use themselves and play the vagabonds . . ."[24]

The new focal concern is continued in 1 Ed. 6. c. 3 (1547) and in fact is made more general so as to include:

> Whoever man or woman, being not lame, impotent, or so aged or diseased that he or she cannot work, not having whereon to live, shall be lurking in any house, or loitering or idle wandering by the highway side, or in streets, cities, towns, or villages, not applying themselves to some honest labour, and so continuing for three days; or running away from their work; every such person shall be taken for a vagabond. And . . . upon conviction of two witnesses . . . the same loiterer (shall) be marked with a hot iron in the breast with the letter V, and adjudged him to the person bringing him, to be his slave for two years . . .

Should the vagabond run away, upon conviction, he was to be branded by a hot iron with the letter S on the forehead and to be thenceforth declared a slave forever. And in 1571 there is modification of the punishment to be inflicted, whereby the offender is to be "branded on the chest with the letter V" (for vagabond). And, if he is convicted the second time, the brand is to be made on the forehead. It is worth noting here that this method of punishment, which first appeared in 1530 and is repeated here with somewhat more force, is also an indication of a change in the type of person to whom the law is intended to apply. For it is likely that nothing so permanent as branding would be applied to someone who was wandering but looking for work, or at worst merely idle and not particularly dangerous *per se*. On the other hand, it could well be applied to someone who was likely to be engaged in other criminal activities in connection with being "vagrant."

By 1571 in the statute of 14 El. C. 5 the shift in focal concern is fully developed:

> All rogues, vagabonds, and sturdy beggars shall . . . be committed to the common gaol . . . he shall be grievously whipped, and burnt thro' the gristle of the right ear with a hot iron of the compass of an inch about; . . . And for the second offense, he shall be adjudged a felon, unless some person will take him for two years in to his service. And for the third offense, he shall be adjudged guilty of felony without benefit of clergy.

And there is included a long list of persons who fall within the statute: "proctors, procurators, idle persons going about using subtil, crafty and unlawful games or plays; and some of them feigning themselves to have knowledge of . . . absurd sciences . . . and all fencers, bearwards, common players in interludes, and minstrels . . . all juglers, pedlars, tinkers, petty chapmen . . . and all counterfeiters of licenses, passports and users of the same." The major significance of this statute is that it includes all the previously defined offenders and adds some more. Significantly, those added are more clearly criminal types, counterfeiters, for example. It is also significant that there is the following qualification of this statute: "Provided also, that this act shall not extend to cookers, or harvest folks, that travel for harvest work, corn or hay."

That the changes in this statute were seen as significant is indicated by the following statement which appears in the statute:

> And whereas by reason of this act, the common gaols of every shire are like to be greatly pestered with more number of prisoners than heretofore hath been, for that the said vagabonds and other lewd persons before recited shall upon their apprehension be committed to the said gaols; it is enacted . . . [25]

And a provision is made for giving more money for maintaining the gaols. This seems to add credence to the notion that this statute was seen as being significantly more general than those previously.

It is also of importance to note that this is the first time the term *rogue* has been used to refer to persons included in the vagrancy statutes. It seems, *a priori*, that a "rogue" is a different social type than is a "vagrant" or a "vagabond"; the latter terms implying something more equivalent to the idea of a "tramp" whereas the former (rogue) seems to imply a more disorderly and potentially dangerous person.

The emphasis upon the criminalistic aspect of vagrants continues in Chapter 17 of the same statute:

> Whereas divers *licentious* persons wander up and down in all parts of the realm, to countenance their *wicked behavior;* and do continually assemble themselves armed in the highways, and elsewhere in troops, *to the great terror* of her majesty's true subjects,

the impeachment of her laws, and the disturbance of the peace and tranquility of the realm; and whereas many outrages are daily committed by these dissolute persons, and more are likely to ensue if speedy remedy be not provided. (Italics added)

With minor variations (*e.g.,* offering a reward for the capture of a vagrant) the statutes remain essentially of this nature until 1743. In 1743 there was once more an expansion of the types of persons included such that "all persons going about as patent gatherers, or gatherers of alms, under pretense of loss by fire or other casualty; or going about as collectors for prisons, gaols, or hospitals; all persons playing of betting at any unlawful games; and all persons who run away and leave their wives or children . . . all persons wandering abroad, and lodging in alehouses, barns, outhouses, or in the open air, not giving good account of themselves," were types of offenders added to those already included.

By 1743 the vagrancy statutes had apparently been sufficiently reconstructed by the shifts of concern so as to be once more a useful instrument in the creation of social solidarity. This function has apparently continued down to the present day in England and the changes from 1743 to the present have been all in the direction of clarifying or expanding the categories covered but little has been introduced to change either the meaning or the impact of this branch of the law.

We can summarize this shift in focal concern by quoting from Halsbury. He has noted that in the vagrancy statutes:

> ". . . elaborate provision is made for the relief and incidental control of destitute wayfarers. These latter, however, form but a small portion of the offenders aimed at by what are known as the Vagrancy Laws, . . . many offenders who are in no ordinary sense of the word vagrants, have been brought under the laws relating to vagrancy, and the great number of the offenses coming within the operation of these laws have little or no relation to the subject of poor relief, but are more properly directed towards the prevention of crime, the preservation of good order, and the promotion of social economy."[26]

Before leaving this section it is perhaps pertinent to make a qualifying remark. We have emphasized throughout this section how the vagrancy statutes underwent a shift in focal concern as the social setting changed. The shift in focal concern is not meant to imply that the later focus of the statutes represents a completely new law. It will be recalled that even in the first vagrancy statute there was reference to those who "do refuse labor, giving themselves to idleness and vice and sometimes to theft and other abominations." Thus the possibility of criminal activities resulting from persons who refuse to labor was recognized even in the earliest statute. The fact remains, however, that the major emphasis in this statute and in the statutes which followed the first one was always upon the "refusal to labor" or "begging." The "criminalistic" aspect of such persons was relatively unimportant. Later, as we have shown, the criminalistic potential becomes of paramount importance. The thread runs back to the earliest statute but the reason for the statutes' existence as well as the focal concern of the statutes is quite different in 1743 than it was in 1349.

Vagrancy Laws in the United States

In general, the vagrancy laws of England, as they stood in the middle eighteenth century, were simply adopted by the states. There were some exceptions to this general trend. For example, Maryland restricted the application of vagrancy laws to "free" Negroes. In addition, for *all* states the vagrancy laws were even more explicitly concerned with the control of criminals and undesirables than had been the case in England. New York, for example, explicitly defines prostitutes as being a category of vagrants during this period. These exceptions do not, however, change the general picture significantly and it is quite appropriate to consider the U.S. vagrancy laws as following from England's of the middle eighteenth century with relatively minor changes. The control of criminals and undesirables was the *raison de etre* of the vagrancy laws in the U.S. This is as true today as it was in 1750. As Caleb Foote's analysis of the application of vagrancy statutes in the Philadelphia court shows, these laws are presently applied indiscriminately to persons considered a "nuisance." Foote suggests that ". . . the chief significance of this branch of the criminal law lies in its quantitative impact and administrative usefulness."[27] Thus it appears that in America the trend begun in England in the sixteenth, seventeenth and eighteenth centuries has been carried to its logical extreme and the laws are now used principally as a mechanism for "clearing the streets" of the derelicts who inhabit the "skid roads" and "Bowerys" of our large urban areas.

Since the 1800's there has been an abundant source of prospects to which the vagrancy laws have been applied. These have been primarily those persons deemed by the police and the courts to be either actively involved in criminal activities or at least peripherally involved. In this context, then, the statutes have changed very little. The functions served by the statutes in England of the late eighteenth century are still being served today in both England and the United States. The locale has changed somewhat and it appears that the present day application of vagrancy statutes is focused upon the arrest and confinement of the "down and outers" who inhabit certain sections of our larger cities but the impact has remained constant. The lack of change in the vagrancy statutes, then, can be seen as a reflection of the society's perception of a continuing need to control some of its "suspicious" or "undesirable" members.[28]

A word of caution is in order lest we leave the impression that this administrative purpose is the sole function of vagrancy laws in the U.S. today. Although it is our contention that this is generally true it is worth remembering that during certain periods of our recent history, and to some extent today, these laws have also been used to control the movement of workers. This was particularly the case during the depression years and California is of course infamous for its use of vagrancy laws to restrict the admission of migrants from other states.[29] The vagrancy statutes, because of their history, still contain germs within them which make such effects possible. Their main purpose, however, is clearly no longer the control of laborers but rather the control of the undesirable, the criminal and the "nuisance."

Discussion

The foregoing analysis of the vagrancy laws has demonstrated that these laws were a legislative innovation which reflected the socially perceived necessity of providing an abundance of cheap labor to landowners during a period when serfdom was breaking down and when the pool of available labor was depleted. With the eventual breakup of feudalism the need for such laws eventually disappeared and the increased dependence of the economy upon industry and commerce rendered the former use of the vagrancy statutes unnecessary. As a result, for a substantial period the vagrancy statutes were dormant, undergoing only minor changes and, presumably, being applied infrequently. Finally, the vagrancy laws were subjected to considerable alteration through a shift in the focal concern of the statutes. Whereas in their inception the laws focused upon the "idle" and "those refusing to labor" after the turn of the sixteenth century and emphasis came to be upon "rogues," "vagabonds," and others who were suspected of being engaged in criminal activities. During this period the focus was particularly upon "roadmen" who preyed upon citizens who transported goods from one place to another. The increased importance of commerce to England during this period made it necessary that some protection be given persons engaged in this enterprise and the vagrancy statutes provided one source for such protection by re-focusing the acts to be included under these statutes.

Comparing the results of this analysis with the findings of Hall's study of theft we see a good deal of correspondence. Of major importance is the fact that both analyses demonstrate the truth of Hall's assertion that "The functioning of courts is significantly related to concomitant cultural needs, and this applies to the law of procedure as well as to substantive law."[30]

Our analysis of the vagrancy laws also indicates that when changed social conditions create a perceived need for legal changes that these alterations will be effected through the revision and refocusing of existing statutes. This process was demonstrated in Hall's analysis of theft as well as in our analysis of vagrancy. In the case of vagrancy, the laws were dormant when the focal concern of the laws was shifted so as to provide control over potential criminals. In the case of theft the laws were re-interpreted (interestingly, by the courts and not by the legislature) so as to include persons who were transporting goods for a merchant but who absconded with the contents of the packages transported.

It also seems probable that when the social conditions change and previously useful laws are no longer useful there will be long periods when these laws will remain dormant. It is less likely that they will be officially negated. During this period of dormancy it is the judiciary which has principal responsibility for *not* applying the statutes. It is possible that one finds statutes being negated only when the judiciary stubbornly applies laws which do not have substantial public support. An example of such laws in contemporary times would be the "Blue Laws." Most states still have laws prohibiting the sale of retail goods on Sunday yet these laws are rarely applied. The laws are very likely to remain but to be dormant unless a recalcitrant judge or a vocal minority of the population insist that the laws be applied. When this happens we can anticipate that the statutes will be negated.[31] Should there arise a perceived need to curtail retail selling under some special circumstances, then it is likely that these laws will undergo a shift in focal concern much like the shift which characterized the vagrancy laws. Lacking such application the laws will simply remain dormant except for rate instances where they will be negated.

This analysis of the vagrancy statutes (and Hall's analysis of theft as well) has demonstrated the importance of "vested interest" groups in the emergence and/or alteration of laws. The vagrancy laws emerged in order to provide the powerful landowners with a ready supply of cheap labor. When this was no longer seen as necessary and particularly when the landowners were no longer dependent upon cheap labor nor were they a powerful interest group in the society the laws became dormant. Finally a new interest group emerged and was seen as being of great importance to the society and the laws were then altered so as to afford some protection to this group. These findings are thus in agreement with Weber's contention that "status groups" determine the content of the law.[32] The findings are inconsistent, on the other hand, with the perception of the law as simply a reflection of "public opinion" as is sometimes found in the literature.[33] We should be cautious in concluding, however, that either of these positions are necessarily correct. The careful analysis of other laws, and especially of laws which do not focus so specifically upon the "criminal," are necessary before this question can be finally answered.

In conclusion, it is hoped that future analyses of changes within the legal structure will be able to benefit from this study by virtue of (1) the data provided and (2) the utilization of a set of concepts (innovation, dormancy, concern and negation) which have proved useful in the analysis of the vagrancy law. Such analyses should provide us with more substantial grounds for rejecting or accepting as generally valid the description of some of the processes which appear to characterize changes in the legal system.

Notes

1. Hall, J., *Theft, Law and Society*, Bobbs-Merrill, 1939. See also, Alfred R. Lindesmith, "Federal Law and Drug Addiction," *Social Problems* Vol. 7, No. 1, 1959, p. 48.

2. See, for example, Rose, A., "Some Suggestions for Research in the Sociology of Law," *Social Problems* Vol. 9, No. 3, 1962, pp. 281–283, and Geis, G., "Sociology, Criminology, and Criminal Law," *Social Problems* Vol. 7, No. 1, 1959, pp. 40–47.

3. 3 Ed. 1. c. 1.

4. 35 Ed. 1. c. 1.

5. 23 Ed. 3.

6. 25 Ed. 3 (1351).

7. Bradshaw, F., *A Social History of England*, p. 54.

8. *Ibid.*

9. *Ibid.*, p. 57.

10. Foote, C., "Vagrancy Type Law and Its Administration," *Univ. of Pennsylvania Law Review* (104), 1956, p. 615.

11. *Ibid.*

12. 34 Ed. 3 (1360).

13. 12 R. 2 (1388).

14. *Ibid.*

15. 11 H. & C. 2 (1495).

16. As evidenced for this note the expectation that ". . . the common gaols of every shire are likely to be greatly pestered with more numbers of prisoners than heretofore . . ." when the statutes were changed by the statute of 14 Ed. c. 5 (1571).

17. Bradshaw, *op. cit.*, p. 61.

18. 22 H. 8. c. 12 (1530).

19. *Ibid.*

20. *Ibid.*

21. 27 H. 8. c. 25 (1535).

22. Hall, *op. cit.*, p. 21.

23. *Ibid.*, p. 23.

24. 27 H. 8. c. 25 (1535).

25. 14 Ed. c. 5. (1571).

26. Earl of Halsbury, *The Laws of England*, Butterworth & Co., Bell Yard, Temple Bar, 1912, pp. 606–607..

27. Foote, *op. cit.*, p. 613. Also see in this connection, Irwin Deutscher, "The Petty Offender," *Federal Probation*, XIX, June, 1955.

28. It is on this point that the vagrancy statutes have been subject to criticism. See for example, Lacey, Forrest W., "Vagrancy and Other Crimes of Personal Condition," *Harvard Law Review* (66), p. 1203.

29. Edwards *vs* California. 314 S: 160 (1941).

30. Hall, *op. cit.*, p. XII.

31. Negation, in this instance, is most likely to come about by the repeal of the statute. More generally, however, negation may occur in several ways including the declaration of a statute as unconstitutional. This later mechanism has been used even for laws which have been "on the books" for long periods of time. Repeal is probably the most common, although not the only, procedure by which a law is negated.

32. M. Rheinstein, *Max Weber on Law in Economy and Society*, Harvard University Press, 1954.

33. Friedman, N., *Law in a Changing Society*, Berkeley and Los Angeles: University of California Press, 1959.

18

Critical Criminology in the Twenty-First Century

Jock Young, the author of "Critical Criminology in the Twenty-First Century," is one of the original, self-styled "critical criminologists." Working with Ian Taylor and Paul Walton, Jock Young co-authored *The New Criminology* in 1973, and co-edited *Critical Criminology* in 1975. Their general position is captured well in the following excerpt from their co-authored book, *The New Criminology*:

> With Marx, we have been concerned with the social arrangements that have obstructed . . . man's chances of achieving full sociality—a state of freedom from material necessity and (therefore) of material incentive, a release from the constraints of forced production, an abolition of the forced division of labour, and a set of social arrangements . . . in which there would be no politically, economically and socially induced need to criminalize deviance (Taylor, Walton, & Young, 1973:270).

In "Working Class Criminology," a chapter in Taylor, Walton and Young's co-edited book *Critical Criminology*, Jock Young announces that the strategy of radical criminology "is to show up the law . . . . as the instrument of the ruling class," and to demonstrate "that the rule-makers are also the greatest of rule-breakers"(Young, 1975:89).

These were familiar themes in the critical criminology of the 1970s. Richard Quinney argues in *Class, State and Crime* that crime is linked to the capitalist mode of production, saying that predatory crimes such as robbery and drug trafficking are caused by high unemployment and the creation of a large "industrial reserve army" composed of marginalized, unskilled workers who are living from hand-to-mouth (Quinney, 1977:54–58). In his 1977 article "Toward a Marxian Theory of Deviance,"

Steven Spitzer talks about "the production of deviance in capitalist society"(Spitzer, 2005:108–110). Like Quinney, Spitzer describes the "surplus population" that is created by the capitalist mode of production, and says that such populations are targeted by the agencies of social control when they steal from the rich or refuse to work for low wages. Essentially, the critical criminologists were saying that capitalism was the cause of crime, and that if capitalism could be replaced with socialism, crime would be reduced, or would disappear altogether.

This type of radical thinking came to be characterized as "left idealism" by a number of observers (cf. Akers & Sellers, 2009:259; Arrigo & Williams, 2009:409; Rock, 1979:71). The critical criminologists were criticized for ignoring the fact that crime also exists in socialist and communist countries, and for failing to recognize that most crime involves members of the working class victimizing other members of the working class (Williams & McShane, 2010:137). It was said that they romanticized working class crime, whilst taking the position that the only crimes worth talking about were those committed by the rich and powerful (Hackler, 2007:145). Jock Young, one of the original critical criminologists, addresses some of these criticisms of critical criminology in his revised approach, described by Young (and others) as "left realism" (Akers & Sellers, 2009:259; Williams & McShane, 2010:137). He acknowledges that while it may be exaggerated and sensationalized by the media, "crime really is a problem," and that offenders and their victims usually come from the same social class and same ethnic background (Young, 2003:192–193). He says that it is wrong to portray the criminal as a modern day version of "Robin Hood," who according to English legend, stole from the rich and gave to the poor (Young, 2003:193).

In the following reading, "Critical Criminology in the Twenty-First Century," Jock Young argues that critical criminology is still relevant today, and that its existence is necessary to counter the recent shift toward administrative criminology, psychological criminology and cognitive behavioral programs. The "left realist" approach that he is now advocating is more policy-oriented, and more concerned with remedying the problems associated with capitalism than it is with replacing the capitalist system (Arrigo & Williams, 2009:409–410; Young, 2002; Young, 2003:196–197). Young still argues that the main causes of crime are marginalization and economic deprivation, drawing attention to the structural (built-in) unemployment and the continued growth of the "under-class" in capitalist society. He calls for a transformative redistribution of the wealth in capitalist society, to offset marginalization and relative economic deprivation. In this regard, Young suggests raising the minimum wage, creating meaningful job training programs, providing more day care facilities so that single parents can afford to work, and giving financial recognition to the value of housework, raising children and caring for the elderly (Young, 2002). Young also argues that critical criminologists need to demystify (or debunk) the notion that welfare recipients, drug addicts and illegal immigrants are the main sources of crime and social disorder, by demonstrating that crime is more evenly distributed throughout the society.

References

Akers, R. L., & Sellers, C. S. (2009). *Criminological theories: Introduction, evaluation, and application* (5th ed.). New York: Oxford University Press.

Arrigo, B. A., & Williams, C. R. (2009). Conflict criminology: Developments, directions, and destinations past and present. In H. Copes, & V. Topalli (Eds.), *Criminological theory: Readings and retrospectives* (pp. 401–412). New York: McGraw-Hill.

Hackler, J. C. (2007). *Canadian criminology: Strategies and perspectives* (Fourth ed.). Toronto: Pearson Prentice-Hall.

Quinney, R. (1977). *Class, state and crime: On the theory and practice of criminal justice.* New York: David McKay Company, Inc.

Rock, P. (1979). The sociology of crime, symbolic interactionism and some problematic qualities of radical criminology. In D. M. Downes, & P. E. Rock (Eds.), *Deviant interpretations* (pp. 52–84). Oxford: Martin Robertson.

Spitzer, S. (2005). Toward a Marxian theory of deviance. In H. N. Pontell (Ed.), *Social deviance: Readings in theory and research* (Fifth ed., pp. 108–112). Upper Saddle River, NJ: Pearson Prentice Hall.

Taylor, I., Walton, P., & Young, J. (1973). *The new criminology: For a social theory of deviance.* London: Routledge & Keegan Paul.

Williams, F. P., & McShane, M. D. (2010). *Criminological theory* (5th ed.). Upper Saddle River, N.J.: Pearson/Prentice Hall.

Young, J. (1975). Working class criminology. In I. Taylor, P. Walton & J. Young (Eds.), *Critical criminology* (pp. 63–94). London: Routledge & Kegan Paul.

Young, J. (2002). Critical criminology in the twenty-first century: Critique, irony and the always unfinished. In K. Carrington, & R. Hogg (Eds.), *Critical criminology: Issues, debates and challenges* (pp. 251–274). Cullompton, Devon: Willan Publishers.

Young, J. (2003). The failure of criminology. In C. M. Renzetti, D. J. Curran & P. J. Carr (Eds.), *Theories of crime: A reader* (pp. 192–199). Boston: Allyn and Bacon.

Critical Criminology in the Twenty-First Century: Critique, Irony and the Always Unfinished

JOCK YOUNG

"I do not wish to end this account without mentioning a rather amusing episode. Right in the middle of the Third National [Criminology] Conference, taking place in Cambridge in July 1968, a group of seven young social scientists and criminologists, participants of the Conference, met secretly and decided to establish an independent 'National Deviancy Conference' and soon afterwards they duly met in York. At the time, it reminded me a little of naughty schoolboys, playing a nasty game on their stern headmaster. It was not necessary to go 'underground' because we were not in

Reprinted from *Critical Criminology*, edited by K. Carrington, R. Hogg and D. Cullompton (2002), Taylor & Francis Books Ltd.

any way opposed to discussing new approaches to the sociology of deviance . . . Although not invited to their conference in York I asked one of my senior colleagues in the Institute to go there as an observer.

"My attitude was by no means hostile or patronizing. As I stated at the time, movements in ideas, like life in general, often lead to seeming unexpected baffling results. Those were the years of dissent, protest and ferment in the United States with their unmistakable echoes in Britain. They affected not only the ways people acted, but also their thinking on many matters relating to social life and its reinterpretations. But it was also a reaction to some extent inevitable and to some extent misguided of the new generation of British criminologists against what appeared to be the stolid establishment of Criminology as personified by the Cambridge Institute and probably also by its first Director."

—*Sir Leon Radzinowicz, 1999, pp. 229–30*

Critical criminology is the criminology of late modernity. Its inception was in the late sixties and early seventies at the cusp of change, its inspiration a world where oppressive relationships of class, age, gender and ethnicity became highlighted and evident (in that historical order) and where the pluralism, ambiguity and shift of values heralded a society where migration and human creativity created a diversity of cultures in close propinquity and interaction. In Britain the key academic organisation which provided a theatre for such debates was the National Deviancy Conference (NDC). Here, as Stan Cohen astutely noted, "well before Foucault and a long way from the Left Bank—our little corner of the human sciences was seized by a deconstructionist impulse" (1998, p. 101). Indeed the NDC was pivoted around deconstruction and anti-essentialism. It dwelt on the social construction of gender, sexual proclivity, crime, suicide, drugs and mental states whilst fiercely criticising the major discourses of modernity, positivism and classicism, and its institutions, whether it was the prison or the clinic. The NDC was anarchistic and antinomian, set deep in the counterculture of the time. My own involvement in it was initially reluctant to say the least. It was a time when we regarded people with 9 to 5 jobs as complete failures, lived in communes and regarded the "straight" world with complete disdain. I was living in Notting Hill where Pink Floyd played weekly at the local parish hall, Jimi Hendrix was at Middle Earth and there was poetry in the streets. Academic conferences were not exactly where it was at. I was persuaded to go to the first NDC in York in 1968. I remember Mike Brake—later to be well known for his books on youth culture (1980, 1985) saying to me the evening we arrived, "What are we doing here, man? Let's get out quick and get to Leeds where there's much better clubs." We stayed all the same and next day I gave my first academic paper, 'The Role of Police as Amplifiers of Deviancy, Negotiators of Reality and Translators of Fantasy' (1971a). A pretentious title but it still captures for me a constant theme of the way in which powerful forces in society create demons out of illusions which then, through stigma and oppression, take on a reality of their own.

The NDC was hectic, irreverent, transgressive and, above all, fun. It took no notice of disciplinary boundaries, it was as important an arena for the emerging field of cultural studies (Stuart Hall, Mike Featherstone, Paul Willis, Dick Heb-didge, all gave papers), anti-psychiatry (Peter Sedgwick, Jeff Coulter) critical legal theory (Boaventura de Sousa Santos and Sol Picciotto), the sociology of sexualities (Ken Plummer, Mary McIntosh), as it was for the sociology of deviance (see the account in Cohen, 1988; Young, 1998). Perhaps, however, it was the pluralism and social constructionism of deviancy theory that gave it such a pivotal role. There was a frenetic quality to the NDC, there were fourteen conferences held between the end of 1968 and the end of 1973 and papers, articles and books seemed to emerge in an endless stream—exciting and excitable.

Within criminology and the sociology of deviance the adversary was clear. Variously named 'positivism' or 'correctionalism' or 'establishment criminology', it was individualistic in focus, technicist in outlook and minimalist in theory—its aim was the social engineering of the 'maladjusted' individual into the ranks of the consensual and contented society. It was summed up by the title of an emblematic text, Barbara Wootton's *Social Science and Pathology*, published in 1959, which, supported by the Nuffield Foundation, sought to review the contribution of the social sciences to "the prevention and cure of the social problems associated with unacceptable forms of deviant behaviour" (p. 9). The intellectual history of this assault on this rather piecemeal ensemble of ideas, which had its institutional centre at the Institute of Criminology at Cambridge, was to involve two stages (Downes, 1988). The first, immediately preceding the first NDC, was the decade of the sixties during which sociology expanded rapidly within the academy and sociologists turned to the extraordinary flourishing American sociology of deviance, both in its subcultural and interactionist variants. In the US, unlike Britain, a longstanding sociological tradition concerned with crime had been extant throughout the century with Vold, Sutherland, The Chicago School, and Merton—themselves inheritors of late and early twentieth century European sociology. The explanatory project which spurred on the sociological involvement in crime and deviance was the rise in crime for, as David Downes put it: "The appeal of American theory was that it addressed the problem, and seemingly furnished a framework for its resolution, of the persistent rise in official crime rates despite the appearance of both greater affluence and diminishing inequality in the major industrial societies." For, "genetics and psychology were seen as offering little purchase on what were perceived as startling differences in crime rates between societies and within societies over relatively short periods of time." (1988, p. 177).

Criminology is, as John Lea (1998) points out, not so much a discipline as a field, its distinctiveness is not its knowledge base but the form of its focus: theories of crime, criminal law and the relation between the two—in this it is a sub-category of the sociology of deviance. It can, and never should be, conceived of as a separate discipline, its categories and processes are social constructs, they have no separate ontological reality. It cannot, therefore, exist separately from social theory as its concerns are inevitably with the nature of social order and disorder. Not only have all of the major social theorists concerned themselves with order, disorder and regulation, but there has been across the century clear links between the great theorists of modernity and the criminological canon. Witness Durkheim, Merton and the anomie theorists; Marx, Engels, Bonger and Marxist criminology; the influence of Simmel and Wirth on the Chicago School and the conflict theorisation of G B Vold; of Schutz and Mead on Becker and labelling theories. Despite this obvious intimacy of intellectual concern, there has been a constant tendency for criminology, particularly in its more practical and administrative manifestations, to cut itself off from grand theory. Such a situation was paramount in Britain in the post-war period and the turn, or should we say *reconnection* of criminology to sociology was a major first step out of empiricism. The second phase which Downes traces was the foundation of the NDC in 1968 and the ten years that followed it, this took on the new American sociology of deviance and considerably radicalised it. It is this phase which gave rise to the 'new' or 'critical' criminology.

This presented itself as a series of 'ironies' which served to turn establishment criminology on its head.

- Self-Fulfilment   That illusions and stereotypes of crime can be real in their consequences and self-fulfilling in reality.
- Seriousness   That crime occurred throughout the social structure and that the crimes of the powerful were more serious in their consequences than the crimes of the poor.
- Ontology   That crime has no ontological reality and that the 'same' behaviour can be constructed totally differently. Thus, for example, a serial killer could be either a psychopathic monster or a hero if dropping bombs daily in the Afghan War.
- Decentring   That the criminal justice system is not the front line defence against crime but a minor part of the system of social control, itself crucially dependent on informal norms of civil society.
- Selectivity   That criminal law, although phrased in a language of formal equality, is targeted in a way that is selective and substantially unequal.
- Counter-   That the prison and the criminal justice system produces criminals rather than defusing criminality.
  Productivity
- Socialisation   That the core values of competitiveness, acquisitiveness, individualism and hedonism are close to the motivations for crime, so that the well socialised person is more likely to offend than the undersocialised.
- Contradiction   That the ideals which legitimate and hold the system together are the very ones which society thwarts and the frustrations generated seem to break the system apart.

- Function

  That 'the criminal', 'the outsider', 'the other', far from destroying the fabric of society, produce stereotypes which hold the fabric together.

- Secondary Harm

  That the primary harm of a social problem is frequently of a lesser order than the secondary harm accruing from the intervention to control it. The prime example of this being the regulation of drug use.

Critical Criminology in the Subsequent Years

"Leaving aside the existence of . . . interesting disputes and divisions, it is clear that the new perspective overall has now become established and institutionalised. In the same way initially outrageous art movements (such as Dado and surrealism) eventually became respectable, so too has the new deviance and criminology become part of the accepted order of things. Its practitioners are ensconced in orthodox academic departments, journals, examining boards and publishing companies. No booklist would be complete without one." (Cohen, 1981, p. 241)

Thus Stan Cohen talks of the institutionalisation of that which was once iconoclastic. Critical criminology has become a staple of textbooks, its concerns form the basis of secondary school sociology exams, it runs conferences, journals and research programmes. Indeed, in Britain, outside of course Cambridge, the majority of centres which teach criminology are within the rubric of critical criminology.

However, in recent years a drastically different version of the subsequent history of critical criminology, and of criminology in general, has gained currency. We have seen an inkling of this in the introductory quote from Sir Leon Radzinowicz's memoirs with his patronising comments (see Cottee, 2001), which present critical commentary as an amusing interlude before getting back to the business of serious criminology. But the most elaborated presentation of such a revisionist history is that of David Garland in a series of pieces from *Punishment and Welfare* (1985) to *The Culture of Control* (2001; see also 1988, 1997, 1999 and with R Sparks, 2000).

1. The Hegemony of the Practical

Garland sees the history of criminology, proper, as a history of the criminology that emerged around the institutions of control. For the first two-thirds of the twentieth century this was correctionalism—with its stress on individual positivism, and then subsequently what he terms the 'crime control complex' with its emphasis on rational choice and situational control. That is a transition from a modern to a late modern criminology, the first sited in the penal-welfare institutions, the second sited in the institutions and practices of private sector crime prevention. It is the latter which is the predominant theory of today—'the criminology of everyday life', but there are two other currents—a residuum of correctionalism and a neo-conservative, anti-modernism. Whereas the criminology of everyday life sees the offenders as normal, rational consumers 'just like us', the criminology of the other sees the offender as 'the other'. It is the criminology of everyday which he sees as going with the grain of everyday life—as being more naturalistically true to reality.

2. The Critical Moment

"In retrospect, the decade of the 1970s appears as a watershed, in which the intellectual, institutional and political assumptions of modern criminology were challenged, often in the name of a more radical social politics. It was during this decade that there arose a more critical and reflexive style of criminology, and a more explicit questioning of criminology's relation to the state, to criminal justice, and to the disciplinary processes of welfare capitalism. Criminology became, at least for a while, concerned to link its ideas and analyses to the broader themes of social thought and less concerned to be an applied discipline. It became more enamoured of sociological theory and more critical of criminal justice practice. In these years, criminology's centre of gravity shifted a little, becoming more reflexive, more critical, and more theoretical. As it happens, this was a short-lived moment [which] did not last long. Before long, new post-correctional forms of crime control emerged and criminology became immersed in applied questions once again . . . " (Garland and Sparks, 2000, pp. 13–14).

Critical criminology is not then seen as a harbinger of the future but a phase which had its moment in the past. Garland does not deny its influence, but it is muted, indeed academic criminology as a whole is strangely marginalized in this account. Rather his focus is on the 'surfaces' concerned with crime control out of which criminology is seen to emerge as power/knowledge bases in a Foucauldian fashion. Thus the move from positivism to control theory, his major transition, is seen as reflecting the change in the *site* of crime control, from the penal-welfare system to private crime prevention—both commercial and amongst the population as a whole.

3. The Critical Midwife

"A movement that initially aimed to enhance prisoners' rights, minimize imprisonment, restrict state power, and end predictive restraint, ultimately ushered in policies that did quote the opposite. How is this strange turn of events to be explained? . . .

"Somehow the anti-correctionalist movement opened the way for a set of changes it could not envisage and could not control . . .

"The processes that undermined the credibility of penal-welfarism were not the same as the ones that subsequently unravelled it. The original damage to the structure came about in the early 1970s as a result of radical and reactionary forces working in tandem, but with the former in the dominant position. The further assault on the system in the 1980s and 1990s occurred in the context of a more regressive public mood and temper . . . and as part of the creation of a new and less inclusive crime narrative." (Garland, 2001, pp. 53, 72, 73).

Although the moment of radical criminology was, in Garland's analysis, short, it was momentous in its impact although this impact was scarcely in the direction intended! The NDC, together with their American counterparts, mounted a scathing criticism of the criminal justice system and the prison in particular, pointing to its counter-productiveness and the utter failure of the rehabilitative ideal. That is as captured in the spirit of the ironies that I have outlined earlier. According to Garland the effect was together with other reformers to undermine the whole intellectual credibility of the penal-welfare basis of modern criminology. In doing this they played into the hand of the reactionary forces which followed them, thus from the 1980s onwards the political success of the New Right rejected the rehabilitative ideal, as they did the notion of social causes of crime, and replaced it with its successor, the 'crime-control complex' with its stress on retribution and incapacitation in prisons and situational crime prevention.

Wait a Moment

My problem with Garland's revisionist history of critical criminology is that it simply does not correspond to reality. The critical tradition both in theory and research palpably flourishes. Textbooks in theory—whatever their political persuasion—all contain chapters on critical criminology and its present developments, whilst the radical textbooks (and there are very many of them) have a standard progression through the canon of criminological theory with critical criminology as the culmination. It is true that varieties of neo-liberal criminology (e.g. Felson, Clarke and Wilson) have emerged in the last fifteen years, but they are still a minor part of academic criminology, are likely to remain so and have a correspondingly small (and much demeaned) role in the textbooks. To this Garland would argue that:

> "Not all criminology is consonant with, or relevant to, the character of contemporary social life. There is a huge inertia built into academic production which ensures the theoretical traditions continue long after they cease to connect to 'the real world'. I have focused upon the criminologies of everyday life because I believe they do connect to the present in an interesting and revealing way." (1999, p. 362).

So much of the academic tradition does not connect. I cannot see how this is true of critical criminology either politically or in terms of its relationship to "the grain" of everyday life. The ten ironies I have listed would seem to me to be as important today as they ever were, in fact all the more so with the growth of the American gulag, the penchant for the scapegoating of the poor, the immigrant and the drug user, and the way in which crime control has become a major currency of politics. As for everyday life, Garland may believe that the rational choice and routine activities theories go with the grain of everyday life in late modernity—indeed his most recent book, *The Culture of Control*, uses such theories as its explanatory basis—but such neo-liberal discourses capture only a limited part of that reality. Contrast this with a critical criminology which insists that out there, in a world of broken narratives where economic and ontological insecurity abounds, where crime, far from being mundane and calculative, is transgressive and sensual, where punishment is frequently vituperative and vindictive and where society, rather than being a one-dimensional scenario of rational contractual atoms, is divisive, contested, contradictory and ironic (see Young, forthcoming; Hayward, 2002).

Finally, as to the role of critical criminology as the midwife to reaction. The criticisms evolved in the seventies were directed against the fact that prisons failed to rehabilitate and that a quasi-medical model of rehabilitation was growing with notions of 'treating' offenders and involving indeterminate sentences to be served until 'cure' was achieved. That is, it was directed against the failure of the prisons and fake notions of rehabilitation. These arguments were not an argument against rehabilitation *per se*, although, as was constantly indicated, if the conditions which led to crime were ameliorated there would be considerably less people in prison needing rehabilitation. That right wing commentators seized upon the obvious inadequacies of the prison was scarcely the 'fault' of critical criminology. The spin they put on the facts of failure was a product of New Right thinking, not of criminological radicals. As it is the extensive expansion in recent years of quasi-medical treatment programmes for drug abuse and various offences, the massive rise of cognitive behavioural programmes within prisons (see Carlen, 2002) and the concomitant emergence of individual positivism in the shape of psychological criminology in the academy not only invalidates Garland's claim of a transition away from penal-welfarism but underscores the need for a renewal of critique on precisely the same lines as before.

The Flourishing of Critical Criminology

My argument so far is that critical criminology in this age of the Gulag and the punitive turn is massively needed, it is the counter-voice to neo-liberalism and conservatism. And what is more, critical criminology is flourishing. The most incisive recent textbooks are all in this genre, witness Mark Lanier and Stuart Henry's *Essential Criminology* (1998), René van Swaaningen's *Critical Criminology: Visions from Europe* (1997), John Lea's *Crime and Late Modernity* (2002), Rob White and Fiona Haines' *Crime and Criminology* (2000), Gregg Barak's *Integrating Criminologies* (1998), John Tierney's *Criminology: Theory and Context* (1996), Wayne Morrison's *Theoretical Criminology: From Modernity to Post-Modernism* (1995), Roger Matthews' *Doing Time* (1999), Russell Hogg and Dave Brown's *Rethinking Law and Order* (1998), Jayne Mooney's *Gender, Violence and the Social Order* (2000) and Ian Taylor's *Crime in Context* (1999). It has produced the most exciting ethnography and critique of the last ten years. Read Phillipe Bourgois' 'Just Another Night in the Shooting Gallery' (1998), Jeff Ferrell's 'Criminological Verstehen: Inside the Immediacy of Crime' (1997), Lois Wacquant's *Les Prisons de la Misère*, Nils Christie's *Crime Control as Industry* (2000), Vincenzo Ruggiero's *Crime and Markets* (2000), Damian Zaitch's (2001) wonderful study of Colombian cocaine dealing in Rotterdam, Pat Carlen's *Jigsaw* (1996), or look at Walter DeKeseredy and his associates' remarkable study of crime and poverty in a Canadian public housing estate with its acute awareness of gender and ethnicity (DeKeseredy *et al*, forthcoming). Critical criminology has been at the cutting edge of the discipline and is international in its scope, think of the burgeoning literature on governmentality (e.g. Stenson, 1998; Rose, 2000; O'Malley, 1999), on masculinity (Jefferson, 2002; Hall, 2002; Messerschmidt, 2000), Phil Scraton's intrepid investigative criminology in the harrowing *Hillsborough: The Truth* (2000), the opening up of the crime prevention discourses to critical analysis by Adam Cawford (1998) and Gordon Hughes (1998), the development of work on youth and justice by John Muncie (1999), Shahid Alvi (2000) and John Pitts (2001), Ruth Jamieson's pioneering work on the criminology of war (1998, 1999), or the extraordinary flourishing of cultural criminology (Ferrell *et al* 2001; Ferrell and Saunders, 1995; Presdee, 2000).

What is of course true, is that the vast expansion of the criminal justice system has resulted in a plethora of evaluative studies, research programmes and vocational courses (see Robinson, 2001) which have generated a substantial institutional base for administrative criminology. All of this further underscores the necessity of a critical voice to counter the minimalist, theoretical 'noise' constantly arising from out of the crime control complex.

The Illegitimacy of Critique

There are, however, writers who maintain that late modernity has brought with it a new predicament wherein the space for fundamental critique is rapidly shrinking. George Pavlich, for example, in an article entitled 'Criticism and Criminology: In search of Legitimacy' (1999), maintains that criticism within critical criminology has been subject to a diluting pragmatism, interesting itself in matters of crime control and technical efficiency, on the one hand, or basing itself on emancipatory rhetoric with an untenable belief in universal 'progress' and the possibilities of a utopian future, on the other. For the uncertainties of postmodern times do not allow us to securely appeal to such emancipatory strategies and when these are absent the danger is that recourse will be made to the technical and the administrative which merely aids the system to work and to continue the status quo. Pavlich, therefore, proposes that to make a critique which has legitimacy we must reject both of these strategies.

So here we are with Phillipe Rushton on the BBC this morning as I shave, telling us how crime and IQ will soon be located in a specific gene and the gene relates to race, whilst yesterday ex-Commissioner Kerik is claiming on national TV the crime drop in New York City as his own, and advising London in the spirit of zero-tolerance to come down heavy on cannabis users, whilst Mayor Ken Livingstone is demanding that the city massively ups its police force to New York levels in order to "win the fight against crime," whilst in the south of the city police are tearing up their rule books and specifically targeting black youth with or without suspicion. Meanwhile, across the Atlantic, a Gulag of an immense size and historical significance has emerged, President Bush II has conflated the war against terror, the war against crime and the war against drugs, whilst vicious farce is being enacted in Camp X-Ray in Guantanamo Bay, Cuba.

Yet amidst all of this we are advised that in order to maintain the legitimacy of our critique we should abstain from narratives which are either emancipatory or follow the "performance logic of techno-administrative reasoning" (*ibid*, p.42). Instead we are advised, via Lyotard, to use "paralogic"—literally that which is against reason. For "paralogy always gestures towards the unknown; it licenses attempts to find new ideas, to formulate new links within language that yield novel enunciations" (*ibid*., p. 43). If this is not too clear Pavlich further elaborates:

> "Yet what critical genres might parology legitimate? No doubt this question would require more detailed elaboration in the context of 'crime-related' discourses than is possible here. However, the concept implies multiple critical practices bound neither to emancipation metanarratives nor to technical formulations of crime."

He clarifies this even further:

> "the point of critique is not to discover the essential or necessary unity of given historical limits; rather, its role is to focus on contingent processes that render such limited 'realities' possible. Accordingly, criticism need not entail the practice of comparing, or judging local 'realities' with 'universal' principles—rather it could develop an ethos that continuously directs itself to absence, the otherness which makes possible the so-called 'realities' contained by given historical limits." (*ibid*., p. 43).

Thus the critical criminologist is advised to dig a deep and impenetrable moat around the ivory tower of the academy within which the "exuberant" discourses of unreason reign—whilst outside a plethora of cruel and insistent practices occur which systematically limit human emancipation whilst being justified by false technical and administrative reasons.

In fact it is important, if we are to critique the practices of the present day system, to demonstrate their technical and administrative incompetence—the exposure of the irony depends on this. It is true, however, that technical critique alone leads to the danger of an autopoetic theory which is internally self-referring and may function just to reduce tension in the system (see Lea, 1998). Hence the need for this critique to be conducted in the context of an emancipatory discourse. It is unclear how paralogic can conceivably provide a methodology by which we can tie the immediate and the technical to the long term and the transformative in a way which effectively expedites reform yet does not succumb to the perils of utopian blueprints. This reduces to two problems: the problem of transformation and the problem of a guiding narrative. The answer to the first question is aided by consideration of the work of Nancy Fraser, the second by reference to Zygmunt Bauman, the major theorist of late/post, or, as he would have it, liquid modernity. To outline this it is necessary to situate the problems of transformation and change and their relationship to crime and punishment within the changed social terrain within which we now live.

The Coordinates of Order:
Class and Identity in the Late Modernity

At this point before mapping the terrain of late modernity I wish to briefly establish coordinates. Nancy Fraser in her influential *Justice Interruptus: Critical Reflections on the Post-Socialist Condition* (1997) outlines two types of politics: those centring around distributive justice and those centring around the justice of recognition— that is class politics and identity politics. In *The Exclusive Society* (1999) I point to the two fundamental problems in a liberal democracy to be the need to distribute rewards fairly so as to encourage commitment to work within the division of labour and the need to encourage respect between individuals and groups so that the self-seeking individualism characteristic of a competitive society does not lead to a situation of war of all against all. Individuals must experience their rewards as fair and just and they must feel valued and respected.

Let us develop the distinction between the sphere of distribution and that of recognition. Central to distributive justice is the notion of fairness of reward and in developed societies this entails a meritocracy, that is where merit is matched to reward. Justice of recognition involves the notion of respect and status allocated to all but if we stretch the concept a little further: it also involves the notion of the level of esteem or social status being related justly. Indeed both the discourses of distributive justice and recognition have the notion of a basic equality (all must receive a base level of reward as part of being citizens) but on top of this rather than a general equality of outcome: a hierarchy of reward and recognition dependant on the individual's achievements.

How does this help inform us as to the genesis of crime and punishment? Firstly, that a major cause of crime lies in deprivation that is, very frequently, the combination of feeling relatively deprived economically (which causes discontent) and misrecognized socially and politically (which causes disaffection). The classic combination is to be marginalized economically and treated as a second rate citizen on the street by the police. Secondly, a common argument is that widespread economic and ontological insecurity in the population engenders a punitive response to crime and deviancy (see for example Luttwak, 1995; Young, 2001).

As we shall see in the process of the transition from modernity to late modernity powerful currents shake the social structure transforming the nature of relative deprivation, causing new modes of misrecognition and exclusion, whilst at the same time being accompanied by widespread economic and ontological insecurity. The purchase of each of these currents impacts differentially throughout the social structure by each of the prime social axes of class, age, ethnicity and gender.

The Journey into Late Modernity

The last third of the twentieth century has witnessed a remarkable transformation in the lives of citizens living in advanced industrial societies. The Golden Age of the post-war settlement with high employment, stable family structures, and consensual values underpinned by the safety net of the welfare state has been replaced by a world of structural unemployment, economic precariousness, a systematic cutting of welfare provisions and the growing instability of family life and interpersonal relations. And where there once was a consensus of value, there is now burgeoning pluralism and individualism (see Hobsbawm, 1994). A world of material and ontological security from cradle to grave is replaced by precariousness and uncertainty and where social commentators of the fifties and sixties berated the complacency of a comfortable 'never had it so good' generation, those of today talk of a risk society where social change becomes the central dynamo of existence and where anything might happen. As Anthony Giddens put it: "to live in the world produced by high modernity has the feeling of riding a juggernaut" (1991, p. 28; see also Beck, 1992; Berman, 1983).

Such a change has been brought about by market forces which have systematically transformed both the sphere of production and consumption. This shift from Fordism to Post-Fordism involves the unravelling of the world of work where the primary labour market of secure employment and 'safe' careers shrinks, the secondary labour market of short-term contracts, flexibility and insecurity increases as does the growth of an underclass of the structurally unemployed.

Secondly, the world of leisure is transformed from one of mass basic consumption, to one where choice and preference is elevated to a major ideal and where the constant stress on immediacy, hedonism and self-actualisation has had a profound effect on late modern sensibilities (see Campbell, 1987; Featherstone, 1985). These changes both in work and leisure, characteristic of the late modern period, generate a situation of widespread relative deprivation and heightened individualism. Market forces generate a more unequal and less meritocratic society, market values encourage: an ethos of every person for themselves, together these create a combination which is severely criminogenic. Such a process is combined with a decline in the forces of informal social control, as communities are disintegrated by social mobility of them and left to decay as capital finds more profitable areas to invest and develop. At the same time, families are stressed and fragmented by the decline in communities systems of support, the reduction of state support and the more diverse pressures of work (see Currie, 1997; Wilson, 1996). Thus, as the pressures which lead to crime increase, the forces which attempt to control it decrease.

The journey into late modernity involves both a change in perceptions of the fairness of distributive justice and in the security of identity. There is a shift in relative deprivation from being a comparison between groups (what Runciman, 1966, calls 'fraternal' relative deprivation) to that which is between individuals (what Runciman terms 'egoistic' relative deprivation). The likely effect on crime is, I would suggest, to move from a pattern committing crimes *outside* of one's neighbourhood onto other richer people to committing crimes in an internecine way *within* one's neighbourhood. That is the frustrations generated by relative deprivation become focused inside the 'community' rather than, as formerly, projected out of it.

But it is also in the realm of identity that relative deprivation is increased and transformed. For here, on one side, you have raised expectations: the spin off of the consumer society is the market in *lifestyles*. On the other hand, both in work and in leisure, there has been a disembeddedness. That is identity is no longer secure; it is fragmentary and transitional—all of which is underscored by a culture of reflexivity which no longer takes the world for granted. The identity crisis permeates our society. As the security of the lifelong job, as the comfort of stability in marriage and relationship fade, as movement makes community a phantasmagoria where each unit of the structure stays in place but each individual occupant regularly moves, where the structure itself expands and transforms and where the habit of reflexivity itself makes choice part of everyday life and problematises the taken for granted—all of these things call into question the notion of a fixed, solid sense of self. Essentialism offers a panacea for this sense of disembeddedness.

The Identity Crisis and the Attractions of Essentialism

In *The Exclusive Society* I discuss the attractions of essentialism to the ontologically insecure and denigrated. To believe that one's culture, "race," gender or community has a fixed essence which is valorised and unchanging is, of course, by its very nature the answer to a feeling that the human condition is one of shifting sands, and that the social order is feckless and arbitrary. To successfully essentialise oneself it is of great purchase to negatively essentialise others. That is to ascribe to the *other* either features which *lack* one's own values (and solidity) or which are an *inversion* of one's own cherished beliefs about one's self. To seek identity for oneself, in an essentialist fashion, inevitably involves denying or denigrating the identity of others.

Crime and its control is a prime site for essentialisation. Who, by definition, could be a better candidate for such a negative 'othering' than the criminal and the culture that he or she is seen to live in? Thus the criminal underclass replete with single mothers and living in slum estates or ghettos, drug addicts committing crime to maintain their habits and the immigrants who commit crime to deceitfully enter the country and continue their lives of crime, in order to maintain themselves become the three major foci of emerging discourses around law and order—that is the welfare "scrounger," the "junkie," and the "immigrant."

This triptych of deviancy, each picture reflecting each other in a late modern portrait of degeneracy and despair, comes to dominate public discussion of social problems. As the discourse develops their ontologies become distinct and different from 'normal' people, their social norms absent or aberrant, their natures frequently racialised and rendered inferior. Crime a product of our society becomes separated from the social structure: it is viewed as a result of distinct aetiologies, it embodies differing values, it emanates from distinct and feared areas of the city and these areas that are contrasted with the organic community where social trust and harmony are seen to reside.

Nancy Fraser: Affirmative and Transformative Politics

The problem of crime is inevitably one of order, and the problem of order that of justice. To tackle predatory crime and punitive responses we must, therefore, involve the politics of distribution and the politics of recognition. We must, in short, intervene both upon a material and a symbolic level. Discussion of reform is usually concerned with the former for without some form of redistribution any considerable reduction in crime is unlikely. The significance of the symbolic level is less explored and has changed remarkably with the transition to late modernity. First of all a more individualistic society generates greater and greater demands for self-actualisation and recognition, secondly, the increased sense of disembeddedness makes, at the same time, a sense of secure identity more and more precarious, thirdly, a potent solution to this ontological uncertainty is that of essentialism, fourthly such a fake sense of solidity is more easily achieved by regaling others, lastly such a dehumanisation of others can be a potent facilitation both of crime (particularly violence) and a punitive attitude towards the criminal. It is therefore crucial that we attend to the problems of identity, arguing for policies which ensure a sense of self-worth and actualisation yet which do not rest upon the fake premises of essentialism where others are systematically denigrated and then abused.

Nancy Fraser in *Justice Interruptus* develops an extremely useful typology of the politics of reform based on the two dimensions of redistribution and recognition. Reform, she argues, must recognise the necessity of changes in both these areas assuaging both the failings of distributive justice and misrecognition and devaluation. But to this dichotomy she adds a further distinction: between the politics of affirmation and the politics of transformation. Affirmative politics merely involves the surface transfer of resources without changing the basic underlying divisions whereas transformative politics seek to eliminate the basic underlying structures of injustice (see Young, 1999; Mooney, 2000). Thus in the area of redistribution affirmative remedies involve, for example, coercing the underclass into the labour market at extremely low wages. Their underclass position is merely reproduced this time within the lower reaches of the market place (see Levitas, 1996). This dragooning of people from one category of exclusion to another ("getting the people to work," as the Social Exclusion Unit—1999—put it, with its cheerless *double entendre*) is experienced all too frequently not as inclusion but as exclusion, not as the 'free' sale of labour but as straightforward coercion. Relative deprivation would, of course, not be solved by such 'inclusionary' politics and the sources of discontent which are liable to generate high crime rates would be unabated. Transformative redistribution, on the other hand, would involve such measures as retraining so that jobs could be gained and then rewarded on a meritocratic basis—thus putting a genuine element of equality into equal opportunity policies, the recognition of non-paid work (e.g. child rearing, caring for ageing parents) as of vital importance for social reproduction, the creation of viable childcare infrastructures for women with children, and the enforcement of a minimum wage on a level which allows the individual an existence which is neither demeaning nor severely straitening in circumstance. Above all it would not fetishize paid work—it would not view such work as the vital prerequisite for full citizenship, for acceptance and inclusion in society.

An affirmative politics of recognition does not question the various essential-isms of difference. That is, in the case of conventional multiculturalism, what is stressed is the need for the positive recognition of various groups on equal terms, for example: Irish, African-Caribbean, Gays, Women, etc. In contrast, transformative politics seek to break down and destabilise and deconstruct the categories by questioning the very notion of fixed identity and essence. Thus the invented notion of tradition is challenged, the overlapping, interwoven nature of what are supposedly separate cultures stressed, and the ambiguity and blurred nature of boundaries emphasised. Diversity is encouraged and, where non-oppressive, celebrated, but difference is seen as a phenomenon of cultures in flux not essences which are fixed.

In the case of crime and punishment, the critique of essences both in criminal victimisation and in punishment is a high priority. The category of hate crimes must be widened out in the realisation that a considerable proportion of acts of violence involve vocabularies of motive which debase and dehumanise the victim (see I Young, 1990). Thus not only crimes against gays and blacks, but against women, the elderly, the poor etc. In terms of our response to crime it is vital that the essentialism which runs through the discourses about crime and its causes is thoroughly debunked. Important, here, is to confront and shatter the triptych which locates crime spatially and socially in three loci—the underclass, the drug user and the immigrant. Such a combination, portrayed as interdependent and very frequently racialised, is presented as the major source of crime and disorder in our society. Against this we must emphasise that crime occurs throughout the structure of society and that its origins lie not in a separate aetiology but in the structure of society and its core values. The identification of a distinct criminal class is an endeavour bound to failure.

Thus Fraser points us to the understanding that what may seem the most obvious of responses to a problem may result in the opposite and that what is seemingly progressive can be counterproductive. She indicates, if you want, ironies in social intervention. Let me conclude this section by briefly examining drug control. As is well documented, the Conservative, punitive, 'obvious' approach to illicit drug use raises drug prices, creates a base for organised crime, encourages dilution and adulteration of drugs, increases crime, violence and mortality. It generates, as critical criminology indicated, the irony in which the primary harm of drugs (the problem before intervention) is considerably less than the secondary harm of drugs (the problem after intervention). Let us turn now to medicalisation, a response which on the surface looks progressive and indeed is touted as the liberal alternative to the 'drug wars'. The irony here is the provision of a sick role model with a social script attached which predicts a perpetual problem of relapse is self-fulfilling. And indeed drugs clinics are scandalous for their recidivism rates and individuals in desperate social and personal predicaments queue up to take on the addict role. For the sick role provides an essence which gives a fake solidity or identity and a series of 'excuses' which absolves and distances the individual from his or her predicament (see Auld *et al*, 1986; Young, 1971b).

From a critical perspective, the first task is to deconstruct the legal-illegal division between psychoactive drugs and situate the effects and harm of drugs within social situations and predicaments. You cannot read the essence of a drug from a pharmacopoeia. The very same drugs can be a grave risk, good fun or a blessing depending on social context. Secondly, we must expose the wrong of punitive sanctions and the war against drugs whilst combating the essentialism of the medical approach. Then finally, we must turn to the social context focusing *only* on those drug users whose dire social predicament drives them to highly risky use. Here the task becomes to transform the social situation and involves the problematic that Fraser has developed. Namely that we oppose reforms whether punitive or medical which serve to capture the drug user in his or her role and social predicament and we support those which genuinely change the social predicament and de-essentialise drug use.

The Unfinishable: An Endless Narrative

I have pointed to the two major components of a transformative politics but this still leaves us the problem of the narrative which guides such a transformation. In the past emancipatory politics have set out endpoints, detailed utopias which are markers to where the programme seeks to arrive and sets itself at rest. The history of such social democratic and communist metanarratives has involved, invariably, the problem of what conceivably could be the endnote and what debatably is the compass of justice and, at worst, the enmeshment of such ideals in state bureaucracy and totalitarianism. Zygmunt Bauman has been centrally concerned with the concept of justice in contemporary times. He starts with his notion of postmodernity; for him it is not the end of modernity, but it is 'modernity without illusion'. Commentating on his change in position he writes:

"At the time that I wrote *Socialism: The Active Utopia* [1976], something had broken once for all: the vision of socialism (or, for that matter, of the 'good society') as a state to be achieved, a state bound to become at some point 'the final state' of humanity. Instead, there emerged the vision of socialism (and more generally of utopia) as a horizon, constantly on the move, perpetually receding, but guiding the travel; or like a spike prodding the conscience, a nagging rebuke that cast complacency and self-adoration out of bounds and out of question. It was now the utopia itself, not the state of affairs it was meant to bring about, that bore the mark of eternity. Its attraction was not in the promise of rest, but in keeping humans forever on the move, in calling them to fight ever new injustices and to take the side of the successive echelons of the left behind, injured, humiliated." (Bauman and Tester, 2001, p. 49).

He envisages instead an endless narrative, a project which is a continuous unfinishable process and a utopian ideal which is constantly contested, yet nags and persists, it is in his phrase a "knife pressed at the future":

"In our times, the concept of injustice is more hotly contested than at any other time in history. It prompts daily reconnaissance skirmishes and recognition wars on ever new fronts. No iniquity is likely to be accepted as 'part of life' for long and borne meekly and placidly. By proxy, also, the idea of justice has become hazier than ever before, and given the mind-boggling pace at which seemingly uncontroversial patterns are rebranded as manifestations of injustice and iniquity, few people would risk committing themselves to blueprints of the 'just society' in the sense of a society thoroughly cleansed of old injustices and giving birth to no new ones.

"This is one aspect of the emerging 'liquid modernity' which gives morality grounds for hope. Ever more forms of human misery are reclassified from 'necessary' into 'super-numerary' and excessive, and we all grow ever more impatient with everything so classified. Does this mean that we move closer to the state of 'ultimate justice'? . . . Today's justices tend to be tomorrow's injustices and this 'until-further-noticeness' is bound to mark them all. A just society as I understand it . . . a society perpetually vigilant for injustice and never sure that its arrangements are just enough . . . justice is a horizon which a just society tries to reach, a horizon which moves further away with every step forward that society makes. Insisting on taking such steps and not relenting in this insistence, come what may, are what make a society just." (*ibid.*, pp. 64–5).

The Necessity of Critique

David Matza in his pivotal book *Becoming Deviant*, published in 1969, which of all texts heralds the shift into late modernity, points to the need for 'naturalism'; the necessity of replacing the 'correctionalist' approach to deviance with an 'appreciative one': to be faithful to the nature of the phenomenon under study. And if one does this, he notes, rather than the social world seeming clear cut and delineated, "the distinction between deviant and conventional phenomena [is seen as] blurred, complicated and sometimes devious" (*Op.cit.*, p.68). He uses two concepts to sum-marise the relationship between the conventional and the deviant: *overlap* and *irony*. Overlap stresses the ultimate convergence between the *normatively* good and the bad, between virtue and evil, the way that one often looks like the other, the way one runs into another in an unbroken narrative line, the way in which one conceals the other. Irony runs on from this, it is the inversion of the conventional view that over time good and evil run in separate sequences: whereas in fact vice can result from virtue and virtue from vice. "The key element is . . . inherent qualities of phenomena that despite their hidden nature, culminate in outcomes that mock the expected result . . . " (*ibid.*, p. 70).

I believe that recognition of the blurred, devious and ironic nature of reality—although true of all time, presents itself all the more clearly in late modernity where the shift and pluralism of values encourage the double take, threatening daily what Alfred Schutz called the 'taken for granted world of everyday life' (see Young, 1999). Further, that it is such a questioning of the solidity of the social world and the stated purposes of its institutions which comes close to what we mean by the word 'critical'. Zygmunt Bauman in recent interviews ponders on the nature of critical theory: "What I understand by that term is the kind of theorising which accepts that, first, 'things are not necessarily what they seem to be' and second that 'the world may be different from what it is' . . . ." And Bauman is fiercely dismissive of those who would view human culture as a thing of inertia, the place of habit, routine, absence of reflection—a sort of stabilising 'preservative' of humanity. As we have seen, the taken for granted world begins to disintegrate in late modernity, reflex gives way to reflexivity. In contrast, he says: "Once you accept culture with its endemic restlessness and its inborn inclination to transcendence as the fundamen-tal characteristic of the human mode of being, the idea of 'critical theory' appears pleonastic, like 'buttery butter' or 'metallic iron'. Theory which wants to be faithful and adequate to its object cannot but be 'critical'." (Bauman and Tester, 2001, p. 33).

All good sociology is critical, as is all competent criminology. It is my belief that critical criminology is more relevant today than ever and that the critical attitude fits the experience of later modernity. If we return to the themes of the ten ironies it is striking how the problems faced in the 1970s are built larger today and how the con-cerns are more a harbinger of the present than a moment of the past. Every single one of the ironies, from the counterproductive nature of the prison to the role of stigmati-sation and othering in law and order politics, are of immense relevance. We are privi-leged to work in an area which has its focus on the fundamental dislocations of justice that occur throughout our social order, a place of irony and contest, of vituperation and transgression. Those who would seek to marginalise critical criminology fail to comprehend its purchase on the grain of social reality, those in our own camp who would narrow their definition of the 'critical' to the sectarian or the esoteric, fail to understand the central position of critique as a counterbalance to neo-liberalism and its administrative discourses. Let us set about our task keeping in mind the urgency of opposition, yet with an eye for irony imbued, as always, with a sense of fun.

References

Alvi, S (2000), *Youth and the Canadian Criminal Justice System.* Cincinnati OH: Anderson Publishing

Auld, J; Dorn, N and South, N (1986), 'Irregular Work, Irregular Pleasures', in R Matthews and J Young (eds.) *Confronting Crime.* London: Sage

Barak, G (1998), *Integrating Criminologies.* Boston: Allyn and Bacon

Bauman, Z (1976), *Socialism: The Active Utopia.* London Allen and Unwin

Bauman, Z (2000), *Liquid Modernity.* Cambridge: Polity

Bauman, Z and Tester, K (2001), *Conversations with Zygmunt Bauman.* Cambridge: Polity Press

Beck, U (1992), *Risk Society.* London: Sage

Berman, M (1983), *All That's Solid Melts Into Air.* London: Verso

Bourgois, P (1998), 'Just Another Night in a Shooting Gallery', *Theory, Culture and Society* 15(2), pp. 37–66

Brake, M (1980), *The Sociology of Youth Culture and Youth Subcultures.* London: Routledge and Kegan Paul

Brake, M (1985), *Comparative Youth Culture.* London: Routledge and Kegan Paul

Campbell, C (1987), *The Romantic Ethic and the Spirit of Modern Consumerism.* Oxford: Blackwells

Carlen, P (1996), *Jigsaw: A Political Criminology of Youth Homelessness.* Buckingham: Open University Press

Carlen, P (2002), 'Carceral Clawback', *Punishment and Society* 4(1) pp. 115–21

Christie, N (2000), *Crime Control as Industry* (3rd ed). London: Routledge

Cohen, S (1981), 'Footprints in the Sand' in M Fitzgerald, G McLennan and J Pawson (eds) *Crime and Society.* London: Routledge and Kegan Paul

Cohen, S (1998), 'Intellectual Scepticism and Political Commitment: The Case of Radical Criminology' in P Walton and J Young (eds) *The New Criminology Revisited.* London: Macmillan

Cottee, S (2001), 'Adventures in Criminology: Radzinowicz, A Review Essay', *Theoretical Criminology* 5(2) pp. 253–64

Crawford, A (1998) *Crime Prevention and Community Safety.* London: Longman

Currie, E (1997), 'Market, Crime and Community', *Theoretical Criminology* 1(2), pp. 147–172

deKeseredy, W; Alvi, S; Schwartz, M; Tomaszewski, A (forthcoming), *Under Siege: Poverty and Crime in a Canadian Public Housing Estate.* Toronto: University of Toronto Press

Downes, D (1988), 'The Sociology of Crime and Social Control in Britain 1960–1987' in P Rock (ed) *The History of British Criminology.* Oxford; Oxford University Press

Featherstone, M (1985), 'Lifestyle and Consumer Culture', *Theory, Culture and Society*, 4, pp. 57–70

Ferrell, J (1997) 'Criminological Verstehen: Inside the Immediacy of Crime', *Justice Quarterly*, 14(1) pp. 3–23

Ferrell, J and Saunders, C (eds.) (1995), *Cultural Criminology.* Boston: Northeastern University Press

Ferrell, J; Milovanovic, D and Lyng, S (2001), 'Edgework, Media Practices and the Elongation of Meaning', *Theoretical Criminology*, 5(2), pp. 177–202

Fraser, N (1997), *Justice Interruptus: Critical Reflections on the Post-Socialist Condition.* New York: Routledge

Garland, D (1985), *Punishment and Welfare.* Aldershot: Gower

Garland, D (1988), 'British Criminology Before 1935' in P Rock (ed.) *The History of British Criminology.* Oxford: Oxford University Press

Garland, D (1995), 'Penal Modernism and Postmodernism' in T Bloomberg and S Cohen (eds) *Punishment and Social Control.* New York: Aldine De Gruyer

Garland, D (1997), 'The Development of British Criminology' in M Maguire, R Morgan and R Reiner (eds.) *The Oxford Handbook of Criminology* (2nd ed.). Oxford: Clarendon Press

Garland, D (1999), 'The Commonplace and the Catastrophic', *Theoretical Criminology*, 3(3), pp. 353–64

Garland, D (2001), *The Culture of Control.* Oxford: Oxford University Press

Garland, D and Sparks, R (2000), 'Criminology, Social Theory and the Challenge of Our Times' in D Garland and R Sparks (eds.) *Criminology and Social Theory*. Oxford; Oxford University Press

Giddens, A (1991), *Modernity and Self-Identity*. Cambridge: Polity

Gorz, A (1999), *Reclaiming Work: Beyond the Wage-Based Society*. Cambridge: Polity Press

Hall, S (2002), 'Daubing the Drudges of Fury', *Theoretical Criminology* 6(1), pp. 35–61

Hobsbawm, E (1994), The Age of Extremes. London: Michael Joseph

Hogg, R and Brown, D (1998), *Rethinking Law and Order*. Awnandale, NSW: Pluto Press

Hughes, G (1998), *Understanding Crime Prevention*. Buckingham: Open University

Jamieson, R (1998), 'Towards a Criminology of War in Europe', in V Ruggiero, N South and I Taylor (eds.) *The New European Criminology*. London: Routledge

Jamieson, R (1999), 'Genocide and the Social Production of Immorality', Theoretical Criminology, 3(2), pp. 131–146

Jefferson, T (2002), 'Subordinating Hegemonic Masculinity', *Theoretical Criminology*, 6(1), pp. 63–88

Katz, J (1988), *The Seductions of Crime*. New York: BasicBooks

Lanier, M and Henry, S (1998), *Essential Criminology*. Boulder, CO: Westview

Lea, J (1998), 'Criminology and Postmodernity', in P Walton and J Young (eds) *The New Criminology Revisited*. London: Macmillan

Lea, J (2002), *Crime and Late Modernity*. London: Sage

Levitas, R (1996), 'The Concept of Social Exclusion and the New Durkheimian Hegemony', *Critical Social Policy*, 16, pp. 5–20

Luttwak, E (1995), 'Turbo-Charged Capitalism and Its Consequences', *London Review of Books*, 17 (21), 2 November, pp. 6–7

Matthews, R (1996), *Doing Time*. London: Macmillan

Matza, D (1969), *Becoming Deviant*. New Jersey, Englewood Cliffs: Prentice Hall

Messerschmidt, J (2000), Nine Lives; *Adolescent Masculinities, The Body and Violence*. Boulder, CO: Westview

Mooney, J (2000), *Gender, Violence and The Social Order*. London: Macmillan

Muncie, J (1999), *Youth and Crime*. London: Sage

O'Malley, P (1999), 'Volatile Punishments: Contemporary Penality and Neo-Liberal Government', *Theoretical Criminology*, 3(2), pp. 175–96

Pavlich, G (1999), 'Criticism and Criminology', *Theoretical Criminology* 3(1), pp. 29–51

Pitts, J (2001), *The New Politics of Youth Crime*. London: Palgrave

Presdee, M (2000), *Cultural Criminology and the Carnival of Crime*. London: Routledge

Radzinowicz, L (1999) *Adventures in Criminology*. London: Routledge

Robinson, M (2001), 'Wither Criminal Justice: An Argument for a Reform of Discipline', *Critical Criminology* 10(2), pp. 97–106

Rose, N (2000), 'Government and Control' in D Garland and R Sparks (eds.) *Criminology and Social Theory*. Oxford: Oxford University Press

Ruggiero, V (2000), *Crime and Markets*. Oxford: Oxford University Press

Runciman, W (1966), *Relative Deprivation and Social Justice*. London: Routledge and Kegan Paul

Scraton, P (2000), *Hillsborough: The Truth*. Edinburgh: Mainstream Publishing

Social Exclusion Unit (1999), *Bringing Britain Together: A National Strategy for Neighbourhood Renewal*. London: The Stationery Office

Stenson, K (1998), 'Beyond Histories of the Present', *Economy and Society*, 27(4), pp. 333–52

Stenson, K and Edwards, A (2001) 'Rethinking Crime Control in Advanced Liberal Government' in K Stenson and R Sullivan (eds.) *Crime, Risk and Justice*. Cullompton, Devon: Willan Publishing

Taylor, I (1999), *Crime in Context*. Oxford: Polity

Tierney, J (1996) *Criminology: Theory and Context*. Hemel Hempstead: Prentice Hall van Swaaningen, R (1997), *Critical Criminology: Visions from Europe*. London: Sage

Wacquant, L (1999), *Les Prisons de la Misére*. Paris: Éditions: Rasions d'agir

White, R and Haines, F (2000), Crime and Criminology (2nd ed.). Melbourne: Oxford University Press

Wilson, W J (1996), *When Work Disappears*. New York: Knopf

Wootton, B (1959), *Social Science and Pathology*. London: Allen and Unwin

Young, I M (1990), *Justice and the Politics of Difference*. Princeton, NJ: Princeton University Press

Young, J (1971a), 'The Role of the Police as Amplifiers of Deviancy, Negotiators of Reality and Translators of Fantasy' in S Cohen (ed) *Images of Deviance*. Harmondsworth: Penguin

Young, J (1971b), *The Drugtakers*. London: Paladin

Young, J (1998), 'Breaking Windows: Situating the New Criminology', in P Walton and J Young (eds) The New Criminology Revisited. London: Macmillan

Young, J (1999), *The Exclusive Society*. London: Sage

Young, J (2001), 'Identity, Community and Social Exclusion' in R Matthews and J Pitts (eds) *Crime, Disorder and Community Safety*. London: Routledge

Young, J (forthcoming) 'Searching for a New Criminology of Everyday Life', Review Article, *The Culture of Control* D Garland, in British Journal of Criminology

Zaitch, D (2001), *Traquetos*. Amsterdam School for Social Science Research

Gender-Based Theories

As noted in the introduction to Section VI, many of the gender-based and feminist theories could be considered forms of conflict or critical criminology (Deutschmann, 2002:357). This does not mean that all are conflict- or Marxist-oriented—there is a wide variety of feminist and gender-based theories, including liberal theories, radical theories, Marxist or socialist theories, post-modernist or post-structuralist theories, and multicultural theories, to mention a few (Burgess-Proctor, 2009:432; Chesney-Lind & Faith, 2001:290). A number of such theories are written by males— e.g., James Messerschmidt's masculinities theory and John Hagan's power-control theory. It could be argued that both of these theories fall somewhere between the Marxist feminist and socialist feminist perspectives (Akers & Sellers, 2009:277, 280; Hackler, 2007:210–211; Simpson, 1991:122). James Messerschmidt talks primarily about male crime, the unequal distribution of power, and the intersection between race, class and gender (Messerschmidt, 1993:63). John Hagan talks primarily about female crime, the manner in which power relationships in the workplace are reproduced in the family, and the interplay between class, state and the household (Hagan, 2003:217–218). Messerschmidt's (2005) synopsis of current work in the area of masculinities theory, entitled "Males, Masculinities and Crime," appears as the second (and final) reading in this section. The first reading in this section, Sally Simpson's (1991) article on "Caste, Class and Violent Crime," analyzes John Hagan's power-control theory at considerable length.

Feminist theory began to make inroads into criminological thinking in the mid-1970s, at about the same time that Taylor, Walton and Young were publishing *The New Criminology* and *Critical Criminology* (Burgess-Proctor, 2009:440; Williams & McShane, 2010:191). Prior to that, criminological theories were developed almost exclusively by male criminologists, with the principal goal of explaining male criminality (Burgess-Proctor, 2009:440; Chesney-Lind & Faith, 2001:287). Most earlier theorists simply assumed that females committed fewer crimes than males. To the extent that females did engage in crime, it was often attributed to their sexuality— to whether they were "good women" or "bad women" (Deutschmann, 2002:356;

Lilly, Cullen, & Ball, 2011:234–235). In the early 20th Century, girls were routinely charged for "waywardness" or "immorality," and were more likely than boys to be sent to reform school or training school "for their own good" (Chesney-Lind, 2005:188; Hackler, 2007:206). Indeed, this type of paternalistic attitude remains on display in today's criminal justice system, with girls in some cases more likely than boys to be placed in custody or placed on probation, primarily because they are seen as "unruly," "uncooperative" or "defiant" (Bell, 2002:145–146).

Feminist theory often focuses on patriarchy—how females are economically and socially disadvantaged, and how female sexuality and labor power are expropriated and exploited by males (Lilly et al., 2011:240; Messerschmidt, 1993:55–56). An example of patriarchy would be the long standing monarchical practice of passing the crown down to a son, with a daughter being the last in line to receive such consideration. In any number of societies, property and money are traditionally passed along to the male heirs, bypassing wives and daughters altogether. There are still religions that do not permit females to worship with males, or to conduct religious ceremonies. There are still countries where females are not allowed to work or attend school. This is not to suggest that North American society is significantly more enlightened—in 1982, Bertha Wilson became the first woman ever to be appointed to the Supreme Court of Canada (Burtch, 2003:152). Power inequalities of this nature, woven into the fabric of the political, economic, social class and family structure, have given males a considerable advantage—not to mention a high degree of control—over females throughout the years (Williams & McShane, 2010:189–190). As feminist criminologists point out, the majority of female "criminals" are stuck at the bottom of this chain of oppression and exploitation, often working at menial, part-time jobs that pay poorly and offer minimal prospects for job security or future advancement (Chesney-Lind, 2005:190–192; Williams & McShane, 2010:192).

While there have always been gender-based explanations of crime, most—e.g., Sutherland's differential association theory, Shaw and McKay's social disorganization theory, Hirschi's social bond theory—have attempted to explain male delinquency. Recently, more scholars have begun to question why it is that males commit more crimes than females, and at the same time, why females commit fewer (and less serious) crimes than males. John Hagan's power-control theory attempts to address this issue through an examination of how the patriarchal—male-dominated and paternalistic—structure of many families results in girls being overly protected and discouraged from taking risks, while boys receive less supervision and experience a greater degree of independence (Akers & Sellers, 2009:277–278; Hagan, 2003:216–217). James Messerschmidt approaches the same issue from a different angle, by arguing that boys and men are constructing masculinity (doing gender) by engaging in delinquent or criminal activities, and that they go about this differently, depending upon their race and social class (Messerschmidt, 2005:197–198). The first reading in this section, Sally Simpson's "Caste, Class and Violent Crime," approaches the issue from yet another angle, asking why it is that some females are more likely than other females to engage in violent crime (Simpson, 1991:117–118).

References

Akers, R. L., & Sellers, C. S. (2009). *Criminological theories: Introduction, evaluation, and application* (5th ed.). New York: Oxford University Press.

Bell, S. J. (2002). Girls in trouble. In B. Schissel, & C. Brooks (Eds.), *Marginality and condemnation: An introduction to critical criminology* (pp. 129–152). Halifax, N.S.: Fernwood Pub. Co.

Burgess-Proctor, A. (2009). Looking back, looking ahead: Assessing contemporary feminist criminology. In H. Copes, & V. Topalli (Eds.), *Criminological theory: Readings and retrospectives* (pp. 431–443). New York: McGraw-Hill.

Burtch, B. E. (2003). *The sociology of law: Critical approaches to social control* (2nd ed.). Toronto: Nelson Thomson Learning.

Chesney-Lind, M. (2005). Girl's crime and woman's place: Toward a feminist model of female delinquency. In H. N. Pontell (Ed.), *Social deviance: Readings in theory and research* (Fifth ed., pp. 181–196). Upper Saddle River, NJ: Pearson Prentice Hall.

Chesney-Lind, M., & Faith, K. (2001). What about feminism? Engendering theory-making in criminology. In R. Paternoster, & R. Bachman (Eds.), *Explaining criminals and crime: Essays in contemporary criminological theory* (pp. 287–302). Los Angeles, Calif.: Roxbury Pub. Co.

Deutschmann, L. B. (2002). *Deviance and social control* (Third ed.). Scarborough, Ontario: Nelson Thomson Learning.

Hackler, J. C. (2007). *Canadian criminology: Strategies and perspectives* (Fourth ed.). Toronto: Pearson Prentice-Hall.

Hagan, J. (2003). A power-control theory of gender and delinquency. In C. M. Renzetti, D. J. Curran & P. J. Carr (Eds.), *Theories of crime: A reader* (pp. 214–221). Boston: Allyn and Bacon.

Lilly, J. R., Cullen, F. T., & Ball, R. A. (2011). *Criminological theory: Context and consequences* (5th ed.). Thousand Oaks: SAGE Publications.

Messerschmidt, J. W. (1993). *Masculinities and crime: Critique and reconceptualization of theory*. Lanham, Md.: Rowman & Littlefield.

Messerschmidt, J. W. (2005). Men, masculinities and crime. In M. S. Kimmel, J. Hearn & R. W. Connell (Eds.), *Handbook of studies on men and masculinities* (pp. 196–212). Thousand Oaks, CA: SAGE Publications.

Simpson, S. S. (1991). Caste, class and violent crime: Explaining difference in female offending. *Criminology, 29*(1), 115–135.

Williams, F. P., & McShane, M. D. (2010). *Criminological theory* (5th ed.). Upper Saddle River, N.J.: Pearson/Prentice Hall.

19

Caste, Class and Violent Crime: Explaining Difference in Female Offending

There has been an ongoing debate about whether female criminality is increasing, and whether females are becoming more prone to violence than they were in the past. Some observers have argued that while there has been an increase in female violence, most of it is "low level" violence, such as common assault, and that at least part of the increase can be explained by the introduction of zero tolerance policies targeted toward violence in schools (Savoie, 2003:83–84). Others have suggested that while the rate of violent crimes committed by females may be going up, the actual seriousness of those crimes is going down, and that any increases in arrest and charge rates are attributable to shifts in official and public attitudes toward youth crime and female criminality (Chesney-Lind & Paramore, 2001:157, 162). Still others have contended that young females are more likely than young males to be arrested, charged and placed in custody or on probation because of rampant paternalism in the criminal justice system—young females are thought to require a greater degree of control and "protection" than young males (Bell, 2002:145–146). In the following reading, however, Sally Simpson states that underclass Black females are indeed more prone to engage in violent crimes than White, Hispanic and Asian underclass females, and that in some cases, the rates of violence amongst underclass Black females approaches that of White males (Simpson, 1991:117).

In her explanation of violent female offending, Sally Simpson employs many of the same factors that James Messerschmidt (see the second reading in this section) does in his analysis of the relationship between the construction of masculinity and male offending—i.e., race, class and gender (Messerschmidt, 1993:67–68; Messerschmidt, 1997:3; Simpson, 1991:116). However, Simpson adds a new factor to the mix, which she calls "caste." Caste—a term which she applies specifically to Black females in the United States who are members of the "underclass"—is a combination of gender and race (Simpson, 1991:116–117). Simpson says this underclass consists primarily of young individuals living in urban centers, who are uneducated or undereducated, unskilled, unemployed or underemployed, and often welfare dependent (1991:119). According to Simpson, these underclass Black females (caste members) are more affected than their White, Hispanic and Asian counterparts by patriarchy, poverty and racism. The majority of the underemployed caste members work in what is known as "the pink collar ghetto"—service, sales and clerical jobs that provide poverty-level pay (Simpson, 1991:119; Williams & McShane, 2010:192).

Simpson explores three possible theoretical explanations for the high level of violence amongst underclass Black females—neo-Marxian theory, power-control theory and socialist-feminist theory—and decides that none are capable on their own of explaining this phenomenon. She observes that neo-Marxian theory has failed to explain differences in gender violence for juveniles who come from the same social class, and that it has not given adequate consideration to the unique position of Blacks in the social structure (Simpson, 1991:121–122). According to Simpson, power-control theory has not properly addressed how patriarchy (male dominance) has a different impact on underclass Black females than it does on White females or females from other ethnic backgrounds and social classes (122–124). Finally, she argues that socialist-feminism tends to view crimes committed by the underclass as crimes of resistance or crimes of accommodation (cf. Quinney, 1977), whilst ignoring the high level of violent crime actually committed by underclass Black females. Thus, she concludes that "theoretical inclusivity" is the best way to go—she combines elements of all three theoretical approaches in her effort to explain why underclass Black females engage in more violent crime than underclass females of White, Hispanic or Asian descent (Simpson, 1991:125).

Sally Simpson frames her analysis in terms of power, control and culture. Using a combination of race and gender, she points out that White males are more powerful than White females, and that White females are more powerful than Black males. Upper-class Black males are more powerful than lower-class Black males, but less powerful than upper-class Whites. She adds that even lower-class White males have power over other ethnicities (Simpson, 1991:125). Male economic power is less of a factor in Black families than in White families, because a significant number of underclass Black females earn as much as their male counterparts. Moreover, many of the underclass Black males are drug addicted, in prison, unemployed, or simply absent due to high divorce rates and the high percentage of "single-parent mothers" (Simpson, 1991:119, 126). The absence of so many Black males from the family structure (and the presence of so many single-parent mothers) leads to a breakdown in informal social controls—there is less parental bonding and less modeling of gender-appropriate behavior. Instead, many of the underclass Black females live in extended domestic networks consisting of family and friends, where social controls tend to be diffused, inconsistent and unpredictable (Simpson, 1991:126–127). Simpson invokes the Marxian notion of the "surplus population"—also referred to by some Marxists as "the surplus labor pool" or "the industrial reserve army" (e.g., Quinney, 1977:56–57)—in explaining cultural definitions and beliefs about the acceptability of violence that she claims are unique amongst underclass Black females. These Black females and their children live under oppressive economic and social conditions, and are exposed to violence on a daily basis. Thus, violence gains cultural legitimacy as a response to racial bias, poverty, unemployment and marginalization (Simpson, 1991:128–129).

References

Bell, S. J. (2002). Girls in trouble. In B. Schissel, & C. Brooks (Eds.), *Marginality and condemnation: An introduction to critical criminology* (pp. 129–152). Halifax, N.S.: Fernwood Pub. Co.

Chesney-Lind, M., & Paramore, V. V. (2001). Are girls getting more violent? Exploring juvenile robbery trends. *Journal of Contemporary Criminal Justice, 7*(2), 142–166.

Messerschmidt, J. W. (1993). *Masculinities and crime: Critique and reconceptualization of theory.* Lanham, Md.: Rowman & Littlefield.

Messerschmidt, J. W. (1997). *Crime as structured action: Gender, race, class and crime in the making.* Thousand Oaks, Calif.; London: Sage Publications.

Quinney, R. (1977). *Class, state and crime: On the theory and practice of criminal justice.* New York: David McKay Company, Inc.

Savoie, J. (2003). Yes! youth violent crime. In R. Hinch (Ed.), *Debates in Canadian criminology* (pp. 80–99). Toronto: Prentice Hall.

Simpson, S. S. (1991). Caste, class and violent crime: Explaining difference in female offending. *Criminology, 29*(1), 115–135.

Williams, F. P., & McShane, M. D. (2010). *Criminological theory* (5th ed.). Upper Saddle River, N.J.: Pearson/Prentice Hall.

Caste, Class, and Violent Crime: Explaining Difference in Female Offending*

SALLY S. SIMPSON

During the past decade, criminological research has targeted gender as an important discriminator of criminal participation and persistence. Yet, the research question too often contrasts the criminality of males and females without taking into account key differences among female populations. In this paper, race and class combine to produce uniquely situated populations of females (e.g., "underclass" black females)

*An earlier version of this paper was presented at the 1988 annual meeting of the American Society of Criminology. I wish to thank the Center for the Study of Women and Society at the University of Oregon for its support of this project, along with Gary Hill, Dorie Klein, Coramae Richy Mann, Charles Wellford, and two anonymous reviewers for their helpful comments on earlier drafts.

Reprinted from *Criminology* 29, no. 1 (1991), American Society of Criminology.

who, when compared with their gender and racial counterparts, also appear to have unique patterns of criminality. Using the extant literature, black female violent crime is juxtaposed against that of white females and black males in order to show how crime varies across groups and the potential sources of those differences. Three theoretical perspectives (neo-Marxian, power-control, and socialist-feminist theory) are reviewed and evaluated for their intragender/racial inclusivity. Directions for further empirical research and theoretical development are suggested.

Class-oppressed men, whether they are white or black, have privileges afforded them as men in a sexist society. Similarly, class-oppressed whites, whether they are men or women, have privileges afforded them as whites in racist society. . . . Those who are poor, black, and female have all the forces of classism, racism, and sexism bearing down on them (Mantsios, 1988:66–67).

Violent criminality provokes an imagery that borders on caricature but one that is reinforced through official statistics and scholarly investigations. Serious street crime is a lower-class phenomenon (Elliott and Huizinga, 1983; Silberman, 1978; Wolfgang, 1958), disproportionately enacted by young (Greenberg, 1979), black (Hindelang, 1978; Tracy et al., 1991; Wolfgang et al., 1972), males (Hindelang, 1981; Tracy et al., 1991; Steffensmeier and Cobb, 1981). Studies and reports that support this portrait rely heavily on official arrest statistics, victimization surveys, and offender self-reports. With few exceptions, these data are not conducive to analyses of the often complex, interactive effects of caste (gender and race) and class. Consequently, comparisons of violence within or between certain subgroups in the population, say lower-class white females versus lower-class black females, are typically neglected.

There has been intense debate among scholars regarding the "true" relationship between social class and crime (lucid summaries are provided by Braithwaite, 1981; Fagan et al., 1986; Hindelang et al., 1981; Tittle and Meier, 1990; see also Tittle et al., 1978), but there is little disagreement about the relationship between gender and violence. The violent female offender is an anomaly—both in the United States and cross-culturally (Harris, 1977; Weiner and Wolfgang, 1985). On those rare occasions when women are violent, their victims tend to be intimates (Bowker, 1981; Mann, 1987; Norland and Shover, 1977).

Recent evidence has done little to challenge this general truism; yet, there are unique patterns and trends in female criminal violence that bear investigation. Specifically, if females are not as a group violent, what accounts for variations in rates of criminal violence among them—particularly between blacks and whites (Hindelang, 1981; Laub and McDermott, 1985; Tracy et al., 1991)? As will be demonstrated, black females, especially those in the "underclass," engage in what might be considered anomalous behavior for their gender (i.e., violent crimes) but not for their race (Lewis, 1977). On the other hand, given the high level of violence among black males, black female rates of violent crime are relatively low.

Black females appear to respond differently to conditions of poverty, racism, and patriarchy than their class, gender, and racial counterparts. Race and gender merge into a theoretically interesting and important case, one that deserves more systematic inquiry (Hill and Crawford, 1990).

The purpose of this review is not to propose and develop a new theoretical perspective. My aims are more modest. Rather, violent crime among under-class black females is taken as illustrative of vertical (power) and horizontal (affiliative) differences between blacks and whites, males and females, and social classes (Hagan and Palloni, 1986). The degree to which extant theory can accommodate these caste and class differences in violent crime is assessed.[1] More specifically, three perspectives (neo-Marxian, power-control, and socialist-feminist theories of crime) are evaluated as to their sensitivity to intraracial and intragender variations in violent crime. To this end, the paper is divided into three parts: a review of the empirical literature on gender and violent crime; a theoretical section in which each perspective is described and criticized; and finally, recommendations for theory modification, including cultural analysis.

The Violent Female Offender

Making an Empirical Case: Problems of Identification

Distinguishing violent crime rates among females of different social classes and races is a difficult empirical task. Many studies employ noncomplimentary instruments and measures that preclude comparisons, or often, one or more of the key demographic variables is missing. For instance, Laub and McDermott (1985) and Laub (1983) compare racial and gender rates of offending, but class is ignored. Brownfield (1986) tests the relationship between several measures of social class and violent crime; yet, race and gender are not considered. Even the exceptions to this exclusionary rule (such as Ageton, 1983), test mostly for direct, not interactive effects; or when variable interactions are calculated, racial and class rather than racial and gender effects are the focus (Elliott and Huizinga, 1983).

In some cases, attempts to compare findings across the same variable are problematic. As Brownfield (1986) and others (Tittle and Meier, 1990) note, class may be calculated as relational (Colvin and Pauly, 1983; Hagan et al., 1985); common characteristics (Matza, 1966; Wilson, 1982); graduational (Elliott and Ageton, 1980; Hirschi, 1969; or social-ecological (Shaw and McKay, 1942). Race is typically dichotomized into white and black or the nonwhite category is broadened to include groups other than blacks (e.g., Hispanic and Asian). The only variable that seemingly defies this definitional drift is gender.

Patterns and Trends

Race

Clearly, extrapolation and interpretation from these data about violent female crime are speculative at best. But caveats aside, piecing together "apparent" patterns and trends from Uniform Crime Reports (UCRs) and victimization and self-report data does yield intriguing and remarkably consistent relationships. Black females have higher rates of homicide and aggravated assault than whites (Mann, 1987; McClain, 1982; Steffensmeier and Allen, 1988; Von Hentig, 1942). For certain types of personal crime victimizations, black female rates for both adults and juveniles are more similar to those for white males than those for white females (Hindelang, 1981; Laub and McDermott, 1985; Young, 1980).[2]

Among juveniles, black females are consistently more involved in assaultive crimes than whites (Ageton, 1983).[3] A recent cohort study (Tracy et al., 1991) found nonwhite female participation in UCR violent offenses to be 5.5 times that of white females. They are also more apt to be chronic offenders. Less dramatic, but similar patterns, were found by Sheldon (1987).

Black female participation in violent criminality does not compare with the high rates among their male counterparts; yet, "black women constitute well over half of all incarcerated women and are a higher proportion of all female offenders than are black men of all male offenders" (Lewis, 1981:69).[4] In light of these findings, gender alone does not account for the variation in criminal violence. Race as constitutive of structural and/or cultural difference demands greater conceptual and empirical attention (Chilton and Datesman, 1987; Hill and Crawford, 1990).[5]

Race and Class

Of the variables most often related to violent crime, class position is important for both blacks and whites (Elliott and Ageton, 1980; Tracy et al., 1991), but underclass status for blacks may be essential. A number of criminologists and sociologists (Blau and Blau, 1982; Currie, 1985; Silberman, 1978; Wilson, 1987) assert that economic inequality—especially the increasing marginalization and social isolation of underclass blacks—is correlated with high levels of criminal violence.

Changes in divorce laws, occupational segregation coupled with low pay for women, and the rise of single-parent mothers (Goldberg and Kremen, 1987; Norris, 1984; Weitzman, 1985) have significantly lowered the objective class position of many women. Since the 1960s, the major increase in poverty has occurred among those living in households headed by a single-parent mother (Goldberg and Kremen, 1987). Of these women, one-third are black (Norris, 1984). One out of three white children and three out of four black children can expect to spend some of their childhood in a single-parent family (New York Times, April 29, 1983). Like the crime statistics, black women and children are overrepresented.

The majority of single-parent mothers work, but most work within the pink-collar ghettos of clerical, service, and sales. Their average weekly earnings place them under the poverty level, which has earned them the title "the working poor" (Norris, 1984).

The Underclass

The lower class, while disproportionately female and black, is relatively heterogeneous. Yet, the bottom of the lower class is more racially homogeneous. Wilson (1982:157) characterizes this population as *underclass*: "In underclass families, unlike other families in the black communities, the head of the household is almost invariably a woman. The distinctive make-up of the underclass is also reflected by the very large number of adult males with no fixed address."

The underclass is poorly educated, unskilled, and chronically under- or unemployed (Lichter, 1988; Wilson, 1987). Its single-parent mothers (often teenagers) are typically welfare dependent (Norris, 1984). The question of how an underclass is created and sustained is debatable. But whether its origins lie in large-scale, race-neutral structural change (Wilson, 1987) or in institutional racism (Duster, 1988; Lichter, 1988), its demographic characteristics are without refute. The face of the underclass is young and black; its geographical terrain is center-city urban.

Violence and the Underclass

Rates of violent crime vary significantly with the economic characteristics of communities. Some researchers suggest that violence is caused by relative economic deprivation (i.e., ascriptive inequality; Blau and Blau, 1982; Blau and Golden, 1984); others argue the violence is correlated with absolute poverty (Messner and Tardiff, 1986) or some interaction of class with race and urbanism (Blau and Blau, 1982; Laub, 1983; Wilson, 1987). Once again, causation is refutable but empirical patterns are more straightforward. Violent crime rates are highest in underclass communities—urban communities that are disproportionately black (Wilson, 1987).

In a recent study of underclass violence (Sampson, 1987), "disrupted" families (female-headed households) increase juvenile and adult robbery offending for both blacks and whites, but they have a greater effect on black homicide rates.[6] Although gender differences in the use of violence are not taken into account, Sampson does suggest that underclass position, particularly labor marginality of black males and its accompanying economic marginalization, has profound negative consequences for black women with children.

In a similar vein, Matsueda and Heimer (1987) discover a positive relationship between broken homes and delinquency, an effect that is much stronger among blacks than whites. Moreover, black delinquency is more likely to be affected by "neighborhood trouble" than white. The authors conclude that "broad historical trends have led to different patterns of social organization among the urban underclass which influence rates of delinquency" (p. 837).

Given the significant impact of family structure on violent criminality among males, researchers must ask (1) whether this same pattern holds for females and (2) what it is about single-parent families that contributes to such a relationship. Both are empirical questions but neither, given the paucity of data, currently is within empirical grasp. Consequently, the answers offered here are necessarily speculative.

Two types of family structure emerge from poverty: (1) extended domestic networks (Stack, 1974; Valentine, 1978) and (2) isolated single-parent units (Miller, 1986). The structure of one's family of origin may influence whether females become involved in criminal activity and in what types of illegality they may engage. Miller's (1986) study of deviant street networks in Milwaukee found poorer women, especially blacks, to be members of shifting households composed of kin, nonkin, and pseudokin.

The extensive and shifting domestic networks in which black females are found are closely associated with criminal recruitment. According to Miller (1986:67),

> Because of the severe limitations that poverty places upon the control exercised by parents and guardians, young women from poor families are more likely to be recruited to deviant networks than those from families that are better off. Moreover, because of the greater frequency of highly developed and far reaching domestic networks among poor blacks than among poor whites, black girls appear to be differentially recruited to the fast life of the street.

The fast life described by Miller heightens female exposure to all types of crime, especially property, but personal offenses as well (e.g., robbery and assault). Yet, because much violent crime is irrational and noninstrumental, exposure to criminal opportunities through deviant street networks may only partially explain the violent crime gap between black and white females. And given that both males and females participate in deviant networks and share similar class experiences, why is there not greater gender convergence in violent crime rates? Obviously, other elements are operative.

Feminists were among the first to call for greater sensitivity to class and racial differences among females, but feminist criminology has yet to produce a cohesive perspective that accounts for intragender racial differences in criminal offending (see, e.g., Messerschmidt, 1986). Similarly, most theories of crime are class (see Meier, 1985), but not gender and race, sensitive. In this next section, three criminological perspectives are assessed as to their ability to account for gender, class, and racial differences in violent offending. The three theories are examined precisely because they tie illegality to class and/or gender *oppression*[7] and because feminist critics of androcentric criminological theory suggest that Marxian and control perspectives are, relative to others, more amenable to the "gender variable" (Leonard, 1982; Naffine, 1988).

Theoretical Considerations

Neo-Marxian Theory

Neo-Marxian explanations formulate the crime problem by examining the objective class position of workers. Depending on the type of employment and employer (e.g., skilled worker/monopoly capitalist versus unskilled worker/competitive capitalist), workers will be disciplined differently and develop different bonds to authority (Colvin and Pauly, 1983). Parents who experience alienative bonding to authority in coercive work situations reproduce those relations with their children. Alienative bonding in juveniles is reinforced through the educational system (through such practices as tracking) and peer relations. The alienated youths who emerge from this process are more apt to be violently delinquent than youths who experience other types of discipline and bonding (e.g., remunerative/calculative or symbolic/moral).

> The more coercive the control relations encountered in these various socialization contexts tend to be, the more negative or alienated will be the individual's ideological bond and the more likely is the individual to engage in serious, patterned delinquency (Colvin and Pauly, 1983:515).

Therefore, children whose parents are least skilled and subject to coercive discipline at work are more likely to act out in criminally violent ways.[8]

This theory adds conceptual precision to the class-violent delinquency relationship, but it fails to account for gender differences among juveniles whose parents are similarly located. A recent empirical test of Colvin and Pauly's theory finds mixed support for both males and females, especially the class-delinquency relationships (Messner and Krohn, 1990). However, these findings may be due to questionable operationalization of concepts such as Marxian class categories and serious patterned delinquency. Also, blacks are excluded from the analysis. Finally, if violence is highest among underclass populations who are increasingly isolated from the labor market, then the processes that are deemed essential to the production of violent crime (i.e., discipline and bonding in the workplace) are not in place. Recognizing some of these failures, John Hagan and his associates construct a theory that is class based, but also sensitive to how patriarchy may structure familial (1985, 1988) and workplace (1987) relations.

Power-Control Theory

Power-control theory builds on the idea that workplace-family power relations affect how parental discipline operates (mother or father as instrument of control) as well as which child is most apt to be disciplined by which parent (male or female as object of control). According to this theory, delinquency will be gendered only under certain class and familial structures. Patriarchal families (which reflect the unequal authority positions of parents in the workplace) produce greater rates of "common" delinquency by sons than daughters, because within the family males are socialized to have a greater taste for risk than females. In more egalitarian families (i.e., both parents share similar work positions or households are female headed), delinquency is not patterned (or as patterned) by gender. "As Mothers gain power relative to husbands, daughters gain freedom relative to sons" (Hagan et al., 1987:792). Ostensibly, under these conditions, females become more risk prone and consequently more delinquent.

In framing power-control theory, Hagan and his associates (1979, 1985:1153-1154) clearly limit their focus to "common" forms of delinquency.[9] Yet, there is no reason that power-control theory cannot be modified to account for class and gender differences in violent crime. In fact, one permutation of power-control theory nestles the concept of power in the same neo-Marxian class categories that Colvin and Pauly (1983) theoretically link to "serious patterned delinquency." Additionally, the inclusion of personal assaults in Hagan et al.'s (1985, 1988) measure of common delinquency raises the question of whether all juvenile assaults are benign enough to be viewed as not serious, or "common."

Appropriate modifications of the theory should focus on how violence is related to freedom to deviate, an absence of controls, and/or socialized risk preferences. For example, Colvin and Pauly (1983) and Hagan and colleagues (1985) claim that discipline and control within the family reproduce workplace authority structures. Common delinquency is expected to be positively related to class position (because freedom to deviate is associated with upperclass socialization and power position), but violent offending should vary negatively with class. Alienative bonding coupled with coercive discipline in the workplace will produce inconsistent bonding to authority and high levels of frustration and alienation in families. Following the original logic of power-control theory, one would expect greater gender differences in violent offending in patriarchal rather than in nonpatriarchal families. Patriarchal power within the family supports and reinforces traditional gender role socialization (i.e., male as aggressive/female as passive). Gender differences in violent offending should decrease with class position, partially because of the disproportionate representation of "egalitarian" single-parent mothers among lower-class families, but also as a result of the deteriorating authority of male and female workers, which is reproduced in parental relations with children.

Risk preference is expanded to include (a) the functionality of risk and (b) the perceived costs if one is caught. In employer classes, violence is apt to be dysfunctional for most males because it does not prepare them for careers nor, given the increased likelihood that this behavior is more apt to come to the attention of authorities than common delinquency, are the costs worth it.[10] For upper-class females, violence is neither functional nor legitimate. And, considering that countertype criminality by females (i.e., masculine crime) may be more harshly viewed by authorities (Bernstein et al., 1977; Schur, 1984; Visher, 1983), the costs of violence for this population of females may be especially high. As one moves down the class ladder, however, definitions of violence and its legitimacy may change. Violence as a means of achieving desired ends—whether pecuniary or interpersonal (power and dominance)—is apt to be more commonplace and less gender-role defined.

Power-control theory has been relatively unsuccessful in subsequent empirical tests (Singer and Levine, 1988),[11] perhaps because it fails to address how patriarchy varies across racial groups and social class lines. Male dominance and control do not necessarily operate similarly for black and white females, nor for racial groups across different classes. The relationship between black women and black men is not "the same or necessarily analogous to that which white women have to white men . . . these relationships are patriarchal and oppressive . . . [but] their form can be very different" (Brittan and Maynard, 1984:64). Consequently, power-control theory may offer insights into class and gendered delinquency, but as currently conceived its insensitivity to race is a major weakness.[12]

Socialist-Feminist Theory[13]

Socialist-feminist approaches to crime, although also unable to link race and racism systematically with class and patriarchy, are at least concerned with such conceptual failures. Messerschmidt (1986:xi) acknowledges that "racial oppression is as important as class and gender oppression, [but] socialist feminism has not linked it systematically with patriarchy and capitalism." Even with these confessed flaws, socialist-feminist approaches provide helpful ways in which to think about class and gender differences in crime.[14]

The strengths of socialist-feminism for this analysis are twofold. First, the criminality of males and females varies in frequency and type due to the gendered social organization of productive (class) and reproductive (family) spheres. Neither sphere is privileged over the other as a source of oppression; they are mutually reinforcing. Consequently, the economic base of capitalist society and its ideological superstructure (social institutions and culture) are seen as dynamic and dialectical. Second, personality and individual consciousness are seen to reflect the dominance/subordination relations found in production and reproduction (Messerschmidt, 1986:30–31).

Patriarchal capitalism creates two distinct groups: the powerful (males and capitalists) and the powerless (females and the working class). Opportunities to commit crime vary according to one's structural position. For the powerful, criminality is a means to maintain domination over the control of the powerless. Conversely, crimes by the powerless are interpreted as forms of resistance and accommodation to their structural position (Messerschmidt, 1986:42). From this perspective, the most costly and deleterious crimes are committed by capitalist males (e.g., corporate offenses). Lower-class and female crime reflects a powerless status, but because of gendered social organization (crime opportunities are distributed unequally and males are apt to resist while females accommodate their powerlessness), male and female criminality takes entirely different forms. Under patriarchal capitalism, powerless males commit violent street crime; powerless females engage mostly in nonviolent property and/or vice offending (primarily drugs and prostitution).

As noted earlier, one of the flaws of socialist-feminism is its neglect of how racial oppression and racism interact with other forms of oppression to produce distinct patterns of criminal offending. A related problem is its insensitivity to intragender variations in violent offending. To suggest that males are violent and females are not ignores the empirical reality of black female crime. In the next section, key concepts and theoretical insights from neo-Marxian, power-control, and socialist-feminist perspectives are used to address intraclass, gender, and racial differences in violent offending.

Toward Theoretical Inclusivity

Power

Class, gender, and race are best understood as intersecting systems of dominance and control. Power is ascribed and compliance determined by how these characteristics cluster across productive and reproductive spheres. Within the workplace, white females are less powerful than white males, but more powerful than black females. Bourgeois blacks are more powerful than lower-class blacks, but less powerful than bourgeois whites, and "white working class men are given at least a vicarious power over third-world peoples" (Silverstein, 1977:178).

In the family, it is less clear how class and race may affect gender relations. Some studies find greater middle-class attitudinal subscription to gender equality, but more equality in practice within working-class families (as measured by decision-making power, Blood and Wolfe, 1960).[15] Because there is greater economic parity between black males and females than there is between whites (black female wage earnings are closer to those of black males than white female earnings are to those of white males; The Wall Street Journal, April 17, 1989), male economic power within black families is less. At the bottom end of the class structure, black males are often unavailable for family participation due to violent death, drug addiction, prison, or unemployment (Wilson, 1982). Here, interpersonal male power is negated by absence, but replaced with the patriarchal state (e.g., through female interactions with Aid for Dependent Children, children's services, the criminal justice system, and so on).

The shared experience of racism also can affect the intrafamilial operation of patriarchy. Although black women recognize their own subordination to men, they keenly feel the racism that keeps black males "in their place." Racism changes the features of male privilege and dominance within the black family.

Control

On the control end, ideology (constraining belief systems that reflect the interests of the powerful)[16] and culture (the symbolic-expressive dimensions of human action; Wuthnow, 1987) determine who gets controlled and how. In traditional working- and upper-class families, control operates through patriarchal structures.

> Individuals are enmeshed in class and gender structures that organize the way people think about their circumstances and devise solutions to act upon them. Gender and class shape one's possibilities. The conditions individuals confront and the manner in which they choose to "handle" those conditions are socially regulated. Just as conforming behavior is socially regulated and intimately related to one's class/gender status, so is nonconforming behavior (Messerschmidt, 1986:41).

Yet, membership in the underclass is disruptive of this process. For blacks, social controls within the family (i.e., parental bonding and learning of "gender-appropriate" behaviors) are attenuated across extensive domestic networks.

The disruption of intrafamilial patriarchal reproduction occurs within a system stratified by racial privilege and framed by race-conscious ideologies. Underclass position, because of alienation and the breakdown of traditional social control in the family, should produce higher crime rates for both black and white females compared with other classes, but blacks—because they have little invested in a racist system or less to gain through conformity with that system—should be more criminal than similarly positioned white women.[17]

White women are more apt to be deterred from crime because of its perceived consequences (e.g., loss of status, negative labeling, and rejection by a system that benefits whites). They will take fewer risks because they have more to lose in a system that accords privilege to whites. Moreover, they can mitigate their powerlessness by "attaching" themselves to a more powerful group in patriarchal racist society (e.g., white males).[18] As Lorde (1988:355) points out, "In a patriarchal power system where white skin privilege is a major prop, the entrapments used to neutralize black women and white women are not the same." White females, under the pretense of sharing power, may be seduced into joining the oppressor.[19]

For the white poor, racist ideology provides a psychologically nonthreatening explanation for their poverty and a language of collective resentment. MacLeod's (1987) study of working/lower-class boys in Clarendon Heights (a low-income housing development) describes how white boys believe blacks and the wealthy are favored at school and in employment. MacLeod notes that these boys exhibit dual contradictory consciousness, embodying "both progressive, counterhegemonic insights and reactionary, distorting beliefs" (p. 123). In a system in which failure is attributable to individual weakness and white skin confers greater value than black skin, it makes sense that white males and females do not reject the system but blame others' privileges for their failures. Psychologically, they cannot afford to do so. Moreover, family structure among impoverished whites is more likely either to be nuclear or isolated, single-parent units (Miller, 1986; Wilson, 1987). These structures are less conducive of breakdowns in patriarchal control, and violent crime opportunities are fewer than in the extended and integrative domestic networks of underclass blacks.

Culture

Power and hierarchy determined by class, patriarchy, and race cannot be separated from horizontal relations of affiliation and solidarity (Hagan and Palloni, 1986). These relations are reciprocal and reinforcing. As structural conditions increasingly preclude mobility for the bottom of the surplus population, cultural redefinitions and adjustments may influence perceptions of, and beliefs about, the emergence and appropriateness of violence (Wilson, 1987).

Although power-control, neo-Marxian, and socialist-feminist perspectives link micro and macro factors to crime, none sufficiently develops the cultural processes that drive interpretation and social action. Most criminological theories that are attentive to cultural forces (e.g., Cloward and Ohlin, 1961; Miller, 1958; Wolfgang and Ferracuti, 1967) are primarily concerned with male criminality. Consequently, they fail to explain how culture either restricts or patterns female criminality (Leonard, 1982). They also tend to employ a narrow and static definition of culture—a system of norms, beliefs, and values that impose on individual actions. This conception divorces cultural production from its situated context and tends to see culture as a distinct and imposing force.

Yet, "culture is not composed of static, discrete traits moved from one locale to another. It is constantly changing and transformed, as new forms are created out of old ones" (Mullins, 1986:13). To understand the unique positioning of black women between two dominant groups in society (Lewis, 1977:343), it makes sense to discern how their material conditions affect how culture is created, interpreted, and reproduced, as well as culture's relation to power and hierarchy.

Collins (1986:524) calls attention to an essential relationship between structural/ material conditions, black women's subjective consciousness, and social action:

> Oppressive structures create patterns of choices which are perceived in varying ways by black women. Depending on their consciousness of themselves and their relationship to these choices, black women may or may not develop black-female spheres of influence where they develop and validate what will be appropriate . . . sanctioned responses.

Although Collins is interested in explaining how black females politically mobilize, criminal behavior can be seen as emerging from similar cultural processes. Class is an oppressive structure for both black and white females, but black women's experiences of their material circumstances and their perceptions of self and choice vary qualitatively from those of whites.

The lives of black women and children are "stitched with violence and hatred . . . [and] violence weaves through the daily tissues of . . . living" (Lorde, 1988:355). Living daily with the fact of violence leads to an incorporation of it into one's experiential self. Men, women, and children have to come to terms with, make sense of, and respond to violence as it penetrates their lives. As violence is added to the realm of appropriate and sanctioned responses to oppressive material conditions, it gains a sort of cultural legitimacy. But not for all. The observed gender differences in how violence is interpreted and incorporated into one's behavioral repertoire emerge from the contradictory cultural tendencies of caste (i.e., female = nonviolent, black = violent; Lewis, 1981). Black females, given their dedication to keeping home and community together (Joseph, 1981) are more apt than black males to delegitimate violence. However, given their racial oppression and differential experience of patriarchy in the family, black females are perhaps less apt to delegitimate violence than their white counterparts.

Summary and Conclusions

Criminologists have been mistaken to ignore important variations in criminal behavior among females. The simplistic assertion that males are violent and females are not contains a grain of truth, but it misses the complexity and texture of women's lives. A review of the empirical literature on violence reveals the confounding effects of gender, race, and class. Although their combined influences are difficult to tease out, a firm understanding of how they interact is fundamental for a more inclusive and elegant criminological theory. Neo-Marxian, power-control, and socialist-feminist perspectives offer some help in this regard.

Before criminologists launch into a major revision of current theory, however, further research is clearly necessary. Extant research yields only a murky picture of essential differences between and among males and females of different classes and races. Until large-scale quantitative designs can readily and meaningfully sort out differences in crime rates and qualitative research can offer subjective accounts of how violence is interpreted and understood by different subpopulations of interest, criminological theory will continue to be only vaguely relevant to the real world.

Notes

1. The focus on violent crime is justified on two counts. First, studies using self-report, victimization, and police reports suggest that gender and racial differences are most acute in personal crime categories (Ageton, 1983; Hindelang, 1981; Steffensmeier and Allen, 1988; Tracy et al., 1991). There are also reasons to suspect that violent crime emerges from different etiological processes than does more instrumental crime (Blau and Blau, 1982; Coser, 1968).

2. In the case of personal crimes (rape, robbery, assault, and larceny from the person), the black female rate of offending among 12- to 17-year olds exceeds that of their white male counterparts (Hindelang, 1981:465; see also Steffensmeier and Allen, 1988).

3. The sole exception is hitting parents. Here, white female participation exceeds that of blacks.

4. See French's discussion of the North Carolina female prison population (1977, 1978).

5. Crime data on other women of color (e.g., Chicanas, Indians, Asians, other Hispanics) are exceedingly difficult to come by. Therefore, in this review, "race" is operationalized as black and white. This does not, nor should it be interpreted to, imply that black female experiences somehow represent those of all women of color. More qualitative and historical studies (e.g., Campbell, 1984 Miller, 1986; Ross, 1988) offer evidence that different historical and cultural experiences of oppressed groups, intersecting with material conditions, influence whether, how, and to what degree group members are apt to act criminally.

6. Although it is important to note the relationship between family structure and crime, intra-familial dynamics and female roles within particular family types are equally important to study. As Brittan and Maynard (1984:120) remind us, "not only do . . . family forms differ in organization, . . . it cannot be assumed that women's involvement in them is everywhere the same."

7. Oppression (as opposed to inequality or subordination) bases stratification in a complex combination of ideological, political, and economic forces (Phillips, 1987).

8. Some may raise concerns that Colvin and Pauly's (1983) neo-Marxian perspective is a theory of delinquency, not adult crime. However, the processes they identify as promoting delinquency (i.e., coercive discipline and alienative bonding to authority) begin in the workplace with adults. It

is reasonable to assume that negative adult bonding to authority also may produce a criminal outcome, but how coercive discipline and alienative bonding are reproduced and reinforced through other relationships and organizations theoretically is unspecified.

9. They justify their choice by suggesting that crime seriousness may be a theoretical issue to be explained rather than assumed and that an exclusive focus on serious offending may limit theoretical development for other, less serious, crime types.

10. However, violence may prove functional for some upper-class males in order to maintain dominance and power within interpersonal relationships. Moreover, given that upper-class intimate violence is more hidden than its lower-class counterpart, its costs may be less.

11. Discrepant findings may be due to differences in sample populations, cohort or temporal effects, or to the addition of new variables (e.g., a measure of group risk taking is added to Singer and Levine's analysis).

12. Feminists note other weaknesses as well. Naffine (1988) argues that power-control theory stereotypically characterizes the process that keeps females from violating the law. Its image of a dependent, controlled, risk-avoiding, law-abiding female does not take into account the degree to which females are (1) tied to the conventional social order and (2) rational and calculating in their assessment of the personal costs of illegality. Further, power-control theory privileges the workplace over the family as the primary source of dominance. Although this approach may be applauded by Marxist-feminists, it is based on assumptions that are not shared by most feminists (c.f., Daly and Chesney-Lind, 1988; Messerschmidt, 1986; Simpson, 1989).

13. For this section, I rely almost exclusively on the work of Messerschmidt (1986). It is by far the most developed representation of this perspective.

14. Like power-control theory, socialist-feminist approaches typically ignore female participation in violent crime. For instance, Messerschmidt (1986:51–98) carefully distinguishes typical male from typical female crime types. In the case of conventional offending, powerless males commit violent crimes and powerless females engage in nonviolent offending.

15. Blood and Wolfe's (1960) study is roundly criticized by feminist scholars, who argue that power in the family is not determined by different levels of economic resources brought into it by males and females. Rather, the marriage contract itself implicitly defines male and female roles; and beyond that, "we cannot ignore the sexism that characterizes heterosexual relations in general" (Johnson, 1988:251).

16. As Thompson (1984) and Larrain (1977) use the concept, ideology retains its critical edge (i.e., tied to a critique of domination). In my case, ideology reflects the interests of upper-class white males.

17. Collins (1986:519) offers an important insight as to why black males in the underclass have higher rates of crime than black females. She argues that being poor, black, and female offers "a clearer view of oppression than other groups who occupy contradictory positions vis-à-vis white male power." Black males can always attempt to negate their oppression through a "questionable appeal to manhood." The source of this appeal is ideological. Patriarchy provides males (white and black) with a "manhood" typescript (Harris, 1977). This typescript defines male-appropriate reactions to stress and frustration (i.e., they act out against others). The dominant "womanhood" typescript is just the opposite. Stress and anger are internalized into self-destructive behaviors like suicide, depression, and other types of mental illness (Piven and Cloward, 1979).

18. See Hook's discussion of white women's pragmatic use of their sex and race to "realize personal gains from the system" (1984:199).

19. There is certainly historical precedent for these speculations. As black abolitionists and suffragists jointly struggled for civil rights in the middle 1800s. political expediency and racism drove many white middle-class feminists to side with their white male brethren against black enfranchisement (Hook, 1984).

References

Ageton, Suzanne S. (1983). The dynamics of female delinquency, 1976–1980. *Criminology* 21:555–584.

Bernstein, Ilene, Edward Kick, Jan Leung, and Barbara Schultz (1977). Charge reduction: An intermediary stage in the process of labeling criminal defendants. *Social Forces* 56:362–384.

Blau, Peter M. and Judith R. Blau. (1982). The cost of inequality: Metropolitan structure and violent crime. *American Sociological Review* 47: 114–129.

Blau, Peter M. and Reid M. Golden. (1984). Metropolitan structure and criminal violence. Paper presented at the annual meeting of the American Sociological Association, San Antonio, Texas.

Blood, Robert O. and Donald M. Wolfe. (1960). *Husbands and Wives: The Dynamics of Married Living.* Glencoe, N.Y. Free Press.

Bowker, Lee. (1981). *Women and Crime in America.* New York: Macmillan.

Braithwaite, John (1981). The myth of social class and crime reconsidered. *American Sociological Review* 46:36–57.

Brittan, Arthur and Mary Maynard. (1984). *Sexism, Racism, and Oppression.* Oxford: Basil Blackwell.

Brownfield, David. (1986). Social class and violent behavior. *Criminology* 24:42–1438.

Campbell, Anne. (1984). *The Girls in the Gang.* New York: Basil Blackwell.

Chilton, Roland and Susan K. Datesman (1987). Gender, race, and crime: an analysis of urban arrest trends, 1960–1980. *Gender and Society* 1:152–171.

Cloward, Richard A. and Lloyd E. Ohlin. (1961). *Delinquency and Opportunity.* Glencoe, N.Y.: Free Press.

Cohen, Albert. (1955). *Delinquent Boys.* Glencoe, N.Y.: Free Press.

Collins, Patricia Hill. (1986). Learning from the outsider within: The sociological significance of black feminist thought. *Social Problems* 33:514–532.

Colvin, Mark and John Pauly. (1983). A critique of criminology: Toward an integrated structural-Marxist theory of delinquency production. *American Journal of Sociology* 89:513–551.

Coser, Louis A. (1968). Conflict: Social aspects. In David L. Sills (ed.), *International Encyclopedia of the Social Sciences.* Vol. 3. New York: Macmillan.

Currie, Elliott. (1985). *Confronting Crime.* New York: Pantheon.

Daly, Kathleen and Meda Chesney-Lind. (1988). Feminism and criminology. *Justice Quarterly* 5:497–538.

Duster, Troy. (1988). From structural analysis to public policy. A review of William J. Wilson's, The Truly Disadvantaged. *Contemporary Sociology* 17:287–290.

Elliott, Delbert S. and Suzanne S. Ageton. (1980). Reconciling race and class differences in self-reported and official estimates of delinquency. *American Sociological Review* 45:95–110.

Elliott, Delbert S. and David Huizinga. (1983). Social class and delinquent behavior in a national youth panel. *Criminology* 21:149–177.

Fagan, Jeffery, Elizabeth Piper, and Melinda Moore. (1986). Violent delinquents and urban youths. *Criminology* 24:439–471.

French, Lawrence. (1977). An assessment of the black female prisoner in the South. Signs 3:483–488.

———. 1978 The incarcerated black female: The case of social double jeopardy. *Journal of Black Studies* 8:321–335.

Goldberg, Gertrude S. and Eleanor Kremen. (1987). The feminization of poverty: Only in America? *Social Policy* 17:3–14.

Greenberg, David. (1979). Delinquency and Age Structure of Society. Pp. 586–620 in Sheldon L. Messinger and Egon Bittner (eds.) *Criminology Review Yearbook.* Beverly Hills, CA: SAGE.

Hagan, John and A. Palloni. (1986). Toward a structural criminology: Method and theory in criminological research. *Annual Review of Sociology* 12:431–449.

Hagan, John, A.R. Gillis, and John Simpson. (1985). The class structure of gender and delinquency: Toward a power-control theory of common delinquent behavior. *American Journal of Sociology* 90:1151–1178.

Hagan, John, John Simpson, and A.R. Gillis. (1979). The Sexual Stratification of Social Control. *British Journal of Sociology* 30:25–38.

———. (1987). Class in the household: A power-control theory of gender and delinquency. *American Journal of Sociology* 92:788–816.

———. (1988). Feminist scholarship, relational and instrumental control, and a power-control theory of gender and delinquency. *British Journal of Sociology* 39:301–336.

Harris, Anthony R. (1977). Sex and theories of deviance. *American Sociological Review* 42:3–16.

Hindelang, Michael. (1981). Variations in sex-race-age-specific incidence rates of offending. *American Sociological Review*, 46:461–474.

———. (1978). Race and involvement in common-law personal crimes. *American Sociological Review* 43:93–109.

Hindelang, Michael, Travis Hirschi and Joseph G. Weis. (1981). *Measuring Delinquency*. Beverly Hills, CA: SAGE.

Hill, Gary D. and Elizabeth M. Crawford. (1990) Women, race, and crime. *Criminology* 28:601–623.

Hirschi, Travis. (1969). *Causes of Delinquency*. Berkeley, CA: University of California Press.

Hook, Elizabeth F. (1984). Black women, white women: Separate paths to liberation. In Allison M. Jagger and Paula S. Rothenberg (eds.), *Feminist Frameworks*. 2nd ed. New York: McGraw-Hill.

Johnson, Miriam M. (1988). *Strong Mothers, Weak Wives*. Berkeley: University of California Press.

Joseph, Gloria I. (1981). Black mothers and daughters. In Gloria I. Joseph and Jill Lewis (eds.), *Common Differences: Conflicts in Black and White Feminist Perspectives*. Boston: South End Press.

Larrain, Jorge. (1977). *The Concept of Ideology*. Athens: University of Georgia Press.

Laub, John. (1983). Urbanism, race, and crime. *Journal of Research in Crime and Delinquency* 20:183–198.

Laub, John and M. Joan McDermott. (1985). An analysis of serious crime by young black women. *Criminology* 23:89–98.

Leonard, Eileen B. (1982). *Women, Crime, and Society*. New York: Longmans, Green.

Lewis, Diane. (1977). A response to inequality: Black women, racism, and sexism. *Signs* 3:339–361.

———. (1981). Black women offenders and criminal justice: Some theoretical considerations. In Marguerite Warren (ed.), *Comparing Female and Male Offenders*. Beverly Hills, Calif.: SAGE.

Lichtern, David T. (1988). Racial differences in underemployment in American cities. *American Journal of Sociology* 13:771–792.

Lorde, Audre. (1988). Age, race, class, and sex: Women redefining difference. In Paul S. Rothenberg (ed.), *Racism and Sexism: An Integrated Study*. New York: St. Martin's Press.

MacLeod, Jay. (1987). *Ain't No Makin' It*. Boulder, Colo.: Westview Press.

Mann, Coramae Richey. (1987). Black female homicide in the United States. Paper presented at the Conference on Black Homicide and Public Health.

Mantsios, Gregory. (1988). Class in America: Myths and realities. In Paula S. Rothenberg (ed.), *Racism and Sexism: An Integrated Study*. New York: St. Martin's Press.

Matsueda, Ross and Karen Heimer. (1987). Race, family structure, and delinquency: A test of differential association and social control theories. *American Sociological Review* 52:826–840.

Matza, David. (1966). The disreputable poor. In Reinhard Bendix and Seymour M. Lipset (eds), *Class, Status and Power*. Glencoe, N.Y.: Free Press.

McClain, Paula D. (1982). Black females and lethal violence: Has time changed the circumstances under which they kill? *Omega* 13:13–25.

Meier, Robert. (1985). *Theoretical Methods in Criminology*. Beverly Hills, CA: SAGE.

Messerschmidt, James W. (1986). *Capitalism, Patriarchy, and Crime*. Totowa, N.J.: Rowman and Littlefield.

Messner, Steven F. and Marvin D. Krohn. (1990). Class compliance structures and delinquency: Assessing integrated Structural-Marxist Theory. *American Journal of Sociology* 96:300–328.

Messner, Steven F. and Kenneth Tardiff. (1986). Economic inequality and levels of homicide: An analysis of neighborhoods. *Criminology* 24:297–316.

Miller, Eleanor M. (1986). *Street Woman*. Philadelphia: Temple University Press.

Miller, Walter B. (1958). Lower class culture as a generating milieu of gang delinquency. *Journal of Social Issues* 14:5–19.

Mullings, Leith. (1986). Anthropolitical perspectives on the Afro-American family. *American Journal of Social Psychiatry* 6:11–16.

Naffine, Ngaire. (1988). *Female Crime: The Construction of Women in Criminology*. Boston: Allen and Unwin.

Norland, Stephen and Neal Shover. (1977). Gender roles and female criminality. *Criminology* 15:87–104.

Norris, Pippa. (1984). Women in poverty: Britain and America. *Social Policy* 14:4–43.

Phillips, Anne. (1987). *Feminism and Equality*. Oxford: Basil Blackwell.

Piven, Frances Fox and Richard A. Cloward. (1979). Hidden protest: The channeling of female innovation and resistance. *Signs* 4:461–470.

Ross, Luana K. (1988). Toward an Indian Study of Indian deviance. Unpublished manuscript, Montana State University, Bozeman.

Sampson, Robert J. (1987). Urban black violence: The effect of male joblessness and family disruption. *American Journal of Sociology* 93:348–382.

Schur, Edwin. (1984). *Labeling Women Deviant*. New York: Random House.

Shaw, Clifford and Henry McKay. (1942). *Juvenile Delinquency and Urban Areas*. Chicago: University of Chicago Press.

Sheldon, Randall. (1987). The chronic delinquent: Gender and racial differences. Paper presented at the annual meeting of the American Society of Criminology. Montreal, Quebéc, Canada.

Silberman, Charles. (1978). *Criminal Violence, Criminal Justice*. New York: Random House.

Silverstein, M. (1977). The history of a short, unsuccessful academic career. In J. Snodgrass (ed.), *For Men Against Sexism*. Albion, Calif.: Times Change Press.

Simpson, Sally S. (1989). Feminist theory, crime , and justice. *Criminology* 27:607–631.

Singer, Simon I. and Murray Levine. (1988). Power-control theory, gender, and delinquency: A partial republication with additional evidence on the effects of peers. *Criminology* 26:627–647.

Stack, Carol B. (1974). *All Our Kin: Strategies for Survival in a Black Community*. New York: Harper Colophon Books.

Steffensmeier, Darrell, T. and Emilie Anderson Allen. (1988). Sex disparities in arrest by residence, race, and age: An assessment of the gender convergence/crime hypothesis. *Justice Quarterly* 5:53–80.

Steffensmeier, Darrell J. and Michael J. Cobb. (1981). Sex differences in urban arrest patterns, 1934–1979. *Social Problems* 28:37–50.

Thompson, John B. (1984). *Studies in the Theory of Ideology*. Berkeley: University of California Press.

Tittle, Charles R., Wayne J. Villemez, and Douglas A. Smith. (1978). The myth of social class and criminality: An empirical assessment of the empirical evidence. *American Sociological Review* 43:643–656.

Tittle, Charles R. and Robert F. Meier. (1990). Specifying the SES delinquency relationship. *Criminology* 28:271–299.

Tracy, Paul E., Marvin E. Wolfgang, and Robert M. Figlio. (1991). *Delinquency in Two Birth Cohorts*. New York: Springer Press

Valentine, Bettylou. (1978). *Hustling and Other Hard Work*. Glencoe, N.Y.: Free Press.

Visher, Christy. (1983). Gender, police arrest decision, and notions of chivalry. *Criminology* 21:5–28.

Von Hentig, Hans. (1942). *The criminality of the colored woman*. University of Colorado Studies (Series C1):231–260.

Weiner, Neil Alan and Marvin E. Wolfgang. (1985). The extent and character of violent crime in America. In Lynn A. Curtis (ed.), *American Violence and Public Policy*. New Haven: Yale University Press.

Weitzman, Lenore J. (1985). *The Divorce Revolution: The Unexpected Social and Economic Consequences for Women and Children in America*. Glencoe, N.Y.: Free Press.

Wilson, William J. (1982). *The Declining Significance of Race*. Chicago: University of Chicago Press.

————. (1987). *The Truly Disadvantaged*. Chicago: University of Chicago Press.

Wolfgang, Marvin. (1958). *Patterns of Criminal Homicide*. Philadelphia: University of Pennsylvania Press.

Wolfgang, Marvin and Franco Ferracuti. (1967). *The Subculture of Violence*. New York: Barnes and Noble.

Wolfgang, Marvin E., Robert M. Figlio, and Thorsten Sellin. (1972). *Delinquency in a Birth Cohort*. Chicago: University of Chicago Press.

Wuthnow, Robert. (1987). *Meaning and Moral Order: Explorations in Cultural Analysis*. Berkeley: University of California Press.

Young, Vernetta D. (1980). Women, race, and crime. *Criminology* 18:26–34.

Sally S. Simpson is an assistant professor of Criminal Justice and Criminology at the University of Maryland, College Park. Her current research interests include testing neo-marxian, power-control, and socialist-feminist perspectives for their gender-race inclusivity; corporate crime etiology and control; and female drug trafficking networks.

20

Men, Masculinities, and Crime

James Messerschmidt is one of the most well known theorists in the area of masculinities and crime. His 1993 and 1997 books *Masculinities and Crime* and *Crime as Structured Action* both made significant contributions to gender-based theory (Akers & Sellers, 2009:281–282; Lilly, Cullen, & Ball, 2011:247–249; Williams & McShane, 2010:194). In *Masculinities and Crime*, Messerschmidt argues that criminologists mistakenly ask why women commit fewer crimes, rather than (correctly) asking why men and boys are the perpetrators of most crimes, and have virtual monopolies on some kinds of crime (Messerschmidt, 1993:1). According to Messerschmidt, the belief that men are naturally aggressive is also wrong. He says that men learn to be aggressive, just like they learn other behavior. He calls for a new "sociology of masculinity," that will offer insight into why men and boys are disproportionately involved in crime, and why they commit different kinds of crime, depending upon their race and social class (Messerschmidt, 1993:25, 62–64).

To understand Messerschmidt's work, it is essential to grasp his concepts of "hegemonic masculinity" and "subordinate masculinity." Hegemonic masculinity is the type of masculinity that is culturally idealized and encouraged by schools and the mass media—it involves money, power, strength, athletic ability, heterosexuality, or simply put, being a "manly man" (Akers & Sellers, 2009:282; Messerschmidt, 1993:82, 94–95; Messerschmidt, 2005:198). "Subordinate masculinity" is the type of masculinity that is discouraged by the mass media and the schools—lack of physical strength, lack of interest in sports, the presence of feminine traits, or not being a manly man. According to Messerschmidt, most males will try to meet with the demands of hegemonic masculinity, but not all have equal power or equal access to normative self-enhancement structures.

Messerschmidt says that social class and race are important determinants when it comes to the construction of masculinity. Upper- and middle-class White males have greater access to power and normative self-enhancement structures. They are able to perform well at school and sports, and have better access to higher education and well-paying jobs. Thus, they are less likely to engage in violent crime, yet more likely (because of opportunity structures) than lower-class or ethnic minority males to become involved in white collar or corporate crime (Messerschmidt, 1993:95–96, 134–136). Lower-class White males do not have the same access to power and normative self-enhancement structures as upper or middle-class White males. Messerschmidt observes that lower-class White males are disproportionately involved in hate crimes, which they use to demonstrate their male dominance over subordinated masculinities and ethnic minorities (Messerschmidt, 1993:99). Gang membership is more important for lower-class minority males, because they do not have the money to subsidize their desired life styles, nor do they have access to high-paying jobs. Realizing that they cannot achieve hegemonic masculinity through normal channels, they construct a violent oppositional masculinity, and are more likely to engage in gang warfare or armed robbery to demonstrate their toughness and dominance over others (Messerschmidt, 1993:105–107).

In the following reading, "Men, Masculinities and Crime," Messerschmidt returns to a number of the themes that he introduced in his earlier works—e.g., hegemonic masculinity, the construction of masculinity, and his view of crime as structured action (the manner in which crime is shaped by the interplay between race, class and gender) (Messerschmidt, 2005:197–198). However, Messerschmidt's main purpose here is to address two recent additions to theories of masculinities and crime—the introduction of psychoanalytic explanations, and the inclusion of physical differences (body types). Messerschmidt argues that recent psychoanalytic explanations of masculinity do not adequately take into consideration the effects of social structure and social situation. Moreover, he characterizes psychoanalytic constructs like "the unconscious" or "projection" as unobservable, unmeasurable, and hence, unprovable (2005:200, 203–204).

Messerschmidt does, however, find merit in considering physical differences when analyzing the relationship between masculinities and crime. As evidence, he presents two life histories that he collected though research interviews. He talks about Hugh and Zack, who lived in the same working class neighborhood and went to the same school. Both also learned from adult role models that "real males" were expected to be tough and masculine (Messerschmidt, 2005:204). Hugh was "tall and muscular for his age," and soon found that his ability to win fights was regarded as "cool" by his peers at school. As a consequence, Hugh developed what Messerschmidt describes as "a physically confrontational masculinity," and engaged in progressively assaultive behavior (2005:205). On the other hand, Zack was overweight, and was often teased by his peers about his physical appearance. He tried to get himself into shape and join the school football team, but was unsuccessful. Zack was also rejected by the girls at school. As a way of overcoming his "subordinate masculinity," he sexually assaulted a young female cousin over a period of several years (Messerschmidt, 2005:207–208). As Messerschmidt points out, Hugh and Zack both used their bodies (albeit differently) to exert male dominance over other individuals.

References

Akers, R. L., & Sellers, C. S. (2009). *Criminological theories: Introduction, evaluation, and application* (5th ed.). New York: Oxford University Press.

Lilly, J. R., Cullen, F. T., & Ball, R. A. (2011). *Criminological theory: Context and consequences* (5th ed.). Thousand Oaks: SAGE Publications.

Messerschmidt, J. W. (1993). *Masculinities and crime: Critique and reconceptualization of theory.* Lanham, Md.: Rowman & Littlefield.

Messerschmidt, J. W. (1997). *Crime as structured action: Gender, race, class and crime in the making.* Thousand Oaks, Calif.: London: Sage Publications.

Messerschmidt, J. W. (2005). Men, masculinities and crime. In M. S. Kimmel, J. Hearn & R. W. Connell (Eds.), *Handbook of studies on men and masculinities* (pp. 196–212). Thousand Oaks, CA: SAGE Publications.

Williams, F. P., & McShane, M. D. (2010). *Criminological theory* (5th ed.). Upper Saddle River, N.J.: Pearson/Prentice Hall.

Men, Masculinities, and Crime

JAMES MESSERSCHMIDT

In recent years, there has emerged a new and growing interest in the relationship among men, masculinities, and crime. Since the early 1990s, numerous works have been published, from individually authored books (Collier, 1998; Hobbs, 1995; Messerschmidt, 1993, 1997, 2000; Polk, 1994; Winlow, 2001), to edited volumes (Bowker, 1998; Newburn & Stanko, 1994; Sabo, Kupers, & London, 2001), to special issues of academic journals (Carlen & Jefferson, 1996). This is not the first time criminologists have been interested in masculinity and its relationship to crime. Such luminaries as Edwin Sutherland and Albert Cohen can be credited with actually placing masculinity on the criminological agenda by perceiving the theoretical importance of the gendered nature of crime. Yet these criminologists understood gender through a biologically based sex-role theory, the weaknesses of which are now well understood: It provides no grasp of gendered power, human agency, and the varieties of masculinities and femininities constructed historically, cross-culturally, in a given society, and throughout the life course (Connell, 1987). Moreover, the social and historical context in which Sutherland and Cohen wrote embodied a relative absence of feminist theorizing and politics and a presumed natural difference between women and men (Messerschmidt, 1993).

The social situation today is dramatically different. Second-wave feminism—originating in the 1960s—challenged the masculinist nature of academia by illuminating the patterns of gendered power that to that point social theory had all

Reprinted by permission from *Handbook of Studies on Men and Masculinities*, edited by Michael S. Kimmel, Jeff Hearn and R. W. Connell (2005).

but ignored. In particular, feminism secured a permanent role for sexual politics in popular culture and moved analysis of gendered power to the forefront of much social thought. Moreover, feminist research—within and without criminology—spotlighted the nature and pervasiveness of violence against women. Since the mid-1970s, feminist scholars have examined girls' and women's crime, the social control of girls and women, and women working in the criminal justice system (see Daly & Chesney-Lind, 1988; Naffine, 1995). The importance of this feminist work is enormous. It has contributed significantly to the discipline of criminology and has made a lasting impact. Not only is the importance of gender to understanding crime more broadly acknowledged within the discipline, but it has led, logically, to the critical study of masculinity and crime. Boys and men are no longer seen as the "normal subjects"; rather, the social construction of masculinities has come under careful criminological scrutiny.

Feminism has exerted a major impact on my life personally, and academically it has influenced me to concentrate my work on masculinities and crime. Two issues were critical in my decision. First, as R. W. Connell taught us, when we think about gender in terms of power relations, as with any structure of power and inequality (such as race and class), it becomes necessary to study the powerful (men!). It is particularly important if we are committed to constructing a more equal society. Indeed, we must examine the advantaged, analyze how they act to reproduce that advantage, and probe what interest they may have in changing. Thus one reason for studying differences among men and diversity of masculinities is to promote possibilities for change.

Additionally, the gendered practices of men and boys raise significant questions about crime. Men and boys dominate crime. Arrest, self-report, and victimization data reflect that men and boys perpetrate more of the conventional crimes, including the more serious of these crimes, than do women and girls. Moreover, men have a virtual monopoly on the commission of syndicated, corporate, and political crime. Indeed, gender has been advanced consistently by criminologists as the strongest predictor of criminal involvement. Consequently, studying masculinities provides insights into understanding the highly gendered ratio of crime in industrialized societies and, perhaps, how to achieve a more equal society.

What follows is a "progress report" on current criminological thinking about men, masculinities, and crime. I begin with a brief outline of my initial approach to masculinities and crime and then critically examine several new directions in the criminological literature.

Masculinities and Crime as Structured Action

In *Masculinities and Crime* (Messerschmidt, 1993), I combined the theoretical work of Connell (1987), West and Zimmerman (1987), and Giddens (1981) to achieve a perspective that emphasized both the meaningful actions of individual agents and the structural features of social settings. Following West and Zimmerman (1987), I argued that gender is a situated, social and interactional accomplishment that grows out of social practices in specific settings and serves to inform such practices in reciprocal relation—we coordinate our activities to "do" gender in situational ways. Crucial to this conceptualization of gender as situated accomplishment is West and Zimmerman's (1987) notion of "accountability." Because individuals realize that they may be held accountable to others for their behavior, they configure and orchestrate their actions in relation to how these might be interpreted by others in the particular social context in which they occur. Within social interaction, then, we facilitate the ongoing task of accountability by demonstrating that we are male or female through concocted behaviors that may be interpreted accordingly. Consequently, we do gender differently depending on the social situation and the social circumstances we encounter. "Doing gender," then, renders us accountable for our social action in terms of normative conceptions, attitudes, and activities appropriate to one's sex in the specific social situation in which one acts (West & Zimmerman, 1987).

Nevertheless, "doing gender" does not occur in a vacuum but is influenced by the social-structural constraints we experience. Social structures are regular and patterned forms of interaction over time that constrain and enable behavior in specific ways; therefore, social structures "exist as the reproduced conduct of situated actors" (Giddens, 1976, p. 127). Following Connell (1987) and Giddens (1976), I pointed out that these social structures are neither external to social actors nor simply and solely constraining; on the contrary, structure is realized only through social action, and social action requires structure as its condition. Thus, as people do gender, they reproduce and sometimes change social structures. Not only, then, are there many ways of doing gender—we must speak of masculinities and femininities—gender must be viewed as *structured action*, or what people do under specific social-structural constraints.

In this way, gender relations link each of us to others in a common relationship: We share structural space. Consequently, shared blocks of gendered knowledge evolve through interaction in which specific gender ideals and activities play a part. Through this interaction, masculinity is institutionalized, permitting men to draw on such existing, but previously formed, masculine ways of thinking and acting to construct a masculinity for specific settings. The particular criteria of masculinity are embedded in the social situations and recurrent practices whereby social relations are structured (Giddens, 1989).

Accordingly, men are positioned differently throughout society, and socially organized power relations among men are constructed historically on the basis of class, race, and sexual orientation. That is, in specific contexts, some men enjoy greater power than do other men. In this sense, masculinity can be understood only as a relational construct. Connell's (1987) notion of "hegemonic masculinity" is crucial to understanding the power relations among men. Hegemonic masculinity is the culturally idealized form of masculinity in a given historical and social setting.

It is culturally honored, glorified, and extolled situationally—such as at the broader societal level (e.g., through the mass media) and at the institutional level (e.g., in school)—and is constructed in relation to "subordinated masculinities" (e.g., homosexuality) and in relation to women. Hegemonic masculinity influences, but does not determine, masculine behavior—the cultural ideals of hegemonic masculinity do not correspond to the actual identities of most men (Connell, 1987, pp. 184–185). Thus, masculinity is based on a social construct that reflects unique circumstances and relationships—a social construction that is renegotiated in each particular context. In this way, men construct varieties of masculinities through specific practices as they simultaneously reproduce, and sometimes change, social structures.

Following this approach, I conceptualized masculinity and crime in new ways—ways that enabled criminologists to explore how and in what respect masculinity is constituted in certain settings at certain times, and how that construct relates to crime (Messerschmidt, 1993). I have argued that one crucial way (not the only way) to understand the "making of crime" by men is to analyze "the making of masculinities." Of course, men's resources for accomplishing masculinity vary depending on position within class, race, age, and gender relations. These differences are reflected in the salience of particular crimes available as resources for accomplishing masculinity. Accordingly, different crimes are chosen as means for doing masculinity and for distinguishing masculinities from each other in different social settings. My work not only criticized traditional criminological theory and radical and socialist feminism but explained class and race differences in male adolescent crimes and in a variety of adult male crimes, from domestic violence to corporate crime (Messerschmidt, 1993).

Recently, two new directions in masculinities and crime literature have emerged: (a) psychoanalysis and (b) difference, the body, and crime. I discuss each of these directions in turn.

Psychoanalysis

Tony Jefferson (1996b, p. 340) noted 8 years ago that contemporary work on masculinity and crime fails to address a crucial criminological question: "why only particular men from a given class or race background (usually only a minority) come to identify with the crime option, while others identify with other resources to accomplish their masculinity" (p. 341). More recently, John Hood-Williams (2001, p. 43) echoed Jefferson by observing that most crime is not committed by men but, rather, by a "highly specific sub-group of the category 'men' "—even though the group's members do not form a unified subgroup. Thus he asks this question: Why is it that "only a minority of men need to produce masculinity through crime rather than through other, noncriminal, means?" (p. 44). Both are fair and provocative questions. Hood-Williams did not offer an argument to resolve these questions, but Jefferson, in sketchy form, has advanced what he calls a "psychosocial theory." Let us then scrutinize Jefferson's perspective.

Jefferson combines the postmodernist notion of discourse with such psycho-analytic concepts as anxiety and the alleged unconscious defenses of "splitting" and "projection" to understand the discursive positions adopted by individuals.[1] Jefferson (1996b, p. 341) argues that social structures are "dissolved into a plethora of discourses" and criticizes postmodernism for making the individual an effect of discourse, as this simply reproduces the determinism of structuralism. In contrast, Jefferson contends that to break from this "deterministic impasse," criminology must conceptualize how individuals position themselves in relation to the discur-sive choices facing them and how they come to adopt particular positions and not others: "how people become invested in, motivated by, or identified with particular [discursive] positions" (p. 341).

A return to psychoanalysis, Jefferson maintains, would allow such an under-standing of the relationship among subjects, discourses, masculinity, and crime. Jefferson turns to the work of the Austrian child psychoanalyst Melanie Klein (1882–1960) on how behavior allegedly is related to unconscious defenses against anxiety. Following Klein, Jefferson argues that the key to understanding the dis-cursive choices made by individuals—which are choices that collectively consti-tute a person's "identity"—is "to be found in the defensive attempts people make to ward off anxiety, to avoid feelings of powerlessness" (Jefferson, 1996a, p. 158). Application of this perspective has involved deconstructions of various journalistic accounts of sensational crimes, as well as interviews with men and women on the fear of crime, highlighting how anxieties result from feelings of powerlessness and, thus, how individuals choose masculine "subject positions" that permit them to gain sufficient power over other people to protect their anxiety-driven, insecure selves.

The world heavyweight boxing champion Mike Tyson, and his involvement in crime as a young boy, is a case in point. In a number of papers, Jefferson (1996a, 1996c, 1997b, 1998) examined the life of Tyson from a "little fairy boy" to "the complete destroyer." Although Jefferson provides an account of Tyson's life from childhood to boxing career, our interest here is his analysis of Tyson's eventual involvement in youth crime. Thus what follows is a brief synopsis of Jefferson's account of Tyson "becoming delinquent."

Jefferson (1996a) reports that as a child, Tyson experienced chronic poverty, emotional malnourishment (his father was absent and his mother drank, fought with her boyfriend, and eventually could not cope), "and a genetic endowment that gave him a body and a head too big and bulky for either his years or his soft, lisping voice, the kind of combination that made him a constant target of bullying" (p. 155). It is not surprising that for most of his childhood, Tyson was passive and withdrew into a less-threatening "inner world," but that withdrawal did not save him from continued peer abuse. One particular bullying incident was a turning point in Tyson's life. One day an older local bully assumed Tyson was a safe tar-get for abuse because of his reputation for passivity and, consequently, the bully proceeded to rip the head off one of Tyson's beloved pigeons (which he kept as pets). In this specific situation, Tyson did not remain docile as he had in the past;

not only did he choose to fight back, he was successful in physically defeating the older bully. From that time on, Tyson no longer was compliant and reserved in interaction with his peers, and he eventually became a "badass" member of the Jolly Stompers, a Brooklyn street gang. How does Jefferson explain this movement from "little fairy boy" to "badass" gang member? Because Tyson now embraced a "tough guy" discourse that denoted the ability to survive on the street through the capacity to meet and resist physical challenges. Not explaining why Tyson at this particular time chose to favor this specific discourse—nor if the endorsement of this discourse was prior to or after the successful assault of the bully—Jefferson (1996c, p. 102) does argue that, given Tyson's powerless position, based on his own unique biography, such a discourse offered Tyson an attractive masculine subject position because it protected him from the anxiety of powerlessness and vulnerability. As Jefferson (1996c) notes, Tyson's childhood experiences were "symptomatic of an unhealthy level of anxiety for a young child" (p. 94). Consequently, these "anxiety-inducing" discourses became the object of splitting and projection. In other words, the "little fairy boy" is

> split off and projected outwards, onto the new victims who then become despised (hence legitimate victims) for "possessing" the bad, weak parts which had become too painful for Tyson to accommodate in himself. This bullying, and the accompanying crime, took Tyson from the ghetto to the reformatory and, we can assume, new anxieties. But, rather than "own" these, his recidivism and growing reputation as a hardcore delinquent suggests a continuation of the splitting. (p. 102)

In sum, Tyson experienced a specific set of social and psychic consequences that "add up to a compelling satisfaction in or desire to inflict punishment and thereby triumph over the threat of having it inflicted" (Jefferson, 1998, p. 94).

Jefferson's psychosocial theory of masculinity and crime clearly has intuitive appeal and is a provocative contribution to the literature. Nevertheless, serious problems seem inherent in his perspective. Let me highlight a few.

Although Jefferson (1997b) acknowledges that "the social world is traversed by relations of power (class, gender, race, etc.)" (p. 286), such power relations quickly vanish from Jefferson's analysis because allegedly they "can only signify, and hence be understood by individual subjects, through available discourses." Consequently, in Jefferson's theory of masculinity and crime, there is scant discussion of gendered power relations (either between men and women or among men) and how such power is connected to race and class and, eventually, crime.

Because of this lack of theoretical attention to power, Jefferson argues that social meaning is only and always the product of available discourses, not social structures. Indeed, for Jefferson, social structures disappear into an overabundance of discourses. Jefferson is interested in how individuals allegedly position themselves in relation to all of the so-called discursive choices facing them—that is, how they come to adopt particular "subject positions" and not others. The problem with this theoretical beginning is that we never learn from where all these alleged discourses come and, therefore, never learn of all the so-called available subject positions. In other words, what is the empirical base of discourse? In the Tyson example, where did the "tough guy" discourse originate? Jefferson ignores the fact that discourse is constructed through practice, is structurally connected with other practices, and has much in common with other forms of practice (Connell, 1987). Jefferson's perspective seems unable to demonstrate—indeed, is glaringly uninterested in—the source of the discourse in relation to which individuals allegedly position themselves. This is a major difficulty, because without such empirical verification, literally anything could be defined as discourse, depending on how the theorist chooses to interpret it.

Even within individual case studies such as that of Tyson, we do not learn specifically *how* the particular individual becomes "invested in" or "identified with" a certain discourse but not others or *when* that investment or identification takes place. What does it actually mean to become invested in or identified with a particular discourse? How does this investment or identification actually occur? What is the particular process? Because Tyson is part of the "specific sub-group of the category 'men'" that engages in crime, it seems imperative to grasp the various discourses available to the adolescent Tyson and why, when, and how he chose the "tough guy" discourse and rejected others. However, there is nothing built into Jefferson's perspective that permits selection among the various possibilities of discourse in a particular social situation or when or how the subject invests or identifies with such discourses.

I agree that it is important to explain why particular men identify with the crime option and other men, from similar milieux, do not. Given Jefferson's parallel concern with this issue, one would expect this to be a priority in his research agenda. Surprisingly, he makes no attempt to address this topic. Other than his efforts at theory construction (e.g., Jefferson, 1994), in all of his published work to date, we are simply provided with individual case studies of boys' or men's involvement in crime, specifically, interpersonal violence. Consequently, Jefferson is unable to explain why individuals with very similar backgrounds—that is, positioned similarly with regard to available discursive choices and suffering similar anxieties—chose not to engage in crime. In other words, following the logic of Jefferson's perspective, it is not sufficient to point out that Tyson, for example, is anxiety driven and chose to adopt the "tough guy" discourse—it is necessary to specify why people in the same milieu as Tyson responded to similar anxieties in *noncriminal* ways. Fortunately, the vast majority of male youth in the ghetto who suffer similar biographical powerlessness and emotional malnourishment do not join gangs or engage in violence. Why don't they? What discourse do they adopt, and why did Tyson not adopt that alternative discourse? In short, Jefferson fails to investigate the effects of childhood powerlessness and emotional malnourishment on nonviolent boys and men, and he simultaneously ignores the range of masculine paths in Tyson's childhood milieu and the interconnections among these differing masculinities. Indeed, masculinity can only be understood in relation to the variety of masculinities in each social situation.

An additional problem is the psychoanalytic angle Jefferson attaches to discourse. As with his conception of discourse, he does not subject the "unconscious" process by which individuals allegedly split and project to empirical verification; he simply infers it. How then do we know that such splitting and projection take place? The only possible answer is that Jefferson says so. Arguably, such so-called psychic processes as the "unconscious," "splitting," and "projection" can never be the objects of direct observation. Therefore, these concepts can be constructed only by Jefferson, who, by giving a name and form to them (following Klein), does not discover them but simply creates them. Thus, as with most psychoanalytic theories, the alleged psychic processes can, for Jefferson, only be hypothetical and speculative, and therefore their validity is highly questionable. It is Jefferson who imagines (and thus contrives) what the empirical evidence cannot supply: that anxious individuals—like Mike Tyson—"unconsciously split and project." In short, Jefferson's identified psychoanalytic terms are nonmeasureable, and, consequently, his theory is nonfalsifiable.

Moreover, because (according to Jefferson) anxieties result from feelings of powerlessness, it should not be surprising to find that when he discusses men, he examines only those who at some point in their lives experienced extreme masculine powerlessness and subsequently became involved in interpersonal violence rather than those who experienced feelings of powerfulness and subsequently became involved in interpersonal violence. Because Jefferson concentrates on powerlessness (but, as stated earlier, ignores a reciprocal conception of power), his perspective is unable to account for boys and men who do not fit this stereotype—the powerful male who is full of self-confidence (and does not "feel" powerlessness) yet also engages in violence. Research shows that certain forms of violence may be associated with, for example, threatened egotism: "highly favorable views of self that are disputed by some person or circumstance" (Baumeister, Smart, & Boden, 1996, p. 5). When individuals who regard themselves as "superior beings" are challenged in some way, they may respond with physical violence. As Baumeister and colleagues (1996) have shown,

> Aggression emerges from a particular discrepancy between two views of self: a favorable self appraisal and an external appraisal that is much less favorable. That is, people turn aggressive when they receive feedback that contradicts their favorable views of themselves and implies that they should adopt less favorable views. More to the point, it is mainly people who refuse to lower their self-appraisals who become violent. (p. 8)

Consequently, although perhaps unintentionally, Jefferson's work reads as though no such self-confident males exist and therefore appears to assume that only certain males are "deviantly" anxiety driven, and that it is "those guys" who commit violence. Jefferson asks us to assume that all crimes committed by boys and men result from splitting and projection because of anxious powerlessness. In doing so, he reifies masculinity by arguing that it results from anxious powerlessness common to all violent men. Clearly, a satisfactory theory requires a more thoroughgoing appreciation of the varieties of masculinities and their relation to violence.

Moreover, Jefferson's concentration exclusively on interpersonal violence is problematic. Other crimes that arc predominantly "male"—such as robbery, burglary, syndicated crime, and the varieties of corporate and political crimes—are underrepresented and therefore undertheorized in Jefferson's work. Thus, one is left with the impression that masculinity (and thus gender) matters only in crimes involving interpersonal violence. Or are we to assume that boys and men involved in crimes other than those involving interpersonal violence similarly experience anxious powerlessness and subsequently split and project prior to committing such crimes?

In addition, Jefferson only speaks of men and masculinity, ignoring the reality that women and girls sometimes do masculinity (as well as violence). As Hood-Williams (2001) asks, "Are we to believe that the genders really do constitute coherent, uniform categories whose social and psychic consequence is a perfect, homogenous binary?" (p. 39). In other words, there is nothing built into Jefferson's perspective that allows for the conceptualization of women, girls, masculinities, and crime. Consequently, his perspective reifies gender difference.

Finally, although Jefferson attempts a psychoanalytic interpretation of masculinity, the concepts he uses to analyze "unconscious" psychic processes—anxiety, splitting, and projection—have nothing to do with gender (Hood-Williams, 2001). As Hood-Williams points out, there is "nothing in the character or structuring of the psyche that explains sexual difference. That must come from elsewhere" (p. 52). And that elsewhere is, according to Hood-Williams, found in the social realm: Masculinity "does not express an inner, psychic, core" but is the "performative work of acts, gestures, enactments" and, consequently, "this means recognizing that masculinity must be understood phenomenologically" (p. 53).

Jefferson (2001) most recently recognized that the Kleinian concepts he employs are gender-neutral terms, and, as he states, this forces him "into the realm of the social to explain sexual difference, but without denying the (irreducible) significance of the psyche" (p. 11). To connect psychic processes with the performance of masculinity (which means, for Jefferson, masculine practices by men, *not* by women), Jefferson initially turns to the work of Nancy Chodorow (1978) on the differential significance of maternal separation for boys and girls. Chodorow argues that because women typically are the primary caretakers of children—because of the unequal gender division of labor in child care—both boys and girls develop early, intense relations with the mother. When the time comes to separate from her, however, this separation process occurs in different ways for boys and girls. According to Chodorow, girls remain closer to the mother than do boys and, therefore, girls do not experience a sharp break from Mom. Consequently, girls achieve femininity by being like their mothers and internalize "feminine" characteristics, such as a capacity for empathy with, and dependence on, others—first their mother, later their spouse. For boys, becoming masculine requires their becoming different from mother and separating completely from her by repudiating all that is feminine. Consequently, boys fail to learn empathy for others and become fearful of intimacy and dependence. Boys' psyches, then, are well suited to being achievement oriented; girls' psyches are well adapted to emotional work. In this way, the gender division of labor in parenting is reproduced as boys become the breadwinners and girls become the primary caretakers of children. The unequal gender division of labor in parenting is reproduced in the psyches of individuals, and masculine dominance is reinforced.

Feminists have criticized Chodorow's thesis for being ahistorical, for falsely universalizing childhood experience, for ignoring differences of race and class, and for being incomplete as a theory of women's subordination because it does not explain how the gender division of labor in parenting emerged (Jaggar, 1983). In addition, Connell (1998, p. 457) points out that the reasons for the reproduction of this specific division of labor probably have little to do with psychology; more likely, they involve the economic costs to families from the loss of a man's wage. Connell goes on to point out—as has Chodorow (1994, 1999)—that a gender division of labor in parenting does not necessarily produce dichotomous gender patterns in later life.

It is perplexing why Jefferson now suddenly supports Chodorow's thesis. As is evident, Chodorow's work is a theory of the reproduction of a specific *social structure* and has nothing to say about *discourse*. This is particularly problematic because Jefferson, as stated earlier, argues that social structures disappear into an overabundance of discourses. Additionally, Jefferson (1998, p. 92) had previously rejected Chodorow's position as a much too general and sociological account of gender formation even though it retained psychoanalytic terminology. Although Jefferson (2001) more recently agreed that Chodorow's thesis is reductive and generalizing, he nevertheless feels that as "an internal process early psychic separation provides the (psychic) preconditions for entry into the (social) world of male domination" (p. 12). In an attempt to save his theory by overcoming the reductive character of Chodorow's perspective, unexpectedly, Jefferson turns to the work of Jessica Benjamin (1998) rather than Chodorow's (1999) most recent reformulation of her thesis.[2]

Benjamin (1998) argues that separation from mother into masculine dominance is but one path the boy may take, and it must be supplemented by an account of the father and the child's identification with him: "This redefines the preoedipal position as one characterized by multiple identifications with both mother and father (or substitutes) and what they symbolize" (Jefferson, 2001, p. 13). The universal task of the child now is not one-dimensional, but rather involves

> separating from a particular mother (and her particular relationship to gender) and learning to share her with a particular father (and his particular relationship to gender) against a backdrop of managing the inevitable excitement and anxiety generated by loving attachments, both the desire for (object love) and the desire to be like

(identificatory love). The timing and management of these universal tasks will determine how any particular individual relates to questions of sexual difference. (p. 13)

Curiously, Jefferson's perspective abruptly ends here without showing how such "timing and management" of the so-called "universal tasks" result in different types of masculinity and how such masculinities eventually are related to crime. Moreover, Jefferson seems to assume a unilateral influence from individual parental figures in childhood to specific constructions of gender without providing any theoretical space for influences outside the family context—such as peers and teachers— or what agency the infant has in this interaction. Indeed, Jefferson neglects research on agency that specifically shows how infants are born into a world populated by self-regulating participants in the interactional achievement of masculinities and femininities. For example, this research suggests that through interaction with others, infants are exposed to gender "contingencies of reinforcement" and, as a result, infants exhibit specific but differentiated patterns of gendered behavior (Cahill, 1986, p. 170). In other words, for some time, research has explained early gender development in infancy not through separation anxiety but as a reflexive process between the infant and others' (parents', children's, and adults') mutual reinforcement.

Consequently, Jefferson's psychosocial theory begs the question: Does a psychoanalytic dimension add a necessary explanatory level to our understanding of masculinities and crime? Because of its sketchy and incomplete nature, as well as the numerous inherent problems associated with his perspective, as outlined, we can only conclude that it does not. (Indeed, Jefferson's [2003] most recent statement of his theory ignores gender altogether.) Instead, a satisfactory theory of masculinities and crime requires an understanding of the meanings boys and men attach to their social actions and how these actions are related to conscious choice and specific social structures in particular settings. It is to the latter that we now turn our attention.

Difference, the Body, and Crime

Despite the problems inherent in psychoanalysis, Jefferson raises an important limitation of past masculinity and crime research: the failure to inquire why some boys and men engage in crime and other boys and men from the same milieu do not, and why those who do engage in crime commit different types of crimes. In addition, Collier (1998) pointed to a second oversight: the importance of the body and its relation to crime. To these beneficial criticisms, it should be added that earlier work on masculinities and crime has not addressed adequately the relationship among masculinities, race, and class. In other words, to understand crime, we must comprehend how gender, race, and class relations are part of all social existence and not view each relation as extrinsic to the others. Because crime operates through a complex series of gender, race, and class practices, crime usually is more than a single activity. In this final section, then, I discuss some recent criminological work that has begun to address these criticisms.

For some time, criminologists have been attempting to conceptualize the "intersection" of gender, race, class, and crime. For example, 8 years ago, an edited volume by Schwartz and Milovanovic (1996) examined, as the title suggests, *Race, Gender, and Class in Criminology: The Intersection*. As well, Marino Bruce's (1997) work on youth crime specifically investigated the interrelation of race and class with the construction of masculinities by delinquent lower working class boys. Similarly, Mark Lettiere's (1997) ethnographic study of masculinities among African American, white, and Latino men in a homeless heroin-addict community showed how "doing begging" and "doing crime" are resources for "doing" different racialized masculinities and thus for constructing a power hierarchy among these men. Most recently, Barak, Flavin, and Leighton (2001) show how gender, race, and class affect the nature and functioning of the criminal justice system, and Jurik and Martin (2001) demonstrate historically how gender, race, class, and sexuality frame and organize work, specifically in policing and corrections. One of the difficulties criminological theorists have experienced is conceptualizing how gender, race, and class are linked or how they actually intersect. The attraction of Jurik and Martin's (2001) work is that they have shown conclusively how workplace social interaction constructs and reaffirms gender, race, and class differences.

A specific method for connecting social interaction with gender, race, class, and crime is the life history. The life history is an important qualitative method because it necessitates a close consideration of the meaning of social life for those who enact it as a way of revealing their experiences, choices, practices, and social world. No other social science method provides as much detail about social development and change as does a life-history study of practices over time.

In *Crime as Structured Action* (Messerschmidt, 1997), I explore, for example, the changes in Malcolm X's masculinities within a range of race and class social contexts: a childhood in which he constantly battled for acceptance as a young man; a zoot-suit culture that embraced him without stigma as a "hipster" and "hustler"; and a spiritual and political movement that celebrated him as father, husband, and national spokesperson. Across these sites and through shifting currencies of his sense of gender, race, and class, Malcolm X moved in and out of crime. Malcolm X simply appropriated crime as a resource for doing masculinity at a specific moment in his life, a period when gender, race, and class relations were equally significant. In this way, the life-history method provides data not only about why people engage in crime at certain stages of their lives but how that engagement relates to the salience of various combinations of gender, race, and class.[3]

My most recent research involves life-history interviews of violent and nonviolent boys and addresses the following questions: Why is it that some boys engage in violence and some boys do not? and Why do the boys who engage in violence commit different types of violence? (Messerschmidt, 2000). The goal of each interview was an attempt to reflect the situational accomplishment of masculinities and the eventual use of violence (or nonviolence) as an outcome of specific choices in a subject's personal life history.

Because of space constraints, I cannot discuss all of the life stories. However, for a taste of the data, I present the life stories of two of the boys interviewed—Hugh and Zack—who simultaneously lived in the same working class neighborhood and attended the same high school, yet took different paths: One became a sex offender and the other an assaultive offender. These two cases, then, are juxtaposed nicely because they report data as to why boys from the same social milieu come to engage in different types of violence. What follows is a brief outline of their life stories and how their differing forms of violence are related to their body, structured action, and masculinity.

Both boys grew up in working class homes that articulated for them a practiced definition of masculine power. In their separate families, Hugh and Zack found themselves in milieux in which they were attached to an adult male—Hugh to his grandfather and Zack to his uncle—who both emphasized hegemonic masculinity through practice. This attachment led both boys consciously to undertake to practice what was being preached and represented. Connell (1995) defines this proactive adoption of "family values" (such as manual and athletic skills and male power and control of others) as the "moment of engagement" with hegemonic masculinity, "the moment at which the boy takes up the project of hegemonic masculinity as his own" (p. 122). Although constructed in different ways, such moments of engagement occurred in both boys' lives through interaction—junctures when the individual boys consciously chose to engineer a newly professed masculinity. Moreover, for both Hugh and Zack, an important part of this engagement with hegemonic masculinity entailed a commitment to the "family value" that use of physical violence is an appropriate means to solve interpersonal problems. In other words, both boys chose to embrace the practice (constructed within their families and the school attended) that physical violence is the fitting and well-chosen masculine response to threat—a "real man" was obligated to respond in this fashion.[4] Although both boys were similar in the sense of accepting that the legitimate response to threat is physical retaliation, the differences between them surfaced during interactions at school.

We begin our examination of these differences with the case of Hugh, an assaultive, tall, and well-built 15-year-old. Hugh was rewarded with favorable appraisal from others for his physicality—at home from his grandfather, at school from other kids, and from his peers in the gang he joined. Consider the following dialogue about Hugh's fighting ability at school:

Q.   What did the other kids think about you fighting?

A.   Since I was a good fighter, everybody my age looked up to me, you know. I wasn't afraid to fight. I liked it. I was the only one my age who fought the older kids.

Q.   How did that make you feel?

A.   Better than the others.

Q.   Why?

A.   Always, ever since I can remember, I'd say I wasn't going to let anybody push me around. I was going to be like Gramps—a force in this world.

Q.   Did you want to be like Gramps? Was he a force?

A.   Yeah. He didn't let people push him around.

Q.   Did the other kids think of you as a force?

A.   They looked up to me, as I said. Because it wasn't about beating the older kids up or them beating me up. It was that I held my own. I didn't let people walk all over me. And they thought that was cool.

Q.   Did you develop a reputation?

A.   Yeah. I became that force, you know. In the back of kids' minds it would always be like, "Man, is this kid going to hit me?" So they didn't mess with me. I was strong and good with my fists, you know. (Messerschmidt, 2000, p. 53)

This dialogue discloses the intricate interplay of Hugh's body with the social processes of becoming a "force" at school. The social requirement to validate one as a masculine force—that is, physically fighting—is an embodied practice that connects specific bodily skill and competence ("good with my fists") with a predictable consequence to that practice ("they looked up to me" and "they thought that was cool"). Hugh consciously responded to masculinity challenges by constructing a bodily presence in school ("I held my own") that was revered by his classmates.

This construction of being a "force" eventually led Hugh to attacking teachers physically. Hugh expressed to me that the physical power he exerted on the playground gave him the confidence to challenge a teacher's power in the classroom under certain conditions. I asked Hugh for an example of when such violence might occur:

> The teacher told me to do my work and I'd say: "I don't want to do my work." And then the teacher would say I had to, and then I'd throw my desk at him. I couldn't stay in class and do what I had to do. I was always getting in trouble. I was the one getting detention and stuff. I'd throw my desk and walk out, sayin' "Fuck you." (Messerschmidt, 2000, p. 54)

When I asked Hugh how it made him feel to respond that way, he stated,

> It felt good. It was a sense of retaliation, you know. I was doing something about it. And after I got out of the principal, kids would pat me on the back. They all wanted to be my friend, you know. I had a reputation of not being pushed around by teachers, and I liked that. So I did it more. (Messerschmidt, 2000, p. 54)

Being tall and muscular for his age, Hugh's bodily resources empowered him to implement physically confrontational practices when he encountered masculinity challenges. His body served, in part, as agent and resource in his practice of embodied force; thus, Hugh embodied power at school through a calculated effort to present his body in a specific way.

For Hugh, then, his body *facilitated* masculine agency. In the face of masculinity challenges from other students and teachers, he successfully constructed himself as a "tough guy" who was "superior" to his victims—his assaultive acts enforced and shaped masculine boundaries. Indeed, his physical ability to fight when provoked convinced him of his own eminent masculine self-worth. His bodily resources empowered him to implement a physically confrontational masculinity, permitted him to resist the school physically, and enabled him to construct specific behavior patterns—acting out in class, bullying other students, and assaulting students and teachers. Thus, within the social setting of the school, Hugh's body became his primary resource for masculine power and esteem and simultaneously constructed his victims as subordinate.

In certain ways, Hugh was following the bodily dictates of the school social structure in which he was embedded. Research shows that in junior high and high school, the tallest and strongest boys are usually the most popular, admired by peers (and parents and teachers) for their size and athletic prowess (Thorne, 1993). In the context of school, a boy's height and musculature increase self-esteem and prestige, thus creating a more positive body image (Thorne, 1993). Research on male adolescent development reveals that boys are acutely aware of the changes in themselves during puberty, as well as other people's responses to those changes (Petersen, 1988). Boys who participate in sports, for example, state that "they take pleasure in their agency and their bodies simultaneously. They feel like they accomplish things in their bodies and in their lives" (Martin, 1996, p. 55).

As the testimonial indicates, Hugh had a very similar response to his embodied practices. Most of the time, Hugh's attention did not focus on his own embodiment; it was simply taken for granted. However, in times of verbally antagonistic and physically confrontational interactions at home and school—that is, during masculinity challenges—the body now became the central aspect of Hugh's attention and experience. Indeed, for Hugh, the body seized center stage and acted—because of its physical size, shape, and skill—according to his chosen masculine goal of being a force in the world. In other words, during these interactions entailing masculinity challenges, both gender and body were highly salient—they became the object of his practice. Moreover, his body facilitated masculine social action—it was a successful masculine resource—by creating boundaries between Hugh and his numerous victims.

Additionally, the embodied practices of Hugh show that such practices are intersubjective. That is, the space in which Hugh's assaultive actions occurred was occupied by others; and it is these others, in part, toward whom the assaultive actions were intended. As Crossley (1995) argues, embodied social action is "other oriented" and derives its sense or meaning from its participation in shared situations: Embodied action is "not only acting-towards-others; it is acting-towards-others in a way that is acceptable to others (in general) by virtue of its reliance upon commonly held rules and resources, and its observance of ritual considerations" (pp. 141–142). Hugh's assaultive actions, then, were accomplished in accordance with a shared masculine subjectivity of others who populated the same school and home space where the assaultive actions occurred.

But boys unlike Hugh—specifically, boys who do not possess the appropriate body shape and size and thus are unable to use their bodies in the physical ways proposed by the school social structure—frequently experience distress (Petersen, 1988). In the teen world, bodies are subject increasingly to inspection and surveillance by peers; and less muscular, nonathletic boys are often labeled "wimps" and "fags" (Kindlon & Thompson, 1999). In junior high and high school, masculine social hierarchies develop in relation to somatic type. Such somatic differentiation affirms inequality among boys, and in this way, diverse masculinities are constructed in relation to biological development (Canaan, 1998; Connell, 1987, 1995; Thorne, 1993). The relationship among these masculinities forms a specific social structure within the social setting of the school. For example, in most secondary schools, we are likely to find power relations between hegemonic masculinities (i.e., "cool guys," "tough guys," and "jocks") and subordinated masculinities (i.e., gay boys, "wimps," and "nerds"). Ethnographies of secondary education in Britain, Australia, and the United Sates consistently report such masculine power relationships, which construct a specific social structure in secondary schools (see Connell, 1996, for a review). In short, today the body increasingly has become crucial to self-image, especially among teenage youth. Through interaction at school, adolescents make bodies matter by constructing some bodies as more masculine than other bodies; thus, social structures are embodied.

Although Hugh's embodied practices represent hegemonic or exemplary masculinities at school, I found subordinate school masculinities in several of the adolescent male sex offenders I interviewed. Consider the case of Zack, who was 15 years old when I interviewed him. When he was in third grade, he gained a considerable amount of weight, and other students considered him "fat," as did he. The "cool guys" at school consistently verbally and physically abused Zack: "They'd call me 'fatty,' 'chubby cheeks,' 'wimp,' and stuff like that. I got pushed down a lot and stuff. I got beat up a lot in the schoolyard" (Messerschmidt, 2000, p. 42). The abuse for being overweight and the constant physical assault extended through grade school and middle school. Unlike some other kids at school, Zack chose not to respond physically to these masculinity challenges because he felt he would be "beat up." As Zack stated,

> I felt like I was a "wimp" 'cause I couldn't do what other boys did. I never could in my life. I couldn't do anything. Other people always told me what to do, I never told anybody. I felt pretty crappy about myself. (Messerschmidt, 2000, p. 43)

Consequently, the peer abuse at school exerted a masculinity challenge, and, subsequently, Zack attempted to invalidate his status as a "wimp" by joining the junior high football team. As Zack stated, "It would make me feel like I was actually worth something, like other guys, you know" (Messerschmidt, 2000, p. 43). However, during the summer, between fifth and sixth grades, Zack broke his wrist while attempting to "get in shape." He remained overweight, and although he tried out for the team in his sixth grade year, he was soon cut.

Also during his sixth grade year, Zack developed a sexual interest in girls. He learned this not from the adults in his life but through interaction at school. Because of the frequent "sex talk" at school, Zack wanted to experience sex to be like the other boys. Because Zack had never been able to arrange a date, he felt extremely "left out" and identified himself as a "virgin." The continual rejection by girls made Zack feel discontented: "I didn't really like myself 'cause girls didn't like me. I was fat and I just didn't seem to fit in. Like I'm the only virgin in the school."

Q.   Did you want to fit in?

A.   Yeah. And I tried really hard. I tried to play football so the popular guys would like me. I tried to dress differently, dress like they [popular kids] did. I tried going on diets. I tried to get girls. (Messerschmidt, 2000, p. 45)

Prior to the masculinity challenges he faced at school, Zack did not think much about his body. However, Zack's body became *much more a part of* his lived experience. This resulted in his body becoming a site of intersubjective disdain through interaction at school that led inevitably to his negative self-conceptualization. In turn, Zack made the conscious choice—to help fulfill his goal to be masculine—to attempt to "fit in" by reconstructing his body: He tried to get into shape to play football, dress "cool at school," and go on diets. In other words, Zack's body became an object of his practice as a result of its socially constructed subordinated presence. Zack actively worked on his body in an attempt to mold it into an "appropriate" gendered body for the particular school setting. Thus, his physical sense of masculinity was in part derived from his attempt to transform his body through social practices (Connell, 1987). In addition to this disciplined management of his body, Zack consciously attempted to obtain heterosexual dates. In all such attempts, however, he failed miserably.

Unable to be masculine like the "cool guys," the masculinity challenges exerted greater pressure on Zack, and he eventually turned to expressing control and power over his youngest female cousin through sex. During his sixth grade year—a time when he experienced the distressing events just described and "discovered" heterosexuality—Zack consciously chose to seek out his cousin: "I wanted to experience sex, like what other boys were doing. I wanted to do what they were talking about but I was rejected by girls at school" (Messerschmidt, 2000, p. 46). Zack sexually assaulted (fondling and oral penetration) his youngest cousin over a 3-year period by using a variety of seemingly nonviolent manipulative strategies. I asked Zack how it made him feel when he manipulated his cousin, and he stated, "It made me feel real good. I just felt like finally I was in control over somebody. I forgot about being fat and ugly. She was someone looking up to me, you know. If I needed sexual contact, then I had it. I wasn't a virgin anymore" (Messerschmidt, 2000, p. 47).

Zack saw himself as not "measuring up" physically to the school view of the ideal masculine body. Consequently, his body was a *restraint* on his agency—he could not do the masculine practices the "cool guys" were doing, including "fighting back" when bullied and engaging in sex with peers. Moreover, his immediate situation at school was seen by him as a dangerous place, as he inhabited the most subordinate position in the masculine power social structure of the school. Consequently, the embodied practices activated by the contextual interactions at school could be directed only outside the school situation. Zack's body became party to a surrogate practice that directed him toward a course of social action that was physically and sexually realizable. For Zack, then, the dominant masculine practices in school were not rejected. Rather, physical and sexual subordination directed Zack toward consciously fixating not only on his body, but on a specific site (the home) and a particular form of embodied conduct (sexual violence) where such masculine practices could be realized. Given that Zack was removed from any type of recognized masculine bodily status in school, the available sexual "outlet" at home was especially seductive and captivating, became an obsession, and was a powerful and pleasurable means of being masculine. In attempting to masculinize and heterosexualize his body within the captivating conceptualization of "cool guy" masculinity, Zack engendered a powerful sense of self by consciously "taking charge" at home and conquering his cousin's body through sexual violence. The choice to be sexually violent, then, was a situational masculine resource in which Zack could be dominant, powerful, and heterosexual through bodily practice. Thus, it was in this way that Zack's body shared in his social agency by shaping and generating his course of action toward sexual violence.

For Zack, then, the peer abuse and inability to "be a man" according to the social structure of the school brought about an absolute split between his subordinate masculinity and the masculinity of other boys—in particular, the "cool guys"— at school. Such, however, is not the case for Hugh. Although engaging in assaultive violence—as Hugh did—placed the body at center stage, it did not disrupt his masculine reality but rather confirmed it; his body was a superordinate masculine presence at school. Indeed, within the social context of Hugh's and Zack's school, such practices as physically fighting are experienced as part of masculine life, not placed outside it. Consequently, these acts maintain intentional links with other boys and reproduce the masculine school social structure of power—their success at assaultive actions enforced the boundary between hegemonic and subordinate masculinities. In contrast, Zack's habitual masculine world was disrupted and correlated with a new relation to his body—it now became a subordinate masculine presence at school. Thus, although Hugh's embodied violent actions are interwoven with others in a common masculine project, Zack constituted embodied subordination in the masculine power hierarchy at school. The result is that Zack experienced social isolation and a telic demand to be free from his subordinate masculine situation—which he "satisfied" through sexual violence.

In short, the interactions experienced by Hugh and Zack at school were situational moments marked by masculinity challenges in which each boy was defined as a rival to other boys, entailing a socially distant, hostile, and power relationship among them. For Zack, however, heterosexual meanings added to the power divide among boys. Yet in the brief, illusory moment of each sexually violent incident—in which the sex offender practiced spatial and physical dominance over his cousin—Zack was a "cool guy"; the subordinate was now the dominant.

Conclusion

Psychoanalysis provides little help in understanding these life stories and embodied practices. The goal for both Hugh and Zack was hegemonic masculinity and being a "cool guy" who could solve problems through interpersonal violence. In Sartre's (1956) words, this was their "fundamental choice," or the gendered attitude they took toward the world. Accordingly, both boys engaged in a *conscious choice* to pursue hegemonic masculinity (defined by the practices in their particular milieu of home and school) as their project, or the fundamental mode by which they chose to relate to the world and express themselves in it. Hugh and Zack's behavior, then, is best understood from the point of view of their socially structured, consciously chosen project rather than from some alleged yet spurious "unconscious" motivation. To appreciate why Hugh and Zack engaged in violence, we must first discover the planned project for both. This is the basic difference between the method employed here and that of Jefferson. Jefferson attempts to comprehend the person in light of "unconscious" antecedents; following Sartre (1956, 1963), I understand the person in light of his conscious choices—in particular, social situations—as he pursues future-oriented projects.

Additionally, the case studies of Hugh and Zack demonstrate that the materiality of bodies often matters in the pursuit of a project. Bodies participate in social action by delineating courses of social conduct: "Bodies in their materiality have both limits and capacities which are always in play in social processes" (Connell, 1998a, p. 6). Indeed, our bodies constrain or facilitate social action and therefore mediate and influence social practices. It is not surprising that it was through masculinity challenges—that is, when both body and gender became highly salient as organizing principles of interaction—and subsequent bodily and sexual subordination (Zack) or superordination (Hugh) that choice and behavior became focused in the specific direction of sexual violence (Zack) or assaultive violence (Hugh). The masculine social structure of the school each boy attended defined both physical and sexual performance as essential criteria for "doing masculinity." Thus, these dominant criteria—within the context of a body either able or unable to construct such criteria—directed the boys' ultimate choices of a specific type of violence and victimization. Nevertheless, both boys viewed their bodies as instruments—weapons in the service of a desire to dominate and control another body through a particular type of interpersonal violence. Accordingly, these two case studies help us understand the relationship among the body, masculinities, and differing types of violence.

Although not generalizable, these two case studies provide additional justification for structured action theory. It was the social structural power relations among differing masculinities at school that made the masculinity challenges and differing forms of violence possible, but not necessarily inevitable. The agency of Hugh and Zack, their interactions within that structure, and their ultimate conscious choices made the masculinity challenges and interpersonal violence happen—which, in turn, reproduced that masculine power social structure. Indeed, one way gender is built into institutions—such as schools—is through hierarchical divisions of masculine power. This particular power hierarchy was a regular and patterned form of interaction that constrained and channeled how the two boys conceptualized and chose to practice masculinity. The school masculine power relations became a constitutive principle of their masculine "identity" through being adopted as a personal project. Thus, the masculine personality of Hugh and Zack existed only as social actions fashioned in accordance with the school power hierarchy. Hugh reproduced a specific form of hegemonic masculinity through assaultive violence. Zack, although choosing to passively maintain his subordinate status within the confines of the school, actively attempted to invalidate that status for himself through sexual violence at home.

In closing, let me suggest some avenues for future research.

First, the current movement in criminology toward conceptualizing the interrelationship among gender, race, class, sexualities, and crime is an important direction for future research. Structured action theory provides *one* way to examine that interrelationship. Others will emerge. Moreover, we need a variety of methodological approaches, from historical and documentary research to ethnographies and life histories, to examine how gender, race, class, and sexuality differently affect crime.

Second, I do not suggest that the body is always salient to the commission of crime. Thus, we should investigate empirically when the body becomes salient to crime and when it does not. In other words, an important question for future research is, What is the relationship among the body, masculinities, and crime?

Third, because Connell (2000) correctly notes that "gender is social practice that constantly refers to bodies and what bodies do, it is not social practice reduced to the body" (p. 27), it follows that masculinities occasionally are enacted by girls and women. Consequently, an important research direction is the relationship between masculinities and crime by girls and women. Indeed, Jody Miller's (2001) important book *One of the Guys* points in this direction by showing how some gang girls consider the gang a "masculine enterprise" in which they participate in practices similar to those of the boys.[5]

Fourth, a new area of criminological study is globalization and crime. Criminological research on gender can contribute to this subject matter by examining how masculinities are related to crime in different societies and how they are linked to historical and contemporary conditions of globalization. Moreover, understanding masculinities and crime in industrialized societies (such as the United States) can be enhanced through a conceptualization of how globalization affects social conditions and thus crime in such societies. Simon Winlow's (2001) book, *Badfellas*, which examines the changes in masculinities and crime in the northeast of England since the 1880s and how those changes are related to globalization, has initiated the research in this area.

Fifth, how gender is constructed by criminal justice personnel is essential to understanding social control in industrialized societies. Jurik and Martin (2001), for example, have been prominent in this regard by showing specifically how the transformation of policing and corrections into professional occupations evinces a modification of hegemonic masculinity from being interpersonally and physically aggressive to wielding control through technical expertise. Moreover, in the important new book *Prison Masculinities*, Sabo et al. (2001) demonstrate, through the words of prisoners and academies, the varieties of masculinities constructed within that closed social setting.

Sixth, postmodern feminist criminologists have disclosed the importance of discourse analysis to the understanding of cultural conceptions of gender and crime (Collier, 1998; Young, 1996). The results of these researches are important, but it is essential to recognize, as stated earlier, that discourse is the result of practice. The work of Gray Cavender (1999) is prominent in this regard. For example, in "Detecting Masculinity," Cavender (1999) shows how masculinities are constructed differently in feature films by reason of historical context—1940s versus 1980s—and discourses that male actors practice as "detectives" in each of the films. We need more research that is similarly sensitive to how practice in particular social settings constructs discourse.

Finally, it is important to examine why some people engage in crime and others do not. A significant task, then, for future research is to discover what type of masculinity people construct who do not commit crime and how it is different from the gender of those who do commit crime.

In short, I recommend these as the chief areas of focus for those working in the area of masculinities and crime. All such studies seek to engage the demanding empirical inquiries that confidently will lead to theoretical reappraisal and, inevitably, to advances in theory.

Notes _____

1. For a postmodern position on masculinities and crime, see Collier (1998). For a critique of this position, see Messerschmidt (1999).

2. Either Jefferson does not know about this work or he rejects it simply because Chodorow is critical of discourse analysis.

3. *Crime as Structured Action* discusses numerous cases in which race, class, and masculinities affect crime. Additionally, the chapter on "lynchers" is unique in criminology through its examination of the role "whiteness" may play in crime.

4. "Violence to solve problems" clearly is a discourse but is rooted—for Hugh and Zack—in the structured actions of home and school.

5. See Messerschmidt (2004) for an examination of the similarities and differences of violent and nonviolent masculinities by both boys and girls.

References _____

Barak, G., Flavin, J. M., & Leighton, P. S. (2001). *Class, race, gender, and crime: Social realities of justice in America.* Los Angeles: Roxbury.

Baumeister, R. F., Smart, L., & Boden, J. M. (1996). Relation of threatened egotism to violence and aggression: The dark side of high self-esteem. *Psychological Review, 103*(1), 5–33.

Benjamin, J. (1998). *Shadow of the other: Intersubjectivity and gender in psychoanalysis.* New York: Routledge.

Bowker, L. (Ed.). (1998). *Masculinities and violence.* Thousand Oaks, CA: Sage.

Bruce, M. (1997, November). *Party animals and badasses: Evidence of the gender, race and class nexus.* Presented at the Annual Meeting of the American Society of Criminology, San Diego, CA.

Cahill, S. E. (1986). Childhood socialization as a recruitment process: Some lessons from the study of gender development. In P. A. Adler & P. Adler (Eds.), *Sociological studies of child development* (pp. 163–186). Greenwich, CT: JAI Press.

Canaan, J. (1998). Is "doing nothing" just boys' play? Integrating feminist and cultural studies: Perspectives on working-class young men's masculinity. In K. Daly & L. Maher (Eds.), *Criminology at the crossroads: Feminist readings in crime and justice* (pp. 172–187). New York: Oxford University Press.

Carlen, P., & Jefferson, T. (1996). (Eds.). Masculinities and crime. *British Journal of Criminology, 33*(6, Special issue).

Cavender, G. (1999). Detecting masculinity. In J. Ferrell & N. Websdale (Eds.), *Making trouble: Cultural constructions of crime, deviance, and control* (pp. 157–175). New York: Aldine de Gruyter.

Chodorow, N. J. (1978). *The reproduction of mothering.* Berkeley: University of California Press.

Chodorow, N. J. (1994). *Femininities, masculinities, sexualities: Freud and beyond.* Lexington: University of Kentucky Press.

Chodorow, N. J. (1999). *The power of feelings: Personal meaning in psychoanalysis, gender, and culture.* New Haven, CT: Yale University Press.

Coleman, J. S. (1988). Social capital in the creation of human capital. *American Journal of Sociology, 94* (Supplement: Organizations and Institutions: Sociological and Economic Approaches to the Analysis of Social Structure), S95–S120.

Collier, R. (1998). *Masculinities, crime and criminology: Men, heterosexuality and the criminal(ised) other.* London: Sage.

Connell, R. W. (1987). *Gender and power: Society, the person, and sexual politics.* Stanford, CA: Stanford University Press.

Connell, R. W. (1995). *Masculinities.* Berkeley: University of California Press.

Connell, R. W. (1996). Teaching the boys: New research on masculinity and gender strategies for schools. *Teachers College Record, 98*(2), 206–235.

Connell, R. W. (1998a). *Bodies, intellectuals, and world society.* Plenary address to British Sociological Association and Annual Conference, Edinburgh, Scotland.

Connell, R. W. (2000). *The men and the boys.* Sydney: Allen & Unwin.

Crossley, N. (1995). Body techniques, agency and intercorporeality: On Goffman's *Relations in Public. Sociology, 29*(1), 133–149.

Daly, K., & Chesney-Lind, M. (1988). Feminism and criminology. *Justice Quarterly, 5*(4), 497–538.

Giddens, A. (1976). *New rules of sociological method: A positive critique of interpretive sociologies.* New York: Basic Books.

Giddens, A. (1981). Agency, institution, and time-space analysis. In K. Knorr-Cetina & A. V. Cicourel (Eds.), *Advances in social theory and methodology: Toward an integration of micro- and macro-sociologies* (pp. 161–174). Boston, MA: Routledge.

Giddens, A. (1989). A reply to my critics. In D. Held & J. B. Thompson (Eds.), *Social theories of modern societies: Anthony Giddens and his critics* (pp. 249–301). New York: Cambridge University Press.

Hobbs, D. (1995). *Bad business: Professional crime in modern Britain.* New York: Oxford University Press.

Hood-Williams, J. (2001). Gender, masculinities and crime: From structures to psyches. *Theoretical Criminology, 5*(1), 37–60.

Jaggar, A. (1983). *Feminist politics and human nature.* Totowa, NJ: Rowman and Allanheld.

Jefferson, T. (1994). Theorizing masculine subjectivity. In T. Newburn & E. A. Stanko (Eds.), *Just boys doing business? Men, masculinities and crime* (pp. 10–31). New York: Routledge.

Jefferson, T. (1996a). From "little fairy boy" to "the complete destroyer": Subjectivity and transformation in the biography of Mike Tyson. In M. Mac an Ghaill (Ed.), *Understanding masculinities* (pp. 153–167). Philadelphia, PA: Open University Press.

Jefferson, T. (1996b). Introduction. *British Journal of Criminology, 36*(6), 337–347.

Jefferson, T. (1996c). "Tougher than the rest": Mike Tyson and the destructive desires of masculinity. *ARENA Journal, 6,* 89–105.

Jefferson, T. (1997a). Masculinities and crime. In M. Maguire, R, Morgan, & R. Reiner (Eds.), *The Oxford handbook of criminology* (pp. 535–557). Oxford, England: Clarendon Press.

Jefferson, T. (1997b). The Tyson rape trial: The law, feminism and emotional "truth." *Social and Legal Studies, 6*(2), 281–301.

Jefferson, T. (1998). "Muscle," "hard men," and "iron" Mike Tyson: Reflections on desire, anxiety, and the embodiment of masculinity. *Body and Society, 4*(1), 77–98.

Jefferson, T. (2001, January). *Subordinating hegemonic masculinity.* Keynote address presented at the Australian and New Zealand Annual Criminology Conference, Melbourne, Australia.

Jefferson, T. (2003). For a psychosocial criminology. In K. Carrington & R. Hogg (Eds.), *Critical criminology: issues, debates, challenges* (pp. 145–167). London: Willan.

Jurik, N. C., & Martin, S. E. (2001). Femininities, masculinities, and organizational conflict: Women in criminal justice occupations. In C. M. Renzetti & L. Goodstein (Eds.), *Women, crime and criminal justice: Original feminist readings* (pp. 264–281). Los Angeles: Roxbury.

Kindlon, D., & Thompson, M. (1999). *Raising Cain: Protecting the emotional life of boys.* New York: Ballantine.

Lettiere, M. (1997, November). *"I'm gettin' a lick 'cus I ain't no white bitch": Racialized masculinities and crime among San Francisco's homeless heroin addicts.* Paper presented at the Annual Meeting of the American Society of Criminology, San Diego, CA.

Martin, K. A. (1996). *Puberty, sexuality, and the self: Boys and girls at adolescence.* New York: Routledge.

Messerschmidt, J. W. (1993). *Masculinities and crime: Critique and reconceptualization of theory.* Lanham, MD: Rowman & Littlefield.

Messerschmidt, J. W. (1997). *Crime as structured action: Gender, race, class, and crime in the making.* Thousand Oaks, CA: Sage.

Messerschmidt, J. W. (1999). *Masculinities, Crime and Criminology* by Richard Collier (Review). *Theoretical Criminology, 3*(2), 246–249.

Messerschmidt, J. W. (2000). *Nine lives: Adolescent masculinities, the body, and violence.* Boulder, CO: Westview.

Messerschmidt, J. W. (2004). *Embodied masculinities, embodied violence: Boys, girls, the body, and assault.* Lanham, MD: Rowman & Littlefield.

Miller, J. (2001). *One of the guys: Girls, gangs, and gender.* New York: Oxford University Press.

Naffine, N. (Ed.). (1995). *Gender, crime, and feminism.* Brookfield, MA: Dartmouth University Press.

Newburn, T., & Stanko, E. A. (1994). *Just boys doing business? Men, masculinities and crime.* London: Routledge.

Petersen, A. C. (1988). Adolescent development. *Annual Review of Psychology, 39,* 583–607.

Polk, K. (1994). *When men kill: Scenarios of masculine violence.* New York: Cambridge University Press.

Sabo, D., Kupers, T. A., & London, W. (Eds.). (2001). *Prison masculinities.* Philadelphia, PA: Temple University Press.

Sartre, J. P. (1956). *Being and nothingness.* New York: Washington Square Press.

Sartre, J. P. (1963). *Search for a method.* New York: Alfred A. Knopf.

Schwartz, M. D., & Milovanovic, D. (Eds.). (1996). *Race, gender, and class in criminology: The intersection.* New York: Garland.

Thorne, B. (1993). *Gender play: Girls and boys in school.* New Brunswick, NJ: Rutgers University Press.

West, C., & Zimmerman, D. H. (1987). Doing gender. *Gender and Society, 1*(2), 125–151.

Winlow, S. (2001). *Badfellas: Crime, tradition and new masculinities.* New York: Berg.

Young, A. (1996). *Imagining crime: Textual outlaws and criminal conversations.* Thousand Oaks, CA: Sage.

References

Adler, P. A., & Adler, P. (2003). Preface. In P. Adler, & P. Adler (Eds.), *Constructions of deviance: Social power, context and interaction* (Fourth ed., pp. xv–xxviii). Belmont, CA: Thomson Wadsworth.

Agnew, R. (1985). A revised strain theory of delinquency. *Social Forces, 64*(1), 151–167.

Agnew, R. (1995). The contribution of social-psychological strain theory to the explanation of crime and delinquency. In F. Adler, W. S. Laufer & R. K. Merton (Eds.), *The legacy of anomie theory* (pp. 113–137). New Brunswick, U.S.A.: Transaction Publishers.

Agnew, R. (2006). General strain theory: Current status and directions for further research. In F. T. Cullen, J. P. Wright & K. R. Blevins (Eds.), *Taking stock: The status of criminological theory* (pp. 101–123). New Brunswick, N.J.: Transaction Publishers.

Ahmed, E., Harris, N., Braithwaite, J., & Braithwaite, V. (2001). *Shame management through reintegration.* Cambridge: Cambridge University Press.

Akers, R. L. (1990). Rational choice, deterrence, and social learning theory in criminology: The path not taken. *The Journal of Criminal Law & Criminology, 81*(3), 653–676.

Akers, R. L. (1998). *Social learning and social structure: A general theory of crime and deviance.* Boston: Northeastern University Press.

Akers, R. L. (2001). Social learning theory. In R. Paternoster, & R. Bachman (Eds.), *Explaining criminals and crime: Essays in contemporary criminological theory* (pp. 192–210). Los Angeles, Calif.: Roxbury Pub. Co.

Akers, R. L., & Jensen, G. F. (2006). The empirical status of social learning theory of crime and deviance: The past, present and future. In F. T. Cullen, J. P. Wright & K. R. Blevins (Eds.), *Taking stock: The status of criminological theory* (pp. 37–76). New Brunswick, N.J.: Transaction Publishers.

Akers, R. L., & Matsueda, R. L. (1989). Donald R. Cressey: An intellectual portrait of a criminologist. *Sociological Inquiry, 59*(4), 423–438.

Akers, R. L., & Sellers, C. S. (2009). *Criminological theories: Introduction, evaluation, and application* (5th ed.). New York: Oxford University Press.

Arrigo, B. A., & Williams, C. R. (2009). Conflict criminology: Developments, directions, and destinations past and present. In H. Copes, & V. Topalli (Eds.), *Criminological theory: Readings and retrospectives* (pp. 401–412). New York: McGraw-Hill.

Bandura, A. (1977). *Social learning theory.* Englewood Cliffs, NJ: Prentice-Hall.

Becker, H. S. (1951). The professional dance musician and his audience. *American Journal of Sociology, 57*(2), 136–144.

Becker, H. S. (1953). Becoming a marihuana user. *American Journal of Sociology, 59*(3), 235–242.

Becker, H. S. (1963). *Outsiders: Studies in the sociology of deviance.* London: Free Press of Glencoe.

Becker, H. S. (1964). Introduction. In H. S. Becker (Ed.), *The other side: Perspectives on deviance* (pp. 1–6). New York: Free Press of Glencoe.

Bell, S. J. (2002). Girls in trouble. In B. Schissel, & C. Brooks (Eds.), *Marginality and condemnation: An introduction to critical criminology* (p. 129). Halifax, N.S.: Fernwood Pub. Co.

Bernard, T. J. (1995). Merton versus Hirschi: Who is faithful to Durkheim's heritage? In F. Adler, W. S. Laufer & R. K. Merton (Eds.), *The legacy of anomie theory* (pp. 81–90). New Brunswick, U.S.A.: Transaction Publishers.

Bernard, T. J., Snipes, J. B., & Gerould, A. L. (2010). *Vold's theoretical criminology* (Sixth ed.). New York: Oxford University Press.

Bernburg, J. G. (2009). Labeling and secondary deviance. In H. Copes, & V. Topalli (Eds.), *Criminological theory: Readings and retrospectives* (pp. 340–350). New York: McGraw-Hill.

Best, J. (1990). *Threatened children: Rhetoric and concern about child-victims*. Chicago: University of Chicago Press.

Best, J. (1994). *Troubling children: Studies of children and social problems*. New York: Aldine de Gruyter.

Best, J. (1995). Typification and social problems construction. In J. Best (Ed.), *Images of issues: Typifying contemporary social problems* (Second ed., pp. 3–10). New York: Aldine de Gruyter.

Best, J. (1999). *Random violence: How we talk about new crimes and new victims*. Berkeley; London: University of California Press.

Best, J. (2003). Deviance: The constructionist stance. In P. Adler, & P. Adler (Eds.), *Constructions of deviance: Social power, context and interaction* (Fourth ed., pp. 90–105). Belmont, CA: Thomson Wadsworth.

Braithwaite, J. (2001). Reintegrative shaming. In R. Paternoster, & R. Bachman (Eds.), *Explaining criminals and crime: Essays in contemporary criminological theory* (pp. 242–251). Los Angeles, Calif.: Roxbury Pub. Co.

Burgess, R. L., & Akers, R. L. (1966). A differential association-reinforcement theory of criminal behavior. *Social Problems, 14*(2), 128–147.

Burgess-Proctor, A. (2009). Looking back, looking ahead: Assessing contemporary feminist criminology. In H. Copes, & V. Topalli (Eds.), *Criminological theory: Readings and retrospectives* (pp. 431–443). New York: McGraw-Hill.

Burns, R., & Crawford, C. (1999). School shootings, the media and public fear: Ingredients for a moral panic. *Crime, Law and Social Change, 32*(2), 147–168.

Bursik, R. J., & Grasmick, H. G. (1993). Economic deprivation and neighborhood crime rates, 1960-1980. *Law & Society Review, 27*(2), 263–283.

Bursik, R. J. J. (1988). Social disorganization and theories of crime and delinquency: Problems and prospects. *Criminology, 26*(4), 519–551.

Burtch, B. E. (2003). *The sociology of law: Critical approaches to social control* (2nd ed.). Toronto: Nelson Thomson Learning.

Cassel, E., & Bernstein, D. A. (2001). *Criminal behavior*. Needham Heights, MA: Allyn and Bacon.

Chambliss, W. J. (1964). A sociological analysis of the law of vagrancy. *Social Problems, 12*(1), 67–77.

Chambliss, W. J. (1975). The political economy of crime: A comparative study of Nigeria and the USA. In I. Taylor, P. Walton & J. Young (Eds.), *Critical criminology* (pp. 167–179). London: Routledge & Kegan Paul.

Chambliss, W. J. (1985). Toward a political economy of crime. In S. H. Traub, & C. B. Little (Eds.), *Theories of deviance* (3rd ed., pp. 423–441). Itasca, Ill.: F. E. Peacock Publishers.

Chambliss, W. J. (2003). The Saints and the Roughnecks. In P. Adler, & P. Adler (Eds.), *Constructions of deviance: Social power, context and interaction* (Fourth ed., pp. 169–182). Belmont, CA: Thomson Wadsworth.

Chesney-Lind, M. (2005). Girl's crime and woman's place: Toward a feminist model of female delinquency. In H. N. Pontell (Ed.), *Social deviance: Readings in theory and research* (Fifth ed., pp. 181–196). Upper Saddle River, NJ: Pearson Prentice Hall.

Chesney-Lind, M., & Faith, K. (2001). What about feminism? Engendering theory-making in criminology. In R. Paternoster, & R. Bachman (Eds.), *Explaining criminals and crime: Essays in contemporary criminological theory* (pp. 287–302). Los Angeles, Calif.: Roxbury Pub. Co.

Chesney-Lind, M., & Paramore, V. V. (2001). Are girls getting more violent? Exploring juvenile robbery trends. *Journal of Contemporary Criminal Justice, 7*(2), 142–166.

Clinard, M. B. (1964). The theoretical implications of anomie and deviant behavior. In M. B. Clinard (Ed.), *Anomie and deviant behavior: A discussion and critique* (pp. 1–56). New York: Free Press of Glencoe.

Cloward, R. A., & Ohlin, L. E. (1960). *Delinquency and opportunity: A theory of delinquent gangs.* New York: Free Press.

Cohen, A. K. (1955, 1964). *Delinquent boys: The culture of the gang.* Glencoe, IL: Free Press of Glencoe.

Cohen, A. K. (1985). The sociology of the deviant act: Anomie theory and beyond. In S. H. Traub, & C. B. Little (Eds.), *Theories of deviance* (3rd ed., pp. 158–171). Itasca, Ill.: F. E. Peacock Publishers.

Cohen, S. (1987). *Folk devils & moral panics: The creation of the Mods and Rockers.* Oxford: Basil Blackwell.

Coleman, J. S. (1988). Social capital in the creation of human capital. *American Journal of Sociology, 94* (Supplement: Organizations and Institutions: Sociological and Economic Approaches to the Analysis of Social Structure), S95–S120.

Cooley, C. H. (2005). The social self. In H. N. Pontell (Ed.), *Social deviance: Readings in theory and research* (Fifth ed., pp. 72–73). Upper Saddle River, NJ: Pearson Prentice Hall.

Cullen, F. T., Wright, J. P., & Blevins, K. R. (Eds.). (2004). *Taking stock: The status of criminological theory.* New Brunswick, N.J.: Transaction Publishers.

Cullen, F. T., Wright, J. P., Gendreau, P., & Andrews, D. A. (2003). What correctional treatment can tell us about criminological theory: Implications for social learning theory. In R. L. Akers, & G. F. Jensen (Eds.), *Social learning theory and the explanation of crime: A guide for the new century* (pp. 339–362). New Brunswick, N.J.: Transaction.

Deutschmann, L. B. (2002). *Deviance and social control* (Third ed.). Scarborough, Ontario: Nelson Thomson Learning.

Durkheim, É. (1951). *Suicide: A study in sociology* (J. A. Spaulding, G. Simpson Trans.). Glencoe, Ill.: Free Press.

Durkheim, É. (1964a). The dualism of human nature and its social conditions. In K. H. Wolff (Ed.), *Essays on sociology & philosophy by Émile Durkheim et al.* (C. Blend Trans.). (pp. 325–340). New York: Harper & Row.

Durkheim, É. (1964b). In Catlin G. E. G. (Ed.), *The rules of sociological method* (J. H. Mueller, S. A. Solovay Trans.). (8th ed.). New York: The Free Press of Glencoe.

Durkheim, É. (1965). *The division of labor in society* (G. Simpson Trans.). New York: Free Press.

Erikson, K. T. (1962). Notes on the sociology of deviance. *Social Problems, 9*(4), 307–314.

Erikson, K. T. (1964). Notes on the sociology of deviance. In H. S. Becker (Ed.), *The other side: Perspectives on deviance* (pp. 9–21). New York: Free Press of Glencoe.

Erikson, K. T. (2005). *Wayward puritans: A study in the sociology of deviance.* Boston: Allyn and Bacon.

Garfinkel, H. (1956). Conditions of successful degradation ceremonies. *American Journal of Sociology, 61*(5), 420–424.

Garland, D. (2001). *The culture of control: Crime and social order in contemporary society.* Chicago: University of Chicago Press.

Goffman, E. (2005). Stigma and social identity. In H. N. Pontell (Ed.), *Social deviance: Readings in theory and research* (Fifth ed., pp. 77–96). Upper Saddle River, NJ: Pearson Prentice Hall.

Goode, E. (1994). Round up the usual suspects: Crime, deviance, and the limits of constructionism. *The American Sociologist, 25*(4), 90–104.

Goode, E. (2005). On behalf of labeling theory. In H. N. Pontell (Ed.), *Social deviance: Readings in theory and research* (Fifth ed., pp. 96–106). Upper Saddle River, NJ: Pearson Prentice Hall.

Goode, E., & Ben-Yehuda, N. (1994). MORAL PANICS: Culture, politics, and social construction. *Annual Review of Sociology, 20*(1), 149–171.

Gottfredson, M. R., & Hirschi, T. (1990). *A general theory of crime.* Stanford, Calif.: Stanford University Press.

Gove, W. (1980). The labelling perspective: An overview. In W. R. Gove (Ed.), *The labelling of deviance: Evaluating a perspective* (2nd ed., pp. 9–26). Beverly Hills, Calif.: Sage Publications.

Gusman, J. R. (1955). Social structure and moral reform: A study of the Woman's Christian Temperance Union. *American Journal of Sociology, 6*(3), 221–223.

Hackler, J. C. (2007). *Canadian criminology: Strategies and perspectives* (Fourth ed.). Toronto: Pearson Prentice-Hall.

Hagan, J. (2003). A power-control theory of gender and delinquency. In C. M. Renzetti, D. J. Curran & P. J. Carr (Eds.), *Theories of crime: A reader* (pp. 214–221). Boston: Allyn and Bacon.

Hinkle, R. C. (1964). Durkheim in American sociology. In K. H. Wolff (Ed.), *Essays on sociology and philosophy* (pp. 267–295). New York: Harper.

Hirschi, T. (1969). *Causes of delinquency.* Berkeley: University of California Press.

Hirschi, T. (1980). Labelling theory and juvenile delinquency: An assessment of the evidence. In W. R. Gove (Ed.), *The labelling of deviance: Evaluating a perspective* (2nd ed., pp. 271–293). Beverly Hills, Calif.: Sage Publications.

Hirschi, T. (2002). *Causes of delinquency.* New Brunswick, N.J.: Transaction Publishers.

Hunter, A. J. (1985). Private, parochial and public social order: The problem of crime and incivility in urban communities. In M. Janowitz, G. D. Suttles & M. N. Zald (Eds.), *The challenge of social control: Citizenship and institution building in modern society: Essays in honor of Morris Janowitz* (pp. 230–242). Norwood, NJ: Ablex Pub.

Jeffery, C. R. (1965). Criminal behavior and learning theory. *Journal of Criminal Law, Criminology, and Police Science, 56*(3), 294–300.

Jeffery, C. R. (1978). Criminology as an interdisciplinary behavioral science. *Criminology, 16*(2), 149–169.

Jensen, G. F., & Akers, R. L. (2003). "Taking social learning global": Micro-macro transitions in criminological theory. In R. L. Akers, & G. F. Jensen (Eds.), *Social learning theory and the explanation of crime: A guide for the new century* (pp. 9–37). New Brunswick, N.J.: Transaction.

Kitsuse, J. I. (1964). Societal reaction to deviant behavior: Problems of theory and method. In H. S. Becker (Ed.), *The other side: Perspectives on deviance* (pp. 87–102). New York: Free Press of Glencoe.

Kornhauser, R. R. (1978). *Social sources of delinquency: An appraisal of analytic models.* Chicago: University of Chicago Press.

Laub, J. H., & Sampson, R. J. (1993). Turning points in the life course: Why change matters to the study of crime. *Criminology, 31*(3), 301–325.

Lemert, C. C. (1993). *Social theory: The multicultural and classic readings.* Boulder, Colo.: Westview Press.

Lemert, E. M. (2005). Primary and secondary deviation. In H. N. Pontell (Ed.), *Social deviance: Readings in theory and research* (Fifth ed., pp. 74–77). Upper Saddle River, NJ: Pearson Prentice Hall.

Liazos, A. (2005). The poverty of the sociology of deviance: Nuts, sluts and preverts. In H. N. Pontell (Ed.), *Social deviance: Readings in theory and research* (Fifth ed., pp. 112–126). Upper Saddle River, NJ: Pearson Prentice Hall.

Lilly, J. R., Cullen, F. T., & Ball, R. A. (2011). *Criminological theory: Context and consequences* (5th ed.). Thousand Oaks: SAGE Publications.

Lowenkamp, C. T., Cullen, F. T., & Pratt, T. C. (2003). Replicating Sampson and Groves's test of social disorganization theory: Revisiting a criminological classic. *Journal of Research in Crime and Delinquency, 40*(4), 351–373.

Lynch, M. J., & Stretesky, P. B. (2001). Radical criminology. In R. Paternoster, & R. Bachman (Eds.), *Explaining criminals and crime: Essays in contemporary criminological theory* (pp. 267–286). Los Angeles, Calif.: Roxbury Pub. Co.

Mailer, N. (1979). *The executioner's song.* Boston: Little, Brown.

Matsueda, R. L. (2001). Labeling theory: Historical roots, implications, and recent developments. In R. Paternoster, & R. Bachman (Eds.), *Explaining criminals and crime: Essays in contemporary criminological theory* (pp. 223–241). Los Angeles, Calif.: Roxbury Pub. Co.

Merton, R. K. (1938). Social structure and anomie. *American Sociological Review, 3*(5), 672–682.

Merton, R. K. (1985). Social structure and anomie. In S. H. Traub, & C. B. Little (Eds.), *Theories of deviance* (3rd ed., pp. 107–138). Itasca, Ill.: F. E. Peacock Publishers.

Merton, R. K. (1993). Manifest and latent functions. In C. C. Lemert (Ed.), *Social theory: The multicultural and classic readings* (pp. 328–334). Boulder, Colo.: Westview Press.

Messerschmidt, J. W. (1993). *Masculinities and crime: Critique and reconceptualization of theory.* Lanham, Md.: Rowman & Littlefield.

Messerschmidt, J. W. (1997). *Crime as structured action: Gender, race, class and crime in the making.* Thousand Oaks, Calif.; London: Sage Publications.

Messerschmidt, J. W. (2005). Men, masculinities and crime. In M. S. Kimmel, J. Hearn & R. W. Connell (Eds.), *Handbook of studies on men and masculinities* (pp. 196–212). Thousand Oaks, CA: SAGE Publications.

Messner, S. F., & Rosenfeld, R. (2007). *Crime and the American Dream* (Fourth ed.). Belmont, CA: Thomson Wadsworth.

Mutchnick, R. J., Martin, R., & Austin, T. W. (2009). *Criminological thought: Pioneers past and present.* Upper Saddle River, NJ: Prentice Hall.

Neyer, J. (1964). Individualism and socialism in Durkheim. In K. H. Wolff (Ed.), *Essays on sociology and philosophy* (pp. 32–76). New York: Harper.

Osgood, D. W., & Chambers, J. M. (2000). Social disorganization outside the metropolis: An analysis of rural youth violence. *Criminology, 38*(1), 81–115.

Passas, N. (1995). Continuities in the anomie tradition. In F. Adler, W. S. Laufer & R. K. Merton (Eds.), *The legacy of anomie theory* (pp. 91–112). New Brunswick, U.S.A.: Transaction Publishers.

Passas, N. (2003). Anomie, reference groups, and relative deprivation. In C. M. Renzetti, D. J. Curran & P. J. Carr (Eds.), *Theories of crime: A reader* (pp. 97–113). Boston: Allyn and Bacon.

Paternoster, R., & Bachman, R. (2001a). Control theories of crime. In R. Paternoster, & R. Bachman (Eds.), *Explaining criminals and crime: Essays in contemporary criminological theory* (pp. 80–191). Los Angeles, Calif.: Roxbury Pub. Co.

Paternoster, R., & Bachman, R. (Eds.). (2001b). *Explaining criminals and crime: Essays in contemporary criminological theory.* Los Angeles, Calif.: Roxbury Pub. Co.

Paternoster, R., & Bachman, R. (2001c). Labeling or social reaction theories of crime. In R. Paternoster, & R. Bachman (Eds.), *Explaining criminals and crime: Essays in contemporary criminological theory* (pp. 211–222). Los Angeles, Calif.: Roxbury Pub. Co.

Pfohl, S. J. (1985). *Images of deviance and social control: A sociological history.* New York: McGraw-Hill.

Piquero, N. L., Tibbetts, S. G., & Blankenship, M. B. (2005). Examining the role of differential association and techniques of neutralization in explaining corporate crime. *Deviant Behavior, 26*(2), 159–188.

Plummer, K. (1979). Misunderstanding labelling perspectives. In D. M. Downes, & P. E. Rock (Eds.), *Deviant interpretations* (pp. 85–121). Oxford: Martin Robertson.

Pratt, T. C., Cullen, F. T., Sellers, C. S., Winfree, L. T., Madensen, T. D., Daigle, L. E., & Gau, J. M. (2010). The empirical status of social learning theory: A meta-analysis. *Justice Quarterly, 27*(6), 765–802.

Putnam, R. D. (2007). E Pluribus Unum: Diversity and community in the Twenty-first Century. The 2006 Johan Skytte Price lecture. *Scandinavian Political Studies, 30*(2), 137–174.

Quinney, R. (1975). Crime control in capitalist society: A critical philosophy of legal order. In I. Taylor, P. Walton & J. Young (Eds.), *Critical criminology* (pp. 181–201). London: Routledge & Kegan Paul.

Quinney, R. (1977). *Class, state and crime: On the theory and practice of criminal justice.* New York: David McKay Company, Inc.

Quinney, R. (2003). Conflict theory of crime. In P. Adler, & P. Adler (Eds.), *Constructions of deviance: Social power, context and interaction* (Fourth ed., pp. 84–89). Belmont, CA: Thomson Wadsworth.

Renzetti, C. M., Curran, D. J., & Carr, P. J. (2003a). Crime and stigma: Labeling theory. In C. M. Renzetti, D. J. Curran & P. J. Carr (Eds.), *Theories of crime: A reader* (pp. 166–167). Boston: Allyn and Bacon.

Renzetti, C. M., Curran, D. J., & Carr, P. J. (Eds.). (2003b). *Theories of crime: A reader*. Boston: Allyn and Bacon.

Rock, P. (1979). The sociology of crime, symbolic interactionism and some problematic qualities of radical criminology. In D. M. Downes, & P. E. Rock (Eds.), *Deviant interpretations* (pp. 52–84). Oxford: Martin Robertson.

Rosenfeld, R., & Messner, S. F. (1995). Crime and the American Dream: An institutional analysis. In F. Adler, W. S. Laufer & R. K. Merton (Eds.), *The legacy of anomie theory* (pp. 159–181). New Brunswick, U.S.A.: Transaction Publishers.

Sacco, V. F., & Kennedy, L. W. (2008). *The criminal event: An introduction to criminology in Canada* (Fourth ed.). Toronto: Thomson Nelson.

Sampson, R. J. (2006). Collective efficacy theory: Lessons learned and directions for future inquiry. In F. T. Cullen, J. P. Wright & K. R. Blevins (Eds.), *Taking stock: The status of criminological theory* (pp. 149–167). New Brunswick, N.J.: Transaction Publishers.

Sampson, R. J., & Groves, W. B. (1989). Community structure and crime: Testing social-disorganization theory. *American Journal of Sociology, 94*(4), 774–802.

Sampson, R. J., & Laub, J. H. (1990). Crime and deviance over the life course: The salience of adult social bonds. *American Sociological Review, 55*(5), 609–627. doi:10.2307/2095859

Sampson, R. J., & Laub, J. H. (1992). Crime and deviance in the life course. *Annual Review of Sociology, 18*(1), 63–84.

Sampson, R. J., & Laub, J. H. (2001). A life-course theory of cumulative disadvantage and the stability of delinquency. In A. Piquero, & P. Mazerolle (Eds.), *Life-course criminology: Contemporary and classic readings* (pp. 146–169). Toronto: Wadsworth Thomson Learning.

Savoie, J. (2003). Yes! youth violent crime. In R. Hinch (Ed.), *Debates in Canadian criminology* (pp. 80–99). Toronto: Prentice Hall.

Schissel, B. (1997). *Blaming children: Youth crime, moral panic and the politics of hate*. Halifax, N.S.: Fernwood.

Scully, D., & Marolla, J. (2003). Convicted rapists' vocabulary of motive." In P. Adler, & P. Adler (Eds.), *Constructions of deviance: Social power, context and interaction* (Fourth ed., pp. 247–271). Belmont, CA: Thomson Wadsworth.

Sellin, T. (1994). Culture conflict and crime. In J. E. Jacoby (Ed.), *Classics of criminology* (2nd ed., pp. 188–192). Prospect Heights, Illinois: Waveland Press Inc.

Shaw, C. R., & McKay, H. D. (1969). *Juvenile delinquency and urban areas: A study of rates of delinquency in relation to differential characteristics of local communities in American cities* (Rev. ed.). Chicago: University of Chicago Press.

Simpson, S. S. (1991). Caste, class and violent crime: Explaining difference in female offending. *Criminology, 29*(1), 115–135.

Spector, M., & Kitsuse, J. I. (1977). *Constructing social problems*. Menlo Park, Calif.: Cummings Pub. Co.

Spitzer, S. (2005). Toward a Marxian theory of deviance. In H. N. Pontell (Ed.), *Social deviance: Readings in theory and research* (Fifth ed., pp. 108–112). Upper Saddle River, NJ: Pearson Prentice Hall.

Sutherland, E. H. (1940). White-collar criminality. *American Sociological Review, 5*(1), 1–12.

Sutherland, E. H. (1950). The diffusion of sexual psychopath laws. *American Journal of Sociology, 56*(2), 142–148.

Sutherland, E. H. (1994). The professional thief. In J. E. Jacoby (Ed.), *Classics of criminology* (2nd ed., pp. 9–12). Prospect Heights, Illinois: Waveland Press Inc.

Sutherland, E. H., & Cressey, D. R. (1985). The theory of differential association. In S. H. Traub, & C. B. Little (Eds.), *Theories of deviance* (3rd ed., pp. 176–182). Itasca, Ill.: F. E. Peacock Publishers.

Sykes, G. M., & Matza, D. (1957). Techniques of neutralization: A theory of delinquency. *American Sociological Review, 22*(6), 664–670.

Tannenbaum, F. (1985). The dramatization of evil. In S. H. Traub, & C. B. Little (Eds.), *Theories of deviance* (3rd ed., pp. 280–284). Itasca, Ill.: F. E. Peacock Publishers.

Taylor, I., Walton, P., & Young, J. (1973). *The new criminology: For a social theory of deviance*. London: Routledge & Keegan Paul.

Taylor, R. B. (2001). The ecology of crime, fear, and delinquency: Social disorganization versus social efficacy. In R. Paternoster, & R. Bachman (Eds.), *Explaining criminals and crime: Essays in contemporary criminological theory* (pp. 124–139). Los Angeles, Calif.: Roxbury Pub. Co.

Thornberry, T. (1987). Toward an interactional theory of delinquency. *Criminology, 25*(4), 863–891.

Thornberry, T. P., & Krohn, M. D. (2005). Applying interactional theory to the explanation of continuity and change in antisocial behavior. In D. P. Farrington (Ed.), *Integrated developmental & life-course theories of offending* (pp. 183–209). New Brunswick, NJ: Transaction Publishers.

Tittle, C. R. (1980). Labelling and crime: An empirical evaluation. In W. R. Gove (Ed.), *The labelling of deviance: Evaluating a perspective* (2nd ed., pp. 241–269). Beverly Hills, Calif.: Sage Publications.

Traub, S. H., & Little, C. B. (1985). *Theories of deviance* (3rd ed.). Itasca, Ill.: F. E. Peacock Publishers.

Veysey, B. M., & Messner, S. F. (1999). Further testing of social disorganization theory: An elaboration of Sampson and Groves's "community structure and crime." *Journal of Research in Crime and Delinquency, 36*(2), 156–174.

Vold, G. B., & Second edition prepared by Thomas J. Bernard. (1979). *Theoretical criminology* (2nd ed.). New York: Oxford University Press.

Warr, M. (2001). The social origins of crime: Edwin Sutherland and the theory of differential association. In R. Paternoster, & R. Bachman (Eds.), *Explaining criminals and crime: Essays in contemporary criminological theory* (pp. 182–191). Los Angeles, Calif.: Roxbury Pub. Co.

Williams, F. P., & McShane, M. D. (2010). *Criminological theory* (5th ed.). Upper Saddle River, N.J.: Pearson/Prentice Hall.

Winfree, L. T., & Abadinsky, H. (2010). *Understanding crime: Essentials of criminological theory* (Third ed.). Belmont, CA: Wadsworth, Cengage Learning.

Wolfgang, M. E., & Ferracuti, F. (1967). *The subculture of violence: Towards an integrated theory in criminology*. London: Tavistock Publication.

Young, J. (1975). Working class criminology. In I. Taylor, P. Walton & J. Young (Eds.), *Critical criminology* (pp. 63–94). London: Routledge & Kegan Paul.

Young, J. (2002). Critical criminology in the twenty-first century: Critique, irony and the always unfinished. In K. Carrington, & R. Hogg (Eds.), *Critical criminology: Issues, debates and challenges* (pp. 251–274). Cullompton, Devon: Willan Publishers.

Young, J. (2003). The failure of criminology. In C. M. Renzetti, D. J. Curran & P. J. Carr (Eds.), *Theories of crime: A reader* (pp. 192–199). Boston: Allyn and Bacon.

Zeitlin, I. M. (2001). *Ideology and the development of sociological theory* (7th ed.). Upper Saddle River, N.J.: Prentice Hall.